Human Development Report 2016

Human Development for Everyone

Published for the
United Nations
Development
Programme
(UNDP)

ered lives.
nt nations.

Human Development Report 2016 Team

Director and lead author

Selim Jahan

Deputy director

Eva Jespersen

Research and statistics

Shantanu Mukherjee (Team Leader). Milorad Kovacevic (Chief Statistician), Botagoz Abdreyeva, Astra Bonini, Cecilia Calderon, Christelle Cazabat, Yu-Chieh Hsu, Christina Lengfelder, Patrizia Luongo, Tanni Mukhopadhyay, Shivani Nayyar and Heriberto Tapia

Production and web

Admir Jahic and Dharshani Seneviratne

Outreach and communications

Jon Hall, Sasa Lucic, Jennifer O'Neil Oldfield and Anna Ortubia

Operations and administration

Sarantuya Mend (Operations Manager), Fe Juarez Shanahan and May Wint Than

Foreword

Human development is all about human freedoms: freedom to realize the full potential of every human life, not just of a few, nor of most, but of all lives in every corner of the world—now and in the future. Such universalism gives the human development approach its uniqueness.

However, the principle of universalism is one thing; translating it into practice is another. Over the past quarter-century there has been impressive progress on many fronts in human development, with people living longer, more people rising out of extreme poverty and fewer people being malnourished. Human development has enriched human lives—but unfortunately not all to the same extent, and even worse, not every life.

It is thus not by chance but by choice that world leaders in 2015 committed to a development journey that leaves no one out—a central premise of the 2030 Agenda. Mirroring that universal aspiration, it is timely that the 2016 Human Development Report is devoted to the theme of human development for everyone.

The Report begins by using a broad brush to paint a picture of the challenges the world faces and the hopes humanity has for a better future. Some challenges are lingering (deprivations), some are deepening (inequalities) and some are emerging (violent extremism), but most are mutually reinforcing. Whatever their nature or reach, these challenges have an impact on people's well-being in both present and future generations.

At the same time, however, the Report reminds us what humanity has achieved over the past 25 years and gives us hope that further advances are possible. We can build on what we have achieved, we can explore new possibilities to overcome challenges and we can attain what once seemed unattainable. Hopes are within our reach to realize.

Given that broader context, the Report then raises two fundamental questions: who has been left out in progress in human development and how and why did that happen. It emphasizes that poor, marginalized and vulnerable groups—including ethnic minorities, indigenous peoples, refugees and migrants—are being left furthest behind. The barriers to universalism include, among others, deprivations and inequalities, discrimination and exclusion, social norms and values, and prejudice and intolerance. The Report also clearly identifies the mutually reinforcing gender barriers that deny many women the opportunities and empowerment necessary to realize the full potential of their lives.

To ensure human development for everyone, the Report asserts that merely identifying the nature of and the reasons for the deprivation of those left out is not enough. Some aspects of the human development analytical framework and assessment perspectives must be brought to the fore to address issues that prevent universal human development. For example, human rights and human security, voice and autonomy, collective capabilities and the interdependence of choices are key for the human development of those currently left out. Similarly, quality of human development outcomes and not only quantity, going beyond the averages and disaggregating statistics (particularly gender-disaggregation)—must be considered to assess and ensure that human development benefits reach everyone.

The Report forcefully argues that caring for those left out requires a four-pronged policy strategy at the national level: reaching those left out using universal policies (for example, inclusive growth, not mere growth), pursuing measures for groups with special needs (for example, persons with disabilities), making human development resilient and empowering those left out.

The Report rightly recognizes that national policies need to be complemented by actions at the global level. It addresses issues related to the mandate, governance structures and work of global institutions. It draws our attention to the fact that even though we have grown accustomed to heated debates winding up in gridlock at the national, regional and global levels, underneath the rumble of all that, consensus has been emerging around many global challenges to ensure a sustainable world for future generations. The landmark Paris

Agreement on climate change, which recently came into force, bears testimony to this. What was once deemed unthinkable must now prove to be unstoppable.

The Report complements the 2030 Agenda by sharing the principle of universalism and by concentrating on such fundamental areas as eliminating extreme poverty, ending hunger and highlighting the core issue of sustainability. The human development approach and the 2030 Agenda can be mutually reinforcing by contributing to the narrative of each other, by exploring how human development and Sustainable Development Goal indicators can complement each other and by being a forceful advocacy platform for each other.

We have every reason to hope that transformation in human development is possible.

What seem to be challenges today can be overcome tomorrow. The world has fewer than 15 years to achieve its bold agenda of leaving no one out. Closing the human development gap is critical, as is ensuring the same, or even better, opportunities for future generations. Human development has to be sustained and sustainable and has to enrich every human life so that we have a world where all people can enjoy peace and prosperity.

Helen Clark
Administrator
United Nations Development Programme

Acknowledgements

The 2016 Human Development Report is the product of the Human Development Report Office (HDRO) at the United Nations Development Programme (UNDP).

The findings, analysis and policy recommendations of the Report are those of HDRO alone and cannot be attributed to UNDP or to its Executive Board. The UN General Assembly has officially recognized the Human Development Report as "an independent intellectual exercise" that has become "an important tool for raising awareness about human development around the world."

We owe a lot to Nobel Laureate Professor Amartya Sen for his continued inspirational intellectual advice, guidance and thoughts. HDRO is also privileged to receive a series of contributions by eminent people and organizations. Particular appreciation is due for the signed contributions from Professor Dan Ariely (James B. Duke Professor of Psychology and Behavioral Economics at Duke University), Carol Bellamy (chair of the Governing Board of the Global Community Engagement and Resilience Fund and former executive director of the United Nations Children's Fund), Mirna Cunningham Kain (Nicaraguan Miskitu, indigenous peoples rights activist and former chairperson of the United Nations Permanent Forum on Indigenous Issues), Olafur Eliasson (artist and founder of Little Sun), Melinda Gates (co-chair of the Bill & Melinda Gates Foundation), Dr. Angela Merkel (chancellor of the Federal Republic of Germany) and Juan Manuel Santos (president of Colombia and 2016 Nobel Peace Prize Laureate). We are especially thankful to Martin Santiago and the UNDP Country Office in Colombia for facilitating President Santos's contribution.

Appreciation is also extended for contributions from the following authors: Paul Anand, Ayesha Banu, Flavio Comim, Giovanni Andrea Cornia, Juliana Martinez Franzoni, Stephany Griffith-Jones, Irene Khan, Peter Lunenborg, Manuel Montes, Siddiqur Osmani, Enrique Peruzzotti, Robert Pollin, Diego Sanchez-Ancochea, Anuradha Seth, Frances Stewart and Florencia Torche.

We are thankful for think pieces contributed by Oscar A. Gomez, Sachiko G. Kamidohzono and Ako Muto of the Japan International Cooperation Agency Research Institute; Mara Simane of the Cross Sectoral Coordination Centre of the Latvia Cabinet of Ministers; and HOPE XXL, a civil society organization. Two UNDP Global Policy Centres—one in Seoul on global development partnerships and one in Nairobi on resilient ecosystems and desertification—contributed think pieces to the Report, and our thanks go to Balazs Hovarth and Anne-Gertraude Juepner.

Invaluable insights and guidance were received from a distinguished Advisory Panel: Olu Ajakaiye, Magdalena Sepúlveda Carmona, Giovanni Andrea Cornia, Diane Elson, Heba Handoussa, Richard Jolly, Ravi Kanbur, Yasushi Katsuma, Ella Libanova, Justin Yifu Lin, Leticia Merino, Solita Monsod, Onalenna Doo Selolwane and Frances Stewart.

For providing expert advice on methodologies and data choices related to the calculation of the Report's human development indices, we would also like to thank the Report's Statistical Advisory Panel members: Lisa Grace S. Bersales, Albina Chuwa, Koen Decancq, Enrico Giovannini, Pascual Gerstenfeld, Janet Gornick, Gerald Haberkorn, Haishan Fu, Robert Kirkpatrick, Jaya Krishnakumar and Michaela Saisana.

The Report's composite indices and other statistical resources rely on the expertise of the leading international data providers in their specialized fields, and we express our gratitude for their continued collegial collaboration with the HDRO. To ensure accuracy and clarity, the statistical analysis has benefited from discussions of statistical issues with Gisela Robles Aguilar, Sabina Alkire, Kenneth Hartggen and Nicolas Fasel and his team from the Office of the United Nations High Commissioner for Human Rights.

The consultations held during the preparation of the Report relied on the generous support of many institutions and individuals who are too numerous to mention here (participants and partners are listed at http://hdr.undp.org/2016-report/consultations). Formal multistakeholder consultations were held between April and September 2016 in Geneva, Paris, Istanbul, Nairobi, Singapore and Panama. We are grateful to the UNDP Office in Geneva, the Organisation for Economic Co-operation and Development and UNDP regional service centres and global policy centres for organizing these consultations and in particular to Rebeca Arias, Max Everest-Phillips, Anne-Gertraude Juepner, Alexis Laffittan, Marcos Neto and Maria Luisa Silva. Informal consultations were also held on the side of the launch of the 2015 Human Development Report in Beijing, Bonn, Colombo, Dhaka, Helsinki, London, Manila, Reykjavik and Vienna. Contributions, support and assistance from partnering institutions, including UNDP regional bureaus and country offices, are acknowledged with much gratitude.

Special thanks are extended to UNDP colleagues who constituted the Readers Group for the Report: Mandeep Dhaliwal, Priya Gajraj, George Ronald Gray, Anne-Gertraude Juepner, Sheila Marnie, Ayodele Odusola, Thangavel Palanivel, Sarah Poole, Mounir Tabet, Claire Van der Vaeren and Claudia Vinay. The political read of the Report was done by Patrick Keuleers, Luciana Mermet and Nicholas Rosellini, and their advice is thankfully acknowledged.

Former HDRO colleagues and friends of the Report, including Moez Doraid, Sakiko Fukuda-Parr, Terry McKinley, Saraswathi Menon, Siddiqur Osmani, Stefano Pettinato and David Stewart, were kind enough to spend a day with us and share their insights, views and experiences, which are invaluable.

We further benefited on Report-related topics from discussions with and inputs from Saamah Abdallah, Helmut K. Anheier, Michelle Breslauer, Cosmas Gitta, Ronald Mendoza, Eugenia Piza-Lopez, Julia Raavad, Diane Sawyer and Oliver Schwank. We would like to thank members of the public who participated in online surveys for Report-related topics on our website.

Several talented young people contributed to the Report as interns: Ellen Hsu, Mohammad Taimur Mustafa, Abedin Rafique, Jeremías Rojas, Prerna Sharma, Weijie Tan and Danielle Ho Tan Yau. They deserve recognition for their dedication and contributions.

We are grateful for the highly professional editing and production by Communications Development Incorporated—led by Bruce Ross-Larson, with Joe Caponio, Mike Crumplar, Christopher Trott and Elaine Wilson—and designers Gerry Quinn and Phoenix Design Aid.

Most of all, on a personal note, I am, as always, profoundly grateful to UNDP Administrator Helen Clark for her leadership and vision as well as her commitment to the cause of human development and her solid support to our work. My thanks also go to the entire HDRO team for their dedication in producing a report that strives to further the advancement of human development.

Selim Jahan
Director
Human Development Report Office

Contents

SPECIAL CONTRIBUTIONS

BOXES

FIGURES

TABLES

Overview

Human development for everyone

Infographic 1 Human development for everyone

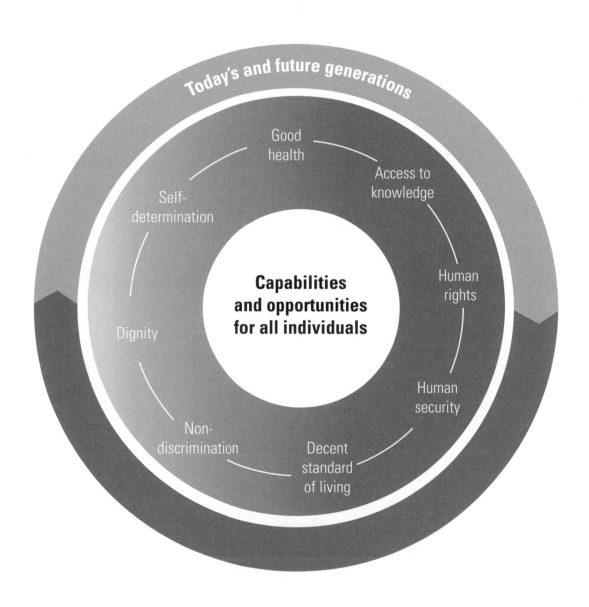

Overview
Human development for everyone

Over the past quarter-century the world has changed—and with it the development landscape. New countries have emerged, and our planet is now home to more than 7 billion people, one in four of them young.[1] The geopolitical scenario has also changed, with developing countries emerging as a major economic force and political power. Globalization has integrated people, markets and work, and the digital revolution has changed human lives.

Progress in human development has been impressive over the past 25 years. People now live longer, more children are in school and more people have access to basic social services.[2] The Millennium Declaration and the Millennium Development Goals—global commitments at the turn of the century to end basic human deprivations within 15 years—added to the momentum.

Yet human development has been uneven, and human deprivations persist. Progress has bypassed groups, communities, societies—and people have been left out. Some have achieved only the basics of human development, and some not even that. And new development challenges have emerged, ranging from inequalities to climate change, from epidemics to desperate migration, from conflicts to violent extremism.

The 2016 Human Development Report focuses on how human development can be ensured for everyone—now and in the future (see infographic 1 on the facing page). It starts with an account of the achievements, challenges and hopes for human progress, envisioning where humanity wants to go. Its vision draws from and builds on the 2030 Agenda for Sustainable Development that the 193 member states of the United Nations endorsed last year and the 17 Sustainable Development Goals that the world has committed to achieve.[3]

The Report explores who has been left out in the progress in human development and why. It argues that to ensure human development for everyone, a mere mapping of the nature and location of deprivations is not enough. Some aspects of the human development approach and assessment perspectives have to be brought to the fore. The Report also identifies the national policies and key strategies that will enable every human being to achieve basic human development and to sustain and protect the gains. And addressing the structural challenges of the current global system, it presents options for institutional reforms.

Key messages

This Report conveys five basic messages:
- Universalism is key to human development, and human development for everyone is attainable.
- Various groups of people still suffer from basic deprivations and face substantial barriers to overcoming them.
- Human development for everyone calls for refocusing some analytical issues and assessment perspectives.
- Policy options exist and, if implemented, would contribute to achieving human development for everyone.
- A reformed global governance, with fairer multilateralism, would help attain human development for everyone.

Human development is all about enlarging freedoms for every human being

Human development is about enlarging freedoms so that all human beings can pursue choices that they value. Such freedoms have two fundamental aspects—freedom of well-being, represented by functionings and capabilities, and freedom of agency, represented by voice and autonomy (figure 1).
- Functionings are the various things a person may value being and doing—such as being happy, adequately nourished and in good

Universalism is key to human development, and human development for everyone is attainable

FIGURE 1

Human development—the analytical approach

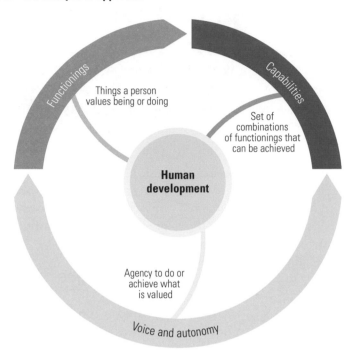

Source: Human Development Report Office.

Human development
focuses on the
richness of human
lives rather than on the
richness of economies

health, as well as having self-respect and taking part in the life of the community.

- Capabilities are the various sets of functionings (beings and doings) that a person can achieve.
- Agency is related to what a person is free to do and achieve in pursuit of whatever goals or values he or she regards as important.

Both types of freedoms are absolutely necessary for human development.

The first Human Development Report, in 1990, presented human development as a people-centred approach to development (box 1).[4] The human development approach shifted the development discourse from pursuing material opulence to enhancing human well-being, from maximizing income to expanding capabilities, from optimizing growth to enlarging freedoms. It focused on the richness of human lives rather than on simply the richness of economies, and doing so changed the lens for viewing development results (box 2).

BOX 1

Human development—a comprehensive approach

Human development is a process of enlarging people's choices. But human development is also the objective, so it is both a process and an outcome. Human development implies that people must influence the processes that shape their lives. In all this, economic growth is an important means to human development, but not the end.

Human development is the development of the people through building human capabilities, by the people through active participation in the processes that shape their lives and for the people by improving their lives. It is broader than other approaches, such as the human resource approach, the basic needs approach and the human welfare approach.

Source: Human Development Report Office.

BOX 2

Measuring human development

The composite Human Development Index (HDI) integrates three basic dimensions of human development. Life expectancy at birth reflects the ability to lead a long and healthy life. Mean years of schooling and expected years of schooling reflect the ability to acquire knowledge. And gross national income per capita reflects the ability to achieve a decent standard of living.

To measure human development more comprehensively, the Human Development Report also presents four other composite indices. The Inequality-adjusted HDI discounts the HDI according to the extent of inequality. The Gender Development Index compares female and male HDI values. The Gender Inequality Index highlights women's empowerment. And the Multidimensional Poverty Index measures nonincome dimensions of poverty.

Source: Human Development Report Office.

The human development approach also provided the analytical bedrock of the Millennium Declaration and the Millennium Development Goals—the timebound development objectives and targets agreed on in 2000 by 189 heads of states and governments to reduce basic human poverty by 2015. And it informed and influenced the 2030 Agenda and the Sustainable Development Goals.

Human development for everyone is attainable

As universalism is the centrepiece of human development, human development must be and can be attained for everyone. The positive evidence is encouraging.

By 2015 the world had achieved some of what seemed to be daunting challenges 25 years ago. Even though the global population increased by 2 billion—from 5.3 billion in 1990 to 7.3 billion in 2015—more than 1 billion people escaped extreme poverty, 2.1 billion gained access to improved sanitation and more than 2.6 billion gained access to an improved source of drinking water.[5]

The global under-five mortality rate was more than halved between 1990 and 2015—from 91 per 1,000 live births to 43. The incidence of HIV, malaria and tuberculosis declined between 2000 and 2015. The proportion of seats held by women in parliaments worldwide rose to 23 percent in 2016—up 6 percentage points over the preceding decade. The global net loss of forested areas fell from 7.3 million hectares a year in the 1990s to 3.3 million during 2010–2015.[6]

Yet, even with all this commendable progress, the world still faces many complex development challenges. Some challenges are lingering (deprivations), some deepening (inequalities) and some emerging (violent extremism). Some are global (gender inequality), some regional (water stress) and some local (natural disasters). Most are mutually reinforcing—climate change reduces food security; rapid urbanization marginalizes the urban poor. Whatever their reach, these challenges have a negative impact on people's well-being.

Despite all these challenges, what humanity has achieved over 25 years gives hope that fundamental changes are possible. In fact, some of the impressive achievements have been in regions or areas that once were lagging. All over the world people are increasingly engaged in influencing the processes that shape their lives. Human ingenuity and creativity have initiated technological revolutions and translated them into the way we work, think and behave.

Gender equality and women's empowerment are now mainstream dimensions of any development discourse. And there is no denying that with an intention to overcome them constructively, space for discussions and dialogues on issues once taboo is slowly opening—as with sexual orientation; discriminations faced by lesbian, gay, bisexual, transgender and intersex people; and female genital mutilation and cutting.

Awareness of sustainability has been growing. The 2030 Agenda and the Paris Agreement on climate change are prime examples. They also show that under the rumble of debate and gridlock, a nascent global consensus is emerging around many global challenges and ensuring a sustainable world for future generations.

> What humanity has achieved over 25 years gives hope that fundamental changes are possible. Some of the impressive achievements have been in regions or areas that once were lagging

Closing the human
development gaps
is critical, but so is
ensuring that future
generations have
the same, or even
better, opportunities

All these promising developments give the world the hope that things can be changed and that transformations are possible. The world has less than 15 years to achieve its inspirational agenda to leave no one behind. Closing the human development gaps is critical, but so is ensuring that future generations have the same, or even better, opportunities.

And fulfilling the 2030 Agenda is a critical step towards enabling all people to reach their full potential. In fact, the human development approach and the 2030 Agenda have three common analytical links (figure 2):

• Both are anchored in universalism—the human development approach by emphasizing the enhancement of freedoms for every human being and the 2030 Agenda by concentrating on leaving no one behind.

• Both share the same fundamental areas of focus—eradicating extreme poverty, ending hunger, reducing inequality, ensuring gender equality and so on.

• Both have sustainability as the core principle.

The links among the human development approach, the 2030 Agenda and the Sustainable Development Goals are mutually reinforcing in three ways. First, the 2030 Agenda can see what analytical parts of the human development approach strengthen its conceptual foundation. Similarly, the human development approach can review the narrative of the 2030 Agenda and examine parts that can enrich it.

Second, the Sustainable Development Goal indicators can use the human development indicators in assessing progress towards the Sustainable Development Goals. Similarly, the human development approach can supplement the Sustainable Development Goal indicators with additional indicators.

Third, the Human Development Reports can be an extremely powerful advocacy instrument for the 2030 Agenda and the Sustainable Development Goals. And the Sustainable Development Goals can be a good platform

FIGURE 2

Analytical links between the human development approach and the 2030 Agenda

Source: Human Development Report Office.

for the greater visibility of the human development approach and the Human Development Report for the coming years.

Yet basic deprivations abound among various groups of people

One person in nine in the world is hungry, and one in three is malnourished.[7] About 15 million girls a year marry before age 18, one every two seconds.[8] Worldwide 18,000 people a day die because of air pollution,[9] and HIV infects 2 million people a year.[10] Every minute an average of 24 people are displaced from their home.[11]

Such basic deprivations are common among various groups. Women and girls, ethnic minorities, indigenous peoples, persons with disabilities, migrants—all are deprived in the basic dimensions of human development.

In all regions women have a longer life expectancy than do men, and in most regions girls' expected years of schooling are similar to those of boys. Yet in all regions women consistently have, on average, a lower Human Development Index (HDI) value than do men. The largest difference is in South Asia, where the female HDI value is 20 percent lower than the male HDI value.

There are group-based disadvantages, as shown in Nepal. Brahmans and Chhetris have the highest HDI value (0.538), followed by Janajatis (0.482), Dalits (0.434) and Muslims (0.422). The greatest inequalities are in education, with pronounced long-lasting effects on capabilities.[12]

Shortfalls in basic human development among various groups often persist because of discrimination. Women are particularly discriminated against with respect to opportunities and end up with disadvantaged outcomes (figure 3). In many societies women are discriminated against with respect to productive assets, such as the right to land and property. As a result only 10–20 percent of landholders in developing countries are women.[13]

Ethnic minorities and other groups are often excluded from education, employment and administrative and political positions, resulting in poverty and higher vulnerability to crime, including human trafficking. In 2012, 51 percent of ethnic minorities in Viet Nam were living in multidimensional poverty, compared with only 17 percent of Kinh or Hoa people, the ethnic majority.[14]

More than 370 million self-identified indigenous peoples in 70 countries also face discrimination and exclusion in the legal framework, in access to education in their own language and in access to land, water, forests and intellectual property rights.[15]

More than a billion people are estimated to live with some form of disability and are among the most marginalized in most societies. They face stigma, discrimination and inaccessible physical and virtual environments.[16]

Today 244 million people live outside their home countries.[17] Many are economic refugees hoping to enhance their livelihoods and send money back home. But many migrants, especially the world's 65 million forcibly displaced people, face extreme conditions—lacking jobs, income and access to health care and social services beyond emergency humanitarian assistance. They often face harassment, animosity and violence in host countries.

Human deprivations are also dynamic. Moving above the low human development threshold does not necessarily ensure that people will be protected from emerging and future threats. Even where people have more choices than before, there may be threats to the security of these choices.

Epidemics, violence, climate change and natural disasters can quickly undermine the progress of those who have moved out of poverty. They can also generate new deprivations. Millions of people around the world are exposed to climate-related natural disasters, droughts and associated food insecurities, subsisting on degraded land.

The deprivations of the current generation can carry over to the next generation. Parents' education, health and income can greatly affect the opportunities available to their children.

Substantial barriers persist for universal human development

Groups of people who remain deprived may be the most difficult to reach—geographically, politically, socially and economically. Surmounting the barriers may require greater

> Human deprivations are dynamic. Moving above the low human development threshold does not necessarily ensure that people will be protected from emerging and future threats

FIGURE 3

Women are discriminated against with respect to opportunities

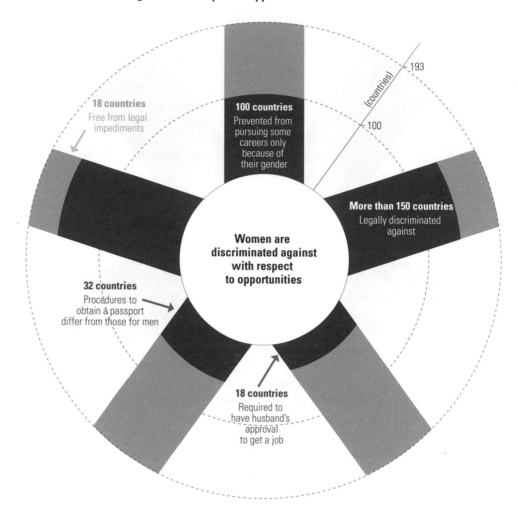

18 countries
Free from legal
impediments

100 countries
Prevented from
pursuing some
careers only
because of
their gender

193

(countries)

100

More than 150 countries
Legally discriminated
against

Women are
discriminated against
with respect
to opportunities

32 countries
Procedures to
obtain a passport
differ from those for men

18 countries
Required to
have husband's
approval
to get a job

Source: Human Development Report Office.

Realizing universal
human development
in practice is possible,
but the key barriers
and forms of exclusion
must first be overcome

fiscal resources and development assistance, continuing gains in technology and better data for monitoring and evaluation.

But some barriers are deeply embedded in social and political identities and relationships —such as blatant violence, discriminatory laws, exclusionary social norms, imbalances in political participation and unequal distribution of opportunities. Overcoming them will require putting empathy, tolerance and moral commitments to global justice and sustainability at the centre of individual and collective choices. People should consider themselves part of a cohesive global whole rather than a fragmented terrain of rival groups and interests.

Moving towards universal human development requires an awareness and understanding

of the drivers and dynamics of how groups are marginalized, which inevitably varies across countries and regions. Realizing universal human development in practice is possible, but the key barriers and forms of exclusion must first be overcome (figure 4).

Whether intentional or unintentional, exclusion can have the same results—some people will be more deprived than others, and not all people will have equal opportunities to realize their full potential. Group inequalities reflect divisions that are socially constructed and sustained because they establish a basis for unequal access to valued outcomes and scarce resources. The dimensions and mechanisms of exclusion are also dynamic, as are the characteristics groups use as a basis for exclusion.

FIGURE 4

Barriers to universalism

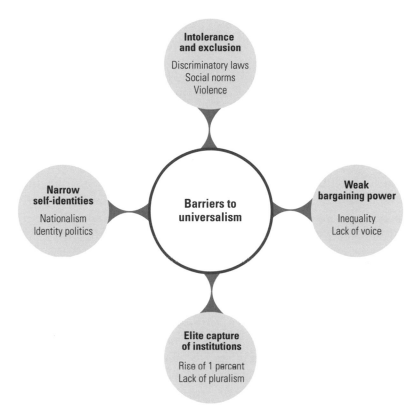

Source: Human Development Report Office.

Legal and political institutions can be used and abused to perpetuate group divisions. An extreme case relates to the rights of the lesbian, gay, bisexual, transgender and intersex community in the 73 countries and five territories where same-sex sexual acts are illegal.[18] Laws are discriminatory in other cases because they prevent certain groups from access to services or opportunities.

Some social norms can be helpful for harmonious coexistence within societies, but others can be discriminatory, prejudicial and exclusive. Social norms in many countries reduce the choices and opportunities for women and girls, who are typically responsible for more than three-quarters of unpaid family work.[19] The presence of women as customers in cafés or restaurants may also be discouraged, and in some cases it is taboo for women to travel in public without being accompanied by a man.[20]

Perhaps the most direct mechanism of exclusion is violence. Motivations include consolidating political power, safeguarding the well-being of elites, controlling the distribution of resources, seizing territory and resources and favouring ideologies based on the supremacy of one identity and set of values.

The top 1 percent of the global wealth distribution holds 46 percent of the world's wealth.[21] Inequalities in income influence inequalities in other dimensions of well-being, and vice versa. Given today's inequality, excluded groups are in a weak position to initiate the transformation of institutions. They lack agency and voice and so have little political leverage to influence policy and legislation through traditional means.

At a time when global action and collaboration are imperative, self-identities are narrowing. Social and political movements linked to identity, whether nationalist or ethnopolitical, seem to be getting stronger. Brexit is one of the most recent examples of a retreat to nationalism when individuals feel alienated in a changing world.

Inequalities in income influence inequalities in other dimensions of well-being, and vice versa

Intolerance of others in all its forms—legal, social or coercive—is antithetical to human development and to principles of universalism.

Human development for everyone calls for refocusing some analytical issues

Human development involves expanding choices, which determine who we are and what we do. Several factors underlie these choices: the wide range of options that we have to choose from—our capabilities; the social and cognitive constraints and social norms and influences that shape our values and choices; our own empowerment and the agency we exercise individually and as part of groups in shaping our options and opportunities; and the mechanisms that exist to resolve competing claims in ways that are fair and conducive to realizing human potential.

The human development approach provides a systematic way to articulate these ideas. It can be especially powerful in illuminating the interplay among factors that can operate to the disadvantage of individuals and groups in different contexts.

Human rights are the bedrock of human development. Human rights offer a useful perspective for analysing human development. Duty holders support and enhance human development and are accountable for a social system's failures to deliver human development. These perspectives not only go beyond the minimal claims of human development, but can also serve as a powerful tool in seeking remedies.

The notion of human security should emphasize a deep understanding of threats, risks and crises for joint action in the human development and human security approaches. The challenges are to balance the shock-driven response to global threats and the promotion of a culture of prevention.

Voice and autonomy, as parts of freedom of agency and freedom of well-being, are integral to human development. The ability to deliberate, participate in public debates and be agents in shaping one's life and environment is fundamental to human development for everyone. The primary focus of the human development

approach has largely been on the freedom of well-being. But as well-being was realized, emphasizing freedom of agency has become more important.

Human development is a matter of promoting not only the freedoms of individuals, but also the freedoms of groups or collectives. For the most marginalized and most deprived people collective agency can be much more powerful than individual agency. An individual is unlikely to achieve much alone, and power may be realized only through collective action.

Identity influences agency and autonomy. People have the liberty of choosing their identities, an important liberty to recognize, value and defend. Individuals deserve options in choosing among different identities that they value. Recognizing and respecting such options are preconditions for peaceful coexistence in multiethnic and multicultural societies.

Three identity issues have implications for universal human development. First, the space for multiple identities is more limited among people who are marginalized, and those people may lack the freedom to choose the identity they value. Second, the insistence on a single irrefutable identity and the denial of reasoning and choice in selecting identities may lead to extremism and violence and thus pose a threat to human development. Third, identity groups compete for limited economic and political resources and power, and deprived and marginalized people lose out. In most cases society's values and norms go against the most disadvantaged, with preferences often formed by social traditions of privilege and subordination. But changing values and norms can transform this bias against disadvantaged people.

Freedoms are interdependent, and such interdependence may be reinforcing. For example, a worker exercising the freedom to green the workspace may contribute to the freedom of co-workers to have clean air. But the freedom of one may also impinge on the freedom of others. A wealthy person has the freedom to construct a multistory house, but that may deprive a poor neighbour of sunlight and an airy environment.

Limiting the freedom of others may not be the intended consequence of exercising one's freedom, but some actions that curb others' freedom may be deliberate. Rich and powerful groups may try to curtail the freedom of others.

Voice and autonomy, as parts of freedom of agency and freedom of well-being, are integral to human development

This is reflected in the affluence bias of the policy options in many economies, in the way the legal system is built and in the way institutions work. All societies have to make tradeoffs and, following reasoned debate, determine the principles for settling issues, dynamically, as they develop and realize a more just society.

Sustainable development is an issue of social justice. It relates to intergenerational equity—the freedoms of future generations and those of today. The human development approach thus considers sustainability to be a matter of distributional equity, both within and across generations.

Specific assessment perspectives can ensure that everyone is reached

Development practitioners agree in principle that enabling all people to benefit from progress in human development demands disaggregated data on such characteristics as region, gender, rural–urban location, socioeconomic status, race and ethnicity. But they are less clear about ensuring the availability of such data. Determining which lines of disaggregation are needed to reveal inequalities along particular dimensions can be difficult without already having some understanding of society's processes of exclusion and marginalization. And political, social and cultural sensitivities can promote exclusions and deprivations.

Disaggregating data by gender is crucial for gender equality and women's empowerment. This is precisely why the 2030 Agenda, particularly Sustainable Development Goal 5 on achieving gender equality and empowering all women and girls, focuses on targets that facilitate gender-disaggregated data.

Even though freedom of agency is an integral part of human development, the human development approach has traditionally focused more on well-being than on agency. Just look at the HDI. But agency is inherently more difficult to measure than well-being.

The relationship between freedom of well-being and freedom of agency is generally positive. This supports the notion that the two aspects of human development, if not perfectly correlated, are complementary. In other words, societies might have achieved high average capabilities or well-being without achieving agency (in voice and autonomy).

Other measures of human well-being, such as the Social Progress Index,[22] the World Happiness Index[23] and the Better Life Index,[24] can usefully assess whether well-being is reaching everyone. Some countries also support subjective measures of well-being or happiness, as with Bhutan's Gross National Happiness Index.[25]

Human development for everyone also implies compiling and presenting data from innovative perspectives, such as real-time data and dashboards. A dashboard approach, in colour-coded tables, can show the levels and progress on various development indicators. It can thus be effective in assessing human well-being. It also implies an inclusive process bringing in more people to generate and disseminate information using new technologies.

In 2013 the UN Secretary-General's High-Level Panel on Sustainable Development called for a Data Revolution for sustainable development, with a new international initiative to improve the quality of information and statistics available to citizens.[26] Big Data describes the large volume of data—both structured and unstructured—that various organizations collect using new technologies and can bring new perspectives to traditional data and statistics.

FIGURE 5

National policies to care for those left out— a four-pronged strategy

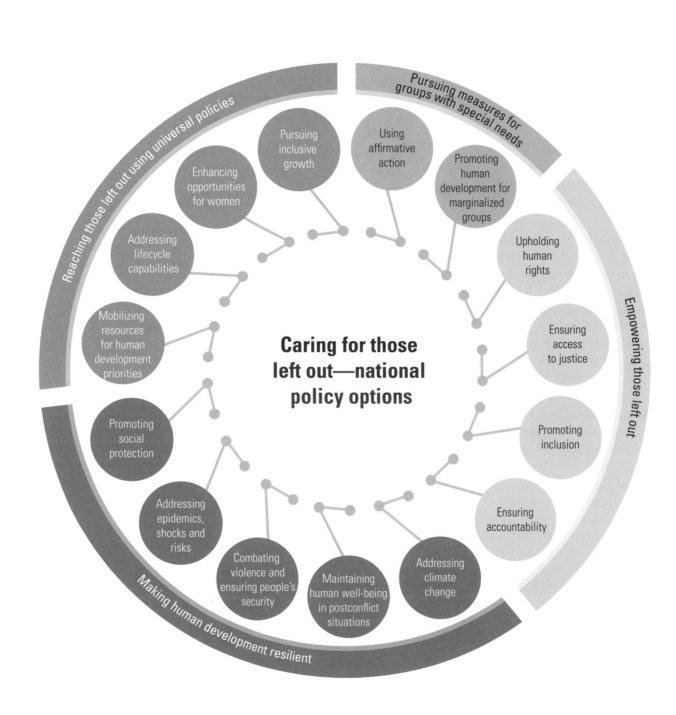

Reaching those left out using universal policies

Pursuing measures for groups with special needs

Empowering those left out

Making human development resilient

Caring for those left out—national policy options

- Pursuing inclusive growth
- Enhancing opportunities for women
- Addressing lifecycle capabilities
- Mobilizing resources for human development priorities
- Promoting social protection
- Addressing epidemics, shocks and risks
- Combating violence and ensuring people's security
- Maintaining human well-being in postconflict situations
- Addressing climate change
- Ensuring accountability
- Promoting inclusion
- Ensuring access to justice
- Upholding human rights
- Promoting human development for marginalized groups
- Using affirmative action

Key policy options

A four-pronged national policy approach can ensure that human development reaches everyone (figure 5). First, universal policies are needed to reach those left out, but practical universalism in policy is challenging. For example, a country may be committed to universal health care, but difficult geography may prevent it from establishing health care centres that are accessible to all localities. So universal human development policies need to be reoriented to reach those left out.

Second, even with the new focus on universal policies, some groups of people have special needs that would not be met. Their situations require specific measures and attention. For example, persons with disabilities require measures to ensure their mobility, participation and work opportunities.

Third, human development achieved does not mean human development sustained. Progress in human development may be slowed or even reversed because of shocks and vulnerabilities, with implications for people who have only achieved the basics in human development and for people who have yet to achieve the basics. Thus human development will have to be resilient.

Fourth, people who have been left out will have to be empowered, so that if policies and the relevant actors fail to deliver, these people can raise their voice, demand their rights and seek to redress the situation.

In a globalized world national policies for universal human development must be complemented and supplemented by a global system that is fair and that enriches human development.

Reaching those left out using universal policies

Appropriate reorientation of universal policies can narrow the deficits in human development among those left out. Essential to this are pursuing inclusive growth, enhancing opportunities for women, addressing lifecycle capabilities and mobilizing resources for human development priorities.

Pursuing inclusive growth

For human development to reach everyone, growth has to be inclusive, with four mutually supporting pillars—formulating an employment-led growth strategy, enhancing financial inclusion, investing in human development priorities and undertaking high-impact multidimensional interventions (win-win strategies).

An employment-led growth strategy would focus on such measures as removing barriers to employment-centred development, designing and implementing a conducive regulatory framework to tackle informal work, strengthening the links between large and small and medium-size enterprises, focusing on sectors where poor people live and work, especially rural areas, and adjusting the distribution of capital and labour in public spending to create jobs.

Several measures can enhance the financial inclusion of poor people, such as expanding banking services to disadvantaged and marginalized groups, relying on simple procedures and harnessing modern technology to promote financial inclusion. In Sub-Saharan Africa 12 percent of adults have mobile bank accounts, compared with 2 percent globally.[27]

Investments focused on human development priorities can provide low-cost but high-quality services and infrastructure to disadvantaged and marginalized groups.

Effective access to services by poor people requires affordability in cost and adaptability in cultural practices. In Nicaragua low-cost ultrasonogram machines, which can be carried on bicycles, are monitoring the health of pregnant women.[28] The presence of only male doctors in rural mother and child care centres would be a disincentive for women and girls to use the centres.

Some priority human development investments have strong and multiple impacts. Take school meal programmes, which provide multiple benefits: social protection by helping families educate their children and protect their children's food security in times of crisis; nutrition, because in poor countries

For human development to reach everyone, growth has to be inclusive

school meals are often the only regular and nutritious meal; and strong incentive to send children to school and keep children in schools. Evidence from Botswana, Cabo Verde, Côte d'Ivoire, Ghana, Kenya, Mali, Namibia, Nigeria and South Africa bears testimony to these benefits.[29]

Rural infrastructure, especially roads and electricity, is another area. Building rural roads reduces transport costs, connects rural farmers to markets, allows workers to move more freely and promotes access to schools and health care clinics. Electrification in rural communities in Guatemala and South Africa has helped increase employment among marginalized groups.[30]

Redistributing assets can also bring those left out into the growth process. Human capital is an asset, and differences in educational attainment prevent poor people from becoming part of the high-productivity growth process. Democratizing education, particularly tertiary education, would benefit people from poorer backgrounds.

Similarly, doing things locally may bring multiple development impacts. Providing autonomy to local governments in formulating and implementing local development plans allows the plans to reflect the aspirations of local communities. Fiscal decentralization can also empower local governments to collect their own revenues and depend less on central government grants. But if the local approach is to ensure human development for those left out, it will also require people's participation and greater local administrative capacity.

Enhancing opportunities for women

Gender equality and women's empowerment are fundamental dimensions of human development. Because half of humanity is not enjoying progress in human development, such development is not universal.

Investing in girls and women has multidimensional benefits—for example, if all girls in developing countries completed secondary education, the under-five mortality rate would be halved.[31] Women also need support to pursue higher education, particularly in science, technology, engineering and mathematics, where much future demand for high-level work will be.

Women also have to juggle paid employment outside the home and unpaid care work inside the home as well as balance their productive and reproductive roles. Flexible working arrangements and enlarged care options, including daycare centres, afterschool programmes, senior citizen homes and long-term care facilities, can help women broaden their choices.

Measures to encourage women's entrepreneurship include establishing a legal framework that removes barriers to women owning land, a critical asset, especially in agriculture. So land policies, legislation and administration need to be changed to accommodate women—and the new rules must be enforced.

The glass ceiling, though cracked in many places, is far from being shattered. Gender requirements in selection and recruitment and incentive mechanisms for retention can enhance women's representation in the public and private sectors. The criteria for promoting men and women into senior management positions should be identical, based on equal pay for equal work. Mentoring, coaching and sponsoring can empower women in the workplace by using successful female senior managers as role models and as sponsors.

Addressing lifecycle capabilities

To ensure that human development reaches those left out, building capabilities should be seen through a lifecycle lens as people face various types of vulnerabilities in different phases of their lives.

Sustained human development is more likely when all children can acquire the skills that match the opportunities open to young people joining the workforce. Much attention is correctly focused on what is needed to ensure that all children, everywhere, complete a full course of schooling, including preschooling. The World Bank has found that every dollar spent on preschool education earns $6–$17 in public benefits, in the form of a healthier and more productive workforce.[32] Ghana now includes two years of preschool in the education system. China is contemplating providing preschool facilities for all youngsters.[33]

Empowering young people requires actions on both the political and the economic fronts. On the political front at least 30 countries have

Because half of humanity is not enjoying progress in human development, such development is not universal

FIGURE 6

21st century skills

Ways of thinking	Tools for working	Ways of working	Skills for living in the world
Creativity Critical thinking Problemsolving Decisionmaking Learning	Information and communication technology Information literacy	Communication Collaboration	Citizenship Life and career Personal and social responsibility

Source: Human Development Report Office.

some kind of nonadult parliamentary structure, nationally or in cities, villages or schools.[34] So young people's opinions in various forms of participation—in government-sponsored advisory roles, youth parliaments and roundtable discussions—are being integrated into policymaking.

On the economic front creating new opportunities for young people and preparing young people with the skills they need to take advantage of the opportunities are required. More than one third of the skills important in today's economy will have changed by 2020.[35] Acquiring skills for the 21st century has to be part of lifelong learning of the four C's—critical thinking, collaborating, creating and communicating (figure 6).

For the aged and infirm, key measures include establishing a combination of public and private provisioning of elder care, strengthening social protection for older people through basic noncontributory social pensions (as in Brazil)[36] and creating opportunities for the older people to work where they can contribute, including teaching children, care work and voluntary work.

Mobilizing resources for human development priorities

Options for mobilizing resources for human development priorities range from creating fiscal space to using climate finance, and from cutting subsidies not beneficial to poor people to using resources efficiently.

Fiscal space has four pillars: official development assistance, domestic revenue, deficit financing (through domestic and external borrowing) and variations in spending priorities and efficiency. The choice of which pillar to use to increase or rebuild fiscal space depends mainly on country characteristics. In 2009 Ghana considered improving revenue collection to increase the health budget, even though the share of the total government budget allocated to health was stable.[37]

Consolidating and streamlining remittances could make them a funding source for human development priorities. Remittance banks can be set up in countries where the flows are large, such as Bangladesh, Jordan and the Philippines. Easy and transparent legal remittance-sending mechanisms can be put in place in consultation with host countries.

In the least developed countries, where emissions are low, climate finance can expand climate-resilient livelihoods, improve water and sanitation systems and ensure food security. These investments go beyond climate adaptation programmes in the narrow sense and focus more on achieving human development by increasing the long-term climate resilience of economies and societies.

Ending subsidies for fossil fuels can free resources for human development. And efficiency in resource use is equivalent to generating additional resources. For example, telemedicine can deliver medical advice and treatment options to patients irrespective of their location—and reduce the cost of service provision.

Options for mobilizing resources for human development priorities range from creating fiscal space to using climate finance, and from cutting subsidies not beneficial to poor people to using resources efficiently

Pursuing measures for groups with special needs

Because some social groups (ethnic minorities, indigenous peoples, persons with disabilities) are systematically discriminated against and thereby left out, specific measures are needed so they may achieve equitable outcomes in human development.

Using affirmative action

Affirmative action has been important in redressing historical and persistent group disparities and group discriminations. It may take the form of enrolment quotas for ethnic minorities in tertiary education or preferential treatment of female entrepreneurs in obtaining subsidized credit through the banking system.

Affirmative action has made a difference in women's representation in parliament. Following the Beijing Declaration and Platform for Action at the United Nations Fourth World Conference in 1995, some countries adopted a gender quota to increase the proportion of seats held by women, providing confidence and incentives for women to run for elected office and win. Rwanda, where women account for 64 percent of representatives in the House of Deputies, is a shining example.[38]

Promoting human development for marginalized groups

Despite the great diversity in identities and needs, marginalized groups such as ethnic minorities, indigenous peoples, persons with disabilities, people living with HIV and AIDS, and lesbian, gay, bisexual, transgender and intersex individuals often face similar constraints, such as discrimination, social stigma and risk of being harmed. But each group also has special needs that must be met if they are to benefit from progress in human development.

For some vulnerable groups, such as ethnic minorities or persons with disabilities, anti-discrimination and other rights are guaranteed in constitutions and other legislation. Similarly,

special provisions often protect indigenous peoples, as in Canada and New Zealand.[39] Yet in many cases effective mechanisms for implementation and full equality in law are lacking. National human rights commissions or commissions for specific groups can provide oversight and ensure that the rights of these groups are not violated. And overcoming the discrimination and abuse of members of the lesbian, gay, bisexual, transgender and intersex community requires a legal framework that can defend their human rights.

Participation in the processes that shape the lives of disadvantaged groups needs to be ensured. For example, quotas for ethnic minorities and representation of indigenous peoples in parliaments are ways to help them raise their concerns. Some indigenous peoples have their own parliaments or councils, which are consultative bodies. New Zealand has the longest history of indigenous representation in a national legislature.[40]

For persons with disabilities, inclusion and accommodation are critical to empowering them to live independently, find employment and contribute to society. Specific vocational training initiatives should be undertaken to develop their skills. Increasing access to productive resources, such as finance for self-employment, and providing information over mobile devices can help them in self-employment. Appropriate infrastructure including technology can enable persons with disabilities to be more mobile.

Migrants and refugees are vulnerable in host countries, and national actions are needed to address the new nature of migration and its evolution. Countries should pass laws that protect refugees, particularly women and children, a big part of the refugee population and the main victims. Transit and destination countries should provide essential public goods in catering to the displaced, such as schooling refugee children. And destination countries should formulate temporary work policies and provisions for refugees.

Marginalized groups often face similar constraints, such as discrimination. But each group also has special needs that must be met if they are to benefit from progress in human development

Making human development resilient

Progress in human development often stagnates or dissipates if threatened by shocks —such as global epidemics, climate change, natural disasters, violence and conflicts. Vulnerable and marginalized people are major victims.

Addressing epidemics, shocks and risks

Much progress has been made in scaling up antiretroviral therapy, but 18 million people living with HIV still do not have access to it.[41] Young women, who may be exposed to gender-based violence and have limited access to information and health care, are among the most exposed, as are prisoners, sex workers, drug users and transgender people. Still, there have been successes in reducing infection rates among women and children and in expanding their access to treatment.

In an increasingly interconnected world, being prepared for possible health crises has become a priority. The recent epidemic of the Zika virus provides a good example. Countries have reacted in different ways to the spread of the Zika virus. Countries with an ongoing virus transmission, such as Colombia, the Dominican Republic, Ecuador and Jamaica, have advised women to postpone pregnancy.[42] In Brazil a new mosquito strain was released to try to fight the Zika virus, and members of the armed forces were sent across the country to educate people about mosquito control and to warn them of the risks linked to the virus.[43]

More recently, the revised strategic response plan designed by the World Health Organization in collaboration with more than 60 partners focuses on research, detection, prevention, and care and support.[44]

Building disaster resilience into policies and programmes at all levels can reduce the risk and mitigate the effects of disasters, particularly for poor people. Innovative programmes are at the heart of the Sendai Framework for Disaster Risk Reduction endorsed by the UN General Assembly following the 2015 Third UN World Conference on Disaster Risk Reduction.

Combating violence and ensuring people's security

The drivers of violence are complex and thus call for a multipronged approach that includes promoting the rule of law based on fairness and zero tolerance for violence; strengthening local governments, community policing and law enforcement personnel in hotspots of violence; and developing response and support services to address violence and its victims.

Viable policy options include developing high-quality infrastructure, improving public transit in high-crime neighbourhoods, building better housing in the poorest areas of cities and providing socioeconomic alternatives to violence, particularly to young people, engaging them in strengthening social cohesion.

Maintaining human well-being in postconflict situations

On the political front transformation of institutions is key. It would ensure people's security through community policing, pursuing rapid governance actions (such as faster caseload processing) and reintegrating ex-combatants by disarming and demobilizing them.

On the economic front reviving basic social services, supporting work in the health sector to cover many goals, initiating public works programmes and formulating and implementing targeted community-based programmes (such as makeshift schools so that children do not lose access education) are key for moving forward on the development continuum.

Addressing climate change

Climate change jeopardizes the lives and livelihoods of poor and marginalized people. Addressing it requires three initial policy measures. Putting a price on carbon pollution —through an emissions trading system or a carbon tax—brings down emissions and drives investment into cleaner options. Approximately 40 countries and more than 20 cities, states and provinces use carbon pricing.[45]

Taxing fuel, removing fossil fuel subsidies and incorporating "social cost of carbon" regulations

Progress in human development often stagnates or dissipates if threatened by shocks. Vulnerable and marginalized people are major victims

are more indirect ways of accurately pricing carbon. By phasing out harmful fossil fuel subsidies, countries can reallocate their spending to where it is most needed and most effective, including targeted support for poor people.

Getting prices right is only one part of the equation. Cities are growing fast, particularly in developing countries. With careful planning in transport and land use and the establishment of energy efficiency standards, cities can avoid locking in unsustainable patterns. They can open access to jobs and opportunities for poor people, while reducing air pollution.

Increasing energy efficiency and renewable energy is crucial. The Sustainable Energy for All initiative sets out three goals for 2030: achieve universal access to modern energy, double the rate of improvement in energy efficiency and double the share of renewable energy in the global energy mix. In many countries developing utility-scale renewable energy is now cheaper than, or on par with, fossil-fuel plants.[46]

Climate-smart agricultural techniques help farmers increase their productivity and resilience to the impacts of climate change while creating carbon sinks that reduce net emissions. Forests, the world's lungs, absorb carbon and store it in soils, trees and foliage.

Focusing on the poverty–environment nexus, which is complex but critical for marginalized people, is also important. Poor people bear the brunt of environmental damage, even though they seldom create it. Policies that protect community commons (such as common forests), ensure the rights and entitlements of poor people and provide renewable energy to poor people would improve biodiversity on which poor people's lives depend and reverse the downward spiral of poverty and environmental damage.

Promoting social protection

Policy options to expand social protection to marginalized groups include pursuing social protection programmes, combining social protection with appropriate employment strategies and providing a living income.

A social protection floor can secure minimum health care, pensions and other social rights for everyone. Creating jobs through a public works programme can reduce poverty through income generation, build physical infrastructure and protect poor people against shocks. The Rural Employment Opportunities for Public Assets programme in Bangladesh is a prime example.[47]

A guaranteed basic income for citizens, independent of the job market, is also a policy option that countries (such as Finland[48]) are experimenting with as an instrument for social protection, particularly for disadvantaged groups.

Empowering those left out

If policies do not deliver well-being to marginalized and vulnerable people and if institutions fail to ensure that people are not left out, there must be instruments and redress mechanisms so that these people can claim their rights. They have to be empowered by upholding human rights, ensuring access to justice, promoting inclusion and ensuring accountability.

Upholding human rights

Human development for all requires strong national human rights institutions with the capacity, mandate and will to address discrimination and ensure the protection of human rights. Human rights commissions and ombudsmen handle complaints about rights abuses, educate civil society and states about human rights and recommend legal reforms.

But state commitments to upholding these rights vary, national institutions have different implementation capacities, and accountability mechanisms are sometimes missing. Institutional shortcomings aside, treating development as a human right has been instrumental in reducing deprivations in some dimensions and contexts.

In an integrated world the state-centred model of accountability must be extended to the obligations of nonstate actors and to the state's obligations beyond national borders. Human rights cannot be realized universally without well established domestic mechanisms and stronger international action.

People will have to be empowered by upholding human rights, ensuring access to justice, promoting inclusion and ensuring accountability

Ensuring access to justice

Access to justice is the ability of people to seek and obtain remedy through formal or informal judicial institutions.

Poor and disadvantaged people face immense obstacles, including their lack of awareness and legal knowledge, compounded by structural and personal alienation. Poor people lack adequate access to public services, which are often expensive and cumbersome and have few resources, personnel and facilities. Police stations and courts may not be available in remote areas, and poor people can rarely afford the cost of legal processes. Quasi-judicial mechanisms may also be inaccessible or prejudicial.

Obstacles to justice for indigenous peoples and for racial and ethnic minorities stem from their historically subordinate status and from sociopolitical systems that reinforce bias in the legal framework and the justice system.

Promoting inclusion

Human development for everyone requires inclusion of all in the development discourse and process.

New global forms and methods of organization and communication are facilitated by technology and social media. They have mobilized grassroots activism and brought in people and groups to voice their opinions, as through cyberactivism. Improving the quality and scope of citizen engagement in public institutions involves civic education, capacity development and political dialogue.

Ensuring accountability

Accountability is central to ensuring that human development reaches everyone, especially in protecting the rights of those excluded.

One major instrument for ensuring accountability of social institutions is the right to information. Since the 1990s more than 50 countries have adopted new instruments that protect the right to information, often due to democratic transitions and to the active participation of civil society organizations in public life.[49]

The right to information requires the freedom to use that information to form public opinions, call governments to account, participate in decisionmaking and exercise the right to freedom of expression. Information and communication technology is increasingly being used to ensure accountability.

Participatory exercises to hold state institutions accountable, such as public expenditure tracking surveys, citizen report cards, score cards, social audits and community monitoring, have all been used to develop direct accountability relationships between service users and service providers.

Global institutional reforms and a fairer multilateral system would help attain human development for everyone

We live in a globalized world where human development outcomes are determined not only by actions at the national level, but also by the structures, events and work at the global level. The shortcomings in the current architecture of global systems pose challenges for human development on three fronts. The distributional consequences of inequitable globalization have promoted the progress of some segments of the population, leaving poor and vulnerable people out. Globalization is also making those left out economically insecure. And people are suffering in lingering conflicts. In short, all these undermine and limit national efforts and pose as barriers to human development for everyone.

Global institutional reforms should encompass the broader areas of regulation of global markets, the governance of multilateral institutions and the strengthening of global civil society with each area reflecting specific actions.

Stabilizing the global economy

Reforms should focus on regulating currency transactions and capital flows and coordinating macroeconomic policies and regulations. One option is a multilateral tax on cross-border

> Global institutional reforms should encompass the broader areas of regulation of global markets, the governance of multilateral institutions and the strengthening of global civil society

transactions; another is the use of capital controls by individual countries.

Applying fair trade and investment rules

The international agenda should be to set rules to expand trade in goods, services and knowledge to favour human development and the Sustainable Development Goals. The key reforms to advance this agenda include finalizing the World Trade Organization's Doha Round, reforming the global intellectual property rights regime and reforming the global investor protection regime.

Adopting a fair system of migration

Measures are needed to strengthen strategies that protect the rights of and promote the opportunities for migrants, to establish a global mechanism to coordinate economic (voluntary) migration and to facilitate guaranteed asylum for forcibly displaced people. The International Organization for Migration officially joined the UN System in September 2016, and its work and actions are expected to expand and advance.

Assuring greater equity and legitimacy of multilateral institutions

The time has come to examine the representation, transparency and accountability of multilateral institutions. Some policy options to move these institutions towards greater equity and legitimacy are increasing the voice of developing countries in multilateral organizations, improving transparency in appointing heads of multilateral organizations and increasing coordination and effectiveness to achieve people-centred goals.

Coordinating taxes and monitoring finance globally

A move towards a global automatic exchange of information (such as a global financial register) would facilitate the work of tax and regulatory authorities tracking income and detecting illicit financial flows, which may be mobilized for human development. This would require increasing technical capacity of countries to process information and implement active policies against tax evasion, tax avoidance and illicit flows.

Making the global economy sustainable

Sustainable development activities at the national level must be complemented with global actions. Curbing global warming is possible. Coordinated global action has worked well in the past, as in moves to halt ozone depletion in the 1990s.

Continuing advocacy and communication on the need to address climate change and protect the environment are essential to gather support from various stakeholders (including multilateral development banks). The recently created New Development Bank has explicitly committed to giving priority to clean energy projects.

Ensuring well funded multilateralism and cooperation

Multilateral and regional development banks can do more to address several challenges of globalization. Increasing official development assistance from traditional donors, expanding the participation of developing countries through South–South and triangular cooperation, and exploring innovative options for financing would be useful.

Globally defending people's security

From a human development perspective, assistance in human emergencies and crises is an ethical obligation. In such cases, proposed solutions include restructuring current mechanisms towards prevention in addition to short-term responses to shocks, prioritizing field operations and coordinating better internally and externally with civil society and the private sector.

Promoting greater and better participation of global civil society

Tapping civil society's potential requires expanding mechanisms for it to participate in multilateral institutions; enhancing the transparency and accountability of multilateral institutions; promoting and supporting inclusive global civil society networks focused on such groups as women, young people and ethnic minorities; increasing the free flow of information and knowledge through active transparency mechanisms; and protecting the work of international investigative journalism.

> The time has come to examine the representation, transparency and accountability of multilateral institutions

An action agenda

Human development for everyone is not a dream; it is a realizable goal. We can build on what we have achieved. We can explore new possibilities to overcome challenges. We can attain what once seemed unattainable, for what seem to be challenges today can be overcome tomorrow. Realizing our hopes is within our reach. His Excellency Juan Manuel Santos, President of Colombia and the 2016 Nobel Peace Prize Laureate confirms the hope of attaining a peaceful and prosperous world (see special contribution).

The 2030 Agenda and the Sustainable Development Goals are critical steps towards human development for everyone. Building on its analysis and findings, the Report suggests a five-point action agenda to ensure human development for everyone. The actions cover policy issues and global commitments.

Identifying those who face human development deficits and mapping where they are

Identifying those who have been left out of the progress in human development and mapping their locations are essential for useful advocacy and effective policymaking. Such mapping can help development activists demand action and guide policymakers in formulating and implementing policies to improve the well-being of marginalized and vulnerable people.

Pursuing a range of available policy options with coherence

Human development for everyone requires a multipronged set of national policy options: reaching those left out using universal policies, pursuing measures for groups with special-needs, making human development resilient and empowering those left out.

Country situations differ, so policy options have to be tailored to each country. Policies in every country have to be pursued in a coherent way through multistakeholder engagement, local and subnational adaptations and horizontal (across silos) and vertical alignment (for international and global consistency).

Closing the gender gap

Gender equality and women's empowerment are fundamental dimensions of human development. Gender gaps exist in capabilities as well as opportunities, and progress is still too slow for realizing the full potential of half of humanity.

At a historic gathering in New York in September 2015 some 80 world leaders committed to end discrimination against women by 2030 and announced concrete and measurable actions to kickstart rapid changes.[50] Now is the time to act on what has been promised and agreed.

Implementing the Sustainable Development Goals and other global agreements

The Sustainable Development Goals, critical in their own right, are also crucial for human development for everyone; the 2030 Agenda and the human development approach are mutually reinforcing. Further, achieving the Sustainable Development Goals is an important step for all human beings to realize their full potential in life.

The historic Paris Agreement on climate change is the first to consider both developed and developing countries in a common framework, urging them all to make their best efforts and reinforce their commitments in the coming years. The UN Summit for Refugees in September 2016 made bold commitments to address the issues facing refugees and migrants and to prepare for future challenges. The international community, national governments and all other parties must ensure that the agreements are honoured, implemented and monitored.

Working towards reforms in the global system

To move towards a fairer global system, the agenda for global institutional reforms should focus on global markets and their regulation, on the governance of multilateral institutions and on the strengthening of global civil society. That reform agenda should be advocated vigorously and consistently by bolstering public advocacy, building alliances among stakeholders and pushing through the agenda for reform.

The 2030 Agenda and the Sustainable Development Goals are critical steps towards human development for everyone

Peace in Colombia is also peace for the world

In Colombia we are more determined than ever to end the longest running and only remaining internal armed conflict in the Americas.

Colombians were divided over the agreement that was negotiated between the Government and the FARC guerrillas. And so, we undertook efforts to reach a new peace accord that would dispel doubts and garner nationwide support. Almost simultaneously we announced the beginning of peace talks with the ELN, the last remaining guerrillas. We hope this will bring a definitive end to the armed conflict in our country.

For five decades the war has had a very high price for Colombia and has, undoubtedly, hurt the nation's prospect. A study by Los Andes University estimates that households who have been victims of forced displacement and violence saw their income reduced by half. This is exacerbated when one considers that these people are likely to have difficulty recovering and are at risk of living in conditions of chronic poverty.

Beyond the effect on our economy, the greatest impact of the war falls on 250,000 or more casualties—and their families—and the 8 million victims and internally displaced people. Every life lost, as well as each and every one of the personal and family tragedies of those who were affected by the armed conflict and survived, both saddens us and also strengthens our commitment.

We agree with the spirit of this Human Development Report, which is that the "wealth of human lives" must be considered before the wealth of economies when judging the prosperity of society. In that sense we understand that peace is a basic condition for enriching the lives of Colombians. And I am referring to a broader concept of peace that transcends the end of the conflict and brings harmony and well-being.

A family with insufficient income does not live in peace, nor does a family without decent housing or access to education. This is why we have focused on fostering economic growth that benefits everyone and that reduces social gaps.

The progress we have made to date is in line with the Sustainable Development Goals that Colombia championed and began working towards, even before they were adopted by the United Nations. Indeed, we were the first country to include these goals in our National Development Plan.

Thanks to our early efforts, we have been able to reap the benefits of our work ahead of schedule. For example, over the past five years we have reduced extreme poverty by nearly half—from 14.4 percent to 7.9 percent —a very significant achievement that allows us to envisage its eradication by 2025, if not sooner.

That jump, beyond the numbers, means that millions of Colombians have improved their quality of life. We are certain of this because, together with traditional income-based measures of poverty, we have pioneered the Multidimensional Poverty Index, which assesses other variables, such as access to public services or the type of family housing. Today, without a doubt, more Colombians have a better life.

We have also made early progress in the quality of education— another of the Sustainable Development Goals. Not only do all children and young people study in public schools for free, we are increasing their class hours and improving the quality of learning through different programmes and initiatives. As a result of these efforts, our students have significantly improved the average scores on tests that measure their knowledge and skills.

With our focus on peacebuilding, the emphasis on education is perhaps the best example of what we can do in this new phase without the burden of the armed conflict. For the first time ever, the education budget is greater than that for security and defence, which is consistent with our goal to become the most educated country in Latin America by the year 2025.

Peace, equity and education are three areas that Colombians have been deprived of historically. Peace, equity and education have been the three pillars of our main efforts over the past few years.

However, if our goal is to achieve "human development for everyone," our efforts cannot stop here: Climate change is the greatest threat ever faced by humankind.

In this regard Colombia has decided to play an active part in tackling this phenomenon. As guardians of one of the most biodiverse regions on the planet, with exceptional forests, water resources and soil fertility, we have an enormous responsibility to both Colombians and the world.

The concept of "green growth" is part of our economic development model and has been mainstreamed into all sectors of the economy. We are convinced that growth and environmental sustainability are perfectly compatible. In addition, the demarcation of our *paramos* (moorland ecosystems) and the declaration of protected areas—which by 2018 should reach 19 million hectares, an area larger than Uruguay—are proof of our resolve.

Under the Paris Agreement on climate change, Colombia has set out a goal: to reduce projected greenhouse gas emissions by 20 percent by 2030. And we have already begun to take decisive action to achieve this ambitious objective: We have presented a bill to Congress for the creation of a carbon tax on various fuels. We will be the first Latin American country—and one of the first in the world—to apply such a measure. With this single initiative we expect to meet half of our commitment established in the Paris Climate Change Conference.

Peace—understood, as I mentioned before, in the broader sense of well-being and harmony—opens the door to the possibility of a viable world for future generations, one in which their very existence is not threatened by global warming. We are proud to confirm that these efforts, in addition to the end of the armed conflict, improved education and increased equity, are a contribution to the world.

With the end to the conflict, people from around the globe can enjoy the natural wonders and tourism in Colombia, which had been restricted for decades—even for Colombians themselves. Also, foreign business people can discover new opportunities in sectors and regions that were previously off limits because of violence.

In terms of equity we are strengthening the middle class that will create an opportunity for investors in search of new markets. And with quality education we are preparing a new generation that in the future will be able to put its skills and knowledge into practice anywhere in the world.

"Human development for everyone" is a commitment that transcends our country, and we want our work to impact and enrich the lives of citizens from other nations. Similarly, we feel that the support of the international community has had a positive impact on Colombians. We are convinced that, in a spirit of solidarity and collaboration, we will continue working together, Colombians and non-Colombians, to build peace in Colombia and peace for the rest of the world.

Juan Manuel Santos
President of Colombia and 2016 Nobel Peace Prize Laureate

*　　*　　*

From a human development perspective, we want a world where all human beings have the freedom to realize their full potential in life so they can attain what they value. In the ultimate analysis, development is of the people, by the people and for the people. People have to partner with each other. There needs to be a balance between people and the planet. And humanity has to strive for peace and prosperity.

Human development requires recognizing that every life is equally valuable and that human development for everyone must start with those farthest behind.

The 2016 Human Development Report is an intellectual contribution to resolving these issues. We strongly believe that only after they are resolved will we all reach the end of the road together. And when we look back, we will see that no one has been left out.

Chapter **1**

Human development— achievements, challenges and hopes

Infographic 1.1 The world we want

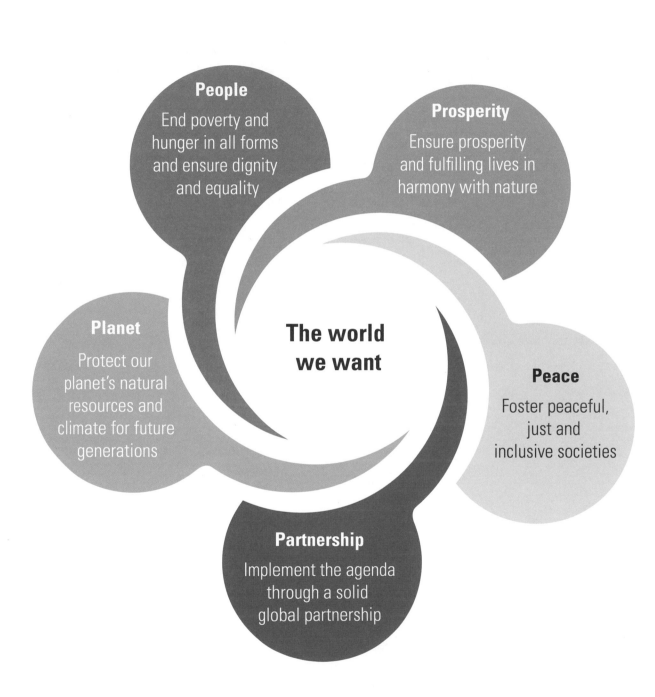

People
End poverty and hunger in all forms and ensure dignity and equality

Prosperity
Ensure prosperity and fulfilling lives in harmony with nature

Planet
Protect our planet's natural resources and climate for future generations

The world we want

Peace
Foster peaceful, just and inclusive societies

Partnership
Implement the agenda through a solid global partnership

1.

Human development—achievements, challenges and hopes

Human development is all about people—expanding their freedoms, enlarging their choices, enhancing their capabilities and improving their opportunities. It is a process as well as an outcome. Economic growth and income are means to human development but not ends in themselves—because it is the richness of people's lives, not the richness of economies, that ultimately is valuable to people. With such a simple but powerful notion, the first Human Development Report, appearing in 1990, put people at the centre of the development discourse, changing the lens for assessing development policies and outcomes (box 1.1).[1]

Over the ensuing 10 years the Human Development Reports extended the frontiers of thought leadership, public policy advocacy and influence on development agendas. The 1994 Human Development Report introduced the notion of human security, going beyond the traditional concept of national and territorial security.[2] The 1995 Human Development Report—which strongly argued that development, if not engendered, is endangered—contributed to the Beijing Declaration and Platform of Action at the Fourth World Conference on Women.[3] The 1997 Human Development Report introduced a multidimensional concept of poverty, known as human poverty, and an associated composite measure—the Human Poverty Index, an analytical breakthrough to elevate the discussion of human deprivations beyond income poverty.[4]

In addition to contributing to development thinking, these reports, with their policy recommendations and innovative data presentations, had policy impacts. The proposal to create Honesty International in the 1992 Human Development Report led to the establishment of Transparency International.[5] And the disaggregation of Egypt's Human Development Index (HDI) value in the 1994 Human Development Report led to an increased allocation of public resources to Upper Egypt, a less well developed area of the country.[6]

At the turn of the century 189 heads of state and government endorsed the Millennium Declaration and the Millennium Development Goals to overcome basic human deprivations by 2015, all solidly anchored in the human development approach.

> The Human Development Reports have extended the frontiers of thought leadership, public policy advocacy and influence on development agendas

---

BOX 1.1

Human development—a people-centred approach

Human development is about acquiring more capabilities and enjoying more opportunities to use those capabilities. With more capabilities and opportunities, people have more choices, and expanding choices is at the core of the human development approach. But human development is also a process. Anchored in human rights, it is linked to human security. And its ultimate objective is to enlarge human freedoms.

Human development is development of the people through the building of human resources, for the people through the translation of development benefits in their lives and by the people through active participation in the processes that influence and shape their lives. Income is a means to human development but not an end in itself.

The human development approach in the 1990 Human Development Report also introduced a composite index, the Human Development Index (HDI), for assessing achievements in the basic dimensions of human development. Those dimensions of human development are to lead a long and healthy life, measured by life expectancy at birth; to acquire knowledge, measured by mean years of schooling and expected years of schooling; and to achieve a decent standard of living, measured by gross national income per capita.

Source: Human Development Report Office.

During the last decade Human Development Reports covered such themes as deepening democracy (2002), cultural diversity (2004), climate change (2008), sustainability and equity (2011) and work for human development (2015).[7]

The global reports have been complemented over the years by more than three dozen regional and subregional Human Development Reports and more than 700 national Human Development Reports.[8] Subnational reports have also been produced, including 19 state-level reports in India and a municipal HDI in Brazil.[9]

Over the last quarter century all these reports have added momentum to human progress, and thus some of what seemed to be a daunting challenge in 1990 was largely achieved by 2015. Extreme poverty is estimated to have been below 11 percent globally in 2013, a drop of more than two-thirds since 1990.[10] So even though the global population increased by 2 billion—from 5.3 billion in 1990 to 7.3 billion in 2015—the number of people in extreme poverty fell by more than a billion.

Yet not all the news is good news. Substantial human deprivations persist despite the progress. One person in nine in the world is hungry, and one person in three is malnourished.[11] Eleven children under age 5 die every minute, and 35 mothers die during childbirth every hour.[12] About 15 million girls a year marry before age 18, one every two seconds.[13] Worldwide 18,000 people a day die because of air pollution, and HIV infects 2 million people a year.[14] Every minute an average of 24 people are displaced from their home.[15]

And new development challenges have emerged. Conflicts, disasters and natural resources can no longer be considered national concerns; they have become global concerns. More than 21.3 million people—roughly the population of Australia—are refugees.[16] More than 100 million people could be affected by the combined impact of El Niño and La Niña, a double shock.[17] Insecurity because of violent extremism has spread throughout the globe. The cost of violence globally is about $1,900 per person.[18] Water scarcity and climate change have added to international tensions. Epidemics such as Ebola and Zika pose serious threats to people, and about 20,000 children have become Ebola orphans.[19]

Human ingenuity has opened promising new arenas, but human suffering also abounds. Violence, not dialogue, has become a common human language. Isolationism, not diversity, is gaining currency. Despite the challenges, what humanity has achieved over the past 25 years and our desire to aspire to even more give us hope on many fronts. Challenges also offer rays of hope, and hopes face daunting challenges before they can be realized. This link needs to be kept in mind as we pursue our goal to overcome the challenges and realize the hopes.

The achievements we have made

The levels of human development have improved all over the world. Every developing region's HDI value increased considerably between 1990 and 2015, although progress has been slowing since 2010 (figure 1.1). This reflects important advances not only in income, but also in health and education. Between 1990 and 2015 the aggregate HDI value of the least developed countries increased 46 percent, and the aggregate HDI value for low human development countries increased 40 percent.[20]

Reduced poverty and hunger

The global extreme poverty rate ($1.90 a day) was estimated at less than 11 percent in 2013, a drop of more than two-thirds from the 35 percent in 1990.[21] The decrease has been particularly remarkable in East Asia and the Pacific, where the proportion of people living on less than $1.90 a day fell from 60.2 percent in 1990 to 3.5 percent in 2013, and in South Asia, where the proportion fell from 44.6 percent to 15 percent.[22] China's extreme poverty rate plummeted from 66.5 percent in 1990 to 1.9 percent in 2013. The working poor, who work and live on less than $1.90 a day, accounted for 10 percent of workers worldwide in 2015, nearly two-thirds less than in 2000.[23] The global population suffering from hunger declined from 15 percent in 2000–2002 to 11 percent in 2014–2016.[24]

Every developing region's HDI value increased considerably between 1990 and 2015, although progress has been slowing since 2010

FIGURE 1.1

Regional trends in Human Development Index values

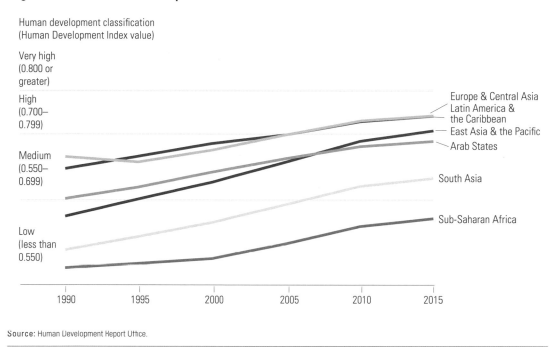

Source: Human Development Report Office.

Decreased mortality

The global under five mortality rate was more than halved between 1990 and 2015.[25] The steepest decline was in Sub-Saharan Africa, where the challenge was the greatest. While children in the poorest households are far less likely to survive to their fifth birthdays, the mortality rate is declining faster for children in poor households than for other children. Maternal mortality rates have also declined considerably since 1990: 45 percent globally and 64 percent in South Asia, as of 2013.[26] Access to professional health care has improved: in 2014 more than 71 percent of births worldwide were attended by skilled health personnel, up from 59 percent in 1990. In North Africa the proportion of pregnant women who receive at least four antenatal medical visits rose from 50 percent in 1990 to 89 percent in 2014, the largest improvement worldwide.[27] Globally, nearly two-thirds of women ages 15–49 who are married or in union use contraception, up from 55 percent in 1990.

Global health is also improving. In developing regions the proportion of undernourished people has been nearly halved since 1990.[28] In 2013 measles-containing vaccines reached 84 percent of children worldwide. Global coverage of two doses of the measles vaccine increased from 15 percent in 2000 to 53 percent in 2013, resulting in a 67 percent decline in the number of annual reported measles cases. An estimated 15.6 million lives were saved through measles vaccination between 2000 and 2013.[29] These positive developments have led to a dramatic decline in preventable child deaths.

Overall mortality rates are falling in part because of actions to tackle malaria, tuberculosis, measles, and HIV and AIDS. Between 2001 and 2015 more than 6.8 million malaria deaths, many of them in children, were prevented.[30] The number of new HIV infections also fell, from an estimated 3.5 million in 2000 to 2.1 million in 2013. From 1995 to 2013 increasing use of antiretroviral therapy averted 7.6 million deaths from AIDS.[31] Tuberculosis mortality rates also fell in response to efforts to prevent, diagnose and treat the disease, with 37 million lives saved between 2000 and 2013.[32]

Improved access to basic social services

Access to basic social services has been greatly expanded worldwide. Between 1990 and 2015,

While children in the poorest households are far less likely to survive to their fifth birthdays, the mortality rate is declining faster for children in poor households than for other children

2.1 billion people gained access to improved sanitation, halving the number of people resorting to open defecation, a major source of transmittable diseases such as cholera.[33] More than 2.6 billion people gained access to an improved source of water, and the Millennium Development Goal target of halving the proportion of the population without access to safe drinking water was reached five years ahead of schedule.[34] The improvement has been impressive in Sub-Saharan Africa, where the proportion of the population with access to an improved drinking water source rose from 48 percent in 1990 to 68 percent in 2015, and in East Asia, where the proportion rose from 68 percent in 1990 to 96 percent in 2015. And despite rapid urbanization across the globe, the proportion of the urban population living in slums fell almost 10 percentage points between 2000 and 2014 in developing regions.[35]

In developing regions 91 percent of primary school–age children were enrolled in 2015, up from 83 percent in 2000, and the number of out-of-school children worldwide fell by almost half over the same period.[36] The greatest progress has been in Sub-Saharan Africa, where the net primary school enrolment rate rose from 52 percent in 1990 to 80 percent in 2015. As a result, a larger proportion of young people can now read and write: The global literacy rate among people ages 15–24 was 91 percent in 2015, up from 83 percent in 1995. The gap in literacy between young men and young women has also narrowed, to an estimated 3 percentage points in 2015. North Africa and South Asia showed the greatest improvement in youth literacy, pushed by a strong increase in literacy among young women.

Increased people's participation

People's participation in public and political life, another essential aspect of human development, has also improved over the past 25 years. The average share of parliamentary seats held by women worldwide rose from 11 percent in 1995 to 22 percent in 2015, and two-thirds of developing countries have achieved gender parity in primary education, allowing girls and women to better voice their concerns and interests.[37] Civil society organizations have expanded considerably, helping individuals exercise agency, express their opinion and defend their interests on the national and international scenes.

Improved environmental sustainability

Environmental protection, which has become a key global issue, has shown encouraging successes as well. The degradation of the ozone layer, a major concern in the 1990s, has been halted, and by 2050 the ozone layer will have fully recovered from the damages caused by ozone-depleting substances.[38] The share of marine biodiversity areas that are protected increased from 15 percent in 2000 to 19 percent in 2016.[39] The global net loss in forest area declined from 7.3 million hectares a year in the 1990s to 3.3 million in 2010–2015, and the share of terrestrial areas that are protected increased from 16.5 percent in 2000 to 19.3 percent in 2016. Communication and information on the need to protect nature and the impact of climate change have reached more people than ever before, raising awareness in every corner of the world.

Advances in technology

New technologies are one of the most apparent changes in our current lives. They have lifted economies up, facilitated transportation and communication, led to major advances in health and education, expanded information and participation and created new security tools. Green technologies may be the key to a more sustainable future, where resources are available to all without harming the environment. Information and communication technology has spread exponentially. In 2016, 94.1 percent of the population in developing countries own a mobile phone, and 40.1 percent have access to the Internet, up from 7.8 percent in 2005.[40] In developed countries access to the Internet and to smartphones is nearly universal.

The impact of technology on the economy is undeniable. Global high-technology exports have more than doubled in the last 15 years, from $987 billion in 1999 to $2,147 billion in 2014.[41] Cloud technology, three-dimensional printing, advanced robotics, energy storage and digital assistants hold great potential for creating new jobs and new areas of work. People with the skills and resources to use

Communication and information on the impact of climate change have reached more people than ever before, raising awareness in every corner of the world

technology and create value can thrive in today's digital world, as discussed in the 2015 Human Development Report.

New technologies have also changed the way governments interact with their citizens, increasing the reach and efficiency of public service delivery.[42] Several countries use mobile phones to extend basic social services, including health care and education, to hard-to-reach populations.[43] The Internet allows much more information to be shared than any other means of communication has. The amount of digital data has doubled every three years since 2000, and today less than 2 percent of stored information is offline.[44]

Though there is far to go before all people can live their lives to their full potential, cooperation and commitments to eliminating deprivations and promoting sustainable human development have improved the lives of billions of people over the past 25 years. The Republic of Korea has sustained progress in human development for even longer (box 1.2).

The challenges we face

Some challenges are lingering (deprivations), some are deepening (inequalities) and some are emerging (violent extremism). Some are global

(gender inequality), some are regional (water stress) and some are within national boundaries (natural disasters). Most are mutually reinforcing: Climate change reduces food security, and rapid urbanization marginalizes poor people in urban areas. Whatever their nature or reach, these challenges have an impact on people's well-being.

Lingering deprivations and inequalities

Even with all the impressive progress in reducing poverty over the past 25 years, 766 million people,[45] 385 million of them children,[46] lived on less than $1.90 a day in 2013. Poor nutrition causes 45 percent of the deaths among children under age 5.[47] Children born in developing countries in 2016 will lose nearly $177 billion in potential lifetime earnings because of stunting and other delays in physical development.[48]

Yet one-third of the world's food is wasted every year.[49] If one-fourth of the food wasted across the globe could be recovered, it could feed 870 million people.[50] Unless the world tackles deprivation today, 167 million children will live in extreme poverty by 2030, and 69 million children under age 5 will die of preventable causes.[51] These outcomes will definitely shrink the capabilities of future generations. About 758 million adults, including

Even with all the impressive progress in reducing poverty over the past 25 years, 766 million people, 385 million of them children, lived on less than $1.90 a day in 2013

BOX 1.2

Human development in the Republic of Korea — a longer term perspective

The Republic of Korea has travelled a highly successful path of human development over the past six decades. And the major drivers behind the country's sustained trajectory of high human development include successful land reforms, rural development, extensive human resources development and rapid equitable economic growth. Export orientation, sustainable domestic resource mobilization with strong redistribution policies, and public infrastructure development also played major roles. Needless to say, effective institutions and governance were also key.

The main dynamics of the Republic of Korea's progress was a virtuous cycle between economic and social policies, which—while maintaining the primacy of the growth objective—adapted flexibly to evolving constraints and opportunities and successfully harnessed

major currents in the human development space, such as globalization, technological change and urbanization.

The Republic of Korea attained a critical mass of policies conducive to human development in the face of multiple challenges. Doing so allowed the country to remain on a path of rapid and socially inclusive human development for so long—and to serve as a model for other countries. The country, assisted by the United Nations Development Programme Seoul Policy Centre for Global Development Partnerships, is already conveying its knowhow (such as that gleaned from the Seoul government's Clean Construction System) to partner countries, duly adapted to the realities of partner countries, whose policymakers and political leaders are aiming for similarly rapid and sustained improvements in human development.

Source: UNDP Seoul Policy Centre for Global Development Partnerships.

114 million young people, still lack basic reading and writing skills.[52] Lingering deprivations are evident in various aspects of human development (figure 1.2).

Poverty is no longer a problem of developing regions only; it is also on the rise in developed countries. The International Labour Organization estimates that in 2012 more than 300 million people in developed countries lived in poverty.[53]

Children and women are the most affected by poverty, and 36 percent of children in developed countries live under the relative poverty line, in households with an income below 60 percent of the national median household income. In the United States 32 million adults are functionally illiterate, and in the United Kingdom 8 million.[54]

Rising incomes around the world have been accompanied by widening inequality. Measures of the gaps in income equality include the Gini coefficient (where a value of 0 means that everyone has the same income, and a value of 1 means that one person has all the income) and quintile ratios (the ratio of the average income of the wealthiest 20 percent of the population to the average income of the poorest 20 percent of the population).

Although income inequality across households has risen in many countries, some estimates show that it has narrowed across the world as a whole because the incomes of developing and developed regions have been converging. Relative global inequality has declined steadily over the past few decades, from a relative Gini coefficient of 0.74 in 1975 to

FIGURE 1.2

Human deprivation lingers in some indicators of well-being

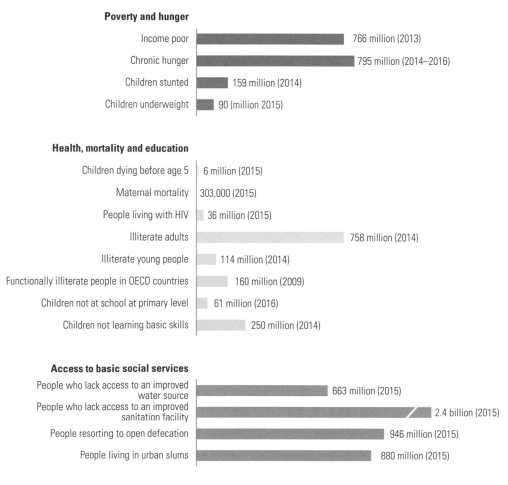

Poverty and hunger

Income poor	766 million (2013)
Chronic hunger	795 million (2014–2016)
Children stunted	159 million (2014)
Children underweight	90 (million 2015)

Health, mortality and education

Children dying before age 5	6 million (2015)
Maternal mortality	303,000 (2015)
People living with HIV	36 million (2015)
Illiterate adults	758 million (2014)
Illiterate young people	114 million (2014)
Functionally illiterate people in OECD countries	160 million (2009)
Children not at school at primary level	61 million (2016)
Children not learning basic skills	250 million (2014)

Access to basic social services

People who lack access to an improved water source	663 million (2015)
People who lack access to an improved sanitation facility	2.4 billion (2015)
People resorting to open defecation	946 million (2015)
People living in urban slums	880 million (2015)

Source: Human Development Report Office.

0.63 in 2010, driven by declining inequality between countries arising from the extraordinary economic growth in, primarily, China and India.[55] This happened despite an increasing trend towards inequality within countries. By contrast, absolute inequality, measured by the absolute Gini coefficient, has increased dramatically since the mid-1970s (figure 1.3). To understand the absolute and the relative, take an example. In 2000 one person in a country earns $1 a day and another person $10 a day. With economic growth, in 2016 the first person earns $8 a day, and the second person $80 a day. The relative difference between the two remains the same (the second person has 10 times more than the first person), but the absolute difference has gone up from $7 to $72.

The World Bank reports that between 2008 and 2013 income gaps widened in 34 of the 83 countries monitored as income grew more quickly for those in the wealthiest 60 percent of the income distribution than for those in the poorest 40 percent.[56] And in 23 countries people in the poorest 40 percent saw their income decline.

Increases in income have been particularly sharp at the top of the income distribution. Some 46 percent of the total increase in income between 1988 and 2011 went to the wealthiest 10 percent (figure 1.4). Since 2000, 50 percent of the increase in global wealth benefited only the wealthiest 1 percent of the world's population. Conversely, the poorest 50 percent of the world's population received only 1 percent of the increase.[57]

Global wealth has become far more concentrated. The wealthiest 1 percent of the population had 32 percent of global wealth around 2000 and 46 percent around 2010 (figure 1.5). The super-rich—the wealthiest 0.1 percent— loom larger. The share of national wealth among the super-rich in the United States increased from 12 percent in 1990 to 19 percent in 2008 (before the financial crisis) and to 22 percent in 2012 (critics pointed to inequality as one of the key causes of the crisis).[58]

Access to the benefits of the digital revolution is uneven globally. Almost 2 billion people still do not use a mobile phone, and only 15 percent of the world population has high-speed Internet access.[59] Some 89 percent of the planet's urban population has access to 3G mobile broadband, compared with only 29 percent of the rural population.[60]

The inequality discussion often focuses on vertical inequality—such as the inequality between wealthiest 10 percent of the population and the poorest 10 percent—and rarely on horizontal inequality—such as the inequality across ethnic groups. Analysis of horizontal inequality can bring critical insights to the inequality discourse (box 1.3).

> Global wealth has become far more concentrated. The wealthiest 1 percent of the population had 32 percent of global wealth around 2000 and 46 percent around 2010

FIGURE 1.3

Relative global inequality has declined steadily over the past few decades, but absolute inequality has increased dramatically

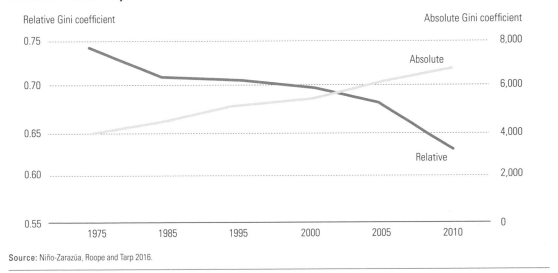

Source: Niño-Zarazúa, Roope and Tarp 2016.

FIGURE 1.4

Some 46 percent of the total increase in income between 1988 and 2011 went to the wealthiest 10 percent

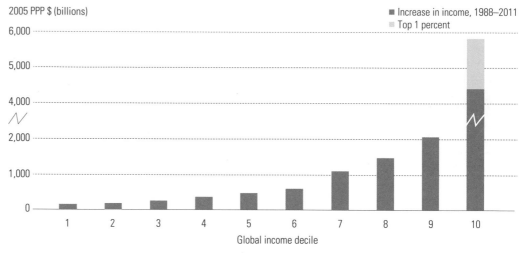

2005 PPP $ (billions)

■ Increase in income, 1988–2011
□ Top 1 percent

Global income decile

Note: PPP is purchasing power parity.
Source: Lawson 2016.

FIGURE 1.5

Global wealth has become far more concentrated

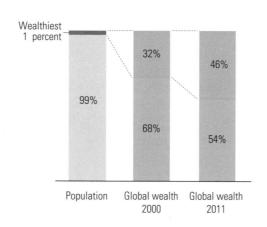

Source: Human Development Report Office estimates based on Milanović (2016).

Multidimensional population dynamics

The planet's surging population is projected to grow to 9.7 billion in 2050 (figure 1.6), with five main implications: widespread urbanization, an ageing population, a growing middle class, migration and a youth bulge.

In 2014 more than half the world's people lived in urban areas, a share expected to reach two-thirds by 2050, when cities will have swollen by another 2.5 billion people.[61] The world is projected to have 41 megacities by 2030, each with more than 10 million inhabitants.[62] Urbanization has been described as a new frontier of development because it is not a passive outcome of development, but a creator of value —the more than half of humanity living in cities generates more than 80 percent of global gross domestic product (GDP).[63]

Not all urbanization is positive, however, especially if it is unplanned. It puts pressure on infrastructure and may lower residents' quality of life. More than 1 billion people live in housing that is below minimum standards of comfort and sanitation, and new houses have to be built for 3 billion people by 2030.[64] Some 880 million people live in slums, and nearly 40 percent of the world's future urban expansion may occur in slums.[65] Almost 700 million urban slumdwellers lack adequate sanitation, which—along with lack of safe

> **Urbanization has been described as a new frontier of development because it is not a passive outcome of development, but a creator of value**

Lingering deprivations and inequalities present serious challenges to human development on at least three fronts. First, they stunt the capabilities of people—not only their well-being, but also their voice and autonomy. Second, they initiate and reinforce a process of exclusion whereby poor people and others at the bottom of the social ladder are excluded from influencing the processes that shape their lives. Third, they create a society where rights and opportunities are denied to poor people—and that is unjust.

BOX 1.3

Insights based on horizontal inequalities

A common argument in discussions about horizontal inequality is that people would be more favourable to redistribution within their own group and less favourable to redistribution between groups because the former is perceived by the group as just and fair.

But Ghana and Uganda showed far higher approval ratings for redistribution between ethnic groups, even though ethnic identity was just as strong as in other countries. High approval for redistribution is clearly compatible with a strong ethnic identification.

Redistribution is critical in addressing horizontal inequality and can form the core of public policy to ensure

rights, justice and equality in a multiethnic society. Such policies would have constitutive benefits (such as enhancing human capabilities in various groups) as well as consequential benefits (such as improving social cohesion).

Deprivation is a denial of human rights (which have intrinsic value), and overcoming it is also instrumental in enjoying other rights and freedoms. Equality has intrinsic value (anchored in the notion of justice) as well as instrumental value because it affects other accepted objectives. Inequality is justified only if it improves the position of the poorest or if it arises through legitimate processes.

Source: Cornia and Stewart 2014.

FIGURE 1.6

The planet's surging population is projected to grow to 9.7 billion in 2050

World population (billions)

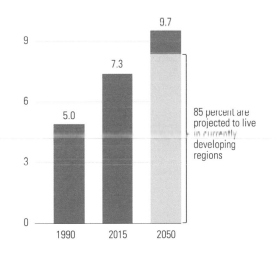

85 percent are projected to live in currently developing regions

Source: UNDESA 2015b.

drinking water—raises the risk of communicable diseases such as cholera and diarrhoea, particularly among children.[66] Violence, drugs and crime also increase with rapid urbanization. And urbanization is linked to climate change. Along with prosperity and innovation, global cities are the principal sources of the carbon dioxide emissions that are warming the earth.[67] Many larger cities are in low-lying coastal areas,

leaving them exposed to the dangers of flooding associated with rising sea levels and storm surges.

As a result of declining fertility and greater longevity, older people now make up an increasing proportion of national populations. The number of people ages 60 and older is expected to reach 1.4 billion in 2030 and 2.1 billion in 2050.[68] That would raise the global old-age dependency ratio (the ratio of the number of people ages 65 and older to the number of people of working age, generally ages 15–64) in developing countries from 13 percent in 2015 to 26 percent in 2050.[69] And that will have major implications for retirement ages, health services, elder care, social protection and family relationships. In developed countries ageing populations are challenging retirement systems and requiring adaptations to work arrangements and long-term care services.[70]

The global middle class—households with a daily expenditure of $10–$100 per capita in purchasing power parity terms—is expected to expand to 3.2 billion people in Asia and the Pacific and to 1.7 billion people elsewhere by 2030.[71] Its rapid expansion stems from the rise in countries such as China, where middle-class households (with an annual income of $11,500–$43,000) increased from 5 million in 2000 to 225 million in 2015.[72] But country definitions of the middle class differ, both through the lenses of income and expenditure and in relative terms compared with a societal mean.[73]

The global middle class is expected to expand to 3.2 billion people in Asia and the Pacific and to 1.7 billion people elsewhere by 2030

How might the growth of the middle class affect human development? The larger middle class is more of an economic middle class than the traditional intellectual middle class, and its approach to social debate, intellectual leadership and social cohesion may differ from that of its predecessors, which acted as the conscience of society, provided intellectual leadership in social and cultural movements and championed the poor and the marginalized. In most societies younger people will constitute an economic middle class that strives for innovation and creativity in life as well as in work. They are also more likely to see themselves as global citizens, with positive implications for human capabilities and opportunities.

But the new middle class may show consumption patterns that have adverse impacts on sustainable consumption. It may have its own social agenda (such as social entrepreneurship) but be motivated more by personal economic advancement. It may also be more insular and be more intimately linked to a Twitter community or a Facebook community than to a physical community or neighbourhood. It may have many digital connections but few human connections.

Population dynamics will continue to change because of migration to developed countries. The population of the European Union was 507 million in 2013. Without migration it would drop to 399 million by 2080, but with migration it would rise to 520 million.[74] The population of the United States was 324 million in 2015. Without migration it would have risen to 338 million by 2016, but with migration it reached 441 million. Population shifts associated with migration will change not only the demographic profile of these and other societies, but also their values, norms, culture and political and social institutions, possibly creating tensions and conflicts. One human development challenge will thus involve forging peaceful and cohesive multicultural societies in many parts of the world.

Today young people ages 10–24 account for about 1.8 billion of the world's 7.3 billion people.[75] Around 90 percent of these young people live in developing countries. A third of the world's population is under age 20, and in about 40 African countries more than half the population is under age 20.[76] There are more young people alive today than at any other time in human history.[77] Young people are active users of information and communication technology, and 30 percent are digital natives, young people ages 15–24 who have been using the Internet for five years or more.[78]

Yet 73.3 million young people are out of work, and 40 percent of young people in the global labour force are either unemployed or poorly paid.[79] Young people are three times more likely than adults to be out of work.[80] Nearly 156 million young people in emerging and developing countries are working poor—working but living in extreme poverty on less than $1.90 a day or in moderate poverty on $1.90–$3.10 a day.[81] In the next 15 years young people worldwide will need 600 million jobs.[82]

Millennials—people ages 18–34 in 2015—are expected to work longer hours (nearly a quarter work more than 50 hours a week) and retire much later (a quarter expect to retire after age 70) than their grandparents—the silent generation, mostly in their 70s and 80s (box 1.4).[83]

Globalization—a double-edged sword

Globalization has been heralded over the years as an engine of growth. In China and India opening up the economy to the world accelerated growth, which in turn helped address human development challenges—reducing poverty, improving health outcomes and extending access to basic social services. Thanks largely to China, the extreme poverty rate in East Asia dropped from 60 percent in 1990 to 3.5 percent in 2013.[84] In 40 countries analysed

BOX 1.4

Millennials versus the silent generation

- Millennials are better educated.
- Female millennials are much more likely to be working.
- Millennials face tougher job markets.
- Millennials are less likely to marry.
- Millennials are more likely to be an ethnic minority.
- Millennials are far less likely to be war veterans.
- Female millennials are better educated than male millennials.

Source: Patten and Fry 2015.

in 2013, 453 million people—190 million of them women—were working in global value chains, up from 296 million in 1995.[85] A study of 40 countries, 13 of them developing countries, found that trade generally favours the poorest people because they spend more in traded sectors.[86]

Globalization has been accelerated by the technological revolution, particularly the digital revolution. Global trade in merchandise and services amounted to almost $24 trillion in 2014, up from $13 trillion in 2005.[87] And knowledge-intensive flows increased 1.3 times faster than labour-intensive flows.[88]

But globalization has not delivered the expected shared prosperity. Unskilled workers lost jobs in many economies, and manufacturing jobs disappeared. Productivity may have increased, but this did not always translate into higher wages, and the inequality in pay between unskilled and highly skilled labour has widened considerably.[89]

People have struggled during the process of globalization: Those who have recently crossed the poverty line in developing countries face vulnerable employment and informality, and the traditional middle class in high income countries faces stagnant wages and reductions in social services. This pattern is shaping global social attitudes towards globalization: People self-defined as part of the lower middle class and working class feel less engaged by the concept of global citizenship (figure 1.7). The causes are invisible in indicators such as overall GDP growth or progress out of poverty by extremely poor people, yet the frustration can create political and institutional instability if left addressed.

There seems to be a widespread view that globalization is good for a small elite but not for the broad masses of people.[90] Even many academics and policymakers who welcomed globalization are revising their opinion. It was always thought that globalization would not benefit everyone but that the benefits would eventually outweigh the losses.[91] The backlash against globalization is reshaping politics in various countries. But it cannot be rolled back, so the challenge is to ensure that globalization leaves no one behind.

People on the move

Millions of people are on the move because of conflicts, disasters or a search for better economic opportunities. Conflicts, violence and human rights violations have prompted massive displacements of people within or outside their countries.

At the end of 2015 more than 65 million people worldwide had been forcibly displaced (internally displaced persons, refugees and asylumseekers) the most since the Second World War and more than the population of France or the combined populations of Australia, Canada and New Zealand (figure 1.8).[92] Some 86 percent of them are hosted in developing countries, making refugees less of a burden on developed countries (box 1.5).[93]

> Globalization cannot be rolled back, so the challenge is to ensure that it leaves no one behind

FIGURE 1.7

People self-defined as part of the lower middle class and working class feel less engaged by the concept of global citizenship

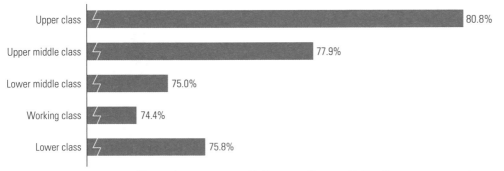

Upper class — 80.8%
Upper middle class — 77.9%
Lower middle class — 75.0%
Working class — 74.4%
Lower class — 75.8%

(% strongly agree or agree with "I see myself as a world citizen")

Note: Data are for 59 countries.
Source: Human Development Report Office estimates based on World Values Survey, wave 6, (www.worldvaluessurvey.org/wvs.jsp).

FIGURE 1.8

At the end of 2015 there were more than 65 million people worldwide who had been forcibly displaced

Children are among the major victims of forced displacement

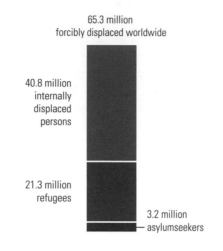

65.3 million
forcibly displaced worldwide

40.8 million
internally
displaced
persons

21.3 million
refugees

3.2 million
asylumseekers

Source: Statista 2016.

BOX 1.5

Five common myths about refugees

Refugees are a European problem
Europe is home to only 6 percent of global refugees; 86 percent are in developing countries. The six richest nations host only 9 percent of refugees worldwide.

Refugees are not desperate—they are choosing to migrate
By definition refugees are people who flee across borders to escape violent conflict or persecution.

Most refugees are young, able-bodied men
Worldwide nearly 50 million children have migrated or been forcibly displaced. These children may be refugees, interally displaced persons or migrants.

Refugees and migrants bring terrorism
Over the past few years the deadliest terrorist attacks around the world have been perpetrated by citizens born in the targeted countries.

Developed countries are overcrowded and cannot take any more people
The size of the population in most developed countries is actually declining, and the demographic dividend in these countries is being exhausted. Migration can be crucial in addressing this issue.

Source: Human Development Report Office.

Children are among the major victims of forced displacement. Of the nearly 50 million children who have migrated across borders or been forcibly displaced, 28 million fled violence and insecurity.[94] More than 98,000 children are unaccompanied in migration or have been separated from their family.[95]

People on the move also face dangers during their journeys and afterwards. The global count of migrant deaths was more than 10,000 in 2014 and 2015, and many more were unaccounted for.

Widespread conflict and violent extremism

Widespread conflict and violent extremism have become a challenge of our time. Conflict-related deaths are a proxy measure for the absence of peace. Since the end of the Second World War there has been a downward trend in such deaths, except in 2000, when the Eritrean–Ethiopian war alone caused at least 50,000 deaths.[96] With the escalation of conflict and extreme violence in the Syrian Arab Republic, 2014 saw the highest number of battle-related deaths since 1989: more than 50,000 (figure 1.9).[97] In 17 countries affected by prolonged conflicts, more than

FIGURE 1.9

2014 saw the highest number of battle-related deaths since 1989: more than 50,000

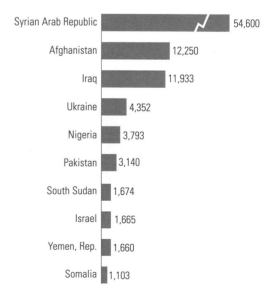

Syrian Arab Republic	54,600
Afghanistan	12,250
Iraq	11,933
Ukraine	4,352
Nigeria	3,793
Pakistan	3,140
South Sudan	1,674
Israel	1,665
Yemen, Rep.	1,660
Somalia	1,103

Source: Purdie and Khaltarkhuu 2016.

56 million people are trapped in a vicious cycle of violence and hunger.[98]

In 2000 UN Security Council resolution 1325 recognized that war affects women differently and stressed the need to increase women's participation in peace talks.[99] But from 1992 to 2011 only 9 percent of participants in peace negotiations were women.[100] Globally, fewer than 5 percent of peacekeepers are women.[101]

Incidents of violent extremism and terrorism worldwide rose from fewer than 5,000 in 2006 to nearly 15,000 in 2014.[102] There has been a nearly tenfold increase in deaths from violent extremism and terrorism since 2000—from 3,329 victims to 32,685 in 2014.[103] And the death toll keeps rising. In Iraq an estimated 50,000 people have died since 2003.[104] In 2016 more than 20,000 people died during internal conflict in Afghanistan, and more than 10,000 died in Yemen.[105]

Economic losses from conflict are estimated at $742 billion a year, dwarfing the $167 billion in annual gross disbursements of official development assistance.[106] But the costs of conflicts and violence are not limited to economic costs. People are uprooted because of conflicts and violence, they lose their belongings, they are on the run, their families are broken up—and too many die. About 600 million young people live in fragile and conflict-affected situations with no work and little hope.[107] Despair sometimes leads them to violent extremism. Refugee children and adolescents are five times more likely than nonrefugee children and adolescents to be out of school, with serious implications for building their capabilities.[108]

Broader peace, stability and security are linked not only to the end of wars and conflicts, but also to the end of violence within societies and human security in personal and community life. Violence has become a human language in many societies, and intolerance has become the reaction (box 1.6).

Rising shocks, expanding vulnerabilities

Although human beings are extremely resilient, the system in which they live and operate has to be resilient as well. Pandemics, natural disasters, climate change, economic and financial crises and other shocks can slow, reverse or completely derail human development. The effects on human development are

BOX 1.6

Human security, as people see it

Human security to me means that my children and grandchildren will never see killing of human beings because of their colour or tribe as I witnessed in 1994 during the genocide of Tutsi in Rwanda.
— *A female professional from Rwanda*

Human security to me means that I can walk on any street, anywhere, at any time using any clothes that I want—and with no fear. — *A man from Brazil*

To me personally, human security means being free to be myself as a transwoman who came from the very oppressive continent of Africa, to be free from that violence and feeling safe and functional.
— *A former student from the United States*

Human security is good nutrition, health and education, stability and peace, prosperity of the country and a robust state, freedoms, justice, democratic government. — *A male government official from Yemen*

For me, human security means equality between people no matter what age, race, gender, social status or preferences they have. It means mutual respect between the people in the whole wide world.
— *A female student from Belarus*

Human security for me is to have a voice. It means the right to participate in political process, the right to criticize injustice. — *A male professor from India*

Human security is not to worry or think about my day-to-day needs and safety.
— *A gay male government official from the Philippines*

Human security for me is the future health and well-being of my children and grandchildren.
— *A female retired social worker from New Zealand*

Source: Human Development Report Office.

not transitory; they may become permanent. Recovering from shocks takes a long time. Even six years after the economic and financial crisis of 2008–2009, at least 61 million fewer jobs were available globally than expected.[109] Five years of war in the Syrian Arab Republic and the spillover in Egypt, Iraq, Jordan, Lebanon and Turkey have cost close to $35 billion— equivalent to the GDP of the Syrian Arab Republic in 2007.[110] It will take time to return to the prewar GDP.[111] Restoring Libya's infrastructure will cost an estimated $200 billion over the next 10 years.[112]

Broader peace, stability and security are linked not only to the end of wars and conflicts, but also to the end of violence within societies and human security in personal and community life

Eighteen million people living with HIV, mostly young and adolescent, do not receive antiretroviral treatment.[113] Young women ages 15–24 are at higher risk of HIV infection and account for 20 percent of new HIV infections among adults globally.[114] About 1.8 million children live with HIV, and only half of them receive lifesaving treatment.[115] More than 50 percent of people living with HIV do not know that they are infected,[116] and only 30 percent of young women have comprehensive and correct knowledge about HIV.[117]

Noncommunicable diseases lead to 38 million deaths a year, 28 million of them in low- and middle-income countries.[118] Cancer causes 8.2 million deaths a year, 5.7 million of them in developing countries.[119] Almost 2.1 billion people worldwide are overweight or obese, 62 percent of them in developing countries.[120] The number of overweight children is projected to double by 2030.[121]

Ebola and Zika have emerged as epidemics going beyond a country or group of countries. And infectious diseases are developing resistance to the antimicrobial drugs used to treat them. Overprescription and failure to complete courses of treatment allow resistance to develop and microbial infections to become a human health threat. Some 700,000 deaths are attributed to antimicrobial resistance each year;[122] that number could skyrocket to 10 million a year by 2050 and cause global GDP to drop 1.1–3.8 percent. Some 28 million more people are projected to slide into poverty because of antimicrobial resistance.[123]

Some 218 million people a year are touched by natural disasters.[124] The total direct costs of disasters and major diseases are equivalent. Between 1980 and 2012 an estimated 42 million human life-years were lost to disasters, and 80 percent of them in developing countries.[125] Fragile and conflict-affected states are home to more than 1.4 billion people and half the world's extremely poor, a number that will grow 82 percent by 2030 if no action is taken.[126]

Imbalances between the needs of people and the capacity of the planet

Every year, 24 billion tonnes of fertile soils are lost to erosion, and 12 million hectares of land are lost to drought and desertification, affecting the lives and livelihoods of 1.5 billion people.[127] Desertification could displace up to 135 million people by 2045.[128] Biodiversity is below safe levels across more than half the world's lands.[129] Every year, 300 million tonnes of plastic are manufactured, but only 15 percent is recycled, leaving 46,000 floating pieces of plastic per square mile of ocean.[130] But this is a minuscule fraction of the total amount of waste held in the seas, which affects nearly 700 marine species.[131]

In 2012 an estimated 8.4 million people died from air, water or land pollution.[132] At least 6.5 million people a year are believed to be dying from air pollution, with many more injured.[133] The cost of air pollution in welfare losses has been estimated at $5 trillion, 60 percent of which is in developing regions.[134] About 2.7 billion people still depend on wood or waste fires that cause indoor air pollution, affecting women and children the most.[135] Indoor air pollution leads to around 3.5 million deaths a year.[136]

Forests and trees provide vital resources to 1.3 billion people, and in developing countries, forest income is second only to farm income among rural communities.[137] Between 60 million and 200 million indigenous peoples rely on forests for survival.[138] Acting as the lungs of the world, forests also slow climate change, and acting as carbon sinks, they increase resilience. Yet in tropical countries the annual net forest loss is 7 million hectares—the size of Ireland.[139]

Water stress is a major challenge affecting more than 4 billion people worldwide.[140] The combined effects of growing populations, rising incomes and expanding cities will cause the demand for water to rise exponentially, while supply becomes more erratic and uncertain. Water is becoming scarcer in the Arab States and in the African Sahel, where it is already in short supply, and may start disappearing in Central Africa or East Asia, where it is currently abundant. These regions could see declines of as much as 6 percent of GDP by 2050 because of water-related impacts on agriculture, health and income.[141]

In 2012 more than 80 percent of the world's primary energy supply came from fossil fuels, and only 16 percent came from renewable energy.[142] In 2015 fossil fuels accounted for 55 percent of global energy investment, and today fossil fuel companies benefit from global subsidies of $10 million a minute.[143] About

The combined effects of growing populations, rising incomes and expanding cities will cause the demand for water to rise exponentially, while supply becomes more erratic and uncertain

1 billion people worldwide lack access to electricity.[144] By 2040 the planet's energy system will need to serve 9 billion people, and much of the energy will have to be renewable.

Climate change will aggravate land degradation—especially in drylands, which occupy 40 percent of global land area, are inhabited by some 2 billion people and support half the world's livestock.[145] By 2030 climate change is expected to cause an additional 250,000 deaths a year from malaria, diarrhoea, heat stress and malnutrition.[146]

The poorest people are more exposed than the average population to climate-related shocks and are at high risk of floods, droughts and heat waves; crop failures from reduced rainfall; spikes in food prices after extreme weather events; and increased incidence of diseases after heat waves and floods. Poor people are also more exposed to higher temperatures and live in countries where food production is expected to decrease. If climate-smart action is not taken now, more than 100 million additional people could be living in poverty by 2030.[147] Climate change can have the most disastrous effects on indigenous peoples, who rely more on natural resources and agriculture.

The hopes we have

What humanity has achieved over 25 years despite all the challenges it has faced gives hope that fundamental change is possible. Yes, progress on many fronts has been uneven and deprivations linger, yet what has been achieved can become a foundation for progress in many areas. We can explore new possibilities for overcoming challenges and attain what once seemed unattainable. Realizing our hopes is within our reach.

Rapid progress is possible

Some of the impressive achievements in human development over the last 25 years have been in regions and areas that once were lagging. South Asia, where extreme poverty is rampant, reduced the extreme poverty rate from 44.5 percent in 1990 to 15 percent in 2013.[148] Average incomes rose among the poorest 40 percent between 2008 and 2013 despite the financial crisis.[149] And between 2011 and 2014,

700 million people worldwide became account holders in banks, other financial institutions or mobile money service providers.[150]

Africa boosted life expectancy by six years in the 2000s. Latin America and the Caribbean reduced the under-five mortality rate by 70 percent between 1990 and 2015.[151] The Americas have been declared free of measles.[152] Guatemala has joined three other Latin American countries that were already free of river blindness.[153] Southeast Asia cut the share of the population living in slums from 40 percent in 2000 to 27 percent in 2014.[154]

In 2005 India aimed to connect every community with more than 1,000 people (and every community with more than 500 people in hilly, tribal and desert areas) to an all-weather road.[155] Four years later, 70 percent of the target communities were connected. In 2005 Ethiopia launched Sub-Saharan Africa's largest social protection programme.[156] Four years later 7.5 million people were supported in times of food insecurity. In 2010 Senegal targeted 191 rural villages for improved access to electricity, boosting the number of people with access from 17,000 to 90,000 in 2012.[157]

All these gains are reasons for hope that rapid progress is possible, even in areas previously lagging. The world has the resources, the technology and the expertise to overcome human deprivations. And the notion of sharing prosperity gives us hope that we are ready to tackle human deprivations together. Inaction is not an option.

The resounding voices of the people

People everywhere want to influence the processes that shape their lives. They are vocal in raising concerns—such as those related to waste recycling and extractive industries, ethical sourcing and fair practices in trade, citizen safety and the public health implications of agribusiness and pharmaceuticals. Other examples include antiglobalization protests and the Occupy movement against wealth and income inequality. Technology and social media have mobilized grassroots activism and included people and groups previously unable to exercise voice and opinion (box 1.7).

The Internet brings people together through offline protests as well. In 2014 the platform Avaaz.org coordinated a gathering of more than

The world has the resources, the technology and the expertise to overcome human deprivations. And the notion of sharing prosperity gives us hope that we are ready to tackle human deprivations together

400,000 people in Manhattan—and hundreds of thousands more in other cities—for the "biggest climate march in history."[158] Crowdfunding allows individuals to contribute small amounts of money towards a philanthropic project that requires larger funds. Donors can fund local projects through civic crowdfunding or projects in other countries through charity crowdfunding.[159] Spacehive, a civic crowdfunding platform in the United Kingdom, specializes in raising funds for small community projects such as improving a playground or renovating a school. It has raised nearly £5 million (more than $6 million) since its launch in 2011.[160]

Although petitions, protests, fundraising and political publications have always existed, the Internet has allowed them to reach an unprecedented level and bring together people across the world. Mobile phones have multiplied the impact of popular movements. The broadcasting on Facebook of police attacks during pro-democracy demonstrations was instrumental in the 2011 Arab Spring.[161] Smartphones and subscription-free mobile phones will likely accelerate this trend, creating new opportunities for people to express themselves freely, even under authoritarian regimes.

As more people raise their voices to express their hopes and aspirations as well as their despair and frustration, mobilizing to demand what they want will become easier. People's voices can thus become a more powerful force, giving others hope in shaping the world they want.

Expanding human ingenuity and creativity

Human ingenuity and creativity have initiated technological revolutions and translated these revolutions into the way we work, think and behave. Technology is all around us, and sometimes in us—biotech, digital tech, nanotech, neurotech, green tech and so on. The digital revolution has been going on for some time. The number of connected devices worldwide was projected to increase from 9 billion in 2012 to 23 billion in 2016.[162] Some estimates put the Internet's contribution to global GDP at as much as $4.2 trillion in 2016.[163]

The innovations of the technological revolution have ranged from three-dimensional technology to digital banking, from e-books to e-commerce, from the sharing economy to crowdworking. Economies have become individualized to match demand and supply peer-to-peer. The labour market does not require a traditional workplace, and the process has opened opportunities for many while making work precarious or even vulnerable for many others.

Mobile phones and mobile Internet services offer many new opportunities for

As more people raise their voices to express their hopes and aspirations as well as their despair and frustration, mobilizing to demand what they want will become easier

BOX 1.7

Cyberactivism—a new form of participation

Cyberactivism is political engagement by means of the Internet. Netizens are individuals who work to create online communities to realize social or political goals. But the Internet also brings together individuals who do not otherwise engage in political or public life and simply feel concerned by a specific issue.

On several occasions in recent years, large numbers of people have signed online petitions to draw the attention of policymakers to their opinions. In 2010, 2 million petitioners succeeded in banning politicians convicted of crimes from running for office in Brazil. In 2012 an online petition received 1.8 million signatures in support of the recognition of Palestine as a state by the United Nations. In 2014, 2.3 million people signed an online petition to oppose the eviction of the Maasai people from their ancestral lands by the Tanzanian government. Since 2010 the United Kingdom has provided the opportunity for citizens to petition Parliament on an issue by gathering 100,000 signatures.

In 2003 online mobilization led protests in several countries against the war in Iraq. Over the past 10 years this trend has encompassed protests by civil society organizations and protests prompted by individuals who join together over a specific issue and then disengage from political discourse. An important aspect of these protests is their geographic scope, sometimes spanning several cities and sometimes several countries.

Source: Human Development Report Office.

people—access to dynamic price information (as in Niger), productivity gains (as in Morocco), job creation in technology-based industries and labour-market services. They have helped poor female entrepreneurs through marketing information (as in Bangladesh) and contributed to the financial inclusion of poor people through mobile banking (as in Kenya).[164]

The digital revolution raises the hope of addressing such daunting challenges as ensuring food security, overcoming health concerns, combating climate change and meeting energy needs. The development of immunotherapy has opened opportunities for successfully battling different types of cancers, such as breast cancer. Three-dimensional printing can produce industrial prototypes and human tissue. Cloud technology has the potential to improve access to online information technology services for businesses and governments at low cost and to enable new online products and services for millions of producers and billions of consumers.

Continuing the progress in women's empowerment

Women have made major strides in all walks of life. Gender equality and women's empowerment are not add-on issues in the development dialogue, but a mainstream dimension of the development discourse locally, nationally and globally.

Women have proved to be productive economic actors, prudent decisionmakers, visionary leaders, compassionate volunteers and constructive peacekeepers. And many women are expanding their horizons.

Focusing primarily on girls and disadvantaged groups, Nepal's Welcome to School Initiative led to an increase in net enrolment of 470,000 children, 57 percent of them girls, within a year of its implementation in 2005.[165] Nepal's policy on adolescent girls was initially centred on health and education but now encompasses needs in employment, skills development and civic participation.[166]

Access to employment opportunities and to finance has opened opportunities for many poor women. The Women Development Act in the Philippines allows women to borrow money, obtain loans, execute security and credit arrangements and access loans in agrarian reform and land resettlement programmes under the same conditions as men.[167] Financial services in South Africa and the United States are similarly regulated to avoid gender discrimination.[168]

Romania's Order No. 473/2014 supports female entrepreneurs by financing their best business plans.[169] It aims to cultivate entrepreneurship among woman-owned businesses. Bangladesh is encouraging female participation in the workforce, with the ambition of bringing the share of women in the workforce up from 34 percent to 82 percent by 2026, thus adding 1.8 percentage points to GDP.[170] In the Democratic Republic of Congo a new family code is being drafted to support women in business.[171] All these efforts contribute to women's economic empowerment, which needs to be appropriately conceptualized (box 1.8).

Women have become active in areas where they were not traditionally active, and they have excelled in every aspect of life where they are engaged, even in societies where women have faced great obstacles in overcoming their traditional roles. Consider the success of Kimia Alizadeh, the Iranian female athlete at the 2016 Olympics, who not only competed but won a medal.[172] There is now a female fighter pilot in the United Arab Emirates.[173]

Women are demanding gender equality in all walks of life. Nearly 15,000 people recently signed an online petition in Saudi Arabia calling on the government to abolish the country's guardianship system, which prevents women from engaging in fundamental tasks without the permission of a male relative or without being accompanied.[174]

Society is gradually accepting and appreciating what women can achieve and contribute. Norms, values and legal frameworks are evolving. Côte d'Ivoire is tackling legal discrimination against women.[175] While in the 1990s very few countries legally protected women from violence, today 127 do. This is partly the result of successful awareness-raising on the human and economic cost of such violence.[176] Lebanon now penalizes domestic violence. Peru prohibits sexual harassment in public spaces. Hungary criminalized economic violence as a form of domestic violence. Cabo Verde adopted a new law in 2011 to fight gender-based violence.[177] The State of Palestine recently elaborated the Arab region's first national strategy to fight violence against women, with the participation of survivors of violence.

Women have become active in areas where they were not traditionally active, and they have excelled in every aspect of life where they are engaged

BOX 1.8

Five misconceptions about women's economic empowerment

- *Women's economic contribution is limited when women are not employed.* Globally, women are less engaged in paid employment than men. In 2015, 36 percent of women and 44 percent of men worked full time for an employer. However, women's economic contribution in unpaid care and domestic work is remarkable: a 2011 survey in 46 countries found that, on average, 28 percent of women and 6 percent of men spent three to five hours a day on household work.

- *Women's economic participation equals women's economic empowerment.* Increasing the number of women in the workforce is an important objective, but if they enter it under poor conditions, their empowerment may not be improved. Exploitation, dangerous or stigmatized work, low pay and job insecurity are unfavourable terms often encountered by women.

- *There is an automatic win-win between gender equality and wider development outcomes.* Gender equality has been found to promote economic growth, household poverty reduction and human development. But the reverse is not always true. This means that governments need to pay

dedicated attention to gender equality and not rely solely on growth to achieve it.

- *What works for one group of women will work for another.* Women across the world often face similar obstacles, such as limited access to property and financial services, lack of social protection and unpaid care burden. Yet demographic, economic and cultural contexts also contribute to these barriers and make each woman's experience different from others'. Policymakers cannot consider women to be a homogeneous group and apply standardized solutions to gender issues. Tailored approaches are required.

- *Increasing women's individual skills and aspirations is the main challenge.* Women's capacity to seize economic opportunities can be substantially improved through individual support such as training in business management skills, but structural causes of gender inequality must be addressed simultaneously. A survey of 67 countries in 2009 showed that 20 percent of men believed that women should not be allowed to hold any job that they are qualified for outside of their home.

Source: Hunt and Samman 2016.

Countries where the rule of law is applied also have more gender-equal laws

El Salvador obtained its first conviction in a case of femicide after a national protocol to guide investigations was adopted.[178] In Latin America and the Caribbean the United Nations Entity for Gender Equality and the Empowerment of Women is working with the Office of the High Commissioner for Human Rights to promote the adoption of a regional model protocol for investigating femicide.[179] Gambia and the United Republic of Tanzania have banned child marriage, raising the legal age of marriage for both boys and girls to 18.[180] And in Mozambique, marrying the survivor of rape is no longer a defence option for rapists.[181]

Countries where the rule of law is applied also have more gender-equal laws.[182] Specialized courts that tackle acts of violence against women can help provide effective legal action. Domestic and family violence courts were created in Brazil through the Maria da Penha Law. The Indian inheritance law reform improved the economic freedom of women, who were thereby able to double their spending on

their daughters' education thanks to increased savings.

Slowly opening the space for action on some taboos

Several issues that were once rarely discussed and poorly addressed have received increased attention from the general public, civil society and policymakers over the last two decades. Among the groups of people who have benefited from breaking these taboos are lesbian, gay, bisexual, transgender and intersex people, women and girls who suffered female genital mutilation and cutting, and survivors of gender-based violence. Same-sex marriage is performed in nearly two dozen countries.[183] Numerous countries recognize civil unions, registered partnership and unregistered cohabitation. Even though lesbian, gay, bisexual, transgender and intersex people have equal constitutional rights in only five countries, at least their existence is recognized and their problems are discussed in various platforms, including the United Nations.[184] According to a report by GLSEN, the situation of lesbian, gay, bisexual, transgender and intersex students in the United Sates may be gradually improving, but it remains troublesome.[185] Many civil society organizations such as OutRight Action International have been working to address these issues.

Several countries have implemented legal reforms to reduce female genital mutilation and cutting, femicide, acid violence and honour violence. Gambia has outlawed female genital mutilation and cutting.[186] El Salvador and Mexico have enacted legal reforms that define femicide as a criminal offence and have adopted measures to prevent and punish the crime.[187]

The first law banning acid violence was passed in Bangladesh in 2002, and the death penalty was introduced later as punishment for the crime.[188] Acid attacks in Bangladesh fell from 494 incidents in 2002 to 59 in 2015. The Indian Penal Code was amended in 2013 to recognize acid violence as a criminal act.[189] Female parliamentarians, political leaders and nongovernmental advocates in Pakistan have actively supported new legislation to prevent acid attacks against women.[190] About 100 acid attacks in Colombia occur each year, so the country strengthened its legislative framework and enacted a law in January 2016 to impose sentences of 12–50 years imprisonment for perpetrators.[191]

The Acid Survivor Foundation, active in Bangladesh, Cambodia and India, provides support to acid violence survivors.[192] A dedicated helpline in the State of Palestine, including online counselling and referral mechanisms, has already provided information to and potentially saved the lives of 18,000 callers.[193]

Increasing awareness of sustainability

Awareness of sustainability has been increasing. It is much more visible in the global development agenda today than it was in the 1990s (box 1.9). Both the 2030 Agenda and the Paris Agreement on climate change bear this out. This increased visibility results from changes in the environment, natural resources and the climate that we can now all perceive. These changes have made it necessary to transform the way we produce, consume and function to protect our ability—and the ability of future generations—to live on the planet.

Realization is growing that natural resources are everybody's responsibility, from individuals to global institutions. They are global common-pool resources, meaning that they are limited (overuse reduces the availability for other users) and that anyone can access them relatively freely (regulating their consumption is difficult). So their management must be global, but national and local actions can have considerable impacts. The pollution of a river by a single factory can deplete natural resources along the riverbanks for kilometres downstream and pollute underground water reserves over an even larger area. Positive individual actions, if repeated by millions of people, can likewise make a difference.

Several countries have implemented legal reforms to reduce female genital mutilation and cutting, femicide, acid violence and honour violence

The growing recognition of the importance of environmental sustainability

In 1992 a milestone summit was organized in Rio de Janeiro that led to the United Nations Framework Convention on Climate Change. In 2000 environmental sustainability was included as one of the eight Millennium Development Goals and subsequently integrated into most international and national development strategies. At the World Summit on Social Development in 2005, environmental sustainability was recognized as one of the three pillars of sustainable development, along with economic development and social development.

The year 2015 was a turning point with the adoption of the 2030 Agenda, which gives unprecedented attention to environmental sustainability and climate change, and the Paris Agreement on climate change, through which 195 member states committed to reducing carbon emissions. Three of 17 Sustainable Development Goals are dedicated to environmental sustainability, and all of the others call for environmentally sustainable practices in their respective fields. Increasingly perceptible resource depletion and climate change highlight the importance of integrating environmental sustainability in development strategies for the good of present and future generations.

Source: Human Development Report Office.

The power of culture to prompt action

My son recently asked me whether he had saved much CO_2 from being emitted into the air by using the Little Sun solar lamp I designed. He also wanted to know why, if a tonne of CO_2 weighs so much, it does not drop to the ground. And where is it? To him, a tonne is heavy and physical and not an intangible mass distributed in the atmosphere. His questions made me realize how little I myself know about CO_2.

When I was my son's age, back in the late seventies, there was no discussion of climate change. Nature was where I spent my summers, in a tent in the Icelandic highlands, a stark contrast to the Copenhagen I lived in. These natural and manmade realms could not be more separate. But today, there is no nature outside of human activity. Our survival and future depend on understanding the effects of CO_2 consumption and acting on that understanding.

But what do we understand? What, for instance, is a tonne of CO_2? Is it hot or cold, wet or dry? Perhaps it would help to know that one tonne of CO_2 could be imagined as a cube the size of a three-storey house or that, when frozen, it would form a block of dry ice about 0.67 cubic metres in size. But what does that actually tell me if I do not know how much CO_2 I produce in a year or on an average day? What does it tell me if I do not sense my interrelationship with planet Earth?

We need science to tell us that the weight of CO_2 is based on the atomic mass of the molecules. A scientist can tell me that a tonne of CO_2 is equal to the energy expenditure of a house for about a month, a small car driven for two days nonstop or a 747 flying for less than two minutes and that because of the greenhouse effect, excessive amounts of CO_2 in the atmosphere lead to global warming.

But for many people, science alone is not enough to compel action. It struck me, when I was looking up this data, that it was familiar, that I had seen it more than once in the media and that I somehow knew most of it. So I asked myself why does knowing not translate into doing when so much is at stake?

This is where culture has something to offer. Culture can help us make sense of abstract concepts and information in ways which resonate. The visual arts, theatre, poetry, literature, dance, architecture and creativity in a broad sense help us build a relationship with abstract ideas, making them concrete, felt. Culture can add motivational impetus to the knowledge we gain from science. Importantly, however, culture can bring people to the point of action without prescribing the actual action. It does not tell us what to do or how to feel, but rather empowers us to find out for ourselves. Today, in politics, we are bombarded with emotional appeals, often linked to polarizing, populist ideas. The great thing about the arts and culture, on the other hand, is that they allow spaces to emerge in which people can disagree and still be together, where they can share individual and collective experiences, and, in the process, form diverse communities based on inclusion rather than exclusion. Experiences like these can become exercises in democracy, inspiring trust, in ourselves and in society.

When I work in my studio, I draw inspiration from the fact that neuroscientists and psychologists recognize that the brain has two different systems for processing perceptions: one is analytical and deals with facts and data, and the other is experiential and deals with emotions and instincts. The experiential system—activated when you encounter art, for instance—tends to be the stronger motivator. Much of the communication on climate change, however, is focused on the analytical, attempting to reason with people to change their behaviour. Although it is clearly important to ground action in knowledge and rational thought, we also need to understand the central role of our experiential system in motivating action.

Ice Watch, an artistic intervention that I created with Minik Rosing, a geologist and expert on Greenland, takes an experiential approach by bringing people into direct contact with the physical reality of climate change. In 2015, during COP21 in Paris, we brought almost 100 tonnes of glacial ice from Greenland to the Place du Panthéon. Visitors touched the blocks of ice as they melted, put their ear to them and even tasted the ice. When we asked people about their responses, most described feelings; they felt touched. Some spoke about the sounds of the melting ice, like miniature explosions—as if the small pockets of compressed air, frozen inside the turquoise ice for millennia, were speaking to us from the past. Contact with the ice afforded an experience of its fragility, of time and of the distant Arctic. It was both concrete, physical and spatial as well as abstract and contemplative. Together, the emotional and intellectual experience allowed each of us to host the climate debate in our bodies, paving the way for an embodied understanding of our changing environment and planet.

Culture can inspire people to move from thinking to doing, and it holds the potential to inspire great social change. It is only by connecting the head and the heart that we will succeed in building a future for the planet shaped by positive, powerful climate action.

Olafur Eliasson
Artist and founder of Little Sun

Climate-smart agriculture and climate-smart development are gaining currency. For example, about 500,000 solar panels were installed every day in 2015, an unprecedented growth that meant that renewable energy had become the world's top source of installed power capacity.[194] On a single day—11 July 2016—India planted 50 million trees to take on climate change.[195] In 2015, 247,000 electric cars were sold in China.[196] Globally, 13 percent of greenhouse gas emissions are now covered by carbon pricing initiatives.[197] The value of the trade in environmental goods almost tripled between 2001 and 2012, from $231 billion to $656 billion.[198] According to some estimates, the value of the environmental goods and services market will reach $1.9 trillion by 2020. Trade can also do more to spread green technology. A clear shift in spending towards cleaner energy was seen in 2015—$313 billion in renewable energy sources and $221 billion in energy efficiency.[199]

But awareness about sustainability has to take a broader view. For example, climate change is not only an environmental issue or a science issue. Olafur Eliasson, artist and founder of Little Sun, argues that to internalize and act on the vital data of climate change, culture has something to offer (see special contribution).

Stronger global commitments

Over the years people have grown accustomed to heated debates leading to bitter gridlock at the national, regional and global levels. But through the rubble the tender shoots of a global consensus are emerging to ensure a sustainable world for future generations. The 2030 Agenda adopted by 193 member states of the United Nations on 25 September 2015 is among the most important platforms for efforts to end poverty by 2030 and pursue a sustainable future.[200] The agenda includes 17 Sustainable Development Goals, 169 targets and 230 indicators (box 1.10).

Similarly, parties to the United Nations Framework Convention on Climate Change reached a landmark agreement on 12 December 2015 in Paris, charting a fundamentally new course in the two-decade-old global climate efforts. After four years of negotiations the treaty is the first to consider both developed and developing countries in a common framework, urging them all to make their best efforts and reinforce their commitments in the coming years.[201] All parties should now report regularly on emissions and on efforts to implement their commitments and submit to international review. The Paris Agreement on climate change came into force on 4 November 2016. More than 70 countries, which account for nearly 60 percent of global emissions, have ratified it.[202]

The first UN Summit for Refugees, held in September 2016, brought member states together to agree on a more humane and coordinated way to respond to the risks faced by refugees and migrants and to prepare for future challenges. It resulted in the New York Declaration, a series of national and international commitments (see chapter 6).

A recent groundbreaking ruling by the International Criminal Court in The Hague sentenced an Islamic militant from Mali who helped destroy the fabled shrines of Timbuktu to imprisonment for nine years.[203] The trial was unique on two fronts: it was the first at the court to focus solely on cultural destruction as a war crime, and it was the court's first prosecution of an Islamic militant.

The human development approach and the 2030 Agenda

The human development approach and the 2030 Agenda have three common analytical links (figure 1.10):

- Both are anchored in universalism—the human development approach by emphasizing the enhancement of freedoms for every human being and the 2030 Agenda by concentrating on leaving no one behind.
- Both share the same fundamental areas of focus—eradicating extreme poverty, ending hunger, reducing inequality, ensuring gender equality and so on.
- Both have sustainability as the core principle.

The links among the human development approach, the 2030 Agenda and the Sustainable Development Goals are mutually reinforcing in three ways. First, the conceptual foundation of the 2030 Agenda is strengthened by the analytical elements of the human development approach strengthen its conceptual foundation. Similarly, the human development approach is enriched by elements in the narrative of the 2030 Agenda.

Second, the Sustainable Development Goal indicators can be used with the human development indicators in assessing progress towards the Sustainable Development Goals. Similarly, the human development approach can supplement the Sustainable Development Goal indicators with additional indicators.

In spite of heated debates leading to bitter gridlock at the national, regional and global levels, through the rubble the tender shoots of a global consensus are emerging to ensure a sustainable world for future generations

BOX 1.10

Sustainable Development Goals

Goal 1
End poverty in all its forms everywhere

Goal 2
End hunger, achieve food security and improved nutrition and promote sustainable agriculture

Goal 3
Ensure healthy lives and promote well-being for all at all ages

Goal 4
Ensure inclusive and equitable quality education and promote lifelong learning opportunities for all

Goal 5
Achieve gender equality and empower all women and girls

Goal 6
Ensure availability and sustainable management of water and sanitation for all

Goal 7
Ensure access to affordable, reliable, sustainable and modern energy for all

Goal 8
Promote sustained, inclusive and sustainable economic growth, full and productive employment and decent work for all

Goal 9
Build resilient infrastructure, promote inclusive and sustainable industrialization and foster innovation

Goal 10
Reduce inequality within and among countries

Goal 11
Make cities and human settlements inclusive, safe, resilient and sustainable

Goal 12
Ensure sustainable consumption and production patterns

Goal 13
Take urgent action to combat climate change and its impacts[1]

Goal 14
Conserve and sustainably use the oceans, seas and marine resources for sustainable development

Goal 15
Protect, restore and promote sustainable use of terrestrial ecosystems, sustainably manage forests, combat desertification, and halt and reverse land degradation and halt biodiversity loss

Goal 16
Promote peaceful and inclusive societies for sustainable development, provide access to justice for all and build effective, accountable and inclusive institutions at all levels

Goal 17
Strengthen the means of implementation and revitalize the Global Partnership for Sustainable Development

1. Acknowledging that the United Nations Framework Convention on Climate Change is the primary international, intergovernmental forum for negotiating the global response to climate change.
Source: United Nations 2015c.

> The links among the human development approach, the 2030 Agenda and the Sustainable Development Goals are mutually reinforcing

Third, the Human Development Report can be an extremely powerful advocacy instrument for the 2030 Agenda and the Sustainable Development Goals. And the Sustainable Development Goals can be a good platform for the greater visibility of the human development approach and the Human Development Report through 2030.

Universalism is at the core of human development. And given the progress in human development over the past 25 years and the hope it presents, human development for everyone must be and can be attained. But there are considerable challenges and barriers to universal human development So universalism of human development must not remain a philosophical tenet. It must become a practical reality to analyse the who and where of why human development not reaching everyone—a task for chapter 2.

FIGURE 1.10

Analytical links between the human development approach and the 2030 Agenda

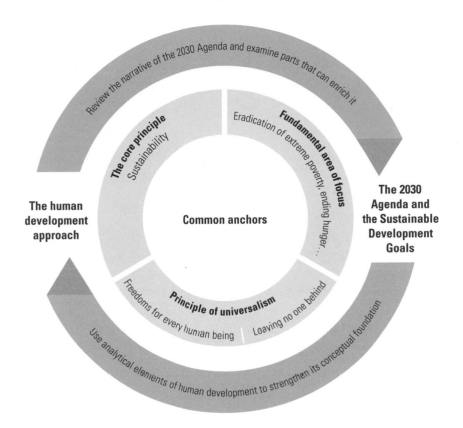

Chapter **2**

Universalism— from principles to practice

Infographic 2.1 Barriers to universalism

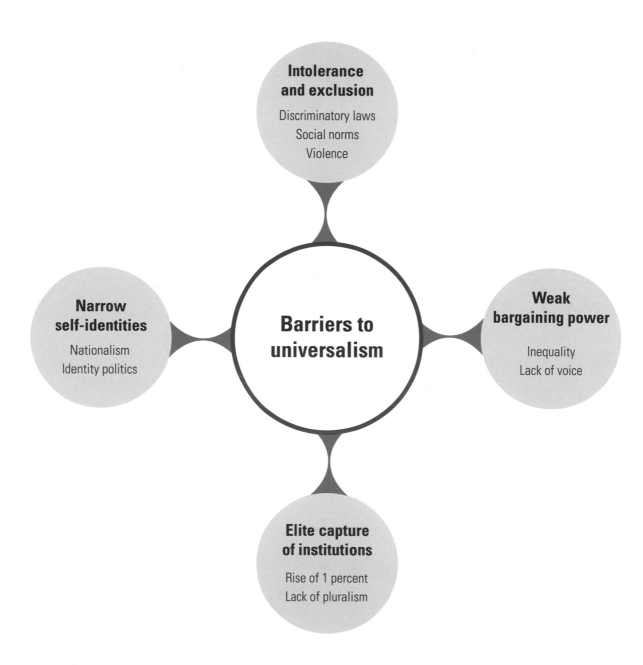

2.

Universalism—from principles to practice

The progress in human development over the past 25 years has been impressive on many fronts. More children are going to school, people are living longer, incomes are higher and people have greater potential to shape their societies and their future under democratic forms of government. But the gains have not been universal, and not all lives have been lifted. This reality was the impetus for the intergovernmental agreement on the 2030 Agenda, which aims to leave no one behind. Millions of people are indeed unable to reach their full potential in life because they suffer deprivations in multiple dimensions of human development—lacking income and secure livelihoods, experiencing hunger and malnutrition, having no or limited access to social services, fearing violence and discrimination and being marginalized from the political processes that shape their lives. There are imbalances across countries; socioeconomic, ethnic and racial groups; urban and rural areas; and women and men. Some groups are more deprived than others, and the most deprived individuals belong to multiple disadvantaged groups—an older, ethnic minority woman in a least developed country, for example.

The absolute deprivations in basic human development remain pronounced and demand urgent attention. But being left behind is a dynamic and relative process, so universalism—human development for everyone—requires a forward-looking approach. As gains are achieved, other deprivations may become more critical, and new groups may bear the burden of being left behind. Many people appear to be doing well according to measures such as minimum schooling and income, but the quality of education and of work conditions are low for many millions of people. Likewise, people are living longer and healthier lives, but many face deficits in political freedom and in opportunities for political participation.

Demographic shifts, transitions from peace to insecurity and other macro threats such as epidemics, financial crises, natural disasters and climate change all generate new forms of advantage and disadvantage. In this digital age a lack of reliable access to information, infrastructure or technology can severely curtail opportunities, even in developed countries, reshaping patterns of deprivation. And even as restrictive social norms—such as restrictions on women working outside the home—lose force in some societies, others—such as discrimination against older people—become more powerful. Who is left behind, how and why are questions with different answers in different places at different times.

Enabling all human beings to realize their full potential demands urgent attention to inequality and to relative capabilities and opportunities. It is not enough to enable those with the least capabilities to move above minimum thresholds. For instance, even if extreme poverty were to be eradicated globally or universal primary school enrolment attained, the wealthy and highly educated could simultaneously accrue enormous economic resources or achieve higher tertiary enrolment rates, thereby maintaining or even widening gaps in key capabilities. Despite absolute gains for all people, the possibilities for those with the least wealth and education to realize their full potential would continue to lag.

Because the starting points vary widely across individuals, more equitable outcomes may require greater attention and support for the people who are farthest behind. It is particularly important to close the gaps in voice and agency. Institutions and policies may otherwise disproportionately reflect the values and interests of elites, who often have greater voice. There is a risk that gaps could become self-perpetuating and ever more difficult to eradicate. And extreme inequalities in voice and agency can breed economic, social and political instability and conflict.

Human development embodies a commitment to ensure rights, voice, security and freedom—not to most, but to all people in every corner of the world. It also stresses the importance of sustaining capabilities and opportunities throughout an individual's lifecycle and for subsequent generations.

> As gains are achieved, other deprivations may become more critical, and new groups may bear the burden of being left behind

One of the main challenges of practical universalism—advancing from ideas to actions and institutions—is reaching those who experience the most extreme deprivations and those who are the most socially marginalized and excluded. Technical and financial barriers can be overcome, and there are indeed strong collective efforts in this direction. But deep-seated barriers to universalism, including discriminatory social norms and laws and inequalities in agency and voice, require more attention. There is also a need to appreciate the dynamic nature of deprivations and exclusion—that gains can be reversed by health or financial shocks, that new barriers can emerge if conflict erupts or community security and services deteriorate and that new groups without reliable access to the Internet can be marginalized when that access becomes central to livelihoods.

The goal is not only to reach the most deprived and ensure that no one is left behind today, but also to protect those at risk of being left behind tomorrow. Universalism is a principle of the human development approach, and now is the time to translate it into practice by identifying and breaking down barriers that exclude certain groups, narrowing the wide gaps in life chances among different groups, proposing policy options that fit contexts and levels of development and identifying institutional shortcomings. This is practical universalism.

Momentum towards universalism

Space is opening for the practice of universalism and the extension of human development to everyone. The 2030 Agenda takes a universal approach. Its Sustainable Development Goals embody a shared vision of progress towards a safe, just and sustainable world in which all human beings can thrive. The goals reflect principles of universality that no one and no country should be excluded and that everyone and every country share a common—albeit differentiated—responsibility for the outcomes of all. Global momentum is thus in place to enable policymakers and advocates to move in ways that may have been much more difficult in the past.

Translating principle into policy and institutional practice requires mapping out who the

deprived are, where they live, what the extent of their deprivation is and what the risks of new deprivations are. The *Report on the World Social Situation 2016* noted that universalism is possible only after those who are being left behind have been identified.[1] With this reasoning, this chapter:

- Looks beyond national averages and existing measures.
- Comprehends the development barriers that often block particular groups, such that some groups are disproportionately marginalized and more at risk of emerging threats.
- Contextualizes human development, identifying deprivations and inequalities across the spectrum of countries with different incomes and human development profiles and mapping out how new barriers can emerge, even as some deprivations are overcome.
- Analyses the barriers to practical universalism so that steps can be taken to eliminate them.

Beyond averages—using the family of human development indices

Human development is about improving the life chances of individuals. However, the measures used to monitor progress in human development often cover only countries and not individuals or groups. Disaggregated measures are therefore needed that show who is deprived, where they live and the nature of their deprivations. National, subregional and regional Human Development Reports have identified deprivations by analysing data disaggregated by age, gender, subnational units, ethnicity and other parameters. Disaggregating and analysing the family of human development indices— the Human Development Index (HDI), the Inequality-adjusted Human Development Index (IHDI), the Gender Development Index (GDI), the Gender Inequality Index (GII) and the Multidimensional Poverty Index (MPI)— are early steps towards quantifying the scale of deprivations globally.

Human Development Index

The HDI is one tool for identifying deprivations in a selection of essential capabilities (a long and healthy life, knowledge and a decent standard of living). Country-level trends on the HDI have been impressive over the past 25 years: Between 1990 and 2015 the number of countries classified as having low human development fell from 62 to 41, and those classified as having very high human development rose from 11 to 51.[2] These shifts reflect improvements in the life conditions of millions of people. But the trends also reflect average national progress. The unfortunate reality is that millions of people fall on the wrong side of the average and struggle with hunger, poverty, illiteracy and malnutrition, among other deprivations. Making human development work for everyone requires a greater understanding of who these people are and where they live.

Disaggregated HDI values within countries confirm that many people live with unacceptably high deprivation, even though their country appears to have improved in HDI value and rank. Panama is classified as having high human development, but 2 of its 12 provinces are classified as having low human development, while the capital province is classified as having very high human development.[3] Ethiopia is classified as having low human development, as are 9 of its 11 regions, but 2 regions are classified as

having medium human development.[4] In both countries the split is between capital provinces and more rural areas.

Disaggregation at the global level suggests that a third of the world's population lives in low human development (figure 2.1). Many of these people are severely deprived in education, health and income. Medium, high and very high human development countries are home to hundreds of millions of people living in low human development.[5] Many people are being left behind in countries across the development spectrum.

Inequality-adjusted Human Development Index

Unequal concentrations of well-being mean that indicators of average human development like the HDI do not reflect the well-being of a vast portion of the population. The IHDI quantifies the effects of inequality on human development, measured in terms of the HDI.

Some 22 percent of the world's human development is lost because of inequality.[6] Inequality in education contributes the most to overall inequality, followed by inequality in income and inequality in life expectancy. Sub-Saharan

Disaggregated HDI values within countries confirm that many people live with unacceptably high deprivation, even though their country appears to have improved in HDI value and rank

FIGURE 2.1

A third of the world's population lives in low human development

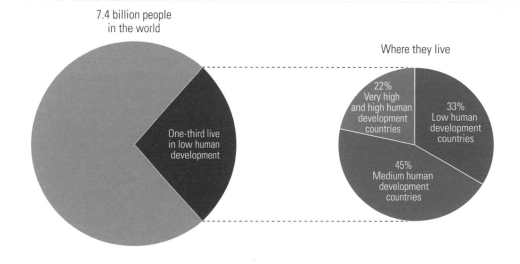

7.4 billion people in the world

One-third live in low human development

Where they live

22% Very high and high human development countries

33% Low human development countries

45% Medium human development countries

Source: Human Development Report Office.

Africa has the highest loss of human development because of inequality (32 percent).[7]

At the country level unequal distribution of human development occurs both in low human development countries, such as Comoros (where 46 percent of human development is lost because of inequality) and in very high human development countries, such as Chile (where 18 percent of human development is lost because of inequality).[8] The IHDI indicates that human development for everyone will require considerable interventions to overcome unequal distributions in key capabilities within countries.

Gender Development Index and Gender Inequality Index

Women are more likely than men to suffer from low human development.[9] Many groups are disadvantaged, but the systemic deprivations of women relative to men deserve to be highlighted because women constitute half the world's population. The deprivations facing women are the most extreme barrier to global progress in human development.

Despite the fact that in all regions women have longer life expectancy than do men and the fact that in most regions the expected number of years of schooling for girls is similar to that for boys, women consistently have a lower HDI value than do men. The largest differences captured by the GDI are in South Asia, where the HDI value for women is 17.8 percent lower than the HDI value for men, followed by the Arab States with a 14.4 percent difference and Sub-Saharan Africa with 12.3 percent.

Much of the variation in HDI between women and men is due to lower income among women relative to men and to lower educational attainment among women relative to men. Part of the variation in the HDI between men and women is generated by barriers to women working outside the home, to accessing education, to voicing their concerns in political arenas, to shaping policies and to receiving the benefits of high-quality and accessible health care.

The GII is a composite index that captures the inequality that many women face in reproductive health, secondary education, political representation and the labour market (figure 2.2). Women are the most disadvantaged in low human development countries.[10]

> The deprivations facing women are the most extreme barrier to global progress in human development

FIGURE 2.2

Women are the most disadvantaged in low human development countries

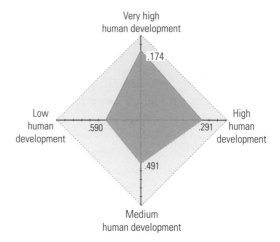

Note: 1 indicates absolute inequality, as measured by the Gender Inequality Index, and 0 indicates perfect equality.
Source: Human Development Report Office.

A challenge to global progress in human development across all regions and groups, gender inequality is most severe in low and medium human development countries and in the Arab States, South Asia and Sub-Saharan Africa.[11] As countries' human development improves, women's choices and opportunities must be equal to those of men so that everyone benefits from advances in human development.

Multidimensional Poverty Index

Deprived people often lack capabilities and opportunities across multiple dimensions. The MPI, which is calculated for 102 developing countries, reveals more about the depth and overlapping nature of people's nonincome deprivations than do one-dimensional measures of poverty. Based on 10 indicators, the MPI identifies households that are acutely deprived by their health, education and standard of living. Almost 1.5 billion people in the developing countries for which the MPI is calculated live in multidimensional poverty, 53.9 percent of them in South Asia and 33.5 percent in Sub-Saharan Africa.[12] People are also deprived in developed countries (box 2.1).

Some systematic patterns of deprivation can be inferred from poverty measures. People in rural areas are far more likely than people in urban areas to be multidimensionally poor (29

BOX 2.1

Poverty is also a developed country problem

Deprivations are a universal problem afflicting people in developed and developing countries alike. An average of 11 percent of the population in Organisation for Economic Co-operation and Development (OECD) countries were below the income poverty line in 2014.[1] As of 2012 there were 633,000 homeless people in the United States and 284,000 in Germany.[2] OECD countries have the highest incarceration rates of any group of countries: an average of 274 people per 100,000, isolated from society in prison.[3] An average of 15 percent of young people ages 15–29 are neither employed nor in education or training and are struggling to find their place in society.[4] Health deprivations caused by obesity are also high. The most recent survey data indicate that an average of 53.8 percent of the adult population in OECD countries is overweight or obese and faces high risks of cardiovascular disease, respiratory illnesses, diabetes and other diseases.[5]

The data make clear that not all people in countries classified as having very high human development are able to achieve their full life potential. Poverty can take different forms in developed countries and in developing countries, but it is no less debilitating to the choices and the future of individuals and households experiencing the deprivations.

Notes
1. OECD 2016a. 2. OECD 2015a. 3. Based on UNODC (2016). 4. OECD 2016e. 5. OECD 2015b.
Source: Human Development Report Office.

---

percent versus 11 percent), though there is variation across regions (figure 2.3).

Nearly half of people in rural areas worldwide lack access to improved sanitation facilities, compared with a sixth of people in urban areas.[13] And twice as many rural children as urban children are out of school.[14] At the same time, slumdwellers account for 48 percent of the urban population in developing countries and are deprived of many services and opportunities —the very benefits that many deprived people migrated from rural areas to obtain.[15]

There is a high likelihood that if a household is deprived in one of the 10 indicators used to calculate the MPI, it will also be deprived in others. To improve the conditions of the most

> There is a high likelihood that if a household is deprived in one of the 10 indicators used to calculate the MPI, it will also be deprived in others

FIGURE 2.3

People in rural areas are far more likely than people in urban areas to be multidimensionally poor

Population in multidimensional poverty (%)

Rural population
Urban population

	Rural	Urban
Developing countries	29	11
Sub-Saharan Africa	74	31
South Asia	64	25
Arab States	29	8
Latin America & the Caribbean	19	3
East Asia & the Pacific	8	2
Europe and Central Asia	3	1

Source: Human Development Report Office.

deprived, a more comprehensive cross-sectoral approach to policy may thus be more effective than interventions that separately target particular elements of poverty.

Poverty rates differ between men and women. Although at the global level households headed by men and those headed women are almost equally likely to be multidimensionally poor—29 percent of man-headed households and 28 percent of woman-headed households are multidimensionally poor—there is considerable variation across countries and regions.[16] Because the MPI is calculated at the household level rather than at the individual level, complementary research may be needed to clarify the relationship between gender and poverty.

People are more likely to fall into multidimensional poverty during conflict, and people in conflict areas face particular barriers to moving out of multidimensional poverty. An average of 49 percent of the population in 24 countries in conflict for which the MPI is calculated lives in multidimensional poverty, and another 16 percent live in near-poverty. An average of 27 percent of people in these countries live in severe multidimensional poverty.

Deprivations also vary across socioeconomic groups. In Sub-Saharan Africa poor people, especially women attending school in rural communities, are far less likely than nonpoor people to be learning critical skills such as reading, writing and mathematics.[17] In Chad the richest quintile of the population averages 6.7 years of schooling, compared with 1.0 for the poorest quintile. The story is similar in Ethiopia—7.5 years for the richest quintile and 1.6 years for the poorest quintile—and in Madagascar—9.8 years and 1.7 years.[18] In South Africa HIV prevalence is higher among the poorest socioeconomic groups. Access to basic social services of acceptable quality is often limited among people living in poverty, intensifying the disparities in well-being. In Zambia poor people are less likely to use public hospitals because of financial and physical barriers, despite having greater need than other income groups.[19]

Too many people are still missing out

The HDI, GII, GDI and MPI indicate that not everyone is lifted as countries progress on these average measures. Despite the overall progress, about one-third of people in the world live in unacceptably low human development. Many of them—especially women and girls, people in rural areas and people in countries in conflict—suffer multiple and overlapping deprivations.

Viewing the nation as the primary unit of analysis for policymaking and measurement has value, but looking directly at the conditions of individuals is essential for identifying who is being left behind. Countries' human development may improve, but this does not mean that entire populations are better off or benefit equally. Supplementing national measures with subnational measures is important for policymaking. Data disaggregation is critical for identifying the integrated actions needed to support universalism and the full realization of life potential among all people (see chapter 3). Melinda Gates, co-chair of the Bill & Melinda Gates Foundation, argues that getting a clearer picture of poverty and deprivation is a fundamental first step towards designing and implementing more effective policies and interventions (see special contribution).

A look at disadvantaged groups

All people in all circumstances are not equally disadvantaged. People with certain characteristics, in certain locations or at particularly vulnerable stages of the lifecycle are more likely than other people to lack access to capability-enhancing resources and opportunities to suffer deprivations. These groups are also disproportionately exposed and vulnerable to emerging threats such as epidemics, climate change and natural disasters, so progress may be less sustainable among these groups even when gains in human development are achieved. Group distinctions such as ethnicity or religion can serve as dividing lines to support discrimination and restrict access to resources and opportunities. The result can be differences in the human development outcomes of particular groups. The following subsections identify some of the groups that are missing out on progress in human development and show how deprivations may take shape in particular contexts and conditions.

mlinda Gates

Getting a clearer picture of poverty

I was asked last year to select one photograph that has profoundly influenced my life. I chose an image known as Migrant Mother—a haunting picture of a woman named Florence Owens Thompson sitting with three of her children in their makeshift home, a rudimentary tent. The photograph was taken in California in 1936 as millions of American families struggled through the Great Depression. Florence and her family are destitute and desperate.

That iconic photograph, which I first came across in high school, still comes to mind whenever poverty is the topic of conversation. Poverty as a category of analysis is an abstraction. Migrant Mother captures its harsh, biting reality better than any other image—and any dictionary definition or economic indicator—that I have ever seen. And what motivates me is that, 70 years on, this struggle is still daily life for more than a billion people around the world.

In my work I have seen that struggle firsthand. I have seen how lack of family planning advice and contraceptives leaves parents with more mouths to feed than they can afford; how not getting the right food and nutrients leaves people unable to fulfil their potential; and how disease leaves adults too weak to work, and children too sick for school.

So while there are robust and legitimate debates going on about the methodology and measurements we use to classify poverty, first and foremost we must remember what it actually means to be poor. Essentially, being poor is about deprivation. Poverty not only deprives people of food, shelter, sanitation, health, income, assets and education, it also deprives them of their fundamental rights, social protections and basic dignity. Poverty also looks different in different places. While in East Africa it is related mostly to living standards, in West Africa child mortality and lack of education are the biggest contributors.

All this complexity and variation is impossible to capture in a definition of poverty as simplistic as living on less than $1.90 a day. If we really mean to "end poverty in all its forms everywhere," as laid out in the first Sustainable Development Goal (SDG), then it fits that we have to know what all those forms are. We need to have a far clearer picture of the most marginalized and most vulnerable. Not just those who are financially poor, but those facing a number of distinct disadvantages, such as gender, race and ethnicity, that taken together deprive them of the chance to lead healthy, productive lives.

One of the reasons I find Migrant Mother so powerful is that it focuses on the plight of a woman and how she is scarred by deprivation, at a time when their hardship and suffering was sometimes overlooked by politicians and policymakers. It is critical to know more about the lives of today's Florence Owens Thompsons since women and girls are widely recognized as one of the most disregarded and disenfranchised groups in many developing countries. Indeed, the World Bank argues that a "complete demographic poverty profile should also include a gender dimension," given that most average income measurements miss the contribution and consumption of women and girls within households entirely.

For a long time, for example, when data collectors in Uganda conducted labour force surveys, they only asked about a household's primary earner. In most cases, the main breadwinner in Ugandan households was the man, so the data made it look like barely any women were participating in the workforce. When the data collectors started asking a second question—who else in the household works?—Uganda's workforce immediately increased by 700,000 people, most of them women. Obviously, these women had existed all along. But until their presence was counted and included in official reports, these women and the daily challenges they faced were ignored by policymakers. Similarly, because many surveys tend to focus solely on the head of household—and assume that to be the man—we have less idea of the numbers of women and children living in poverty and the proportion of woman-headed households in poverty.

Getting a clearer picture of poverty and deprivation is a fundamental first step towards designing and implementing more effective policies and interventions, as well as better targeting scarce resources where they will have the greatest impact. That's why our foundation is supporting partners to better identify who and where the poorest and most vulnerable are, collect better information on what they want and need to improve their lives and develop a better understanding of the structural barriers they face. The findings will then be used to develop strategies that specifically target those identified within the first 1,000 days of SDG implementation.

This report is a welcome contribution to these efforts, along with the United Nations Development Programme's ongoing work to revamp the Human Development Index (HDI), including an explicit focus on women and girls. Since its creation in 1990 the HDI has been a central pillar of multidimensional poverty and a key instrument to measure both how much we have achieved and the challenges ahead. The report is also a timely addition to the calls made by the Commission on Global Poverty, the Organisation for Economic Co-Operation and Development and others for incorporating quality of life dimensions into the way we understand and determine human deprivation.

I am excited by the prospect of a broader, more sophisticated approach to determining poverty. But all the best data in the world won't do us much good if they sit on a shelf collecting dust. They must be used to influence decisionmaking and accountability, and ultimately to transform the lives of the world's most vulnerable people. The last 15 years have shown us that progress on poverty is possible. But we also know that it is not inevitable—nor has it been universal. My hope is that this report will catalyse the global community to ensure that, this time, no one is left behind. Let's not squander this momentum.

Melinda Gates
Co-chair of the Bill & Melinda Gates Foundation

Women and girls

Women and girls are not able to live their lives to their full potential in many countries. Gender disparities in human development, while narrowing slowly, are embedded in social norms and long-standing patterns of exclusion from household and community decision-making that limit women's opportunities and choices (box 2.2).

Gender-based discrimination starts before school, even before birth. The preference for a son can lead to sex-selective abortions and missing women, particularly in some South Asian countries. Discrimination continues in families through intrahousehold resource allocation. The gender politics of food—nurtured by the assumptions, norms and values about women needing fewer calories—can push women into a perpetual state of malnutrition and protein deficiency. Women and girls sometimes eat last and least within the household. Early marriage among girls limits their long-term capabilities and potential. Each year, 15 million girls in developing countries marry before age 18, and if there is no reduction in the incidence of early marriage among girls, by 2050, 18 million girls will be married before age 18.[20] Worldwide, one out of eight age-eligible girls does not attend primary or secondary school.[21] Only 62 of 145 countries have achieved gender parity in primary and secondary education.[22]

As highlighted in the 2015 Human Development Report, women face numerous disadvantages in paid and unpaid work. The global labour force participation rate is 49.6 percent among women and 76.2 percent among men.[23] Women employed in vulnerable work or the informal economy may lack decent work conditions, social security and voice and have lower earnings than do other workers. Women also suffer discrimination in relation to productive assets, such as the right to land and property. Women are barred from owning land because of customary laws and social norms and practices. Only 10–20 percent of landholders

BOX 2.2

Gender-based inequalities in South Asian households

Women in South Asia are often excluded from decision-making, have limited access to and control over resources, are restricted in their mobility and are often under threat of violence from male relatives. These deprivations are linked strongly to patriarchal social norms and attitudes that impede equitable gender relationships within households. They have consequences for health, education and community participation.

Discrimination at each stage of the female lifecycle contributes to health disparities—from sex-selective abortions (particularly common in India and Pakistan) to lower nutrition intake and the neglect of health care among girls and women. A girl between her first and fifth birthdays in India or Pakistan has a 30–50 percent greater chance of dying than a boy. The maternal mortality ratio in South Asia is also stubbornly high, second only to that in Sub-Saharan Africa. This is partly because many births are not attended by skilled health personnel (44 percent in Bangladesh). Decisions about seeking care are made largely by husbands or older male and female household members, and mistrust or misinformation about modern health facilities for child delivery restricts access by women.

Inequality in work and education begins in childhood. Girls in South Asia learn domestic skills in the household and begin to take on domestic duties and child care. There are strong beliefs in rural areas that sons should be educated because they will remain in the family and support ageing parents, while daughters are likely to serve other families after marriage. Cultural beliefs that the role of a woman is to be a wife and mother have direct consequences on parents' incentives to invest in expanding their daughters' capabilities through education and preparation for paid work. Another common perception is that education for girls beyond primary school will make it harder for a woman to find a husband.

Legislation promoting gender equality is vital for women in South Asia. But households are where most decisionmaking takes place, and norms and values continue to perpetuate inequalities between men and women across generations, even when such laws are in place. If women are not encouraged to work outside the home, labour laws will not reach them. If families do not allow girls to attend school, scholarships and school gender quotas will not support them. And if violence against women is overlooked in the home, women will not feel empowered to voice their concerns.

Source: Banu 2016.

in developing countries are women.[24] Women take on a disproportionate amount of unpaid work in the home, forgoing opportunities for other activities, including education, visits to health centres and work outside the home. There are more women than men living in poverty. In 2012 in Latin America and the Caribbean there were 117 women in poor households for every 100 men, an 8 percent increase since 1997.[25]

In many countries outcomes in educational attainment and health are worse for girls than for boys. Globally, 60.3 percent of adult women have at least some secondary education, compared with 69.2 percent of adult men.[26] Maternal mortality ratios and adolescent birth rates are declining but remain high in Sub-Saharan Africa, at 551 deaths per 100,000 live births and 103 births per 1,000 women ages 15–19.[27]

One of the most brutal forms of women's disempowerment is violence against women, including in the home, in all societies, among all socioeconomic groups and at all levels of education. According to a 2013 global review, one-third of women—and more than two-thirds in some countries—have experienced physical or sexual violence inflicted by an intimate partner or sexual violence inflicted by a nonpartner. Some 20 percent of women experienced sexual violence as children.[28] Nearly a quarter of girls ages 15–19 worldwide reported having been victims of violence after turning 15.[29]

Violence against women can be perpetuated through social norms. For example, female genital mutilation and cutting remain widespread. New estimates indicate that 200 million women and girls living today have undergone female genital mutilation, even though the majority of men and women oppose the practice in many countries where it is performed.[30] Acid attacks against women are a heinous form of violence common in communities where patriarchal gender orders are used to justify violence against women. In the last 15 years more than 3,300 acid-throwing attacks have been recorded in Bangladesh, Colombia, Pakistan, Uganda and the United Kingdom.[31] The true number is likely much higher because many cases go unrecorded. In some societies women are also targets of honour-based violence, where the concept of honour and shame is fundamentally bound

up with the expected behaviours of women, as dictated by their families or societies. Worldwide, 5,000 women a year are murdered in such honour killings.[32]

When women are discriminated against, society suffers. Even in a narrow economic sense, gender gaps in women's entrepreneurship and labour force participation account for estimated economywide income losses of 27 percent in the Middle East and North Africa, 19 percent in South Asia, 14 percent in Latin America and the Caribbean and 10 percent in Europe.[33] In Sub-Saharan Africa annual economic losses because of gender gaps in effective labour (the labour force participation rate and years of schooling) are estimated at $95 billion.[34]

Ethnic minorities

In many developing and developed countries ethnic minority status is associated with lower capabilities and opportunities. More than 250 million people worldwide face discrimination solely on the basis of caste or inherited status.[35] In Viet Nam there are gaps between the capabilities of ethnic or linguistic minorities and the Kinh-Hoa majority. In 2012, 50.9 percent of the ethnic minority population was living in multidimensional poverty, compared with only 16.5 percent of the Kinh-Hoa population. In 2008 the poverty rate was 51 percent among ethnic minorities and 54 percent among non-Vietnamese speakers, compared with only 26 percent among the Kinh-Hoa population. Some 84.6 percent of Kinh-Hoa children ages 12–23 months were fully immunized in 2014, compared with 69.4 percent of ethnic minority children.[36]

Evidence from Nepal shows similar patterns of disadvantages among ethnic minority groups. The 2014 Nepal National Human Development Report found wide variations in HDI values across population groups, although the trends are towards less inequality. The Newar people have the highest HDI value, 0.565, followed by the Brahman-Chhetris (0.538), followed by Janajatis (0.482), Dalits (0.434) and Muslims (0.422; figure 2.4). The variations in HDI values are significant within these groups, depending on location. The highest inequalities are in education, and this may have pronounced long-term effects on capabilities later in life.

In many developing and developed countries ethnic minority status is associated with lower capabilities and opportunities

FIGURE 2.4

Variations in Human Development Index values are wide across population groups in Nepal

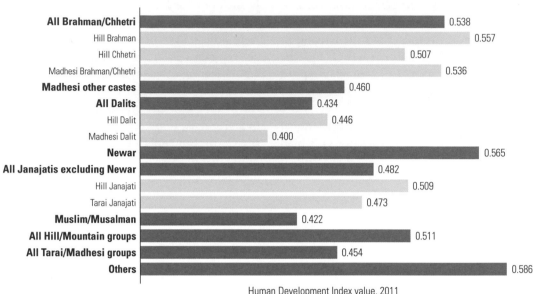

All Brahman/Chhetri	0.538
Hill Brahman	0.557
Hill Chhetri	0.507
Madhesi Brahman/Chhetri	0.536
Madhesi other castes	0.460
All Dalits	0.434
Hill Dalit	0.446
Madhesi Dalit	0.400
Newar	0.565
All Janajatis excluding Newar	0.482
Hill Janajati	0.509
Tarai Janajati	0.473
Muslim/Musalman	0.422
All Hill/Mountain groups	0.511
All Tarai/Madhesi groups	0.454
Others	0.586

Human Development Index value, 2011

Source: UNDP 2014e.

Deprivations among ethnic minorities are also apparent in very high human development countries

Deprivations among ethnic minorities are also apparent in countries classified as having very high human development. Measure of America produces an HDI value that is disaggregated by ethnic group for each state in the United States. The country's average HDI value (scaled from 0 to 10) is 5.03; the HDI value for Latinos (4.05), African Americans (3.81) and Native Americans (3.55) are below this average, while the HDI values for Whites (5.43) and Asian Americans (7.21) are above it (figure 2.5). Box 2.3 focuses on the issue of human

FIGURE 2.5

In the United States the Human Development Index value is below the country average for some ethnic groups but above it for others

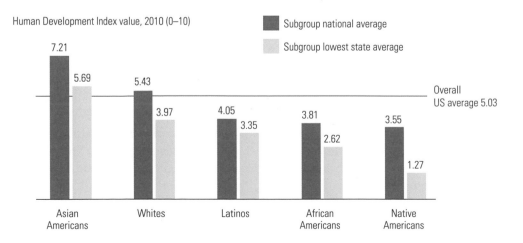

Human Development Index value, 2010 (0–10)

Subgroup national average
Subgroup lowest state average

	Asian Americans	Whites	Latinos	African Americans	Native Americans
Subgroup national average	7.21	5.43	4.05	3.81	3.55
Subgroup lowest state average	5.69	3.97	3.35	2.62	1.27

Overall US average 5.03

Note: Data refer to the Human Development Index produced by Measure of America, which differs from teh Human Development Index produced by hte Human Developme Report Office.
Source: Human Development Report Office estimates based on Lewis and Burd-Sharps (2013).

BOX 2.3

Human development among African Americans in the United States

African Americans' life expectancy is shorter than that of other ethnic and racial groups in the United States. African Americans also trail Whites and Asian Americans in education and wages: Whites earn 27 percent more on average. In some metropolitan areas the disparity is particularly striking. The life expectancy of African Americans in Baltimore, Chicago, Detroit, Pittsburgh, St. Petersburg and Tampa is now close to the national average in the late 1970s.[1] The reasons are complex but linked to a long history of legal and social discrimination.

Policies that improve educational achievement can expand opportunities for African Americans and other racial and ethnic minorities in work and other areas. Equalizing educational achievement could reduce disparities in employment between African Americans and Whites by 53 percent, incarceration by 79 percent and health outcomes by 88 percent.[2]

Differences in wages between African Americans and Whites are also related to discrimination in the job market. Discrimination accounts for an estimated one-third of wage disparities, all else (including education) being equal.[3] This indicates that policies are needed to ensure that skills and education are rewarded equally. Social pressures within the African American community can limit choices and later life chances among adolescents. Being labelled as "acting White" —whereby high-achieving African American students are shunned in some contexts by their peers for doing well academically—can discourage good performance in school.[4] Reducing the stigmatization of academic achievement among African American youth could be a step towards reducing inequalities in human development outcomes.

Notes
1. Lowis and Burd Sharps 2013. 2. Curto, Fryer and Howard 2011. 3. Fryer, Pager and Spenkuch 2013. 4. Fryer 2006.
Source: Human Development Report Office.

---

development among African Americans in the United States.

Deprivations in capabilities linked to ethnicity can be exacerbated by greater exposure to external pressures such as climate change. In Cambodia indigenous peoples are disadvantaged by higher poverty rates, limited access to education and health, and fewer representatives in national and subnational decisionmaking institutions. The same groups are doubly deprived because their livelihoods rely more heavily on natural resources and agriculture than those of other population groups, and the impact of climate change on their livelihoods has been high.

People in vulnerable locations

Where individuals are born has an immense effect on their potential capabilities and opportunities. People born in the least developed countries, fragile states and countries in conflict suffer huge disadvantages relative to people born in stable, highly developed countries. Citizenship, an ascribed group characteristic, can tie individuals to place-based conditions of violence and insecurity, under-resourced public programmes or vulnerability to environmental

change and economic shocks, with devastating effects on life chances (box 2.4).

The resources available to individuals to enhance their capabilities vary by country. For example, public spending on health care programmes and insurance in Organisation for Economic Co-operation and Development (OECD) countries averages 7.7 percent of GDP, while public health expenditures in the least developed countries average only 1.8 percent of GDP.[37] Public expenditure on education is 5.1 percent of GDP in OECD countries but 3.3 percent in the least developed countries.[38] In 2010 the share of the population living on degraded land (land with limited productive capacity) was only 3.4 percent in OECD countries but 23.5 percent in the least developed countries.[39] These statistics suggest why people in different countries face different means of reaching their full potential.

Individuals born into communities that are geographically isolated, predominantly home to politically and socially excluded minorities or disproportionately exposed to environmental pressures have fewer opportunities. Whole communities risk being left behind unless unbalanced service distribution is rectified.

Individuals born into communities that are geographically isolated, predominantly home to politically and socially excluded minorities or disproportionately exposed to environmental pressures have fewer opportunities

BOX 2.4

Limitations in opportunities among young people in small island developing states

Small island developing states face several economic challenges stemming from the limited resource base, remoteness from markets and barriers to economies of scale. Extreme vulnerabilities to climate change place additional stress on economic activity, particularly in tourism, fisheries and agriculture. The economic vulnerabilities translate into limited choices and opportunities among citizens. The obstacles are especially high for young people looking for decent work. The youth unemployment rate ranges from 18 percent to 47 percent among countries in the Caribbean, with the exception of Trinidad and Tobago, and the jobs available to working young people are often in low-skill areas with limited mobility.[1] Likewise, in the Pacific Islands, youth unemployment is estimated at 23 percent but reaches 63 percent in the Republic of the Marshall Islands, 54 percent in Kiribati and 46 percent in the Solomon Islands.[2] The lack of stable employment opportunities is detrimental to income generation and

poverty reduction efforts and negatively affects security by exacerbating crime and violence. Indeed, in 2012, 17–24 percent of male school-age young people in 10 Caribbean countries admitted to having been involved in gangs.[3] High rates of crime and violence can contribute to a vicious cycle whereby youth imprisonment and declines in revenues from tourism reduce overall economic activity and opportunities.

There are formidable challenges to expanding choices among young people and other vulnerable groups in small island developing states, but some of these challenges could be transformed into opportunities with the right mix of policies. Investments in climate-resilient infrastructure could turn climate change into a generator of employment. Investments in high-quality education and youth training programmes could increase entrepreneurship and remittances from labour migration and invigorate sectors such as telecommunication, tourism and creative industries.[4]

Notes
1. UNDP 2016b. 2. ILO 2014b. 3. UNDP 2016b. 4. ILO 2014b.
Source: Human Development Report Office.

People in conflict-affected countries experience severe and immediate impacts on human development. Modelling of the losses in each dimension of the HDI by the United Nations Relief and Works Agency for Palestine Refugees in the Near East in 2013 suggested that over two conflict years the Syrian Arab Republic lost the equivalent of 35 years of progress in human development.[40]

Conflict limits the availability of essential human development–enhancing services such as health care and education. Children in conflict-affected countries accounted for half of all children denied an education in 2011, even though they made up only 22 percent of the world's primary school–age children.[41] The United Nations Educational, Scientific and Cultural Organization reported in 2013 that 28.5 million children in conflict-affected countries were out of school.[42] Livelihoods are similarly disrupted when violence interferes with trade, infrastructure and service provision.

The distribution of opportunities and social services is uneven between and within countries. The ability to access health care, education, water and housing can vary greatly by region in

a country, as can the quality of these services.[43] Financial support—national and official development assistance—also varies across regions, with different effects on development outcomes. Thus, a far greater proportion of people are poor in rural areas than in urban areas, and in urban areas poor people are often clustered in slums.

Health care in India exemplifies the extreme geographic differences in health services. In the mid-2000s, 39 percent of children overall and 59 percent in urban areas benefited from full immunization coverage, theoretically provided by the public sector. Kerala had one public hospital bed per 1,299 people, but Uttar Pradesh only one bed per 20,041. Almost all births in Kerala were attended by health personnel, compared with just 27 percent in Uttar Pradesh.[44]

Geography in Tunisia counts much more than wealth, gender or the education level of the household head in determining access to some opportunities. Whether a person was born in a rural or urban area explains 30 percent of the inequality in school attendance and almost 50 percent of the inequality in access to sanitation. The pattern is similar in other Arab States, including Egypt and Morocco.[45] And in

The ability to access health care, education, water and housing can vary greatly by region in a country, as can the quality of these services

Sudan in the mid-2000s the use of antenatal health care services was five times greater in urban areas than in rural areas.[46]

The 2016 Mongolia National Human Development Report highlights differences in levels of inequality in human development across *aimags*, first-level administrative subdivisions.[47] Likewise, the HDI in China varies considerably across regions: from the equivalent of a medium human development country in some provinces (for example, Gansu, at 0.689) to the equivalent of a high human development country in other provinces (for example, Fujian, at 0.758) and to the equivalent of a very high human development country in Beijing (at 0.869).[48]

Migrants and refugees

Individuals born into disadvantage—in conflict-affected situations, countries at risk of environmental disaster or areas with few economic opportunities—have few strategies available to better their conditions. One option may be to leave their home and community in search of more physically and economically secure environments despite the risks the journey presents and the potential obstacles to be faced.

The United Nations Population Fund reported in 2015 that 244 million people were living outside their home countries.[49] Many are seeking better economic opportunities and hope to enhance their livelihoods and send money back home. A 2012 survey in Somalia reported that more than 60 percent of young people intended to leave the country in search of better work opportunities.[50] In 2010/2011 one person in nine born in Africa who had obtained a tertiary diploma lived in an OECD country.[51]

Not all migrants move because of hardship, and not all move because of a lack of choices at home. Many migrants return with new skills and experience as opportunities for employment at home increase, particularly in emerging economies. But many migrants, especially the world's nearly 23 million refugees, asylumseekers and stateless people, are fleeing extreme conditions.[52] And there are 50 million irregular migrants who seek better conditions at great risk, often relying on smugglers for travel.[53] People migrating to flee conflict and insecurity usually experience declines in their overall human development, but migration is still a better

choice than exposure to the harms they would face by staying home. Migrants who leave without the push of violence typically improve their human development potential by migrating.[54]

Migrants fleeing conflict are cut off from their main sources of income and may lack access to health care and social services beyond emergency humanitarian assistance (box 2.5). They frequently face harassment, animosity and violence in receiving countries. Trying to find work and earn an income is the single greatest challenge. In many countries refugees are not permitted to work; when they are, they see few opportunities. Many also lack identification papers, limiting access to formal jobs and services. People fleeing conflict are especially vulnerable to trafficking, forced labour, child labour, sex work and work in other exploitative, high-risk activities.

Migrants also confront barriers to participation in political and public life. Numerous countries impose restrictions on noncitizens in voting and holding elected public office. The restrictions may be based on the duration of the stay of the migrants, reciprocal laws in the country of origin or the scope of the election—most countries grant noncitizens the right to vote at communal but not regional or national elections. Language barriers can also be a key obstacle to community engagement. Newspapers, websites, television and radio programmes covering host country political and public issues in the migrants' native language can encourage civil participation.

As migrant and refugee flows surge, the infrastructure and services of host countries are challenged to absorb the newcomers. The pressure is especially intense in Jordan, Lebanon and Turkey, which have taken in the vast majority of refugees from the conflict in the Syrian Arab Republic.[55] All basic services in Lebanon are under stress, especially the education system, which has welcomed refugee children from the Syrian Arab Republic but is now stretched thin.[56]

Indigenous peoples

Indigenous peoples are characterized by distinct cultures and close relationships with the land they inhabit. There are more than 370 million self-identified indigenous peoples in some 70 countries. Latin America alone numbers more than 400 groups, and Asia and the Pacific

Individuals born into disadvantage have few strategies available to better their conditions. One option may be to leave their home and community in search of more physically and economically secure environments

BOX 2.5

Disadvantages facing migrants

Migrants face barriers in accessing services to maintain their capabilities. They may not have the legal or financial resources to access health care in their host countries and may therefore develop physical or mental problems that are aggravated by poor transit and living conditions. When they are able to access health care, they may not find health practitioners experienced in treating diseases that are uncommon in the host country, such as tropical diseases in northern latitudes or the psychological trauma associated with migration. They may also face discrimination from health practitioners or be unable to express themselves in the same language. Health care provided in refugee camps is not always of adequate quality and quantity, and people in transit may not be available for long-term treatments. The poor living conditions and the high population density in most camps can propagate communicable diseases. Women often confront threats of violence and physical insecurity.

Education is another challenge among migrants. Migrant children often have difficulty adapting in the host country's classrooms, where the teaching methods, curriculum and language are unfamiliar. An Organisation for Economic Co-operation and Development study in 23 countries showed that first-generation immigrant students have much lower scores than do local students; second-generation immigrant students do slightly better.[1] The variations across host countries are important, which may indicate that policies to integrate migrant students affect these students' outcomes. Migrant children may be experiencing school for the first time in the host country at an age when their peers have already been in school. Besides the stress of adapting to a new country, migrant children must catch up to become integrated in their new schools. Some migrant children do not have access to education in their host country, especially if they are undocumented.

Note
1. Keeley 2009.
Source: Human Development Report Office.

---

an estimated 705.[57] Indigenous peoples account for around 5 percent of the world's population but 15 percent of people living in poverty.[58] Indigenous peoples face deprivations caused by social, economic and political exclusion. In Africa indigenous peoples are more vulnerable to HIV and AIDS because of a range of factors, including stigmatization, structural racism and discrimination, and individual and community disempowerment.[59] In the United States Native Americans die at rates higher than the national average, especially as a result of liver disease, diabetes, accidents, homicide, suicide and chronic lower respiratory diseases.[60]

Indigenous children are challenged in education systems by daily schedules that do not accommodate nomadic movement, and curricula rarely incorporate their history, culture and language.[61] In many countries this leads to substantial gaps in years of schooling between indigenous children and nonindigenous children (table 2.1). In Guatemala nonindigenous children average twice as many years of schooling as indigenous children. Income-generating opportunities are more difficult to access when indigenous young people have low educational attainment.

Calls for self-determination through self-government have been at the forefront of the relationship between states and indigenous communities since the mid-20th century. Because indigenous self-determination is explicitly limited by the right of states to territorial integrity, the representation of indigenous groups in parliament is a powerful symbol of self-determination and of inclusion more widely.

In some cases, indigenous peoples have established their own parliaments or councils that act as consultative bodies—for example, the Sami people of Finland, Norway and Sweden. In other cases, such as the Maori in New Zealand, parliamentary seats are allocated for indigenous representatives.[62]

Lesbian, gay, bisexual, transgender and intersex individuals

In many countries people who are lesbian, gay, bisexual, transgender and intersex suffer extreme discrimination and insecurity that deprive them of dignity, basic rights and opportunities. Statistics on sexual orientation are scarce, especially in countries where same-sex sexual acts are illegal or socially invisible. But recent surveys in

> Because indigenous self-determination is explicitly limited by the right of states to territorial integrity, the representation of indigenous groups in parliament is a powerful symbol of self-determination and of inclusion more widely

TABLE 2.1

Years of schooling, indigenous and nonindigenous children, selected countries

Country	Nonindigenous	Indigenous	Difference
Bolivia	9.6	5.9	3.7
Ecuador	6.9	4.3	2.6
Guatemala	5.7	2.5	3.2
Mexico	7.9	4.6	3.3
Peru	8.7	6.4	2.3

Source: UNDESA 2009.

developed countries give some indication of the size of the population. In Australia 3 percent of the adult population self-identified as gay, lesbian or "other" in 2014.[63] In the United Kingdom 545,000 adults identified as gay or lesbian, and 220,000 identified as bisexual in 2012.[64] In the United States 3.4 percent of adults identified as lesbian, gay, bisexual or transgender.[65] In these surveys younger respondents were more likely than older respondents to self-report as lesbian, gay, bisexual, transgender or intersex, suggesting that social norms influence the likelihood of higher response rates.

Same-sex sexual acts are illegal among men in 73 countries and among women in 45. In 13 countries people who engage in such acts can face the death penalty.[66] Even in countries where lesbian, gay, bisexual, transgender and intersex people are not considered criminals, their prospects for human development are limited by discrimination in social and economic life. Unlike other minorities the lesbian, gay, bisexual, transgender and intersex community is often hidden. Sexual minorities may not disclose their identity for fear of legal punishment, social abuse, hostility and discrimination by society or by close friends and family members. Because differences in sexual orientation are not openly recognized in many societies, data on discrimination are not widely available, and evidence-based policymaking is difficult.

For 25 countries with data, attitudes towards the lesbian, gay, bisexual, transgender and intersex community have become more tolerant since the 1990s (figure 2.6). Social acceptance has increased as the adoption of antidiscrimination legislation has moved forward. Social norms and legislation have positively reinforced one another. Where intolerance remains high, legislation is critical to pushing back against hostile and discriminatory behaviour that limits the choices of a large global population.

Older people

Given that many countries have an ageing population, what are the deprivations facing older people? By 2020 the number of people ages 60 and older will be greater than the number of children under age 5. The proportion of the world's population over age 60 will double between 2015 and 2050, to 22 percent.[67] Few countries are prepared to cope with this demographic transition. Without adequate health systems, social protection, and work and retirement schemes in place, older people are deprived of opportunities to maintain and expand their capabilities. They also suffer from prejudicial attitudes and discriminatory policies and practices, often referred to as ageism.[68]

These issues may be particularly pertinent for women, because the life expectancy of women usually exceeds that of men. Pensions may be unavailable to women who have performed unpaid care work for much of their lives or who have worked in the informal sector. Older men are more likely to have pensions as a benefit of their paid formal work. Poverty rates are higher among older women than among older men.[69] In the European Union older women are 37 percent more likely than older men to live in poverty.[70]

Women are often expected to continue well into old age unpaid care work for spouses and grandchildren. This can be a source of fulfilment but also takes a physical toll and may come with little recognition. Many older people,

Even in countries where lesbian, gay, bisexual, transgender and intersex people are not considered criminals, their prospects for human development are limited by discrimination in social and economic life

FIGURE 2.6

Since the 1990s attitudes towards the lesbian, gay, bisexual, transgender and intersex community have become more tolerant, and the number of antidiscrimination laws has increased

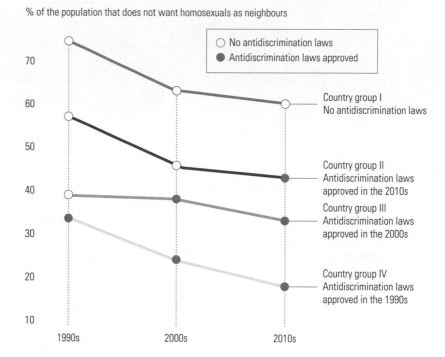

% of the population that does not want homosexuals as neighbours

○ No antidiscrimination laws
● Antidiscrimination laws approved

Country group I
No antidiscrimination laws

Country group II
Antidiscrimination laws
approved in the 2010s

Country group III
Antidiscrimination laws
approved in the 2000s

Country group IV
Antidiscrimination laws
approved in the 1990s

Source: Human Development Report Office estimates based on ILGA (2016a) and WVSA (2016).

particularly women, are also constrained by psychological and physical abuse that reduces their sense of security and dignity. A HelpAge International study found that two-thirds of older people who experience emotional, economic and physical abuse in Moldova are women.[71]

The general increase in life expectancy means that older people have many healthy, productive years ahead of them. In 2014, 11 percent of entrepreneurs in the United States were in the 55–64 age group.[72] Many older people are still capable and willing to work, and many need to continue working if adequate retirement schemes are not in place. But hiring practices that discriminate against older people limit their opportunities for work, and a mandatory retirement age may force older people to leave the labour market.

Deprivations suffered in old age are generally accumulated through the lifecycle. Children in poorer households may suffer from malnutrition, have poorer health, have less schooling and end up in a low-skilled, low-paid job

without health insurance or retirement benefits. In the United Kingdom people in wealthier neighbourhoods live six years longer than people in poor neighbourhoods and spend 13 more years without disability.[73]

Persons with disabilities

Physical and social barriers may deprive persons with disabilities of the chance to achieve their full life potential. Special facilities allow persons with disabilities, older people and other groups with limited mobility to fully participate in public life. Although around 1 billion people worldwide live with some form of disability, adequate infrastructure for persons with disabilities is still underdeveloped, making independent mobility a challenge for many.[74] Remote rural areas present severe mobility challenges. Additional impediments may remain even when infrastructure is in place—such as discriminatory hiring practices that limit access to jobs for persons with disabilities.

Deprivations suffered in old age are generally accumulated through the lifecycle

People with mental health conditions are particularly vulnerable to social exclusion. In 27 European countries the gap in unemployment rates between individuals with mental health conditions and those without widened between 2006 and 2010 (before and after the financial crisis), and social stigmatization was an important factor contributing to job insecurity.[75] In Germany the unwillingness to recommend an individual with depression for a job increased between 1990–2000 and 2000–2010.[76] An estimated 350 million people worldwide are affected by depression, about 60 million are affected by bipolar affective disorders, 21 million by schizophrenia and other psychoses and 47.5 million by dementia.[77] The fact that half a billion people suffer from these conditions means that the exclusion of people with mental health conditions from work and social activities is a major barrier to universalism.[78]

Deprivations in human development as a dynamic process

The universal achievement of some basic capabilities will not enable all people to realize their full life potential. Many dimensions of human development may still be lacking, including agency, security and sustainability. And the capabilities that matter most vary in different contexts and at different stages of the lifecycle. Security may be at the top of the list for a household in a conflict-affected country, while interesting work opportunities may be the top priority of an educated young person. Nor does rising above the low human development threshold ensure that people are protected from emerging and future threats to human development. Indeed, 900 million people live close to the threshold of multidimensional poverty and risk falling into poverty after even a minor setback in health, education or livelihood.[79] The condition of being deprived is therefore dynamic.

Deprivations can materialize when development leads to new needs and new mechanisms of exclusion. Political transitions, demographic shifts and outbreaks of violence put pressure on achieved gains. Climate change, financial crises and epidemics push people into multidimensional poverty. People in developed countries can lack opportunities for work, education and access to information, despite extensive information and communication technology infrastructure because broadband Internet systems do not reach some rural areas or carry prohibitive costs. This section elaborates on important but perhaps underemphasized issues of human development—quality, information access, security, and lifecycle and intergenerational deprivations—that are increasingly central to people's life potential.

From quantity to quality in human development

Over the last quarter-century, assessments of human development have focused primarily on quantitative achievements. But with substantial progress in human development linked to measures of quantity, such as years of schooling or life expectancy, there are questions about whether quality has also improved. Has quality in education, health and standards of living been enhanced? Quality is an important yardstick against which the progress in human development across countries and individuals should be examined. Large variations in the quality of human development across groups can become the basis for inequality and the perpetuation of deprivations throughout an individual's lifecycle and across generations. Within the human development approach, the concept of quality can be explored in opportunities for public participation, the enforcement of rights and the quality of work. As a starting point, the analysis is directed at the quality of education, health and living standards—the dimensions of human development that compose the HDI.

Many countries have made gains in access to education, but improvements in the quality of education have not kept pace. One-third of primary school–age children are not learning basic mathematics and reading even though half of them have spent at least four years in school.[80] Girls' enrolment in primary education has increased, but the results in terms of literacy are not encouraging. In half of 53 developing countries with data, the majority of adult women who completed four to six years of

Deprivations can materialize when development leads to new needs and new mechanisms of exclusion

People are living
longer but also
spending more years
suffering because of
illness and disability

primary school are illiterate.[81] These outcomes are linked partly to the quality of teaching. The number of primary school teachers trained according to national standards is below 75 percent in around a third of the countries for which data are available.[82] High pupil–teacher ratios are also a challenge to quality of education. Ratios in primary education were above 40 to 1 in 26 countries (23 in Sub-Saharan Africa) in 2011.[83] Such lack of support diminishes the prospects of learning and raises the likelihood of dropping out of school.

Health is improving worldwide. People are living longer. Life expectancy at birth globally was four years longer in 2015 than in 2000.[84] This is due in part to declines in death and illness caused by HIV and AIDS and malaria in the past decade as well as to advances in treating communicable, maternal, neonatal and nutritional disorders. Improvements in sanitation and indoor air quality, greater access to immunization and better nutrition have also enabled children in poor countries to live longer.[85] But are the added years of life expectancy healthy years or years with illnesses and disability? The World Health Organization has examined healthy life expectancy by measuring the years lived in good health without disability. Analysis for 188 countries in 1990, 2005 and 2013 indicates that there have been increases in healthy life expectancy but that they have not been as dramatic as the increase in overall life expectancy.[86] The difference between life expectancy and healthy life expectancy can be interpreted as years that are burdened with illness and disability. In 2015 the difference was more than 10 years in nine countries (table 2.2). People are living longer but also spending more years suffering because of illness and disability.

It is assumed that people's living standards improve when incomes rise. However, the quality of people's lives can vary greatly even as per capita income rises. Per capita income measures can rise when goods and services that are consumed in response to social malaise and problems—such as police protection, prison systems, legal services and mental health services—increase. Per capita income likewise excludes some goods and services that may raise the quality of people's lives, such as unpaid care work and ecological services. Qualitative improvements in people's standard of living thus need to be assessed beyond quantitative growth in per capita income.

Inequality in access to advanced, high-quality education, health care and other services restricts the ability of some people to expand their capabilities. It also affects the distribution of income in the long run. Inequality in the quality and quantity of education is directly related to unequal income. Segregated education systems can reinforce class distinctions and the intergenerational perpetuation of inequalities.[87] Governments can take steps to reduce differences in service quality between

TABLE 2.2

The difference between life expectancy and healthy life expectancy in selected countries

Country	Relative difference between life expectancy and healthy life expectancy (percent)	Absolute difference between life expectancy and healthy life expectancy (years)
Nicaragua	14.8	11.1
Qatar	13.4	10.5
Saudi Arabia	13.4	10.0
Australia	13.2	10.9
United States	12.9	10.2
Sweden	12.6	10.4
Spain	12.6	10.4
Chile	12.5	10.1
Finland	12.5	10.1

Source: Human Development Report Office estimates based on WHO (2016e).

private and public providers and standardize costs, including by taxing private suppliers to support public services (box 2.6). The key is to build the support across all population groups for good-quality, universal services so that all classes, genders and ethnicities have an interest in fair and adequate provision to all.

Expanding digital access

Broadband coverage and variations in access to computers and smartphones could generate new forms of exclusion. Inexpensive and reliable access to the Internet is becoming essential to the development of capabilities in other areas, such as education, work and political participation. Access to information is crucial for high-quality education and thus for expanding opportunities among children and youth. The biggest challenge is to make these benefits available to all people everywhere. However, the digital divide continues to impede universal benefits and could push people who are already deprived in other areas further behind.

Less than half the world's population (47 percent) uses the Internet. Only 25 percent of people in Sub-Saharan Africa are users, and only 42 percent of people in Asia and the Pacific and the Arab States are. In contrast, two-thirds of the population is online in the Americas and in the Commonwealth of Independent States. The rate in Europe is 79 percent.[88]

Prices in many regions make connecting to the Internet prohibitively expensive. Basic mobile or fixed broadband plans cost much more in developing countries than in developed countries and cost the most in the least developed countries (figure 2.7). But digital divides exist even in developed countries.

To enable all people to benefit from the opportunities that information and communication technology holds for human development, striving for universal access to free Wi-Fi may be needed. Combined with access

> The digital divide continues to impede universal benefits and could push people who are already deprived in other areas further behind

BOX 2.6

The challenge of a two-tier public and private system for universal access to quality services

Despite advances towards universal public education, health care and social protection in many countries, people are still being left behind in accessing high-quality services. Quality differs greatly between public and private services in some cases. Access to high-quality services is too often a privilege reserved for well-off populations. Highly unequal societies face the risk of segmentation between a universal public system and a smaller private system for elites.

Take Argentina. Despite expanded investment in public schools between 2003 and 2011, enrolment in private schools increased from 22 percent to 39 percent.[1] In Latin America and the Caribbean on average 50 percent of children of households in the highest income quintile attended private primary and secondary schools in 2010, compared with less than 4 percent of children of households in the lowest income quintile.[2] In Turkey expansion among private health care providers has resulted in more social stratification in the consumption of health services because higher income patients are abandoning public services for private services that are often better in quality.[3]

The use of private services by middle and upper segments of the welfare distribution across countries increases the likelihood of poor-quality public services because large segments of the population do not have a vested interest in public service quality, social pressure is insufficient to maintain good-quality, universally accessible public services and public services are becoming less cost-efficient because of user flight. The sustainability of funding for public programmes is at risk if the middle class does not have a vested interest in the programmes.

A two-tier public and private service system is not inherently negative. It is problematic only if there are extreme variations in quality between the two options that reinforce inequalities in opportunity among those who can pay and those who cannot. There are wide disparities in quality between public and private education services in many developing countries. A recent review of 21 studies in Ghana, India, Kenya, Nepal, Nigeria and Pakistan found that students in private schools tend to achieve better learning outcomes than do students in state schools. Teaching is also often better in private schools than in state schools—for example, in India, Kenya, Nigeria, Pakistan, South Africa and Tanzania.[4]

Notes
1. Martinez-Franzoni and Sánchez-Ancochea 2016. 2. Daude 2012. 3. Agartan 2012. 4. Day Ashley and others 2014.
Source: Human Development Report Office.

FIGURE 2.7

Basic mobile or fixed broadband plans cost much more in developing countries than in developed countries and cost the most in the least developed countries

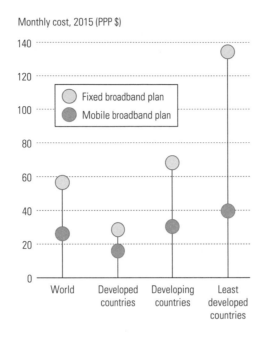

Monthly cost, 2015 (PPP $)

Source: ITU 2016b.

to high-quality education, universal Internet access could greatly increase opportunities and reduce inequalities everywhere.

Security threats

There may be threats to the security of the more abundant choices and opportunities available to people today. Epidemics, violence, climate change and natural disasters can quickly undermine the progress of individuals who have exited poverty and push poor people into more extreme poverty. They can also generate new deprivations. Millions of people around the world are exposed to climate-related natural disasters, droughts and associated food insecurities and subsist on degraded land. Between 1995 and 2014 more than 15,000 extreme weather events resulted in more than 525,000 deaths worldwide and economic losses of more than $2.97 trillion.[89]

Some groups are more exposed to threats than others. Many women depend on agriculture for their livelihoods and are therefore disproportionately exposed to climate pressures on food production. Children are physiologically and metabolically less able than adults to adapt to heat and other climate-related exposure and are more likely to be injured or killed during natural disasters.[90] They may also be kept out of school following disasters. During the Ebola outbreak in 2014 an estimated 5 million children were deprived of education in Guinea, Liberia and Sierra Leone because schools were closed for months.[91] Women were also disproportionately affected by the Ebola outbreak: they faced higher risks of infection because of their role caring for the sick, and they suffered from less antenatal, perinatal and postnatal care. In Sierra Leone's Kenema District avoidance of hospitals and birthing centres for fear of exposure to Ebola resulted in 29 percent fewer antenatal care visits and 21 percent fewer postnatal care visits.[92]

Voicing concerns about these emerging threats can carry risk. Defenders of land and the environment around the world suffer from threats and physical violence, criminalization and restrictions on their freedoms. As environmental pressures have increased, so have physical threats against environmental activists. A record number of environmentalists were killed in 2015—185 in 16 countries, up 59 percent from 2014. Members of indigenous groups, who accounted for 40 percent of the deaths in 2015, are among the most at risk.[93]

The physical insecurity of those who speak out about environmental pressures is part of a larger condition of physical insecurity and violence that severely restrict the choices and freedoms of individuals around the world. Many people feel insecure in their homes and communities. One billion girls and boys ages 2–17 worldwide experienced physical, sexual or psychological violence in the prior year, according to one study.[94] Some 25 percent of children suffer physical abuse, and nearly 20 percent of girls are sexually abused at least once in their life.[95] Elder abuse remains a hidden problem:[96] 10 percent of older adults were abused in the prior month.[97] Homicide is also a major social concern. In 2012, 437,000 people worldwide were the victims of intentional homicide.[98] Average homicide rates in Latin America and the Caribbean between 2010 and 2014 exceeded 20 per 100,000 people.[99]

Freedom from violence was one of the most frequently cited concerns among respondents

> Epidemics, violence, climate change and natural disasters can quickly undermine progress in human development

to a survey on human security carried out by the Human Development Report Office. Physical security and freedom from the threat of violence were particular concerns among female respondents (box 2.7). For women, real or perceived physical and emotional violence is a major barrier to meeting their full human potential and feeling free to move about.

Deprivations throughout the lifecycle and across generations

Lifelong deprivations among children and adults can begin even before birth (figure 2.8). Starting at conception, the environment to which pregnant women are exposed and the choices available to them shape the future skills and abilities of their children in ways that are difficult to alter as the children grow. A lack of medical attention, poor nutrition and heavy physical demands put unborn children at risk.

Poor children are more likely than their more affluent peers to experience myriad environmental risks before birth, including household disruption, pollution and violence. These antenatal exposures to stress have been found to mould life trajectories in health and cognitive and socioemotional development—precisely the areas of development that might otherwise allow individuals to be productive members of society (box 2.8). For instance, children in Canada who had been exposed in the womb to a strong winter storm in 1998 later exhibited lower levels of cognitive development, language functioning and motor functioning than did children who had not been exposed. Antenatal exposure to a 2005 earthquake in Chile has been negatively associated with children's future cognitive ability. Such exposure to stress can play a role in the intergenerational transmission of disadvantage by constraining development potential early in life.[100]

Lifelong deprivations among children and adults can begin even before birth

Human security from a woman's point of view

A survey conducted by the Human Development Report Office asked women of all ages and occupational backgrounds around the world, "What does human security mean to you?" Many women responded that they were concerned with physical and psychological violence.

"Human security is the right to move freely in your town without worrying about whether you will return home unharmed and unthreatened."
    —A female teacher from Brazil

"It is impossible to feel safe as a human being if our own existence is not recognized or respected, even if we have access to all sorts of opportunities."
    —A female economist from Mauritania

"Human security means being able to go about alone outside any time of the day or night and not fear any possible violence. It means that I should not consider my gender, religion or any other distinctive features when making a decision to spend time outdoors for fear of malicious intent."
    —A female development worker from Kazakhstan

"Human security for me is freedom from fear, fear of being looked down at because of being a woman and being assaulted and disrespected because of the same"
    —A female student from India

"Human security is being able to sleep peacefully, not being afraid of getting home late at night because of violators, not driving with closed windows for fear that someone will grab my bag, going to the supermarket without being afraid of having my belongings stolen from the car, going to the Yaoundé market without hiding my money in my bra, and walking freely along Kennedy Avenue."   —A woman from Cameroon

"Human security is the freedom to live your life free from hate crimes, sexism, racism and other kinds of oppression, freedom to express yourself and be active in society."   —A female activist from Sweden

"Human security means freedom from abuse and violence, particularly child abuse, domestic violence, interpersonal violence and intimate partner violence. It is about the protection of children, youth, elderly, persons with disabilities and women from violence and crime."
    —A female researcher from Trinidad and Tobago

Source: Human Development Report Office.

FIGURE 2.8

Deprivations among women can accumulate throughout life

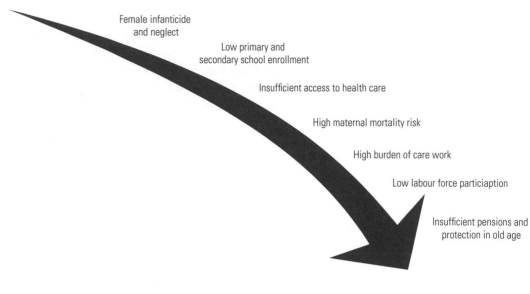

Female infanticide
and neglect

Low primary and
secondary school enrollment

Insufficient access to health care

High maternal mortality risk

High burden of care work

Low labour force particiaption

Insufficient pensions and
protection in old age

Source: Human Development Report Office.

BOX 2.8

Antenatal stress and intergenerational deprivation

Educational attainment is a central mechanism for perpetuating socioeconomic stratification across generations. Advantaged parents can afford more and better education for their children, which has many benefits in the labour market. There is also a direct transmission of economic advantage through inheritance and the use of job referral networks to favour children. These mechanisms affect later stages of the lifecycle, when children have reached school age or working age. But a growing body of research suggests that the intergenerational perpetuation of deprivation begins before birth and that the intergenerational transmission of advantage may already be advanced when children enter the education system.

Exposure to environmental stressors in the womb has been connected to poor birth outcomes such as lower birthweight and higher probability of preterm birth. It has also been connected to children's developmental outcomes such as motor skills, cognitive ability, emotional stability, attention deficit disorder and early educational achievement. Given that birth outcomes and early childhood development predict educational and economic attainment in adulthood, the higher probability that poor people will be exposed to risks in the womb may constitute the first injustice and may play a central role in the persistence of disadvantage across generations.

Why does antenatal exposure have such persistent effects over the lifecycle? The antenatal period includes critical and sensitive developmental stages in which the effect of the environment on future capabilities is especially strong and potentially irreversible, regardless of subsequent interventions. During the antenatal period the central nervous system and the brain undergo a cascade of critical developmental processes that are particularly susceptible to the environment and that shape later abilities in a cumulative fashion. An antenatal shock can result in reduced language ability in the first years of life, which may affect the ability to read and to succeed in school overall.

Abundant research in the biological and behavioural sciences highlights the importance of investing in the well-being of populations in the early stages of life, starting at conception. An economic perspective suggests that investments in capabilities early in life are much more cost-effective than investments later on.

Source: Torche 2016.

> Educational attainment
> is a central mechanism
> for perpetuating
> socioeconomic
> stratification across
> generations

Parents' educational attainment and earnings are strong predictors of children's educational attainment.[101] A study in South Africa found that fathers with high educational attainment pass on three-fifths of their earnings advantage to sons.[102] Daughters who inherit the low educational attainment of their parents are more disadvantaged as adults: They are 9 percent more likely to be in the bottom of the occupation distribution relative to the overall population.[103] In the United Kingdom people whose father had low educational attainment are 7.5 times more likely to have little education than are people with a highly educated father; in turn, people with low educational attainment are 11 times more likely to be deprived of material assets than are people with higher educational attainment.[104]

As the 2015 Human Development Report stressed, increasing women's access to education and paid work may have effects on the choices of subsequent generations of girls. Girls are more likely to be employed and to earn more as adults if their mother was employed. In the United States the daughters of mothers who are employed earn 23 percent more than the daughters of mothers who do not work outside the home.[105] In Senegal the parents'

education is positively associated with the offspring's adult living standards, and maternal education has a much larger positive effect than does paternal education.[106] Interventions to overcome deprivations today need to be viewed as opportunities to prevent deprivations among future generations.

Interventions for women early in life can prevent deprivations later in the lifecycle (figure 2.9). When investments in life capabilities occur sooner rather than later, as through early childhood education and care, the prospects improve for education and work.[107] This is because capabilities at any stage in life are path dependent and reflect the challenges and opportunities encountered at earlier stages. Children who do not have access to early childhood education may not do as well in primary and secondary school. Young people who have an education but live in an area with a sluggish labour market may resort to informal work or remain unemployed, which can lead to an insufficient pension in old age. Older people may suffer illnesses and disabilities accumulated over years of strenuous physical labour and insufficient preventive health care. The barriers facing marginalized groups may emerge at various points throughout the lifecycle and lead to

> Interventions to overcome deprivations today need to be viewed as opportunities to prevent deprivations among future generations

FIGURE 2.9

Interventions for women early in life can prevent deprivations later in the lifecycle

More sufficient pensions and social protection for women in old age

More women in parliament and upper managment positions

Higher likelihood of labour force participation and paid work

Lower likelihood of child marriage and adolescent pregnancies

Equitable access to primary and secondary education for girls

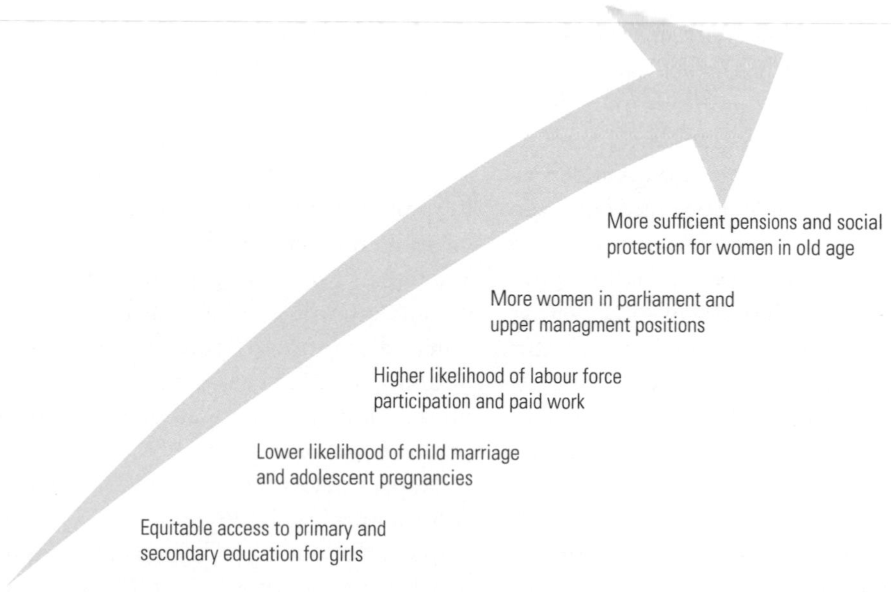

Source: Human Development Report Office.

severe deprivations in old age. Early interventions can prevent subsequent limitations, along with interventions that help individuals recover from past deprivation.

What do people value in human development beyond the basics?

Fulfilling basic needs is an essential part of expanding capabilities but is insufficient to enable people to reach their full potential. This is especially so in a world characterized by new and often more precarious forms of work, escalating violence and mounting environmental crises. Many people are deprived of a sense of security that they will be able to retain tomorrow the gains they have made today. Many are deprived of voice and opportunities to participate in the collective valuation of policies and priorities. Others lack access to good-quality services and to information and communication technology. Practical universalism requires attention to these and other dimensions of human development in which people in both developed and developing countries remain deprived.

Development in some of these dimensions may not have appeared so urgent in the past simply because of the scale of the deprivation in basic needs. Parents of children who lack access to schooling may not worry about the quality of secondary education. Families that are trying to get by on less than $1.90 a day may not prioritize the prevention of environmental crises. But as the types of deprivations captured in the HDI and MPI are reduced for individuals and societies, other deprivations become more prominent. People have more choices and freedoms, but there are still constraints that limit life potential.

Surveys based on subjective evaluations provide insights into the diversity of values across populations and suggest links between the surroundings and the development priorities of individuals. For example, the My World global survey being conducted by the United Nations in support of the 2030 Agenda assessed development issues that matter most to people.[108] More than 9 million responses have prioritized action issues from 16 options, ranging from securing a good education and ensuring political freedom to tackling climate change. The top three priorities are good education, better health care and better job opportunities. A disaggregation of the survey data by development status, age, gender, citizenship and region shows more variation in the top priorities. There are thus differences in the aggregate priorities of individuals in countries at different levels of human development (figure 2.10). Good education is the top priority across all human development groups, and the top three priorities are similar in the low, medium and high human development countries. But an honest and responsive government and access to clean water and sanitation are among the top three priorities in very high human development countries, where better health care and better job opportunities are not even among the top five priorities.

A survey by the Pew Research Center reinforces the context specificity of people's priorities and concerns. Some 83 percent of respondents in 34 developing countries considered crime to be the biggest problem in their country.[109] Corruption, lack of health care, poor schools and water pollution were also viewed as major problems. The percentage of respondents who listed crime as a concern was 93 percent) in Tunisia, compared with only 31 percent in Poland, where 59 percent of respondents listed health care as a very big problem (which compares with only 17 percent in China).

Income can also shape people's priorities. Respondents in a nationwide opinion survey in Chile were asked what was most important to them in order to have a happy life. The answers of respondents in the highest and lowest income quintiles varied substantially. Respondents in the highest income quintile most often cited the achievement of life goals and targets, whereas respondents in the lowest income quintile cited a peaceful life without much disruption (figure 2.11). Leading a meaningful life and enjoying the good things in life were less of a priority among respondents in the lowest income quintile.

People's priorities and values appear to be context specific. In Algeria, where youth unemployment rates are high, a young woman may value employment most. Once integrated into the labour market and at the peak of her career, she may value free time the most. A

FIGURE 2.10

There are differences in the aggregate priorities of individuals in countries at different levels of human development

	Low human development	Medium human development	High human development	Very high human development
A good education	1	1	1	1
Better health care	2	2	3	
Better job opportunities	3	3	2	
An honest and responsive government	4	5	4	2
Affordable and nutritious food	5			5
Access to clean water and sanitation		4		3
Protection against crime and violence			5	4

Source: Human Development Report Office estimates based on United Nations (2015b).

FIGURE 2.11

The priorities of Chileans vary by income

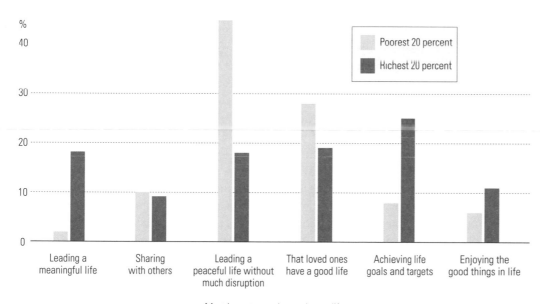

Source: UNDP 2012a.

healthy older man in Norway may value good interpersonal relationships with friends and family the most, despite having valued free time more when he was younger and working, like his Algerian counterpart. Because values evolve and shift according to the context, the human development approach remains relevant even as basic needs are met.

Because values evolve and shift according to the context, the human development approach remains relevant even as basic needs are met

Barriers to universalism

Deprivations can be eliminated. The progress since the first Human Development Report in 1990 demonstrates this. The global HDI value has increased 20 percent since then, from 0.597 to 0.717. The increase in the HDI value for the least developed countries is 46 percent.[110]

Progress has not come easily, but the path to progress may have been easier than the path to the goal of leaving no one behind. Individuals who are still deprived may be the most difficult to reach—geographically, politically, socially and economically. It is time to push to eradicate the remaining deprivations not only in access to health care, education and livelihoods, but also in other dimensions of well-being, such as security, freedom of participation in political life and access to advanced, high-quality services.

The realization of this vision will face challenges. Some barriers may require technical solutions—greater fiscal resources and development assistance, gains in technology and improved data resources for monitoring and evaluation (see chapter 3). These barriers can be addressed, albeit not easily, through changes in national policies (see chapter 4) and in international systems (see chapter 5).

Other barriers are deeply embedded in social and political relationships and identities. The context in which many individuals make choices is fraught with insecurity, glaring inequalities and competition for scarce resources. Discriminatory laws, exclusionary social norms, violence, imbalances in political participation and unequal distribution of opportunities all stand in the way of progress. Exclusion can be intentional or unintentional, but the results are the same—some people will be more deprived than others, and not all people will have an equal chance to realize their full potential. Men have more choices than women, rich people have more choices than poor people, citizens have more choices than migrants and some ethnicities have more choices than others.

Progress towards universal human development requires a deep awareness and understanding of the drivers and dynamics of these groups' exclusion. The drivers and the dynamics inevitably vary across countries and regions. Universalism in practice is possible, but key barriers and types of exclusion must be overcome (see infographic 2.1 at the beginning of the chapter).

Intolerance and exclusion and the related mechanisms

Whether intentional or unintentional, one group excluding another group from opportunities is often the root of deprivation and disadvantage. Membership in a group fulfils a basic desire to belong to a family, a community, a religion or a race. Individuals have multiple group affiliations at any one time and belong to different groups throughout life. Groups allow individuals to identify with others based on a shared characteristic or interest, but they also permit exclusion.

Group inequalities reflect divisions that are socially constructed and sustained because they establish a basis for unequal access to valued outcomes and scarce resources. Once inequalities are established, the organizational focus becomes how to maintain the distinctions and ensure group loyalty and solidarity so that those who benefit from membership in the group are able to maintain their advantageous positions. At the same time the dimensions and mechanisms of exclusion are dynamic, as are the characteristics that groups use as a basis for exclusion. An ethnic minority group may penetrate the political space that has been occupied by the majority—a success from the perspective of equity in political participation —but the members of the ethnic minority who occupy the space may then use class divisions to exclude others in the same ethnic minority from participating in policy decisions. It is thus important to recognize that group identity and barriers of exclusion tend to shift under strategies to protect advantages.

Many dynamics have a bearing on group formation and protection strategies. Today, trends in global income distribution present challenges to collective agreements and cooperation across countries and population segments. Voters in the lower middle class in developed countries are frustrated with the lower than average growth in their living standards relative to elites (box 2.9). The frustration is coupled with an awareness of high income growth in emerging economies such as China and India,

Whether intentional or unintentional, the exclusion from the opportunities of one group by another group is often the root of deprivation and disadvantage

BOX 2.9

From the champagne glass to the elephant curve

The 1992 Human Development Report showed that global income distribution followed a champagne glass pattern, where the bulk of income is concentrated at the top of the distribution, and the global income distribution in 1998 and 2008 reflected that pattern (see left panel of figure). One might conclude that the people who are not at the top of the distribution have a collective interest in redistributing resources. But there seems to be a different lived experience across the stem of the glass. The rate of change in the real income between

1988 and 2008 follows an elephant curve (see right panel of figure).[1] The percentage change in real income favoured those who were in the bottom half and the top decile of the global income distribution, whereas the real income of the lower middle class in developed countries—grew only modestly. For example, in Germany the real income of the poorest 50 percent grew 0–7 percent, in the United States the poorest 50 percent saw real income growth of slightly over 20 percent and in Japan the poorest 10 percent saw real income decline.

Income gains from 1998 to 2008 have not been even across income deciles

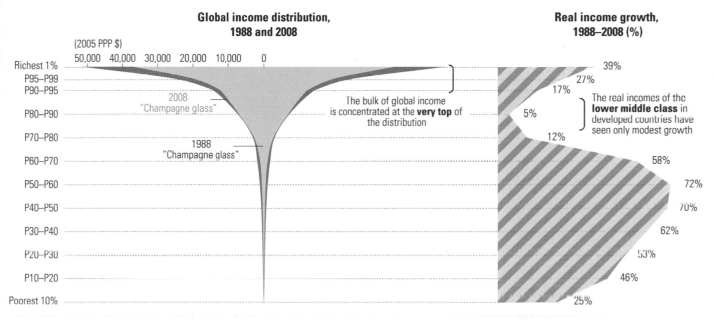

Global income distribution, 1988 and 2008

Real income growth, 1988–2008 (%)

Note
1. Milanović 2016.
Source: Human Development Report Office estimates based on Milanović (2016) and UNDP (1992).

which may become a source of resentment against trade with and migration from developing countries.

The pace of change is rapid and unpredictable, and many people are struggling to find their way. With globalization and greater human mobility, come changes in demographic structures, languages and cultural diversity. From a human development perspective, diversity should be celebrated as a powerful ingredient of human creativity. But there are also risks that social cohesion, mutual respect and tolerance of differences can be strained or break down altogether, resulting in xenophobia, nationalism, discrimination and violence. There can be a lack of recognition or appreciation for different beliefs and views, norms

and cultures, and lifestyles. Historically, people have navigated periods of widespread change and unpredictability, but these periods are often characterized by immense suffering and conflict. Strict and extreme beliefs and views —whether religious or political—breed intolerance and prevent flexibility and adjustability to change. It is therefore crucial to identify and reverse patterns of intolerance during such times, whether discriminatory laws, exclusionary social norms or violence and coercion and to instead respond to emerging global challenges through mutual respect and collaboration. Discrimination, exclusion and intolerance run counter to universalism—the centrepiece of human development and the cornerstone of the world we want.

Discriminatory laws

Legal and political institutions can be used and abused to perpetuate group divisions. An extreme case relates to the rights of the lesbian, gay, bisexual, transgender and intersex community in the 73 countries and five territories where same-sex sexual acts are illegal, including 13 where such acts are punishable by death.[111] Only 10 countries grant lesbian, gay, bisexual, transgender and intersex people equal constitutional rights.[112] Laws are discriminatory in other cases because they prevent certain groups from accessing services or opportunities, such as when host countries legally bar refugees from working. State policies can be discriminatory as well—such as denying citizenship or the right to vote or run for political office. National borders thus become legal instruments that can reinforce inequalities between the citizens of different countries. Within-country inequalities are wide, but the laws and practices in countries of birth can also determine life chances and opportunities.

In some cases women do not have the same legal rights as men. Women's opportunities are impeded by law in 155 out of 173 countries with data. In 100 countries women are prevented from engaging in some professions because of their gender. In 32 countries the procedures that women face to obtain a passport differ from those that men face. In 18 countries women need their husband's approval to take a job. And in 46 countries laws do not protect women from domestic violence.[113] Women also face discrimination if their opportunities and choices are restricted because appropriate protective laws have not been enacted—for example, when paid maternity leave is not mandated or when discriminatory hiring practices are tolerated.

As the 2015 Human Development Report highlighted, far more women would become active in the labour market and have better wages and positions of influence if regulations were in place to reduce workplace harassment against women, ensure equal wages and hiring practices and provide care options for children and older people.[114] Discriminatory laws and the lack of legislation restrict women's freedoms and impede their full participation in public life as equal members of society. These outcomes are linked to the fact that women are often excluded from the political spaces where policies and legislation are agreed. Globally women hold only 22 percent of the seats in parliament, 26 percent of the seats on the highest courts and 18 percent of ministerial positions.

Regulations and the nature of institutions can also indirectly limit the access poor people have to services and resources. For example, banks that require minimum deposits limit access to financial services for poor people. Around 2 billion people worldwide are still unbanked—lacking accounts at banks, other financial institutions or mobile money service providers.[115] Similarly, the absence of birth registrations and lack of identity cards can prevent poor people from gaining access to many public services.

Social norms

Social norms are implicitly established rules of behaviour. Some may be helpful in promoting harmonious coexistence, but others may be discriminatory, prejudicial and exclusive.

For example, prejudice and social perceptions often lead to unequal outcomes among different groups in job markets, which reduces livelihood opportunities for minorities. In employment recruitment in the United States White job applicants are often systematically selected over African American and Latino job applicants, even when the minorities have equal or higher qualifications. African Americans are often rejected solely on the basis of their names (which employers glean from resumes) and receive only half as many job offers as White candidates. Despite Nepal's laws against untouchability, individuals considered of lower caste continue to be excluded from certain jobs and services, and Dalits earn considerably less than non-Dalits. Discriminatory treatment of persons with disabilities is widespread and has implications for their livelihoods. In Mauritius, Panama, Peru, the Russian Federation and the United States the employment gap between persons with disabilities and persons without disabilities is more than 40 percentage points.[116]

In many countries social norms reduce choice and opportunities for women and girls. As the 2015 Human Development Report highlighted, norms and traditions that distribute the bulk of unpaid work in the home to women limit women's participation in the labour market and can prevent girls from attending school.[117] Women are typically responsible for more than three-quarters of unpaid care work in the household.[118] The presence of women as customers in cafés or restaurants may also be discouraged by social norms, and in some cases it is taboo for women to travel in public without being accompanied by a man.[119] Practices such as female genital mutilation and cutting, performed on 200 million girls and women alive today, are also linked to social norms and put girls at extreme and unnecessary health risk.[120]

Social norms in marriage can reduce opportunities and reinforce inequalities. Child marriage is a fundamental violation of human rights, yet it continues because of customs and other normative factors.[121] In South Asia 46 percent of girls become child brides, and many marry before age 15 (figure 2.12). Early marriage limits a girl's future development because it increases the likelihood of early pregnancy, social isolation and leaving school early.

There is also evidence that the choices people make in marriage reinforce socioeconomic hierarchies and ethnic divisions because people tend to marry within their own socioeconomic or ethnic group. A study in the United Kingdom found that 56 percent of the current generation of women have married a partner in the same social class, a rising trend.[122] Some 11 percent of the increase in inequality in developed countries since the 1980s is due to people's choice to marry at a similar socioeconomic level—doctors marrying lawyers, for instance.[123] Marriage also perpetuates social norms and traditions linked to ethnic groups. The preference in Mauritius for marrying within the same ethnic group overrides even class-based considerations.[124]

Violence

Perhaps the most direct and radical mechanism of exclusion is violence. Coercive tools enable one group to force its vision of society on another and to protect its access to resources, outcomes and the power to make decisions. Motivations include consolidating political power, safeguarding the well-being of elites, controlling the distribution of resources, seizing territory and resources and favouring ideologies based on the supremacy of one identity and set of values.[125]

Exclusion breeds violence. One study drawing on global data since 1945 found that a 30 percent increase in the size of the politically excluded population boosted the chance of civil war by 25 percent.[126] Another study found that countries with higher inequality among ethnic groups have lower incomes overall and a more uneven distribution of services and infrastructure and are more prone to conflict and violence.[127]

Intolerance of others—legal, social or coercive—is antithetical to human development and to universalism. Intolerance, exclusion and inequality are nonetheless common and are on the rise in some cases. Overcoming these barriers will require finding ways to link collective interests to equity and justice (see chapter 3).

Elite capture of institutions

Some thrive in a global labour market owing to their advanced skills and education. They retire comfortably with private pension funds and savings. They send their children to the best schools for advanced tertiary education. They

FIGURE 2.12

In South Asia many girls marry before age 18—some before age 15

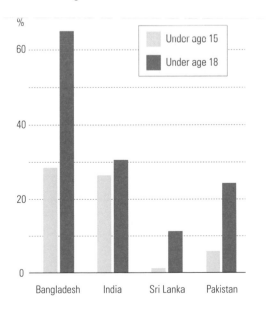

Source: Banu 2016.

> Intolerance of others—legal, social or coercive—is antithetical to human development and to universalism

live in the safest communities. And they have the means to influence the political process in their favour.

There are links among income inequality, inequalities in education and health care and inequalities in political participation and influence. The top 1 percent of the wealth distribution holds 46 percent of the world's wealth.[128] Much of the income gain in recent decades has been at the top: 44 percent of the income earned between 1988 and 2008 went to only 5 percent of the population.[129] Such income inequalities influence inequalities in other dimensions of well-being.

Extreme inequality and the concentration of capabilities and opportunities among a narrow elite are part of a vicious circle. As inequalities become wider, marginalized and excluded groups face growing deficiencies in opportunities to expand and apply their capabilities and to influence the institutions and policies that determine the subsequent distribution. Positive opportunities for political participation and influence are central to breaking the vicious circle.

The interests of the middle class may also sometimes lead to policy decisions that perpetuate deprivations and the exclusion of poorer groups. Antipoverty programmes have been opposed in some countries because they do not benefit the middle class, an important political constituency.[130] One result is that redistribution programmes can have limited coverage among the poorest population and exhibit substantial leakage to the middle class and elites. Some programmes tie eligibility for transfers to employment in the formal sector in order to gain the support of the middle class.[131] In Tanzania distributing vouchers for agricultural inputs disproportionately benefited the households of village officials, who received 60 percent of the vouchers.[132] These approaches increase political support, but miss those who are most in need of support.

Conditional cash transfers have generated impressive reductions in poverty, but their reach has extended beyond poor people. In some cases this has been to ensure that people who are near poverty and people who are vulnerable have access to funds, but there is also leakage to those with less need. The share of nonpoor beneficiaries of conditional cash transfers increased from 46 percent in 2004 to 65 percent in 2010 in Ecuador and from 40 percent in 2002 to 61 percent in 2010 in Mexico.[133]

Elite capture of the benefits of development and the institutions—markets, states and civil society—that guide the distribution of opportunities can widen and perpetuate divisions in capabilities in highly unequal societies.[134] The extreme concentration of capabilities and opportunities at the top can erode democratic governance and reduce pluralism in decision-making. Equity and justice take a back seat to rules that perpetuate divides.

Weak bargaining power

Excluded groups are in a weak position to instigate the transformation of institutions because of the extent of inequality and elite capture. They lack agency and voice and have little political leverage to influence policy outcomes and legislation through traditional means. Over the past three decades, various measures have shown a decline in rights of free association and collective bargaining (figure 2.13).[135] The increasingly flexible and part-time nature of work reduces the ability of traditional worker organizations, such as trade unions, to counter elite interests.

Other, sometimes dangerous and debilitating means of participating become more attractive in highly unequal societies. There has been a steady increase in local and global protests in recent years, including demonstrations and rallies, campaigns of social and political movements and unorganized crowd actions such as riots (843 worldwide between 2006 and 2013).[136] This suggests that people do not feel sufficiently empowered by established political processes and are choosing to voice their concerns in alternative ways.

Groups may be organizing and participating in peaceful marches and rallies, but they are also using civil disobedience to magnify their voices by blocking roads and occupying city streets and public spaces. They are using technology to leak government and corporate data. The global circulation of the Panama Papers drew attention to grievances against offshore tax havens and hidden wealth accumulation among the world's political and corporate leaders.

FIGURE 2.13

Over the past three decades there has been a decline in rights of free association and collective bargaining

Freedom of Association and Collective Bargaining Index

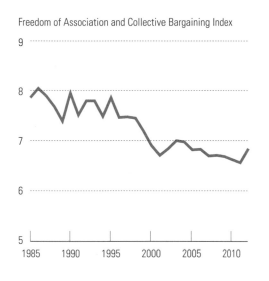

Note: Data are for 73 countries.
Source: Human Development Report Office estimates based on Marx, Soares and Van Acker (2015).

Narrow self-identities

Economic, ecological and technological systems extend across national borders. Decisions in one nation or region can affect individuals on the opposite side of the world. Trade policies in Europe can affect agricultural livelihoods in Latin America. Carbon emissions in Asia can generate climate vulnerabilities in Africa. Financial policies in the United States can shift global capital flows. Universal human development and ensuring opportunities for all thus require a united global effort to reduce inequalities and empower marginalized groups.

At a time when global action and collaboration are imperative, self-identities are narrowing. Social and political movements linked to identity, whether nationalist or ethnopolitical, seem to be increasing in frequency and strength. Identity politics are on the rise. Data from 1816 to 2001 show a peak in 2001 when almost 90 percent of the conflicts in the world were being fought by nationalists seeking to establish separate nation-states or between ethnicities over ethnic balances of power within existing states.[137] The Brexit is one of the most recent examples of a retreat to nationalism among individuals who are feeling alienated in a changing world. This shift towards support for nationalism might have been foreseen.

Breaking down barriers

Divisions and exclusions, while often deep, are not static. Shocks, disasters, crises, political shifts, the spread of technologies, the globalization of information, business and social networks—all open space for new alignments and the redistribution of political and material resources across groups. This is why we need to understand emerging trends that can unite, empower and motivate people to push for change and the potential collective interests of groups that may stand to gain influence and leverage. The 2030 Agenda is momentous in that it focuses on the universal reduction of deprivations. If this intergovernmental agreement can be harnessed to truly shift institutions onto a path that promotes justice, equity and sustainability, remaining deprivations and inequalities can be overcome.

The human development approach has always advocated for the expansion of capabilities and freedoms to the fullest for all people regardless of gender, nationality, ethnicity, sexual orientation or any other group identity. But translating universalism from principle to practice will have to rely on more than mapping the groups that have been bypassed in the human development journey and identifying the barriers to ensure that human development reaches everyone. It will also require refocusing on some elements of the human development analytical approach that have so far been insufficiently considered, such as voice and participation, identity and diversity, inclusion and social justice. Chapter 3 is devoted to such analysis.

> Divisions and exclusions, while often deep, are not static

Chapter **3**

Reaching everyone—analytical and assessment issues

Infographic 3.1 Human development represents freedom of well-being as well as freedom of agency

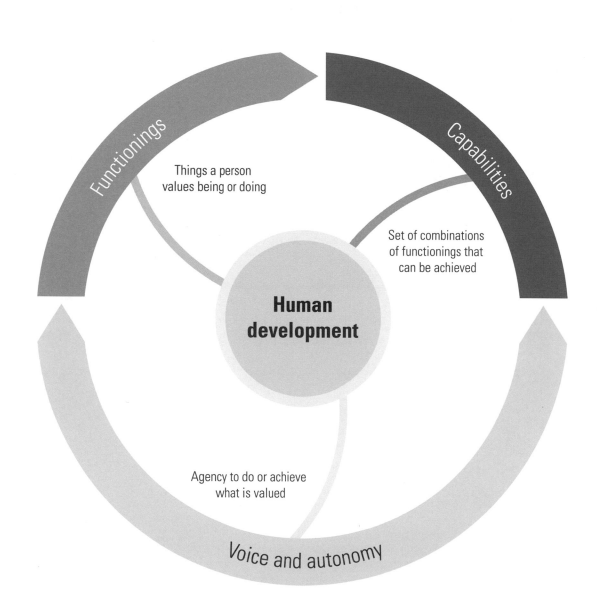

3.

Reaching everyone—
analytical and assessment issues

The human development approach is anchored in the idea of universalism, whereby all people—present and future—can realize their full potential. Two issues stand out. First, practical universalism shows that progress in human development is unbalanced across and within countries, socioeconomic groups, ethnic and racial groups, women and men, and generations and have not always reached the most deprived. Second, the world of today differs from the world of 25 years ago and presents new opportunities and challenges. It is thus necessary to map out those who have been left out of the progress in human development and to understand why. It is equally important—as this chapter outlines—to address analytical and assessment issues that, once resolved, may help the barriers to universal human development be overcome.

The human development approach is based on two fundamental freedoms—the freedom of well-being, including functionings and capabilities, and the freedom of agency, including voice and autonomy. Functionings are the various things that a person may value being and doing, and capabilities are the combinations of functionings that a person can achieve. Agency is related to "what a person is free to do and achieve in pursuit of whatever goals or values he or she regards as important" (see infographic 3.1 on the preceding page).[1]

What aspects need to be analysed

Over the years the Human Development Report has emphasized that human development is about expanding choices. This remains true. Choices determine who we are and what we do. Those choices rest on four foundations: the wide range of options that we have to choose from—our capabilities; the social and cognitive constraints and social norms and influences that shape our values and choices; our own empowerment and the agency we exercise individually and as part of groups in shaping our options and opportunities; and the mechanisms that exist to resolve competing claims in ways that are fair and conducive to realizing human potential (figure 3.1).

Examining these foundations is particularly important to ensuring human development for everyone. The human development approach, grounded in the capability approach, provides

a systematic way to articulate these ideas. It can be especially powerful in illuminating the interplay among factors that can operate to the disadvantage of individuals and groups in different contexts.

This chapter highlights ideas from the human development approach that need to be re-emphasized to ensure that human development reaches everyone. It also presents specific analytical perspectives for examination.

The human development approach has shown continuity but also resilience. It has proven robust but also adaptable to changes in the world over the past quarter-century. The core definitions of the approach have been used in diverse ways. They have been used to describe whether and how much people have a say in matters that concern their lives, a meaningful opportunity to contribute to development and a chance to obtain a fair share of the fruits of development. And they have been simplified by attributing to human development any improvement in the human condition that allows people to live longer and healthier lives. The human development approach is ultimately "simple yet rich, full yet open-ended, flexible yet responsible, normative yet visionary, inspiring yet practical."[2]

Human rights—the bedrock of the human development approach

The definition of human rights consistently used in the Human Development Report is that of the Universal Declaration of Human Rights of 1948, which considers political and

> The human development approach can be especially powerful in illuminating the interplay among factors that can operate to the disadvantage of individuals and groups in different contexts

FIGURE 3.1

Choices rest on four foundations

Source: Human Development Report Office.

socioeconomic rights as well as civil and cultural rights.[3] Human rights thus include the right to life, liberty and security; the freedom of assembly, thought, religion and opinion; the right to work; the right to an adequate standard of living, food, clothing, housing and education; and the right to participate in community life.

Human development and human rights are closely related. The best way to secure human rights may be to consider rights in terms of capabilities. The right to bodily integrity, to associate freely, to political participation and all other rights are secured when the relevant capabilities are available. To secure a right is to enable people to be or do something that they have reason to value. Yet certain fundamental rights may be recognized on paper but not implemented or available in practice.[4] Women may have the right to vote by law but be threatened with violence if they leave the house. They thus lack the capability to exercise the human right of political participation.

Human rights offer a useful perspective for analysing human development such as "the idea that others have duties to facilitate and enhance human development."[5] The 2000 Human Development Report highlighted that "to have a particular right is to have a claim on other people or institutions that they should help or collaborate in ensuring access to some freedom."[6] With invoked duties come the notions of accountability, culpability and responsibility. For example, recognizing the human right

to free basic education means much more than merely agreeing that it is a good thing for everyone to have a basic education—or even that everyone should have an education. Rather, asserting this right is claiming that all people are entitled to a free elementary education and that if some lack access to it, there must be accountability somewhere in the social system.

This focus on accountability for failures within a social system broadens the outlook beyond the minimum claims of human development. This broader perspective can be a powerful tool in seeking remedy, and the analysis of human development can profit from it. Such a perspective spotlights the strategies and actions of various duty bearers to contribute to fulfilling human rights and advancing the corresponding aspects of human development. It also leads to an analysis of the responsibilities of actors and institutions when rights go unfulfilled. This analysis and understanding are essential to achieving progress in human development for everyone.

Voice, participation and democratic practice—an integral part of human development

The ability to deliberate, participate in public debates and be agents in shaping their own lives and environments is a fundamental value of most people. There are three main reasons within the human development approach to value voice and participation (box 3.1). Voice

> Focusing on accountability for failures within a social system broadens the outlook beyond the minimum claims of human development and can be a powerful tool in seeking remedy

and participation are both a means and an end. Truly functional, participatory democracy, which is much broader than a voting process, leads to a virtuous circle. Political freedoms empower people to demand policies that expand their opportunities to hold governments accountable. Debate and discussion help communities shape priorities. A free press, a vibrant civil society and the political freedoms guaranteed by a constitution underpin inclusive institutions and human development. The human development approach views people not only as beneficiaries of development, but also as architects of their own lives.[7]

Related to this is the notion of agency. People who enjoy high levels of agency are engaged in actions congruent with their values. When people are coerced into an action, are submissive or desirous to please or are simply passive, they are not exercising agency.[8]

Well-being and agency—the two fundamental freedoms in the human development approach—are related yet distinct. An agent is someone who acts and brings about change. Agency can advance one's own well-being, but it can also further the well-being of others. People may thus volunteer for causes that do not advance their own well-being, such as protecting the rights or improving the conditions of vulnerable groups or conserving ecosystems, landmarks or historical monuments. People may put themselves in gruelling situations, working to promote causes they believe in at the cost of their own health or security. They are exercising their agency. Human agency thus advances any goals that are important to individuals—for themselves, for their communities or for other entities.

The exponential spread of information and communication technologies, along with rising education and literacy rates, has provided individuals with new tools for participation (box 3.2). Online participation can have a major impact on agency and empowerment. But new forms of participation also face challenges and risks that must be addressed. Equal access to the Internet for all people must be pursued between and within countries. And people must be protected from the risks of misinformation and online violence—such as cyberbullying, online sexual abuse, harassment or hate speech—that target mostly children and women.[9]

The primary focus of the human development approach and of the Human Development Report has largely been on the freedom of well-being. This is reflected in the way the Human Development Index (HDI) has been constructed. This focus may have arisen because basic deprivations were once more widespread, attracting the preponderance of analysis, measurement and policy response. But as well-being was realized, emphasizing freedom of agency has become more important. That freedom has an independent, intrinsic worth, in addition to an instrumental value because it enhances well-being.

> Agency can advance one's own well-being, but it can also further the well-being of others

BOX 3.1

Voice and participation—intrinsic, instrumental and constructive

Voice and participation are intrinsically important, make instrumental contributions and play a constructive role in the human development approach:

- *Intrinsic*. Voice and participation have high intrinsic value to people as key functionings.
- *Instrumental*. Voice and participation enhance democratic political freedoms and thus have instrumental value in expanding capabilities. The functionings of being well fed and free of disease or having an adequate education may appear basic. In practice, even these are difficult to achieve without the ability to participate in society. Being excluded and shut off and not possessing voice are usually the reasons that people and groups lack basic capabilities, sometimes generation after generation.

- *Constructive*. Societies and nations must deliberate and decide, through give and take, their common priorities and agendas. Effective participation ensures that all groups sit at the table. Broad, truly representative participation in civic dialogue is the way to ensure that societies advance towards realizing the concept of justice, the principles of universalism and sustainability, and other values that they hold collectively.

Source: Human Development Report Office.

Facilitating participation through new technologies

The spread of the Internet over the past decades has facilitated the rise of new forms of civil participation. These include e-government, online petitions, mass demonstrations, crowdfunding and blogging. Although petitions, protests, fundraising and political publications have long existed, the Internet has allowed them to achieve unprecedented coverage, bringing people together across physical borders with enormous speed.

Activists can now gather support from millions of people in a few weeks and with limited resources, permitting them to have an impact on public and political life that would have been impossible through traditional means of participation. This has challenged government and party monopolies in politics and effectively broadened civil participation. New technologies have also helped previously excluded groups—such as people with limited mobility, people living in secluded areas and young people—participate in public and political life.

Source: Human Development Report Office.

Human security—a precondition for human development

The concept of human security shifts the attention from interstate conflicts towards people's feelings of insecurity. It encompasses concerns about jobs, income, health, the environment and crime. It also means protection from sudden and harmful disruptions in life. According to the 1994 Human Development Report, "human security is not a concern with weapons—it is a concern with human life and dignity."[10]

Millions of people around the world must cope with the impacts of climate change, natural disasters, economic and health crises, and intolerance and violence (see chapter 1). Because of these new realities and the aspiration of leaving no one behind, the concept of human security remains highly relevant. The emphasis should be on achieving a deep understanding of threats, risks and crises and addressing them through joint action based on the crucial concepts and approaches of human development and human security.[11] Two ideas are relevant:

- *Countering the shock-driven response to global threats.* There is no denying that an inevitable short-term security imperative exists requiring an emergency response. This is understandable from a human agency perspective. The effect of shocks on global attention nonetheless has significance in responding to questions about who is being left behind and why. This is because precisely these forgotten or difficult to reach populations are usually the most at

> Looking at the world only through the lens of threats sometimes imposes the tyranny of the urgent over the essential

risk to shocks. But looking at the world only through the lens of threats sometimes imposes the tyranny of the urgent over the essential. Peaks in attention to emergencies fail to address the gradual and complex process of vulnerability that builds between shocks. The human development and human security approaches, while remaining available to confront short-term security imperatives, should become involved in aligning efforts to shift the emphasis away from shock-driven responses to global threats. People are also left behind when threats are protracted and require a long-term commitment to crisis management.

- *Promoting a culture of prevention.* How should we understand and practise prevention as part of the development process? If one sees the world through the prism of threats, it may appear normal for crises to be considered opportunities. A return to business as usual once the emergency has passed may appear equally normal. Yet, while crisis prevention may receive the least attention in the cycle of crisis management, it is the component that, everybody agrees, should be the most important.

To shift from a shock-driven response to crisis to a needs-driven one, human development strategies must be anchored in the everyday and not rooted in emergencies. Human security emphasizes the centrality of people in the calculations that make us assign importance to some threats over others. This emphasis should also encourage us to pay attention to the full cycle of relief, recovery and prevention in crisis management.

Human decisionmaking—to be examined more closely

The functionings that individuals realize through their capabilities flow from a confluence of conscious or subconscious choices. In making choices, people often fail to take into account the spillovers and long-term consequences. They may follow the herd or fail to correct for cognitive bias. They may simply be overwhelmed and unable to process all the available information—with important implications for human development. Examples include the failure to save for retirement or taking on bad loans although better options are available. Such mistakes are well documented in the literature on behavioural and cognitive science.[12]

People face many decisions, ranging from the trivial to the consequential. They face multiple options and have to make choices, sometimes as part of a group. Development economists and practitioners use standard models to assess how people make choices. Psychologists and experimental and behavioural economists, meanwhile, have been documenting the mistakes in how people make choices.[13] People's decisions seem to be swayed by considerations that should not matter—the default option, the order in which options are presented and sometimes seemingly irrelevant options. Some researchers say that people are irrational or that they make (predictably) irrational choices.[14] Dan Ariely, James B. Duke Professor at Duke University and a leading authority on behavioural economics, shares his thoughts on how to advance human development in a less than rational world (see special contribution).

What seems like irrational behaviour by a group, such as poor people, may at times simply reflect a lack of access to services that everyone else takes for granted. People with stable incomes may fail to save and ensure future financial security. This may appear to be irrational behaviour. But it may simply be that these people lack access to basic services such as savings accounts. In the Philippines about 30 percent of people who were offered a savings account with no option to make a withdrawal for six months accepted. Individuals who used the accounts increased their savings 82 percent more than the control group did.[15]

Some choices seem to irrationally depend on considerations that should not matter—how healthy and unhealthy foods are arranged in the supermarket or whether a company signs up employees automatically for a retirement savings plan. In all walks of life, how the options are presented and experienced can have an effect on the choices made.[16]

In some cases understanding how and under what conditions choices are made may suggest straightforward policy fixes.[17] In many other cases there may be no easy policy fixes. So being aware of the vagaries of human behaviour is essential. Only by being aware of how people make choices can planners design programmes and policies to support decisionmaking appropriately among people who may otherwise be especially prone to mistakes. Policy design involves judgements about default options, how much information to introduce and how the information is framed, presented and disseminated. Understanding how people make choices can enhance the process.[18] Some of these insights are integrated into policymaking. Others are novel, and a large number of researchers around the world are working on uncovering them.[19]

Collective capabilities—helping marginalized groups

Human development is not only a matter of promoting the freedoms that individuals have and have reason to choose and value. It is also a matter of promoting the freedoms of groups or collective entities. Individuals are not the only unit of moral concern; structures of living together are, too.[20] The failure to explicitly include them in evaluating the state of affairs leads to the loss of important information.

Take the example of a society that makes explicit arrangements to include persons with disabilities in the mainstream, allowing them to lead full lives as individuals and members of society. Or a society that is open towards and accepting of refugees, allowing them to find work and integrate in the mainstream. Conversely, a community that discourages lesbian, gay, bisexual, transgender or intersex individuals from marrying or having children limits the fulfilment of these people's lives. Societies vary in the number, functions and effectiveness

Human development is also a matter of promoting the freedoms of groups or collective entities

Dan Ariely (signature)

Predictably irrational—helping advance human development in a less than rational world

How did you get into studying how individuals make decisions or choices? Was this a rational decision?

I got into this following my experience of being in hospital for a very long time. I was badly injured when young. While in hospital, there were a number of things that I thought were very wrong, and I didn't like. One was how the bandages were replaced for burn patients. What is the right approach for doing this—ripping them fast, or taking them out slowly? What is the best way to minimize the pain? The nurses said they knew the best approach, which was to rip them off fast. They followed their intuition. I didn't agree that this was the right way. Despite good intentions, the nurses were wrong about this.

After leaving the hospital, I thought about doing experiments to understand how we sometimes have bad intuitions. Where do these fail us the most? What is the right model of human behaviour? I wanted to understand how people behave, how we make mistakes and also how we can do better.

This was not a "rational" decision. I did not consider all my options and think about them. I found something I liked to do and felt passionate about. I jumped right into it without thinking too much and without thinking for too long.

What have we learned from behavioural economics about how individuals and groups make decisions? How has this changed how economists think about decisionmaking? What are the implications in terms of policies for health, education and well-being?

People, in general, don't make very thoughtful, rational decisions. For example, take texting and driving and our general addiction to cellphones. This is quite irrational. Most of the messages and emails we get do not need immediate attention.

There is the concept of random reinforcement. A rat gets food every 100th time he presses a lever. If the food is given on any random press between 1 and 200, the rat will go on pressing for much longer in hope of a reward. This is why we are addicted to our phones. From time to time we get an email or message that is very exciting, and hence we are hooked. We check our phones way too often, including when we are driving.

Take overeating, underexercising, financial decisionmaking, and there are millions of other places where we fail. In terms of relevant policies, this is not always an information problem. With smoking, for example, the barrier is not lack of good information.

A policy is a tool to get people to behave in a different way. If the model that the policy is based on is wrong, the policy will fail. There are some assumptions in standard models that have to be questioned. For example, people do not usually think long term.

And then, with banking regulation there is a need to understand the model. Bankers are not bad people, but there are conflicts of interest. Policies are introduced, for example, to increase transparency, but they do not achieve much. What is needed is a better theory of how people behave, what the conflicts of interest are and what can be done to bring down these conflicts of interest.

Being able to lead a long and healthy life, being well informed and being able to participate and make decisions are the foundations of well-being in the human development approach. This view holds that the expansion of individuals' choices should be the goal of development. Given what we know from behavioural economics, would you say this view can be qualified, or nuanced, in some way?

This is a beautiful but naïve perspective. Choices are all good when they have no cost. Having choices can lead to what has been called the burden of choice.

We have to ask ourselves: Are we helping people by giving choices? Is it fair? Do you want to choose when to end your parent's life, when to pull life support?

There are tiny choices—where to drink coffee, eat. People have no time to think about those choices. People take what is easily available. They don't make these choices with full agency. There are the middle-range choices, for example, which camera or stereo system to buy. These are the decisions where people can make the right choice—given the right information, if they have the time and they think about it.

Then there are the really huge choices, involving marriage, house, savings, etc. When people get bad news, say about a health condition, they "shut down." Studies show that with people who have prostate cancer, the course of treatment depends on which doctor they see first. If they see a surgeon, they have surgery. If they see a different doctor, they have a different treatment plan, not surgery.

It is with the very small and the very big choices that we have to help people.

We want to explore how individuals act as part of groups. How much are individual decisions impacted by social norms, values, stereotypes and prejudices? How do norms such as those of fairness, cooperation and honesty come to be, and how are they sustained?

With honesty, we have to think about rationalization. There are different aspects of honesty. People ask, how dishonest can I be and yet feel good about myself? This has to do with social norms. In some countries, bribery is ok. People ask themselves, what is acceptable here? They end up saying, ok, this is acceptable. If you live in a country where giving a bribe to a public official is common practice, you tell yourself that this is perfectly acceptable.

In the United States everyone gets away with illegal downloads. This is corruption! There is a big social element to it. People know it is illegal. Because everyone does it, this empties the moral content of it.

How important is self-image, or how we view ourselves, in making decisions? What are some applications of this and some implications for policy design?

Experiments show that people are not completely dishonest. People cheat less than what the theory of rational individuals would suggest. People ask themselves what they will be comfortable with (not what they can get away with). There is a range of goodness. People have a self-image, an internal standard for good behaviour, which is very much a social construct.

Policies that take advantage of the impact of social norms can be very effective. They had this problem in Bogotá, where people would not stop at red lights. The city hired mimes (clowns) to stand at intersections and to make fun of people who wouldn't stop at traffic signals. People started behaving better. If you think about it, it was a beautiful intervention. This underlines the importance of understanding social constructs, changing the words and terms that people use and to get people to start thinking of themselves in different ways.

Dan Ariely
James B. Duke Professor of Psychology and Behavioral Economics at Duke University

of social institutions and thus in the range of social competencies that can promote human freedoms.[21]

What social institutions—family, community, nongovernmental organizations, neighbourhood or social clubs, and cooperatives—can be or do reflects collective capabilities. Such capabilities enhance human development, particularly among people who are marginalized or deprived and whose freedom cannot be enhanced through the actions of individuals alone.

The collective capabilities of social institutions are essential in many cases. Every individual values freedom from hunger, but few individuals have the capability to achieve this freedom through their own efforts. Society must organize resources, technology, expertise, policies and institutions in a way that enables individuals to take action to achieve the freedom. Similarly, people in forced labour may not escape it without collective capabilities or the capabilities of institutions.

Groups and coalitions are a means of exercising collective agency, which is much more powerful than people exercising individual agency. Groups to which individuals belong, including groups that individuals may establish, can expand individual capabilities and afford individuals new freedoms. A leading example is the Grameen Bank experience in Bangladesh, where groups of destitute women helped empower individual woman economically and socially, which individual efforts might not have achieved. Informal workers in many economies have organized to demand their rights to better conditions. Through organization and collective action since 2002, waste pickers in Buenos Aires transformed a hazardous activity based on poor technology into a cooperative system of urban recycling based on decent work conditions, appropriate technology and reduced incidence of child labour.[22]

Social values and norms—key impacts on universalism

Social values and norms influence the parameters of the freedoms that are enhanced through human development. Societies may limit the freedoms that are recognized among individuals who are, say, women, gay, transgender, with disabilities or of a particular race or religion (see chapter 2). For example, a society that expects women to perform only unpaid care work explicitly or implicitly discourages girls from attaining higher education and fulfilling their full potential.

The norms and values of a society may not support the most disadvantaged. Prejudice against some groups is sometimes deeply ingrained in culture and practice. Women face explicit and implicit discrimination in school and working life.[23] This discrimination is found even in environments that would be expected to reward merit objectively, such as higher education and the scientific community.[24] In advanced countries groups may face discrimination and lack of opportunities based on race. In the United States the bias of educators against African American children has an impact as early as preschool.[25] Bias and prejudice thus play a role in almost all important aspects of life. What individuals do and how they act are dictated largely by social traditions of privilege and subordination.

Society must organize resources, technology, expertise, policies and institutions in a way that enables individuals to take action to achieve human freedom

Groups are governed by social norms that also influence the behaviour of individuals and often shape the freedoms individuals articulate, particularly agency. The effect on freedom has been analysed in terms of adaptive preferences, the mechanism people use to adjust their preferences according to their circumstances. The frequently unconscious adaptation of preferences distorts perceptions of freedom so that individuals may not notice that their freedom of choice has been constrained.

The concept of adaptive preferences is especially applicable to the gender debate.[26] The deprivation in agency associated with social norms and culture is evident in the practice of early marriage, the lack of women's control over household resources and the attitudes that expose women to the risk of gender-based violence. Almost half the women surveyed in Africa report agency-related deprivation in more than one area of their lives. Women who are educated, who work or who live in urban areas have more voice and autonomy. In Africa almost 20 percent of women who live in rural areas and have no more than a primary education experience three major deprivations, compared with 1 percent of women who live in urban areas and have higher education.[27]

Social norms, rules and conventions are not created in a vacuum. Norms and expected and accepted behaviour evolve. The circumstances that may have given rise to particular norms may change, but the norms themselves may not. Traditions and norms tend to become entrenched. Once established, a norm can be difficult to dislodge. Many anachronistic and sometimes perverse social norms persist for generations. Traditions, including dowry from the families of brides and child marriage, are maintained by households under social pressure. Violating a norm can cause psychological discomfort, financial loss or worse. In these cases the focus should be how the norms can influence the effects of healthy policies and the identification of ways to alter the norms (box 3.3).

Multiple identities—how they influence agency and well-being

Multiple identities influence an individual's agency and well-being (functionings and capabilities): citizenship, residence, geographic origin, class, gender, politics, profession, employment, social commitments and so on. Each of these groups is associated with a specific aspect of an individual's identity. Group affiliations and identities are more fluid than fixed. Each person belongs to a number of groups at one time. People are born into some groups —a woman, an Asian, lefthandedness. Other groups may be abandoned, such as religion. Still others may be joined, such as citizenship. No single identity can completely define an individual throughout her or his life.

People have the liberty of choosing their identities. Individuals have reason to recognize, value and defend the freedom to choose identities. Liberty is important and valuable because all individuals deserve the space to consider the various facets, nuances and choices associated with their identity. Liberty is also a precondition for peaceful coexistence in multiethnic and multicultural societies.

Three identity issues have implications for human development. First, the space for multiple identities is more limited among people who are marginalized, and those people may lack the freedom to choose the identity they

> People should have the liberty of choosing their identities

BOX 3.3

Strategies for changing social norms

- Rectify mistaken beliefs about what others do or think.
- Use the mechanisms of social pressure.
- Change the symbolic meaning of a social norm.
- Create or exploit conflicts among different norms.
- Change the signalling function of norm compliance.

- Change the incentives for supporting norms among key actors.
- Send countermessages through appropriate messengers.
- Adjust how norms interact with laws.

Source: World Bank 2014.

value. This absence can be a serious deprivation in their lives because it limits their agency.

Second, many people favour a single identity to the disadvantage of all others and deny reasoning and choice in selecting identities. Much extremism and hatred can be undermined by promoting the acceptance of multiple identities over a single identity, such as ethnicity, religion or caste. Embracing single identities may make other groups or identities appear as rivals or even enemies. It misses all the multiple identities that may be shared, such as humanity, parents or neighbours. Multiple identities are essential to the freedom of agency because they provide people with the chance to explore different functionings and capabilities, and they can ensure autonomy.

Third, identity groups interact and compete with each other over limited economic and political resources and power. Groups often seek to obtain more power at the cost of other groups. They are often able to become entrenched in positions of power. The resulting concentration of economic and political control within a single group can be difficult to unravel (see chapter 2). In this process, marginalized groups experiencing deprivations—such as indigenous groups, older people and ethnic minorities—lose out and may become excluded from progress in human development.

Yet groups have the space to interact and share their concerns in a participatory democratic system. They should seek a common understanding of a fair society through negotiation and discussion so all people possess the freedom to explore different identities and choose their own path. Collective values and collective aspirations can be fostered through a collective discourse in which all constituencies truly and effectively participate.

The interdependence of freedoms —the inevitability of tradeoffs

According to the human development approach, all people should be able to lead the kind of life that they have reason to value. But the freedom of one person or group may interfere with the freedom of another person or group. This can be an unintended outcome or a deliberate goal. Given the political economy of societies, there may be attempts by richer and more powerful groups to restrict the freedom of others. This is reflected in the affluence bias of the policy matrix, the way the legal system functions and the way institutions operate in many economies. This elite capture represents an attempt of the rich and the powerful to curb the opportunities of poor and deprived people.

The human development approach recognizes that more must be done than merely calling for the expansion of capabilities and freedoms. All societies need to make tradeoffs, decide among the claims of competing groups on finite resources and establish priorities in a context of unequal distribution of income and wealth, voice and participation, inclusion and diversity, and so on. Following reasoned debate, societies need to determine the principles for settling these issues to realize a more just society.

Sustainable development as social justice

Interdependent freedoms and choices are also characteristic of intergenerational equity—the freedoms of future generations in relation to the freedoms of the present generation. The 2011 Human Development Report defines sustainable human development as "the expansion of the substantive freedoms of people today while making reasonable efforts to avoid seriously compromising those of future generations."[28]

This is similar to many conventional notions of environmental sustainability. But it also reflects the concept of universalism, which goes deeper. Universalism argues that the life experiences of all individuals within and across generations are equally important. The human development approach therefore considers sustainability as a matter of distributional equity both within and across generations. Human Development Reports have consistently advanced this integrated approach to sustainability.

The human development approach reiterates that sustainable development is much broader than the protection of natural resources and the environment; that environmental degradation exerts larger, unequal impacts on poor, marginalized and vulnerable people; and that climate change affects the people and countries the most that have least contributed to it. From

Interdependent freedoms and choices are also characteristic of intergenerational equity

a human development perspective, sustainable development thus embodies social justice.

Gender equality and women's empowerment—vital markers

If human development must reach everyone, gender equality and women's empowerment need to be central. When women are allowed to work in a profession of their choice, when they have access to financial services and when they are protected by law from domestic violence, they are able to lead lives to their full potential. The more command women have over household income, the more they participate in the economy, the more girls are enrolled in secondary school and the larger the benefits for their families, their communities and their countries.

Gender equality and women's empowerment need to be addressed in a mainstreamed and integrated way. Sustainable Development Goal 5 covers gender equality and the empowerment of all women and girls, and it proposes relevant targets and indicators. But gender equality and women's empowerment should not be limited to a single goal. Gender-focused targets are also covered by Sustainable Development Goal 3 (good health and well-being) and Goal 4 (quality education). These goals and targets have catalysing effects on achieving the other Sustainable Development Goals.

Gender parity is often mistaken for gender equality. Gender parity is an equality of numbers. Gender equality, by contrast, refers to the social relationship between men and women and has deeper dimensions. Take the example of women's participation in peacebuilding efforts to end conflicts. At times, female representatives are invited to negotiations in order to meet a formal requirement for equal participation. However, when women are empowered to be effective participants, they can have a great impact.[29] In the recently completed Colombia peace process, one-third of participants in the negotiations were women. Their lobbying ensured that those who committed sexual violence in the conflict would not be eligible for pardons. The women also advocated for economic support for women in rural areas for new development activities.[30] When women are included in the peace process, there is a 20 percent increase in the probability of an agreement lasting at least 2 years and a 35 percent increase in the probability of an agreement lasting at least 15 years.[31]

Checking whether progress in human development reaches everyone—assessment requirements

Averages are not adequate for determining whether everyone benefits from progress in human development; a disaggregated approach is needed. Nor will a purely quantitative assessment succeed; qualitative aspects are needed, too. Data on freedom of agency also need to be reviewed, particularly on voice and accountability. Other indicators of human well-being can provide insights, such as the social progress index.[32] Finally, good generation and dissemination of data are important and require additional in-depth research, experimentation, consultations and alliance-building among stakeholders.

The disaggregated perspective

An assessment of whether progress in human development is reaching everyone requires disaggregated data by region, gender, rural–urban location, socioeconomic status, race, ethnicity and so on. Disaggregated data unmask the averages and show who has been bypassed, where they are and why.

Development barriers often fall along group lines. People with certain characteristics, in certain locations and with certain identities are more likely to lack access to essential services and opportunities and are more prone to be victims of discrimination and other forms of social exclusion.

To include everyone in progress in human development, the excluded and marginalized, as well as the depth of their deprivations, need to be identified, often through data disaggregated in National Human Development Reports. For example, Ethiopia's 2014 National Human Development Report presented HDI values disaggregated by region, Mexico's 2010 National Human Development Report presented HDI values disaggregated by indigenous group and

> The more command women have over household income, the more they participate in the economy, the more girls are enrolled in secondary school and the larger the benefits for their families, their communities and their countries

Somalia's 2012 National Human Development Report presented Multidimensional Poverty Index values disaggregated by area (nomadic, rural, urban and the like).[33] The 2030 Agenda stipulates that progress towards achieving the Sustainable Development Goals will depend on high-quality, accessible, timely and reliable data disaggregated by income, gender, age, race, ethnicity, migration status, disability, geographic location and other characteristics relevant in national contexts.[34]

While there is agreement in principle that enabling all people to benefit from progress in human development demands disaggregated data, there is less clarity about how to ensure data availability. Which survey instruments are the most accurate and cost-effective for collecting these data? And there are questions about how to gather data that may be culturally or politically sensitive but extremely important. Many groups may remain largely invisible in data because of such sensitivities—for example, the lesbian, gay, bisexual, transgender and intersex community. Any group that suffers extreme discrimination or criminalization may hide their identity, making the collection of accurate data nearly impossible. Likewise, data disaggregated by indigenous population or ethnic group may be discouraged. Overcoming these cultural and political barriers to open self-identification

is a great challenge in reaching the most excluded and marginalized groups.

Data on health, education and other aspects of well-being are already available in disaggregated form by gender, age, location and income decile through household surveys, including Demographic and Health Surveys, Multiple Indicator Cluster Surveys and the Living Standards Measurement Study.[35] More can be done to increase the frequency of these surveys and improve their comparability, but using the disaggregated data that already exist is a start towards understanding patterns of exclusion. Investments in national statistical capacities, more financing to support longer and more detailed surveys that target the individual rather than the household and greater use of big data will be needed to strengthen and extend survey coverage.

Disaggregated data can also be mobilized through perception surveys. A 2015 field survey in Nigeria revealed that people's perceptions of threats to security in such areas as ability to support oneself or losing one's bank savings were much more intense in the Federal Capital Territory than in the South-South region (figure 3.2). Such information alerts policymakers to the barriers to a sense of security in the Federal Capital Territory and to the need to undertake remedial action.[36]

> Investments in national statistical capacities, more financing to support longer and more detailed surveys that target the individual rather than the household and greater use of big data will be needed to strengthen and extend survey coverage

FIGURE 3.2

People's perceptions of threats to security were much more intense in Nigeria's Federal Capital Territory than in the South-South region

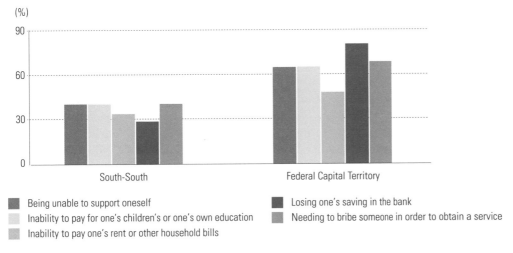

Source: UNDP 2015b.

Determining the types of disaggregation needed to reveal inequalities along particular dimensions can be difficult without understanding the processes of exclusion and marginalization in a society. It is thus important that decisions about data collection be rooted in qualitative and historical research on these processes in each context. For example, in Mongolia, data have been disaggregated by disability. In 2010 the share of people ages 10 or older with no education was three times higher among persons with disabilities than among the rest of the population, and persons with disabilities were also less likely to obtain higher education (8 percent versus 18 percent of the rest of the population).[37]

Disparities in one area may reinforce disparities in other areas and create a dynamic whereby people are left further and further behind in human development. For example, women are generally disadvantaged relative to men in obtaining the benefits of human development. If such women are living in ecologically fragile areas, they are doubly deprived: because of their gender and because of their location. The deprivations may pile up if these women are also poor. The assessment perspective should thus address these dynamics and focus first on those who are furthest behind.

One key dimension of data disaggregation is gender, yet this dimension is missing or opaque in most development indicators. The 2030 Agenda, particularly Sustainable Development Goal 5, focuses on targets that will require gender-disaggregated data, including:[38]

- Ending all forms of discrimination against all women and girls everywhere.
- Eliminating all forms of violence against all women and girls in the public and private spheres, including trafficking and sexual and other types of exploitation.
- Eliminating all harmful practices, such as child, early and forced marriage and female genital mutilation.
- Recognizing and valuing unpaid care and domestic work through the provision of public services.
- Ensuring women's full and effective participation and equal opportunities for leadership at all levels of decisionmaking in political, economic and public life.
- Ensuring universal access to sexual and reproductive health and reproductive rights as

agreed in accordance with the Programme of Action of the International Conference on Population and Development (1994) and the Beijing Platform for Action (1995) and the outcome documents of their review conferences.

Qualitative assessment

Progress in human development has often been widespread and impressive quantitatively but is less impressive when the quality of outcomes is factored in. The differences in quality across groups can also be stark. In terms of people and their lives, low quality implies a lack of the tools necessary to reach one's full potential and express all one's capabilities.

More children are enrolled in and attending school than ever. But 250 million children worldwide do not learn basic skills, even though half of them have spent at least four years in school.[39] In most countries class size, the number of qualified teachers and the availability of improved facilities are more desirable in better-off neighbourhoods than in poorer neighbourhoods, leading to wide differences in learning.

International testing has been conducted since the 1950s to compare cognitive achievement at various levels of schooling across countries and to identify the causes of measured differences (box 3.4). Most of these attempts to assess the quality of education reflect the principle that cognitive development is the main objective of education and thus measure the success of education systems based on this concept. Scholastic test scores provide a gauge of how well the curriculum is learned and of students' learning achievements at the main exit points of school systems.

Global health is also improving. People are living longer. Global life expectancy at birth was 4.9 years longer in 2015 than in 2000, though there were wide variations across regions and countries. The increase in life expectancy at birth from 2000 to 2015 was greatest in Sub-Saharan Africa (8.8 years), followed by South Asia (5.5 years) and Latin America and the Caribbean (3.8 years).[40] But are the added years of life expectancy healthy years or years characterized by illness and disability? The notion of healthy life expectancy helps answer this question (see chapter 2). The increase in

Disparities in one area may reinforce disparities in other areas and create a dynamic whereby people are left further and further behind in human development

BOX 3.4

Test score methods for assessing the quality of education

More than 60 countries and other education systems participate in the Trends in International Mathematics and Science Study, which covers mathematics and science, and 55 education systems took part in the 2011 round of the Progress in International Reading Literacy Study.[1] In 2015 the Organisation for Economic Co-operation and Development's Programme for International Student Assessment (PISA) was conducted in 72 countries and economies, mainly industrialized and middle-income countries. Other initiatives include the 16 country Southern and Eastern African Consortium for Monitoring Educational Quality and the 15 country Latin American Laboratory for the Assessment of Quality in Education.

The question is whether these international tests provide a useful assessment of the quality of education outcomes in a country or remain mainly a measure of how well students have learned a curriculum. PISA is the only one that uses tests not directly linked to curricula. National PISA scores are averages and so conceal variations within a country. PISA and the Latin American Laboratory assessment provide more detail on distribution, such as quartiles, and on standard deviations and scores by parent income quintile.

Note
1. U.S. Department of Education's Trends in International Mathematics and Science Study website (https://nces.ed.gov/timss/) and Progress in International Reading Literacy Study website (https://nces.ed.gov/surveys/pirls/)
Source: Human Development Report Office.

healthy life expectancy has not been as dramatic as the increase in life expectancy, so people are generally living more years, but those years are not free from illness and disability.[41]

Urban-based health facilities provide better health services than do rural health centres. The upshot is that not everyone or every group enjoys high-quality human development; there are differences in the quality of the capabilities achieved and the opportunities available.

Data on freedom of agency

Even though freedom of agency has always been an integral component of the concept of human development, the Human Development Report has usually been much more concerned with well-being than with agency. This is true of the HDI, which does not accord intrinsic value—as distinct from instrumental value—to freedom of agency. The omission is mitigated to some extent by the Gender Empowerment Index and related measures, but agency is not only a gender issue.

One of the problems in assessing freedom of agency is that it is inherently much more difficult than well-being to measure. However, a good deal can be learned about the progress in achieving freedom of agency (or not) around the world without precise measurements. This is particularly relevant to examining who is being left behind and why and who is likely to be left behind as a result of ongoing trends. Groups that suffer absolute and relative deprivations in outcomes are often also deprived in voice, participation and process freedoms.

The extent of agency and participation enjoyed by different groups may change. Advances in technology, government regimes, economic structures and legal frameworks may affect freedom of agency.

There is generally a positive relationship between well-being (measured by the HDI) and agency and participation (as measured by the World Bank's voice and accountability indicator; box 3.5). But it is possible for a country to have a high HDI value and a low score on the voice and accountability index (figure 3.3). This supports the notion that the two measures, if not perfectly correlated, are complementary. In other words, societies may achieve high average freedom of well-being but not freedom of agency. If human development is to reach everyone in its various aspects, freedom of agency must be enhanced. An assessment that combines well-being with agency and participation at the political level may be a more complete assessment of human development.

One aspect of freedom of agency is the extent of women's agency and the extent to which women are able to shape decisions that affect their lives. This is extremely important from a human development perspective but difficult to capture quantitatively in all its

An assessment that combines well-being with agency and participation at the political level may be a more complete assessment of human development

BOX 3.5

Voice and accountability indicator—the World Bank's approach

The voice and accountability indicator is one of six aggregate governance indicators constructed by the World Bank to capture the dimensions of governance in a country—voice and accountability, political stability and absence of violence, government effectiveness, regulatory quality, rule of law and control of corruption. Each indicator is based on information from several data sources, ranging from household and firm surveys to the subjective assessments of multilateral organizations, nongovernmental organizations and providers of commercial business information. The voice and accountability indicator aggregates data from surveys to capture perceptions of "the extent to which a country's citizens are able to participate in selecting their government, as well as freedom of expression, freedom of association and a free media."[1]

The individual variables from the various data sources are rescaled to run from zero to one, with higher values indicating better outcomes, and the rescaled values are then used to construct estimates of voice and accountability. Estimates are available for 214 countries and territories from 1996 to 2015 in units of a standard normal distribution ranging from approximately –2.5 to 2.5. Updated annually, the indicator was first used by the Human Development Report Office in the 2002 Human Development Report.[2]

Notes
1. World Bank 2007, p. 262. 2. UNDP 2002.
Source: Human Development Report Office.

FIGURE 3.3

It is possible for a country to have a high Human Development Index value and a low score on the voice and accountability index

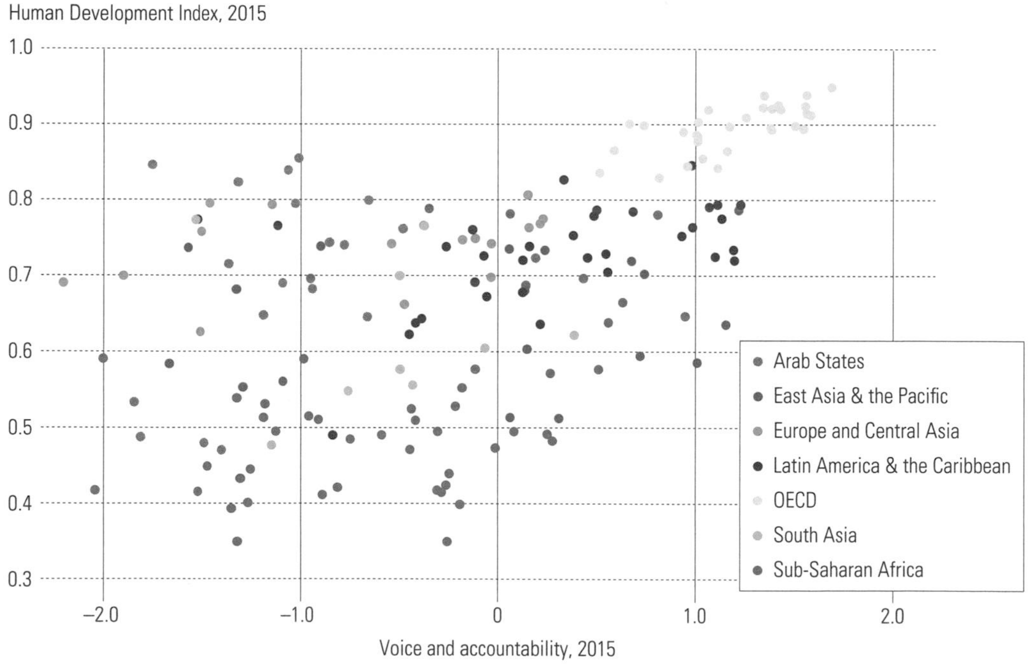

Human Development Index, 2015
1.0
0.9
0.8
0.7
0.6
0.5
0.4
0.3
–2.0
–1.0
0
1.0
2.0
Voice and accountability, 2015
Arab States
East Asia & the Pacific
Europe and Central Asia
Latin America & the Caribbean
OECD
South Asia
Sub-Saharan Africa

Source: The World Bank's Worldwide Governance Indicators website (www.govindicators.org); Human Development Report Office.

One dimension that lends itself to measurement is women's participation in national political life and decisionmaking

dimensions. One dimension that lends itself to measurement is women's participation in national political life and decisionmaking, which is measured using women's share of seats in the national parliament. (This indicator is included in the Gender Inequality Index.) By shedding light on a key dimension of women's agency, this indicator complements the HDI and provides a more complete picture of a nation's progress.

FIGURE 3.4

The trend in nonincome Human Development Index values and in women's and men's shares of seats in parliament is moving in the desired direction in every region

Human Development Index, 1997 and 2015

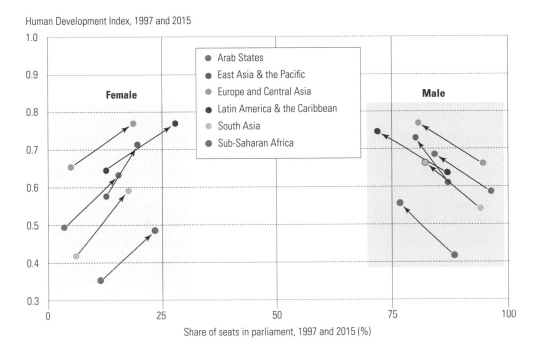

Source: Human Development Report Office.

HDI values can be estimated separately for women and men by estimating education, health and income outcomes among women and men separately. The gender-based differences in well-being outcomes tend to be more pronounced in the education and health outcomes. They are also measured more clearly, are better understood and reflect more robust data. So estimates of nonincome HDI values among women and men are used—that is, HDI values constructed from the education and health dimensions alone.

The trend in nonincome HDI values and in women's and men's shares of seats in parliament is moving in the desired direction in every region, even if initial points and changes over time vary (figure 3.4). Yet all regions have made progress in closing the gap in representation in parliament between women and men. Latin America and the Caribbean has one of the strongest performances, while East Asia and the Pacific has made little progress.

Other measures of well-being

Various measures of human well-being have been proposed and constructed over the years. In the context of human development reaching everyone, this section examines whether some of these measures can provide an assessment framework for capturing universal well-being.

Social progress index

The social progress index ranks countries by social progress—how societies improve in social, political and economic structures so that everyone benefits.[42] Gains may derive from direct human action, such as through social enterprise or social activism, or as a natural progression in sociocultural evolution. The index measures the extent to which countries provide for the social and environmental needs of their citizens. Fifty-three indicators on basic human needs, the foundations of well-being and opportunity to progress show the relative performance of nations.

All regions have made progress in closing the gap in representation in parliament between women and men

World happiness index

The world happiness index annually surveys numerous people in various countries around the world to identify the country with the happiest population.[43] Rankings are based on responses to a life evaluation questionnaire that is based on Cantril's ladder. It asks respondents to think of a ladder on which their best possible life would be step 10, while their worst possible life would be step 0. Respondents are then asked to rate their lives at the present moment as a step on the ladder. The researchers identify the result as the perception respondents have of their own happiness. The responses are weighted based on six other factors: level of gross domestic product (GDP), life expectancy, generosity, social support, freedom and corruption.

Better life index

The better life index is a composite index computed for the 35 Organisation for Economic Co-operation and Development countries plus Brazil, the Russian Federation and South Africa. It measures well-being according to 11 themes in living conditions (housing, income and jobs) and quality of life (community, education, environment, civic engagement, health, life satisfaction, safety and work–life balance).[44]

It involves citizens in constructing the index, so people have a say in its value.

Subjective measures of well-being

Some countries support subjective measures of well-being or happiness. For example, Bhutan has a gross national happiness index.[45] The United Kingdom, through the Office for National Statistics, is one of the first countries to officially embrace the measurement of life satisfaction and happiness, with measures of national well-being.[46] Proponents note that a single measure of happiness, which arguably summarizes people's feelings about many aspects of well-being, avoids the need to weight components. Others note that an individual's happiness may also be related to his or her relative—rather than absolute—level of well-being in a society, which may hinder cross-country comparisons. Many people, including young people, are thinking of a long-term vision of the future in terms of achieving a life that can be graded "good" (box 3.6).

Human development indicators and Sustainable Development Goal indicators

Human development indicators and Sustainable Development Goal indicators may support each other (figure 3.5). For example,

> Various measures of human well-being have been proposed and constructed over the years

---

BOX 3.6

A long-term vision of the future—the Leimers List

In 1967 Martin Luther King, Jr., called for a world perspective. The young people of HOPE XXL are trying to answer that call. HOPE XXL wants to ensure that all people can achieve a life they grade as "good" (at least a 8 on a scale of 0 to 10).

HOPE XXL started in 2009 in The Netherlands. Ten young people from the Liemers region developed the first version of the Liemers List: a long-term vision of the future. HOPE XXL has since grown into an international movement with thousands of young people joining and sharing their ideas. During a series of international events, including the 2012 European conference with Kofi Annan, the Liemers List was developed further. The Liemers List was finalized by young people from all over the world at the HOPE XXL Global Summit in Costa Rica in January 2015

and presented to the United Nations in February 2015. HOPE XXL challenges everyone to contribute.

To implement the Liemers List, HOPE XXL has proposed a new approach to international cooperation called the People's Partnership. It is an essential element in the young people's vision of the future and a new approach to international cooperation. In the People's Partnership all countries are paired together to realize the goal of all persons grading their lives as good. HOPE XXL believes that the number 8 encompasses the greater goal of the UN Global Goals and is therefore the perfect symbol to communicate to reach a wider audience.

The first partnership is between Bangladesh and The Netherlands, and HOPE XXL is focusing on strengthening the relationship between the two countries.

Source: HOPE XXL 2015.

FIGURE 3.5

Human development indicators and Sustainable Development Goal indicators may support each other—an example in health

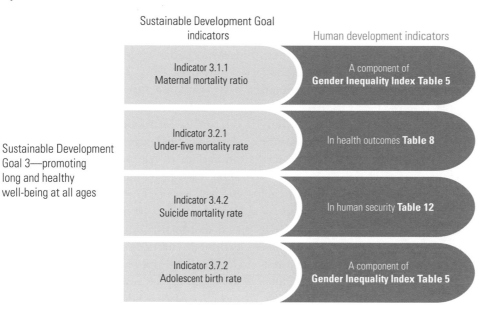

Source: Human Development Report Office.

Data need to be generated and disseminated on the basis of innovative perspectives to encourage the participation of more people, use of new technologies and reliance on more aspects of people's perceptions

Sustainable Development Goal indicator 3.2.1 on the under-five mortality rate can draw on data in the Human Development Report (see *Statistical table 8*) and be used to track progress. Similar examples can be drawn from such areas as poverty and inequality, education and gender equality. Human development indicators in the Human Development Report may also identify and integrate Sustainable Development Goal indicators in the Human Development Report statistical tables, particularly those on sustainability, urbanization and governance.

New ways to generate and disseminate data

Data need to be generated and disseminated on the basis of innovative perspectives—to encourage the participation of more people, use of new technologies and reliance on more aspects of people's perceptions. In a survey of existing projects that use new sources of data and their suitability for measurement of the Sustainable Development Goals, the most common sources of new data were mobile phones, satellite imagery and social media (figure 3.6).[47]

FIGURE 3.6

New data sources for Sustainable Development Goals

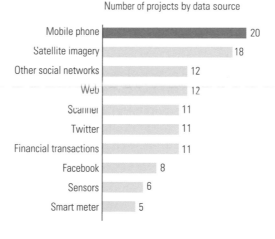

Source: Ballivian 2015.

One issue in the data generation and the dissemination process is Big Data. Big Data is about data characterized by high volume, high velocity, great variety and often also significant veracity.[48] It is as much associated with how, where and why it is generated, whether collected purposely by official or private entities or as byproducts of data generated for other purposes. Granularity—detail—is a particular strength, enabling deeper, more nuanced analysis and tracking, but it is also associated with elements of risk, particularly pertaining to the protection of individuals or groups who may not be aware that they are being monitored. The World Economic Forum obtained data from LinkedIn to add granularity to analysis of tertiary education for its 2016 Human Capital Report.[49] In the international context Big Data has wide application in humanitarian situations and for data on community behaviour as part of programme and project implementation.

The UN Secretary-General's High-Level Panel on Sustainable Development called for a data revolution for sustainable development in 2013 through a new international initiative to improve the quality of statistics and information available to citizens.[50] It asked stakeholders to take advantage of new technology, crowdsourcing and improved connectivity to empower people with information on the progress towards the Sustainable Development Goal targets. It maintained that better data and statistics would help governments track progress and ensure that decisions were based on evidence. These enhanced data and statistics can also strengthen accountability. A true data revolution would draw on existing and new sources of data to integrate statistics into decisionmaking, promote open access to and use of data and ensure increased support for statistical systems.

Particularly important in the call for a data revolution is the focus on empowering citizens through information, including through the transparency and openness of official statistics

and through government accountability. The call was also recognition that the trajectory of progress in internationally available official statistics was inadequate and needed new momentum, despite the efforts of the Partnership in Statistics for Development in the 21st Century and other bilateral, regional and global initiatives.

A dashboard approach has become a common approach for measuring development outcomes. It provides colour-coded tables that show the levels and progress of humanity on various development indicators. Such an approach can be effective in presenting data on well-being. This edition of the Human Development Report experiments with two dashboards, one on the environmental, economic and social aspects of sustainable development and one on gender equality and women's empowerment (see the statistical annex). A dashboard does not convey a definitive conclusion on country achievements, merely an indication. But if useful, dashboards could be extended to other areas of human development.

*   *   *

The human development approach recognizes that the choices people make are the ways in which they realize their aspirations, though the claims of individuals are interdependent and can compete with one another. A practical realization of universal outcomes thus requires considering not only the ways choices are made, but also the ways those choices can be enhanced not for a few, not for the most, but for everyone. And that is where policies become important—a theme taken up in chapter 4.

Chapter **4**

Caring for those left out—national policy options

Infographic 4.1 National policies to care for those left out—a four-pronged strategy

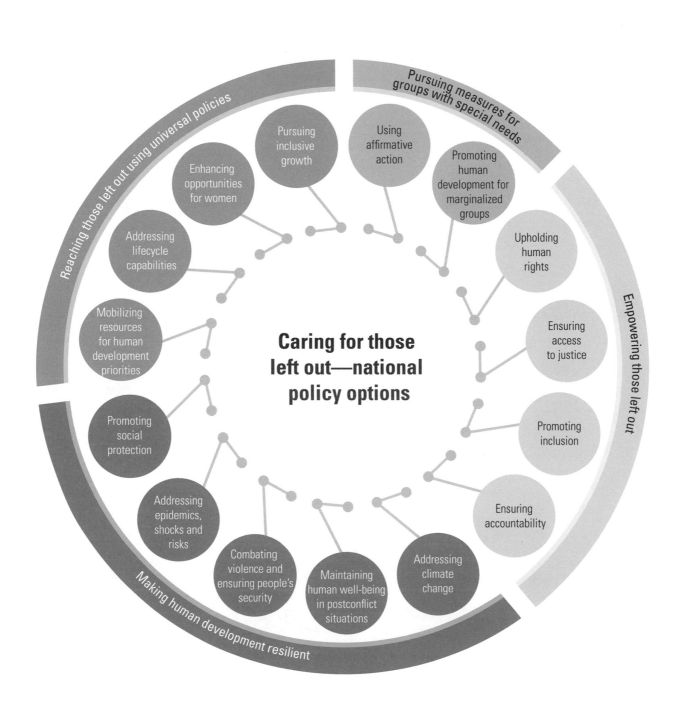

4.

Caring for those left out— national policy options

Basic human development has progressed well on average in all regions of the world. But not everyone has benefited from this progress—at least not equitably. Some have been left out, and some have been left behind. Given the challenges of today's world, this chapter identifies the key national policies and strategies that need to be pursued to achieve basic human development for everyone and to protect the gains that have been made.

Ensuring that human development reaches everyone calls for a four-pronged policy approach (see infographic 4.1 on the facing page). First, universal policies are needed to reach those left out. There are three important aspects of universal policies. One, universalism is an idea, but as chapter 2 shows, practical universalism is another matter, particularly in policy areas. For example, a country may be committed to universal health care, but difficult geography may prevent it from establishing health care centres that are accessible to all localities. Two, even with universal outcomes, there may be disparities. For instance, a country may attain universal primary education, but the quality of learning may vary between schools in rich neighbourhoods and schools in poor neighbourhoods. Three, because of these factors, universal human development policies need to be reoriented to reach those left out. Thus, economic growth is an important means to achieve human development, but if the benefits of growth are to reach disadvantaged and marginalized people, growth will have to be inclusive such that poor and disadvantaged people actively participate in the generation of growth and have an equitable share in the outcome.

Second, even with the new focus on universal policies, some groups of people have special needs that would not be met (see chapter 2). Their situations require specific measures and attention. For example, persons with disabilities require measures to ensure their mobility, participation and work opportunities.

Third, human development achieved does not mean human development sustained. Particularly in today's world, with all the risks and vulnerabilities (see chapter 1), progress in human development may be slowed or even reversed. This makes it essential to protect the gains and avoid reversal, especially for people who have achieved only the basics in human development and for people who have yet to achieve the basics. The first group could fall back below the threshold of basic human development, and the second might make no headway towards reaching it. Thus human development has to be resilient.

Fourth, people who have been left out will have to be empowered so that if policies and the relevant actors fail to deliver, these people can raise their voice, demand their rights and seek to redress the situation. That requires a framework for human rights and access to justice, a space for dialogue and effective participation, and a mechanism for demanding accountability.

Reaching those left out using universal policies

Some policies that enhance human development, especially universal ones, can have more than proportionally positive impacts on marginalized and vulnerable people. Identifying and reorienting these policies can narrow the human development deficits of those left out. Essential in this are pursuing inclusive growth, enhancing opportunities for women, addressing lifecycle capabilities and mobilizing resources for human development priorities —because universal policies are resource intensive.

Pursuing inclusive growth

For human development to reach everyone, growth has to be inclusive. This means that

Some policies that enhance human development, especially universal ones, can have more than proportionally positive impacts on marginalized and vulnerable people

people who are willing and able to participate in the growth process must be able to do so and to derive equitable benefits. Inclusive growth has four mutually supporting pillars: formulating an employment-led growth strategy with an emphasis on creating productive and remunerative employment opportunities in sectors where poor people live and work; enhancing inclusion in productive resources, especially finance; investing in human development priorities relevant to those who are left out; undertaking high-impact multidimensional interventions (win-win strategies).

Formulating an employment-led growth strategy

The major elements of an employment-led growth strategy are:

- *Removing barriers to employment-centred development.* For example, small- and medium-size enterprises often face bias in market entry and access to credit, and entrepreneurs may lack access to information and marketing skills. Removing these barriers requires multiple levels of support to improve the productivity and income of such enterprises.
- *Designing and implementing a conducive legal and regulatory framework to tackle informal work.* Informal workers are among the most vulnerable and insecure, and a regulatory framework can provide protection, which increases security and incentives to enhance productivity and value added.
- *Strengthening the links between large firms (typically capital intensive) and small and medium-size enterprises (typically labour intensive).* Industrial clusters supported by public investment can increase access to capital and technology and promote transfers of skills. Those actions can shift resources to sectors with greater potential for creating jobs and adding value.
- *Focusing on sectors where poor people live and work, especially in rural areas.* Policy measures to sustain and generate jobs in agriculture can improve productivity (without displacing jobs) through intensive cultivation, regular changes in cropping patterns, integrated input packages and better marketing. As the 2015 Human Development Report indicated, low-cost, sustainable technologies are

available in agriculture and can be transferred to and adapted in various economies through collaboration across developing countries.[1]

- *Adjusting the distribution of capital and labour in public spending to create jobs.* Public spending can support job creation by favouring technologies and sectors that enhance human development. It can also have a demonstration effect, signalling to the rest of the economy the many ways of using more labour-intensive technologies.

Securing decent work opportunities and better jobs for all people around the world with the notion of just jobs—those with fair remuneration, rights at work and opportunities for economic mobility—is the main feature of the Global Deal launched in September 2016 (box 4.1).[2]

Enhancing financial inclusion

People who are left out lack access to productive resources, including land, inputs and technology. But lack of access to finance has been identified as a major constraint to their economic opportunities and to becoming a part of the inclusive growth process. From 2011 to 2014, 700 million additional people worldwide became bank account holders, yet 2 billion people are still unbanked.[3] Financial services can be a bridge out of poverty and vulnerability. Several measures can enhance the financial inclusion of the poor.

- *Expanding banking services to disadvantaged and marginalized groups.* Opening bank branches in rural areas, offering easy banking services, using group solidarity as collateral (as with the Grameen Bank in Bangladesh) and having simple procedures that can be followed by people with low literacy can all reach people now unbanked. The former Yugoslav Republic of Macedonia has a model for others to emulate (box 4.2).
- *Steering credit towards unserved remote areas and sectors.* Investment banks in Argentina, Brazil, Malaysia and the Republic of Korea have directed credit to industrial sectors specializing in exports.[4]
- *Reducing interest rates and providing credit guarantees and subsidized credit to small and medium-size enterprises.* In Nigeria an agricultural lending facility provided incentives

> Lack of access to finance has been identified as a major constraint to an inclusive growth process

The Global Deal—a triple-win strategy

Decent work and good labour relations contribute to greater equality and more inclusive economic development, benefiting workers, companies and societies (a triple win). The Global Deal—initiated by the Prime Minister of Sweden and designed with the Organisation for Economic Co-operation and Development and the International Labour Organization—aims to enhance dialogue among like-minded national governments, companies, employer associations, trade unions and broader civil society to improve employment conditions and boost productivity.

It aims to develop a platform for parties to collaborate and to strengthen existing cooperation structures. It will build on established initiatives and projects, providing political direction and impetus to overall development and systematizing and scaling up existing processes. The expectation is that it will contribute to inclusive growth, reduce inequalities and become a step towards achieving the Sustainable Development Goals and the ultimate goal of eradicating extreme poverty.

Source: Dewan and Randolph 2016; Global Citizen 2016.

Providing finance to rural farmers in the former Yugoslav Republic of Macedonia

Two-thirds of the poor people in the former Yugoslav Republic of Macedonia, mostly subsistence farmers, unemployed people and pensioners, live in rural areas, where they lack the finance for investment and rural financial and technical services.

A 2008 Agricultural Financial Services Project that was aligned with the country's rural development policy concentrated on two basic services. In one, groups of clients were formed, their financial literacy was enhanced and the technical and managerial skills of service providers were improved. In the other, only agricultural financial services and technical support were provided through agricultural investments.

In a simple but focused approach, the project provided 2,745 loans, lifting the average participant household's annual business income from €5,166 to €8,050 in two years. Project-linked branches offering credit and credit officers expanded fivefold.[1]

Note
1. IFAD 2009, 2016.
Source: Human Development Report Office.

to banks to allocate a large share of their credit to agribusiness, particularly small entrepreneurs. Such loans accounted for 1 percent of total bank loans in 2010 and are expected to reach 10 percent by 2020.[5]

- *Harnessing modern technology to promote financial inclusion.* In Africa 12 percent of adults have mobile bank accounts, compared with 2 percent globally.[6] Kenya leads the way at 58 percent, followed by Somalia, the United Republic of Tanzania and Uganda at 35 percent.[7] M-Pesa in Kenya is a prime example of how mobile phone technology can reach the unbanked. BKash, a mobile banking system in Bangladesh, has changed the way poor people transfer money, including remittances by garment workers, bill payments and the purchase of daily necessities.

Investing in human development priorities

In 2014 public expenditure as a percentage of such basic social services as health care was 3 percent in developing countries; the share in education was 4.7 percent between 2005 and 2014.[8] Yet a major part of this expenditure may not reach those who need the services the most. Most disadvantaged and marginalized groups lack universal primary education, universal health care, improved sanitation and decent housing. But simply increasing social spending is not enough because in many instances such spending goes for modern health facilities for well-off groups in urban areas rather than to mother and child care centres in rural areas. Focused investments in human development

Financial services can be a bridge out of poverty and vulnerability

Focused investments in human development priorities can deliver high-quality services to disadvantaged and marginalized groups

priorities can produce human development benefits by delivering services along with infrastructure, thereby directing high-quality services to disadvantaged and marginalized groups (figure 4.1).

Investing in human priorities is intended to reach those who lack basic social services such as education and health care that are essential for enhancing human capital so that these people can not only be part of inclusive growth, but also enhance their capabilities, which are intrinsically valuable.

But there are four relevant policy considerations. First, the mere availability of services or access to them is not enough; the effective use of services also requires affordability and adaptability. Low-cost but good services are possible and can be affordable for poor people. In Nicaragua compact ultrasound machines that can be carried on bicycles are being used to monitor the health of pregnant women, improving antenatal care at relatively low cost.[9] Similarly, services must be sensitive to the cultural and social norms of the contexts in which they are provided. For example, the presence of only male doctors in rural mother and child

care centres would be a disincentive for women and girls to use the centres.

Second, mere provisioning of services without considering quality is detrimental to poor people. Many services in poor areas are low quality—partly because of the perception that poor people do not want to pay for high-quality services and partly because of the perception that it is enough that poor people have some services, regardless of the quality. The result: Most high-quality services are enjoyed by the affluent. But poor people are usually ready to pay for high-quality and affordable services. In 2004 poor parents in Chad paid for schooling both in cash ($2 is the average annual contribution) and in kind (volunteering at community or government schools).[10] Parents also covered the cost of books and other supplies.

High-quality services can indeed be provided to poor people, as in Burkina Faso. The Office National de l'Eau et de l'Assainissement (the National Office of Water and Sanitation), the utility in charge of water and wastewater services in the capital, Ouagadougou, and other urban areas, provides piped water only to formal settlements.[11] But about 16 percent

FIGURE 4.1

Investments in priority human development to ensure human development for everyone

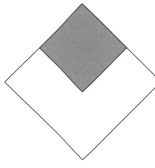

Public expenditure ratio
Government share of GNP

Social allocation ratio
Social services share of
government spending

Social priority ratio
Human priority share of
social sector spending

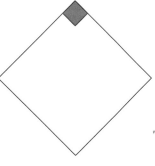

Human expenditure ratio
Human priority share of GNP

The human expenditure ratio is the product of three ratios:

E/Y = public expenditure as a proportion of national income

S/E = the proportion of public expenditure going to the social sector—the social allocation ratio

P/S = the proportion of expenditure in the social sectors going to human development priorities—the social priority ratio

Put differently, the human expenditure ratio is E/Y x S/E x P/S

Source: Human Development Report Office based on UNDP (1991).

of Ouagadougou's nearly 2 million inhabitants live in informal settlements, which are beyond the utility's mandate.[12] To skirt this problem, the utility designed five-year concession contracts for private firms to build and operate water networks in five informal settlements, beginning in 2013.[13] The utility sells bulk water to the operators and regulates the tariffs. The model has been so successful that the utility added two more concessions in Ouagadougou and three in Houndé in 2015. Another should be ready by the end of 2016 in Bobo-Dioulasso.

Third, nongovernmental organizations have become major actors in many countries by providing such basic social services as health care, education and safe drinking water. The BRAC nonformal education system in Bangladesh is a prime example.[14] Following an innovative curriculum but providing education in a cost-effective way has boosted both school attendance and retention. Two major measures that BRAC schools have initiated are separate toilets and two free sets of school uniforms for girls. These measures have contributed immensely to the education of girls in Bangladesh. BRAC also leads in providing basic social services, particularly in conflict and postconflict countries such as Afghanistan.[15] In many countries nongovernmental organizations and foundations (for instance, the Bill & Melinda Gates Foundation) are working with governments and other agencies on immunization drives for children.[16] Public–private partnerships and alliances may thus be an effective mechanism for providing services.

Fourth, innovative services rarely include poor people, even though poor people often need these services the most. As the UN Secretary-General's High-Level Panel on Access to Medicines highlighted, medical innovations have saved and improved millions of lives around the world, but access to them is highly unequal. Vulnerable groups are prevented from fully benefiting from the innovations because of multiple factors, including limited resources, stigma, discrimination, poor health education, unavailability of health insurance, regulatory barriers and exclusive marketing rights.[17]

One stark example: The international nongovernmental organization Médecins Sans Frontières validated new tests for tuberculosis to be used in low-income, humanitarian settings.[18] Yet the cost was too high for affected developing countries, which obtained the tests only after a dedicated public–private partnership was created. Economic and political choices around the funding and support of innovations often result in such barriers to access. Identifying gaps in the protection of target populations, determining the best new ways to address persistent challenges and providing evidence of the efficiency of the new methods may convince decisionmakers to scale up innovations and ensure inclusiveness.[19]

Since 2000, governments around the world have increasingly used the Internet to engage with their populations, publishing official documents and data on websites, allowing citizens to undertake administrative procedures online and sometimes inviting them to provide feedback or even participate in political decisionmaking (box 4.3).[20] But with a digital divide and without a digital dividend, few marginal and vulnerable groups can take advantage of these services.

Undertaking high-impact multidimensional interventions—win-win strategies

Universal human development could be accelerated if some multidimensional high-impact interventions are pursued. Measures such as providing school meals, redistributing assets and prioritizing local actions are a crucial part of the answer because such interventions have strong and multiple impacts; they are win-win strategies.

Providing school meals. School meal programmes provide multiple benefits: social protection by helping families educate their children and protect their children's food security in times of crisis; nutrition, because in poor countries school meals are often the only regular and nutritious meal a child receives; education, because a daily school meal provides a strong incentive to send children to school and keep them there; and a boost to local agriculture, because food is often bought locally, benefiting local farmers. Evidence from Botswana, Cabo Verde, Côte d'Ivoire, Ghana, Kenya, Mali, Namibia, Nigeria and South Africa bears testimony to all the benefits of school feeding programmes.[21]

Universal human development could be accelerated if some multidimensional high-impact interventions are pursued

BOX 4.3

E-governance

Digital identification systems, a new area of development for civil participation, have great potential. They have increased the efficiency of public services in Belgium, Estonia, Finland, France, the Republic of Korea and Singapore, where citizens can pay taxes or request official documents online.[1] In developing countries digital identification can expand civil registration systems. Nigeria piloted a new voter authentication system in the 2015 elections, using fingerprint-encoded cards to avoid duplicate votes.[2]

E-government can reduce costs and expand reach to even the most secluded areas of a country, as long as the Internet is accessible. In 2000 the United States launched the government's official web portal to provide information and services to the public. Today 159 governments publish information online on finance, 151 on health, 146 on education, 132 on labour, 130 on the environment and 123 on social welfare.[3] Another rapidly developing area is open government data—freely accessible on websites with raw data, giving people the opportunity to follow their government's results and to hold it accountable.

Notes
1. World Bank 2016p. 2. World Bank 2016p. 3. UNDESA 2014a.
Source: Human Development Report Office.

Rural infrastructure, especially roads and electricity, is another area. Building rural roads reduces transport costs, connects rural farmers to markets, allows workers to move more freely and promotes access to schools and health care clinics. More than 1 billion people worldwide lack electricity.[22] Electrification in rural communities in Guatemala and South Africa has helped increase employment among marginalized groups.[23] Low-cost options such as mini-grids have been successful in Kenya (green mini-grid), Senegal (smaller community projects) and the United Republic of Tanzania (good consumer tariff) and can be easily replicated elsewhere.[24] Mini-grids—often supplied by hybrid generation systems and incorporating smart technologies—are also connecting rural households.

Cost-effective nutritional interventions can address deficiencies in iodine and micronutrients—deficiencies common among disadvantaged and marginalized groups.[25] Adding iodine to salt, removing taxes on micronutrients and fortifying staples and condiments have improved the nutrition status of poor people.[26] Such easy low-cost interventions can be readily scaled up and replicated elsewhere.

Redistributing assets. Redistributive policies are often framed as reducing inequalities in outcomes (such as income) or providing social protection (as in cash transfers). But redistributing assets can also bring those left out into the growth process. For example, land reform has been advocated as a prerequisite for levelling the playing field so that growth is equitable. But customary laws for property tenure are still the norm in many societies. Such laws cover more than 75 percent of the land in most African countries and deprive women in particular.[27] Appropriate land legislation can be formulated to supersede customary laws.

Human capital is an asset, and differences in educational attainment, one aspect of this asset, prevent poor people from becoming part of the high-productivity growth process. And the outcome of that difference becomes stark in tertiary education. In the United States in 2015 the median weekly income of a person with a master's degree was $1,341, but that of a person with only a high school diploma was roughly half that, at $678.[28] (The 2015 Human Development Report called for democratizing tertiary education both nationally and globally.)[29]

Subsidizing inputs for poor people enhances their productivity and contributes to the growth process. For example, subsidizing green energy would be both poverty reducing and environment friendly. Bangladesh's central bank has financed environmentally sustainable initiatives through a low-cost refinancing window.[30] Jordan and Morocco have followed suit.

Prioritizing local actions. Local approaches can limit conflict, protect minority rights, improve service delivery and be more responsive to local needs and citizen preferences.

> Differences in educational attainment prevent poor people from becoming part of the high-productivity growth process

Providing autonomy to local governments in formulating and implementating local development plans allows plans to reflect the aspirations of local communities. Fiscal decentralization can also empower local governments to collect their own revenues and depend less on central government grants, under a formula for revenue generation between the central government and local governments. In Latin America decentralization increased local government spending from 20 percent of total government spending in 1985 to about 30 percent in 2010.[31] But the share of own-source revenue remained unchanged, at about 10 percent of the national total, making local government finances more vulnerable and less predictable, undermining long-term planning. Indonesia's big bang decentralizations provide resources to meet local needs (box 4.4).

But if the local approach is to ensure human development for those left out, it will also require people's participation and greater local administrative capacity. A transparent and accountable mechanism should be in place to monitor human development outcomes. With community involvement and support from the central government and other development partners, local approaches can contribute much to human development in the poorest areas, as in Moldova (box 4.5).[32] The participatory model has worked so well that 70 towns and communities have adopted it, and 350,000 Moldovans are involved in improving local development.

Enhancing opportunities for women

Creating opportunities for women requires ensuring women's empowerment in the economic, political and cultural spheres (figure 4.2). Investing in girls and women has multidimensional benefits—for example, if all girls in developing countries completed secondary education, the under-five mortality rate would be halved.[33]

As more girls finish primary and secondary education, they can carry on to higher education, enabling them to do the work of the future and move up the career ladder. But more women should be in science, technology, engineering and mathematics, where much future demand for high-level work will be. Only one-fifth of countries had achieved gender parity in research by 2015, meaning that 45–55 percent of researchers were women.[34] Increasing women's enrolment in tertiary education and in science, technology, engineering and mathematics requires such incentives as scholarships, admission quotas and internships with research institutions and technology firms.

> Local approaches can contribute much to human development in the poorest areas

BOX 4.4

Fiscal decentralization in Indonesia—improving service delivery

Starting in 2000, when devolution to cities and districts became a focus of government reforms, decentralization was especially strong on the expenditure side in Indonesia. Subnational governments now manage almost a third of total public spending and about half of development outlays. Local governments are obliged to provide health care, education, and environmental and infrastructure services. Some of the major steps of the reforms:

- Local governments were given budget autonomy. The next higher administrative level was mandated to review legality. Law 32/2004 expanded higher-level oversight of local budgeting.
- Local and provincial assemblies are now elected every five years.

- Provincial governors and local mayors have been directly elected since 2005.
- The Public Information Disclosure Act, passed in 2008, promised better access to public information as well as more transparency.
- Citizens provide input into local government planning, and there are mechanisms for providing small-scale community services.

The positive outcomes of the reforms include a substantial increase in local public spending on services and better service delivery in some sectors. But there have been issues with spending efficiency in some areas, as well as disputes over the extent of gains. And more attention has to be paid to developing effective local accountability mechanisms.

Source: Smoke 2015.

BOX 4.5

How local government makes a difference in Moldova

Telenesti, a town of 9,000, was once one of Moldova's poorest. For 20 years basic water, sewerage and garbage services were a rare luxury for most people. Then Telenesti's municipal government teamed with local residents to improve basic services under a national participatory initiative.

A long-standing problem was that local governments had little experience in guiding local development. Under socialism they depended on the distant central government for direction. So more than 10,000 local officials—80 percent of the national total—were trained in how to engage with community members and better manage public services.

Telenesti has since renovated its water network, added street lighting and built new roads. It became the first town in the country to provide all residents with access to a sewerage system.

Source: UNDP 2013a.

FIGURE 4.2

Factors that enable or constrain women's empowerment—six direct and four underlying factors

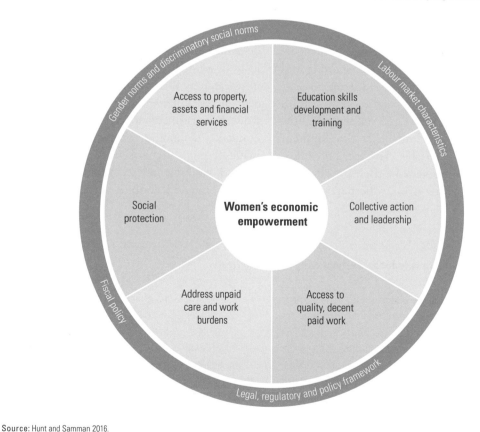

Source: Hunt and Samman 2016.

Investing in girls and women brings multidimensional benefits—for example, if all girls in developing countries were to complete secondary education, the under-five mortality rate would be halved

Women also have to juggle paid employment outside the home and unpaid care work inside the home as well as balance their productive and reproductive roles. Reserving jobs for women on maternity leave for up to a year and flexible working arrangements, including telecommuting, can allow women to return to work after giving birth. Women could also be offered salary increases to return to work.

Reducing the burden of unpaid care work among women can also give women more choices. Enlarging care options, including day care centres, afterschool programmes, homes for senior citizens and long-term care facilities could help. Another option is to subsidize unpaid care work through vouchers or credits. Improved access to clean water and sanitation, energy services and public infrastructure, including transport, can greatly reduce the burden of unpaid care work, leaving more time for paid work, if women choose to pursue it. Parental leave for mothers and fathers can balance the distribution of unpaid care work and reduce wage gaps in paid work when fathers are included and have incentives to use it. A more equitable distribution of reproductive roles between mothers and fathers would also benefit men, who often miss out on important family time with their children.

Encouraging and supporting female entrepreneurs

Measures to encourage women's entrepreneurship include establishing a legal framework that removes barriers to women owning land, a critical asset, especially in agriculture. Farms managed by woman-headed households are between half and two-thirds the size of farms run by man-headed households.[35] So, land policies, legislation and administration need to be changed to accommodate women—and the new rules must be enforced. These measures should cover formal and informal legal systems. In some countries legal reforms are already under way that may provide opportunities for women that have been heretofore unavailable (box 4.6).

Breaking the glass ceiling

The glass ceiling, though cracked in many places, is far from being shattered. Women in business hold 24 percent of senior management positions globally, but 33 percent of businesses have no women in those posts.[36] Gender requirements in selection and recruitment and incentive mechanisms for retention can enhance women's representation in the public and private sectors. The criteria for promoting men and women into senior management positions should be identical, based on equal pay for equal work.

In developing countries business leadership positions that are open to women are often limited to micro or small enterprises. In such contexts, policies promoting women's entrepreneurship and supporting the participation of women-led small and medium-size enterprises in public sector procurement can be particularly relevant.

Women's representation can be increased through affirmative action, such as quotas for women on corporate boards, as in the European Union. Such efforts are even more effective when accompanied by policies that raise retention rates. Mentoring, coaching and sponsoring can empower women in the workplace by using successful senior female managers as role models and as sponsors. All these approaches can change norms and promote women to positions of seniority and responsibility. A complementary approach is to encourage men to join professions traditionally dominated by women.

Mentoring, coaching and sponsoring can empower women in the workplace by using successful senior female managers as role models and as sponsors

BOX 4.6

Arab States—opening opportunities for women

Business associations are emerging to support female entrepreneurs through training, research, networking and other services. Examples include the MENA Businesswomen's Network Association in Bahrain, the Occupied Palestinian Territory Business Women's Forum and the National Association of Women Entrepreneurs of Tunisia.[1]

Female labour force participation may increase in the Arab States as businesses and governments recognize the financial benefits of employing women,

especially given women's higher educational attainment and purchasing power.

In Saudi Arabia the number of women employed has increased 48 percent since 2010, thanks partly to petitions and legal reforms that enable women to work in formerly closed sectors, including law, to go outside unaccompanied by men, to exercise voting rights and to be elected at certain levels of government.[2] In Jordan the online platform for engineering contractors, Handasiyat.net, has attracted female engineers seeking to work from home.[3]

Notes
1. ILO 2016b. 2. Chew 2015. 3. ILO 2016b.
Source: Human Development Report Office.

The Norwegian quota law requires all public (limited) companies listed on the Norwegian Stock Exchange as well as state-owned, municipal, intermunicipal and cooperative companies to appoint boards that include at least 40 percent women. Women made up 6 percent of the boards of public limited liability companies in 2002 and 40 percent only six years later.[37]

Addressing lifecycle capabilities

Capabilities built over a lifetime have to be nurtured and maintained. And vulnerabilities that people face in various phases of their lives must be overcome. To ensure that human development reaches those left out, building capabilities should be seen through a lifecycle lens.

Helping children prepare for the future

Universally fulfilling outcomes are more likely when all children can acquire the skills that match the opportunities open to young people joining the workforce. Much attention is correctly focused on what is needed to ensure that all children, everywhere, complete a full course of schooling.

But the formal education system is only part of a continuum of influences that connects a newborn to adulthood. Social and cultural influences operate inside and outside the school system. Factors critical to learning and life outcomes make themselves felt even in the womb and are cumulative, so that a shortfall at one stage can be compounded later and become harder—if not impossible—to address.

At one level, school systems have to be flexible enough to accommodate divergent cultures. At another, promoting school readiness—creating capabilities that promote learning—is as important as schooling for producing positive life outcomes, such as increased productivity, higher income, better health and greater upward mobility. Traditional methods of remediation, such as public on-the-job training or adult literacy programmes to boost the skills of disadvantaged young people, have lower returns than early childhood programmes. A better choice is early interventions in the preschool years that promote learning and retention in school. Early childhood education services have expanded considerably

since 2000, but the gaps, still large, require urgent attention.

The World Bank has found that every dollar spent on preschool education earns $6–$17 in public benefits in the form of a healthier and more productive workforce.[38] Many developing countries seem to have accepted this. Ethiopia says that it will increase preschool enrolment to 80 percent by 2020, from 4 percent in 2009. Ghana now includes two years of preschool in the education system. China is contemplating providing preschool facilities for all youngsters.[39]

Empowering young people

Voting is often the main avenue to influencing a political process, but it seems to be less attractive to younger voters than to older voters. In Canada 35–50 percent of voters ages 18–34 voted in 2004–2011, compared with 65–78 percent of voters ages 55–74.[40] Young people also seem disenchanted with traditional politics. That should not be interpreted as a lack of interest in public life.

Millennials are seeking alternative ways to improve their communities, both locally and globally. Sixty-three percent of them have donated to charity, 52 percent have signed petitions and 43 percent have volunteered for civil society organizations.[41] They are also looking to social movements and community organizations as platforms for their political interests and action. In Egypt, the Syrian Arab Republic and Tunisia young protesters used their mobile phones to post comments, photos and videos of events during the Arab Spring live on social media, to generate national and international support for their demands.[42]

The challenge in these areas is integrating into policymaking the opinions and convictions of young people expressed through alternative forms of participation. One approach might be through government-sponsored advisory roles, youth parliaments and roundtable discussions. At least 30 countries have some kind of non-adult parliamentary structure, nationally or in cities, villages or schools.[43] Government agendas developed for children and youth, such as those in New Zealand, can also promote participation.

On the economic front creating new opportunities for young people and preparing

Universally fulfilling outcomes are more likely when all children can acquire the skills that match the opportunities open to young people joining the workforce

young people with the skills needed to take advantage of those opportunities are required. More than one-third of the skills important in today's economy will have changed by 2020.[44] Acquiring skills for the 21st century has to be part of lifelong learning of the four C's—critical thinking, collaborating, creating and communicating (figure 4.3).

Unbridling young people's creativity and entrepreneurship requires policy support for sectors and enterprises in new areas of the economy, for young entrepreneurs involved in startups or crowdsourcing, for instance, and for social entrepreneurs (box 4.7).

Protecting vulnerable workers

Three of the world's ten largest employers are replacing workers with robots, and an estimated 57 percent of jobs in Organisation for Economic Co-operation and Development countries are at risk because of automation (figure 4.4).[45] The world is also moving towards a knowledge economy, so that low-skilled or marginal workers are losing their livelihoods. The European Union is expected to add 16 million new jobs between 2010 and 2020, but the number of jobs available for people with little or no formal education is anticipated to decline by around 12 million.[46]

As some jobs disappear, new jobs will appear in nontradables such as education, health care and public services, which are also fundamental to enhancing human development. Workers should be educated for and guided towards such jobs. For example, skills can be developed so workers can transition to sustainable employment in the green economy, solar energy and wind power.

A fit-for-the-future skill-learning system can be designed and implemented starting in secondary school and continuing in tertiary education. An emphasis on science, technology, engineering and mathematics may be necessary. But flexibility in the curricula of the learning

> As some jobs disappear, new jobs will appear in nontradables such as education, health care and public services, which are also fundamental to enhancing human development

FIGURE 4.3

21st century skills

Ways of thinking	Tools for working	Ways of working	Skills for living in the world
Creativity	Information and communication technology	Communication	Citizenship
Critical thinking		Collaboration	Life and career
Problemsolving	Information literacy		Personal and social responsibility
Decisionmaking			
Learning			

Source: Human Development Report Office.

BOX 4.7

Social businesses attract young people

Social businesses are emerging as new areas of work among young people. They are cause-driven entities designed to address a social problem—nonloss, non-dividend companies, financially self-sustainable, the primary aim of which is not to maximize profits (though profits are desirable) but social benefits.

Inspired by a particular cause and by the desire to give back to society, numerous successful young commercial entrepreneurs around the world are transitioning from for-profit ventures to engage in social change. A survey of 763 commercial entrepreneurs in India who made the transition from commercial to social entrepreneurship between 2003 and 2013 and a quantitative analysis of 493 entrepreneurs indicated that 21 percent of successful entrepreneurs shifted to social change efforts. Most are skilled organization builders, independently wealthy, often establishment outsiders, and some from the diaspora.

Source: UNDP 2015a.

FIGURE 4.4

Navigating the fourth industrial revolution

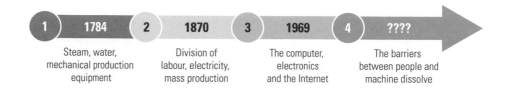

Source: Schwab 2016.

---

system is crucial, and training should provide multitasking skills and the agility to move from one line of activity to another. Workers whose livelihoods are threatened can transition to jobs at similar and higher levels with the aid of wage subsidies and temporary income support.

Caring for older people

Older people form a particularly vulnerable group that often suffers from deprivations in health, income and social life (see chapter 2). They require dedicated attention from policymakers to ensure that their human rights are respected and that opportunities are available so they can enjoy self-realization and contribute to society. Some appropriate measures include:

- *Establishing a combination of public and private provisioning of elder care.* Public provision of health care can be strengthened through affordable but high-quality health services targeted exclusively at older people. Because of changing family structures and women's increasing economic activity, market mechanisms can enable private provision of such care (such as the employment of private caregivers) or innovative collective community-based systems. Under the Fureai Kippu system in Japan, people earn credits for caring for older people that they can use later when they need care or that they can transfer to others.[47]
- *Strengthening the social protection for older people through basic noncontributory social pensions (as in Brazil).*[48] Countries should also explore fully funded contributory pensions and social pensions.[49]
- *Creating opportunities for older people to work where they can contribute, including teaching*

children, care work and voluntary work. Older relatives may provide care for children whose parents are working or have migrated for work or where the children have become orphans. In Denmark and the Netherlands more than 60 percent of women and more than 40 percent of men ages 60–65 provide care for their grandchildren.[50] In the United Kingdom 30 percent of people ages 65–74 engage in voluntary work.[51]

Mobilizing resources for human development priorities

Public policies for human development priorities require domestic and external resources. One of the critical issues is how resources are mobilized for such investments. The domestic revenue base in many developing countries is generally low. For example, in 2002 tax revenue as a share of GDP was about 7.2 percent in low human development countries, compared with nearly 15 percent in very high human development countries.[52] Foreign direct investment favours certain countries (such as China and India), but not so much other countries. The economic lifeline of some poor countries is official development assistance, the prospect of which is rather dim because of the global political economy situation. Given such diverse circumstances, there are at least five options that developing countries can explore to generate the necessary resources.

Creating fiscal space

Fiscal space is the financing available to governments through policy actions aimed at enhancing resource mobilization and reforms

> Older people require dedicated attention to ensure that their human rights are respected

to improve the governance, institutional and economic environment. Fiscal space has four pillars: official development assistance, domestic revenue, deficit financing (through domestic and external borrowing) and variations in spending priorities and efficiency.[53]

The choice of which pillar to use to increase or rebuild fiscal space depends mainly on country characteristics. In 2009 Ghana considered improving revenue collection to increase the health budget, even though the share of the total government budget allocated to health was stable.[54] In 2006 Chile identified higher revenue and greater borrowing as channels to expand the fiscal space.[55] In the mid-2000s Brazil and India identified higher expenditure efficiency in areas where stronger revenue efforts were identified as a means to boost the fiscal space.[56]

Expanding the per capita fiscal space allows for greater spending on sectors of the economy that directly enhance human development. And the stability of the fiscal space during economic downturns can also help maintain or even increase expenditure on social services as a countercyclical measure.

Macroeconomic stability can help boost the fiscal space. Fiscal rules, stabilization funds and a medium-term expenditure framework can strengthen fiscal governance and bolster the fiscal space, as can more efficient use of resources. For example, developing countries might take advantage of lower commodity prices to reform subsidies. Broadening the tax base and reducing tax distortions also help.

Consolidating remittances

In 2016 remittances to developing countries—a lifeline for many societies—were expected to reach $442 billion.[57] They enter through various channels (not all legal) for a raft of purposes, from pure consumption to education and asset purchases, including land. But the transfer costs are steep, averaging nearly 8 percent worldwide to send $200 internationally in 2015.

Consolidating and streamlining remittances could make them a funding source for human development priorities. Remittance banks can be set up in countries where the remittance flows are large, such as Bangladesh, Jordan and the Philippines. Easy and transparent legal remittance-sending mechanisms can be instituted in consultation with host countries. And digital remittance transfers can be modelled after M-Pesa and BKash.

Using climate finance as human development priority financing

The 2030 Agenda and the Paris Climate Change Agreement mark the global community's commitment to take action to end poverty, confront inequality and tackle climate change, which impact marginalized and vulnerable people the most. Climate finance has thus emerged as a major resource to help countries tackle climate change. Given the differences in concerns in middle-income countries and the least developed countries, there has been a debate about the appropriate relationship between development finance and climate finance.

Concerns vary across countries. Developed and middle-income countries that emit the majority of the carbon dioxide into the atmosphere are seeking financing and technologies to reduce emissions and mitigate climate change. But in the least developed countries, where emissions are low, climate finance can expand climate resilient livelihoods, improve water and sanitation systems and ensure food security. These investments go beyond climate adaptation programmes in the narrow sense to focus on achieving human development by increasing the long-term climate resilience of economies and societies.

Exploiting other means

An estimated $1 trillion flows illegally out of developing and emerging economies each year, more than these economies receive in foreign direct investment and official development assistance.[58] Beyond depriving the world's needy countries, this propels crime, corruption and tax evasion. Most of the money is lost through trade invoicing—changing prices to secretly move money across borders. If exporting and importing countries collaborate to monitor invoicing through trade rules and other mechanisms, such flows can be identified and seized.

Development impact bonds can be floated to open revenue streams from private investors and allow public entities to transfer risk. They also force policymakers to measure the benefits of interventions. But they need clear goals—such as building 1 million toilets. A clear quantitative goal may sound great and be easily measurable, but the toilets would make little difference if they are not part of a locally led sustainable sanitation system.

Stopping corruption and capital flight can also provide resources for human development. In 2010, $21 trillion worth of financial assets were transferred to offshore tax havens.[59] Nigeria is estimated to have lost over $400 billion to corruption between independence and 1999.[60] A small fraction of that could do much to reach those left out.

Ending subsidies to the rich or for commodities such as fossil fuel can free resources for human development. In 2014 the richest 20 percent of India's population enjoyed subsidies of $16 billion thanks to six commodities and services—cooking gas, railways, power, aviation fuel, gold and kerosene—and exempt-tax treatment under the public provident fund.[61] The International Monetary Fund estimates that fossil fuel companies benefit from global subsidies of $10 million a minute largely because polluters are not charged for the cost of the environmental damage they cause.[62] That cost includes the harm to local populations by air pollution as well as to people across the globe affected by the floods, droughts and storms driven by climate change.

In the 1990s a 20:20 compact was proposed for basic human development—developing countries would devote 20 percent of their domestic budget to human development priorities, complemented by 20 percent of official development assistance.[63] Given the 2030 Agenda, such ideas should be revived.

Using resources efficiently

Efficiency in resource use is equivalent to generating additional resources. For example, telemedicine can deliver medical advice and treatment options to patients irrespective of their location, thereby reducing the cost of service provision. Frontline health workers have difficulty diagnosing pneumonia, which kills more than 1 million children a year, and pre-eclampsia, the second-leading cause of maternal deaths. To change this, the Phone Oximeter mobile health platform uses a low-cost sensor powered by a mobile phone to measure blood oxygen levels and then displays informed advice for diagnosis and treatment.[64]

Pursuing measures for groups with special needs

Because some groups in society are systematically discriminated against and thereby left out, only positive discriminatory measures can achieve more equitable outcomes in human development. To ensure that human development reaches everyone, measures are needed for some groups with special needs—such as women, ethnic minorities, indigenous peoples, persons with disabilities, people living with HIV and AIDS and vulnerable workers.

One of these measures is to collect disaggregated data on all these groups (see chapter 3). Other policy measures are affirmative action and specific interventions to promote human development for marginalized groups.

Using affirmative action

Affirmative action—positive discrimination for distributive justice—has been important in redressing historical and persistent group disparities and group discrimination and in reiterating that every human being has equal rights. Women, ethnic minorities and persons with disabilities face various forms of discrimination because of their sex, ethnicity or circumstances (see chapter 2). Stigma and norms also contribute to the disparities and discrimination affecting indigenous peoples or people living with HIV and AIDS. Affirmative action may take the form of enrolment quotas for ethnic minorities in tertiary education or preferential treatment for female entrepreneurs in obtaining subsidized credit through the banking system.

Affirmative action such as quotas not only reserves jobs for persons with disabilities, but also provides an opportunity for the rest of society to observe the capabilities and achievements of these people, changing bias, attitudes and social norms. One area where affirmative action has made a difference is in women's representation in parliament (box 4.8).

Ending subsidies to the rich or for commodities such as fossil fuel can generate resources for human development

India's affirmative action programme—launched in 1950, making it the world's oldest —was originally intended to benefit Scheduled Castes, which include Dalits, or untouchables, who had been oppressed for centuries under the caste system and accounted for about 16 percent of the population, and Scheduled Tribes, the historically neglected tribal groups that accounted for about 8 percent of the population.[65] The programme was expanded in the early 1990s to include the Other Backward Classes, lower castes of socially and educationally disadvantaged people encompassing about 25 percent of the population. The programme has not remedied caste-based exclusions, but it has had substantial positive effects. In 1965, for example, Dalits held fewer than 2 percent of senior civil service positions, but the share had grown to 11 percent by 2001.

In 2013, 32 of the 38 state universities and 40 of the 59 federal universities in Brazil had some form of affirmative action policy.[66] Between 1997 and 2011 the share of Afro-Brazilians of college age enrolled in university rose from 4 percent to 20 percent.

Promoting human development for marginalized groups

Despite the great diversity in identities and needs (see chapter 2), marginalized groups, such as ethnic minorities, indigenous peoples, persons with disabilities, people living with HIV and AIDS, and lesbian, gay, bisexual, transgender and intersex individuals, often face similar constraints in their efforts to enhance their capabilities and freedoms, such as marginalization in basic well-being, voice and autonomy, or rights and privileges. They often face discrimination, social stigma and risk of being harmed. But each group also has special needs that must be met for the group to benefit from progress in human development.

First, for some vulnerable groups, such as ethnic minorities or persons with disabilities, anti-discrimination and other rights are guaranteed in constitutions and other legislation. Similarly, special provisions often protect indigenous peoples, as in Canada and New Zealand. Yet in many cases effective mechanisms for full equality in law are lacking. National human rights commissions or commissions for specific groups can provide oversight and ensure that the rights

> Despite the great diversity in identities and needs, marginalized groups must confront common constraints in their efforts to enhance their capabilities and freedoms

BOX 4.8

Affirmative action has helped increase women's representation in parliament

Gender-based quotas in senior positions and parliaments have gained prominence since the adoption of the Beijing Declaration and Platform for Action at the United Nations Fourth World Conference in 1995 and the Committee on the Elimination of Discrimination against Women's general recommendation 25 (2004) on special temporary measures, including quotas. Governments have increasingly adopted quotas since the conference to boost women's participation, counter discrimination and accelerate change.

In countries with some type of parliamentary gender quota a higher share of parliamentary seats are held by women. Women average 26 percent of the seats in lower houses and in single houses of parliament in countries with voluntary party quotas, 25 percent in countries with legislated candidate quotas and 23 percent in countries with reserved seats for women.[1] Compare this with 16 percent in countries with no such quotas. Countries with quotas for female parliamentarians have provided confidence and incentives for women to contest general parliamentary seats and win those seats.

Rwanda, with female representation of 64 percent in the House of Deputies, is a shining example. The 2003 constitution set aside 30 percent of legislative seats for women. Each election since has increased the seats held by women, both those reserved for women and some of the nonreserved seats. Women's representation in the House of Deputies rose to 64 percent in 2013. Today, women account for over 60 percent of the members of parliament.[2] Since the introduction of quotas, women have not only increased their number of representatives, they have also used their positions to pass laws empowering women, including preventing and punishing violence against women, increasing property rights for women and promoting women in the labour force.

Notes
1. United Nations 2015d. 2. UN Women 2016a.
Source: Human Development Report Office.

of these groups are not violated. Some of these groups are not recognized as marginalized in many countries. Only five countries recognize the rights of lesbian, gay, bisexual, transgender and intersex people (box 4.9; see also chapter 2).

Second, recognition of the special identity and status of marginalized groups, such as ethnic minorities or indigenous peoples, is necessary. Thus, because recognizing the right to self-determination sends a powerful message about the need for protection, recognizing the right of self-determination among indigenous communities is crucial. The special relationship of many indigenous peoples and the land should likewise be recognized, with measures to advance human development among these people reflecting an awareness of this reality. Ethnic minorities and indigenous peoples have distinct cultures and languages that need to be taken into consideration in expanding access to health care facilities and education opportunities. Education in their native language not only recognizes the importance of distinct native languages, but is also conducive to greater learning among children.

Third, effective participation by disadvantaged groups in the processes that shape their lives needs to be ensured. Quotas for ethnic minorities and indigenous peoples in parliaments are thus a means not only to foster self-determination, but also to help them raise their concerns. Some indigenous peoples have their own parliaments or councils, which are consultative bodies (see chapter 2). New Zealand has the longest history of indigenous self-representation in a national legislature (box 4.10). Mirna Cunningham Kain, activist for the rights of the Nicaraguan Miskitu indigenous peoples rights activist and former chairperson of the United Nations Permanent Forum on Indigenous Issues, emphasizes that the there is much to learn from indigenous peoples' quest for peace and development in a plural world (see special contribution).

> Quotas in favour of ethnic minorities and the representation of indigenous peoples in parliaments are a means not only to foster self-determination, but also to raise issues of special concern

BOX 4.9

Overcoming discrimination against lesbian, gay, bisexual, transgender and intersex individuals

Overcoming the discrimination and abuse of lesbian, gay, bisexual, transgender and intersex (LGBTI) individuals requires a legal framework that can defend the relevant human rights. Where LGBTI people are criminalized, they are widely discriminated against. In countries with no basic legal tolerance for LGBTI people, there is almost no room for a defence based on the principle of antidiscrimination: The main protection is for LGBTI people to deny their sexual preference. Awareness campaigns need to be launched in households, communities, schools and workplaces so that acceptance becomes easier. Nonacceptance within households often leads teenagers to run away or drift and encourages harassment in schools and discrimination in hiring. Help centres, hotlines and mentoring groups can assist this community.

Source: Human Development Report Office.

BOX 4.10

Maori representation in New Zealand's parliament

The Maori Representation Act of 1867 introduced a dual constituency system in New Zealand whereby members of parliament are elected from two sets of single-member electorates, one for people of Maori descent and the other for people of European descent—now referred to as general electorates. In 1975 the act was amended to introduce a Maori Electoral Option, which gave electors of Maori descent the right to choose whether they enrolled in the Maori or the general electorates.

Electoral reform in the 1990s affected Maori representation in two ways. First, it allowed the number of Maori electorates, which had remained fixed at four since 1867, to vary up or down depending on the numbers of voters of Maori descent who elected to enroll to vote in those electorates. Second, it introduced proportional representation, which allowed Maori and other groups to be elected from party lists. This resulted in the election of Maori from a wider range of political parties and a much higher number of Maori members of parliament (currently 25 out of 121 total members of parliament).

Source: Edwards 2015; Forbes 2015.

The world has much to learn from indigenous peoples

From my lifelong experiences, being an advocate for the rights of some of the most marginalized peoples, allow me to share what I have learned and come to see as essential elements to ensure peaceful societies and sustainable development in a plural world.

Celebrating diversity

Indigenous peoples contribute to diversity, and their history emphasizes the importance of revitalizing and celebrating ancient cultures, music, languages, knowledge, traditions and identities. Living in an era where xenophobia, fundamentalism, populism and racism are on the rise in many parts of the world, celebrations and positive messages about the value of diversity can contribute to counter negative stereotypes, racism and discrimination and instead foster tolerance, innovation and peaceful coexistence between peoples. This is essential to safeguard the inherent belief in human beings' equal worth, as reflected in the fundamental principles of the Universal Declaration on Human Rights.

Taking special measures to ensure equality and combat discrimination

The world today is more unequal than ever before—yet, there is an increasing recognition of the crucial importance of addressing systematic inequalities to ensure sustainable development. To address inequalities, a first step is to repeal discriminatory policies and laws that continue to exist in many countries, preventing particular groups of peoples from fully realizing their potential. For indigenous peoples, it is necessary to adopt positive or special measures to overcome discrimination and ensure the progressive achievement of indigenous peoples' rights, as emphasised in the UN Declaration on the Rights of Indigenous Peoples (article 21.2). This includes measures to safeguard cultural values and identities of indigenous peoples (article 8.2) or to ensure access to education in their own languages (article 14). Further, nondiscrimination for indigenous peoples is strongly related to the right to self-determination and cultural integrity. These principles should be promoted in the context of addressing target 16b of the 2030 Agenda, promoting and enforcing nondiscriminatory laws and policies.

Getting down to the root causes of conflicts

No solution to conflicts and injustices will be possible without addressing the root causes for these conflicts. For indigenous peoples, root causes most often relate to violations against their human rights, in particular rights related to their lands, territories and resources. Across the world, indigenous peoples increasingly experience militarization, armed conflict, forced displacements or other conflicts on their lands, which have become increasingly valuable in light of globalization and the continued quest for resource extraction. Indigenous human rights and environmental defenders, who mobilize to protect their rights, face death threats, harassment, criminalization and killings. According to an Oxfam Report, 41 percent of murders of human rights defenders in Latin America were related to the defence of the environment, land, territory and indigenous peoples. The essential and first step to prevent conflict and ensure peaceful development is hence to protect, promote and ensure the basic rights of all peoples, including their free, prior and informed consent on development activities taking place on their lands. In that light the 2030 Agenda's goal 16 on peaceful societies and strong institutions is essential. In particular, the focus on transparency, the rule of law and equal access to justice will be crucial to ensure accountability to the rights of all peoples.

Bringing in the voices, world views and power of indigenous peoples

Indigenous peoples have called for their rights to be at the negotiating table and have a voice in decisionmaking processes. "Nothing about us, without us" goes one of the mottoes, that is being repeated. Consistent with the UN Declaration on the Rights of Indigenous Peoples article 7, indigenous peoples have the collective right to live in freedom, peace and security as distinct peoples. Furthermore, in postconflict societies, states should ensure the participation of indigenous peoples through their own representative institutions in peace negotiations, peacebuilding, peacekeeping, humanitarian assistance and reconciliation processes. By strengthening indigenous peoples' own institutions and governance systems and ensuring their inclusion in essential decisionmaking processes at the local, national and global levels, just solutions to conflicts can be found, and the structural root causes that led to the conflicts can be addressed. Indigenous peoples can also contribute to peace processes through their ancient wisdom and approaches to reconciliation and peace. Indigenous approaches to reconciliation often go beyond legal solutions with an essential focus on forgiveness, coexistence and harmony, which can inspire in a conflict situation that might otherwise seem protracted. The world has much to learn from indigenous peoples in the quest for peace and development in a plural world, as the one we are living in.

Mirna Cunningham Kain
Nicaraguan Miskitu, indigenous peoples rights activist and former chairperson of the United Nations Permanent Forum on Indigenous Issues

Fourth, among marginalized groups inclusion and accommodation are fundamental human rights and are critical to empowering them to live independently, find employment and participate in and contribute to society on an equal basis. An environment conducive to productivity and creativity is essential among persons with disabilities, though finding and sustaining employment may be difficult. Ensuring skill and vocational training among persons with disabilities, expanding their access to productive resources (such as finance for self-employment) and providing information over mobile devices are positive steps. More efficient information flows and infrastructure can help persons with disabilities obtain work and help employers take advantage of this wealth of human ingenuity. Some countries are relying on these techniques to enlarge employment choices among persons with disabilities (box 4.11).

There is also a need to encourage behavioural shifts in favour of persons with disabilities. Changing social norms and perceptions to promote the perception that persons with disabilities are differently abled and should be given a fair opportunity in work is fundamental and should be backed by a legal framework that discourages discrimination.

Technology can enhance the capacities of persons with disabilities. Indonesia instituted a legal requirement for Braille templates for blind voters or voters with visual impairments at all polling stations.[67] Cambodia has made such templates available since 2008.[68] The Philippines offers special voter registration facilities before election day and express lanes for voters with disabilities.[69]

> Persons with disabilities are differently abled

Fifth, migrants and refugees—often compelled to leave their home countries by violent conflict and consequently a desperate form of migration—are vulnerable in host countries (see chapter 2). Although a cross-border issue (chapter 5 analyses it as a global challenge), the problem also needs to be addressed locally. And actions need to reflect the new nature of migration and its context. Countries should pass laws that protect refugees, particularly women and children, a big part of the refugee population and the main victims. Transit and destination countries should provide essential public goods in catering to displaced people, such as schooling for refugee children; refugees will otherwise become a lost generation. Destination countries should formulate temporary work policies and provisions for refugees because work is the best social protection for these people (box 4.12).

A comprehensive set of indicators measuring human development among migrant families should be created. Governments should establish comprehensive migration policy regimes, given that migration boosts national economies, as in Sweden (box 4.13). Because the refugee problem is global, collaboration among national and international actors would represent a step forward.

Making human development resilient

Progress in human development can stagnate or even be reversed if threatened by shocks from environmental degradation, climate

BOX 4.11

Enlarging employment choices among persons with disabilities in Serbia

Living with a disability in Serbia has often meant being poor and unemployed and facing prejudice and social exclusion. More than 10 percent of the population has disabilities, more than 70 percent of persons with disabilities live in poverty, and only 13 percent of persons with disabilities have access to employment.[1]

In 2009 the government introduced the Law on Professional Rehabilitation and Employment of Persons with Disabilities. The law established an employment quota system that legally obliged all employers with 20–50 employees to hire at least one person with disabilities and one more for every 50 additional employees. Private companies could opt not to comply with the quotas, but then had to pay a tax that would fund services for persons with disabilities. Almost 3,700 persons with disabilities found employment in 2010, up from only 600 in 2009.[2]

Notes
1. UNDP 2011a. 2. UNDP 2011a.
Source: Human Development Report Office.

Providing work to Syrian refugees in Jordan

In Jordan the presence of Syrian refugees in host communities has bolstered the informal economy, depressed wages, impeded access to public services and increased child labour.

Efforts are under way to improve the access of Syrian refugees and members of local host communities to Jordan's formal labour market. Early in 2016 Jordan agreed to accommodate a fixed number of Syrians in the labour market in return for better access to European markets,

greater European investment in Jordan and access to soft loans. As a followup, Syrian refugees were given a three-month grace period to apply for work permits.

The focus then became finding a practical means to increase Syrian refugees' access to the labour market in a way that would fill labour shortfalls, benefit host communities and contribute to Jordan's economy. By June 2016, 12,000 new work permits had been issued to Syrian refugees.

Source: ILO 2016a.

---

change, natural disasters, global epidemics and conflicts. Vulnerable and marginalized groups —those already left out—are the major victims.

Promoting social protection

Social protection provides support for those left out, but it can also have an impact on development by enhancing capabilities. Social protection includes social security, social assistance and social safety nets. Only 27 percent of the world's population is covered by a comprehensive social protection system—about 5.2 billion people are not.[70] Policy options to expand social protection include:

- *Pursuing well designed, well targeted and well implemented social protection programmes.* A social protection floor—a nationally defined set of basic social security guarantees— launched within the UN system in 2009 and updated with concrete recommendations in 2012 aims to secure a minimum level of health care, pensions and other social rights for everyone.[71] Countries are exploring ways to finance the floor, ranging from restructuring current public expenditures to extending social security contributions, restructuring debt and using the foreign exchange reserves of central banks.
- *Combining social protection with appropriate employment strategies.* Creating jobs through a public works programme targeted at poor people can reduce poverty through income generation, build physical infrastructure and protect poor people against shocks. The National Rural Employment Guarantee Programme in India and the Rural Employment Opportunities for Public

The Swedish economy is being boosted by immigration

Immigration has helped fuel Sweden's biggest economic boom in five years. In 2015 Sweden took in more refugees per capita than any other country in Europe. The National Institute of Economic and Social Research indicates that the economy has benefited from the larger workforce, but emphasizes the difference between immigrants and refugees. There is a perception that a large influx of refugees is an impossible burden on the state even in the short term, but it increases growth. Still, the government needs a long-term strategy to integrate refugees and continue the economic expansion.

Source: Witton 2016.

Assets Programme in Bangladesh are prime examples.[72]

- *Providing a living income.* A guaranteed basic minimum income for all citizens, independent of the job market, is also a policy option. Finland is about to launch an experiment whereby a randomly selected group of 2,000– 3,000 citizens already on unemployment benefits will receive a basic monthly income of €560 (approximately $600), which would replace their existing benefits. The amount is the same as the country's guaranteed minimum social security support. A pilot study to run in 2017–2018 will assess whether this basic income transfer can reduce poverty, social exclusion and bureaucracy, while increasing employment.[73] Switzerland held a

Progress in human development can stagnate or even be reversed if threatened by shocks from environmental degradation, climate change, natural disasters, global epidemics and conflicts

Human development will never be resilient in the fight against HIV and AIDS unless everyone who needs help can be reached

referendum on a basic minimum income in 2016, but only 23 percent of voters backed the measure.[74] The main criticism is the enormous cost; the counterargument is that a large portion of the cost would be offset by the elimination of other social programmes. Another criticism is that a living income would be a disincentive to work, but the goal is not to enhance the incentive to work for pay, but to enable people to live if there is no paid work.

- *Tailoring programmes to local contexts.* The lessons learned through highly successful Latin American experiences show that cash transfers can provide effective social protection. The conditional cash transfer programme in the Philippines reached 4.4 million families in 2015, covering 21 percent of the population; 82 percent of the benefits went to the poorest 40 percent of the population.[75] The programme's success can be linked to careful targeting and regular assessments to update the list of recipients and ensure that the programme effectively matches the needs of the most vulnerable. Madagascar, where 60 percent of the population lives in extreme poverty, has a simple cash transfer programme. Beneficiaries, mostly women,

receive regular cash payments and training in nutrition, early childhood development and leadership skills.[76]

Addressing epidemics, shocks and risks

Human development will never be resilient in the fight against HIV and AIDS unless everyone who needs help can be reached. Yes, much progress has been made in scaling up antiretroviral therapy, but 18 million people living with HIV still do not have access to it.[77] Particular populations are left out; young women, who may be exposed to gender-based violence and have limited access to information and health care, are among the most exposed.[78] Still, there have been successes in reducing infection rates among women and children and in expanding their access to treatment (box 4.14).

In an increasingly interconnected world, in which people move around more and more easily and frequently, being prepared for possible health crises has become a priority in both developed and developing countries. The recent epidemic of the Zika virus provides a good example of why countries should be prepared for health shocks. The outbreak of the virus

BOX 4.14

Reaching those left out in the fight against HIV and AIDS

Malawi is a leader in the fight against HIV and AIDS with a game-changing approach known as Option B+, adopted in 2011. The programme provides antiretroviral therapy to all pregnant women with HIV in a treat-all approach, which removes the delays and hurdles involved in determining eligibility. Early treatment helps women stay healthy, protects their next pregnancies from infection and reduces the risk of transmitting HIV to their partners. A year after Option B+ was introduced, the number of pregnant and breastfeeding women living with HIV who were on antiretroviral therapy had risen from 1,257 in the second quarter of 2011 to 10,663 in the third quarter of 2012.[1] Following this success, Malawi launched the 2015–2020 National HIV and AIDS Strategic Plan in 2014 to reach populations missed by previous initiatives.

Brazil opened its first clinic for transgender people in São Paulo in 2010 and has since opened nine more

primary health care services in the city centre. In Kigali, Rwanda, the Women's Equity in Access to Care and Treatment Clinic, dedicated to working with women and vulnerable young people and adolescents living with HIV, supports nearly 400 young people living with HIV, 90 percent of them on antiretroviral therapy. In Dar es Salaam, United Republic of Tanzania, the faith-based organization Pastoral Activities and Services for People with AIDS Dar es Salaam Archdiocese offers testing and counselling to increase enrolment in care, treatment and support among children and adolescents living with HIV. In Nairobi, Kenya, the Mathari hospital provides antiretroviral therapy for those living with HIV who inject drugs. And Support for Addiction, Prevention and Treatment in Africa provides psychosocial counselling, testing for HIV and other sexually transmitted infections, and needle and syringe programmes at two facilities.[2]

Notes
1. CDC 2013; UNAIDS 2016f. 2. UNAIDS 2016c.
Source: UNAIDS 2016f.

occurred at the beginning of 2015 in Brazil, and the virus spread rapidly across countries in the Americas. The spread of the virus has been so rapid and alarming that in February 2016 the World Health Organization declared the virus a Public Health Emergency of International Concern.

Countries have reacted in different ways to the spread of the Zika virus. Countries with an ongoing virus transmission such as Colombia, the Dominican Republic, Ecuador and Jamaica have advised women to postpone pregnancy.[79] In Brazil a new mosquito strain was released to try to fight the virus, and members of the armed forces were sent across the country to educate people about mosquito control and to warn them of the risks linked to the virus.[80] The revised strategic response plan designed by the World Health Organization, in collaboration with more than 60 partners, focuses on research, detection, prevention, and care and support.[81]

The Ebola epidemic that tore through West Africa in 2014 claimed 11,310 lives. A combination of factors contributed to its savagery, including a mobile population, crumbling public health systems, official neglect and hazardous burial practices. A genetic mutation may have made Ebola more deadly by improving the virus's ability to enter human cells. This suggests that the scope of the epidemic was expanded. According to one alarming finding, patients infected with mutated versions of Ebola are much more likely to die.[82]

Natural disasters—earthquakes, floods, tsunamis, volcanic eruptions and the like—can generate enormous loss of life, drive people into poverty and even reverse progress in human development. The effects of disasters on human well-being can be greatly reduced, especially among the groups that are most exposed. Building disaster resilience into policies and programmes can reduce the associated risks and greatly mitigate the effects.

This is the approach at the heart of the Sendai Framework for Disaster Risk Reduction agreed in March 2015. Several programmes illustrate the innovations involved in the approach. In Azerbaijan meteorological stations are being modernized with automatic alarm systems to alert authorities when critically high water levels are reached.[83] The system also collects data that can be used to predict seasonal flooding. Sri Lanka has implemented projects to improve the resilience of school buildings that can jointly serve as community facilities during disasters such as the 2004 tsunami.[84] The buildings are designed with storm-resilient toilets, solar systems for electricity, high foundations to reduce flood vulnerability and flat concrete roofs to resist high winds. The success of these and similar programmes requires cooperation and collaboration among various stakeholders and affected groups (government, civil society, scientific research institutions, the private sector, women, migrants, poor people and children). It also requires communication and shared resources among institutions at all levels and an understanding of the different roles these institutions play in disaster monitoring and response.

Combating violence and ensuring people's security

Violence endangers people's security. The drivers of violence are complex and thus call for a multipronged approach that includes:

- *Promoting the rule of law based on fairness and zero tolerance for violence.* This approach needs a civic space for dialogue and participatory decisionmaking against violence and close collaboration with local leaders and credible intermediaries to promote dialogue with gangs and alienated groups.
- *Strengthening local governments, community policing and law enforcement personnel in hotspots of violence* not only to address violence, but also to fight corruption.
- *Developing high-quality infrastructure, improving public transit in high-crime neighbourhoods and building better housing in the poorest urban areas to enhance the trust between the authorities and people left out.* The Medellín miracle in Colombia's second largest city is a prime example of how a multipronged approach can turn a city once notorious for its homicide rate (about 6,000 a year in 1991) into a thriving and agreeable place to live.[85]
- *Providing socioeconomic alternatives to violence, particularly among young people, by building social cohesion.*
- *Developing response and support services to address violence and aid its victims.*

The drivers of violence are complex and thus call for a multipronged approach

Maintaining human well-being in postconflict situations

Many societies, especially those with low human development, face great difficulty in achieving progress in well-being because they are in the grips of violent conflict or its aftermath. Human development policies in such situations must include both political and economic measures.

On the political front a three-pronged approach to transforming institutions is needed during postconflict relief, recovery and reconstruction. First is to ensure people's security. This needs to be done through citizen protection and community policing, including the vetting and redeployment of security forces accountable to the public. The need to immediately deploy an effective police force—national or international—trained in dealing with violence against women is urgent.

Second is to pursue faster caseload processing to ensure social accountability, especially in delivering humanitarian relief and establishing the groundwork for future powersharing.

Third is to reintegrate ex-combatants. Disarmament, demobilization and reintegration of ex-combatants are early steps in the transition from war to peace. Disarmament and demobilization require security, the inclusion of all warring parties, political agreement, a comprehensive approach and sufficient resources. Reintegration focuses on reinsertion, addressing the economic needs of ex-combatants and economic reintegration. Successful programmes in disarmament,

demobilization and reintegration must recognize that ex-combatants are a heterogeneous group and often include child soldiers, so a targeted, phased approach is needed.

On the economic front, the following policy interventions are necessary:

- *Reviving basic social services.* This has social and political benefits, and positive results can be achieved even in the direst situations (box 4.15). Communities, nongovernmental organizations and public–private partnerships can be good catalysts in such situations.
- *Supporting work in the health system to cover many goals.* In many conflict-afflicted countries the health system has collapsed, converting health services into a life-threatening challenge for helpers and the wounded. International aid becomes indispensable in this setting, but local volunteers can contribute substantially to providing crucial health services and saving lives.
- *Initiating public works programmes.* Emergency temporary jobs and cash for work can provide much-needed livelihoods and contribute to the building of critical physical and social infrastructure.
- *Formulating and implementing targeted community-based programmes—for example by continuing to use makeshift schools so that children do not lose access to education.* Through such initiatives, the capabilities of future generations can be maintained. Economic activities can be jumpstarted by reconnecting people, reconstructing networks and helping restore the social fabric.

> Successful programmes in disarmament, demobilization and reintegration must recognize that ex-combatants are a heterogeneous group and often include child soldiers, so a targeted, phased approach is needed

BOX 4.15

Success in reducing maternal and child mortality in Afghanistan

After the collapse of the Taliban in 2002, Afghanistan adopted a new development path and, with the help of donors, invested billions of dollars in rebuilding the country's economy and health systems. These investments have improved maternal and child health and reduced maternal and under-five mortality.

The 2010 Afghanistan Mortality Survey estimated that there were 327 maternal deaths per 100,000 live births and 97 deaths among children under age 5 per 1,000 live births.

Decreases in the maternal mortality ratio and the under-five mortality rate are consistent with changes in key determinants of mortality, including higher age at marriage, greater contraceptive use, lower fertility, better immunization coverage, improvements in the share of women delivering in health facilities, more widespread antenatal and postnatal care, greater involvement of community health workers and increased access to the basic package of health services.

Source: Rasooly and others 2014.

Addressing climate change

Climate change jeopardizes the lives and livelihoods of poor and marginalized people through food insecurity, health and other risks. Addressing it requires three initial policy measures.

Putting a price on carbon pollution and ending fossil subsidies

Putting a price on carbon pollution brings down emissions and drives investment into cleaner options. There are several paths governments can take to price carbon, all leading to the same result (box 4.16). The choice of the instrument will depend on national and economic circumstances. There are also more indirect ways of accurately pricing carbon, such as through fuel taxes, the removal of fossil fuel subsidies and regulations that incorporate a social cost of carbon. Greenhouse gas emissions can also be priced through payments for emission reductions. Private or sovereign entities can purchase emissions reductions to compensate for their own emissions (offsets) or to support mitigation activities through results-based finance.

These measures begin to capture what are known as the external costs of carbon emissions —costs that the public pays for in other ways, such as higher food prices because of damage to crops, higher health care costs because of heat waves and droughts, and damage to property because of flooding and sea level rise—and tie them to their sources through a price on carbon.

These options are intended to make those who are responsible for the damage and who are in a position to limit it pay for remediation. Rather than placing formal restrictions on emissions, a price on carbon raises the awareness of polluters while giving them a choice. They can interrupt their polluting activities, find ways to reduce their emissions or agree to pay the price for the pollution they generate. This is the most flexible and least costly way for society to achieve environmental protection. It is also an efficient way to encourage innovations in clean technologies while promoting economic growth.

Approximately 40 countries and more than 20 cities, states and provinces use carbon pricing mechanisms, and more intend to do so in coming years. These mechanisms cover around half of the emissions of these entities, or 13 percent of annual global greenhouse gas emissions.[86] The Paris Agreement on climate change further encourages countries to cooperate internationally on carbon markets and link their respective carbon pricing policies.

Getting prices right is only one part of the equation. Cities are growing fast, particularly in developing countries. Over half the global population is urban today; by 2050 that proportion is expected to reach two-thirds.[87] With careful planning in transport and land use and the establishment of energy efficiency standards, cities can avoid locking in unsustainable patterns. They can open access to jobs and opportunities for poor people, while reducing air pollution.

> Rather than placing formal restrictions on emissions, a price on carbon raises the awareness of polluters while giving them a choice; it is the most flexible and least costly way for society to achieve environmental protection

BOX 4.16

Two paths in carbon pricing

There are two main types of carbon pricing: an emissions trading system and a carbon tax. An emissions trading system—sometimes referred to as a cap-and-trade system—caps the total level of greenhouse gas emissions and allows industries with low emissions to sell their extra allowances to larger emitters. By creating supply and demand for emissions allowances, the system establishes a market price for greenhouse gas emissions. The cap helps ensure that the required emission reductions will take place to keep the emitters (in aggregate) within their preallocated carbon budget.

A carbon tax directly sets a price on carbon by defining a tax rate on greenhouse gas emissions or—more commonly—on the carbon content of fossil fuels. It is different from an emissions trading system in that the reduction in emissions as a result of the tax is not predefined, though the price of carbon is.

Source: World Bank 2016j.

By phasing out harmful fossil fuel subsidies, countries can reallocate their spending to where it is most needed and most effective, including targeted support for poor people. In 2013 global fossil fuel subsidies totalled $550 billion and accounted for a large share of some countries' GDP.[88] Yet fossil fuel subsidies are not about protecting the poor: The wealthiest 20 percent of the population captures six times more benefit from such subsidies than does the poorest 20 percent.[89]

Increasing energy efficiency and the use of renewable energy

About 1.2 billion people worldwide lack access to electricity, and 2.8 billion rely on solid fuels, such as wood, charcoal and coal, which cause noxious indoor air pollution, for cooking.[90] The Sustainable Energy for All Initiative sets out three goals for 2030: achieve universal access to modern energy, double the rate of improvement in energy efficiency and double the share of renewable energy in the global energy mix. More than 20 years of effort in improving energy efficiency have reduced global energy use to one-third less than it otherwise would have been. Choosing renewable energy is more affordable than ever. Prices are falling, and developing utility-scale renewable energy is now less expensive than the cost of fossil fuel facilities in a number of countries.[91]

Focusing on the poverty–environment nexus—complex but critical for marginalized people

The poverty–environment nexus is complex. Environmental damage almost always affects people living in poverty the most. These people become the major victims of air and water pollution, experience drought and desertification and generally live nearest to the dirty factories, busy roads, waste dumps and ecologically fragile lands. There is an irony here. Even though poor people bear the brunt of environmental damage, they are seldom the creators of it. The rich pollute more, generate more waste and put more stress on nature.

Poor people and environmental damage are often caught in a downward spiral. Past resource degradation deepens today's poverty, which

forces poor people to deplete resources to survive. Biodiversity, on which poor people's lives, livelihoods, food and medicine depend, has passed the precautionary threshold in half the world's land.[92]

It would be too simplistic to explain the poverty–environment nexus in terms of income only: Questions about the ownership of natural resources, access to common resources (such as water), the strengths and weaknesses of local communities and local institutions, and ensuring poor people's rights and entitlements to resources are all part of the policy options because they impact people's environmental behaviour.

Climate-smart agriculture supports development while ensuring food security as climate changes. Using this approach, farmers can raise productivity and improve their resilience to climate change. Their farms, along with forests, can absorb and store carbon, creating carbon sinks and reducing overall emissions.[93]

Through a Poverty–Environment Initiative led jointly by the United Nations Development Programme and the United Nations Environment Programme, the mutually reinforcing links between poverty and environment have been mainstreamed into the national and local development strategies of 24 countries and into the sector strategies of 18 countries in an integrated fashion, focusing on multidimensional development issues (box 4.17).

Protecting the gains of human development and stopping the reversals of these gains would model resilience in concentric circles around the individual, the family and tight local groups, the local community, local government, the state and the planet. The government's role is to ensure a balance between the protection and the empowerment of the individual and the concentric circles of security providers, which are either extensions of the individual or, if they are malfunctioning, the threats to the individual. Latvia has been at the forefront of such an approach, which can be replicated in other parts of the world (box 4.18).

Empowering those left out

If policies do not deliver well-being to marginalized and vulnerable people and if institutions fail to ensure that people are not left out, there must be instruments and redress

BOX 4.17

Mainstreaming the poverty–environment nexus

Rwanda has integrated the poverty–environment nexus and climate objectives and targets into 30 district plans, as it institutionalizes mainstream approaches to the poverty–environment nexus and implements poverty–environment objectives into its National Development Plan.

Mongolia's Green Development Policy integrates poverty–environment objectives and indicators. Substantial progress was also made in 17 provincial development plans and in the National Socio-Economic Development Plan (2016–2020), in which sustainable development and inclusive growth are outcomes in support of the country's economic development.

A poverty–environment initiative has helped the government of Guatemala include pro-poor, gender and sustainable natural resource management objectives in its National Development Plan and regional

development plans.[1] The initiative has trained government officials on how ecosystem services and valuation methodologies can contribute to poverty reduction.

Lao People's Democratic Republic has identified foreign direct investment in natural resources, including land, mining and hydropower, as the key poverty–environment nexus issue.[2] Such investment was driving rapid economic growth in the country but degrading the environment of rural communities. The initiative has helped integrate social and environmental safeguards into national development planning and private investment management, including modern guidelines for new investments and improved monitoring capacity, in a signal contribution to Sustainable Development Goal target 17.5, to adopt and implement investment promotion regimes for least developed countries.[3]

Notes
1. UNEP and UNDP 2016. 2. United Nations 2015c. 3. United Nations 2015c.
Source: GC-RED 2016.

BOX 4.18

Resilient human development—lessons from Latvia

First, human resilience must be seen though a combined lens of human development and human security.

Second, human resilience must be embedded in reality, as follows:

- Information technology and human mobility increase the impact of individual and global actions.
- There are many development goals and limited resources. The best development gains result from smart prioritizing and making good choices.
- The emergence of behavioural economics helps policymakers address human perceptions.

Third, to prioritize actions, decisionmakers may take the following steps:

- Ask people to identify the main threats, risks and barriers to their development, collect data on the

risks identified, gauge the intensity of the threats through standard approaches and identify the most vulnerable groups.

- Address objective and subjective factors because both affect behaviour.
- Identify and strengthen the factors with the greatest impact on promoting resilience, remembering that those factors can be specific to individuals and communities.
- Foster the abilities of individuals to develop their own security strategies.
- Ensure efficient security constellations—intersectoral, multilevel cooperation to help the individual, community and country to maintain security.

Source: Simane 2016.

mechanisms so that these people can claim their rights and demand what they deserve.

Upholding human rights

The landscape of human rights tools for addressing deprivations and exclusion across the dimensions of human development is complex. Frameworks are in place to guarantee universal human rights and justice for all people. But state commitments to upholding these rights vary, national institutions have different implementation capacities and accountability mechanisms are sometimes missing. The Universal

> The landscape of human rights tools for addressing deprivations and exclusion across the dimensions of human development is complex

Declaration of Human Rights, adopted in 1948, has served as the foundation for global and national human rights and moral calls for action.[94] It has drawn attention to human rights by influencing national constitutions and prompting international treaties aimed at protecting specific types of rights, including the International Covenant on Civil and Political Rights and the International Covenant on Economic, Social and Cultural Rights.

Governments have been selective in recognizing international treaties and vary in adoption of mechanisms for greater accountability (figure 4.5). Optional protocols have been established to provide individuals with a means to file complaints about rights violations to international committees. These committees are entrusted to conduct inquiries into serious and systematic abuses.

Human development for all entails a full commitment to human rights that, as measured by ratifications of human rights treaties, has yet to be made. It also requires strong national human rights institutions with the capacity, mandate and will to address discrimination and ensure the protection of human rights across multiple dimensions. Such institutions, including human rights commissions and ombudsmen, handle complaints about rights abuses, educate civil society and states about human rights and recommend legal reforms.

Treating development as a human right has been instrumental in reducing deprivations in some dimensions and contexts. For example, under the Indian Constitution the state must provide schools within a reasonable distance to the communities they serve; after this provision became a motive of public litigation against the government in the Supreme Court, such schools were provided.

Treating the full expansion of choices and freedoms associated with human development as human rights is a practical way of shifting highly unequal power balances. Human rights provide principles, vocabularies and tools for defending the rights, help reshape political dynamics and open space for social change.

In an integrated world, human rights require global justice. The state-centred model of accountability must be extended to the obligations of nonstate actors and to the state's obligations beyond national borders. Human rights cannot be realized universally without well established domestic mechanisms and stronger international action (see chapter 5).

Ensuring access to justice

Access to justice is the ability of people to seek and obtain remedy through formal or informal judicial institutions. The justice process has qualitative dimensions and should be pursued in accordance with human rights principles and standards. A central feature of the rule of law is the equality of all before the law—all people have the right to the protection of their rights by the state, particularly the judiciary. Therefore, equal access to the courts and other institutions of justice involved in enforcing the law is important. Access to justice goes beyond access to the formal structures of the courts and the legal system; it is more than legal empowerment alone.

Poor and disadvantaged people face immense obstacles, including their lack of awareness and legal knowledge, compounded by structural and personal alienation. Poor people have limited access to public services, which are often expensive and cumbersome and lack adequate resources, personnel and facilities. Police stations and courts may not be available in remote areas, and poor people can rarely afford the cost of legal processes, such as legal fees. Quasi-judicial mechanisms may also be inaccessible or prejudicial.

Obstacles to justice for indigenous peoples and for racial and ethnic minorities stem from their historically subordinate status and from sociopolitical systems that reinforce bias in the legal framework and the justice system, which may tend to criminalize the actions of and incarcerate members of these minorities disproportionately. This leads to a systemic reinforcement of weaknesses and susceptibility to abuse by law enforcement officials.

The political and legal marginalization of historically oppressed or subordinate groups can still be seen in these groups' limited access to justice. Ethnic minorities, poor rural people and people displaced by conflict have traditionally faced some of the largest barriers to justice.

Universal access to justice is particularly important for marginalized groups. Legal empowerment and knowledge are essential so that people can claim their rights. The weakest in society need them the most. The state-financed

In an integrated world, human rights require global justice

FIGURE 4.5

Many countries have not ratified or signed various international human rights instruments

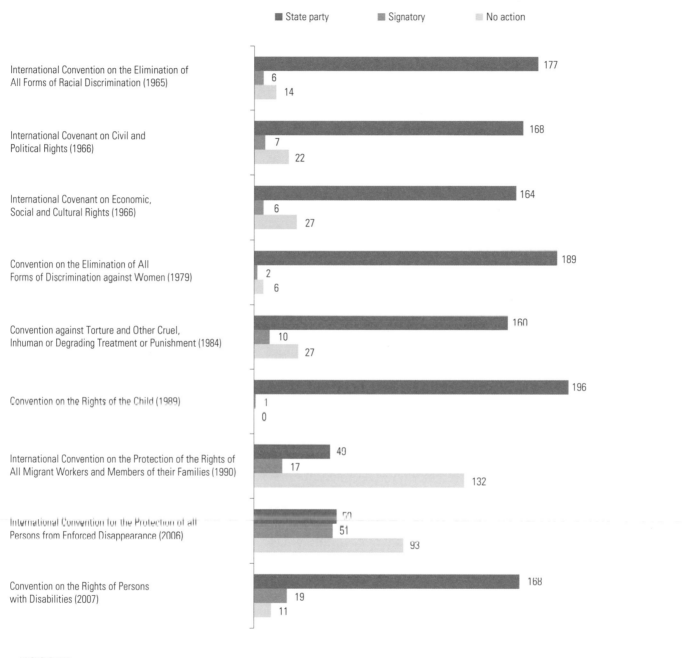

■ State party ■ Signatory ▪ No action

International Convention on the Elimination of
All Forms of Racial Discrimination (1965): 177, 6, 14

International Covenant on Civil and
Political Rights (1966): 168, 7, 22

International Covenant on Economic,
Social and Cultural Rights (1966): 164, 6, 27

Convention on the Elimination of All
Forms of Discrimination against Women (1979): 189, 2, 6

Convention against Torture and Other Cruel,
Inhuman or Degrading Treatment or Punishment (1984): 160, 10, 27

Convention on the Rights of the Child (1989): 196, 1, 0

International Convention on the Protection of the Rights of
All Migrant Workers and Members of their Families (1990): 49, 17, 132

International Convention for the Protection of all
Persons from Enforced Disappearance (2006): 50, 51, 93

Convention on the Rights of Persons
with Disabilities (2007): 168, 19, 11

Source: UNOHCHR 2016.

Legal Aid Service in Georgia is a promising example that has produced timely and tangible results (box 4.19).[95]

Promoting inclusion

Countries have deployed various political approaches in dealing with difference and diversity among their population and within borders. Societies have dealt with cultural diversity and heterogeneous populations through multiple measures that focus on integration, assimilation and multiculturalism.

These approaches have often required an evolving notion of citizenship with sociopolitical features. These features have had varying effects

BOX 4.19

Equality under the law—Georgia's Legal Aid Service

Georgia's state-financed Legal Aid Service was established in 2007 to provide legal advice, particularly to vulnerable groups, as part of a sweeping package of judicial reforms. The service operates as an independent entity accountable to parliament. Its independence and transparency are safeguarded by the Legal Aid Council.

The government has established the High School of Justice to train judicial professionals.[1] Lawyers have gained public outreach skills, particularly on behalf of marginalized groups.

Three-quarters of respondents to a 2010 survey rated the service "very satisfactory," and 71 percent said that they had achieved a favourable outcome in court.[2]

By 2015 the service had expanded to 18 offices across the country and had provided free legal assistance to more than 75,000 people. The majority of beneficiaries were from the most vulnerable groups —57 percent without jobs, 11 percent without the education to understand legal language, 10 percent socially vulnerable and 4 percent ethnic minorities. Fifty-eight percent of users were women.

Notes
1. UNDP 2016g. 2. UNDP 2016g.
Source: Human Development Report Office.

> The right to information requires the freedom to use that information to form public opinions, call governments to account, participate in decisionmaking and exercise the right to freedom of expression

on people's well-being and human development priorities because they have had a broad impact on people's political freedoms, their relative position in markets and their status in social and public life. For example, some 1.5 billion people worldwide cannot prove who they are.[96] Without birth registration, a birth certificate or any other identification document, they face barriers carrying out everyday tasks such as opening a bank account, accessing social benefits and obtaining health insurance. New technologies can help countries build robust and inclusive identification systems.

Where the deprived, excluded group is a demographic majority, democratic institutions may lead to comprehensive policies that reduce socioeconomic inequalities. This was the case in post-apartheid South Africa and in Malaysia following the adoption of the New Economic Policy in 1970.

Inclusion is at the core of the 2030 Agenda. The pledge to leave no one behind is embedded in the vision of a just, equitable, tolerant, open and socially inclusive world in which the needs of the most vulnerable are met.

Ensuring accountability

Holding social institutions publicly and mutually accountable, especially in protecting the rights of excluded segments of a population, requires explicit policy interventions. One major instrument to accomplish this is the right to information.

Since the 1990s more than 50 countries have adopted new instruments that protect the right to information.[97] In 2015 more than 100 countries had national laws or national ordinances and regulations on the right to information.[98] While laws on freedom of information were enacted in advanced industrialized countries to promote good governance, transparency and accountability, they had a somewhat different trajectory in many developing countries (box 4.20).

The right to information requires the freedom to use that information to form public opinions, call governments to account, participate in decisionmaking and exercise the right to freedom of expression. This right of access to information places two key obligations on governments: to publish and disseminate to the public key information on what public bodies are doing and to respond by letting the public view the original documents or receive copies of documents and information.

Participatory exercises to hold state institutions accountable, such as public expenditure tracking surveys, citizen report cards, score cards, social audits and community monitoring, have all been used to develop direct accountability relationships between service users and service providers. They also provide stakeholder inputs in deliberative exercises that prioritize and allocate local services and resources through participatory budgeting, sector-specific budget monitoring and participatory audits, all improving citizen engagement in the management of public finances.

BOX 4.20

Right to information—actions in developing countries

Since 2005 India has introduced progressive acts on the right to socioeconomic entitlements, including information, work, education, forest conservation, food and public service. These acts have been marked by their explicit use of rights-based claims and by the design of innovative governance mechanisms that seek to enhance the transparency, responsiveness and accountability of the state.[1]

Social audits, defined as mechanisms by which information on expenditures and implementation problems is gathered and then presented for discussion in a public meeting, have become popular, thanks to the work of the Indian grassroots group Mazdoor Kisaan Shakti Sangathana.[2]

In Bangladesh the Local Government (Union Parishad) Act 2009 and the Right to Information Act 2009 require disclosure of information on the Union Parishad's proposed budget at open meetings and of current development plans and budgets at citizen gatherings.[3] Mozambique's Conselhos consultivas (consulting councils) comprise citizens elected by their communities, with quotas for community leaders (40 percent), women (30 percent) and young people (20 percent). They are intended to establish a public administration for development as part of a process through which citizens participate and influence the decisionmaking on development.

Notes
1. Ruparelia 2013. 2. Joshi 2010. 3. McGee and Kroesschell 2013.
Source: Human Development Report Office.

Such participation is also well recognized as contributing to human development and to democratic governance—particularly for those left out. Empowered voice and participation have had pro-poor development outcomes as well as democracy building outcomes. People's freedoms, including those associated with voice and accountability, can also have instrumental or indirect value for other development objectives, because different types of freedoms can be complementary. Enhancing voice and accountability can therefore have an impact on poverty and deprivations.

Conclusion

Advancing human development through efforts to reach everyone requires meaningful and well designed policies—including universal policies with appropriate focus and reorientation, measures for groups with specific needs and interventions to protect human development gains and stop reversals. But policies supporting national policies will also involve ensuring people's participation in influencing policies and in evaluating development results, particularly the voice of the marginalized and vulnerable. For this, the quality and use of data for evidence-based policymaking will need to be greatly improved. And the systems and tools for transparency, accountability and evaluation will need to be greatly strengthened.

But the relevance and the effectiveness of national policies depend largely on what happens globally in terms of issues and institutions, given the broader bounds of the global community and global markets. Chapter 5 takes up that issue.

> People's freedoms, including those associated with voice and accountability, can have instrumental or indirect value for other development objectives, because different types of freedoms can be complementary

Chapter **5**

Transforming global institutions

Infographic 5.1 Challenges and reforms in global institutions—a summary

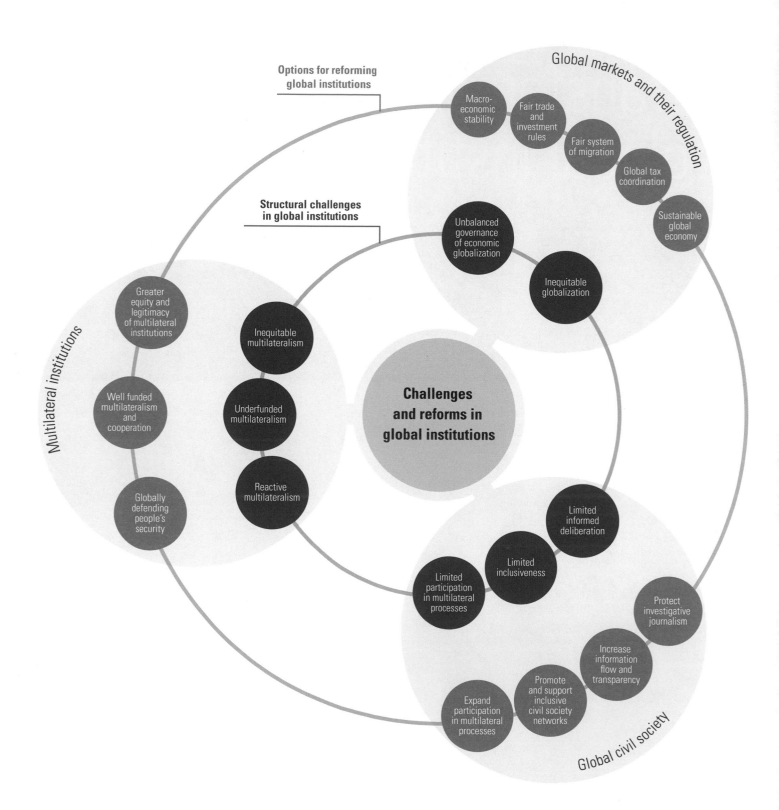

Options for reforming global institutions

Global markets and their regulation

Macro-economic stability

Fair trade and investment rules

Fair system of migration

Global tax coordination

Sustainable global economy

Unbalanced governance of economic globalization

Inequitable globalization

Structural challenges in global institutions

Multilateral institutions

Greater equity and legitimacy of multilateral institutions

Well funded multilateralism and cooperation

Globally defending people's security

Inequitable multilateralism

Underfunded multilateralism

Reactive multilateralism

Challenges and reforms in global institutions

Limited informed deliberation

Limited inclusiveness

Limited participation in multilateral processes

Protect investigative journalism

Increase information flow and transparency

Promote and support inclusive civil society networks

Expand participation in multilateral processes

Global civil society

5.

Transforming global institutions

The current global landscape is very different from what the world faced in 1990. New global challenges threaten the 2030 Agenda for "leaving no one behind." Inequality and exclusion, violence and extremism, refugees and migration, pollution and environmental degradation—all are caused by humans and their interactions, particularly across borders. That is why their solution depends not only on the actions of individual countries, but also on the construction of global collective capabilities to achieve results that no country can on its own.

All these cases involve global public goods and spillovers, which have grown in tandem with globalization and human connectivity. Uncoordinated national policies addressing global challenges—cutting greenhouse gas emissions, protecting labour rights, ensuring minimum incomes, cooperating to strengthen fragile states, providing humanitarian aid and refuge to those extremely endangered—are bound to be insufficient because of the existence of externalities.[1] So global and regional institutions are necessary to bring systematic attention, monitoring and coordination to key global issues.

International institutions and the resulting global order have enabled considerable progress in human development. But these institutions have also coexisted with persistent extreme deprivation—leaving behind large segments of the global population—and persistent human insecurity (see chapters 1 and 2). The mixed success calls for reforms, with an agenda that keeps what works and addresses evident gaps.

The main global social institutions—markets, multilateral organizations and civil society—are the focus of this chapter. They include rules and regulations governing the interchange of goods, services, capital and labour; multilateral organizations setting and enforcing the promotion of global public goods; and global networks of citizens promoting their diverse interests. The chapter addresses the structural challenges for human development, particularly for reaching everyone, and presents reform options.

On the challenges and structural deficiencies, the leitmotif is inequality among countries at different levels of development and among segments of the global population. Asymmetries persist in the way countries participate in global markets, in defining rules, in financing compensatory mechanisms and in

having the capacity to pursue accountability. These inequalities constitute barriers to practical universalism and compromise fairness, as some groups have decisive advantages in defining both the rules of the game and the payoffs. The winners and losers of globalization depend on the way globalization is pursued.

To respond to these challenges, global institutions can enhance collective capabilities. They can expand opportunities for international exchange (including people, knowledge, goods, services and capital), both for cooperation and for participation and accountability. But there is tension between globalization and democratic national policymaking. International rules can constrain some national policies, including those that today's developed countries used in the past. However, it is possible to construct better global institutions and governance along the following lines:

- *Rules that over-restrict development policies are not an inevitable result of globalization.* They are the consequence of a particular path to globalization, where some countries and some voices have had a greater say at the negotiating table. But if broader views are included more systematically and more equitably, it will be possible to enact human development–friendly rules for all. In particular, expanding opportunities requires that countries retain meaningful space for national policymaking under democratic principles.
- *The generation of global public goods demands stronger multilateralism and policy coherence, able to match the common good with the common responsibility, all endowed with legitimacy.* For example, curbing the inflow of migrants cannot be fully separated from the responsibility to protect people facing extreme deprivation abroad.

The winners and losers of globalization depend on the way globalization is pursued

- *Developing countries require enhanced capacities to use globalization for sustainable development.* In the past they have accepted —through democratic processes—the restrictions on national policymaking in investment protection treaties, tax incentives to foreign companies and the liberalization of trade. Some of these commitments later become obstacles for development policies in some countries.

Structural challenges in global institutions

Human development for everyone requires identifying relevant barriers to practical universalism at the level of the main global institutions: markets, multilateral organizations and global civil society.

Governance of economic globalization

Unbalanced governance of economic globalization

The globalization of market institutions regulating the international flow of goods, services, capital and labour is neither spontaneous nor inevitable. The world has previously seen waves of globalization followed by periods of protectionism, a result of collective national, regional and global decisions. Globalization requires minimum standards, rules and trust. For individuals globalization can be seen as intrinsically human development–enhancing, since it opens new opportunities for interacting, travelling and investing (an expansion of individual capabilities). But it also implies exposure to external shocks through interactions with other people and nations. Some shocks will expand capabilities, some will reduce them (table 5.1). Based on these effects, collective decisions shape global institutions—through the interactions of different groups, with varying costs and benefits.

Multilateral and bilateral organizations determine the main rules and standards. For trade in goods and services the World Trade Organization is the main standard-setting entity: Member countries are bound by its norms. For the flow of capital the main mechanisms of protection are international investment agreements and bilateral investment treaties. For the flow of labour there is a mix of bilateral agreements and international conventions.

The multilateral mechanisms protecting foreign goods and foreign capital from

TABLE 5.1

Examples of the social benefits and costs of globalizing market institutions

	Benefits	Costs
Trade	• Access to goods and services at a lower price • Access to larger markets • Upgrading and diversifying economic structures	• Unemployment in import-substituting sectors • Exposure to negative trade shocks • Reduced space for national policies • Race to the bottom (workers)
Finance	• Access to new sources of financing • Ability for firms to diversify risks by accessing other markets	• Financial volatility (exposure to financial shocks) • Reduced space for national policies • Race to the bottom (workers, tax systems and regulations)
Migration	• Access to a broader labour market for host countries • Access to better working and living conditions than in source countries for migrants • Remittances for source countries • Flow of knowledge and culture	• Vulnerability of migrants and their families • Potential imbalances in service provision in host countries, particularly in the face of a migration shock • Gaps in skills and care for countries of origin ("brain drain")

Source: Human Development Report Office.

discriminatory treatment are much more prevalent than those protecting foreign workers from discrimination (figure 5.1). The World Trade Organization has 164 members subject to its standards and rules; 181 countries have signed investment protection treaties, which provide legal mechanisms for affected corporations to sue states. But fewer than 50 countries are committed to protecting migrants, their basic rights as human beings and their economic rights as workers.

The asymmetry in multilateral and bilateral institutions regulating international markets has affected patterns of globalization. The globalization of trade has surged since 1990, averaging 6.7 percent growth a year. The globalization of finance has expanded even faster. Foreign direct investment increased 8.9 percent a year over 1990–2015.[2] Meanwhile the number of migrants has grown 1.9 percent a year, keeping the share of migrants in the world population stable over the last 25 years, at around 3 percent.[3]

Mobility differs for goods, services, capital and labour. It is more limited for workers than for goods or for capital, which can move in seconds. But there has been little progress in policies favouring labour mobility. About 73 percent of surveyed countries had migration policies consistent with keeping migration constant (typically no intervention), 16 percent had policies to lower migration and only 11 percent had policies to increase it.[4]

One of the main costs of globalization is the transmission of "major" external shocks, those beyond "normal" cycles. A collapse in terms of trade because of global recession, a sudden stop of capital flows or a surge in migrants caused by a conflict in a neighbouring country are external events with the potential to create large cross-border crises. From the point of view of a particular country, these external shocks are typically exogenous, but from the point of view of the international community, they are endogenous human-caused events. So in many cases they are preventable. Similarly, once the shock starts, individual countries rarely have the capacity to affect its magnitude and duration. Instead, the coordinated action of many countries must contain and reduce the negative effects.

Mobility is more limited for workers than for goods or for capital. But there has been little progress in policies favouring labour mobility

FIGURE 5.1

The number of countries subscribing to multilateral instruments varies

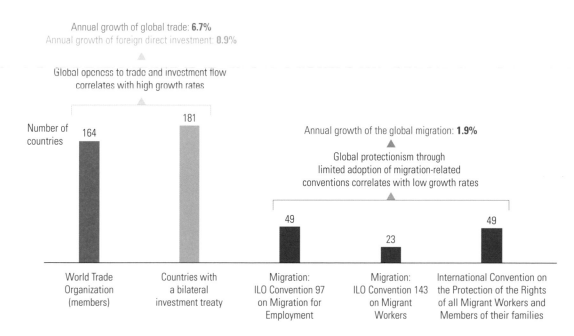

Annual growth of global trade: **6.7%**
Annual growth of foreign direct investment: **8.9%**

Global openness to trade and investment flow correlates with high growth rates

Number of countries

164

181

Annual growth of the global migration: **1.9%**

Global protectionism through limited adoption of migration-related conventions correlates with low growth rates

49

23

49

| World Trade Organization (members) | Countries with a bilateral investment treaty | Migration: ILO Convention 97 on Migration for Employment | Migration: ILO Convention 143 on Migrant Workers | International Convention on the Protection of the Rights of all Migrant Workers and Members of their families |

Note: Growth rates are for 1990–2015.
Source: World Trade Organization, United Nations Conference on Trade and Development, United Nations Department of Economic and Social Affairs, International Labour Organization and United Nations Treaty Collection.

Inequitable globalization

The current architecture of international institutions and unbalanced evolution of global markets present challenges to human development

The current architecture of international institutions and unbalanced evolution of global markets present challenges to human development on two fronts. Some population segments have progressed, leaving others behind. And unregulated financial globalization has increased people's economic insecurity (see chapters 1 and 2).

Capital tends to be concentrated in the wealthiest segment of the population, which enjoys the benefits of mobility and the increasingly flexible forms of production (global value chains). Some of the gains are transmitted to the rest of society, but the positive effects cannot be taken for granted (box 5.1). The increasingly complex global economy has also created loopholes that might accommodate illegal activities and tax evasion, undermining government effectiveness (box 5.2).

Barriers to migration undermine one path to development for people in poor countries. Orderly migration increases opportunities for people in developing countries. Individuals generally see moving to another country as a way to increase their well-being and human development. More than 75 percent of international migrants move to a country with higher human development than in their home country.[5] In some cases they discover choices they did not have at home. For instance, women may be allowed to study and work more freely. Refugees can escape violence and persecution and hope that their human rights will be respected. International migrants are a source of money, investment and trade for their home country.[6]

But the costs of migration can be unacceptably high. They derive from the lack of protection of migrants' basic rights, resulting in,

---

BOX 5.1

Transnational corporations and human development—no automatic link

Transnational corporations have been one of the most notable faces of globalization. The stock of foreign direct investment grew from $2 billion in 1990 to $25 billion in 2015.[1] This increase has been associated with investment treaties (see figure 5.1) and national investment policies liberalizing or promoting foreign direct investment. An underlying promise is that foreign direct investment can enhance human development, through different channels: the increase in productive capacity (particularly in developing countries, which are capital scarce), the transfer and diffusion of technology and knowhow, the creation of employment and skill development and increases in tax revenues. But these positive links should not be taken for granted.

- A significant share of foreign direct investment is devoted to mergers and acquisitions related to existing assets. In those cases, there is no direct creation of productive capacity. In 2015, 41 percent of foreign direct investment inflows were for mergers and acquisitions.[2]
- Foreign direct investment tends to come from and go to high-income countries. In such economies the stock of foreign direct investment was 37 percent of GDP in 2015, compared with 31 percent in transition countries and 28 percent in developing countries.[3]
- Transnational corporations often operate protected by investment treaties that might prevent the

correction of negative externalities rooted in their operations. For example, legislative reform in the renewable energy sector was the top activity by states pursuing investment arbitration in 2015. Similarly, the Energy Charter Treaty is by far the most frequently invoked international investment agreement.[4]

- Transnational corporations have been changing the global pattern of production through global value chains, geographically fragmenting production processes. Today around 80 percent of global exports are nested within global value chains.[5] If a country imports all high value-added inputs, it might end up exporting sophisticated final goods with relatively low value-added. One consequence is that for developing countries, engaging in a manufacturing global value chain does not necessarily upgrade the productive and social structure.
- Transnational corporations often use geographical fragmentation to avoid taxes.[6]
- Another effect of global value chains is the rising share of value added generated by capital and high-skilled labour, with pervasive consequences for the distribution of income across and within countries (between investors and workers and between different segments of the population, in general).[7] For example, in Latin America foreign direct investment widened income gaps.[8]

Notes
1. UNCTAD 2016. 2. UNCTAD 2016. 3. UNCTAD 2016. 4. UNCTAD 2016. 5. Montes and Lunenborg 2016. 6. Zucman 2015. 7. Timmer and others 2014. 8. Herzer, Huhne and Nunnenkamp 2014; Suanes 2016.

BOX 5.2

Loopholes of globalization—tax avoidance and illegal financial flows

The mobility of capital in a world of uneven rules has created loopholes that erode the capacities of national governments to perform such basic tasks as collecting taxes and regulating and restricting illegal activities.

Large firms and high-income groups take advantage of regulatory loopholes on international financial markets to avoid paying national taxes. Corporations producing at global scale can shift profits to places with lower taxes (through transfer pricing and debt restructuring). For example, in August 2016 the European Commission determined that the effective corporate tax rate that Apple paid was 0.005 percent in fiscal 2014, thanks to a special tax regime in Ireland, where profits from sales across Europe could be recorded.[1] Similarly, high-income people can use offshore centres to hide their money and reduce their tax burden. The wealth in offshore centres was estimated at $7.6 trillion in 2014, more than the capitalization of the world's 20 largest companies, and the accumulated assets of the wealthiest 1,645 people (see figure). In April 2016 the "Panama Papers" offered a glimpse into the mechanisms that wealthy people use in offshore centres. The fiscal cost to national governments: more than $190 billion a year.[2]

Illicit financial flows—money illegally earned, transferred or used—present a big challenge for developing countries, particularly those in Africa. The flows weaken governance and reduce consumption, investment and social spending, hurting the long-term construction of collective capabilities and the expansion of human development. In Africa an estimated $30–$60 billion

Transferring wealth offshore

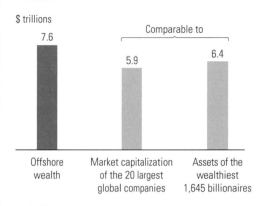

Source: Zucman 2015; Forbes FT 500.

a year is lost because of laundering criminal proceeds associated with human trafficking—corruption that leads to the theft of state assets, tax abuse and commercial abuse. In 2001–2010 Africa lost around $400 billion to trade mispricing alone. The size of illicit financial flows are in the range of total official development assistance to the region.[3] There are multiple drivers of illicit financial flows, but the main ones are lack of transparency, lack of monitoring systems, heterogeneous tax systems, limited national capacities, incomplete international architecture and insufficient coordination among countries, all in a context of economies based on extractive industries operating under weak institutions.[4]

1. European Commission 2016. 2. Zucman 2015. 3. Over the last 50 years Africa lost an estimated $1 trillion dollars because of illicit financial flows, which is roughly the level of official development assistance (African Union and Economic Commission for Africa 2015). 4. African Union and Economic Commission for Africa 2015.
Source: Human Development Report Office.

for example, a high death toll among refugees and widespread human trafficking (as the 2015 Human Development Report documented). Such costs undermine the globalization of labour as a vehicle for human development. The growth in the stock of voluntary migrants (excluding refugees) fell from 3 percent in 2005–2010 to 1.5 percent in 2010–2015.[7]

Imbalances in the governance of multilateral institutions

Inequitable multilateralism

The governance of multilateral institutions is important not only for achieving their key functions, but also for expanding the collective capabilities among nations. An appropriate structure ensures the legitimacy and the quality of the work of such institutions.

The International Monetary Fund (IMF) helps solve information, commitment and coordination problems that might affect the stability and soundness of the global monetary system. In practical terms it performs surveillance work (having access to sensitive information) and acts as a trusted advisor. Its effectiveness depends on how trustworthy, competent and impartial countries see it.

The IMF's governance structure (which is dominated by Group of 7 countries) matters. After reforms agreed on in 2010 and

> The governance of multilateral institutions is important not only for achieving their key functions, but also for expanding the collective capabilities among nations

implemented in January 2016, the United States alone has veto power, with almost 17 percent of the voting power. Brazil, China, India, the Russian Federation and South Africa combined have 14 percent of the voting power.[8] There are some complaints that lending decisions have been connected to the borrower's alignment with the main shareholders' interests.[9] For example, the systemic exemption clause—in effect during 2010–2015 to assist Greece—allowed the IMF to provide loans to countries with unsustainable debts if the countries' problems could pose a threat to international financial stability.[10] The policy has pros (defending global financial stability) and cons (creating moral hazard). Such a case also raises an alert about possible tension at the geopolitical level.

The IMF's Independent Evaluation Office found that trust in the organization was variable, "with authorities in Asia, Latin America and large emerging markets the most sceptical, and those in large advanced countries the most indifferent."[11] Limited trust affects its role not only as advisor, but also as lender in times of crisis.[12] It is argued that as a result of this limited trust, developing economies have chosen to accumulate very large reserves as self-insurance, a choice that is costly for countries and inefficient (with a recessionary bias) for the world.[13]

The World Bank is also governed by shareholders, predominately Group of 7 countries, though China became the third largest voter after the United States and Japan since a 2010 reform.[14] There may be tension between the goal of eradicating poverty and the goal of overcoming failures in capital markets and providing global public goods.[15]

The governance of international trade is dominated by rules—the General Agreement on Tariffs and Trade and its successor, the World Trade Organization. They have favoured trade expansion[16] in a context of generalized trade liberalization in developing countries as a result of structural adjustment in the 1980s and 1990s.[17] However, the rules affect national space to define public policies.[18] In particular, they limit the use of trade policy to support sectoral or industrial development (policies used in the past by today's developed countries to promote their industries).[19] In addition, some rules can restrict the use of social policy, such as India's National Food Security Act (box 5.3).

The World Trade Organization's Doha Development Round offered some space for rebalancing the rules, this time towards a development-oriented perspective. But progress on the key issues of this round, negotiated since 2001, has been limited.[20] With the Doha Round stalled, international trade rules have been dominated by regional and bilateral trade agreements, where protecting investments and intellectual property rights have become central. In practice, industrial countries (the main source of foreign direct investment and

The rules that govern international trade affect national space to define public policies

BOX 5.3

The World Trade Organization and India's national development policies

India's National Food Security Act of 2013 grants the "right to food" in the biggest ever food safety net programme, distributing highly subsidized food grain (61 million tonnes) to 67 percent of the population. The scale of buying grain from poor farmers for sale to poorer consumers put India at risk of violating its World Trade Organization obligations in agriculture. World Trade Organization members are subject to trade sanctions if they breach a ceiling on their agricultural subsidies. But the method of calculating the ceiling is fixed on the basis of 1986–1988 prices and in national currency, an unusually low baseline.

This clear asymmetry in international rules reduces national space for development policy. India, as other developing countries, did not have large agricultural subsidies when the rules were originally agreed. The act—which aims to stave off hunger for 840 million people and which can play a pivotal role in the UN agenda to end hunger everywhere—is being challenged because it raises India's direct food subsidy bill from roughly $15 billion a year to $21 billion. In comparison, the United States increased its agricultural domestic support from $60 billion in 1995 to $140 billion in 2013.

The matter has not been resolved, except for a negotiated pause in dispute actions against countries with existing programmes that notify the World Trade Organization and promise to negotiate a permanent solution.

Source: Montes and Lunenborg 2016.

patents) use such agreements to obtain benefits. The payments of royalties and licences from developing to developed countries (particularly to the United States) have grown immensely since 1990 (figure 5.2).[21]

International investment agreements and bilateral investment treaties might restrict governments' ability to define national policies and standards.[22] These agreements often define expropriation as an action that reduces investors' expected profits—a very broad definition that is ripe for litigation.[23] An international entity, in most cases the International Centre for Settlement of Investment Disputes, resolves disputes related to these instruments. Proper regulation of foreign corporations might become difficult (box 5.4). Most countries have signed some of the 2,958 bilateral investment treaties recorded by the United Nations Conference on Trade and Development (see figure 5.1).

With 193 member states and most resolutions decided by one country one vote, the United Nations is perhaps the international organization with the greatest international legitimacy. However, asymmetries exist, notably between developed and developing countries, tied to two elements.

First, the five permanent members of the Security Council—China, France, the Russian Federation, the United Kingdom and the United States—have veto power. As the only UN body with the capacity to issue binding resolutions, the Security Council has a decisive role in selecting the UN Secretary-General (appointed by the General Assembly but only on the recommendation of the Security Council, according to Article 97 of the UN Charter).

Second, the expenditures of both operational and peacekeeping activities are funded largely by a few donor countries. For the UN system as a whole, 55 percent of resources are earmarked by donors, meaning that they have to be spent on specific, predetermined activities.[24] For its operational activities (62 percent of UN expenditure), core resources (those not restricted) represent a small and declining proportion of total funding, falling from 32 percent in 2003 to 24 percent in 2014 (figure 5.3).

The expenditures of UN operational and peacekeeping activities are funded largely by a few donor countries

FIGURE 5.2

Net payments of royalties and licences from developing to developed countries have grown immensely since 1990

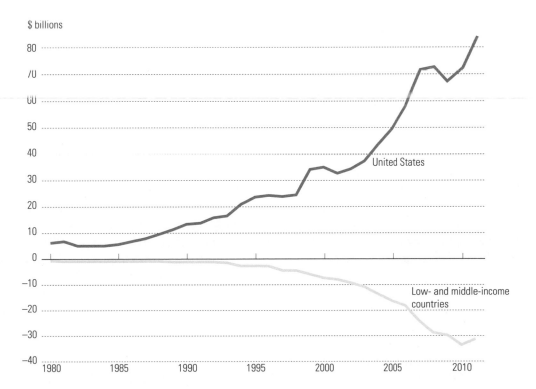

Source: Montes and Lunenborg 2016.

Bilateral investment treaties and national policies in Ecuador

In October 2012 an arbitration tribunal of the International Centre for Settlement of Investment Disputes ruled against Ecuador in a case brought by Occidental Petroleum Corporation and Occidental Exploration and Production Company under the United States–Ecuador Bilateral Investment Treaty. It imposed a penalty on Ecuador of $1.8 billion plus compound interest and litigation costs, bringing the award to $2.3 billion.

What legal observers found striking about this judgement is that the tribunal recognized that Ecuador cancelled its contract because the company violated a key clause (selling 40 percent of the concession to another company without permission) but found that Ecuador violated the obligation of "fair and equitable treatment" under the United States–Ecuador Bilateral Investment Treaty.

Source: Montes and Lunenborg 2016; Wallach and Beachy 2012.

FIGURE 5.3

The share of core resources in UN operational activities is low and declining

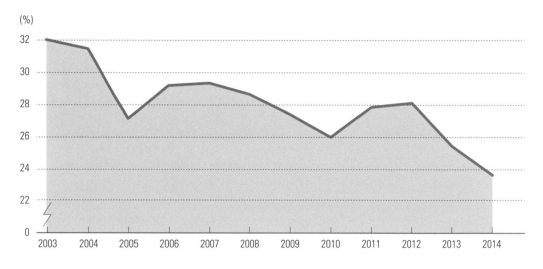

Source: Human Development Report Office based on ECOSOC (2016).

Noncore resources, typically earmarked to a certain thematic or geographical area, have been increasing, resulting in UN development agencies having to compete for funding from donors. While earmarked funds can in some cases expand the resource envelope, they have generally crowded out core resources.

Underfunded multilateralism

The resources channelled through the main global institutions are modest. In 2014 official development assistance was a mere 0.17 percent of global GDP.[25] UN spending in 2014 was 0.06 percent of global GDP.[26] Lending from the main international financial institutions

has also been limited: IMF disbursements were 0.04 percent of global GDP,[27] and multilateral development bank disbursements were 0.09 percent of global GDP.[28] If directed to one goal, these resources make a difference. But they are often directed to multiple fronts, some associated with deprivations and some with global public goods (with increasing demand, as for peace and security). The European Union, facing fewer deprivations, manages around 1 percent of its members' GDP.[29]

The funding of global institutions appears inadequate for achieving international targets. The Sustainable Development Goals, far broader than the Millennium Development Goals, require investments in developing

The funding of global institutions appears inadequate for achieving international targets

countries of $3.3–4.5 trillion over the next 15 years. Subtracting current annual investments of $1.4 trillion, the resource gap is around $2.5 trillion (around 3 percent of global GDP in current prices).[30] The global agenda also demands a strong global approach. The United Nations—leading this agenda, which includes several issues intrinsically global, particularly those related to the environment and climate change—has a budget that is very small (around 2 percent of the resource gap for achieving the Sustainable Development Goals in developing countries[31]).

Nor is the Sustainable Development Goals' more ambitious agenda matched by resources provided by traditional donor countries through official development assistance. The typical contribution of developed countries has with a few exceptions been consistently below 0.7 percent of gross national income (GNI), a mark established in 1970 and reaffirmed by the Monterrey Consensus in 2002 and by the Sustainable Development Goals last year. In 2014 the average contribution of donor countries through this channel was 0.39 percent of GNI.[32]

Two problems demand a strong economic role of global institutions: the underprovision of public goods when left to voluntary decentralized decisions, and the imperfections in capital markets. Reducing carbon dioxide emissions under the Paris Agreement on climate change would require annual clean energy investments equivalent to 1.5 percent of every country's GDP.[33] The resource gaps are also wide for such urgent issues as forcibly displaced people. Despite record contributions from donors in 2015 ($3.36 billion), the funding gap for the Office of the United Nations High Commissioner for Refugees grew to 53 percent, from 36 percent in 2010.[34] In 2016 its estimated funding need is $6.55 billion[35]—equivalent to 0.4 percent of global military expenditure.[36]

Reactive multilateralism

Over the last few years the number of countries in conflict and the number of casualties have trended upward.[37] Today's armed conflicts are increasingly within countries, reducing the traditional tools of coercive diplomacy and deterrence.[38] But the consequences are felt globally, both because the international community must respond to international terrorism and violations of human rights and because extreme human insecurity can be a source of border tensions and refugee crises. These "new" phenomena have the following characteristics:[39]

- The majority are supported by illegal financing.
- Nonstate actors are much more prominent.
- Civilians account for the vast majority of victims.[40] Of people killed or injured by explosive weapons in populated areas, 92 percent are civilians.[41]

These crises highlight the weakness of global institutions, whether their inadequate response to forced migration or their failure to prevent crises through bolder development programmes. In most cases the surge in international cooperation seems to have waited until the situation reached a global scale.

International cooperation is based on sovereignty. Bilateral cooperation takes place between two sovereign states. Multilateral cooperation through UN entities is demand driven: Programmes are agreed with governments. The underlying assumption is that the nation-state can protect its citizens, which is not always the case. But the envelope of resources also depends on the priorities of donor countries. Therefore, this system of demand and supply leaves some people behind. Consider the three main sources of refugees in 2010–2015 (Afghanistan, Somalia and the Syrian Arab Republic).[42] In the late 1990s they received 0.4 percent of total official development assistance, despite accounting for 0.8 percent of the population of developing countries.[43] In the last few years, after the crisis became a reality affecting other countries, they received around 5 percent,[44] led more by their instability than by the root social conditions causing it.

Untapped potential of global civil society

Limited participation in multilateral processes

One notable institutional change over the past 25 years is the progressive involvement of global civil society movements in formal multilateral processes. In 2000 the United Nations Millennium Declaration encouraged

Today's armed conflicts are increasingly within countries, but the consequences are felt globally

governments to develop strong partnerships with civil society organizations.[45] The Paris Declaration on Aid Efficiency in 2005, the Accra Agenda for Action in 2008 and the Busan Partnership for Effective Development in 2011 all acknowledged civil society's growing responsibilities in pursuing the development agenda. More recently, the post-2015 agenda for sustainable development brought together governmental and nongovernmental actors in dozens of national, regional, global and thematic consultations. The 2030 Agenda now recognizes the role of civil society organizations and philanthropic organizations in its implementation.[46]

The United Nations Economic and Social Council grants consultative status to more than 4,500 nongovernmental organizations, up from 41 at its creation in 1946.[47] Of the nongovernmental organizations with consultative status, 72 percent were admitted after 2000, and 43 percent between 2010 and 2015 (figure 5.4).[48]

Global social movements have spotlighted inequality, sustainability and the globalization of markets. On environmental sustainability they have been particularly successful in raising awareness and promoting policies (box 5.5).

Nongovernmental organizations were among the first stakeholders to bring environmental sustainability to the attention of the general public and policymakers in the 1980s and 1990s. Today, they implement environmental programmes independently or in partnership with governments and multilateral institutions. They also monitor progress and ensure that governments and corporations respect their commitments.

Limited inclusiveness

Information and communication technologies have allowed civil society to gather across borders and share ideas, online or offline, but are unequally spread around the world. Telecommunication infrastructure and online participation tools are positively correlated (figure 5.5).[49] The more a country's telecommunication infrastructure is developed, the more likely the existence of online mechanisms for civil society participation in public and political life.

Although less than 5 percent of the world's people are native English speakers, 53 percent of online content is in English.[50] Around 85 percent of user-generated content on Google today

Global social movements have spotlighted inequality, sustainability and the globalization of markets

FIGURE 5.4

Of the more than 4,500 nongovernmental organizations granted consultative status by the United Nations Economic and Social Council, 72 percent were admitted after 2000

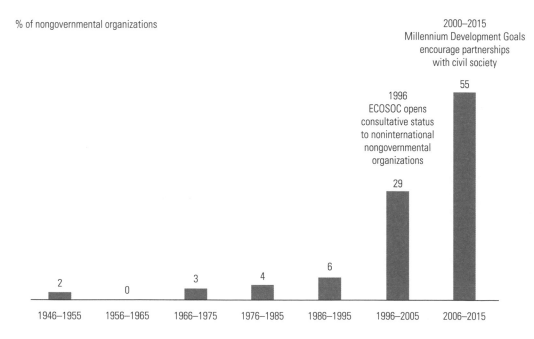

% of nongovernmental organizations

ECOSOC is the United Nations Economic and Social Council.
Source: ECOSOC 2015.

BOX 5.5

Civil society and environment sustainability

The international nongovernmental organization Greenpeace elaborated one of the first scenarios for mitigating climate change as early as 1993 and was instrumental in raising awareness of global warming through protests and other communications.[1] In the early 1990s it developed a new technology, Greenfreeze, to build refrigerators without using chlorofluorocarbons, which deplete ozone. In 1997 the United Nations Environment Programme recognized Greenpeace's contributions to protecting the Earth's ozone layer. Today, more than 800 million of the world's refrigerators use Greenfreeze technology.[2]

Civil society organizations have had a major local, national or global impact on the environment, through their direct action and their advocacy. Highly publicized campaigns, in the media or on the streets, have informed people about environmental issues and pressured governments to take action. For instance, Greenpeace research on deforestation in the Amazon due to the production of soy, followed by protests by the organization's activists, led the Brazilian government to adopt an agreement keeping the rainforest from being destroyed by soybean farming.[3]

Notes
1. IPCC 2000. 2. Greenpeace 2016a. 3. Greenpeace 2016b.
Source: Human Development Report Office.

FIGURE 5.5

Good telecommunication infrastructure means more online participation

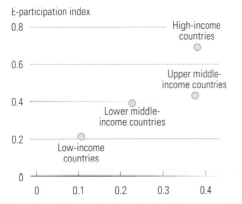

E-participation index

Information and communication technology infrastructure index

Source: UNDESA 2016d.

is produced in Canada, Europe or the United States.[51] Individuals unable to read or write English are thus excluded from most of the opportunities for participation on the Internet.

Limited informed deliberation

New forms of participation—particularly though social networks with global reach—are increasingly important in policymaking. They are based on fast and decentralized interactions, which do not always allow proper fact-checking and analysis. So the policy debate can be too reactive and based on a short-term news cycle. Computer-generated fake accounts (bots) can alter the information that governments and the media extract from social networks.

Social media can also spread false information. User-created content allows anyone to publish anything regardless of its veracity. Aggregating users by their identity, tastes and beliefs into "echo chambers" makes it easier to persuade groups of people.[52] This is reinforced by a confirmation bias that leads people to focus on information matching their own opinion rather than be open to other arguments.

Options for institutional reform

The global order and its effects on human development depend on the quality of global institutions. While national policies can facilitate a country's insertion in global society, a good economic, social and political order requires institutions to coordinate the collective actions of all countries. The following options for reform aim to make better global institutions by promoting global public goods.

Stabilizing the global economy

The history of financial crises shows how capital markets tend to underestimate risks in times of liquidity and to overreact in times of trouble.

New forms of participation—particularly though social networks with global reach—are increasingly important in policymaking

Coordinate macroeconomic policies and regulations

Macroeconomic coordination among larger economies is key to preserving the public good of stability. Global imbalances could be more systematically addressed with greater participation of the United Nations in Group of 7 and Group of 20 meetings, on behalf of developing countries with small economies but great exposure to external shocks.

The 2008 financial crisis triggered a wide array of coordination efforts, led by the Group of 20, around a consensus for countercyclical fiscal and monetary policy. An important measure was the heavy capitalization of multilateral development banks. And the IMF approved the largest issuance of special drawing rights in its history ($250 billion), allocating 60 percent to high-income countries.[53]

After the crisis the main central banks (US Federal Reserve, Bank of Canada, European Central Bank, Bank of England, People's Bank of China and Bank of Japan) used currency swaps to provide liquidity and stabilize exchange rate markets, working among themselves and with some central banks from developing countries.[54] Such coordination should be enhanced and made more systematic. One proposal is a global international reserve system based on special drawing rights and managed by the IMF, allowing countries to deposit unused special drawing rights at the IMF, which could finance its lending operations, facilitating countercyclical policy and efficient risk sharing.[55]

Regulate currency transactions and capital flows

To help capital markets channel resources from savers to investors and facilitate the smoothing of consumption, regulation has become well accepted, but mainly in the space of banks. The Financial Stability Board coordinates national financial authorities and international standard-setting in their efforts to come up with regulatory and supervisory policies. But there has been reluctance to regulate nonbank international capital flows.[56]

One option is to tax international transactions. A multilateral tax on the four major trading currencies (with a very small rate of 0.1 percent) could raise roughly 0.05 percent of global GDP.[57] Such transaction taxes in France curtail trading volumes and intraday volatility with negligible effect on liquidity.[58] A multilateral tax could reduce speculation and the associated short-term volatility and strengthen the longer term segments of capital markets, linked to productive investment.

Another option is to use capital controls. Even the IMF (which in 1997 attempted to make capital account liberalization mandatory for all its members) has recently acknowledged their benefits,[59] highlighting that they reduced vulnerabilities (overheating and excessive indebtedness) before the financial crisis in 2008.[60]

Applying fair trade and investment rules

A fair system regulating the flow of goods, services, knowledge and productive investment is a global public good. International trade has been a strong engine of development for many countries, particularly in Asia. But two problems are now crucial. First, trade rules—including their extension to intellectual property rights and investment protection treaties—tend to favour developed countries. Second, global trade has slowed in recent years, which might reduce opportunities for developing countries.[61] The international agenda should be to set rules to expand trade of goods, services and knowledge to favour human development and the Sustainable Development Goals.

Finalize the World Trade Organization's Doha Round

For developing countries, one of the most important global public goods would be a fair and well functioning World Trade Organization. There is hope: As developing countries have gained negotiating power, multilateral agreements can, despite their limitations, become a tool for fairer trade. The Doha Round intends to add development principles to trade rules, by introducing implementation issues to ease the ability of developing countries to perform World Trade Organization obligations, by addressing imbalances in agricultural subsidy regimes and by strengthening and operationalizing special and differential treatment (see Sustainable Development Goal target 17.10).

Macroeconomic coordination among larger economies is key to preserving the public good of stability

Reform the global intellectual property rights regime

Assessing the usefulness of the current intellectual property rights regime to meet the Sustainable Development Goals could be a basis for reform. Two Sustainable Development Goals are particularly sensitive to property rights: the promotion of healthy life and well-being for all (Sustainable Development Goal 3) and the technology facilitation mechanism, introduced in the Addis Ababa Action Agenda (Sustainable Development Goal 17).

The UN Secretary-General's High-Level Panel on Access to Medicines has recommended that World Trade Organization members revise agreements on Trade-Related Aspects of Intellectual Property Rights to enable a swift and expeditious export of essential medicines produced under compulsory license to countries that cannot produce them themselves.[62] In practice, priority should be given to medicines on the World Health Organization Model List of Essential Medicines. A similar principle should be used with the technology facilitation mechanism: Every year technologies critical to achieving the Sustainable Development Goals should be identified (in a forum proposed by the Addis Agenda), as should the obstacles to their adoption. In this context, if intellectual property rights enforced through World Trade Organization mechanisms prove to be an obstacle to the timely diffusion of required technology, the international community must take a hard look at reshaping the way such assets are protected and remunerated internationally.[63] Progress in this direction could be particularly important in fighting climate change, since technology diffusion is essential to decouple GDP growth from greenhouse gas emissions.

Reform the global investor protection regime

While investors and their property rights have to be properly defended against arbitrariness, most bilateral investment treaties with developing countries have been negotiated asymmetrically. Developing countries should use the available legal space to reassess and change the models of these treaties (box 5.6).

Adopting a fair system of migration

Strengthen strategies that protect the rights of and promote opportunities for migrants

A first step in implementing a human rights–based approach to protect migrants is to ratify the 1990 UN Convention on Migrant Workers and Their Families. Since migration is also part of a global economy, its rules should be the counterpart to fair trade and investment rules, establishing nondiscriminatory treatment of national workers. This market-based view should be subject to negotiation in bilateral and regional agreements, taking advantage of similarities among countries.

Migration can continue to be a source of human development if the long-term needs of host countries match the interests of migrants. Voluntary global mobility could benefit from better coordination among countries of origin, transit and destination. International agreements could ensure migrants' security and increase their productivity. Training and information could be provided to migrants in their country of origin on the opportunities and challenges they will encounter in their host country.

Governments could exchange administrative information on migrants to facilitate their integration. For example, the Bulgarian city of Kavarna signed an agreement with Polish cities, where most of its Roma population is employed,

> Migration can continue to be a source of human development if the long-term needs of host countries match the interests of migrants

to ensure their right to work, allow them to start companies and facilitate tax collection.[64] The Romas' economic success improved how the host community perceived them.

Establish a global mechanism to coordinate economic migration

The International Organization for Migration joined the UN system in September 2016 (box 5.7). Long-term migration policies, with a human development perspective, require continuous and consistent coordination and cooperation at all levels. As part of the UN system the International Organization for Migration becomes a permanent member of the Chief Executives Board, the highest entity for UN coordination, and its subsidiary bodies. The International Organization for Migration is now formalized in UN country teams as part of the UN Development Assistance Framework. It is poised to be the main supporter of negotiations to adopt the Global Compact for Safe, Orderly and Regular Migration, scheduled for 2018.

Facilitate guaranteed asylum for forcibly displaced people

The 1951 Refugee Convention and its 1967 Protocol oblige countries to welcome asylumseekers on their territories and to not send them back where their lives may be at risk.

Only 148 of 193 UN member states are party to the convention or its protocol.

The safety of forcibly displaced people during their journey must also be ensured through humanitarian aid or organized transportation. Since displacement lasts on average 17 years, their journeys require international coordination and agreement to share the responsibility of care in times of emergency and in the longer term.[65] In the Kenyan refugee camp of Kalobeyei, refugees have been granted plots of land and the right to sell their produce and to open businesses for more sustainable livelihoods.[66]

Coordinating taxes and monitoring finance, globally

One of the pillars of human development is a system of taxation to finance key human development priorities. But the recent wave of globalization has been weakening governments' ability to collect taxes and curb illicit financial flows.

Move towards a global automatic exchange of information from financial institutions

A global financial register, recording ownership of all financial securities in circulation in the world, would facilitate the work of tax and regulatory authorities tracking income and

BOX 5.7

International Organization for Migration—a new member of the UN family

The International Organization for Migration—the lead global agency on migration—joined the UN system as a related organization in September 2016, precisely when the international community faced the task of coordinating a holistic approach to the global challenge of large movements of migrants and refugees. It embraces areas as diverse as migration, humanitarian assistance (including food security), public health and labour markets. With its new status, cooperation with UN agencies, funds and programmes will be deepened on substantial issues as well as in such areas as administrative cooperation, reciprocal representation and personnel arrangements.

As part of a regional response to the Syrian crisis, the International Organization for Migration provided assistance for 4 million people in Iraq, Jordan, Lebanon, the Syrian Arab Republic and Turkey.[1] It has room for cooperation with the Office of the High Commissioner for Refugees and other specialized UN agencies, funds and programmes. It is expected to play a key role from a migration perspective in the long-term normalization of the crisis, providing services in prescreening, counselling, medical processing, training, transport, reception and integration.[2]

Notes
1. IOM 2016a, 2016b. 2. UNHCR 1997.
Source: Human Development Report Office.

detecting illicit flows. This is feasible if existing registries from main markets are centralized and expanded to include derivatives.[67]

On-demand information (for example, one government requesting information about some taxpayer) is not effective, since it has to go through an investigation with limited information (precisely why information is being requested). But an active global mechanism is feasible. In 2010 the US Congress passed the Foreign Account Tax Compliance Act, which requires financial institutions in the world to inform US tax authorities of assets held by US citizens.[68]

Integrated information systems can reduce illicit financial flows, enabling authorities at both ends of the flows to act against them. For instance, the destination of illicit flows from Africa is concentrated in its main trading partners (Canada, China, Europe, India, Japan, the Republic of Korea and the United States).[69] Given the institutional weakness of most African countries, their trading partners could boost transparency.

Increase technical capacity of countries to process information and implement active policies against tax evasion, tax avoidance and illicit flows

To make the globalization of information work in favour of public policies, governments require preparation. Even if information about foreign assets becomes readily available as the result of a data revolution, its effectiveness will depend on adequate and systematic analysis. So international cooperation should support the development of technical capacity in this area.

Making the global economy sustainable

The Paris Agreement on climate change is a milestone but will not be enough in itself. Experts agree that countries' current pledges to reduce greenhouse gas emissions (intended nationally determined contributions) will not keep global warming below the critical level of 1.5°–2°C above preindustrial levels.[70] In fact, if all countries were to keep to their pledges, the global mean temperature would rise 2.4°–2.7°C by 2100.[71]

Yet curbing global warming is possible. Coordinated global action has worked well in the past, as in moves to halt ozone depletion in the 1990s. The 1987 Montreal Protocol on Substances That Deplete the Ozone Layer and subsequent compliance by signatory states led to a sharp decline in atmospheric chlorine, which depletes the ozone layer.[72] Then, however, both the problem and the solution appeared much more straightforward. Now the world has a clear diagnosis of the problem associated with greenhouse gases, but the solution is not as clear and even less incentive-compatible. Still, things may be changing: A proposed plan to raise global investment in energy efficiency and to expand renewable energy from the current 0.4 percent of GDP a year to 1.5–2 percent of GDP a year would reduce carbon dioxide emissions 40 percent over 20 years, to levels consistent with a limited increase in temperatures, and have positive net macroeconomic effects.[73] With enough political commitment, these targets are feasible.

Technological development has already allowed the decoupling of economic growth and carbon dioxide emissions in 21 countries, including Germany, Spain, Sweden, the United Kingdom and the United States.[74] World economic growth in 2014 and 2015 was not accompanied by emissions growth.[75] So there is space for a good equilibrium. If countries have access to those technologies through new investments, a decisive investment plan can overcome the feared tradeoff between faster economic development and lower greenhouse gas emissions.

Environmentally sustainable policies are not only the right thing to do for future generations, they are also an effective way of promoting human development now. An aggressive investment plan is likely to have a positive effect on job creation, based on estimates in Brazil, China, Germany, India, Indonesia, the Republic of Korea, South Africa, Spain and the United States. In India increasing clean energy investments by 1.5 percent of GDP a year for 20 years will generate a net increase of about 10 million jobs annually, after factoring in job losses from retrenchments in the fossil fuel industries.[76]

Continuing advocacy and communication on the need to address climate change and protect the environment are essential to gather

> Technological development has already allowed the decoupling of economic growth and carbon dioxide emissions in 21 countries

Today's new realities
and aspirations
call for improved
representation of
developing countries
in the governance
of multilateral
organizations

support from governments, corporations and individuals. Technological advances and better knowledge of impacts on the environment have provided the tools to correct ways of living, consuming and producing. This correction will come with a cost, including inevitable job losses in polluting industries. But the 2015 Human Development Report exposed different ways to respond to this challenge, such as targeted social policies and the development of new professional skills for affected workers.[77]

A good balance requires access to technology, economic incentives aligned with green investment, and resources to invest. Indeed, efficiency and sustainability depend on identifying the "right" social costs of the different types of energy and on tackling failures in credit markets.

One promising option is to expand access to credit through national and multilateral development banks. Germany is a world leader in energy efficiency thanks to the decisive action of Germany's state-owned development bank, KfW. Its loans and subsidies for investment in energy-efficiency measures in buildings and industry have leveraged voluminous private funds. And the recently created New Development Bank, which is expected to emphasize sustainable development and renewable energy, has explicitly committed to giving priority to clean energy projects. In 2016 it approved its first package of loans worth $811 million to Brazil, China, India and South Africa.

Assuring greater equity and legitimacy of multilateral institutions

With today's new realities the time has come to examine the governance structures of multilateral institutions.

Increase the voice of developing countries in multilateral organizations

There has been progress over the last few years with the recapitalization of the IMF and multilateral development banks to face the financial crisis, but most developing countries remain under-represented. The UN Security Council should open more space for developing countries. Today's new realities and aspirations call for improved representation of developing countries in the governance of multilateral organizations.

Improve transparency in appointing heads of multilateral organizations

The appointment process of heads of multilateral organizations should be more transparent. The lack of transparency limits the opportunity to shape each organization for future challenges. In 2016 the United Nations made some progress on this front, with the election of the Secretary-General preceded by public declarations of candidacies and public informal dialogues with member states. This progress should continue with more robust processes in all multilateral organizations.

Increase coordination and effectiveness to achieve people-centred goals

The performance of multilateral institutions should be assessed on people's agency and well-being. The multilateral system is committed to achieving the Sustainable Development Goals by 2030. This powerful agenda might require institutional adjustments, such as reshaping entities to strengthen coherence, increase accountability and ensure synergy, or binding mechanisms to make effective the common but differentiated responsibility of countries. The advancement of disadvantaged groups in many parts of the world depends heavily on the consistent work of multilateral organizations (box 5.8).

Ensuring well funded multilateralism and cooperation

The international community should expand the resource envelope for global action, including global financing for national development and for institutional public goods.

Strengthen multilateral and regional development banks

Multilateral and regional development banks can address the lack of resources to support poverty eradication, the knowledge gaps in policymaking, the market failures affecting the financing of socially valuable projects

BOX 5.8

Global institutional developments promoting women's inclusion

Global institutions supporting gender equality and women's empowerment have evolved over the last three decades. In addition to the continuing work of the Commission on the Status of Women (since 1946) and the 1979 Convention on the Elimination of all Forms of Discrimination against Women, two important processes have been under way.

First, the institutional architecture has been expanded since the 1995 Beijing Platform for Action, which defined strategic objectives and actions by governments, regional organizations, multilateral organizations and private sector and civil society organizations. In July 2010 the United Nations Entity for Gender Equality and the Empowerment of Women, also known as UN Women, was created to consolidate the mandates of four previously separate entities in the UN system and to lead, coordinate and promote the accountability of the UN system in its work on gender equality and women's empowerment.

Second, the normative work on gender equality and women's empowerment has been progressively mainstreamed through different instruments, following the rights-based and evidence-based premise that improving the situation of women is not only a moral imperative, but also a prerequisite and an effective—and indispensable—development tool. In 2000 the UN Security Council approved the landmark resolution 1325, stressing the key role of women in preventing and resolving conflicts through peace negotiations, peacebuilding, peacekeeping, humanitarian responses and postconflict reconstruction. In 2015 it approved resolution 2242, strengthening the agenda for Women, Peace and Security within the UN system and defining the accountability of all peace actors, including UN peacekeepers.

The dual role of gender equality and women's empowerment—as a means and end of human development—has been consistently reflected in the global development agenda. In the Millennium Development Goals and in the 2030 Agenda and the Sustainable Development Goals, gender equality and women's empowerment appear both as standalone goals and part of most development objectives. This view, in turn, has trickled down to other multilateral, regional, national and local government entities, supported by a global network of civil society organizations.

A majority of developing regions have achieved gender parity in primary education, and gaps have narrowed in secondary and tertiary education. But in most areas progress has been too slow and uneven.[1] One important global institutional challenge is to generate accurate and updated sex-disaggregated statistical data and information for all countries, particularly in lagged statistical areas such as time use, essential for comprehensive analysis of the economic and noneconomic situation of women and men in a rapidly changing world.

Note
1 UNDESA 2015e.
Source: Human Development Report Office.

(local, national, regional or global) and financial instability.

The World Bank Group is the most important multilateral development bank (with around 50 percent of multilateral development bank disbursements over 2004–2012).[78] Founded to address market failures in international capital markets, it now has the primary goal of reducing extreme poverty. It is also a knowledge bank, collecting and disseminating data and ideas.

Multilateral and regional development banks played an active countercyclical role in the financial crisis of 2008, a role to be strengthened. For example, the multilateral development banks increased their lending to developing and emerging countries 72 percent between 2008 and 2009, precisely when private capital markets were contracting their flows of resources.[79]

They reacted quickly to the paralysis in private trade financing, committing to $9.1 billion, on top of the $3.2 billion they were already providing. The Group of 20 agreed in 2009 to support the recapitalization of multilateral development banks.[80]

Development banks can catalyse long-term private financing and thus leverage public resources. For example, in 2012 the European Investment Bank doubled its paid-in capital by €10 billion, which increased its lending capacity by €80 billion. Given typical cofinancing of at least 50 percent by private investors, this opened financing space of €160 billion.[81] If multilateral development banks diversify, they can accommodate broader objectives in line with the Sustainable Development Goals. In the last few years two very large multilateral

Multilateral and regional development banks played an active countercyclical role in the financial crisis of 2008, a role to be strengthened

FIGURE 5.6

Developing countries would add $191 billion to official development assistance by meeting their contribution target of 0.7 percent of gross national income

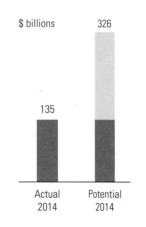

Source: Human Development Report Office calculations based on UNSD (2016).

development banks have been created: the Asian Infrastructure Investment Bank, supporting an infrastructure-led view of development and a regional emphasis (box 5.9), and the New Development Bank, emphasizing sustainable development and renewable energy.

Increase official development assistance from traditional donors

Developed countries should increase their contributions to official development assistance, meeting their commitment of 0.7 percent of gross national income (supported in the Addis Ababa Agenda and a target under Sustainable Development Goal 17). Meeting this target would have added an estimated $191 billion to actual official development assistance in 2014, an increase of 141 percent (figure 5.6). Meeting this Sustainable Development Goal target would be crucial to achieve other Sustainable Development Goals, in particular in the least developed countries—unable to mobilize domestic resources or access private international capital markets.

Expand the participation of developing countries through South–South and triangular cooperation

With the rise of donors that do not form part of the Organisation for Economic Cooperation and Development—Development Assistance Committee, the landscape of development cooperation has been changing, with South-South cooperation and triangular cooperation gaining importance. The first is a long-standing form of international cooperation with its roots in the 1970s; the second emerged at the end of the 1990s. In both forms developing countries share skills, knowledge and resources to meet their development goals. Triangular cooperation includes either a Development Assistance Committee donor or a multilateral institution, facilitating funding, training and management. As suggested by the Paris Declaration for Aid Effectiveness,[82] developing countries should assume ownership of technical cooperation projects and carefully select areas of cooperation and partner countries according to their needs.

BOX 5.9

The new regional development bank—for infrastructure in Asia

Regional development banks provide technical and financial assistance to developing countries through technical cooperation, grants and low-interest loans. Traditionally the regional development banks have included the African Development Bank, the Asian Development Bank, the European Bank for Reconstruction and Development and the Inter-American Development Bank. The Asian Infrastructure Investment Bank, a major new institution, emerged in January 2016.

Considering the substantive challenge of reaching the Sustainable Development Goals by 2030, the regional development banks complement global cooperation. They can disseminate region-specific knowledge, align their programmes and projects to region-specific challenges and appear as more legitimate regional actors than global institutions. The Asian Infrastructure Investment Bank is the first major regional development bank funded mainly by the region's emerging economies. Of $85.9 billion in subscriptions, China contributes 34.7 percent, India 9.7 percent and the Russian Federation 7.6 percent. This reflects a shift towards a

greater role for emerging countries in development finance, with potentially important implications for global governance, including more diverse sources of finance for developing and emerging country borrowers as well as more favourable lending conditions.

The Asian Infrastructure Investment Bank's mandate is slightly different from that of other development banks in that it emphasizes investing in infrastructure and other productive areas rather than directly targeting poverty reduction and social protection.

The expansion of regional development banking is a major step in development policies, but also a management and governance challenge. Griffith-Jones (2016) underscores clear targets in the context of clear development frameworks; good governance to increase efficiency and promote alignment with national development strategies; correct incentives for bank staff and for borrowers to ensure that loans maximize development impact and ensure a minimum commercial return; transparency of operations; and technical assistance to limit adverse social and environmental effects in operations.

Source: Human Development Report Office.

Although financial contributions from most non–Development Assistance Committee donors are not officially reported to the Organisation for Economic Co-operation and Development, some estimates provide insights on the increasing amount of these financial flows to developing countries. Saudi Arabia, as the largest non–Development Assistance Committee donor in financial terms, provided $13.7 billion in 2014, followed by the United Arab Emirates, with $5.1 billion the same year. China increased its aid flows from $2.6 billion in 2010 to $3.4 billion in 2014, and India from $708 million to $1.4 billion. Substantial resources also came from Qatar ($1.3 billion in 2013), the Russian Federation ($876 million in 2014), Mexico ($529 million in 2013), Brazil ($500 million in 2010)[83] and South Africa ($148 million in 2014). Smaller countries such as Chile and Costa Rica have also contributed ($49 million and $24 million, respectively, in 2014), especially in triangular cooperation agreements with other donors.[84]

South–South cooperation has become popular because of several comparative advantages of developing countries. First, given their own very recent path to development, they are more familiar with recent development challenges. Second, many southern countries share the same development contexts and perspectives background as their cooperation partners. Third, some South–South cooperation projects may be more cost-efficient than traditional technical cooperation. Shorter distances between partner countries can reduce travel costs, while fees for translation are saved when the two partner countries speak the same language (table 5.2).

Triangular cooperation has benefits similar to those of South–South cooperation. An example of triangular cooperation is Germany's support for Brazil and Peru to create a Centre for Environmental Technology. The centre trains experts in air technology, the Clean Development Mechanism, regeneration of degraded areas, energy efficiency, renewable energy and innovations in environmental technologies.[85] It was jointly funded by the German Regional Fund for the Promotion of Triangular Cooperation in Latin America and the Caribbean and the Brazilian and Peruvian governments.

Another example of triangular cooperation is Brazil's Centre of Excellence against Hunger. A joint initiative between the World Food

> South–South cooperation has become popular because of several comparative advantages of developing countries

TABLE 5.2

South–South cooperation advantages in Asia and Latin America

Comparative advantage of southern partners	South–South cooperation example
Expertise through recent path to development	Based on India's outstanding capacities in information and communication technology, the Indian government established the Indian Technical and Economic Cooperation Civilian Training Programme. The purpose is to share expertise in information technology, telecommunication, management, renewable energy, small and medium-size enterprise, rural development and other specialized disciplines. Financed with some $32 million by the Indian government, 10,000 participants, mostly from the least developed countries, were trained in 2014–2015.[a]
Alignment thanks to regional background—and cost-efficiency	Argentina and Colombia are cooperating in the peace negotiations between the Colombian government and the Fuerzas Armadas Revolucionarias de Colombia. The two countries are working on a database with genetic profiles of people who disappeared during the conflict to identify and register victims. This work aims at establishing justice and reparation for the victims' families. The common regional background, including the same language and similar culture, can be useful in this delicate work.

a. Asia Foundation 2015.
Source: Human Development Report Office.

Programme and the Brazilian government, the centre makes the successful Brazilian strategy of addressing Zero Hunger available to other developing countries. Brazil had reduced the number of people suffering from hunger from 22.8 million in 1992 to 13.6 million in 2012.[86] The centre, launched in 2011, aims to improve food security, social protection and school attendance (through school feeding) in developing countries—mostly in Africa but also in Asia and Latin America—through training, workshops, technical missions and national consultations.[87]

Explore options for funding global public goods

In view of conflicts, insecurity, financial volatility and environmental degradation, awareness of the need to provide global public goods is increasing, but collective action problems encourage states to free ride. That is why such goods are hugely underfunded.

One option is the traditional mechanism of UN financing, included in the Charter of the United Nations: "The expenses of the organization shall be borne by the Members as apportioned by the General Assembly." In 2014 assessed contributions accounted for around 29 percent of UN system revenues, more than half of which were devoted to peacekeeping operations.[88] Given the growing share of earmarked resources, enhanced mandatory assessed contributions can be explored to increase the global collective capabilities to, for example, deal with crises—such as climate mitigation and adaptation—that have global repercussions. Contributions can be an incentive device, linking them to the generation of negative externalities, such as carbon dioxide emissions.[89]

The Adaptation Fund established under the Kyoto Protocol of the United Nations Framework Convention on Climate Change is financed in part by government and private donors as well as from a 2 percent share of proceeds of Certified Emission Reductions issued under the Protocol's Clean Development Mechanism projects. Since 2010 it has committed almost $360 million to climate adaptation and resilience activities in 61 countries.[90] The collapse of carbon prices has greatly reduced this mechanism's revenues.

A global financial transaction tax to increase funding for developing countries has been proposed by some entities (such as the UN Department of Economic and Social Affairs). As discussed earlier, this would increase the cost of purely speculative financial transactions. Some of the revenues could go towards global public goods.[91] About 30 economies have some form of financial transaction tax. The European Union is the closest to adopting a comprehensive approach, including 10 member states, but has yet to make a final decision.[92]

Other innovative ways to fund global public goods include taxes, fees and levies; funds from private companies; public sources from developing countries (including South–South cooperation); and partnerships that combine sources. UNITAID, established in 2006 by the governments of Brazil, Chile, France, Norway and the United Kingdom, aims to prevent and treat HIV and AIDS, tuberculosis and malaria. Through traditional contributions and an additional tax on airfares, it raises around $300 million a year.[93]

Globally defending people's security

Rising geopolitical instability, challenging globalization and reappearing nationalism and xenophobia in many countries make it more important than ever to bring the world together through multilateral organizations. The existing multilateral institutions have a long-established legitimacy and functioning capacity to convene states around common actions. But they require substantial reforms to address today's issues.

Discussions are under way to ensure that the United Nations provides a forum to reach multilateral decisions promptly in response to major global problems—and that it possesses the means to implement decisions effectively. Some of the proposed solutions are restructuring current mechanisms towards prevention rather than towards mere reaction, prioritizing field operations and coordinating better internally and with civil society and the private sector. In a special contribution, Carol Bellamy, chair of the Governing Board of the Global Community Engagement and Resilience

The existing multilateral institutions have a long-established legitimacy and functioning capacity to convene states around common actions. But they require substantial reforms to address today's issues

Fund and former executive director of United Nations Children's Fund, argues that preventing violent extremism has worked its way onto the global development agenda (see special contribution).

Improve mechanisms to ensure an adequate response to crisis

The 2014 Human Development Report pointed out that today's fragmented global institutions are not accountable or fast-acting enough to address crises. They typically work in an ad hoc manner with neither the mandate nor the resources to tackle modern threats. Each global institution has its own structural problems and drawbacks.[94] For example, the United Nations was founded explicitly to uphold the collective security of sovereign states, a structure that no longer matches today's security threats. It thus suffers from structural legacies of the Cold War—such as Security Council vetoes—that restrict multilateral actions. Humanitarian organizations, which are usually the first to respond to human suffering in the aftermath of natural disasters, see themselves restricted in conflict prevention and resolution because of their need to preserve absolute impartiality towards the belligerents and nondiscrimination towards the victims. They may stay away from peace processes in order to assure their ability to continue their work in case conflict prevention fails.[95]

Such problems highlight first, the need for institutional adequacy and coherence, and second, the need for commensurate resources to tackle these modern threats. Global and multilateral institutions require fundamental reforms that can endow their international efforts with both legitimacy and capacity—boosting their means of implementation.

The international community should be able to act in cases of evident deterioration of human conditions, particularly in crisis situations. The 2014 Human Development Report argues that the responsibility to protect should be expanded beyond mass atrocities to include other intense deprivations in the human security of particular vulnerable groups.[96]

Strengthen global redress mechanisms

For human security the rule of law imposes dual accountability on the state. First, the state has an obligation to victims of violence to bring perpetrators to justice. Second, when agents of the state break the law they too must be held to account. Yet it is precisely in wartorn societies that the rule of law is absent and difficult to rebuild, leaving the demand for justice unmet.

That is why advocates of human rights saw the establishment of the International Criminal Court as one of their major victories. More than a decade later the assessment is sobering. Prosecutions have been few, slow and difficult, with patchy support and cooperation from member states. There is no clear evidence to suggest that the court's action has had a deterrent effect—and enhanced protection and empowerment of victims. On the contrary, the court has encountered severe resistance from governments and local communities.[97] In 2016 Burundi and South Africa announced their withdrawal from it.[98]

Adequate, well equipped and well accepted global redress mechanisms are indispensable for resolving cross-broader issues, such as genocide, ethnic cleansing, refugees, migrant workers, humans trafficked and claims on international or territorial waters. Yet the international forums for deliberating these shared global challenges remain mired with historic deficits in participation and accountability. Global mechanisms to deal with international crimes need to be strengthened, by reasserting country commitments to accountable, collective action at the global level and by holding member states accountable for compliance both in commitments and in action.

Promoting greater and better participation of global civil society in multilateral processes

Greater people's participation should be ensured in multilateral decisionmaking, making it inclusive, equitable and truly global. It should also be based on facts and reason, to produce positive changes in policies.

The international community should be able to act in cases of evident deterioration of human conditions, particularly in crisis situations

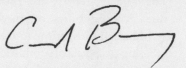

Preventing violent extremism and promoting human development for all: A critical issue on the global development agenda

"Preventing violent extremism" (PVE) has gradually worked its way onto the global development agenda and now seems set to become a permanent fixture.

Initially there was scepticism among many in the development community, but it has gained much wider legitimacy, for example, through the work of the 35 member state Global Counterterrorism Forum (GCTF). At the same time the fact the PVE agenda emerged from a counterterrorism community was a further concern. While welcoming the effort to correct the security-heavy counterterrorism policies of the past, there remained a suspicion that PVE was no more than a fig leaf and that efforts to engage development would simply continue to instrumentalize it.

While the development community is still far from fully converted, a number of recent advances may alleviate concerns. First, the UN Secretary-General has embraced PVE and its relevance to the global development agenda, publishing his Action Plan to Prevent Violent Extremism in January 2016 and calling on all UN agencies to respond. Second, this builds on a clear recognition of the interdependency of security and development in the Sustainable Development Goals. Third, the Development Assistance Committee (DAC) of the Organisation for Economic Co-operation and Development (OECD) has recognized PVE contributions by donors as eligible for official development assistance (ODA) status. As a result, some of the most significant development donors—from the UK Department for International Development (DFID) through the Swiss Agency for Development and Cooperation (SDC) to the US Agency for International Development (USAID)—are now funding PVE activities at scale.

Existing research on what causes and may in turn prevent violent extremism—while still in its infancy—nevertheless points up the potential relevance of development interventions. While one of the challenges of PVE remains that its drivers are context-specific and extremely localized, exclusion and marginalization are constants. How to lift the obstacles to human development generated by exclusion and marginalization is one of the themes for this Human Development Report; and it is clear that doing so

will also help prevent violent extremism. The sorts of interventions that have been demonstrated to be most effective, for example, include empowering women and girls, educating children especially to think critically, and creating positive alternatives such as apprenticeships and jobs.

Beyond the individual and community levels, the linkages between development and violent extremism at the national and global levels are also becoming clearer. Despite media attention to atrocities committed in a growing number of rich countries, it is worth remembering that the impact of violent extremism is felt disproportionately by poor communities in poorer countries. Rapidly developing countries like Egypt, Kenya and Tunisia are losing a significant proportion of their GDP because of the reduction in tourism in response to concerns about extremism and terrorism. The 2015 Global Terrorism Index estimated that the global economic cost of terrorism (including direct and indirect costs) was over $50 billion in 2014, thereby also making a strong business case for private sector engagement.

The Global Community Engagement and Resilience Fund (GCERF) has been at the forefront with initiatives to prevent violent extremism through promoting human development. They are conceived and developed by affected communities and include activities for raising awareness of violent extremism, mobilizing action against it and creating positive alternatives. In its first two years the fund has distributed about $25 million to support local initiatives to build community resilience against violent extremism in Bangladesh, Kenya, Kosovo*, Mali, Myanmar and Nigeria. Such initiatives also seek to bridge different perspectives on security and development among stakeholders and ensure national ownership, doing no harm and protecting the communities that participate.

The challenges of integrating PVE with human development should not be underestimated. But perhaps for the first time in my career, human development for all may actually be attainable. I am strongly committed to contribute to lift a significant barrier that remains in the way of this epochal achievement. Preventing violent extremism is a critical development goal.

Carol Bellamy

Chair of the Governing Board of the Global Community Engagement and Resilience Fund and former executive director of the United Nations Children's Fund

*References to Kosovo shall be understood to be in the context of Security Council Resolution 1244 (1999).

Expand mechanisms for participation of civil society in multilateral institutions

Efforts have already been made to encourage civil society in multilateral institutions, such as including nongovernmental organizations in international debates as observers or consultants. Some civil society organizations participate in international initiatives, alongside governments and intergovernmental organizations. Consider the Busan Partnership for Effective Development Co-operation, which counts the Bill & Melinda Gates Foundation and the civil society network Better Aids among its signatories. Such participation mechanisms should be developed further to ensure that the civil society organizations involved represent a wide range of interests.

Enhance the transparency and accountability of multilateral institutions

Information and communication technologies provide new tools for civil society and concerned individuals from around the world to monitor the commitments and results of multilateral institutions. Some multilateral institutions recently published databases online so that the public could use them for monitoring and advocacy, starting with the United Nations in 2008,[99] the World Bank in 2011[100] and the European Union in 2012.[101] Other mechanisms include online petitions to address multilateral bodies on specific issues. To support these new forms of civil participation, more people must possess computer skills and have access to the Internet.

Promote and support inclusive global civil society networks focused on specific groups

Networks of women; young people; ethnic minorities; persons with disabilities; lesbian, gay, bisexual, transgender and intersex people; and displaced workers make their voices stronger in the global arena and facilitate peer-learning of best practices to promote inclusion in every country. Civil society has been praised for its positive impact on women's participation in public and political life (box 5.10).

Increase the free flow of information and knowledge through active transparency mechanisms

In the long term both market and multilateral institutions will benefit from the accountability ensured by a well informed civil society. Well regulated markets collect and disseminate information about prices, wages, taxes paid and service quality. Similarly, multilateral initiatives are standardizing open government practices, such as the Open Government Partnership, which has 70 member countries.[102] Multilateral organizations must themselves be accountable not only to member states, but also to civil society.

The International Aid Transparency Initiative is a global benchmark for multilateral organizations to publish relevant information on their programmes. Open government data initiatives publish raw data on freely accessible websites; in 2014, 86 countries provided government data in machine-readable structures, such as Microsoft Excel.[103] The United States launched the Open Government Initiative in 2009,[104] joined by the United Kingdom in 2010,[105] Kenya in 2011,[106] Ghana in 2012[107] and Japan in 2013,[108] to cite a few.

Multilateral organizations must themselves be accountable not only to member states, but also to civil society

BOX 5.10

Civil society and women's participation

Women are less represented than men in traditional political forums. In 2015 women held 22.5 percent of national parliamentary seats worldwide. When women face discrimination in formally entering political or public life, civil society presents them with alternatives for participation. Of the 11,554 UN online volunteers who contributed their skills for peace and development in 2015, 59 percent were women.[1] Civil society organizations have been advocating for gender equity and raising awareness of women's rights violations for decades.

The role of civil society in gender initiatives is now fully recognized by multilateral institutions. The United Nations Entity for Gender Equality and the Empowerment of Women regards civil society as one of its most important constituencies, playing "a pivotal role in advancing gender equality and the empowerment of women".[2] In 2016 the Commission on the Status of Women agreed to increase resources and support for women's and civil society organizations to promote gender equality, the empowerment of women and the rights of women and girls. The United Nations Development Programme's 2014–2017 Gender Equality Strategy also plans to support women's networks and civil society movements to bring gender equality perspectives into policymaking and legal reforms.

Notes
1. UNV 2016. 2. UN Women 2014.
Source: Human Development Report Office.

Protect the work of international investigative journalism

Freedoms of expression and of information are fundamental human rights recognized in the Universal Declaration of Human Rights and the International Covenant on Civil and Political Rights. They are also instrumental in human development and human security. Free and competent media can ensure transparency, accountability and the rule of law, promote participation in public and political discourse and contribute to the fight against poverty. Yet freedom of the press has been under attack worldwide in recent years, with investigative journalists risking their freedom and sometimes their lives for their work. The United Nations recommends making freedom of expression possible through:[109]

- A legal and regulatory environment that allows for an open and pluralistic media sector to emerge.
- Political will to support the sector and rule of law to protect.
- Laws ensuring access to information, especially information in the public domain.
- Media literacy skills among news consumers to critically analyse and synthesize the information they receive to use it in their daily lives and to hold the media accountable for its actions.

The media have uncovered war crimes, asymmetries in global markets, abuses of privacy on the Internet and problems in international organizations, information essential for improving national and global institutions.

Conclusion

The transformation of global institutions can expand human development for everyone. It is a process that requires a delicate balance among the regulation of markets, the governance of multilateral organizations and the participation of an increasingly interconnected global civil society. The three are linked, and their reciprocal accountability is crucial to undertake reforms. Global markets are a great source of dynamism, but they need to be properly regulated to work for the majority. These regulations in turn need to be rooted in legitimate multilateral processes, where the interests of developing countries are central and where the voices of people contribute to the deliberative process. These transformations at the global level are essential for achieving human development for everyone.

Chapter 6 builds on the national policies and global reforms to propose a five point action agenda. It also looks forward to identify the substantive work on human development that needs to be undertaken to extend the frontiers of knowledge on human development for everyone..

> The transformation of global institutions can expand human development for everyone

Chapter **6**

Human development for everyone— looking forward

Infographic 6.1 Human development for everyone— a five-point action agenda

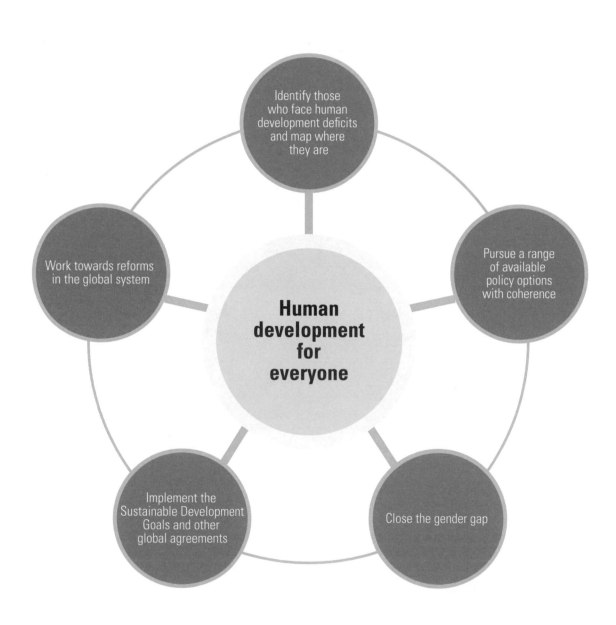

Identify those who face human development deficits and map where they are

Pursue a range of available policy options with coherence

Close the gender gap

Implement the Sustainable Development Goals and other global agreements

Work towards reforms in the global system

Human development for everyone

6.

Human development for everyone— looking forward

We want a world where human development reaches everyone and no one is left behind—now or in the future. In that broader perspective the preceding chapters have articulated the message that since universalism is key to human development, it is both an ethical imperative and a practical requirement. The human development journey will not be universal if we leave anyone behind, and we cannot build a peaceful and prosperous world by excluding people on the path.

Human development for everyone is not a dream; it is a realizable goal. We can build on what we have achieved. We can explore new possibilities to overcome challenges. We can attain what once seemed unattainable, for what seem to be challenges today can be overcome tomorrow. Realizing our hopes is within our reach. The 2030 Agenda and the Sustainable Development Goals are critical steps towards human development for everyone.

But the reality is that the impressive progress on many human development fronts over the past 25 years has bypassed many people, particularly those who are marginalized and vulnerable. Such progress has enriched many lives—but not to the same extent and certainly not for all. The barriers are still substantial— economic, political and social—for all human beings to realize their full potential in life. Such barriers are particularly stark for women and girls, since they are discriminated against just because of their gender.

Overcoming such inequality and barriers is a prerequisite for human development for everyone. Despite the barriers to universalism, a more just, equitable and inclusive world must be viewed as achievable. Particularly where the financial and technological resources exist to eliminate deprivations, the persistence of such injustice is indefensible. A more equal world calls for practical and immediate action on three fronts. First is implementing relevant measures from the range of available policy options. Second is reforming global governance with fairer multilateralism. And third is refocusing on analytical issues, such as disaggregated indicators, voice and autonomy measures and qualitative assessments of human development.

The world has fewer than 15 years to achieve the aspirational and inspirational goals to eradicate poverty, end hunger, achieve gender equality and empower all women and girls. Time is of the essence, as Sub-Saharan Africa shows (figure 6.1). To eliminate extreme poverty by 2030, it must progress twice as fast as its current rate. If nothing happens in the next six years, progress will have to be more than three times faster.[1] If numbers stagnate in the next 11 years, progress will have to be eight times faster.

Human development for everyone—an action agenda

In the context of these aspirations, the Report builds on its analysis and findings to suggest a five-point action agenda for ensuring human development for everyone (see infographic 6.1 on the facing page). These actions cover policy issues and global commitments

Identifying those who face human development deficits and mapping where they are

Identifying those who have been left out of the progress in human development and mapping their locations are not just parts of an academic exercise, they are essential tasks for useful advocacy and for effective policymaking. Such mapping can help development activists demand action and guide policymakers in formulating and implementing policies to improve the well-being of marginalized and vulnerable people. National and subnational Human Development Reports can be useful instruments for identifying those left behind and mapping their locations.

Identifying those who have been left out of the progress in human development and mapping their locations are not just parts of an academic exercise, they are essential tasks for useful advocacy and for effective policymaking

FIGURE 6.1

Reaching everyone—time is of the essence in Sub-Saharan Africa

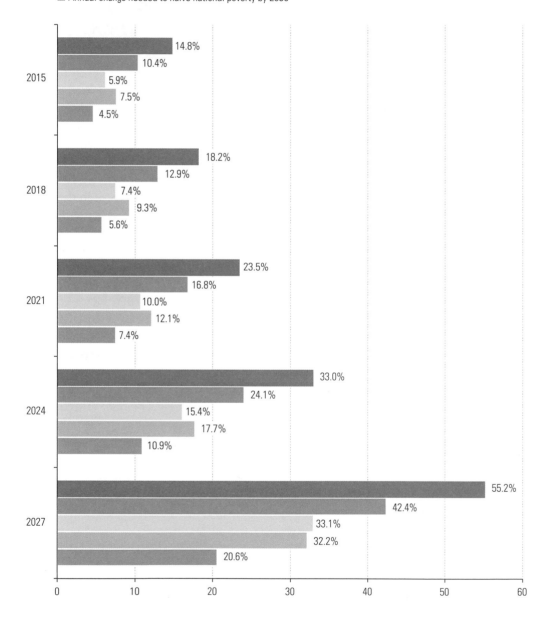

■ Annual change needed to eliminate education poverty by 2030
■ Annual change needed to eliminate ultra poverty[a] by 2030
■ Annual change needed to achieve universal birth registration by 2030
■ Annual change needed to reduce under-five mortality to 25 preventable deaths per 1,000 live births by 2030
■ Annual change needed to halve national poverty by 2030

a. Defined as poverty in which individuals cannot afford to meet daily recommended food requirements.
Source: ODI 2016.

BOX 6.1

Administrative registries in Latin America and the Caribbean

Administrative registries collect multidimensional data on such subjects as time use, income and subjective well-being. A well known example is Brazil's Cadastro Único shared registry, which provides panel data on the vulnerable population, defined as households earning half or less of a minimum wage per person or three minimum wages in all. The database contains information on the characteristics of the household and each family member and on their social and economic circumstances and access to public services.

Run by Caixa Econômica Federal, a public bank, the database covers about 78 million people, mainly to assign benefits for Bolsa Família, the well known cash transfer programme. It has increased the programme's outreach while mitigating the risk of data manipulation, fraud and clientelism, for which Bolsa Família was earlier criticized.

Other countries in Latin America and the Caribbean have followed Brazil's lead. The Dominican Republic's Single Beneficiary Selection System helps identify and classify households eligible for social programmes. This targeting mechanism has been key for channelling resources to the most vulnerable households, while also improving the monitoring and evaluation of social policy programmes.

A single national database for determining eligibility has other benefits, such as preventing duplication (otherwise people may receive benefits from several programmes), reducing administrative costs across programmes and facilitating the monitoring of criteria for time limits and graduation.

Source: Checchi and van der Werfhorst 2014; ILO 2014a; World Bank 2015c.

A critical element of such a mapping exercise is collecting relevant information and data. Rather than traditional census and household surveys, innovative data collection mechanisms —such as administrative registries, as pursued in some countries in Latin America and the Caribbean—can be more effective (box 6.1).

Pursuing a range of available policy options with coherence

Translating universalism from principle to practice will have to go beyond mapping those left out in the human development journey and identifying the barriers they face. Pursuing necessary policies and empowering those left out are a must.

Human development for everyone requires a multipronged set of national policy options (see chapter 4): reaching those left out using universal policies, pursuing measures for groups with special needs, making human development resilient and empowering those left out.

Keep in mind, however, that country situations differ and policy options have to be tailored to each country. Policies in every country have to be pursued in a coherent way through multistakeholder engagement, local and subnational adaptations and horizontal (across silos) and vertical policy coherence (for international and global consistency).

Closing the gender gap

Gender equality and women's empowerment are fundamental dimensions of human development. With half of humanity lacking equal progress in human development, human development is not universal. This simple but a powerful truth is often forgotten in the preoccupation with average human progress.

Gender gaps exist in capabilities as well as opportunities. As the 2016 Global Gender Gap Report indicates, progress is still too slow for realizing the full potential of half of humanity within our lifetimes.[2] On current trends East Asia and the Pacific will take 111 years to close just the economic gender gap (not to speak of other gender gaps), and the Middle East and North Africa, 356 years.

At a historic gathering in New York in September 2015 some 80 world leaders committed to end discrimination against women by 2030 and announced concrete and measurable national actions to kickstart rapid changes. The commitments address the most pressing barriers for women, such as increasing investment in gender equality, reaching parity for women at all levels of decisionmaking, eliminating discriminatory legislation and tackling social norms that perpetuate discrimination and violence against women. Now is the time to act on what has been promised and agreed.

Gender equality and women's empowerment are fundamental dimensions of human development

Implementing the Sustainable Development Goals and other global agreements

The Sustainable Development Goals, critical in their own right, are also crucial for human development for everyone; the 2030 Agenda and the human development approach are mutually reinforcing. Further, achieving the Sustainable Development Goals is an important step for all human beings to realize their full potential in life. In that context the focus should be not only on people who are "just behind and visible," but also on those who are "far behind and invisible." Tracking and monitoring the Sustainable Development Goals are thus important to measure progress, identify gaps in sustainable development and change policies and implementation plans, if development is off track. Her Excellency Angela Merkel, chancellor of the Federal Republic of Germany, argues that all of humanity will have to work together towards realizing the inspirational 2030 Agenda (see special contribution).

The historic Paris Agreement on climate change is the first to consider both developed and developing countries in a common framework, urging them all to make their best efforts and reinforce their commitments in the coming years (box 6.2). All parties should now report regularly on their emissions and their efforts to implement their commitments, submitting to international review. On another front, the New York Declaration, announced at the UN Summit for Refugees in September 2016, contains bold commitments to address the issues facing refugees and migrants and to prepare for future challenges (box 6.3). The international community, national governments and all other parties must ensure that the agreements are honoured, implemented and monitored.

Working towards reforms in the global system

In today's globalized world, national policies for universal human development must be complemented and supplemented by a global system that is fair and that enriches human development. The current architecture of the global system has five glaring shortcomings: the governance of economic globalization is

> The Sustainable Development Goals, critical in their own right, are also crucial for human development for everyone; the 2030 Agenda and the human development approach are mutually reinforcing

---

BOX 6.2

The Paris Agreement on climate change

The key outcomes of the Conference of the Parties of the United Nations Framework Convention on Climate Change were the Paris Agreement and a companion decision known as the 21st Session. Among their provisions:
- Reaffirm the goal of limiting global temperature increase to well below 2°C above preindustrial levels, while urging efforts to limit the increase to 1.5°C.
- Establish binding commitments by all parties to make nationally determined contributions and pursue domestic measures aimed at achieving the contributions.
- Commit all countries to report regularly on their emissions and progress in implementing and achieving nationally determined contributions and to undergo international review.
- Commit all countries to submit new nationally determined contributions every five years, with the clear expectation that they will represent progress beyond the previous contributions.

- Reaffirm the binding obligations of developed countries under the United Nations Framework Convention on Climate Change to support the efforts of developing countries, while encouraging voluntary contributions by developing countries, too.
- Extend through 2025 the current goal of mobilizing $100 billion a year in support by 2020 with a higher goal to be set for the period after 2025.
- Extend a mechanism to address the loss and damage resulting from climate change, which explicitly will not involve or provide a basis for any liability or compensation.
- Require parties engaging in international emissions trading to avoid double counting.
- Call for a new mechanism, similar to the Clean Development Mechanism under the Kyoto Protocol, that enables emission reductions in one country to be counted towards another country's nationally determined contributions.

Source: UNFCCC 2015.

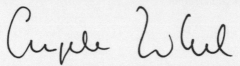

The Sustainable Development Goals—shared vision, collective responsibilities

Human dignity is inviolable. This principle has not changed since 1948 when it was formulated by the United Nations in the Universal Declaration of Human Rights. It does not stop at national borders and applies to everyone regardless of age, gender or religion. However, to what extent have we lived up to this high principle? How far have we progressed in reality towards ensuring that every individual can lead a life in dignity? The Human Development Report sheds light on this regularly. By placing the focus on individuals, it also highlights the necessity of investing in people: in health, in education and training, in economic and social infrastructure.

Poverty and hunger, state fragility and terror—we are aware of these and other existential challenges. However, we also know that good human development is possible. Even in the poorest regions there are not only natural resources, but also tremendous creativity, innovative drive and a willingness to work hard. We have to make the most of these assets in order to seize the opportunities for a life in dignity—regardless of how difficult that might be in some cases.

At a time of increasing globalization, life chances on the different continents are more closely interconnected than ever before. It is therefore all the more important to act jointly on the basis of shared values. That is why we have adopted the 2030 Agenda with its global Sustainable Development Goals. That is why we have concluded a global climate agreement. As a result of these instruments, all states have an obligation and responsibility to tackle the key challenges facing humankind—from the eradication of poverty and the protection of the climate, nature and the environment to ensuring peace.

In many respects, viable answers to such crucial questions require us to fundamentally change how we think and act in the way we live and work. The economy, social issues and the environment have an impact on each other. Economic productivity, social responsibility and protection of the natural resources on our planet therefore have to be reconciled. This is exactly the meaning of the principle of sustainability, which the 2030 Agenda is aiming for. In its essence, it is about nothing less than a life in dignity, justice and peace, a life in an intact environment, social security and the opportunity for every individual to reach their economic potential.

The 2030 Agenda has laid the cornerstone of a new global partnership in which Germany too is assuming an active role. Already in July 2016, at the first High-Level Political Forum in New York, the German government reported on the steps taken towards implementing the agenda at national level, as well as the measures to follow. At the international level we will use our G20 presidency in 2017 in particular to set priorities on the AGENDA.

The consistent implementation of the 2030 Agenda also calls for a transformation of the international system. One key task of the new UN Secretary-General, António Guterres, will therefore be to make the UN structures and institutions fit for purpose. Germany will be happy to support him in this process.

Modern information and communications technologies offer major opportunities for the successful implementation of the 2030 Agenda. They boost the efficiency, effectivity and transparency of measures and processes, thus saving time and money. They open up new possibilities for dialogue and cooperation. They enable everyone to have access to knowledge.

Broader access to information can, not least, promote development policy goals in areas such as good governance and rural development, as well as education, health and the development of financial systems. The development and expansion of digital infrastructure can create new opportunities for economic growth and employment in both industrialized and developing countries. The important thing is to eliminate existing differences not only between industrialized and developing countries, but also within developing countries, for example between urban and rural regions.

Alongside access to modern technologies, there is the question of digital inclusion. The right qualifications are essential if every man and woman is to participate in the digital world on an equal basis in both economic and social terms. This, too, will be one of the focal issues during Germany's G20 presidency.

Not only determination, but also unity are required in order to master the diverse global challenges and in some cases crisis-ridden developments. The 2030 Agenda provides us with a comprehensive and forward-looking approach for shaping our world together—not any old way, not at the expense of people and nature in other regions but for the benefit of everyone in our one world. We all have a responsibility, day in and day out, to make sustainability a guiding principle in action—as responsible politicians and decisionmakers in business and society, as individuals who are truly interested in our future.

Before the adoption of the 2030 Agenda it was the time to negotiate. Now is the time to act. It is up to us to enable everyone to live a life in dignity.

Dr. Angela Merkel
Chancellor of the Federal Republic of Germany

unbalanced, globalization remains inequitable, imbalances exist in the governance of multilateral institutions, multilateralism remains reactive to human security and the potential of global civil society remains untapped.

These shortcomings pose challenges to human development on several fronts. The distributional consequences of inequitable globalization promote the progress of some segments of the population, leaving poor and

The New York Declaration

- Protect the human rights of all refugees and migrants, regardless of status. This includes the rights of women and girls and promoting their full, equal and meaningful participation in finding solutions.
- Ensure that all refugee and migrant children are receiving education within a few months of arrival.
- Prevent and respond to sexual and gender-based violence.
- Support those countries rescuing, receiving and hosting large numbers of refugees and migrants.
- Work towards ending the practice of detaining children for the purposes of determining their migration status.
- Strongly condemn xenophobia against refugees and migrants and support a global campaign to counter it.
- Strengthen the positive contributions made by migrants to economic and social development in their host countries.

- Improve the delivery of humanitarian and development assistance to those countries most affected, including through innovative multilateral financial solutions, with the goal of closing all funding gaps.
- Implement a comprehensive refugee response based on a new framework that sets out the responsibility of Member States, civil society partners and the UN system, whenever there is a large movement of refugees or a protracted refugee situation.
- Find new homes for all refugees identified by the United Nations High Commissioner for Refugees as needing resettlement and expand the opportunities for refugees to relocate to other countries through, for example, labour mobility or education schemes.
- Strengthen the global governance of migration by bringing the International Organization for Migration into the UN system.

Source: United Nations 2016i.

> Voice and autonomy have become more important not only in their own right, but also as critical instruments for the empowerment and well-being of those left out

vulnerable people behind. Such globalization makes those left behind economically insecure. And people suffer in lingering conflicts.

To move towards a fairer global system, the agenda for global institutional reforms should focus on global markets and their regulation, on the governance of multilateral institutions and on the strengthening of global civil society. That reform agenda should be promoted vigorously and consistently by bolstering public advocacy, building alliances among stakeholders and pushing through the agenda for reform.

Human development for everyone —future substantive work

To ensure universal human development, the action agenda for policies and reforms will have to be backed by substantive work on analytical issues and assessment perspectives. The substantive work must begin with the why questions. Why are people discriminated? Why have social norms and values evolved to what they are now? Answering will require not only economic analysis, but also sociological and anthropological studies.

Some issues in the human development approach need to be refocused. So far, the approach has concentrated more on freedom of well-being than on freedom of agency. This may have a historical reason. In earlier years basic deprivations were more significant, deserving the most analysis, measurement and policy response. But as well-being has been realized, freedom of agency has become more important. Voice and autonomy have become more important not only in their own right, but also as critical instruments for the empowerment and well-being of those left out.

The focus also has to be on analysing and understanding collective capabilities. Collective agency is critical for people who are marginalized and vulnerable, who may not be able to achieve much alone. And because poor and disadvantaged people suffer most from insecurities and vulnerabilities, human security needs to be analysed through its links with human development and the balance between short-term responses and long-term prevention.

To ensure human development for everyone, future substantive work should also concentrate on assessing human development. Reaching everyone requires disaggregated data and the pursuit of three other issues.

First, assessments of human development so far have focused on quantitative achievements. But with progress in human development, quality has also become important. For example, more children are enrolled in and attending school, but what are they learning? So along with quantitative monitoring of progress in human development, it is equally important to assess the quality of those achievements.

Second, even though it is more difficult to measure voice and autonomy, research should focus on developing such a measure. Much has been written on this, and human development assessments can build on that work. Such a measure would not only complement the Human Development Index (a measure of well-being), it would also be a powerful instrument to advocate for the voiceless.

Third, various measures of well-being and deprivations have been proposed from different perspectives. Those left out suffer deprivation in multiple aspects of life. So it is crucial that we have a clear idea of multiple deprivations and well-being. Examining how human development measures can benefit from the other measures of well-being would be a worthwhile exercise.

Because universalism is central to the human development approach, some of these analytical and assessment issues would inform and guide the research, analysis and work of future Human Development Reports, including the 2017 Report. This is necessary to extend the frontiers of the human development approach, to better understand human development issues and to address future human development challenges.

Conclusion

From a human development perspective, we want a world where all human beings have the freedom to realize their full potential in life so they can attain what they value. This is what human development is all about—universalism, leaving no one behind. Universal human development must enable all people—regardless of their age, citizenship, religion, ethnicity, gender, sexual orientation or any other identity—to expand their capabilities fully and put those capabilities to use. This also means that capabilities and opportunities are sustainable throughout an individual's lifecycle and across generations. But those less endowed or lagging behind need support from others—from individuals, communities and states—to realize their full potential.

In the ultimate analysis, development is of the people, by the people and for the people. People have to partner with each other. There needs to be a balance between people and the planet. And humanity has to strive for peace and prosperity. Human development requires recognizing that every life is equally valuable and that human development for everyone must start with those farthest behind.

The 2016 Human Development Report is an intellectual contribution to resolving these issues. We strongly believe that only after they are resolved will we all reach the end of the road together. And when we look back, we will see that no one has been left out.

Human development requires recognizing that every life is equally valuable and that human development for everyone must start with those farthest behind

Notes

Overview

1 UNFPA 2014.
2 United Nations 2015a.
3 United Nations 2015c.
4 UNDP 1990.
5 United Nations 2015a.
6 United Nations 2016h.
7 United Nations 2016h.
8 UNICEF 2014a.
9 IEA 2016b.
10 UNAIDS 2016a.
11 UNHCR 2016a.
12 UNDP 2014a.
13 SIDA 2015.
14 UNDP 2016e.
15 UNDESA 2016a.
16 WHO 2011b.
17 UNFPA 2015.
18 ILGA 2016b.
19 Charmes 2015.
20 Abadeer 2015.
21 Human Development Report Office calculation using data from Milanović (2016).
22 The Social Progress Imperative's Social Progress Index website (www.socialprogressimperative.org/global-index/, accessed 12 December 2016).
23 The Sustainable Development Solutions Network's World Happiness Report website (http://worldhappiness.report, accessed 12 December 2016).
24 The Organisation for Economic Co-operation and Development's Better Life Index website (www.oecdbetterlifeindex.org, accessed 12 December 2016).
25 Centre for Bhutan Studies and GNH Research's Gross National Happiness Index website (www.grossnationalhappiness.com/articles/, accessed 12 December 2016).
26 In 2009 the UN Secretary-General created the Global Pulse initiative aiming to harness Big Data as a public good in the service of sustainable development and humanitarian action. In 2014 the UN Statistical Commission formed a Global Working Group on Big Data. The Global Partnership on Sustainable Development Data was formed among governments, corporate, UN and international financial institutions, nonprofits and academic stakeholders. It currently has 150 members.
27 Demirgüç-Kunt and others 2014.
28 Harris and Marks 2009.
29 WFP 2016b.
30 World Bank 2016i.
31 UNESCO 2013b.
32 World Bank 2015b.
33 The Economist 2016c.
34 UNDESA 2016a.
35 WEF 2016a.
36 Cecchini and others 2015.
37 Cashin 2016.
38 UN Women 2016a.
39 UNDESA 2016a.
40 UNDESA 2016a.
41 UNAIDS 2016d.
42 WHO 2016j.
43 The Guardian 2016a.
44 WHO 2016j.
45 World Bank 2015a.
46 World Bank 2015a.
47 UNDP 2015a.
48 Demos Helsinki 2016.
49 United Nations 2013.
50 UN Women 2015b.

Chapter 1

1 Jahan 2010.
2 UNDP 1994.
3 UNDP 1995.
4 UNDP 1997. The Human Poverty Index was replaced by the Multidimensional Poverty Index in 2010.
5 UNDP 1994
6 Jahan 2003.
7 UNDP 2002, 2004, 2007, 2011b, 2015a.
8 UNDP 2017.
9 UNDP and IAER 2013.
10 World Bank 2017.
11 IFPRI 2015; United Nations 2015a.
12 WHO 2015c, 2016b.
13 UNICEF 2014a.
14 IEA 2016b; UNAIDS 2016a.
15 UNHCR 2016a.
16 UNHCR 2016a.
17 FAO 2016a.
18 IEP 2010.
19 Street Child 2014.
20 Human Development Report Office estimates based on data from UNDESA (2015d), UNESCO Institute for Statistics (2016), UNSD (2016), World Bank (2016o), Barro and Lee (2015) and IMF (2016d).
21 World Bank 2016i.
22 World Bank 2017.
23 United Nations 2016h.
24 United Nations 2016h.
25 United Nations 2016h.
26 United Nations 2016h.
27 United Nations 2015a.
28 United Nations 2015a.
29 United Nations 2015a.
30 WHO 2016i.
31 United Nations 2015a.
32 United Nations 2015a.
33 United Nations 2015a.
34 United Nations 2015a.
35 United Nations 2015a.
36 United Nations 2015a.
37 United Nations 2015a.
38 United Nations 2015a.
39 United Nations 2016h.
40 ITU 2016a.
41 World Bank 2016e.
42 UNDESA 2016d.
43 WHO 2011a; UNDESA 2014a.
44 Cukier and Mayer-Schoenberger 2013.
45 World Bank 2017.
46 UNICEF and World Bank 2016.
47 WFP 2016a.
48 Fink and others 2016.
49 FAO 2011a.
50 McKenzie 2014.
51 UNICEF 2016c.
52 UNESCO Institute for Statistics 2016.
53 ILO 2016d.
54 Woosey 2005; Lattier 2015.
55 Niño-Zarazúa, Roope and Tarp 2016.
56 World Bank 2016i.
57 Lawson 2016.
58 Saez and Zucman 2014.
59 World Bank 2016p.
60 United Nations 2016h.
61 DFID 2010.
62 UNDESA 2014b.
63 World Bank 2015g.
64 World Bank 2016d.
65 United Nations 2015a; WEF 2015.
66 WEF 2015.
67 UNDESA 2014b.
68 UNDESA 2015c.
69 UNDESA 2015a.
70 UNDESA 2015b.
71 Kharas and Gertz 2010.
72 The Economist 2016a.
73 Kharas and Gertz 2010.
74 Ehrentreund 2016.
75 UNFPA 2014.
76 UNDESA 2015b.
77 UNFPA 2016.
78 Office of the Secretary-General's Envoy on Youth 2016.
79 ILO 2015a; UNDESA 2016e.
80 UNDESA 2016e.
81 ILO 2016e.
82 S4YE 2015.
83 ManpowerGroup 2016.
84 World Bank 2017.
85 ILO 2015b.
86 Fajgelbaum and Khandelwal 2016.
87 UNCTAD 2015.
88 McKinsey Global Institute 2014.
89 UNDP 2015a.
90 The Economist 2016e.
91 The Economist 2016e.
92 UNHCR 2016a.
93 UNHCR 2016a.
94 UNICEF 2016e.
95 UNHCR 2016a.
96 Purdie and Khaltarkhuu 2016.
97 Purdie and Khaltarkhuu 2016.
98 FAO and WFP 2016.
99 United Nations 2000a.
100 UN Women 2012.
101 United Nations Peacekeeping 2016.
102 IEP 2016.
103 IEP 2015.
104 The Economist 2016b.
105 IEP 2016.
106 IEP 2016.
107 IANYD 2016.
108 UNESCO 2016a.
109 ILO 2015c.
110 World Bank 2016c.
111 World Bank 2016c.
112 World Bank 2016c.
113 WHO 2016h.
114 UNAIDS 2014a.
115 UNAIDS 2016b.
116 UNAIDS 2014b.
117 UNAIDS 2016b.
118 WHO 2015d.
119 WHO 2015b.
120 Ng and others 2014.
121 World Bank 2015d.
122 WHO 2016a.
123 World Bank 2016b.
124 CRED and UNISDR 2015.
125 UNISDR 2015.
126 UNDP 2016f.
127 UNCCD 2015.
128 Braimoh 2015.
129 Newbold and others 2016.
130 Gjerde 2006; Parker 2015; PlasticsEurope 2013.
131 Gall and Thompson 2015.
132 GAHP 2014.
133 IEA 2016b.
134 World Bank and IHME 2016.
135 IEA 2016b.
136 IEA 2016b.
137 World Bank 2016n.
138 Chao 2012.
139 FAO 2016b.
140 Mekonnen and Hoekstra 2016.
141 World Bank 2016a.
142 EIA 2016.
143 Goody and others 2015; IEA 2016c.
144 United Nations 2016h.
145 United Nations 2010.
146 WHO 2016c.
147 Hallegatte and others 2016.
148 World Bank 2017.
149 World Bank 2016i.
150 Demirgüç-Kunt and others 2014.
151 United Nations 2015a.
152 PAHO-WHO 2016a.
153 PAHO-WHO 2016b.
154 United Nations 2015a.
155 Stuart and others 2016.
156 Stuart and others 2016.
157 Peracod 2012.
158 Avaaz 2016.
159 Hollow 2013.
160 Spacehive 2016.
161 Austin 2011.
162 Statista 2016.
163 Dean and others 2012.
164 UNDP 2015a.
165 UNICEF 2004.
166 Watson 2016.
167 Arekapudi 2014.
168 Arekapudi 2014.

169 Arekapudi 2014.
170 Indrawati 2015.
171 Indrawati 2015.
172 IOC 2016.
173 Ford 2016.
174 *New York Times* 2016.
175 Indrawati 2015.
176 Indrawati 2015.
177 UN Women 2016b.
178 UN Women 2016b.
179 UN Women 2013.
180 BBC News 2016b.
181 Indrawati 2015.
182 Indrawati 2015.
183 Pew Research Center 2015b.
184 Raub and others 2016.
185 Greytak and others 2016.
186 Lyons 2015.
187 UN Women 2016b.
188 Le Coz 2016.
189 Ghosh 2016.
190 UN Women 2016b.
191 BBC News 2016a.
192 Avon Global Center for Women and
    Justice and others 2011.
193 UN Women 2016b.
194 Clark 2016.
195 Banerjee 2016.
196 Kynge 2016.
197 World Bank and ECOFYS 2016.
198 ITC 2014.
199 IEA 2016c.
200 United Nations 2015c.
201 C2ES 2015.
202 United Nations 2016e.
203 Bokova 2016.

Chapter 2

1 UNDESA 2016c.
2 HDI classifications are based on HDI
   fixed cutoff points, which are derived
   from the quartiles of distributions of
   the component indicators. The cutoff
   points are less than 0.550 for low
   human development, 0.550–0.699
   for medium human development,
   0.700–0.799 for high human development and 0.800 or greater for very
   high human development.
3 UNDP 2014c.
4 UNDP 2014d.
5 Human Development Report Office
   estimate.
6 Human Development Report Office estimates based on abridged life-tables
   of the United Nations Department of
   Economic and Social Affairs (UNDESA
   2015d) and data of the Luxembourg
   Income Study database (LIS 2016),
   Eurostat's European Union Statistics
   on Income and Living Conditions
   (Eurostat 2016b), the World Bank's
   International Income Distribution
   Data Set (World Bank 2013), United
   Nations Children's Fund Multiple
   Indicator Cluster Surveys (UNICEF
   2016b) and Demographic and Health
   Surveys (ICF International 2016)
   using the methodology described in

Technical note 2 (available at http://
hdr.undp.org/sites/default/files/
hdr2016_technical_notes.pdf).
7 Human Development Report Office
   estimates based on UNDESA (2015d).
8 Human Development Report Office
   estimates based on data from
   UNDESA (2015d), UNESCO Institute
   for Statistics (2016), UNSD (2016),
   World Bank (2016o), Barro and Lee
   (2015) and IMF (2016d).
9 Human Development Report Office
   estimates based on the GDI.
10 Human Development Report Office
   estimates based on data from the UN
   Maternal Mortality Estimation Group
   (2016), UNDESA (2015d), IPU (2016),
   UNESCO Institute for Statistics (2016)
   and ILO (2016c).
11 Human Development Report Office
   estimates based on IPU (2016), ILO
   (2016c), UN Maternal Mortality
   Estimation Group (2016), UNDESA
   (2015d) and UNESCO (2016b).
12 Human Development Report
   Office estimates based on data on
   household deprivations in education,
   health and living standards from
   various household surveys using the
   methodology described in *Technical
   note 1* (available at http://hdr.undp.
   org/sites/default/files/hdr2016_
   technical_notes.pdf).
13 United Nations 2015a.
14 United Nations 2015a.
15 UN-Habitat 2014.
16 Human Development Report Office
   estimates.
17 Agbor 2012.
18 Watkins, van Fleet and Greubel 2012.
19 Phiri and Ataguba 2014.
20 UNICEF 2014a.
21 UNESCO 2015a.
22 UNESCO 2015b.
23 Human Development Report Office
   estimates based on ILO (2016c).
24 SIDA 2015.
25 United Nations 2015a.
26 Human Development Report Office
   estimates based on UNESCO (2016b).
27 Human Development Report Office
   estimates based on UN Maternal
   Mortality Estimation Group (2016) and
   UNDESA (2015d).
28 WHO 2016g.
29 UNICEF 2014b.
30 UNICEF 2016a.
31 Acid Survivors Foundation 2016.
32 Thomson 2016.
33 World Bank 2015h.
34 UNDP 2016a.
35 United Nations 2016g.
36 UNDP 2016e.
37 Human Development Report Office
   estimates based on UNDESA (2015d).
38 Human Development Report Office
   estimates based on World Bank
   (2016o).
39 Human Development Report Office
   estimates based on FAO (2011b).

40 UNRWA 2013.
41 UNESCO and UNICEF 2015.
42 UNESCO 2013a.
43 Much of the data in this section are
   from Martinez-Franzoni and Sánchez-
   Ancochea (2016).
44 Baru and others 2010.
45 Krishnan and others 2016.
46 Kronfol 2012.
47 UNDP 2016i.
48 UNDP 2016c.
49 UNFPA 2015.
50 UNDP 2012b.
51 OECD and UNDESA 2013.
52 UNHCR 2016c.
53 IOM 2014.
54 UNDP 2009.
55 UNHCR 2016b.
56 Watkins 2013.
57 UNDESA 2016a.
58 IFAD 2012.
59 UNDESA 2013a.
60 IHS 2016.
61 IWGIA 2016.
62 UNDESA 2016e.
63 ABC News 2015.
64 ONS 2012.
65 Gates and Newport 2012.
66 ILGA 2016b.
67 WHO 2015e.
68 Butler 1980.
69 Shriver Center 2016.
70 UN Women 2015a.
71 HelpAge International and Center for
   Demographic Research 2015.
72 Kelley and others 2015.
73 UCL Institute of Health Equity 2010.
74 WHO 2011b.
75 Evans-Lacko and others 2013.
76 Angermeyer, Matschinger and
   Schomerus 2013.
77 WHO 2016f.
78 WHO 2016f.
79 Human Development Report
   Office estimates based on data on
   household deprivation in education,
   health and living standards from
   various household surveys using the
   methodology described in *Technical
   note 1* (available at http://hdr.undp.
   org/sites/default/files/hdr2016_
   technical_notes.pdf).
80 UNESCO 2014b.
81 Sandefur 2016.
82 UNESCO 2014b.
83 UNESCO 2014b.
84 Human Development Report Office
   estimates based on UNDESA (2015d).
85 IHME 2016.
86 Murray and others 2015.
87 Checchi and van der Werfhorst 2014.
88 ITU 2016b.
89 Kreft and others 2015.
90 UNICEF 2011.
91 United Nations 2015a.
92 Strong and Schwartz 2016.
93 Global Witness 2016.
94 Hillis and others 2014.
95 End Violence Against Children: The
   Global Partnership 2016.

96 The World Health Organization
   defines elder abuse as an act of commission or of omission (neglect) that
   may be intentional or psychological
   (involving emotional or verbal aggres-
   sion) financial or material, inflicting
   unnecessary suffering, injury or pain.
97 WHO 2015e.
98 UNODC 2013.
99 Human Development Report Office
   estimates based on UNODC (2016).
100 Torche 2016.
101 Blanden 2013; Duncan and Murnane
    2011; Torche 2014.
102 Piraino 2015.
103 Keswell, Girdwood and Leibbrandt
    2013.
104 Serafina and Tonkin 2014.
105 McGinn, Castro and Lingo 2015.
106 Lambert, Ravallion and van de Walle
    2014.
107 UNDP 2014b.
108 At the time of writing, there were
    more than 9.7 million survey votes
    on what matters to respondents. The
    data may not be statistically repre-
    sentative in all countries and subpop-
    ulations, but the results are indicative
    of variations in values. The responses
    are based on subjective evaluations.
    See United Nations (2016a).
109 See Pew Research Center (2014).
    The survey involved face to face
    interviews with approximately 1,000
    respondents in each country, except
    China (3,190) and India (2,464).
110 Human Development Report Office
    estimates based on data from Barro
    and Lee (2015), IMF (2016d), UNDESA
    (2015d, 2016e), UNDP (1990),
    UNESCO (2016b) and World Bank
    (2016o).
111 ILGA 2016c.
112 Raub and others 2016.
113 World Bank 2015h.
114 UNDP 2015a.
115 Demirgüç-Kunt and others 2014.
116 Banning-Lover 2016.
117 UNDP 2015a.
118 Charmes 2015.
119 Abadeer 2015.
120 WHO 2016d.
121 UNICEF 2016b.
122 IPPR 2012.
123 OECD 2011.
124 Nave 2000.
125 United Nations 2014.
126 See Wimmer (2012). The size of the
    politically excluded population is cal-
    culated as a function of the number of
    power sharing elites.
127 Alesina, Michalopoulos and
    Papaioannou 2012.
128 Milanović 2016.
129 Milanović 2016.
130 Desai 2007.
131 Desai 2007.
132 Pan and Christiaensen 2012.
133 Stampini and Tornarolli 2012.

134 Darrow and Tomas 2005; Johnson and Start 2001.

135 See Marx and others (2015), which is based on data from a sample of 73 mostly high- and middle-income countries.

136 Ortiz and others 2013.

137 Wimmer 2012.

Chapter 3

1 Sen 1985, p. 203.

2 Alkire 2010, p. 1.

3 United Nations 1948.

4 Nussbaum 2003.

5 UNDP 2000, p. 21.

6 UNDP 2000, p. 21.

7 UNDP 2010a.

8 Alkire 2009.

9 United Nations Broadband Commission for Digital Development 2015; UNODC 2014b.

10 UNDP 1994, p. 22.

11 Gómez, Muto and Kamidohzono 2016.

12 Kahneman and Tversky 2000.

13 Kahneman and Tversky 2000; Thaler 2015.

14 Ariely 2008, 2015.

15 World Bank 2015i.

16 Ariely 2008; Diamond and Vartiainen 2007.

17 Banerjee and Duflo 2011; Karlan and Appel 2011.

18 Thaler and Sunstein 2008.

19 Thaler and Sunstein 2008; World Bank 2015i.

20 Deneulin 2008.

21 Stewart 2013.

22 Deneulin 2016.

23 United Nations 2016b.

24 Mandavilli 2016; Moss-Racusin and others 2012.

25 Gillian and others 2016.

26 Nussbaum 2003.

27 UNDP 2016a; World Bank 2014.

28 UNDP 2011b, p. 2. See also Sen (2009).

29 United Nations 2015b.

30 Power 2016.

31 UN Women n.d.

32 Social Progress Imperative 2016.

33 UNDP 2010b, 2012b, 2014d.

34 United Nations 2015c.

35 ICF International 2016; UNICEF 2016b; World Bank 2016g.

36 UNDP 2015b.

37 UNDP 2016i.

38 United Nations 2015c.

39 UNESCO 2014a.

40 Based on UNDESA (2015d).

41 Murray and others 2016.

42 The Social Progress Imperative's Social Progress Index website (www.socialprogressimperative.org/global-index/, accessed 12 December 2016).

43 The Sustainable Development Solutions Network's World Happiness Report website (http://worldhappiness.report, accessed 12 December 2016).

44 The Organisation for Economic Co-operation and Development's Better Life Index website (www.oecdbetterlifeindex.org, accessed 12 December 2016).

45 Centre for Bhutan Studies and GNH Research's Gross National Happiness website (www.grossnationalhappiness.com/articles/, accessed 12 December 2016).

46 UK Office for National Statistics's National Wellbeing Website (www.ons.gov.uk/peoplepopulationandcommunity/wellbeing, accessed 12 December 2016).

47 Ballivian 2015.

48 GWG 2016.

49 WEF 2016c.

50 The UN Secretary-General created the Global Pulse Initiative in 2009 to harness Big Data as a public good in the service of sustainable development and humanitarian action. The UN Statistical Commission formed the Global Working Group on Big Data in 2014. The Global Partnership on Sustainable Development Data was formed among governments, corporate partners, the United Nations, international financial institutions, and nonprofit and academic stakeholders. It currently has more than 150 members.

Chapter 4

1 UNDP 2015a.

2 Dewan and Randolph 2016; Global Citizen 2016.

3 Demirgüç-Kunt and others 2014.

4 Epstein 2007.

5 Rizwanul and Iyanatul 2015.

6 Demirgüç-Kunt and others 2014.

7 Demirgüç-Kunt and others 2014.

8 UNDP 2015a.

9 Harris and Marks 2009.

10 Hillman and Jenkner 2004.

11 World Bank 2011a.

12 INSD 2016; Soura 2015.

13 Filou 2014.

14 BRAC Centre 2016.

15 BRAC Afghanistan 2016.

16 Bill & Melinda Gates Foundation 2016.

17 United Nations Secretary General's High-Level Panel on Access to Medicines 2016.

18 CID 2016.

19 United Nations Secretary General's High-Level Panel on Access to Medicines 2016.

20 UNDESA 2014a.

21 WFP 2016b.

22 United Nations 2016h.

23 World Bank 2016i.

24 Wiemann and Eibs-Singer 2016.

25 FAO and ILSI 1997.

26 Allen and others 2006.

27 SIDA 2015.

28 US Bureau of Labor Statistics 2016.

29 UNDP 2015a.

30 UNEP 2016.

31 Bonet and Cibils 2013.

32 UNDP 2013a.

33 UNESCO 2013c.

34 UN Women 2016c.

35 SIDA 2015.

36 Grant Thornton 2016.

37 Teigen 2012.

38 World Bank 2015e.

39 The Economist 2016c.

40 Kembhavi 2013.

41 Deloitte 2014.

42 Austin 2011.

43 United Nations 2016h.

44 WEF 2016a.

45 Schwab 2016; Williams-Grut 2016.

46 UNDP 2015a.

47 UNDP 2015a.

48 Cecchini and others 2015.

49 UNDP 2015a.

50 UNFPA and HelpAge International 2012.

51 UNDP 2015a.

52 See Statistical table 10.

53 Roy, Heuty and Letouzé 2007.

54 Cashin 2016.

55 World Bank 2006.

56 World Bank 2006.

57 World Bank 2016k.

58 Kar and Spanjers 2015.

59 Amundsen 2014.

60 Nnochiri 2012.

61 Nair 2016.

62 Coady and others 2015.

63 UNDP 1991.

64 PATH 2013.

65 Brown and Langer 2015.

66 Lloyd 2015.

67 Mann 2014.

68 Cambodian Disabled People's Organization 2015.

69 Asia Foundation 2013.

70 UNDP 2015a.

71 Rizwanul and Iyanatul 2015.

72 UNDP 2015a.

73 Neuvonen 2016.

74 BBC News 2016c.

75 World Bank 2015f.

76 Rutkowski 2016.

77 UNAIDS 2016e.

78 UNAIDS 2015.

79 WHO 2016j.

80 The Guardian 2016a.

81 WHO 2016j.

82 Zimmer 2016.

83 UNDP 2016h.

84 UNDP 2016j.

85 Brodzinsky 2014.

86 World Bank 2015j.

87 UNDESA 2015f.

88 World Bank 2015a.

89 Coady, Flamini and Sears 2015.

90 World Bank 2015a.

91 World Bank 2015a.

92 Vaughan 2016.

93 World Bank 2015a.

94 United Nations 1948.

95 UNDP 2016g.

96 World Bank 2016f.

97 United Nations 2013.

98 Banisar 2015.

Chapter 5

1 For actions with positive externalities the result is underprovision, as individuals or countries decide to free-ride without contributing to their supply. For actions with negative externalities there is a tendency to overprovision or overexploitation, as some individual or countries do not absorb their direct cost.

2 UNCTAD 2016.

3 UNDESA 2015c.

4 UNDESA 2013b.

5 UNDP 2009.

6 For example, in 2015 remittances to Sub-Saharan Africa amounted to 2.46 percent of GDP, over three times more than in 1990. In Latin America and the Caribbean they almost tripled over the same time period, to 1.43 percent of GDP. In 2015 global remittances came to more than four times global official development assistance (World Bank 2016h). See also UNDP (2015a).

7 Human Development Report Office estimate based on data from the United Nations Department of Economic and Social Affairs, the Office of the United Nations High Commissioner for Refugees and the United Nations Relief and Works Agency for Palestine Refugees in the Near East.

8 IMF 2016a.

9 Thacker 1999; Dreher, Sturm and Vreeland 2009; Reinhart and Trebesch 2016.

10 IMF 2016b.

11 Independent Evaluation Office of the International Monetary Fund 2013, p. 1.

12 Eichengreen and Woods 2016.

13 Ocampo 2015a.

14 World Bank 2016m.

15 Clemens and Kremer 2016; Ravallion 2016.

16 Subramanian and Wei 2007.

17 Seth 2016.

18 Even creating tensions with democratic principles, as described by Rodrik (2011).

19 Chang 2002.

20 Montes and Lunenborg 2016.

21 Protection can go beyond foreign direct investment flows. For instance, the North American Free Trade Agreement introduced clauses to limit potential regulations not only for foreign direct investment , but also for destabilizing short-term speculative flows (Gallager and others 2013).

22 Montes and Lunenborg 2016; Mercurio 2014.

23 Montes and Lunenborg 2016.

24 Jenks and Topping 2016.

25 Equivalent to $135 billion in 2014. UNSD 2016; World Bank 2016o.
26 Equivalent to $48 billion in 2014. Jenks and Topping 2016; World Bank 2016o.
27 Data are the average for the period 2008–2015 to include the response to the global financial crisis (IMF 2016c; World Bank 2016o).
28 Data are for 2012. Ocampo 2015a; World Bank 2016o.
29 European Union 2014.
30 UNCTAD 2014. Similar estimates can be found in Schmidt-Traub (2015).
31 Comparing the UN budget ($48 billion) with the estimated annual resource gap of implementing the Sustainable Development Goals in developing countries ($2.5 trillion).
32 OECD 2016f, table 4.
33 Pollin 2016.
34 UNHCR 2015a.
35 UNHCR 2015b.
36 Perlo-Freeman and others 2016.
37 UCDP 2016.
38 Kaldor 1999.
39 Weiss 2007; Kaldor 2013.
40 Wiist and others 2014.
41 United Nations 2016d.
42 UNHCR 2016a.
43 OECD 2016d.
44 OECD 2016d.
45 United Nations 2000b.
46 United Nations 2015c.
47 UNDESA 2016b.
48 ECOSOC 2015.
49 UNDESA 2016b.
50 W3 Techs 2016.

51 World Bank 2016p.
52 Del Vicario and others 2016.
53 Ocampo 2015a.
54 Council on Foreign Relations 2015.
55 Ocampo 2015b.
56 Ocampo 2015a.
57 Matheson 2011.
58 Becchetti, Ferrari and Trenta 2014.
59 IMF 2012.
60 Ostry and others 2011.
61 Montes and Lunenborg 2016.
62 United Nations Secretary-General's High-Level Panel on Access to Medicines 2016.
63 Montes and Lunenborg 2016.
64 IOM 2015.
65 UNHCR 2014.
66 The Economist 2016d.
67 See details in Zucman (2015).
68 See details in Zucman (2015).
69 African Union and Economic Commission for Africa 2015.
70 Independent Commission on Multilateralism 2016; Pollin 2016; IEA 2016d.
71 IEA 2016d; Pollin 2016.
72 Independent Commission on Multilateralism 2016.
73 Pollin 2016.
74 World Resources Institute 2016.
75 IEA 2016a.
76 Pollin 2016.
77 UNDP 2015a.
78 Ocampo 2015a.
79 Griffith-Jones 2016.
80 Ocampo 2015a.
81 Griffith-Jones and Cozzi 2015.
82 OECD 2008.

83 Brazil's development cooperation is significantly higher according to the official figures published by the Brazilian government. The Organisation for Economic Co-operation and Development uses these data but, for its analysis, only includes in its estimates activities in low- and middle-income countries and contributions to multilateral agencies whose main aim is promoting the economic development and welfare of developing countries (or a percentage of these contributions when a multilateral agency does not work exclusively on development activities in developing countries). The Organisation for Economic Co-operation and Development also excludes bilateral peacekeeping activities. Brazil's official data may exclude some activities that would be included as development cooperation in Development Assistance Committee statistics and so are also excluded from the Organisation for Economic Co-operation and Development estimates that are based on Brazil's own data. (www.oecd.org/dac/dac-global-relations/brazil-development-co-operation.htm).
84 All data are Organisation for Economic Co-operation and Development estimates, except those for the Russian Federation and the United Arab Emirates, which do not report to the Organisation for Economic Co-operation and

Development (www.oecd.org/development/stats/non-dac-reporting.htm).
85 GIZ 2014.
86 WFP 2014.
87 UNOSSC 2016.
88 Jenks and Topping 2016.
89 Sachs 2012.
90 Adaptation Fund 2015; United Nations 2011.
91 UNDESA 2012.
92 Hemmelgarn and others 2015; Council of the European Union 2016.
93 WHO 2013.
94 UNDP 2014b.
95 Tanner 2000.
96 UNDP 2014b.
97 Khan 2016.
98 The Guardian 2016b.
99 UNSD 2008.
100 World Bank 2011b.
101 European Union 2012.
102 Open Government Partnership website (www.opengovpartnership.org, accessed 26 September 2016).
103 UNDESA 2014a.
104 United States of America 2009.
105 United Kingdom 2010.
106 Republic of Kenya 2011.
107 Republic of Ghana 2012.
108 State of Japan 2013.
109 United Nations 2016f.

Chapter 6

1 ODI 2016.
2 WEF 2016b.

References

Abadeer, A.S.Z. 2015. *Norms and Gender Discrimination in the Arab World.* New York: Palgrave Macmillan.

ABC (Australian Broadcasting Corporation) News. 2015. "ABS Collects Data on Sexual Orientation for First Time." *PM* (news broadcast), 6 July. www.abc.net.au/news/2015-07-06/abs-collects-data-on-sexual-orientation-for-first/6599506. Accessed 26 October 2016.

Acid Survivors Foundation. 2016. "Statistics." www.acidsurvivors.org/Statistics. Accessed 11 October 2016.

Adaptation Fund. 2015. "About the Adaptation Fund." www.adaptation-fund.org/about/. Accessed 30 September 2016.

African Union and Economic Commission for Africa. 2015. *Illicit Financial Flows: Report of the High Level Panel on Illicit Financial Flows from Africa.* www.uneca.org/sites/default/files/PublicationFiles/iff_main_report_26feb_en.pdf. Accessed 8 November 2016.

Agartan, T.I. 2012. "Marketization and Universalism: Crafting the Right Balance in the Turkish Healthcare System." *Current Sociology* 60(4): 456–471.

Agbor, J. 2012. "Op-Ed: Poverty, Inequality and Africa's Education Crisis." Brookings Institution, Washington, DC. www.brookings.edu/opinions/poverty-inequality-and-africas-education-crisis/. Accessed 26 October 2016.

Alesina, A.F., S. Michalopoulos and E. Papaioannou. 2012. "Ethnic Inequality." NBER Working Paper 18512, National Bureau of Economic Research, Cambridge, MA. www.nber.org/papers/w18512.pdf. Accessed 27 October 2016.

Alkire, S. 2009. "Concepts and Measures of Agency." In K. Basu and R. Kanbur, eds., *Arguments for a Better World: Essays in Honor of Amartya Sen. Volume I: Ethics, Welfare, and Measurement and Volume II: Development, Society, and Institutions.* Oxford, UK: Oxford University Press.

———. **2010.** "Human Development: Definitions, Critiques, and Related Concepts." Human Development Research Paper 2010/01. United Nations Development Programme, New York.

Allen, L., B. de Benoist, O. Dary and R. Hurrell, eds. 2006. *Guidelines on Food Fortification with Micronutrients.* Geneva: World Health Organization; Rome: Food and Agriculture Organization of the United Nations. www.who.int/nutrition/publications/guide_food_fortification_micronutrients.pdf. Accessed 22 November 2016.

Amundsen, I. 2014. "Corruption and Other Leakages." Paper presented at the 2014 Natural Resource Charter Conference "Strengthening Resource Governance," 12–13 June, Oxford, UK. www.cmi.no/publications/5247-corruption-and-other-leakages. Accessed 7 November 2016.

Angermeyer, M.C., H. Matschinger and G. Schomerus. 2013. "Public Attitudes towards People with Depression in Times of Uncertainty: Results from Three Population Surveys in Germany." *Social Psychiatry and Psychiatric Epidemiology* 48(9): 1513–1518.

Arekapudi, N. 2014. "Credit for All: Increasing Women's Access to Finance." Thomson Reuters Foundation News, 11 November. New York. http://news.trust.org//item/20141111224416-boan9/. Accessed 14 October 2016.

Ariely, D. 2008. *Predictably Irrational: The Hidden Forces That Shape Our Decisions.* New York: HarperCollins.

———. **2015.** *Irrationally Yours: On Missing Socks, Pickup Lines, and Other Existential Puzzles.* New York: HarperCollins.

Asia Foundation. 2013. "The Right to Vote: Filipinos with Disabilities and the 2013 Elections." Manila, The Philippines. https://asiafoundation.org/resources/pdfs/PWDs2013Elections.pdf. Accessed 7 November 2016.

———. **2015.** *50 Years of Indian Technical and Economic Cooperation.* Indian Development Cooperation Research Report. Manila, The Philippines. www.cprindia.org/sites/default/files/working_papers/IDCR%20Report%20-%2050%20years%20of%20ITEC.pdf. Accessed 19 November 2016.

Austin, L. 2011. "The Politics of Youth Bulge: From Islamic Activism to Democratic Reform in the Middle East and North Africa." *SAIS Review of International Affairs* 31(2): 81–96.

Avaaz. 2016. "Climate Change: The Beginning of the End of Fossil Fuels." https://avaaz.org/page/en/highlights/. Accessed 11 October 2016.

Avon Global Center for Women and Justice, New York City Bar Association, Cornell Law School International Human Rights Clinic and Virtue Foundation. 2011. "Combating Acid Violence in Bangladesh, India, and Cambodia." New York. www.nycbar.org/pdf/report/uploads/20072039-CombatingAcidViolenceinBangladeshIndiaandCambodia.pdf. Accessed 14 October 2016.

Ballivian, A. 2015. "Using Big Data for the Sustainable Development Goals." Global Working Group on Big Data for Official Statistics, New York. http://unstats.un.org/unsd/trade/events/2015/abudhabi/presentations/day3/02/2b%20A-Using%20Big%20Data%20for%20the%20Sustainable%20Development%20Goals%2010222015.pdf. Accessed 7 November 2016.

Banerjee, A., and E. Duflo. 2011. *Poor Economics: A Radical Rethinking of the Way to Fight Global Poverty.* Philadelphia: Public Affairs.

Banerjee, B. 2016. "India State Aims to Plant a Record 50 Million Trees in a Day." Associated Press, 11 July. http://bigstory.ap.org/article/6421397504594f6e80a179d07f35f8d3/india-state-aims-plant-record-50-million-trees-day. Accessed 26 August 2016.

Banisar, D. 2015. "National Right to Information Laws, Regulations and Initiatives 2015." Article 19: Global Campaign for Free Expression. http://dx.doi.org/10.2139/ssrn.1857498. Accessed 7 November 2016.

Banning-Lover, R. 2016. "Russia and the US Have the Worst Employment Gaps for Disabled People." *The Guardian*, 23 June. www.theguardian.com/global-development-professionals-network/2016/jun/23/russia-and-the-us-have-the-worst-employment-gaps-for-disabled-people. Accessed 25 August 2016.

Banu, A. 2016. "Human Development, Disparity and Vulnerability: Women in South Asia." Background paper for Human Development Report 2016. United Nations Development Programme, Human Development Report Office, New York.

Barro, R.J., and J.-W. Lee. 2015. *Education Matters: Global Schooling Gains from the 19th to the 21st Century.* New York: Oxford University Press.

Baru, R., A. Acharya, S. Acharya, A.K. Shiva Kumar and K. Nagaraj. 2010. "Inequities in Access to Health Services in India: Caste, Class and Region." *Economic and Political Weekly* 45(38): 49–58.

BBC News. 2016a. "Colombia's President Santos Enacts Tougher Law on Acid Attacks." 19 January. www.bbc.com/news/world-latin-america-35349222. Accessed 14 October 2016.

———. **2016b.** "Gambia and Tanzania Outlaw Child Marriage." 8 July. www.bbc.com/news/world-africa-36746174. Accessed 14 October 2016.

———. **2016c.** "Switzerland's Voters Reject Basic Income Plan." 5 June. www.bbc.com/news/world-europe-36454060. Accessed 7 November 2016.

Becchetti, L., M. Ferrari and U. Trenta. 2014. "The Impact of the French Tobin Tax." *Journal of Financial Stability* 15: 127–148.

Bill & Melinda Gates Foundation. 2016. "What We Do: Vaccine Delivery Strategy Overview." Seattle. www.gatesfoundation.org/What-We-Do/Global-Development/Vaccine-Delivery. Accessed 17 December 2016.

Blanden, J. 2013. "Cross-country Rankings in Intergenerational Mobility: A Comparison of Approaches from Economics and Sociology." *Journal of Economic Surveys* 27(1): 38–73.

Bokova, I. 2016. "At Last, the Destruction of Heritage Has Been Recognised as a Weapon of War." *The Guardian*, 28 September. www.theguardian.com/global-development/2016/sep/28/destruction-of-heritage-weapon-of-war-timbuktu-shrines-irina-bokova?CMP=share_btn_tw#img-1via. Accessed 14 October 2016.

Bonet, J, and V.F. Cibils. 2013. "Expanding Local Revenues for Promoting Local Development." *Urban Public Economics Review* 19(July–December): 64–87.

BRAC Afghanistan. 2016. "BRAC Afghanistan." Kabul. http://brac.net/brac-afghanistan/item/756-education. Accessed 17 December 2016

BRAC Centre. 2016. "Education." Dhaka. http://brac.net/education-programme/item/758-overview. Accessed 17 December 2016.

Braimoh, A. 2015. "To Fight Desertification, Let's Manage Our Land Better." Landscape Approach (Blog), 17 June. World Bank, Washington, DC. http://blogs.worldbank.org/taxonomy/term/13891. Accessed 11 October 2016.

Brodzinsky, S. 2014. "From Murder Capital to Model City: Is Medellín's Miracle Show or Substance?" *The Guardian*, 17 April. www.theguardian.com/cities/2014/apr/17/medellin-murder-capital-to-model-city-miracle-un-world-urban-forum. Accessed 7 November 2016.

Brown, G.K., and A. Langer. 2015. "Does Affirmative Action Work? Lessons from around the World." *Foreign*

Affairs 94(March–April): 49–56. www.foreignaffairs. com/articles/2015-03-01/does-affirmative-action-work. Accessed 7 November 2016.

Butler, R.N. 1980. "Ageism: A Foreword." *Journal of Social Issues* 36(2): 8–11.

C2ES (Centre for Climate and Energy Solutions). 2015. "Outcomes of the U.N. Climate Change Conference in Paris." Arlington, VA. www.c2es.org/international/ negotiations/cop21-paris/summary. Accessed 14 October 2016.

Cambodian Disabled People's Organization. 2015. "Disability Inclusion in the Voter Registration Processes, The Challenges, Lessons Learned and Good Practices: A Pathway of Disability Inclusion in Political Rights." Phnom Penh. www.ifes.org/sites/default/files/cdpo_report_the_ challenges_lessons_learned_and_good_practices.pdf. Accessed 7 November 2016.

Cashin, C. 2016. *Health Financing Policy: The Macroeconomic, Fiscal, and Public Finance Context.* Washington, DC: World Bank. http://elibrary.worldbank. org/doi/abs/10.1596/978-1-4648-0796-1. Accessed 7 November 2016.

CDC (US Centers for Disease Control and Prevention). 2013. "Impact of an Innovative Approach to Prevent Mother-to-Child Transmission of HIV: Malawi, July 2011– September 2012." *Morbidity and Mortality Weekly Report,* 1 March. www.cdc.gov/mmwr/preview/mmwrhtml/ mm6208a3.htm?s_cid=mm6208a3_w. Accessed 7 November 2016.

Cecchini, S., F. Filgueira, R. Martínez and C. Rossel, eds. 2015. *Towards Universal Social Protection: Latin American Pathways and Policy Tools.* Santiago: United Nations Economic Commission for Latin America and the Caribbean.

Chang, H.-J. 2002. *Kicking Away the Ladder: Development Strategy in Historical Perspective.* London and New York: Anthem Press.

Chao, S. 2012. "Forest Peoples: Numbers across the World." Forest Peoples Programme, Moreton-in-Marsh, UK. www. forestpeoples.org/sites/fpp/files/publication/2012/05/ forest-peoples-numbers-across-world-final_0.pdf. Accessed 26 October 2016.

Charmes, J. 2015. "Time Use across the World: Findings of a World Compilation of Time Use Surveys." Background paper for Human Development Report 2015. United Nations Development Programme, Human Development Report Office, New York. www.hdr.undp.org/sites/default/files/ charmes_hdr_2015_final.pdf. Accessed 27 October 2016.

Checchi, D., and H.G. van der Werfhorst. 2014. "Educational Policies and Income Inequality." IZA Discussion Paper 8222. Institute for the Study of Labour, Bonn, Germany. http://ftp.iza.org/dp8222.pdf. Accessed 26 October 2016.

Chew, J. 2015. "Women Are Taking over Saudi Arabia's Workforce." *Fortune,* 10 August. http://fortune. com/2015/08/10/women-saudi-arabia/. Accessed 7 November 2016.

CID (Council for International Development). 2016. "Healthcare Innovations Won't Cure Global Health Inequality: Political Action Will." Wellington. www.cid.org. nz/news/healthcare-innovations-wont-cure-global-health-inequality-political-action-will/. Accessed 7 November 2016.

Clark, P. 2016. "Renewables Overtake Coal as World's Largest Source of Power Capacity." *Financial Times,* 25 October. www.ft.com/content/09a1f984-9a1d-11e6-8f9b-70e3cabccfae. Accessed 1 November 2016.

Clemens, M., and M. Kremer. 2016. "The New Role for the World Bank." *Journal of Economic Perspectives* 30(1): 53–76.

Coady, D., I.W.H. Parry, L. Sears and B. Shang. 2015. "How Large Are Global Energy Subsidies." IMF Working Paper 15/105. International Monetary Fund, Washington, DC. www.imf.org/external/pubs/cat/longres. aspx?sk=42940.0. Accessed 7 November 2016.

Coady, D., V. Flamini and L. Sears. 2015. "The Unequal Benefits of Fuel Subsidies Revisited: Evidence for Developing Countries." IMF Working Paper 15/250. International Monetary Fund, Washington, DC. www.imf. org/external/pubs/ft/wp/2015/wp15250.pdf. Accessed 22 November 2016.

Cornia, G.A., and F. Stewart, eds. 2014. *Towards Human Development: New Approaches to Macroeconomics and Inequality.* Oxford: Oxford University Press.

Council of the European Union. 2016. "Outcome of the Council Meeting, 3475th Council Meeting, Economic and Financial Affairs." Luxembourg. www.consilium.europa. eu. Accessed 30 September 2016.

Council on Foreign Relations. 2015. "Central Bank Currency Swaps." www.cfr.org/international-finance/central-bank-currency-swaps-since-financial-crisis/p36419#!/?cid=from_ interactives_listing. Accessed 8 November 2016.

CRED (Centre for Research on the Epidemiology of Disasters) and UNISDR (United Nations Office for Disaster Risk Reduction). 2015. "The Human Cost of Weather-Related Disasters 1995–2015." Geneva. www. unisdr.org/files/46796_cop21weatherdisastersreport2015. pdf. Accessed 14 October 2016.

Cukier, K.N., and V. Mayer-Schoenberger. 2013. "Rise of Big Data: How It's Changing the Way We Think about the World." *Foreign Affairs* 92(3): 28–40. http://faculty.cord. edu/andersod/The%20Rise%20of%20Big%20Data.docx. Accessed 4 December 2016.

Curto, V.E., R.G. Fryer, Jr., and M.L. Howard. 2011. "It May Not Take a Village: Increasing Achievement among the Poor." In G.J. Duncan and R.J. Murnane, eds., *Whither Opportunity? Rising Inequality, Schools, and Children's Life Chances.* New York: Russell Sage Foundation. http:// scholar.harvard.edu/files/fryer/files/it_may_not_take_a_ village_increasing_achievement_among_the_poor.pdf. Accessed 26 October 2016.

Darrow, M., and A. Tomas. 2005. "Power, Capture, and Conflict: A Call for Human Rights Accountability in Development Cooperation." *Human Rights Quarterly* 27(2): 471–538.

Daude, C. 2012. "Educación, Clases Medias y Movilidad Social en América Latina." In L. Paramio and R. Grynspan, eds., *Clases medias en sociedades emergentes.* Pensamiento Iberoamericano Series 10. Madrid: Fundación Carolina and Agencia Española de Cooperación Internacional para el Desarrollo. www.fundacioncarolina. es/wp-content/uploads/2014/07/PensamientoIbero10.pdf. Accessed 26 October 2016.

Day Ashley, L., C. Mcloughlin, M. Aslam, J. Engel, J. Wales, S. Rawal, R. Batley, G. Kingdon, S. Nicolai and P. Rose. 2014. "The Role and Impact of Private Schools in Developing Countries." Education Rigorous Literature Review. UK Department for International Development, London. www.gov.uk/government/uploads/ system/uploads/attachment_data/file/439702/private-schools-full-report.pdf. Accessed 26 October 2016.

Dean, D., S. DiGrande, D. Field, A. Lundmark, J. O'Day, J. Pineda and P. Zwillenberg. 2012. "BCG Report: The Connected World; The Internet Economy in the G-20: The $4.2 Trillion Growth Opportunity." Boston Consulting Group, Boston, MA. www.bcg.com/documents/file100409. pdf. Accessed 20 October 2016.

Del Vicario, M., A. Bessi, F. Zollo, F. Petroni, A. Scala, G. Caldarelli, H. Stanley and W. Quattrociocchi. 2016. "The Spreading of Misinformation Online." *Proceedings of the National Academy of Sciences of the United States of America* 113(3): 554–559.

Deloitte. 2014. "Big Demands and High Expectations: The Deloitte Millennial Survey." London. http://www2. deloitte.com/content/dam/Deloitte/ru/Documents/ Corporate_responsibility/ru_2014_MillennialSurvey_ ExecutiveSummary.pdf. Accessed 7 November 2016.

Demirgüç-Kunt, A., L.F. Klapper, D. Singer and P. Van Oudheusden. 2014. "The Global Findex Database 2014: Measuring Financial Inclusion around the World." Policy Research Working Paper 7255. World Bank, Washington, DC. http://documents.worldbank.org/curated/ en/187761468179367706/pdf/WPS7255.pdf. Accessed 21 December 2016.

Demos Helsinki. 2016. "Thousands to Receive Basic Income in Finland: A Trial That Could Lead to the Greatest Societal Transformation of Our Time." Helsinki. www. demoshelsinki.fi/en/2016/08/30/thousands-to-receive-basic-income-in-finland-a-trial-that-could-lead-to-the-greatest-societal-transformation-of-our-time/. Accessed 7 November 2016.

Deneulin, S. 2008. "Beyond Individual Freedom and Agency: Structures of Living Together in the Capability Approach." In F. Comim, M. Qizilbash and S. Alkire, eds., *The Capability Approach: Concepts, Measures and Applications.* New York: Cambridge University Press.

———. **2016.** "Expanding Freedoms, Changing Structures: The Human Development Report 2014." *Development and Change* 47(FORUM 2016): 937–951.

Desai, R.M. 2007. "The Political Economy of Poverty Reduction: Scaling Up Antipoverty Programs in the Developing World." Working Paper 2. Brookings Institution, Wolfensohn Center for Development, Washington, DC. www.brookings.edu/wp-content/ uploads/2016/06/11_poverty_desai.pdf. Accessed 27 October 2016.

Dewan, S., and G. Randolph. 2016. "The Global Deal: A New Economic Consensus." *Huffington Post* (Blog), 17 June. www.huffingtonpost.com/sabina-dewan/the-global-deal-a-new-eco_b_7603460.html. Accessed 7 November 2016.

DFID (UK Department for International Development). 2010. *Cities: The New Frontier.* London. www.gov.uk/ government/uploads/system/uploads/attachment_data/ file/67689/cities-new-frontier.pdf. Accessed 25 August 2016.

Diamond, P., and H. Vartiainen, eds. 2007. *Behavioral Economics and its Applications.* Princeton, NJ: Princeton University Press.

Dreher, A., J. Sturm and J. Vreeland. 2009. "Global Horse Trading: IMF Loans for Votes in the United Nations Security Council." *European Economic Review* 53(7): 742–757.

Duncan, G.J., and R.J. Murnane, eds. 2011. *Whither Opportunity? Rising Inequality, Schools, and Children's Life Chances*. New York: Russell Sage Foundation.

The Economist. 2016a. "China's Middle Class: 225m Reasons for China's Leaders to Worry." 9 July. www.economist.com/news/leaders/21701760-communist-party-tied-its-fortunes-mass-affluence-may-now-threaten-its-survival-225m. Accessed 11 October 2016.

———. 2016b. "Daily Chart: Iraq's Deadly War." 8 July. www.economist.com/blogs/graphicdetail/2016/07/daily-chart-4?fsrc=scn/tw/te/bl/ed/iraqsdeadlywar. Accessed 25 August 2016.

———. 2016c. "Early Childhood Development: Give Me a Child." 29 October. www.economist.com/news/international/21709292-boosting-health-toddlers-bodies-and-brains-brings-multiple-benefits-too-often. Accessed 7 November 2016.

———. 2016d. "Special Report on Migration." 28 May–3 June.

———. 2016e. "The World Economy: An Open and Shut Case." 1 October. www.economist.com/news/special-report/21707833-consensus-favour-open-economies-cracking-says-john-osullivan. Accessed 11 October 2016.

ECOSOC (United Nations Economic and Social Council). 2015. "List of Non-governmental Organizations in Consultative Status with the Economic and Social Council as of 1 September 2015." E/2015/INF/5. New York. http://csonet.org. Accessed 18 October 2016.

———. 2016. "Statistical Annex on Funding Data of the 2016 Secretary General's Report on the Implementation of the QCPR." www.un.org/en/ecosoc/qcpr/pdf/statistical_annex_tables_on_funding_flows_2014.xlsx. Accessed 28 July 2016.

Edwards, B. 2015. "2014 NZ General Election Results—The Definitive Stats." Liberation (Blog), 3 March. http://liberation.typepad.com/liberation/2015/03/2014-nz-general-election-results-the-definitive-stats.html. Accessed 2 June 2015.

Ehrenfreund, M. 2016. "This Is How Immigration Will Change Europe during the Rest of This Century." World Economic Forum, Geneva. www.weforum.org/agenda/2016/07/this-is-how-immigration-will-change-europe-over-the-rest-of-this-century. Accessed 11 October 2016.

EIA (US Energy Information Administration). 2016. *International Energy Outlook 2016*. Washington, DC. www.eia.gov/forecasts/ieo/pdf/0484(2016).pdf. Accessed 14 October 2016.

Eichengreen, B., and N. Woods. 2016. "The IMF's Unmet Challenges." *Journal of Economic Perspectives* 30(1): 29–52.

End Violence Against Children: The Global Partnership. 2016. "Global Leaders and Youth Advocates Launch New Partnership and Fund to End Violence against Children Everywhere." Press release, 12 July. New York. www.end-violence.org/press_releases.html. Accessed 27 October 2016.

Epstein, G. 2007. "Central Banks as Agents of Employment Creation." Working Paper 38. Report ST/ESA/2007/DWP/38. United Nations Department of Economic and Social Affairs, New York. www.un.org/esa/desa/papers/2007/wp38_2007.pdf. Accessed 22 November 2016.

European Commission. 2014. "Communication from the Commission on the European Citizens' Initiative 'Water and Sanitation Are a Human Right! Water Is a Public Good, Not a Commodity!'" Brussels. http://ec.europa.eu/transparency/regdoc/rep/1/2014/EN/1-2014-177-EN-F1-1.Pdf. Accessed 7 November 2016.

———. 2016. "State Aid: Ireland Gave Illegal Tax Benefits to Apple Worth up to €13 Billion." Press release, 30 August. http://europa.eu/rapid/press-release_IP-16-2923_en.htm. Accessed 21 December 2016.

European Union. 2012. "European Union Open Data Portal." Brussels. http://open-data.europa.eu/en/data. Accessed 26 September 2016.

———. 2014. "The European Union Explained: Budget." Brussels. https://europa.eu/european-union/topics/budget_en. Accessed 28 November 2016.

Eurostat. 2016a. "Asylum Statistics Source." http://ec.europa.eu/eurostat/statistics-explained/index.php/Asylum_statistics. Accessed 21 October 2016.

———. 2016b. European Union Statistics on Income and Living Conditions (EUSILC). Brussels. http://ec.europa.eu/eurostat/web/microdata/european-union-statistics-on-income-and-living-conditions. EUSILC UDB 2014—version 2 of August 2016.

Evans-Lacko, S., M. Knapp, P. McCrone, G. Thornicroft and R. Mojtabai. 2013. "The Mental Health Consequences of the Recession: Economic Hardship and Employment of People with Mental Health Problems in 27 European Countries." Plos One (Community Blog), 26 July. http://journals.plos.org/plosone/article?id=10.1371/journal.pone.0069792#s2. Accessed 26 October 2016.

Fajgelbaum, P.D., and A.K. Khandelwal. 2016. "Measuring the Unequal Gains from Trade." *Quarterly Journal of Economics* 131(3): 1113–1180.

FAO (Food and Agriculture Organization of the United Nations). 2011a. "Global Food Losses and Food Waste: Extent, Causes and Prevention." Rome. www.fao.org/docrep/014/mb060e/mb060e.pdf. Accessed 24 August 2016.

———. 2011b. *The State of the World's Land and Water Resources for Food and Agriculture: Managing Systems at Risk*. Rome. www.fao.org/docrep/017/i1688e/i1688e.pdf. Accessed 7 November 2016.

———. 2016a. "UN Seeks to Boost Response to El Niño's Dire Impact in Africa and Asia/Pacific, Urges La Niña Preparedness." Rome. www.fao.org/news/story/en/item/423058/icode/. Accessed 23 August 2016.

———. 2016b. *State of the World's Forests 2016, Forests and Agriculture: Land-Use Challenges and Opportunities*. Rome. www.fao.org/3/a-i5588e.pdf. Accessed 23 August 2016.

FAO (Food and Agriculture Organization of the United Nations) and ILSI (International Life Sciences Institute). 1997. *Preventing Micronutrient Malnutrition: A Guide to Food-Based Approaches: A Manual for Policy Makers and Programme Planners*. Rome. www.fao.org/docrep/X5244E/X5244e00.htm. Accessed 22 November 2016.

FAO (Food and Agriculture Organization of the United Nations) and WFP (World Food Programme). 2016. "Monitoring Food Security in Countries with Conflict Situations: A Joint FAO/WFP Update for the United Nations Security Council (July 2016)." Rome. www.fao.org/3/a-c0335e.pdf. Accessed 11 October 2016.

Filou, E. 2014. "The African Water Companies Serving the Poorest and Staying Afloat." *The Guardian*, 4 October. www.theguardian.com/global-development-professionals-network/2016/oct/04/urban-africa-water-companies-poorest-profit. Accessed 22 November 2016.

Fink, G., E. Peet, G. Danaei, K. Andrews, D.C. McCoy, C.R. Sudfeld, M.C.S. Fawzi, M. Ezzati and W.W. Fawzi. 2016. "Schooling and Wage Income Losses Due to Early-Childhood Growth Faltering in Developing Countries: National, Regional, and Global Estimates." *American Journal of Clinical Nutrition* 104(1): 104–112.

Forbes, M. 2015. "A Year of Mixed Fortunes for Maori MPs." Radio New Zealand, 29 December. www.radionz.co.nz/news/national/293124/year-of-mixed-fortunes-for-maori-mps. Accessed 7 November 2016.

Ford, D. 2016. "UAE's First Female Fighter Pilot Led Airstrike against ISIS." CNN, 9 October. www.cnn.com/2014/09/25/world/meast/uae-female-fighter-pilot/. Accessed 14 October 2016.

Fryer, R.G., Jr. 2006. "Acting White: The Social Price Paid by the Best and Brightest Minority Students." *Education Next* Winter: 52–59. http://educationnext.org/files/ednext20061_52.pdf. Accessed 26 October 2016.

Fryer, R.G., Jr., and S.D. Levitt. 2004. "The Causes and Consequences of Distinctively Black Names." *Quarterly Journal of Economics* 119(3): 767–805.

Fryer, R.G., Jr., D. Pager and J.L. Spenkuch. 2013. "Racial Disparities in Job Finding and Offered Wages." *Journal of Law and Economics* 56(3): 633–689.

GAHP (Global Alliance on Health and Pollution). 2014. "Pollution: The Silent Killer of Millions in Poor Countries." New York. www.gahp.net/new/wp-content/uploads/2014/12/GAHP-PollutionSummaryNov2014DRAFT.pdf. Accessed 23 August 2016.

Gall, S.C., and R.C. Thompson. 2015. "The Impact of Debris on Marine Life." *Marine Pollution Bulletin* 92(1–2): 170–179.

Gallagher, K., R. Ffrench-Davis, L. Mah-Hui and K. Soverel. 2013. "Financial Stability and the Trans-Pacific Partnership: Lessons from Chile and Malaysia." GEGI Working Paper. Boston, MA: Global Economic Governance Initiative.

Gates, G.J., and F. Newport. 2012. "Special Report: 3.4% of U.S. Adults Identify as LGBT." Gallup, Politics, 18 October. Washington, DC. www.gallup.com/poll/158066/special-report-adults-identify-lgbt.aspx. Accessed 26 October 2016.

GC-RED (Global Policy Centre on Resilient Ecosystems and Desertification). 2016. "UNDP-UNEP Poverty-Environment Initiative (PEI)." Nairobi. www.undp.org/content/undp/en/home/ourwork/global-policy-centres/sustainable_landmanagement/pei.html. Accessed 7 November 2016.

Geneva Declaration on Armed Violence and Development. 2015. "Executive Summary." *Global Burden of Armed Violence 2015: Every Body Counts*. Geneva. www.genevadeclaration.org/fileadmin/docs/GBAV3/GBAV3_ExecSummary_pp1-10.pdf. Accessed 11 October 2016.

Ghosh, T. 2016. "Acid Attack in India: Where Does the Nation Stand Today?" *Huffington Post*, 29 March. www.huffingtonpost.com/tanushree-ghosh/acid-attack-in-india-wher_b_9559790.html. Accessed 14 October 2016.

Gillian, W.S., A.N. Maupin, C.R. Reyes, M. Accavitti and F. Shic. 2016. "Do Early Educators' Implicit Biases Regarding Sex and Race Relate to Behavior Expectations and Recommendations of Preschool Expulsions and Suspensions?" Research Study Brief. Yale University, Yale Child Study Center, New Haven, CT.

GIZ (Deutsche Gesellschaft für Internationale Zusammenarbeit). 2014. *Developing an Environmental Technology Centre (CTA) in Peru. Triangular Cooperation Brazil–Peru–Germany.* Eschborn, Germany. www.giz.de/en/downloads/giz2014-en-zentrum-umwelttechnologien-peru.pdf. Accessed 8 November 2016.

Gjerde, K.M. 2006. "Ecosystems and Biodiversity in Deep Waters and High Seas." UNEP Regional Seas Reports and Studies No. 178. United Nations Environment Programme, Nairobi. www.unep.org/pdf/EcosystemBiodiversity_DeepWaters_20060616.pdf. Accessed 11 October 2016.

Global Citizen. 2016. "Sweden's New Global Deal Will Boost Employment and the SDGs." 12 October. New York. www.globalcitizen.org/en/content/sweden-new-global-deal/. Accessed 7 November 2016.

Global Initiative to End All Corporal Punishment of Children. 2015. "Towards Non-violent Schools: Prohibiting All Corporal Punishment, Global Report 2015." London. www.endcorporalpunishment.org/assets/pdfs/reports-thematic/Schools%20Report%202015-EN.pdf. Accessed 26 October 2016.

Global Witness. 2016. "On Dangerous Ground." London. www.globalwitness.org/en/reports/dangerous-ground/. Accessed 26 October 2016.

Gómez, O.A., A. Muto and S.G. Kamidohzono. 2016. "Sharing the Journey: The Way Ahead for Human Development and Human Security Frameworks." Background paper for Human Development Report 2016. United Nations Development Programme, Human Development Report Office, New York.

Grant Thornton. 2016. "Women in Business: Turning Promise into Practice." London. www.grantthornton.global/en/insights/articles/women-in-business-2016/.

Greenpeace. 2016a. "Refrigeration that Won't Heat Up the Planet." www.greenpeace.org/international/en/campaigns/climate-change/Solutions/Climate-friendly-refrigeration/. Accessed 8 November 2016.

———. 2016b. "10 Years Ago the Amazon Was Being Bulldozed for Soy—Then Everything Changed." www.greenpeace.org/usa/victories/amazon-rainforest-deforestation-soy-moratorium-success/. Accessed 8 November 2016.

Greytak, E.A., J.G. Kosciw, C. Villenas and N.M. Giga. 2016. "From Teasing to Torment: School Climate Revisited, A Survey of U.S. Secondary School Students and Teachers." GLSEN, New York. www.glsen.org/sites/default/files/TeasingtoTorment%202015%20FINAL%20PDF%5B1%5D_0.pdf. Accessed 14 October 2016.

Griffith-Jones, S. 2016. "Global Governance and Growth for Human Development." Background paper for Human Development Report 2016. United Nations Development Programme, Human Development Report Office, New York.

Griffith-Jones, S., and G. Cozzi. 2015. "Investment-led Growth: A Solution to the European Crisis." *Political Quarterly* 86: 119–133.

The Guardian. 2016a. "Brazil is 'Badly Losing' the Battle against Zika Virus, Says Health Minister." 26 January. www.theguardian.com/world/2016/jan/26/brazil-zika-virus-health-minister-armed-forces-eradication. Accessed 30 November 2016.

———. 2016b. "South Africa to Quit International Criminal Court." www.theguardian.com/world/2016/oct/21/south-africa-to-quit-international-criminal-court-document-shows. Accessed 8 November 2016.

GWG (Global Working Group on Big Data for Official Statistics). 2016. "UN Big Data for Official Statistics." United Nations Department of Economic and Social Affairs, New York. http://unstats.un.org/bigdata/. Accessed 7 November 2016.

Hallegatte, S., M. Bangalore, L. Bonzanigo, M. Fay, T. Kane, U. Narloch, J. Rozenberg, D. Treguer and A. Vogt-Schilb. 2016. *Shock Waves: Managing the Impacts of Climate Change on Poverty.* Climate Change and Development Series. Washington, DC: World Bank. https://openknowledge.worldbank.org/bitstream/handle/10986/22787/9781464806735.pdf. Accessed 25 August 2016.

Harris, R.D., and W.M. Marks. 2009. "Compact Ultrasound for Improving Maternal and Perinatal Care in Low-Resource Settings: Review of the Potential Benefits, Implementation Challenges and Public Health Issues." *Journal of Ultrasound Medicine* 28: 1067–1076.

Heckman, J., R. Pinto and P. Savelyev. 2013. "Understanding the Mechanisms through Which an Influential Early Childhood Program Boosted Adult Outcomes." *American Economic Review* 103(6): 2052–86.

HelpAge International and Center for Demographic Research. 2015. "Breaking the Silence: Elder Abuse in the Republic of Moldova." Chisinau, Moldova. www.refworld.org/pdfid/566a972e4.pdf. Accessed 26 October 2016.

Hemmelgarn, T., G. Nicodème, B. Tasnadi and P. Vermote. 2015. "Financial Transaction Taxes in the European Union." Taxation Papers Working Paper 62. Brussels. www.steuer-gegen-armut.org/fileadmin/Dateien/Kampagnen-Seite/Unterstuetzung_Ausland/EU/2015-2016/1602_EU_Commission.pdf. Accessed 30 September 2016.

Herzer, D., P. Huhne and P. Nunnenkamp. 2014. "FDI and Income Inequality: Evidence from Latin American Economies." *Review of Development Economics* 18(4): 778–793.

Hillis, S., J. Mercy, A. Amobi and H. Kress. 2014. "Global Prevalence of Past-year Violence against Children: A Systematic Review and Minimum Estimates." *Pediatrics* 137(3):e20154079.

Hillman, A.L., and E. Jenkner. 2004. "Educating Children in Poor Countries." Economic Issues 33. International Monetary Fund, Washington, DC. www.imf.org/external/pubs/ft/issues/issues33/. Accessed 7 November 2016.

Hollow, M. 2013. "Crowdfunding and Civic Society in Europe: A Profitable Partnership?" *Open Citizenship* 4(1): 68–73. www.academia.edu/3415172/Crowdfunding_and_Civic_Society_in_Europe_A_Profitable_Partnership. Accessed 11 October 2016.

HOPE XXL. 2015. "The Liemers List: Final Version." Duiven, The Netherlands. www.hope-xxl.com/downloads/liemers-list-final-version.pdf. Accessed 7 November 2016.

Hunt, A., and E. Samman. 2016. "Women's Economic Empowerment: Navigating Enablers and Constraints." Research Report. Overseas Development Institute, London. www.odi.org/sites/odi.org.uk/files/resource-documents/10683.pdf. Accessed 7 November 2016.

IANYD (United Nations Inter-Agency Network on Youth Development). 2016. "Young People's Participation in Peacebuilding: A Practice Note." New York. www.un.org/en/peacebuilding/pbso/pdf/Practice%20Note%20Youth%20&%20Peacebuilding%20-%20January%202016.pdf. Accessed 11 October 2016.

ICAP (International Carbon Action Partnership). 2016. "Korea Emissions Trading Scheme." 26 September, Berlin. https://icapcarbonaction.com/en/?option=com_etsmap&task=export&format=pdf&layout=list&systems[]=47. Accessed 22 November 2016.

ICF International. 2016. "Data." DHS Program. Rockville, MD. www.dhsprogram.com/Data/. Accessed 15 July 2016.

IEA (International Energy Agency). 2016a. "Decoupling of Global Emissions and Economic Growth Confrmed." Press release, 16 March. Paris. www.iea.org/newsroom/news/2016/march/decoupling-of-global-emissions-and-economic-growth-confirmed.html. Accessed 24 October 2016.

———. 2016b. *Energy and Air Pollution: World Energy Outlook Special Report.* Paris. www.iea.org/publications/freepublications/publication/WorldEnergyOutlookSpecialReport2016EnergyandAirPollution.pdf. Accessed 23 August 2016.

———. 2016c. "WEI 2016: Fact Sheet." Paris. www.iea.org/media/publications/wei/WEI2016FactSheet.pdf. Accessed 14 October 2016.

———. 2016d. *World Energy Outlook 2016.* www.iea.org/media/publications/weo/WEO2016Factsheet.pdf. Accessed 1 November 2016.

IEP (Institute for Economics and Peace). 2015. "Global Terrorism Index 2015: Measuring and Understanding the Impact of Terrorism." New York. http://economicsandpeace.org/wp-content/uploads/2015/11/Global-Terrorism-Index-2015.pdf. Accessed 23 August 2016.

———. 2016. "Global Peace Index 2016: Ten Years of Measuring Peace." New York. http://static.visionofhumanity.org/sites/default/files/GPI%202016%20Report_2.pdf. Accessed 23 August 2016.

IFAD (International Fund for Agricultural Development). 2009. "Macedonia: Agricultural Financial Services Project." Project Completion Digests. Rome. http://operations.ifad.org/documents/654016/037e464d-864a-458d-b142-dcdf0086bca8. Accessed 7 November 2016.

———. 2012. "Indigenous Peoples: Valuing, Respecting and Supporting Diversity." Rome. www.ifad.org/documents/10180/0f2e8980-09bc-45d6-b43b-8518a64962b3. Accessed 1 November 2016.

———. 2016. "Rural Poverty Portal." Rome. www.ruralpovertyportal.org/country/statistics/tags/macedonia. Accessed 7 November 2016.

IFPRI (International Food Policy Research Institute). 2015. *Global Nutrition Report 2015: Actions and Accountability to Advance Nutrition and Sustainable*

Development. Washington, DC. http://ebrary.ifpri. org/utils/getfile/collection/p15738coll2/id/129443/ filename/129654.pdf. Accessed 24 August 2016.

IHME (Institute for Health Metrics and Evaluation). 2016. "Rethinking Development and Health: Findings from the Global Burden of Disease Study." IHME University of Washington, Seattle. www.healthdata.org/policy-report/ rethinking-development-and-health-findings-global- burden-disease-study. Accessed 4 November 2016.

IHS (Indian Health Service, Federal Health Program for American Indians and Alaska Natives). 2016. "Disparities." Fact sheet. Rockville, MD. www.ihs.gov/ newsroom/factsheets/disparities/. Accessed 28 October 2016.

IISD (International Institute for Sustainable Development). 2016. "Fossil-Fuel Subsidies." Global Subsidies Initiative, Geneva. www.iisd.org/gsi/fossil-fuel- subsidies. Accessed 7 November 2016.

ILGA (International Lesbian, Gay, Bisexual, Trans and Intersex Association). 2016a. "Global Attitudes Survey on LGBTI People." Geneva. http://ilga.org/what-we-do/ ilga-riwi-global-attitudes-survey-lgbti-logo/. Accessed 2 November 2016.

———. **2016b.** "Sexual Orientation Laws in the World: Criminalisation." Geneva. http://ilga.org/downloads/04_ ILGA_WorldMap_ENGLISH_Crime_May2016.pdf. Accessed 26 October 2016.

———. **2016c.** "Sexual Orientation Laws in the World: Overview." Geneva. http://ilga.org/downloads/03_ILGA_ WorldMap_ENGLISH_Overview_May2016.pdf. Accessed 26 October 2016.

ILO (International Labour Organization). 2012. "ILO Global Estimate of Forced Labour: Results and Methodology." Geneva. www.ilo.org/wcmsp5/groups/ public/---ed_norm/---declaration/documents/publication/ wcms_182004.pdf. Accessed 26 October 2016.

———. **2014a.** "Brazil, Cadastro Único: Operating a Registry through a National Public Bank." Geneva.

———. **2014b.** "Decent Work and Social Justice in Pacific Small Island Developing States: Challenges, Opportunities and Policy Responses." ILO Office for Pacific Island Countries, Suva, Fiji Islands. www.ilo.org/wcmsp5/ groups/public/---dgreports/---nylo/documents/publication/ wcms_242172.pdf. Accessed 28 November 2016.

———. **2015a.** "Global Employment Trends for Youth 2015: Scaling Up Investments in Decent Jobs for Youth." Geneva. www.ilo.org/wcmsp5/groups/public/- --dgreports/---dcomm/---publ/documents/publication/ wcms_412015.pdf. Accessed 23 August 2016.

———. **2015b.** *World Employment and Social Outlook: The Changing Nature of Jobs.* Geneva. www.ilo.org/wcmsp5/ groups/public/---dgreports/---dcomm/---publ/documents/ publication/wcms_368626.pdf. Accessed 11 October 2016.

———. **2015c.** *World Employment and Social Outlook: Trends 2015.* Geneva. www.ilo.org/wcmsp5/groups/ public/@dgreports/@dcomm/@publ/documents/ publication/wcms_337069.pdf. Accessed 14 October 2016.

———. **2016a.** "Our Impact, Their Voices: Helping Syrian Refugees Formalize Their Work Status through Cooperatives." 26 June. Geneva. www.ilo.org/beirut/

media-centre/fs/WCMS_493964/lang--en/index.htm. Accessed 10 November 2016.

———. **2016b.** "Women in Business and Management: Gaining Momentum in the Middle East and North Africa." Regional Office for Arab States, Beirut. www. ilo.org/wcmsp5/groups/public/---arabstates/---ro-beirut/ documents/publication/wcms_446101.pdf. Accessed 7 November 2016.

———. **2016c.** "Women at Work: Trends 2016." Geneva. http://ilo.org/wcmsp5/groups/public/---dgreports/--- dcomm/---publ/documents/publication/wcms_457317.pdf. Accessed 7 November 2016.

———. **2016d.** *World Employment and Social Outlook 2016: Transforming Jobs to End Poverty.* Geneva. https://sustainabledevelopment.un.org/content/ documents/10290ILO%20WESO(2016).pdf. Accessed 11 October 2016.

———. **2016e.** *World Employment and Social Outlook: Trends for Youth 2016.* Geneva. www.ilo.org/wcmsp5/ groups/public/---dgreports/---dcomm/---publ/documents/ publication/wcms_513739.pdf. Accessed 20 October 2016.

IMF (International Monetary Fund). 2012. *The Liberalization and Management of Capital Flows: An Institutional View.* Washington, DC.

———. **2016a.** "IMF Members' Quotas and Voting Power, and IMF Board of Governors." Washington, DC. www.imf. org/external/np/sec/memdir/members.aspx. Accessed 16 December 2016.

———. **2016b.** "IMF Survey: IMF Reforms Policy for Exceptional Access Lending." www.imf.org/external/ pubs/ft/survey/so/2016/pol012916a.htm. Accessed 21 December 2016.

———. **2016c.** "Past IMF Disbursements and Repayments for All Members." Washington, DC. www.imf.org/exter- nal/np/fin/tad/extrep1.aspx. Accessed 10 November 2016.

———. **2016d.** *World Economic Outlook: October 2016: Subdued Demand: Symptoms and Remedies.* World Economic and Financial Surveys. Washington, DC. www. imf.org/external/pubs/ft/weo/2016/02/pdf/text.pdf. Accessed 7 November 2016.

Independent Commission on Multilateralism. 2016. *UN 2030: Rebuilding Order in a Fragmenting World.* New York. www.ipinst.org/wp-content/uploads/2016/08/ IPI-ICM-UN-2030-Chairs-Report2FINAL.pdf. Accessed 26 September 2016.

Independent Evaluation Office of the International Monetary Fund. 2013. *The Role of the IMF as Trusted Advisor.* Evaluation Report. www.ieo-imf.org/ieo/ files/completedevaluations/RITA_-_Main_Report.pdf. Accessed 8 November 2016.

Indrawati, S.M. 2015. "Discriminating against Women Keeps Countries Poorer." Voices: Perspectives on Development (Blog), 10 September. Washington, DC. http://blogs.worldbank.org/voices/discriminating-against- women-keeps-countries-poorer. Accessed 14 October 2016.

INSD (Burkina Faso Institut National de la Statistique et de la Démographie). 2016. "Chiffres clés." Ouagadougou. www.insd.bf/n/. Accessed 22 November 2016.

IOC (International Olympic Committee). 2016. "Kimia Alizadeh: The Yog Star Flying the Flag for Female Athletes

in Iran." 26 August. Lausanne, Switzerland. www.olympic. org/news/kimia-alizadeh-the-yog-star-flying-the-flag-for- female-athletes-in-iran. Accessed 14 October 2016.

IOM (International Organization for Migration). 2014. "Global Migration Trends: An Overview." Geneva. http:// missingmigrants.iom.int/sites/default/files/Global- migration-trends_December-2014_final.pdf. Accessed 26 October 2016.

———. **2015.** *World Migration Report 2015: Migrants and Cities: New Partnerships to Manage Mobility.* Geneva. http://publications.iom.int/system/files/wmr2015_en.pdf. Accessed 26 September 2016.

———. **2016a.** *IOM Regional Response to the Syria Crisis.* Geneva. http://reliefweb.int/sites/reliefweb.int/files/ resources/IOM%20Regional%20Response%20to%20 the%20Syria%20Crisis%20Sitrep%20%28June%20 2016%29.pdf. Accessed 7 November 2016.

———. **2016b.** *IOM Regional Response to the Syria Crisis* [infographic]. Geneva. www.iom.int/sites/default/files/ country/docs/IOM-Regional-Response-to-the-Syria-Crisis- Map-March2016.pdf. Accessed 16 December 2016.

IPCC (Intergovernmental Panel on Climate Change). 2000. *Special Report on Emission Scenarios.* Cambridge, UK: Cambridge University Press.

IPPR (Institute for Public Policy Research). 2012. "Modern Women Marrying Men of the Same or Lower Social Class." 5 April. London. www.ippr.org/news-and- media/press-releases/modern-women-marrying-men- of-the-same-or-lower-social-class. Accessed 27 October 2016.

IPU (Inter-Parliamentary Union). 2016. Women in na- tional parliaments. www.ipu.org/wmn-e/classif-arc.htm. Accessed 19 July 2016.

ITC (International Trade Centre). 2014. "Trade in Environmental Goods and Services: Opportunities and Challenges." Technical Paper. Geneva. www.intracen. org/uploadedFiles/intracenorg/Content/Publications/ AssetPDF/EGS%20Ecosystems%20Brief%20040914%20 -%20low%20res.pdf. Accessed 27 October 2016.

ITU (International Telecommunication Union). 2016a. *End-2016 Estimates for Key ICT Indicators.* Geneva. www. itu.int/en/ITU-D/Statistics/Documents/statistics/2016/ ITU_Key_2005-2016_ICT_data.xls. Accessed 4 December 2016.

———. **2016b.** "ICT Facts and Figures 2016." Geneva. www.itu.int/en/ITU-D/Statistics/Documents/facts/ ICTFactsFigures2016.pdf. Accessed 26 October 2016.

IWGIA (International Work Group for Indigenous Affairs). 2016. "Indigenous Peoples' Education." Copenhagen. www.iwgia.org/culture-and-identity/ indigenous-peoples-and-education. Accessed 28 October 2016.

Jahan, S. 2003. "Evolution of the Human Development Index." In S. Fukuda-Parr and A.K. Shiva Kumar, eds., *Readings in Human Development: Concepts, Measures and Policies for a Development Paradigm.* New Delhi: Oxford University Press.

———. **2010.** *Freedom for Choice: Essays in Human Development.* Dhaka: Shahitya Prakash.

Jenks, B., and J. Topping. 2016. *Financing the United Nations Development System: Current Trends and New Directions.* Uppsala, Sweden: Dag Hammarskjold Foundation and Multi-Partner Trust Fund Office.

Johnson, C., and D. Start. 2001. "Rights, Claims and Capture: Understanding the Politics of Pro-Poor Policy." Working Paper 145. Overseas Development Institute, London. www.odi.org/sites/odi.org.uk/files/odi-assets/publications-opinion-files/2319.pdf. Accessed 27 October 2016.

Joshi, A. 2010. "Review of Impact and Effectiveness of Transparency and Accountability Initiatives: Annex 1 Service Delivery." Paper prepared for the Transparency and Accountability Initiative Workshop, Institute of Development Studies, 14–15 October, Brighton, UK. www.ids.ac.uk/files/dmfile/IETAAnnex1ServicedeliveryJoshiFinal28Oct2010.pdf. Accessed 22 November 2016.

Kahneman, D. 2011. *Thinking, Fast and Slow*. New York: Farrar, Straus and Giroux.

Kahneman, D., and A. Tversky, eds. 2000. *Choices, Values and Frames*. Cambridge: Cambridge University Press; New York: Russell Sage Foundation.

Kaldor, M. 1999. *New and Old Wars: Organized Violence in a Global Era*. Cambridge, UK: Polity Press.

———. 2013. "In Defense of New Wars." *Stability: International Journal of Security and Development* 2(1). www.stabilityjournal.org/articles/10.5334/sta.at/. Accessed 19 December 2016.

Kar, D., and J. Spanjers. 2015. "Illicit Financial Flows from Developing Countries: 2004–2013." Global Financial Integrity, Washington, DC. www.gfintegrity.org/wp-content/uploads/2015/12/IFF-Update_2015-Final-1.pdf. Accessed 22 November 2016.

Karki, M., and A.K. Bohara. 2014. "Evidence of Earnings Inequality Based on Caste in Nepal." *Developing Economies* 52(3): 262–286.

Karlan, D., and J. Appel. 2011. *More Than Good Intentions: How a New Economics Is Helping to Solve Global Poverty*. New York: Dutton Adult.

Keeley, B. 2009. *International Migration: The Human Face of Globalization*. OECD Insights. Paris. www.oecd-ilibrary.org/docserver/download/0109111e.pdf?expires=1460475031&id=id&accname=guest&checksum=600363DC6E73F73CCFACB0DAF7A97E36. Accessed 26 October 2016.

Kelley, D.J., A. Ali, C. Brush, A.C. Corbett, C. Daniels, P.H. Kim, T.S. Lyons, M. Majbouri and E.G. Rogoff. 2015. "Global Entrepreneurship Monitor: 2014 United States Report." Global Entrepreneurship Research Association, London Business School, London. www.babson.edu/Academics/centers/blank-center/global-research/gem/Documents/GEM%20USA%202014.pdf. Accessed 2 November 2016.

Kembhavi, R. 2013. "Political Participation among Seniors." Research Note. Elections Canada, Gatineau, Quebec, Canada. www.elections.ca/res/rec/part/partsen/pdf/sen_e.pdf. Accessed 7 November 2016.

Keswell, M., S. Girdwood and M. Leibbrandt. 2013. "Educational Inheritance and the Distribution of Occupations: Evidence from South Africa." *Review of Income and Wealth* 59(S1): S111–S137.

Keuleers, P. 2016. "Securing Our Societies from the Threat of Senseless Terrorism." Our Perspectives (Blog), 11 April. New York. www.undp.org/content/undp/en/home/blog/2016/4/11/Securing-our-societies-from-the-threat-of-senseless-terrorism-.html. Accessed 11 October 2016.

Khan, I. 2016. "Pathways to Justice: Rule of Law, Human Rights, Sustainable Development and Human Security." Background paper for Human Development Report 2016. United Nations Development Programme, Human Development Report Office, New York.

Kharas, H., and G. Gertz. 2010. "The New Global Middle Class: A Crossover from West to East." In *China's Emerging Middle Class: Beyond Economic Transformation*, Cheng Li, ed. Washington, DC: Brookings Institution Press.

Kim, C.-Y. 2011. *From Despair to Hope: Economic Policy Making in Korea: 1945-1979*. Seoul: Korean Development Institute.

Kim, D.-I. and R.H. Topel. 1995. "Labor Markets and Economic Growth: Lessons from Korea's Industrialization, 1970-1990." In R.B. Freeman and L. Katz, eds., *Differences and Changes in Wage Structures*. Chicago, IL: University of Chicago Press.

Kim, K.S., and J.K. Kim. 1997. "Korean Economic Development: An Overview." In D.-S. Cha, K.S. Kim and D.H. Perkins, *The Korean Economy 1945-1995: Performance and Vision for the 21st Century*. Seoul: Korea Development Institute.

Kim, T.-H. 2011. "Development of a Gender Equality Index and Measurement of Gender Equality in South Korea." *Gender Studies and Policy Review* 4: 80–93.

Kreft, S., D. Eckstein, L. Dorsch and L. Fischer. 2015. "Global Climate Risk Index 2016: Who Suffers Most from Extreme Weather Events? Weather-Related Loss Events in 2014 and 1995 to 2014." Germanwatch Briefing Paper. Bonn, Germany. http://docplayer.net/18855757-Global-climate-risk-index-2016.html. Accessed 3 November 2016.

Krishnan, N., G.L. Ibarra, A. Narayan, S. Tiwari and T. Vishwanath. 2016. *Uneven Odds, Unequal Outcomes: Inequality of Opportunity in the Middle East and North Africa*. Directions in Development: Poverty Series. Washington, DC: World Bank.

Kronfol, N.M. 2012. "Access and Barriers to Health Care Delivery in Arab Countries: A Review." *Eastern Mediterranean Health Journal* 18(12): 1239–1246.

Kynge, J. 2016. "China in Three Numbers." *Financial Times*, 13 July. http://video.ft.com/5032304024001/China-in-three-numbers/World. Accessed 14 October 2016.

Lambert, S., M. Ravallion and D. van de Walle. 2014. "Intergenerational Mobility and Interpersonal Inequality in an African Economy." *Journal of Development Economics* 110(C): 327–344.

Lattier, D. 2015. "32 Million U.S. Adults Are 'Functionally Illiterate': What Does That Even Mean?" 25 August. Intellectual Takeout, Bloomington, MN. www.intellectualtakeout.org/blog/32-million-us-adults-are-functionally-illiterate-what-does-even-mean. Accessed 26 October 2016.

Lawson, M. 2016. "It's Time to Demolish the Myth of Trickle-Down Economics." 19 July. World Economic Forum, Geneva. www.weforum.org/agenda/2016/07/it-s-time-to-demolish-the-myth-of-trickle-down-economics. Accessed 11 October 2016.

Le Coz, C. 2016. "As Acid Attacks Rise against Women, Laws Help to Deter Such Assaults." City University of New York, Ralph Bunche Institute for International Studies, New York. www.passblue.com/2016/02/29/as-acid-attacks-rise-against-women-laws-help-deter-such-assaults/. Accessed 14 October 2016.

Lee, J.H., and D.-I. Kim. 1997. "Labor Market Developments and Reforms in Korea." Working Paper 9703. Korean Development Institute, Seoul.

Lee, K., W. Shin and H. Shin. 2015. "How Large or Small in the Policy Space? WTO Regime and Industrial Policy." In J. Alonso and J. Ocampo, eds., *Global Governance and Rules for the Post-2015 Era: Addressing Emerging Issues in the Global Environment*. New York: Bloomsbury.

Lewis, K., and S. Burd-Sharps. 2013. *American Human Development Report: The Measure of America 2013–2014*. New York: Measure of America. www.measureofamerica.org/wp-content/uploads/2013/06/MOA-III.pdf. Accessed 26 October 2016.

LIS (Luxembourg Income Study). 2016. "LIS Database." Cross-National Data Center in Luxembourg, Luxembourg. www.lisdatacenter.org/our-data/lis-database/. Accessed 15 July 2016.

Lloyd, M. 2015. "A Decade of Affirmative Action in Brazil: Lessons for the Global Debate." In R.T. Teranishi, L.B. Pazich, M. Knobel and W.R. Allen, eds., *Mitigating Inequality: Higher Education Research, Policy and Practice in an Era of Massification and Stratification*. Bingley, UK: Emerald Group Publishing. www.ses.unam.mx/integrantes/uploadfile/mlloyd/Lloyd_ADecadeOffAffirmativeActionInBrazil.pdf. Accessed 22 November 2016.

Lyons, K. 2015. "The Gambia Bans Female Genital Mutilation." *The Guardian*, 24 November. London. www.theguardian.com/society/2015/nov/24/the-gambia-bans-female-genital-mutilation. Accessed 14 October 2016.

Mandavilli, A. 2016. "Female Scientists Turn to Data to Fight Lack of Representation on Panels." *New York Times*, 5 September.

Mann, T. 2014. "Prejudice at the Polling Booth: Disabled Indonesians Face Barriers in Voting." Asia Foundation, Jakarta. http://asiafoundation.org/2014/04/09/prejudice-at-the-polling-booth-disabled-indonesians-face-barriers-in-voting/. Accessed 7 November 2016.

ManpowerGroup. 2016. "Millennial Careers: 2020 Vision, Facts, Figures and Practical Advice from Workforce Experts." Milwaukee, WI. www.manpowergroup.com/wps/wcm/connect/660ebf65-144c-489e-975c-9f838294c237/MillennialsPaper1_2020Vision_lo.pdf?MOD=AJPERES. Accessed 20 October 2016.

Martínez-Franzoni, J. and D. Sánchez-Ancochea. 2016. "Achieving Universalism in Developing Countries." Background paper for Human Development Report 2016. United Nations Development Programme, Human Development Report Office, New York.

Marx, A., J. Soares and W. Van Acker. 2015. "The Protection of International Labour Rights: A Longitudinal Analysis of the Protection of the Rights of Freedom of Association and Collective Bargaining over 30 Years in 73 Countries." In A. Marx, J. Wouters, G. Rayp and L. Beke, eds., *Global Governance of Labour Rights: Assessing the Effectiveness of Transnational Public and Private Policy Initiatives*. Leuven Global Governance Series. Cheltenham, UK: Edward Elgar Publishing.

Marx, A., J. Wouters, G. Rayp and L. Beke, eds. 2015. *Global Governance of Labour Rights: Assessing the Effectiveness of Transnational Public and Private Policy Initiatives*. Leuven Global Governance Series. Cheltenham, UK: Edward Elgar Publishing.

Matheson, T. 2011. "Taxing Financial Transactions: Issues and Evidence." Working Paper WP/11/54. Washington, DC: International Monetary Fund.

McGee, R., and C. Kroesschell. 2013. "Local Accountabilities in Fragile Contexts: Experiences from Nepal, Bangladesh and Mozambique." IDS Working Paper 422. Institute of Development Studies, Brighton, UK. www.ids.ac.uk/download.cfm?objectid=E8A258F0-A82B-11E2-806C005056AA0D87. Accessed 7 November 2016.

McGinn, K.L., M.R. Castro and E.L. Lingo. 2015. "Mums the Word! Cross-National Effects of Maternal Employment on Gender Inequalities at Work and at Home." Harvard Business School Working Paper 15–094. Harvard Business School, Boston, MA. https://dash.harvard.edu/bitstream/handle/1/16727933/15-094%20(2).pdf?sequence=4. Accessed 26 October 2016.

McKenzie, A.D. 2014. "A Billion Tons of Food Wasted Yearly While Millions Still Go Hungry." Inter Press Service, 9 October. www.ipsnews.net/2014/10/a-billion-tons-of-food-wasted-yearly-while-millions-still-go-hungry/. Accessed 24 August 2016.

McKinsey Global Institute. 2012. "Africa at Work: Job Creation and Inclusive Growth." London. www.mckinsey.com/global-themes/middle-east-and-africa/africa-at-work. Accessed 28 November 2016.

———. 2014. "Global Flows in a Digital Age: How Trade, Finance, People, and Data Connect the World Economy." New York. www.mckinsey.com/~/media/mckinsey/global%20themes/globalization/global%20flows%20in%20a%20digital%20age/mgi%20global%20flows%20in%20a%20digial%20age%20executive%20summary.ashx. Accessed 11 October 2016.

Mekonnen, M.M., and A. Hoekstra. 2016. "Four Billion People Facing Severe Water Scarcity." Science Advances 2(2). http://advances.sciencemag.org/content/2/2/e1500323. Accessed 14 December 2016.

Mercurio, B. 2014. "International Investment Agreements and Public Health: Neutralizing a Threat through Treaty Drafting." Bulletin of the World Health Organization 92: 520–525.

Milanovic, B. 2016. Global Inequality: A New Approach for the Age of Globalization. Cambridge, MA: Harvard University Press. www.hup.harvard.edu/catalog.php?isbn=9780674737136. Accessed 20 October 2016.

MINN (Minnesota International NGO Network). 2016. Why Do So Many Developing Countries Fail to Develop? Minneapolis, MN. www.minnesotangos.org/event/why-do-so-many-developing-countries-fail-develop. Accessed 7 November 2016.

Montes, M., and P. Lunenborg. 2016. "Trade Rules and Integration Trends and Human Development." Background paper for Human Development Report 2016. United Nations Development Programme, Human Development Report Office, New York.

Moss-Racusin, C.A., J.F. Dovidio, V.L. Brescoll, M.J. Graham and J. Handelsman. 2012. "Science Faculty's Subtle Gender Biases Favor Male Students." Proceedings of the National Academy of Sciences 109(41): 16474–16479.

Murray, C.J.L., R.M. Barber, K.J. Foreman, A.A. Ozgoren, F. Abd-Allah, S.F. Abera, V. Aboyans and others. 2015. "Global, Regional, and National Disability-Adjusted Life Years (DALYs) for 306 Diseases and Injuries and Healthy Life Expectancy (HALE) for 188 Countries, 1990–2013: Quantifying the Epidemiological Transition." Lancet 386(10009): 2145–2191.

Nair, R. 2016. "Economic Survey Says the Rich Get Implicit Subsidy of More Than Rs1 Trillion." Livemint, 10 December. www.livemint.com/Specials/d4pZ9spLnUtMu55D59GI8I/Why-should-rich-benefit-from-subsidies.html. Accessed 7 November 2016.

Nave, A. 2000. "Marriage and the Maintenance of Ethnic Group Boundaries: The Case of Mauritius." Ethnic and Racial Studies 23(2): 329–352.

Neuvonen, A. 2016. "Thousands to Receive Basic Income in Finland: A Trial That Could Lead to the Greatest Societal Transformation of Our Time." Demos Helsinki, 30 August. www.demoshelsinki.fi/en/2016/08/30/thousands-to-receive-basic-income-in-finland-a-trial-that-could-lead-to-the-greatest-societal-transformation-of-our-time/. Accessed 7 November 2016.

New York Times. 2016. "Thousands Sign Petition to Abolish Guardianship of Women in Saudi Arabia." Women in the World, 27 September. http://nytlive.nytimes.com/womenintheworld/2016/09/27/thousands-sign-petition-to-abolish-guardianship-of-women-in-saudi-arabia/. Accessed 14 October 2016.

Newbold, T., L.N. Hudson, A.P. Arnell, S. Contu, A. De Palma, S. Ferrier, S.L.L. Hill and others. 2016. "Has Land Use Pushed Terrestrial Biodiversity beyond the Planetary Boundary? A Global Assessment." Science 353(6296): 288–291. http://science.sciencemag.org/content/353/0290/200. Accessed 20 October 2016.

Ng, M., T. Fleming, M. Robinson, N. Thomson, N. Graetz, C. Margono, E.C. Mullany and others. 2014. "Global, Regional, and National Prevalence of Overweight and Obesity in Children and Adults during 1980–2013: A Systematic Analysis for the Global Burden of Disease Study 2013." Lancet 384(9945): 766–781.

Niño-Zarazúa, M., L. Roope and F. Tarp. 2016. "Global Inequality: Relatively Lower, Absolutely Higher." Review of Income and Wealth. http://onlinelibrary.wiley.com/doi/10.1111/roiw.12240/full. Accessed 11 October 2016.

Nnochiri, I. 2012. "Nigeria Loses $400bn to Oil Thieves — Ezekwesili." Vanguard, 28 August. www.vanguardngr.com/2012/08/nigeria-loses-400bn-to-oil-thieves-ezekwesili/. Accessed 7 November 2016.

Nussbaum, M.C. 2003. "Capabilities as Fundamental Entitlements: Sen and Social Justice." Feminist Economics 9(2–3): 33–59.

Ocampo, J. 2015a. "Reforming the International Monetary and Financial Architecture." In J. Alonso and J. Ocampo, eds., Global Governance and Rules for the Post-2015 Era: Addressing Emerging Issues in the Global Environment. New York: Bloomsbury.

———. 2015b. A Special Moment for Special Drawing Rights. www.project-syndicate.org/commentary/has-moment-come-for-special-drawing-right-by-jose-antonio-ocampo-2015-10. Accessed 8 November 2016.

ODI (Overseas Development Institute). 2016. Leaving No One Behind: A Critical Path for the First 1,000 Days of the Sustainable Development Goals. London. www.odi.org/sites/odi.org.uk/files/resource-documents/10692.pdf. Accessed 14 October 2016.

OECD (Organisation for Economic Co-operation and Development). 2008. "The Paris Declaration on Aid Effectiveness and the Accra Agenda for Action 2005/2008." Paris. www.oecd.org/dac/effectiveness/34428351.pdf. Accessed 2 December 2016.

———. 2011. "An Overview of Growing Income Inequalities in OECD Countries: Main Findings." In Divided We Stand: Why Inequality Keeps Rising. Paris. www.oecd.org/els/soc/49499779.pdf. Accessed 27 October 2016.

———. 2015a. Health at a Glance 2015: OECD Indicators. Paris. http://apps.who.int/medicinedocs/documents/s22177en/s22177en.pdf. Accessed 28 October 2016.

———. 2015b. Integrating Social Services for Vulnerable Groups: Bridging Sectors for Better Service Delivery. Paris. www.keepeek.com/Digital-Asset-Management/oecd/social-issues-migration-health/integrating-the-delivery-of-social-services-for-vulnerable-groups_9789264233775-en#.WBOInC0rIdU#page8. Accessed 28 October 2016.

———. 2015c. OECD Yearbook 2015. Paris.

———. 2016a. "Education at a Glance 2016: OECD Indicators." Paris. www.oecd.org/edu/education-at-a-glance-19991487.htm. Accessed 28 October 2016.

———. 2016b. How's Life in Korea? Paris.

———. 2016c. OECD Better Life Index. Paris.

———. 2016d. OECD Statistics. Paris. http://stats.oecd.org/#. Accessed 21 October 2016.

———. 2016e. Society at a Glance 2016, OECD Social Indicators: A Spotlight on Youth. Paris. http://static.pulso.cl/20161005/2338198.pdf. Accessed 28 October 2016.

———. 2016f. "Statistics on Resource Flows to Developing Countries." Paris. www.oecd.org/dac/financing-sustainable-development/development-finance-data/statisticsonresourceflowstodevelopingcountries.htm. Accessed 16 December 2016.

OECD (Organisation for Economic Co-operation and Development) and UNDESA (United Nations Department of Economic and Social Affairs). 2013. "World Migration in Figures." Paris. www.oecd.org/els/mig/World-Migration-in-Figures.pdf. Accessed 26 October 2016.

Office of the Secretary-General's Envoy on Youth. 2016. #YouthStats: Information and Communication Technology." New York. www.un.org/youthenvoy/information-communication-technology/. Accessed 11 October 2016.

ONS (United Kingdom Office for National Statistics). 2012. "Integrated Household Survey April 2011 to March 2012: Experimental Statistics." Statistical Bulletin, 28 September. London. http://webarchive.nationalarchives.gov.uk/20160105160709/www.ons.gov.uk/ons/dcp171778_280451.pdf. Accessed 26 October 2016.

Ortiz, I., S. Burke, M. Berrada and H. Cortés. 2013. "World Protests 2006–2013." Working Paper. Initiative for Policy Dialogue and Friedrich-Ebert-Stiftung, New York. http://policydialogue.org/files/publications/World_Protests_2006-2013-Executive_Summary.pdf. Accessed 27 October 2016.

Ostry, J., A. Ghosh, K. Habermeier, L. Laeven, M. Chamon, M. Qureshi and A. Kokenyne. 2011. "Managing Capital Inflows: What Tools to Use?" IMF Staff Discussion Note SDN/11/06. Washington, DC: International Monetary Fund.

Pager, D., B. Western and B. Bonikowski. 2009. "Discrimination in a Low-Wage Labor Market: A Field

Experiment." *American Sociological Review* 74(5): 777–799.

PAHO-WHO (Pan American Health Organization–World Health Organization). 2016a. "Region of the Americas Is Declared Free of Measles." 27 September. Washington, DC. www.paho.org/hq/index.php?option=com_content &view=article&id=12528%3Aregion-americas-declared-free-measles. Accessed 14 October 2016.

———. **2016b.** "Guatemala Is the Fourth Country in the World to Eliminate Onchocerciasis, Known as 'River Blindness'." 26 September. Washington, DC. www.paho.org/hq/index.php?option=com_content&view=article&id =12520%3Aguatemala-eliminates-onchocerciasis-river-blindness&Itemid=135&lang=en. Accessed 14 October 2016.

Pan, L., and L. Christiaensen. 2012. "Who Is Vouching for the Input Voucher? Decentralized Targeting and Elite Capture in Tanzania." *World Development* 40(8): 1619–1633.

Parker, L. 2015. "Ocean Trash: 5.25 Trillion Pieces and Counting, but Big Questions Remain." *National Geographic,* 11 January. http://news.nationalgeographic.com/news/2015/01/150109-oceans-plastic-sea-trash-science-marine-debris/. Accessed 26 October 2015.

PATH. 2013. "Breakthrough Innovations That Can Save Women and Children Now." Washington, DC. www.path.org/publications/files/APP_unga_innovations_rpt.pdf. Accessed 7 November 2016.

Patten, E., and R. Fry. 2015. "How Millennials Today Compare with Their Grandparents 50 Years Ago." Factan, 19 March. Pew Research Center, Washington, DC. www.pewresearch.org/fact-tank/2015/03/19/how-millennials-compare-with-their-grandparents/#!17. Accessed 7 November 2016.

Peracod (Programme for the Promotion of Renewable Energy, Rural Electrification and a Sustainable Supply of Household Fuels). 2012. "The Rural Electrification Senegal (ERSEN) Project: Electricity for over 90,000 Persons." Dakar. https://energypedia.info/images/6/61/Rural_Electrification_Senegal_ERSEN_Project_Factsheet.pdf. Accessed 25 August 2016.

Perlo-Freeman, S., A. Fleurant, P. Wezeman and S. Wezeman. 2016. "Trends in World Military Expenditure, 2015." SIPRI Fact Sheet. Stockholm: Stockholm International Peace Research Institute.

Pew Research Center. 2014. "Crime and Corruption Top Problems in Emerging and Developing Countries." Global Attitudes & Trends. Washington, DC. www.pewglobal.org/2014/11/06/crime-and-corruption-top-problems-in-emerging-and-developing-countries/. Accessed 26 October 2016.

———. **2015a.** "Latest Trends in Religious Restrictions and Hostilities, Sidebar: Religious Hostilities and Religious Minorities in Europe." 26 February. Washington, DC. www.pewforum.org/2015/02/26/sidebar-religious-hostilities-and-religious-minorities-in-europe/. Accessed 26 October 2016.

———. **2015b.** "Gay Marriage around the World." 26 June. Washington, DC. www.pewforum.org/2015/06/26/gay-marriage-around-the-world-2013/. Accessed 14 October 2016.

Phiri, J., and J.E. Ataguba. 2014. "Inequalities in Public Health Care Delivery in Zambia." *International Journal for Equity in Health* 13(24).

Piraino, P. 2015. "Intergenerational Earnings Mobility and Equality of Opportunity in South Africa." *World Development* 67(C): 396–405.

PlasticsEurope (Association of Plastics Manufacturers in Europe). 2013. "Plastics, the Facts 2013: An Analysis of European Latest Plastics Production, Demand and Waste Data." Brussels. www.plasticseurope.de/cust/documentrequest.aspx?DocID=59179. Accessed 20 October 2016.

Pollin, R. 2016. "Global Green Growth for Human Development." Background paper for Human Development Report 2016. United Nations Development Programme, Human Development Report Office, New York.

Power, S. 2016. "Remarks at a UN Security Council Open Debate on Women, Peace, and Security." 25 October. New York. https://usun.state.gov/remarks/7505. Accessed 7 November 2016.

Purdie, E., and B.E. Khaltarkhuu. 2016. "Obstacles to Development: What Data Are Available on Fragility, Conflict and Violence?" The Data Blog, 13 July. World Bank, Washington, DC. http://blogs.worldbank.org/opendata/obstacles-development-what-data-are-available-fragility-conflict-and-violence. Accessed 25 August 2016.

Rasooly, M.H., P. Govindasamy, A. Agil, S. Rutstein, F. Arnold, B. Noormal, A. Way, S. Brock and A. Shadoul. 2014. "Success in Reducing Maternal and Child Mortality in Afghanistan." *Global Public Health* 9(Supplement 1): S29–542.

Raub, A., A. Cassola, I. Latz and J. Heymann. 2016. "Protections of Equal Rights across Sexual Orientation and Gender Identity: An Analysis of 193 National Constitutions." *Yale Journal of Law and Feminism* 28(1): 149–169. www.worldpolicycenter.org/sites/default/files/WORLD_Constitutions_SOGI.pdf. Accessed 25 August 2016.

Ravallion, M. 2016. "The World Bank: Why It Is Still Needed and Why It Still Disappoints." *Journal of Economic Perspectives* 30(1): 77–94.

Reinhart, C., and Trebesch, C. 2016. "The International Monetary Fund: 70 Years of Reinvention." *Journal of Economic Perspectives* 30(1): 3–28.

Republic of Ghana. 2012. "Ghana Open Data Initiative." Accra. http://data.gov.gh. Accessed 26 September 2016.

Republic of Kenya. 2011. "Kenya Open Data." Nairobi. https://opendata.go.ke. Accessed 26 September 2016.

Rizwanul, I., and I. Iyanatul. 2015. *Employment and Inclusive Development.* Routledge Studies in Development Economics Series. New York: Routledge.

Rodrik, D. 2011. *The Globalization Paradox: Democracy and the Future of the World Economy.* New York: Norton.

Roy, R., A. Heuty and E. Letouzé. 2007. "Fiscal Space for What? Analytical Issues from a Human Development Perspective." Paper prepared for the G-20 workshop on fiscal policy, Istanbul, 30 June–2 July. www.undp.org/content/dam/aplaws/publication/en/publications/poverty-reduction/poverty-website/fiscal-space-for-what/FiscalSpaceforWhat.pdf. Accessed 7 November 2016.

Ruparelia, S. 2013. "A Progressive Juristocracy? The Unexpected Social Activism of India's Supreme Court." Helen Kellogg Institute Working Paper 391. University of Notre Dame, South Bend, IN. http://citeseerx.ist.psu.edu/viewdoc/download;jsessionid=12495ED2CD0B6B329183D

D50898008F7?doi=10.1.1.352.2424&rep=rep1&type=pdf. Accessed 17 November 2016.

Rutkowski, M. 2016. "Combating Poverty and Building Resilience through Social Protection." *Voices: Perspectives on Development*, 21 September. World Bank, Washington, DC. http://blogs.worldbank.org/voices/combating-poverty-and-building-resilience-through-social-protection. Accessed 7 November 2016.

S4YE (Solutions for Youth Employment). 2015. "Toward Solutions for Youth Employment: A Baseline for 2015." Washington, DC. www.s4ye.org/sites/default/files/Toward_Solutions_for_Youth_Employment_Full.pdf. Accessed 11 October 2016.

Sachs, J. 2012. "How to Make Rich Countries Pay for Climate Change?" http://jeffsachs.org/2012/10/how-to-make-rich-countries-pay-for-climate-change/. Accessed 8 November 2016.

Saez, E., and G. Zucman. 2014. "Wealth Inequality in the United States since 1913: Evidence from Capitalized Income Tax Data." NBER Working Paper 20625. National Bureau of Economic Research, Cambridge, MA. http://gabriel-zucman.eu/files/SaezZucman2014.pdf. Accessed 1 November 2016.

Sandefur, J. 2016. "Measuring the Quality of Girls' Education across the Developing World." Views from the Center: Education, Gender. Center for Global Development, Washington, DC. www.cgdev.org/blog/measuring-quality-girls-education-across-developing-world?utm_source=261018&utm_medium=cgd_email&utm_campaign=cgd_weekly&utm_&&&. Accessed 31 October 2016.

Schmidt-Traub, G. 2015. "Investment Needs to Achieve the Sustainable Development Goals: Understanding the Billions and Trillions." SDSN Working Paper Version 2. Sustainable Development Solutions Network, Paris. http://unsdsn.org/wp-content/uploads/2015/09/151112-SDG-Financing-Needs.pdf. Accessed 19 November 2016.

Schwab, K. 2016. "How Can We Embrace the Opportunities of the Fourth Industrial Revolution?" World Economic Forum, Geneva. www.weforum.org/agenda/2016/01/how-can-we-embrace-the-opportunities-of-the-fourth-industrial-revolution/. Accessed 7 November 2016.

Sen, A. 1985. "Well-being, Agency and Freedom: The Dewey Lectures 1984." *Journal of Philosophy* 2(4): 169–221.

———. **2009.** *The Idea of Justice.* Cambridge, MA: Harvard University Press.

Serafina, P., and R. Tonkin. 2014. "Intergenerational Transmission of Disadvantage in the UK & EU, 2014." 23 September. UK Office for National Statistics, London. http://webarchive.nationalarchives.gov.uk/20160105160709/www.ons.gov.uk/ons/dcp171766_378097.pdf. Accessed 26 October 2016.

Seth, A. 2016. "Macroeconomic Policies for Human Development." Background paper for Human Development Report 2016. United Nations Development Programme, Human Development Report Office, New York.

Shin, G.-W. 1998. "Agrarian Conflict and the Origins of Korean Capitalism." *American Journal of Sociology* 103(5): 1309–1351.

Shriver Center (Sargent Shriver National Center on Poverty Law). 2016. "Older Women and Poverty." *WomanView* 19(9). Chicago. www.ncdsv.

org/SSNCPL_Woman-View-Older-Women-and-Poverty_3-30-2016.pdf. Accessed 1 November 2016.

SIDA (Swedish International Development Agency). 2015. "Women and Land Rights." Gender Tool Box Brief. Stockholm. www.sida.se/English/contact-us/offices-in-sweden/?epieditmode=true. Accessed 26 October 2016.

Simane, M. 2016. "Human Resilience and Human Security in Latvia." Background paper for Human Development Report 2016. United Nations Development Programme, Human Development Report Office, New York.

Smoke, P. 2015. "Quality Support Facilities in the Field of Decentralization, Local Governance and Local Development: Decentralization in Indonesia." Letter of Contract No. 2, 330793. IBF International Consulting and Local Development International and European Union, Brussels.

Social Progress Imperative. 2016. "2016 Social Progress Index." Washington, DC. www.socialprogressimperative.org/global-index/. Accessed 19 July 2016.

Soura, A.B. 2015. "Climate Variability and Water Availability in Ouagadougou's Informal Settlements." International Development Research Centre of Canada, Climate Change and Water Programme, Ouagadougou. https://idl-bnc.idrc.ca/dspace/bitstream/10625/54180/1/IDL-54180.pdf. Accessed 22 November 2016.

Spacehive. 2016. "Spacehive: About Us." London. www.spacehive.com/Home/AboutUs. Accessed 11 October 2016.

Stampini, M., and L. Tornarolli. 2012. "The Growth of Conditional Cash Transfers in Latin America and the Caribbean: Did They Go Too Far?" Social Sector, Social Protection and Health Division Policy Brief IDB-PB-185. Inter-American Development Bank, Washington, DC. https://publications.iadb.org/handle/11319/1448?locale-attribute=en. Accessed 27 October 2016.

State of Japan. 2013. "Japan's Open Data Initiative." Tokyo. www.data.go.jp. Accessed 26 September 2016.

Statista. 2016. "Refugees and Forced Displacement in Focus: In 2015, 65.3 Million People Were Forcibly Displaced from Their Homes." New York. www.statista.com/chart/5073/forced-displacement-in-focus/. Accessed 8 December 2016

Stewart, F. 2013. "Capabilities and Human Development, Beyond the Individual: The Critical Role of Social Institutions and Social Competencies." Occasional Paper 2013/03, United Nations Development Programme, Human Development Report Office, New York.

Stone, L. 2015. "Quantitative Analysis of Women's Participation in Peace Processes." In M. O'Reilly, A.Ó. Súilleabháin and T. Paffenholz, eds., *Reimagining Peacemaking: Women's Roles in Peace Processes*. New York: International Peace Institute.

Street Child. 2014. "Ebola Orphans: Rays of Hope for 2015, but 30,000+ at Crisis Point Now." London. www.street-child.co.uk/news/2014/12/22/ebola-orphans-rays-of-hope-for-2015-but-30000-at-crisis-point-now. Accessed 11 October 2016.

Strong, A., and D.A. Schwartz. 2016. "Sociocultural Aspects of Risk to Pregnant Women during the 2013–2015 Multinational Ebola Virus Outbreak in West Africa." *Health Care for Women International* 37(8): 922–942.

Stuart, E., K. Bird, T. Bhatkal, R. Greenhill, S. Lally, G. Rabinowitz, E. Samman and M.B. Sarwar. 2016.

"Leaving No One Behind: A Critical Path for the First 1,000 Days of the Sustainable Development Goals." With Alainna Lynch, Overseas Development Institute, London. www.odi.org/sites/odi.org.uk/files/resource-documents/10692.pdf. Accessed 14 October 2016.

Suanes, M. 2016. "Foreign Direct Investment and Income Inequality in Latin America: a Sectoral Analysis." *CEPAL Review* 118, April.

Subramanian, A., and S.-J. Wei. 2007. "The WTO Promotes Trade, Strongly But Unevenly." *Journal of International Economics* 72(1): 151–75.

Swartz, J. 2016. "China's National Emissions Trading System: Implications for Carbon Markets and Trade." Issue Paper 6. International Centre for Trade and Sustainable Development, Geneva. www.ieta.org/resources/China/Chinas_National_ETS_Implications_for_Carbon_Markets_and_Trade_ICTSD_March2016_Jeff_Swartz.pdf. Accessed 16 November 2016.

Tanner, F. 2000. "Conflict Prevention and Conflict Resolution: Limits of Multilateralism." *International Review of the Red Cross* 839.

Teigen, M. 2012. "Gender Quotas on Corporate Boards." Discussion paper presented at the European Commission "Exchange of Good Practices on Gender Equality: Women in Economic Decision-Making," 10–11 May, Oslo. http://ec.europa.eu/justice/gender-equality/files/exchange_of_good_practice_no/no_discussion_paper_no_2012_en.pdf. Accessed 22 November 2016.

Thacker, S. 1999. "The High Politics of IMF Lending." *World Politics* 52: 38–75.

Thaler, R.H. 2015. *Misbehaving: The Making of Behavioral Economics.* New York: W.W. Norton & Company.

Thaler, R.H., and C.R. Sunstein. 2008. *Nudge: Improving Decisions about Health, Wealth, and Happiness.* New Haven, CT: Yale University Press.

Thomson, S. 2016. "5,000 Women a Year Are Still Being Killed in the Name of 'Honour'." World Economic Forum, Geneva. www.weforum.org/agenda/2016/07/honour-killings-pakistan-qandeel-baloch/. Accessed 11 October 2016.

Timmer, M., A. Erumban, B. Los, R. Stehrer and G. de Vries. 2014. "Slicing Up Global Value Chains." *Journal of Economic Perspectives* 28(2): 99–118.

Torche, F. 2014. "Intergenerational Mobility and Inequality: The Latin American Case." *Annual Review of Sociology* 40(1): 619–642.

———. 2016. "Early-Life Exposures and the Intergenerational Persistence of Disadvantage." Background paper for Human Development Report 2016. United Nations Development Programme, Human Development Report Office, New York.

UCDP (Uppsala Conflict Data Program). 2016. "Uppsala Conflict Data Program Database." www.ucdp.uu.se. Accessed 8 November 2016.

UCL Institute of Health Equity. 2010. *Fair Society, Healthy Lives: Marmot Review, Strategic Review of Health Inequalities in England Post-2010.* London. www.instituteofhealthequity.org/projects/fair-society-healthy-lives-the-marmot-review. Accessed 26 October 2016.

UNAIDS (Joint United Nations Programme on HIV/AIDS). 2014a. "The Gap Report 2014: Adolescent Girls and Young Women." In *The Gap Report*. Geneva. www.unaids.org/sites/default/files/

media_asset/02_Adolescentgirlsandyoungwomen.pdf. Accessed 14 October 2016.

———. 2014b. *The Gap Report.* Geneva. www.unaids.org/sites/default/files/media_asset/UNAIDS_Gap_report_en.pdf. Accessed 14 October 2016.

———. 2015. *World AIDS Day 2015: On the Fast-Track to End AIDS by 2030: Focus on Location and Population.* Geneva. www.unaids.org/sites/default/files/media_asset/WAD2015_report_en_part01.pdf. Accessed 14 October 2016.

———. 2016a. *AIDS by the Numbers: AIDS Is Not Over, But It Can Be.* Geneva. www.unaids.org/sites/default/files/media_asset/AIDS-by-the-numbers-2016_en.pdf. Accessed 23 August 2016.

———. 2016b. "Children and HIV." Fact sheet. Geneva. www.unaids.org/sites/default/files/media_asset/FactSheet_Children_en.pdf. Accessed 14 October 2016.

———. 2016c. "Fast-Track Cities: Cities Ending the AIDS Epidemic." Geneva. www.unaids.org/sites/default/files/media_asset/cities-ending-the-aids-epidemic_en.pdf. Access 16 November 2016.

———. 2016d. *Global Aids Update 2016.* Geneva. www.unaids.org/sites/default/files/media_asset/global-AIDS-update-2016_en.pdf. Accessed 25 August 2016.

———. 2016e. "Global HIV Statistics Fact Sheet November 2016." Geneva. www.unaids.org/sites/default/files/media_asset/UNAIDS_FactSheet_en.pdf. Accessed 30 November 2016.

———. 2016f. "On the Fast-Track to an AIDS-Free Generation." Geneva. www.unaids.org/sites/default/files/media_asset/GlobalPlan2016_en.pdf. Accessed 7 November 2016.

UNCCD (United Nations Convention to Combat Desertification). 2015. "Desertification, Land Degradation and Drought (DLDD): Some Global Facts and Figures. Bonn, Germany. www.unccd.int/Lists/SiteDocumentLibrary/WDCD/DLDD%20Facts.pdf. Accessed 11 October 2016.

UNCTAD (United Nations Conference on Trade and Development). 2014. *World Investment Report 2014 Investing in the SDGs: An Action Plan.* Geneva.

———. 2015. UNCTADStat. Geneva. http://unctadstat.unctad.org/wds/ReportFolders/reportFolders.aspx. Accessed 11 October 2016.

———. 2016. *World Investment Report 2016: Investor Nationality: Policy Challenges.* Geneva.

UNDESA (United Nations Department of Economic and Social Affairs). 2009. *State of the World's Indigenous Peoples.* Report ST/ESA/328. New York. www.un.org/esa/socdev/unpfii/documents/SOWIP/en/SOWIP_web.pdf. Accessed 28 October 2016.

———. 2012. *World Economic and Social Survey 2012: In Search of New Development Finance.* New York.

———. 2013a. *Indigenous Peoples' Access to Health Services.* Vol. 2 of *State of the World's Indigenous Peoples.* New York. www.un.org/esa/socdev/unpfii/documents/2015/sowip2volume-ac.pdf. Accessed 28 October 2016.

———. 2013b. *International Migration Policies: Government Views and Priorities.* New York.

———. 2014a. *United Nations E-government Survey 2014: E-Government for the Future We Want.* Report ST/ESA/

PAD/SER.E/188. New York. https://publicadministration. un.org/egovkb/Portals/egovkb/Documents/un/2014-Survey/E-Gov_Complete_Survey-2014.pdf. Accessed 7 November 2016.

———. **2014b.** *World Urbanization Prospects: The 2014 Revision.* New York. https://esa.un.org/unpd/wup/Publications/Files/WUP2014-Report.pdf. Accessed 11 October 2016.

———. **2015a.** "Old-Age Dependency Ratio (Ratio of Population Aged 65+ per 100 Population 15–64)." https://esa.un.org/unpd/wpp/DataQuery/. Accessed 26 October 2016.

———. **2015b.** "Percentage of Total Population by Broad Age Group, Both Sexes (per 100 Total Population)." New York. https://esa.un.org/unpd/wpp/DataQuery/. Accessed 26 October 2016.

———. **2015c.** *Trends in International Migrant Stock: The 2015 Revision.* New York.

———. **2015d.** *World Population Prospects: Key Findings and Advance Tables: 2015 Revision.* New York. https://esa.un.org/unpd/wpp/Publications/Files/Key_Findings_WPP_2015.pdf. Accessed 23 August 2016.

———. **2015e.** *The World's Women 2015: Trends and Statistics.* New York.

———. **2015f.** *World Urbanization Prospects: The 2014 Revision.* Report ST/ESA/SER.A/366. New York. https://esa.un.org/unpd/wup/Publications/Files/WUP2014-Report.pdf. Accessed 16 November 2016.

———. **2016a.** *Global Sustainable Development Report 2016.* New York. https://sustainabledevelopment.un.org/content/documents/2328Global%20Sustainable%20development%20report%202016%20(final).pdf. Accessed 1 November 2016.

———. **2016b.** "NGO Branch." New York. http://csonet.org. Accessed 18 October 2016.

———. **2016c.** *Report on the World Social Situation 2016, Leaving No One Behind: The Imperative of Inclusive Development.* Document ST/ESA/362. New York. www.un.org/development/desa/dspd/2015/12/30/report-on-world-social-situation-2016-2/. Accessed 4 November 2016.

———. **2016d.** *United Nations E-government Survey 2016: E-government in Support of Sustainable Development.* New York. http://workspace.unpan.org/sites/Internet/Documents/UNPAN96407.pdf. Accessed 4 December 2016.

———. **2016e.** *World Youth Report on Youth Civic Engagement.* New York. www.unworldyouthreport.org/images/docs/un_world_youth_report_youth_civic_engagement.pdf. Accessed 23 August 2016.

UNDP (United Nations Development Programme).
1990. *Human Development Report 1990: Concept and Measurement of Human Development.* New York: Oxford University Press. http://hdr.undp.org/sites/default/files/reports/219/hdr_1990_en_complete_nostats.pdf. Accessed 8 December 2016.

———. **1991.** *Human Development Report 1991.* New York: Oxford University Press. http://hdr.undp.org/sites/default/files/reports/220/hdr_1991_en_complete_nostats.pdf. Accessed 7 November 2016.

———. **1992.** *Human Development Report 1992: Global Dimensions of Human Development.* New York. http://hdr.undp.org/sites/default/files/reports/221/

hdr_1992_en_complete_nostats.pdf. Accessed 7 November 2016.

———. **1994.** *Human Development Report 1994: New Dimensions of Human Security.* New York: Oxford University Press. http://hdr.undp.org/sites/default/files/reports/255/hdr_1994_en_complete_nostats.pdf. Accessed 11 October 2016.

———. **1995.** *Human Development Report 1995: Gender and Human Development.* New York: Oxford University Press. http://hdr.undp.org/sites/default/files/reports/256/hdr_1995_en_complete_nostats.pdf. Accessed 11 October 2016.

———. **1997.** *Human Development Report 1997: Human Development to Eradicate Poverty.* New York: Oxford University Press. http://hdr.undp.org/sites/default/files/reports/258/hdr_1997_en_complete_nostats.pdf. Accessed 11 October 2016.

———. **2000.** *Human Development Report 2000: Human Rights and Human Development.* New York: Oxford University Press.

———. **2002.** *Human Development Report 2002: Deepening Democracy in a Fragmented World.* New York: Oxford University Press. http://hdr.undp.org/sites/default/files/reports/263/hdr_2002_en_complete.pdf. Accessed 11 October 2016.

———. **2004.** *Human Development Report 2004: Cultural Liberty in Today's Diverse World.* New York: Oxford University Press. http://hdr.undp.org/sites/default/files/reports/265/hdr_2004_complete.pdf. Accessed 11 October 2016.

———. **2007.** *Human Development Report 2007/2008: Fighting Climate Change: Human Solidarity in a Divided World.* New York: Palgrave Macmillan. http://hdr.undp.org/sites/default/files/reports/268/hdr_20072008_en_complete.pdf. Accessed 11 October 2016.

———. **2009.** *Human Development Report 2009: Overcoming Barriers: Human Mobility and Development.* New York: Palgrave Macmillan. www.hdr.undp.org/sites/default/files/reports/269/hdr_2009_en_complete.pdf. Accessed 26 October 2016.

———. **2010a.** *Human Development Report 2010: The Real Wealth of Nations: Pathways to Human Development.* New York: Palgrave Macmillan.

———. **2010b.** *Informe sobre Desarrollo Humano de los Pueblos Indígenas en México: El reto de la desigualdad de oportunidades.* Mexico City.

———. **2011a.** "Empowering Lives, Building Resilience: Development Stories from Europe and Central Asia." Volume 1. New York. www.scribd.com/doc/153150985/UNDP-development-stories-Europe-and-CIS. Accessed 7 November 2016.

———. **2011b.** *Human Development Report 2011: Sustainability and Equity: A Better Future for All.* New York: Palgrave Macmillan. http://hdr.undp.org/sites/default/files/reports/271/hdr_2011_en_complete.pdf. Accessed 11 October 2016.

———. **2012a.** *Desarrollo Humano en Chile 2012: Bienestar subjetivo: el desafío de repensar el desarrollo.* Santiago. http://desarrollohumano.cl/idh/informes/2012-bienestar-subjetivo-el-desafio-de-repensar-el-desarrollo/. Accessed 26 October 2016.

———. **2012b.** *Somalia Human Development Report 2012: Empowering Youth for Peace and Development.* Mogadishu.

www.hdr.undp.org/sites/default/files/reports/242/somalia_report_2012.pdf. Accessed 26 October 2016.

———. **2013a.** *Annual Report 2012–2013: Supporting Global Progress.* New York. www.undp.org/content/dam/timorleste/img/UNDP_AR2013_English_v11-PRINT-Ready.pdf. Accessed 7 November 2016.

———. **2013b.** *China National Human Development Report 2013: Sustainable and Liveable Cities: Toward Ecological Civilization.* Beijing. www.hdr.undp.org/sites/default/files/china_nhdr_2013_en_final.pdf. Accessed 1 November 2016.

———. **2013c.** *Human Development Report 2013: The Rise of the South: Human Progress in a Diverse World.* New York. http://hdr.undp.org/sites/default/files/reports/14/hdr2013_en_complete.pdf. Accessed 4 December 2016.

———. **2014a.** *Beyond Geography: Unlocking Human Potential.* Kathmandu. www.hdr.undp.org/sites/default/files/nepal_nhdr_2014-final.pdf. Accessed 26 October 2016.

———. **2014b.** *Human Development Report 2014: Sustaining Human Progress: Reducing Vulnerabilities and Building Resilience.* New York. http://hdr.undp.org/sites/default/files/hdr14-report-en-1.pdf. Accessed 26 October 2016.

———. **2014c.** *Informe Nacional de Desarrollo Humano Panamá 2014: El Futuro es ahora: Primera infancia, juventud y formación de capacidades para la vida.* Panama City. www.hdr.undp.org/sites/default/files/idh-panama-ene-10-14-final.pdf. Accessed 26 October 2016.

———. **2014d.** *National Human Development Report 2014: Ethiopia: Accelerating Inclusive Growth for Sustainable Human Development in Ethiopia.* Addis Ababa. www.hdr.undp.org/sites/default/files/nhdr2015-ethiopia-en.pdf. Accessed 26 October 2016.

———. **2014e.** *Nepal Human Development Report 2014: Beyond Geography: Unlocking Human Potential.* Kathmandu. http://hdr.undp.org/sites/default/files/nepal_nhdr_2014-final.pdf. Accessed 26 October 2016.

———. **2015a.** *Human Development Report 2015: Work for Human Development.* New York. http://hdr.undp.org/sites/default/files/2015_human_development_report.pdf. Accessed 11 October 2016.

———. **2015b.** *National Human Development Report 2015: Human Security and Human Development in Nigeria.* Abuja.

———. **2016a.** *Africa Human Development Report 2016: Accelerating Gender Equality and Women's Empowerment in Africa.* New York. www.undp.org/content/dam/undp/library/corporate/HDR/Africa%20HDR/AfHDR_2016_lowres_EN.pdf?download. Accessed 14 October 2016.

———. **2016b.** *Caribbean Human Development Report: Multidimensional Progress: Human Resilience beyond Income.* New York. www.bb.undp.org/content/barbados/en/home/presscenter/articles/2016/09/13/caribbean-human-development-report-2016-launched.html. Accessed 28 November 2016.

———. **2016c.** *China National Human Development Report 2016: Social Innovation for Inclusive Human Development.* Beijing. www.cn.undp.org/content/china/en/home/library/human_development/china-human-development-report-2016.html. Accessed 13 December 2016.

———. **2016d.** *Eurasia: 2015 in Review: Stories across the Region, from the Year that Changed the Global Development Agenda.* https://undpeurasia.exposure.co/eurasia-2015-in-review. New York. Accessed 7 November 2016.

———. 2016e. *Growth that Works for All: Viet Nam Human Development Report 2015 on Inclusive Growth.* Hanoi. www.hdr.undp.org/sites/default/files/nhdr_2015_e.pdf. Accessed 26 October 2016.

———. 2016f. "Helen Clark: Remarks at the Panel on Ensuring that No-One Is Left Behind and the Challenge of Countries in Special Situations at the Ministerial Segment of the ECOSOC High Level Political Forum on Sustainable Development." 18 July. New York. www.undp.org/content/undp/en/home/presscenter/speeches/2016/07/18/helen-clark-remarks-at-the-panel-on-ensuring-that-no-one-is-left-behind-at-the-ministerial-segment-of-the-ecosoc-high-level-political-forum-on-sustainable-development.html. Accessed 11 October 2016.

———. 2016g. "Legal Aid Service in Georgia." New York. www.undp.org/content/undp/en/home/ourwork/democraticgovernance/projects_and_initiatives/georgia_justice_forall.html. Accessed 17 November 2016.

———. 2016h. "Managing Droughts and Floods in Azerbaijan." New York. www.undp.org/content/undp/en/home/ourwork/ourstories/managing-droughts-and-floods-in-azerbaijan-.html. Accessed 16 November 2016.

———. 2016i. *Mongolia Human Development Report 2016: Building a Better Tomorrow: Including Youth in the Development of Mongolia.* Ulaanbaatar. www.hdr.undp.org/sites/default/files/mongolia_human_devlopment_report_2016_english_full_report_2016_06_28.pdf. Accessed 1 November 2016.

———. 2016j. "Together, Sri Lankan Communities Build Back with Rocilionco." New York. www.undp.org/content/undp/en/home/ourwork/ourstories/together-sri-lankan-communities-build-back-with-resilience.html. Accessed 16 November 2016.

———. 2017. Human Development Report Office's Library [online database]. http://hdr.undp.org/en/reports. Accessed 16 January 2017.

UNDP (United Nations Development Programme) and IAER (Institute for Applied Economic Research, João Pinheiro Foundation). 2013. *Human Development Atlas in Brazil.* http://atlasbrasil.org.br/2013/en/o_atlas/o_atlas_/ Accessed 14 December 2016.

UNEP (United Nations Environment Programme). 2016. "Developing Countries Show World Way Forward on Green Finance." UNEP News Centre, 18 July. Geneva. www.unep.org/newscentre/default.aspx?DocumentID=27079&ArticleID=36231&l=en. Accessed 9 November 2016.

UNEP (United Nations Environment Programme) and UNDP (United Nations Development Programme). 2016. "The Poverty-Environment Initiative in the Context of the Sustainable Development Goals: Relevance and Experience for National and Subnational Implementation." UNDP-UNEP Poverty-Environment Facility, United Nations, Nairobi. www.undp.org/content/dam/undp/library/Environment%20and%20Energy/sustainable%20land%20management/Factsheet-PEI.pdf. Accessed 16 November 2016.

UNESCO (United Nations Educational, Scientific and Cultural Organization). 2013a. "Children Still Battling to go to School." Education for all Global Monitoring Report, Policy Paper 10. Montreal. http://unesdoc.unesco.org/images/0022/002216/221668E.pdf. Accessed 26 October 2016.

———. 2013b. *Education for All Global Monitoring Report – Girls' Education – the Facts.* Paris.

———. 2013c. "Girls' Education: The Facts." Education for All Global Monitoring Report, Fact Sheet. Paris. http://en.unesco.org/gem-report/sites/gem-report/files/girls-factsheet-en.pdf. Accessed 7 November 2016.

———. 2014a. *Education for All: Global Monitoring Report 2014: Teaching and Learning: Achieving Quality for All.* Paris.

———. 2014b. *Teaching and Learning: Achieving Quality for All: EFA Global Monitoring Report 2013/4: Summary.* Paris. http://unesdoc.unesco.org/images/0022/002256/225654e.pdf. Accessed 3 November 2016.

———. 2015a. "A Growing Number of Children and Adolescents Are out of School as Aid Fails to Meet the Mark." Policy Paper 22/Fact sheet 31. Paris. www.uis.unesco.org/Education/Documents/fs-31-out-of-school-children-en.pdf. Accessed 25 August 2016.

———. 2015b. *2015 Global Monitoring Report: Education for All 2000-2015: Achievements and Challenges.* Paris. http://unesdoc.unesco.org/images/0023/002322/232205e.pdf. Accessed 14 October 2016.

———. 2016a. *Global Education Monitoring Report 2016: Education for People and Planet. Creating Sustainable Futures for All.* Paris. http://unesdoc.unesco.org/images/0024/002457/245752e.pdf. Accessed 11 October 2016.

———. 2016b. "UNESCO eAtlas of Gender Inequality in Education." UNESCO Institute for Statistics, Montreal. www.tellmaps.com/uis/gender/#!/tellmap/-1195952519. Accessed 10 June 2016.

UNESCO (United Nations Educational, Scientific and Cultural Organization) Institute for Statistics. 2016. "Education: Illiterate Population." Montreal. http://data.uis.unesco.org. Accessed 8 December 2016.

UNESCO (United Nations Educational, Scientific and Cultural Organization) and UNICEF (United Nations Children's Fund). 2015. "Fixing the Broken Promise of Education for All: Findings from the Global Initiative on Out-of-School Children." UNESCO Institute for Statistics, Montreal. http://unesdoc.unesco.org/images/0023/002315/231511e.pdf. Accessed 26 October 2016.

UNFCCC (United Nations Framework Convention on Climate Change). 2015. "Paris Agreement on Climate Change." Paris. http://unfccc.int/paris_agreement/items/9485.php. Accessed on 3 December 2016.

UNFPA (United Nations Population Fund). 2014. *State of World Population 2014: The Power of 1.8 Billion.* New York. www.unfpa.org/sites/default/files/pub-pdf/EN-SWOP14-Report_FINAL-web.pdf. Accessed 20 October 2016.

———. 2015. "Migration." 23 December. New York. www.unfpa.org/migration. Accessed 26 October 2016.

———. 2016. "World Population Day." New York. www.unfpa.org/events/world-population-day. Accessed 11 October 2016.

UNFPA (United Nations Population Fund) and HelpAge International. 2012. *Ageing in the Twenty-First Century: A Celebration and a Challenge.* New York. www.unfpa.org/publications/ageing-twenty-first-century. Accessed 22 November 2016.

UN-Habitat (United Nations Human Settlements Programme). 2014. "Proportion of Urban Population Living in Slums 1990–2014." Nairobi. http://unhabitat.org/wp-content/uploads/2014/03/Table-2.2-Proportion-of-urban-population-living-in-slums-1990-2014.pdf. Accessed 26 October 2016.

UNHCR (United Nations High Commissioner for Refugees). 1997. "Memorandum of Understanding between the United Nations High Commissioner for Refugees and the International Organization for Migration." Geneva. www.unhcr.org/4aa7a3ed9.pdf. Accessed 11 November 2016.

———. 2014. *UNHCR Global Report 2014: Progressing towards Solutions.* Geneva. www.unhcr.org/en-us/publications/fundraising/5575a78813/unhcr-global-report-2014-progressing-towards-solutions.html?query=17years. Accessed 26 September 2016.

———. 2015a. "Funding UNHCR's Programmes." In *Global Report 2015.* Geneva. www.unhcr.org/574ed5574.pdf. Accessed 7 November 2016.

———. 2015b. "Needs and Funding Requirements." In *UNHCR Global Appeal 2016-2017.* Geneva. www.unhcr.org/564da0e20.pdf. Accessed 16 December 2016.

———. 2016a. *Global Trends: Forced Displacement in 2015.* Geneva. https://s3.amazonaws.com/unhcrsharedmedia/2016/2016-06-20-global-trends/2016-06-14-Global-Trends-2015.pdf. Accessed 23 August 2016.

———. 2016b. "Syria Regional Refugee Response." Geneva. http://data.unhcr.org/syrianrefugees/regional.php. Accessed 1 November 2016.

———. 2016c. "UNHCR Statistics: The World in Numbers." Geneva. http://popstats.unhcr.org/en/overview. Accessed 26 October 2016.

UNICEF (United Nations Children's Fund). 2004. "Nepal, Welcome to School: Enrolment and Retention in the Education for All Initiative." New York. www.unicef.org/innovations/files/fa2_nepal_welcome_to_school(1).doc. Accessed 14 October 2016.

———. 2011. "Children's Vulnerability to Climate Change and Disaster Impacts in East Asia and the Pacific." UNICEF East Asia and Pacific Regional Office, Bangkok. www.unicef.org/environment/files/Climate_Change_Regional_Report_14_Nov_final.pdf. Accessed 26 October 2016.

———. 2014a. *Ending Child Marriage: Progress and Prospects.* New York. www.unicef.org/media/files/Child_Marriage_Report_7_17_LR..pdf. Accessed 23 August 2016

———. 2014b. *A Statistical Snapshot of Violence against Adolescent Girls.* New York. www.unicef.org/publications/files/A_Statistical_Snapshot_of_Violence_Against_Adolescent_Girls.pdf. Accessed 25 August 2016.

———. 2016a. "Female Genital Mutilation/Cutting: A Global Concern." New York. www.unicef.org/media/files/FGMC_2016_brochure_final_UNICEF_SPREAD.pdf. Accessed 26 August 2016.

———. 2016b. "Multiple Indicator Cluster Surveys." New York. http://mics.unicef.org. Accessed 15 July 2016.

———. 2016c. *State of the World's Children 2016: A Fair Chance for Every Child.* New York. www.unicef.org/publications/files/UNICEF_SOWC_2016.pdf. Accessed 24 August 2016.

———. 2016d. "UNICEF Data: Monitoring the Situation of Children and Women." New York. http://data.unicef.org/child-protection/child-marriage.html. Accessed 27 October 2016.

———. 2016e. *Uprooted: The Growing Crisis of Migrant Children*. New York. www.unicef.org/publications/files/Uprooted_growing_crisis_for_refugee_and_migrant_children.pdf. Accessed 11 October 2016.

UNICEF (United Nations Children's Fund) and World Bank. 2016. "Ending Extreme Poverty: A Focus on Children." New York. www.unicef.org/publications/files/Ending_Extreme_Poverty_A_Focus_on_Children_Oct_2016.pdf. Accessed 11 October 2016.

UNISDR (United Nations Office for Disaster Risk Reduction). 2015. *Global Assessment Report on Disaster Risk Reduction 2015: Making Development Sustainable: The Future of Disaster Risk Management*. Geneva. www.preventionweb.net/english/hyogo/gar/2015/en/gar-pdf/GAR2015_EN.pdf. Accessed 11 October 2016.

United Kingdom. 2010. "Opening up Government." London. https://data.gov.uk. Accessed 26 September 2016.

United Nations. 1948. "Universal Declaration of Human Rights." Document A/RES/3/217 A. New York.

———. 2000a. "Resolution 1325 (2000) Adopted by the Security Council at its 4213th meeting, on 31 October 2000." New York. https://documents-dds-ny.un.org/doc/UNDOC/GEN/N00/720/18/PDF/N0072018.pdf?OpenElement. Accessed 11 October 2016.

———. 2000b. *United Nations Millennium Declaration, A/RES/55/2*. New York. www.un.org/millennium/declaration/ares552e.htm/. Accessed 26 September 2016.

———. 2010. "Decade for Deserts and the Fight against Desertification: Why Now?" New York. www.un.org/en/events/desertification_decade/whynow.shtml. Accessed 23 August 2016.

———. 2011. *Innovative Mechanisms of Financing for Development*. Report of the Secretary-General. New York. www.un.org/ga/search/view_doc.asp?symbol=A/66/334&Lang=E. Accessed 30 September 2016.

———. 2012. "The Future We Want." General Assembly Resolution 66/288. New York. www.un.org/ga/search/view_doc.asp?symbol=A/RES/66/288&Lang=E. Accessed 1 July 2015.

———. 2013. "Promotion and Protection of the Right to Freedom of Opinion and Expression." Note by the Secretary-General. A/68/362. New York. https://documents-dds-ny.un.org/doc/UNDOC/GEN/N13/464/76/pdf/N1346476.pdf?OpenElement. Accessed 7 November 2016.

———. 2014. "Framework of Analysis for Atrocity Crimes: A Tool for Prevention." United Nations Office on Genocide Prevention and the Responsibility to Protect, New York. www.un.org/en/preventgenocide/adviser/pdf/framework%20of%20analysis%20for%20atrocity%20crimes_en.pdf. Accessed 27 October 2016.

———. 2015a. *The Millennium Development Goals Report 2015*. New York. www.un.org/millenniumgoals/2015_MDG_Report/pdf/MDG%202015%20rev%20(July%201).pdf. Accessed 26 October 2016.

———. 2015b. "Report of the Secretary-General on Women, Peace and Security." Document S/2015/716. UN Security Council, New York.

———. 2015c. *Transforming Our World: The 2030 Agenda for Sustainable Development*. Resolution adopted by the General Assembly on 25 September 2015. New York. www.un.org/ga/search/view_doc.asp?symbol=A/RES/70/1&Lang=E. Accessed 26 September 2016.

———. 2015d. "The World's Women 2015: Trends and Statistics." New York. http://unstats.un.org/unsd/gender/downloads/Ch5_Power_and_decision_info.pdf. Accessed 22 November 2016.

———. 2016a. "Have Your Say." My World Analytics. New York. http://data.myworld2015.org. Accessed 26 October 2016.

———. 2016b. *Leave No One Behind: A Call to Action for Gender Equality and Women's Economic Empowerment*. New York.

———. 2016c. "New York Declaration." New York. http://refugeesmigrants.un.org/declaration. Accessed 7 November 2016.

———. 2016d. *One Humanity: Shared Responsibility*. Report of the Secretary General for the World Humanitarian Summit. New York.

———. 2016e. "Paris Climate Agreement to Enter into Force on 4 November 2016." New York. www.un.org/sustainabledevelopment/blog/2016/10/paris-climate-agreement-to-enter-into-force-on-4-november/. Accessed 14 October 2016.

———. 2016f. "Press Freedom: Freedom of Expression, a Human Right." New York. www.un.org/en/events/pressfreedomday/background.shtml. Accessed 8 December 2016.

———. 2016g. "Report of the Special Rapporteur on Minority Issues." Document A/HRC/31/56. New York. www.refworld.org/docid/56dfde5d4.html. Accessed 14 October 2016.

———. 2016h. "The Sustainable Development Goals Report 2016." New York. http://unstats.un.org/sdgs/report/2016/The%20Sustainable%20Development%20Goals%20Report%202016.pdf. Accessed 23 August 2016.

———. 2016i. "UN Summit for Refugees." New York. http://refugeesmigrants.un.org/summit. Accessed on 3 December 2016.

United Nations Broadband Commission for Digital Development, Working Group on Broadband and Gender. 2015. *Cyber Violence against Women and Girls: A World-wide Wake-up Call*. Geneva.

United Nations Peacekeeping. 2016. "Gender Statistics by Mission for the Month of August." 7 September. New York. www.un.org/en/peacekeeping/contributors/gender/2016gender/aug16.pdf. Accessed 11 October 2016.

United Nations Secretary General's High-Level Panel on Access to Medicines. 2016. *Report of the United Nations Secretary General's High-Level Panel on Access to Medicines: Promoting Innovation and Access to Health Technologies*. New York. https://static1.squarespace.com/static/562094dee4b0d00c1a3ef761/t/57d9c6ebf5e231b2f02cd3d4/1473890031320/UNSG+HLP+Report+FINAL+12+Sept+2016.pdf. Accessed 2 December 2016.

United States of America. 2009. "Open Government." Washington, DC. www.data.gov/open-gov/. Accessed 26 September 2016.

UN Maternal Mortality Estimation Group (World Health Organization, United Nations Children's Fund, United Nations Population Fund and World Bank). 2016. Maternal mortality data. http://data.unicef.org/topic/maternal-health/maternal-mortality/. Accessed 28 April 2016.

UNODC (United Nations Office on Drugs and Crime). 2013. *Global Study on Homicide 2013*. Vienna. www.unodc.org/documents/gsh/pdfs/2014_GLOBAL_HOMICIDE_BOOK_web.pdf. Accessed 14 October 2016.

———. 2014a. *Global Study on Homicide 2013: Trends, Contexts, Data*. Vienna. www.unodc.org/documents/gsh/pdfs/2014_GLOBAL_HOMICIDE_BOOK_web.pdf. Accessed 14 October 2016.

———. 2014b. "Study Facilitating the Identification, Description and Evaluation of the Effects of New Information Technologies on the Abuse and Exploitation of Children." Vienna. www.unodc.org/documents/commissions/CCPCJ/CCPCJ_Sessions/CCPCJ_23/E-CN15-2014-CRP1_E.pdf. Accessed 7 November 2016.

———. 2016. "Statistics, UN-CTS Metadata 2014–2015: Prisons." Vienna. https://data.unodc.org/?lf=1&lng=en#state:6. Accessed 7 November 2016.

UNOHCHR (Office of the United Nations High Commissioner for Human Rights). 2016. "Monitoring the Core International Human Rights Treaties." Geneva. www.ohchr.org/EN/HRBodies/Pages/TreatyBodies.aspx. Accessed 7 November 2016.

UNOSSC (United Nations Office for South-South Cooperation). 2016. *Good Practices in South-South and Triangular Cooperation for Sustainable Development*. New York.

UNRWA (United Nations Relief and Works Agency for Palestine Refugees in the Near East). 2013. *The Syrian Catastrophe: Socioeconomic Monitoring Report*. First Quarterly Report (January–March). Amman. www.unrwa.org/userfiles/2013071244355.pdf. Accessed 26 October 2016.

UNSD (United Nations Statistics Division). 2008. *UNdata: A World of Information*. New York. http://data.un.org/Default.aspx. Accessed 26 September 2016.

———. 2016. "Millennium Development Goals Indicators: The Official United Nations Site for the MDG Indicators." New York. http://mdgs.un.org/unsd/mdg/Data.aspx. Accessed 16 June 2016.

UNV (United Nations Volunteers). 2016. *Annual Report: Delivering at the Grassroots*. New York. www.unv.org/annual-report-2015/pdf/UNV-Annual-report-2015.pdf. Accessed 19 November 2016.

UN Women (United Nations Entity for Gender Equality and the Empowerment of Women). 2012. "Women's Participation in Peace Negotiations: Connections between Presence and Influence." New York. www.unwomen.org/~/media/headquarters/attachments/sections/library/publications/2012/10/wpssourcebook-03a-womenpeace-negotiations-en.pdf. Accessed 11 October 2016.

———. 2013. "Femicide in Latin America." 4 April. New York. www.unwomen.org/en/news/stories/2013/4/femicide-in-latin-america. Accessed 14 October 2016.

———. 2014. *The Premise and Promise of UN Women's Partnerships with Civil Society*. New York. www2.unwomen.org/-/media/headquarters/attachments/sections/partnerships/civil%20society/unwomen-civilsociety-brochure-en.pdf?v=1&d=20141013T121445. Accessed 16 December 2016.

———. 2015a. *Progress of the World's Women 2015–2016: Transforming Economies, Realizing Rights*. New York.

http://progress.unwomen.org/en/2015/. Accessed 1 November 2016.

———. 2015b. "World Leaders Agree: We Must Close the Gender Gap. Historic Gathering Boosts Political Commitment for Women's Empowerment at the Highest Levels." Press release, 27 September. New York. www.unwomen.org/en/news/stories/2015/9/press-release-global-leaders-meeting. Accessed 12 December 2016.

———. 2016a. "Facts and Figures: Leadership and Political Participation, Women in Parliaments." New York. www.unwomen.org/en/what-we-do/leadership-and-political-participation/facts-and-figures. Accessed 22 November 2016.

———. 2016b. "Passing and Implementing Effective Laws and Policies." New York. www.unwomen.org/en/what-we-do/ending-violence-against-women/passing-strong-laws-and-policies. Accessed 14 October 2016.

———. 2016c. "Let's Change These Numbers and Get More Women in STEM." Tweet, 3 October. https://twitter.com/un_women/status/782982362854461442.

———. n.d. "Women at the Forefront of Peacebuilding." New York. www.unwomen.org/en/news/in-focus/women-peace-security. Accessed 7 November 2016.

US Bureau of Labor Statistics. 2016. "Employment Projections." United States Department of Labor, Washington, DC. www.bls.gov/emp/ep_chart_001.htm. Accessed 7 November 2016.

Vaughan, A. 2016. "Biodiversity Is Below Safe Levels across More Than Half of World's Land—Study." The Guardian, 14 July. www.theguardian.com/environment/2016/jul/14/biodiversity-below-safe-levels-across-over-half-of-worlds-land-study. Accessed 7 November 2016.

W3 Techs. 2016. "Usage of Content Languages for Websites." https://w3techs.com/technologies/overview/content_language/all. Accessed 28 November 2016.

Walk Free Foundation. 2016. The Global Slavery Index 2016. Broadway Nedlands, Western Australia. http://assets.globalslaveryindex.org/downloads/Global+Slavery+Index+2016.pdf. Accessed 11 October 2016.

Wallach, L., and B. Beachy. 2012. "Occidental v. Ecuador Award Spotlight Perils of Investor State System." Global Trade Watch. www.citizen.org/documents/oxy-v-ecuador-memo.pdf. Accessed 16 December 2016.

Watkins, K. 2013. "Education without Borders: A Report from Lebanon on Syria's Out-of-School Children." World at School, London. www.odi.org/sites/odi.org.uk/files/odi-assets/publications-opinion-files/8575.pdf. Accessed 26 October 2016.

Watkins, K., J.W. van Fleet and L. Greubel. 2012. "Interactive: Africa Learning Barometer." 17 September. Brookings Institution, Washington, DC. www.brookings.edu/interactives/africa-learning-barometer/. Accessed 4 November 2016.

Watson, C. 2016. "How Communications Can Change Social Norms around Adolescent Girls: Lessons Learned from Year 3 of a Multi-country Field Study." Overseas Development Institute, London. www.odi.org/sites/odi.org.uk/files/resource-documents/10375.pdf. Accessed 20 October 2016.

WEF (World Economic Forum). 2015. "Global Risks 2015, Part 2: Risks in Focus: 2.3 City Limits: The Risks of Rapid and Unplanned Urbanization in Developing Countries." Geneva. http://reports.weforum.org/global-risks-2015/part-2-risks-in-focus/2-3-city-limits-the-risks-of-rapid-and-unplanned-urbanization-in-developing-countries/. Accessed 11 October 2016.

———. 2016a. The Future of Jobs. Employment, Skills and Workforce Strategy for the Fourth Industrial Revolution. Global Challenge Insight Report. Geneva. www3.weforum.org/docs/WEF_Future_of_Jobs.pdf. Accessed 25 August 2016.

———. 2016b. Global Gender Gap Report 2016. Davos. http://reports.weforum.org/global-gender-gap-report-2016/. Accessed 3 December 2016.

———. 2016c. Insight Report: The Human Capital Report 2016. Geneva.

Weiss, T. 2007. Humanitarian Intervention: Ideas in Action. Cambridge: Polity Press.

WFP (World Food Programme). 2014. "Brazil: A Champion in the Fight against Hunger." www.wfp.org/stories/brazil-champions-fight-against-hunger. Accessed 30 September 2016.

———. 2016a. "Hunger Statistics." Rome. www.wfp.org/hunger/stats. Accessed 25 August 2016.

———. 2016b. "School Meals." Rome. www.wfp.org/school-meals. Accessed 7 November 2016.

WHO (World Health Organization). 2011a. mHealth: New Horizons for Health through Mobile Technologies. Geneva. www.who.int/goe/publications/goe_mhealth_web.pdf. Accessed 4 December 2016.

———. 2011b. World Report on Disability. Geneva. www.who.int/disabilities/world_report/2011/en/. Accessed 28 November 2016.

———. 2013. UNITAID Strategy 2013-2016. Geneva.

———. 2015a. "Ageing and Health." Fact sheet 404. Geneva. www.who.int/mediacentre/factsheets/fs404/en/. Accessed 26 October 2016.

———. 2015b. "Cancer." Fact sheet 297. Geneva. www.who.int/mediacentre/factsheets/fs297/en/. Accessed 14 October 2016.

———. 2015c. "Maternal Mortality." Fact sheet 348. Geneva. www.who.int/mediacentre/factsheets/fs348/en/. Accessed 11 October 2016.

———. 2015d. "Noncommunicable Diseases." Fact sheet 355. Geneva. www.who.int/mediacentre/factsheets/fs355/en/. Accessed 14 October 2016.

———. 2015e. World Report on Ageing and Health. Geneva. http://apps.who.int/iris/bitstream/10665/186463/1/9789240694811_eng.pdf?ua=1. Accessed 25 August 2016.

———. 2016a. "Call to Action: Combat Antimicrobial Resistance and Preserve Antimicrobials for Future Generations." Geneva. http://apps.who.int/medicinedocs/documents/s22393en/s22393en.pdf. Accessed 14 October 2016.

———. 2016b. "Children: Reducing Mortality." Fact sheet 178. Geneva. www.who.int/mediacentre/factsheets/fs178/en/. Accessed 11 October 2016.

———. 2016c. "Climate Change and Health." Fact sheet 266. Geneva. www.who.int/mediacentre/factsheets/fs266/en/. Accessed 25 August 2016.

———. 2016d. "Female Genital Mutilation." Fact sheet 241. Geneva. www.who.int/mediacentre/factsheets/fs241/en/. Accessed 27 October 2016.

———. 2016e. "Global Health Observatory (GHO) Data." Geneva. www.who.int/gho/mortality_burden_disease/life_tables/en/. Accessed 3 November 2016.

———. 2016f. "Mental Disorders." Fact sheet 396. Geneva. www.who.int/mediacentre/factsheets/fs396/en/. Accessed 26 October 2016.

———. 2016g. "Violence against Women: Intimate Partner and Sexual Violence against Women." Fact sheet 239. Geneva. www.who.int/mediacentre/factsheets/fs239/en/. Accessed 25 August 2016.

———. 2016h. "WHO Issues New Guidance on HIV Self-testing ahead of World AIDS Day." Press release, 29 November. Geneva. www.who.int/mediacentre/news/releases/2016/world-aids-day/en/. Accessed 5 December 2016.

———. 2016i. World Malaria Report 2016. Geneva. http://apps.who.int/iris/bitstream/10665/252038/1/9789241511711-eng.pdf?ua=1. Accessed 14 December 2016.

———. 2016j. "Zika Strategic Response Plan." Geneva. http://apps.who.int/iris/bitstream/10665/246091/1/WHO-ZIKV-SRF-16.3-eng.pdf?ua=1&ua=1&ua=1&ua=1 Accessed 30 November 2016.

Wiemann, M., and C. Eibs-Singer. 2016. "Renewable Mini-grids: Unlocking Africa's Rural Powerhouse." ESI Africa Issue 1. www.ruralelec.org/sites/default/files/esiafrica-renewablemini-grids.pdf. Accessed 7 November 2016.

Wiist, W., K. Barker, N. Arya, J. Rohde, M. Donohoe, S. White, P. Lubens, G. Gorman and A. Hagopian. 2014. "The Role of Public Health in the Prevention of War: Rationale and Competencies." American Journal of Public Health 104(6). e34–e47 www.ncbi.nlm.nih.gov/pmc/articles/PMC4062030/. Accessed 19 November 2016.

Williams-Grut, O. 2016. "3 of the World's 10 Largest Employers Are Now Replacing Their Workers with Robots." Business Insider, 9 June. www.businessinsider.com/clsa-wef-and-citi-on-the-future-of-robots-and-ai-in-the-workforce-2016-6?r=UK&IR=T. Accessed 7 November 2016.

Wimmer, A. 2012. Waves of War: Nationalism, State Formation, and Ethnic Exclusion in the Modern World. Cambridge Studies in Comparative Politics Series. New York: Cambridge University Press.

Witton, B. 2016. "How Immigration is Fuelling Sweden's Economic Boom." Independent, 5 October. www.independent.co.uk/news/world/europe/sweden-immigration-economic-boom-theresa-may-refugee-crisis-tory-conference-a7347136.html. Accessed 10 November 2016.

Woosey, B. 2005. "The Effect the Eight Million Illiterate Adults on the UK." Where I Live Northhamptonshire, 2 November. BBC Northamptonshire, Northampton, UK. www.bbc.co.uk/northamptonshire/content/articles/2005/02/11/becky_woosey_the_effect_the_eight_million_illiterate_adults_on_the_uk_feature.shtml. Accessed 26 October 2016.

World Bank. 2006. "Fiscal Policy for Growth and Development: An Interim Report." Report DC2006-0003. Washington, DC. http://siteresources.worldbank.org/DEVCOMMINT/Documentation/20890698/DC2006-0003(E)-FiscalPolicy.pdf. Accessed 7 November 2016.

———. 2007. World Development Indicators 2007. Washington, DC.

———. 2011a. "Water Supply and Sanitation in Burkina Faso: Turning Finance into Services for 2015 and Beyond." AMCOW Country Status Overview, Report 74207, Water and Sanitation Program, Nairobi. https://openknowledge. worldbank.org/handle/10986/17756. Accessed 7 November 2016.

———. 2011b. "World Bank Open Data." Washington DC. http://data.worldbank.org. Accessed 26 September 2016.

———. 2013. "The International Income Distribution Data Set (I2D2)." Washington, DC.

———. 2014. *Voice and Agency: Empowering Women and Girls for Shared Prosperity.* Washington, DC.

———. 2015a. "5 Ways to Reduce the Drivers of Climate Change." Washington, DC. www.worldbank.org/en/news/ feature/2015/03/18/5-ways-reduce-drivers-climate-change?cid=CCG_TTccgEN_D_EXT. Accessed 7 November 2016.

———. 2015b. "Boosting the Health of Toddlers' Bodies and Brains Brings Multiple Benefits: But Too Often the Wrong Methods Are Used." Washington, DC. www. worldbank.org/en/topic/earlychildhooddevelopment/ overview. Accessed 7 November 2016.

———. 2015c. "Dominican Republic: Integrated Social Protection and Promotion Project." Report PAD1070. Washington, DC.

———. 2015d. *Ending Poverty and Hunger by 2030: An Agenda for the Global Food System.* Washington, DC. http://documents.worldbank.org/curated/ en/700061468334490682/pdf/95768-REVISED-WP-PUBLIC-Box391467B-Ending-Poverty-and-Hunger-by-2030-FINAL.pdf. Accessed 26 October 2016.

———. 2015e. "Overview." 22 December. Washington, DC. www.worldbank.org/en/topic/earlychildhooddevelopment/ overview. Accessed 7 November 2016.

———. 2015f. "Philippines: CCT Proven to Keep Poor Children Healthy and in School." Press release, 23 September. Washington, DC. www.worldbank.org/en/ news/press-release/2015/09/23/philippines-cct-proven-to-keep-poor-children-healthy-and-in-school. Accessed 7 November 2016.

———. 2015g. "Urban Development: Overview." 10 October. Washington, DC. www.worldbank.org/en/topic/ urbandevelopment/overview. Accessed 11 October 2016.

———. 2015h. *Women, Business and the Law 2016: Getting to Equal.* Washington, DC. http://wbl.worldbank. org/~/media/WBG/WBL/Documents/Reports/2016/ Women-Business-and-the-Law-2016.pdf. Accessed 14 October 2016.

———. 2015i. *World Development Report 2015: Mind, Society, and Behavior.* Washington, DC.

———. 2016a. "Climate-Driven Water Scarcity Could Hit Economic Growth by Up to 6 Percent in Some Regions, Says World Bank." Press release, 3 May. www.worldbank. org/en/news/press-release/2016/05/03/climate-driven-water-scarcity-could-hit-economic-growth-by-up-to-6-percent-in-some-regions-says-world-bank. Accessed 14 October 2016.

———. 2016b. "Drug-Resistant Infections: A Threat to Our Economic Future." Discussion Draft. Washington, DC. http://pubdocs.worldbank.org/en/527731474225046104/ AMR-Discussion-Draft-Sept18updated.pdf. Accessed 14 October 2016.

———. 2016c. "The Economic Effects of War and Peace." MENA Quarterly Economic Brief 6. Washington, DC. http://documents.worldbank.org/curated/ en/644191468191061975/pdf/103013-REPLACEMENT-PUBLIC-MENA-QEB-ISSUE-6-JANUARY-2016.pdf. Accessed 14 October 2016.

———. 2016d. "Eight Stubborn Facts about Housing Policies." Washington, DC. http://blogs.worldbank.org/ sustainablecities/eight-stubborn-facts-about-housing-policies. Accessed 11 October 2016.

———. 2016e. "High-Technology Exports (Current US$)." Washington, DC. http://data.worldbank.org/indicator/ TX.VAL.TECH.CD. Accessed 4 December 2016.

———. 2016f. "I4D, Identification for Development: Strategic Framework." 25 January. Washington, DC. http://pubdocs.worldbank.org/en/21571460567481655/ April-2016-ID4D-Strategic-RoadmapID4D.pdf. Accessed 7 November 2016.

———. 2016g. "Living Standards Measurement Study." Washington, DC. http://go.worldbank.org/IPLXWMCNJ0. Accessed 7 November 2016.

———. 2016h. "Personal Remittances, Received (% of GDP)." http://data.worldbank.org/indicator/BX.TRF.PWKR. DT.GD.ZS. Accessed 2 November 2016.

———. 2016i. *Poverty and Shared Prosperity 2016: Taking on Inequality.* Washington, DC. www.worldbank.org/en/ publication/poverty-and-shared-prosperity. Accessed 22 November 2016.

———. 2016j. "Pricing Carbon." Washington, DC. www. worldbank.org/en/programs/pricing-carbon. Accessed 7 November 2016.

———. 2016k. "Remittances to Developing Countries Edge Up Slightly in 2015." Press release, 13 April. Washington, DC. www.worldbank.org/en/news/press-release/2016/04/13/remittances-to-developing-countries-edge-up-slightly-in-2015. Accessed 7 November 2016.

———. 2016l. "Urban Violence: A Challenge of Epidemic Proportions." 6 September. Washington, DC. www. worldbank.org/en/news/feature/2016/09/06/urban-violence-a-challenge-of-epidemic-proportions. Accessed 11 October 2016.

———. 2016m. "World Bank Group Finances Top 8 Countries Voting Power." Washington, DC. https:// finances.worldbank.org/Shareholder-Equity/Top-8-countries-voting-power/udm3-vzz9/data. Accessed 5 December 2016.

———. 2016n. "World Bank Group: Forest Action Plan FY16–20." Washington, DC. http://documents.worldbank. org/curated/en/240231467291388831/pdf/106467-REVISED-v1-PUBLIC.pdf. Accessed 23 August 2016.

———. 2016o. World Development Indicators database. Washington, DC. http://data.worldbank.org. Accessed 14 October 2016.

———. 2016p. *World Development Report: Digital Dividends.* Washington, DC. www.worldbank.org/en/ publication/wdr2016. Accessed 22 November 2016.

———. 2017. PovcalNet [online database]. http://iresearch. worldbank.org/PovcalNet/povDuplicateWB.aspx. Accessed 5 December 2016.

World Bank and ECOFYS. 2016. "Carbon Pricing Watch 2016." Washington, DC. https://openknowledge. worldbank.org/handle/10986/24288. Accessed 26 August 2016.

World Bank and IHME (Institute for Health Metrics and Evaluation). 2016. "The Cost of Air Pollution: Strengthening the Economic Case for Action." Washington, DC. https://openknowledge.worldbank. org/bitstream/handle/10986/25013/108141. pdf?sequence=4&isAllowed=y. Accessed 20 October 2016.

World Resources Institute. 2016. "The Roads to Decoupling: 21 Countries Are Reducing Carbon Emissions While Growing GDP." www.wri.org/blog/2016/04/roads-decoupling-21-countries-are-reducing-carbon-emissions-while-growing-gdp. Accessed 26 September 2016.

WVSA (World Values Survey Association). 2016. "Data and Documentation." Institute for Comparative Survey Research, Vienna. www.worldvaluessurvey.org/ WVSContents.jsp. Accessed 2 November 2016.

WWF-Korea. 2016. *Korea Ecological Footprint Report 2016: Measuring Korea's Impact on Nature.* Seoul.

Yi, I. 2012. "Economic and Social Development in the Republic of Korea: Processes, Institutions and Actors." Research and Policy Brief 14. United Nations Research Institute for Social Development, Geneva.

———. 2014. "How Could the Enhancement of Education and Health Contribute to Economic Growth in South Korea?" In I. Yi and T. Mkandawire, eds., *Learning from the South Korean Developmental Success: Effective Developmental Cooperation and Synergistic Institutions and Policies.* London: Palgrave Macmillan UK.

Yi, I., C. Olive, H. Rhee and Y.-A. Chung. 2011. "The Korean Experience within the Context of Development Cooperation Effectiveness." Presentation at the 5th Seoul ODA International Conference, 13 Ocotober, Seoul.

Yi, I., O. Cocoman, Y.-A. Chung and H. Rhee. 2014. "Effective Aid and Development Cooperation in South Korea." In I. Yi and T. Mkandawire, eds., *Learning from the South Korean Developmental Success: Effective Development Cooperation and Synergistic Institutions and Policies.* London: Palgrave Macmillan UK.

Zimmer, C. 2016. "Ebola Evolved Into Deadlier Enemy during the African Epidemic." *New York Times*, 3 November. www.nytimes.com/2016/11/04/science/ebola-evolution-african-epidemic.html. Accessed 7 November 2016.

Zucman, G. 2015. *The Hidden Wealth of Nations: The Scourge of Tax Havens.* Chicago, IL: University of Chicago Press.

Human Development Reports 1990–2016

1990	Concept and Measurement of Human Development
1991	Financing Human Development
1992	Global Dimensions of Human Development
1993	People's Participation
1994	New Dimensions of Human Security
1995	Gender and Human Development
1996	Economic Growth and Human Development
1997	Human Development to Eradicate Poverty
1998	Consumption for Human Development
1999	Globalization with a Human Face
2000	Human Rights and Human Development
2001	Making New Technologies Work for Human Development
2002	Deepening Democracy in a Fragmented World
2003	Millennium Development Goals: A Compact among Nations to End Human Poverty
2004	Cultural Liberty in Today's Diverse World
2005	International Cooperation at a Crossroads: Aid, Trade and Security in an Unequal World
2006	Beyond Scarcity: Power, Poverty and the Global Water Crisis
2007/2008	Fighting Climate Change: Human Solidarity in a Divided World
2009	Overcoming Barriers: Human Mobility and Development
2010	The Real Wealth of Nations: Pathways to Human Development
2011	Sustainability and Equity: A Better Future for All
2013	The Rise of the South: Human Progress in a Diverse World
2014	Sustaining Human Progress: Reducing Vulnerability and Building Resilience
2015	Work for Human Development
2016	Human Development for Everyone

Statistical annex

Readers guide

The 17 statistical tables in this annex provide an overview of key aspects of human development. The first six tables contain the family of composite human development indices and their components estimated by the Human Development Report Office (HDRO). The remaining tables present a broader set of indicators related to human development. The two dashboards introduce partial groupings of countries according to their performance on each indicator.

Unless otherwise noted, tables use data available to the HDRO as of 1 September 2016. All indices and indicators, along with technical notes on the calculation of composite indices and additional source information, are available at http://hdr.undp.org/en/data.

Countries and territories are ranked by 2015 Human Development Index (HDI) value. Robustness and reliability analysis has shown that for most countries differences in HDI are not statistically significant at the fourth decimal place. For this reason countries with the same HDI value at three decimal places are listed with tied ranks.

Sources and definitions

Unless otherwise noted, the HDRO uses data from international data agencies with the mandate, resources and expertise to collect national data on specific indicators.

Definitions of indicators and sources for original data components are given at the end of each table, with full source details in *Statistical references*.

Methodology updates

The 2016 Report retains all the composite indices from the family of human development indices—the HDI, the Inequality-adjusted Human Development Index (IHDI), the Gender Development Index (GDI), the Gender Inequality Index (GII) and the Multidimensional Poverty Index (MPI). The methodology used to compute these indices is the same as the one used in the 2015 Report. See *Technical notes 1–5* at http://hdr.undp.org/sites/default/files/hdr2016_technical_notes.pdf for details.

New in this year's Report are two colour-coded dashboard tables, *Life-course gender gap* and *Sustainable development*. The dashboards introduce partial grouping of countries by their performance on each indicator.

Comparisons over time and across editions of the Report

Because national and international agencies continually improve their data series, the data—including the HDI values and ranks—presented in this Report are not comparable to those published in earlier editions. For HDI comparability across years and countries see table 2, which presents trends using consistent data.

Discrepancies between national and international estimates

National and international data can differ because international agencies harmonize national data using a consistent methodology and occasionally produce estimates of missing data to allow comparability across countries. In other cases international agencies might not have access to the most recent national data. When HDRO becomes aware of discrepancies, it brings them to the attention of national and international data authorities.

Country groupings and aggregates

The tables present weighted aggregates for several country groupings. In general, an aggregate is shown only when data are available for at least half the countries and represent at least two-thirds of the population in that classification. Aggregates for each classification cover only the countries for which data are available.

Human development classification

HDI classifications are based on HDI fixed cutoff points, which are derived from the quartiles of distributions of the component indicators. The cutoff points are HDI of less than 0.550 for low human development, 0.550–0.699 for medium human development, 0.700–0.799 for high human development and 0.800 or greater for very high human development.

Regional groupings

Regional groupings are based on United Nations Development Programme regional classifications. Least developed countries and small island developing states are defined according to UN classifications (see www.unohrlls.org).

Developing countries

Aggregates are provided for the group of all countries classified as developing countries, grouped by region.

Organisation for Economic Co-operation and Development

Of the 35 OECD members, 32 are considered developed and 3 developing (Chile, Mexico and Turkey). Aggregates refer to all countries from the group for which data are available.

Country note

Data for China do not include Hong Kong Special Administrative Region of China, Macao Special Administrative Region of China or Taiwan Province of China.

Symbols

A dash between two years, as in 2005–2014, indicates that the data are from the most recent year available during the period specified. A slash between years, as in 2005/2014, indicates that data are the average for the years shown. Growth rates are usually average annual rates of growth between the first and last years of the period shown.

The following symbols are used in the tables:

..	Not available
0 or 0.0	Nil or negligible
—	Not applicable

Statistical acknowledgements

The Report's composite indices and other statistical resources draw on a wide variety of the most respected international data providers in their specialized fields. HDRO is particularly grateful to the Centre for Research on the Epidemiology of Disasters; Economic Commission for Latin America and the Caribbean; Eurostat; Food and Agriculture Organization; Gallup; ICF Macro; Institute for Criminal Policy Research; Internal Displacement Monitoring Centre; International Labour Organization; International Monetary Fund; International Telecommunication Union; International Union for the Conservation of Nature; Inter-Parliamentary Union; Luxembourg Income Study; Office of the United Nations High Commissioner for Human Rights; Office of the United Nations High Commissioner for Refugees; Organisation for Economic Co-operation and Development; Socio-Economic Database for Latin America and the Caribbean; Syrian Center for Policy Research; United Nations Children's Fund; United Nations Conference on Trade and Development; United Nations Department of Economic and Social Affairs; United Nations Economic and Social Commission for West Asia; United Nations Educational, Scientific and Cultural Organization Institute for Statistics; United Nations Entity for Gender Equality and the Empowerment of Women; United Nations Office on Drugs and Crime; United Nations Relief and Works Agency for Palestine Refugees in the Near East; United Nations World Tourism Organization; World Bank; and World Health Organization. The international education database maintained by Robert Barro (Harvard University) and Jong-Wha Lee (Korea University) was another invaluable source for the calculation of the Report's indices.

Statistical tables

The first six tables relate to the five composite human development indices and their components.

Since the 2010 Human Development Report, four composite human development indices—the HDI, the IHDI, the GII and the MPI for developing countries—have been calculated. The 2014 Report introduced the GDI, which compares the HDI calculated separately for women and men.

The remaining tables present a broader set of human development indicators and provide a more comprehensive picture of a country's human development.

Table 1, Human Development Index and its components, ranks countries by 2015 HDI value and details the values of the three HDI components: longevity, education (with two indicators) and income. The table also presents the difference in rankings by HDI and gross national income per capita, as well as the ranking on the 2014 HDI, calculated using the most recently revised historical data available in 2016.

Table 2, Human Development Index trends, 1990–2015, provides a time series of HDI values allowing 2015 HDI values to be compared with those for previous years. The table uses the most recently revised historical data available in 2016 and the same methodology applied to compute 2015 HDI values. The table also includes the change in HDI rank over the last five years and the average annual HDI growth rate across four time intervals: 1990–2000, 2000–2010, 2010–2015 and 1990–2015.

Table 3, Inequality-adjusted Human Development Index, contains two related measures of inequality—the IHDI and the loss in HDI due to inequality. The IHDI looks beyond the average achievements of a country in longevity, education and income to show how these achievements are distributed among its residents. An IHDI value can be interpreted as the level of human development when inequality is accounted for. The relative difference between IHDI and HDI values is the loss due to inequality in distribution of the HDI within the country. The table also presents the coefficient of human inequality, which is an unweighted average of inequalities in three dimensions. In addition, the table shows each country's difference in rank on the HDI and the IHDI. A negative value means that taking inequality into account lowers a country's rank on the HDI. The table also presents three standard measures of income inequality: the ratio of the top and the bottom quintiles; the Palma ratio, which is the ratio of income of the top 10 percent and the bottom 40 percent; and the Gini coefficient.

Table 4, Gender Development Index, measures disparities on the HDI by gender. The table contains HDI values estimated separately for women and men; the ratio of which is the GDI value. The closer the ratio is to 1, the smaller the gap between women and men. Values for the three HDI components—longevity, education (with two indicators) and income—are also presented by gender. The table includes five country groupings by absolute deviation from gender parity in HDI values.

Table 5, Gender Inequality Index, presents a composite measure of gender inequality using three dimensions: reproductive health, empowerment and the labour market. Reproductive health is measured by two indicators: the maternal mortality ratio and the adolescent birth rate. Empowerment is measured by the share of parliamentary seats held by women and the shares of population with at least some secondary education by gender. And labour market is measured by participation in the labour force by gender. A low GII value indicates low inequality between women and men, and vice-versa.

Table 6, Multidimensional Poverty Index: developing countries, captures the multiple deprivations that people in developing countries face in their education, health and living standards. The MPI shows both the incidence of nonincome multidimensional poverty (a headcount of those in multidimensional poverty) and its intensity (the average deprivation score experienced by poor people). Based on deprivation score thresholds, people are classified as multidimensionally poor, near multidimensional poverty or in severe poverty. The contributions of deprivations in each dimension to overall poverty are also presented. In addition, the table provides measures of income poverty—population living below the national poverty line and population living on less than PPP $1.90 per day. MPI estimations for this year use the revised methodology introduced in the 2014 Report, which modified the original set of 10 indicators in several ways. Height-for-age replaced weight-for-age for children under age 5 because stunting is a better indicator of chronic malnutrition. A child death is considered a health deprivation only if it happened in the five years prior to the survey. The minimum threshold for education deprivation was raised from five years of schooling to six to reflect the standard definition of primary schooling used in the Millennium Development Goals and in international measures of functional literacy. And the indicators for household assets were expanded to better reflect rural as well as urban households.

Table 7, Population trends, contains major population indicators, including total population, median age, dependency ratios and total fertility rates, which can help assess the burden of support that falls on the labour force in a country.

Table 8, Health outcomes, presents indicators of infant health (percentage of infants who are exclusively breastfed for the first six months of life, percentage of infants who lack immunization for DTP and measles, and infant mortality rate) and of child health (under-five mortality rate and percentage of children under age 5 whose height is stunted). The table also contains indicators of adult health (adult mortality rates by gender, mortality rates due to malaria and tuberculosis, HIV prevalence rates and life expectancy at age 60). Two indicators of quality of health care are also included: number of physicians per 10,000 people and public health expenditure as a share of GDP.

Table 9, Education achievements, presents standard education indicators along with indicators on education quality. The table provides indicators of educational attainment—adult and youth literacy rates and the share of the adult population with at least some secondary education. Gross enrolment ratios at each level of education are complemented by primary school dropout rates. The table also includes two indicators of education quality—primary school teachers trained to teach and the pupil–teacher ratio—as well as government expenditure on education as a percentage of GDP.

Table 10, National income and composition of resources, covers several macroeconomic indicators such as gross domestic product (GDP), gross fixed capital formation, and taxes on income, profit and capital gain as percentage of total tax revenue. Gross fixed capital formation is a rough indicator of national income that is invested rather than consumed. In times of economic uncertainty or recession, gross fixed capital formation typically declines. General government final consumption expenditure (presented as a share of GDP and as average annual growth) is an indicator of public spending. In addition, the table presents two indicators of debt—domestic credit provided by the financial sector and total debt service, both measured as a percentage of GDP or GNI. The consumer price index is a measure of inflation; two indicators related to the price of food are also presented—the price level index and the price volatility index.

Table 11, Work and employment, presents indicators on two components: employment and unemployment. Two key indicators related to employment are the employment to population ratio and labour force participation rate. The table also reports employment in agriculture and in services and indicators related to vulnerable employment and different forms of unemployment. The table brings together indicators on child labour and the working poor. Two indicators—paid maternity leave and old-age pensions—reflect security stemming from employment.

Table 12, Human security, reflects the extent to which the population is secure. The table begins with indicators of birth registration, refugees by country of origin and internally displaced persons. It then shows the size of the homeless population due to natural disasters, the population of orphaned children and the prison population. Also provided are indicators of homicide and suicide (by gender), violence against women and the depth of food deficit.

Table 13, International integration, provides indicators of several aspects of globalization. International trade is captured by measuring exports and imports as a share of GDP. Financial flows are represented by net inflows of foreign direct investment and flows of private capital, net official development assistance and inflows of remittances. Human mobility is captured by the net migration rate, the stock of immigrants, the net number of tertiary students from abroad (expressed as a percentage of total tertiary enrolment in that country) and the number of international inbound tourists. International communication is represented by the share of the population that uses the Internet, the number of mobile phone subscriptions per 100 people and the percentage change in mobile phone subscriptions between 2010 and 2015.

Table 14, Supplementary indicators: perceptions of well-being, includes indicators that reflect individuals' perceptions of relevant dimensions of human development—education quality, health care quality, standard of living and labour market, personal safety and overall satisfaction with freedom of choice and life. The table also presents indicators reflecting perceptions about community and government.

Table 15, Status of fundamental human rights treaties, shows when the key human rights conventions were ratified by countries. The 11 selected conventions cover civil and political rights; social, economic, and cultural rights; and rights and freedoms related to elimination of all forms of racial and gender discrimination and violence, protection of children's rights, rights of migrant workers and persons with disabilities. They also cover torture and other cruel, inhuman and degrading treatment as well as protection from enforced disappearance.

Dashboard 1, Life-course gender gap, contains a selection of indicators that indicate gender gaps over the life course—childhood and youth, adulthood and older age. The indicators refer to health, education, labour market and work, leadership,

seats in parliament and social protection. Some indicators are presented only for women, and others are presented as a ratio of female to male values. Three-colour coding visualizes partial grouping of countries by indicator. For each indicator countries are divided into three groups of approximately equal size (terciles)—the top third, the middle third and the bottom third. Sex ratio at birth is an exception—countries are divided into two groups: the natural group (countries with a value between 1.04–1.07, inclusive) and the gender-biased group (all other countries). Deviations from the natural sex ratio at birth have implications for population replacement levels, suggest possible future social and economic problems and may indicate gender bias. Countries with values of a parity index concentrated around 1 form the group with the best achievements in that indicator. Deviations from parity are treated equally regardless of which gender is overachieving. The intention is not to suggest thresholds or target values for these indicators. See *Technical note 6* at http://hdr.undp.org/sites/default/files/hdr2016_technical_notes.pdf for details about partial grouping in the table.

Dashboard 2, Sustainable development, contains a selection of indicators that cover environmental, economic and social sustainable development. A mix of level and change indicators is related to renewable energy consumption, carbon-dioxide emissions, forest areas and fresh water withdrawals. Economic sustainability indicators look at natural resource depletion, national savings, external debt stock, government spending on research and development, and diversity of economy. Social sustainability is captured by changes in income and gender inequality and by the old-age dependency ratio. Three-colour coding visualizes a partial grouping of countries by indicator. For each indicator countries are divided into three groups of approximately equal sizes (terciles): the top third, the middle third and the bottom third. The intention is not to suggest thresholds or target values for these indicators. See *Technical note 7* at http://hdr.undp.org/sites/default/files/hdr2016_technical_notes.pdf for more details about partial grouping in the table.

Human development composite indices

Rank	Country	Value
1	Norway	0.949
2	Australia	0.939
2	Switzerland	0.939
4	Germany	0.926
5	Denmark	0.925
5	Singapore	0.925
7	Netherlands	0.924
8	Ireland	0.923
9	Iceland	0.921
10	Canada	0.920
10	United States	0.920
12	Hong Kong, China (SAR)	0.917
13	New Zealand	0.915
14	Sweden	0.913
15	Liechtenstein	0.912
16	United Kingdom	0.909
17	Japan	0.903
18	Korea (Republic of)	0.901
19	Israel	0.899
20	Luxembourg	0.898
21	France	0.897
22	Belgium	0.896
23	Finland	0.895
24	Austria	0.893
25	Slovenia	0.890
26	Italy	0.887
27	Spain	0.884
28	Czech Republic	0.878
29	Greece	0.866
30	Brunei Darussalam	0.865
30	Estonia	0.865
32	Andorra	0.858
33	Cyprus	0.856
33	Malta	0.856
33	Qatar	0.856
36	Poland	0.855
37	Lithuania	0.848
38	Chile	0.847
38	Saudi Arabia	0.847
40	Slovakia	0.845
41	Portugal	0.843
42	United Arab Emirates	0.840
43	Hungary	0.836
44	Latvia	0.830
45	Argentina	0.827
45	Croatia	0.827
47	Bahrain	0.824
48	Montenegro	0.807

2015 Human Development Index

Global State of Human Development

Rank	Country	Value
96	Dominica	0.726
97	Suriname	0.725
97	Tunisia	0.725
99	Dominican Republic	0.722
99	Saint Vincent and the Grenadines	0.722
101	Tonga	0.721
102	Libya	0.716
103	Belize	0.706
104	Samoa	0.704
105	Maldives	0.701
105	Uzbekistan	0.701
107	Moldova (Republic of)	0.699
108	Botswana	0.698
109	Gabon	0.697
110	Paraguay	0.693
111	Egypt	0.691
111	Turkmenistan	0.691
113	Indonesia	0.689
114	Palestine, State of	0.684
115	Viet Nam	0.683
116	Philippines	0.682
117	El Salvador	0.680
118	Bolivia (Plurinational State of)	0.674
119	South Africa	0.666
120	Kyrgyzstan	0.664
121	Iraq	0.649
122	Cabo Verde	0.648
123	Morocco	0.647
124	Nicaragua	0.645
125	Guatemala	0.640
125	Namibia	0.640
127	Guyana	0.638
127	Micronesia (Federated States of)	0.638
129	Tajikistan	0.627
130	Honduras	0.625
131	India	0.624
132	Bhutan	0.607
133	Timor-Leste	0.605
134	Vanuatu	0.597
135	Congo	0.592
135	Equatorial Guinea	0.592
137	Kiribati	0.588
138	Lao People's Democratic Republic	0.586
139	Bangladesh	0.579
139	Ghana	0.579

49 Russian Federation	0.804
50 Romania	0.802
51 Kuwait	0.800
52 Belarus	0.796
52 Oman	0.796
54 Barbados	0.795
54 Uruguay	0.795
56 Bulgaria	0.794
56 Kazakhstan	0.794
58 Bahamas	0.792
59 Malaysia	0.789
60 Palau	0.788

60 Panama	0.788
62 Antigua and Barbuda	0.786
63 Seychelles	0.782
64 Mauritius	0.781
65 Trinidad and Tobago	0.780
66 Costa Rica	0.776
66 Serbia	0.776
68 Cuba	0.775
69 Iran (Islamic Republic of)	0.774
70 Georgia	0.769
71 Turkey	0.767
71 Venezuela (Bolivarian Republic of)	0.767

73 Sri Lanka	0.766
74 Saint Kitts and Nevis	0.765
75 Albania	0.764
76 Lebanon	0.763
77 Mexico	0.762
78 Azerbaijan	0.759
79 Brazil	0.754
79 Grenada	0.754
81 Bosnia and Herzegovina	0.750
82 The former Yugoslav Republic of Macedonia	0.748
83 Algeria	0.745

84 Armenia	0.743
84 Ukraine	0.743
86 Jordan	0.741
87 Peru	0.740
87 Thailand	0.740
89 Ecuador	0.739
90 China	0.738
91 Fiji	0.736
92 Mongolia	0.735
92 Saint Lucia	0.735
94 Jamaica	0.730
95 Colombia	0.727

Very high human development

High human development

Medium human development

Low human development

139 Zambia	0.579
142 Sao Tome and Principe	0.574
143 Cambodia	0.563
144 Nepal	0.558
145 Myanmar	0.556
146 Kenya	0.555
147 Pakistan	0.550
148 Swaziland	0.541
149 Syrian Arab Republic	0.536
150 Angola	0.533
151 Tanzania (United Republic of)	0.531

152 Nigeria	0.527
153 Cameroon	0.518
154 Papua New Guinea	0.516
154 Zimbabwe	0.516
156 Solomon Islands	0.515
157 Mauritania	0.513
158 Madagascar	0.512
159 Rwanda	0.498
160 Comoros	0.497
160 Lesotho	0.497
162 Senegal	0.494
163 Haiti	0.493

163 Uganda	0.493
165 Sudan	0.490
166 Togo	0.487
167 Benin	0.485
168 Yemen	0.482
169 Afghanistan	0.479
170 Malawi	0.476
171 Côte d'Ivoire	0.474
172 Djibouti	0.473
173 Gambia	0.452
174 Ethiopia	0.448
175 Mali	0.442

176 Congo (Democratic Republic of the)	0.435
177 Liberia	0.427
178 Guinea-Bissau	0.424
179 Eritrea	0.420
179 Sierra Leone	0.420
181 Mozambique	0.418
181 South Sudan	0.418
183 Guinea	0.414
184 Burundi	0.404
185 Burkina Faso	0.402
186 Chad	0.396
187 Niger	0.353
188 Central African Republic	0.352

TABLE 1

Human Development Index and its components

TABLE 1

HDI rank	Human Development Index (HDI) Value 2015	Life expectancy at birth (years) 2015	Expected years of schooling (years) 2015[a]	Mean years of schooling (years) 2015[a]	Gross national income (GNI) per capita (2011 PPP $) 2015	GNI per capita rank minus HDI rank 2015	HDI rank 2014
VERY HIGH HUMAN DEVELOPMENT							
1 Norway	0.949	81.7	17.7	12.7	67,614	5	1
2 Australia	0.939	82.5	20.4 [b]	13.2	42,822	19	3
2 Switzerland	0.939	83.1	16.0	13.4	56,364	7	2
4 Germany	0.926	81.1	17.1	13.2 [c]	45,000	13	4
5 Denmark	0.925	80.4	19.2 [b]	12.7	44,519	13	6
5 Singapore	0.925	83.2	15.4 [d]	11.6	78,162 [e]	−3	4
7 Netherlands	0.924	81.7	18.1 [b]	11.9	46,326	8	6
8 Ireland	0.923	81.1	18.6 [b]	12.3	43,798	11	8
9 Iceland	0.921	82.7	19.0 [b]	12.2 [c]	37,065	20	9
10 Canada	0.920	82.2	16.3	13.1 [f]	42,582	12	9
10 United States	0.920	79.2	16.5	13.2	53,245	1	11
12 Hong Kong, China (SAR)	0.917	84.2	15.7	11.6	54,265	−2	12
13 New Zealand	0.915	82.0	19.2 [b]	12.5	32,870	20	13
14 Sweden	0.913	82.3	16.1	12.3	46,251	2	15
15 Liechtenstein	0.912	80.2 [g]	14.6	12.4 [h]	75,065 [e,i]	−11	14
16 United Kingdom	0.909	80.8	16.3	13.3	37,931	10	16
17 Japan	0.903	83.7	15.3	12.5 [c]	37,268	10	17
18 Korea (Republic of)	0.901	82.1	16.6	12.2	34,541	12	18
19 Israel	0.899	82.6	16.0	12.8	31,215	16	19
20 Luxembourg	0.898	81.9	13.9	12.0	62,471	−12	20
21 France	0.897	82.4	16.3	11.6	38,085	4	22
22 Belgium	0.896	81.0	16.6	11.4	41,243	1	21
23 Finland	0.895	81.0	17.0	11.2 [f]	38,868	1	23
24 Austria	0.893	81.6	15.9	11.3 [c]	43,609	−4	24
25 Slovenia	0.890	80.6	17.3	12.1	28,664	13	25
26 Italy	0.887	83.3	16.3	10.9	33,573	6	27
27 Spain	0.884	82.8	17.7	9.8	32,779	7	26
28 Czech Republic	0.878	78.8	16.8	12.3	28,144	11	28
29 Greece	0.866	81.1	17.2	10.5	24,808	16	29
30 Brunei Darussalam	0.865	79.0	14.9	9.0 [f]	72,843	−25	30
30 Estonia	0.865	77.0	16.5	12.5 [c]	26,362	12	31
32 Andorra	0.858	81.5 [g]	13.5 [d]	10.3	47,979 [i]	−18	32
33 Cyprus	0.856	80.3	14.3	11.7	29,459	4	34
33 Malta	0.856	80.7	14.6	11.3	29,500	3	35
33 Qatar	0.856	78.3	13.4	9.8	129,916 [e]	−32	33
36 Poland	0.855	77.6	16.4	11.9	24,117	11	36
37 Lithuania	0.848	73.5	16.5	12.7	26,006	7	37
38 Chile	0.847	82.0	16.3	9.9	21,665	16	38
38 Saudi Arabia	0.847	74.4	16.1	9.6	51,320	−26	38
40 Slovakia	0.845	76.4	15.0	12.2	26,764	1	40
41 Portugal	0.843	81.2	16.6	8.9	26,104	2	41
42 United Arab Emirates	0.840	77.1	13.3 [k]	9.5 [c]	66,203	−35	42
43 Hungary	0.836	75.3	15.6	12.0	23,394	6	43
44 Latvia	0.830	74.3	16.0	11.7 [f]	22,589	7	44
45 Argentina	0.827	76.5	17.3	9.9 [f]	20,945 [l]	12	45
45 Croatia	0.827	77.5	15.3	11.2	20,291	14	46
47 Bahrain	0.824	76.7	14.5 [k]	9.4 [m]	37,236	−19	46
48 Montenegro	0.807	76.4	15.1	11.3 [n]	15,410	24	49
49 Russian Federation	0.804	70.3	15.0	12.0	23,286	1	48
50 Romania	0.802	74.8	14.7	10.8	19,428	11	51
51 Kuwait	0.800	74.5	13.3	7.3	76,075 [e]	−48	50
HIGH HUMAN DEVELOPMENT							
52 Belarus	0.796	71.5	15.7	12.0	15,629	19	51
52 Oman	0.796	77.0	13.7	8.1 [m]	34,402	−21	53
54 Barbados	0.795	75.8	15.3	10.5 [n]	14,952	20	54
54 Uruguay	0.795	77.4	15.5	8.6	19,148	8	54
56 Bulgaria	0.794	74.3	15.0	10.8 [c]	16,261	13	57
56 Kazakhstan	0.794	69.6	15.0	11.7 [f]	22,093	−3	56
58 Bahamas	0.792	75.6	12.7 [k]	10.9	21,565	−3	58
59 Malaysia	0.789	74.9	13.1	10.1	24,620	−13	59
60 Palau	0.788	72.9 [g]	14.3	12.3 [k]	13,771	21	62
60 Panama	0.788	77.8	13.0	9.9	19,470	0	60

HDI rank		Human Development Index (HDI)	Life expectancy at birth	Expected years of schooling	Mean years of schooling	Gross national income (GNI) per capita	GNI per capita rank minus HDI rank	HDI rank
		Value	(years)	(years)	(years)	(2011 PPP $)		
		2015	2015	2015[a]	2015[a]	2015	2015	2014
62	Antigua and Barbuda	0.786	76.2	13.9	9.2 [k]	20,907	−4	61
63	Seychelles	0.782	73.3	14.1	9.4 [k]	23,886	−15	63
64	Mauritius	0.781	74.6	15.2	9.1	17,948	1	64
65	Trinidad and Tobago	0.780	70.5	12.7 [o]	10.9	28,049	−25	64
66	Costa Rica	0.776	79.6	14.2	8.7	14,006	14	66
66	Serbia	0.776	75.0	14.4	10.8	12,202	22	66
68	Cuba	0.775	79.6	13.9	11.8 [m]	7,455 [p]	48	69
69	Iran (Islamic Republic of)	0.774	75.6	14.8	8.8 [f]	16,395	−2	68
70	Georgia	0.769	75.0	13.9	12.2	8,856	38	71
71	Turkey	0.767	75.5	14.6	7.9	18,705	−7	72
71	Venezuela (Bolivarian Republic of)	0.767	74.4	14.3	9.4	15,129	2	70
73	Sri Lanka	0.766	75.0	14.0	10.9 [f]	10,789	21	72
74	Saint Kitts and Nevis	0.765	74.0 [g]	13.7	8.4 [k]	22,436	−22	75
75	Albania	0.764	78.0	14.2	9.6	10,252	24	75
76	Lebanon	0.763	79.5	13.3	8.6 [m]	13,312	8	74
77	Mexico	0.762	77.0	13.3	8.6	16,383	−9	77
78	Azerbaijan	0.759	70.9	12.7	11.2	16,413	−12	77
79	Brazil	0.754	74.7	15.2	7.8	14,145	−1	79
79	Grenada	0.754	73.6	15.8	8.6 [k]	11,502	13	80
81	Bosnia and Herzegovina	0.750	76.6	14.2	9.0	10,091	22	82
82	The former Yugoslav Republic of Macedonia	0.748	75.5	12.9	9.4 [n]	12,405	5	83
83	Algeria	0.745	75.0	14.4	7.8 [c]	13,533	−1	84
84	Armenia	0.743	74.9	12.7	11.3	8,189	28	85
84	Ukraine	0.743	71.1	15.3	11.3 [f]	7,361	34	81
86	Jordan	0.741	74.2	13.1	10.1	10,111	15	85
87	Peru	0.740	74.8	13.4	9.0	11,295	6	89
87	Thailand	0.740	74.6	13.6	7.9	14,519	−11	88
89	Ecuador	0.739	76.1	14.0	8.3	10,536	6	87
90	China	0.738	76.0	13.5	7.6 [c]	13,345	−7	91
91	Fiji	0.736	70.2	15.3 [k]	10.5 [f]	8,245	20	91
92	Mongolia	0.735	69.8	14.8	9.8 [m]	10,449	4	93
92	Saint Lucia	0.735	75.2	13.1	9.3 [m]	9,791	14	90
94	Jamaica	0.730	75.8	12.8	9.6 [f]	8,350	16	94
95	Colombia	0.727	74.2	13.6	7.6 [c]	12,762	−10	95
96	Dominica	0.726	77.9 [g]	12.8 [k]	7.9 [m]	10,096	6	95
97	Suriname	0.725	71.3	12.7	8.3 [m]	16,018	−27	97
97	Tunisia	0.725	75.0	14.6	7.1 [c]	10,249	3	97
99	Dominican Republic	0.722	73.7	13.2	7.7	12,756	−13	101
99	Saint Vincent and the Grenadines	0.722	73.0	13.3 [m]	8.6 [k]	10,372	−1	99
101	Tonga	0.721	73.0	14.3 [m]	11.1	5,284	33	101
102	Libya	0.716	71.8	13.4 [k]	7.3 [c]	14,303	25	100
103	Belize	0.706	70.1	12.8	10.5	7,375	14	103
104	Samoa	0.704	73.7	12.9 [d]	10.3 [d]	5,372	27	104
105	Maldives	0.701	77.0	12.7 [o]	6.2 [q]	10,383	−8	105
105	Uzbekistan	0.701	69.4 [r]	12.2	12.0 [m]	5,748	21	108
MEDIUM HUMAN DEVELOPMENT								
107	Moldova (Republic of)	0.699	71.7	11.8	11.9	5,026	31	105
108	Botswana	0.698	64.5	12.6	9.2 [c]	14,663	−33	107
109	Gabon	0.697	64.9	12.6	8.1 [q]	19,044	−46	109
110	Paraguay	0.693	73.0	12.3	8.1	8,182	3	110
111	Egypt	0.691	71.3	13.1	7.1 [f]	10,064	−7	111
111	Turkmenistan	0.691	65.7	10.8	9.9 [k]	14,026	−32	111
113	Indonesia	0.689	69.1	12.9	7.9	10,053	−8	113
114	Palestine, State of	0.684	73.1	12.8	8.9	5,256	21	115
115	Viet Nam	0.683	75.9	12.6	8.0 [c]	5,335	18	115
116	Philippines	0.682	68.3	11.7	9.3	8,395	−7	114
117	El Salvador	0.680	73.3	13.2	6.5	7,732	−3	115
118	Bolivia (Plurinational State of)	0.674	68.7	13.8	8.2	6,155	6	118
119	South Africa	0.666	57.7	13.0	10.3	12,087	−30	119
120	Kyrgyzstan	0.664	70.8	13.0	10.8 [c]	3,097	32	120
121	Iraq	0.649	69.6	10.1 [k]	6.6 [n]	11,608	−30	121
122	Cabo Verde	0.648	73.5	13.5	4.8 [k]	6,049	3	122
123	Morocco	0.647	74.3	12.1	5.0 [f]	7,195	−4	123

TABLE 1 Human Development Index and its components | 201

TABLE 1 HUMAN DEVELOPMENT INDEX AND ITS COMPONENTS

TABLE
1

HDI rank		Human Development Index (HDI)	Life expectancy at birth	Expected years of schooling	Mean years of schooling	Gross national income (GNI) per capita	GNI per capita rank minus HDI rank	HDI rank
		Value	(years)	(years)	(years)	(2011 PPP $)		
		2015	2015	2015[a]	2015[a]	2015	2015	2014
124	Nicaragua	0.645	75.2	11.7	6.5 [f]	4,747	16	124
125	Guatemala	0.640	72.1	10.7	6.3	7,063	−4	126
125	Namibia	0.640	65.1	11.7	6.7 [f]	9,770	−18	126
127	Guyana	0.638	66.5	10.3	8.4 [c]	6,884	−5	125
127	Micronesia (Federated States of)	0.638	69.3	11.7 [k]	9.7 [d]	3,291	22	126
129	Tajikistan	0.627	69.6	11.3	10.4 [q]	2,601	30	129
130	Honduras	0.625	73.3	11.2	6.2	4,466	11	130
131	India	0.624	68.3	11.7	6.3 [c]	5,663	−4	131
132	Bhutan	0.607	69.9	12.5	3.1 [n]	7,081	−12	132
133	Timor-Leste	0.605	68.5	12.5	4.4 [q]	5,371 [l]	−1	133
134	Vanuatu	0.597	72.1	10.8 [o]	6.8 [n]	2,805	23	134
135	Congo	0.592	62.9	11.1	6.3 [c]	5,503	−7	135
135	Equatorial Guinea	0.592	57.9	9.2 [k]	5.5 [q]	21,517	−79	137
137	Kiribati	0.588	66.2	11.9	7.8 [k]	2,475	23	136
138	Lao People's Democratic Republic	0.586	66.6	10.8	5.2 [n]	5,049	−2	137
139	Bangladesh	0.579	72.0	10.2	5.2 [c]	3,341	8	140
139	Ghana	0.579	61.5	11.5	6.9 [f]	3,839	5	140
139	Zambia	0.579	60.8	12.5	6.9 [f]	3,464	7	139
142	Sao Tome and Principe	0.574	66.6	12.0	5.3	3,070	12	142
143	Cambodia	0.563	68.8	10.9	4.7 [q]	3,095	10	143
144	Nepal	0.558	70.0	12.2	4.1 [n]	2,337	19	144
145	Myanmar	0.556	66.1	9.1 [m]	4.7 [f]	4,943	−6	146
146	Kenya	0.555	62.2	11.1	6.3 [f]	2,881	10	147
147	Pakistan	0.550	66.4	8.1	5.1	5,031	−10	148
LOW HUMAN DEVELOPMENT								
148	Swaziland	0.541	48.9	11.4	6.8 [n]	7,522	−33	149
149	Syrian Arab Republic	0.536	69.7	9.0	5.1 [s]	2,441 [t]	13	145
150	Angola	0.533	52.7	11.4	5.0 [q]	6,291	−27	150
151	Tanzania (United Republic of)	0.531	65.5	8.9	5.8	2,467	10	152
152	Nigeria	0.527	53.1	10.0	6.0 [q]	5,443	−23	151
153	Cameroon	0.518	56.0	10.4	6.1 [c]	2,894	2	154
154	Papua New Guinea	0.516	62.8	9.9 [k]	4.3 [f]	2,712	4	153
154	Zimbabwe	0.516	59.2	10.3	7.7	1,588	20	158
156	Solomon Islands	0.515	68.1	9.6 [m]	5.3 [d]	1,561	19	155
157	Mauritania	0.513	63.2	8.5	4.3 [f]	3,527	−12	155
158	Madagascar	0.512	65.5	10.3	6.1 [n]	1,320	25	157
159	Rwanda	0.498	64.7	10.8	3.8	1,617	14	162
160	Comoros	0.497	63.6	11.1	4.8 [q]	1,335	22	160
160	Lesotho	0.497	50.1	10.7	6.1 [f]	3,319	−12	161
162	Senegal	0.494	66.9	9.5	2.8 [m]	2,250	3	163
163	Haiti	0.493	63.1	9.1 [k]	5.2 [c]	1,657	9	164
163	Uganda	0.493	59.2	10.0	5.7 [m]	1,670	8	165
165	Sudan	0.490	63.7	7.2	3.5	3,846	−22	165
166	Togo	0.487	60.2	12.0	4.7 [q]	1,262	18	167
167	Benin	0.485	59.8	10.7	3.5 [c]	1,979	1	168
168	Yemen	0.482	64.1	9.0	3.0 [c]	2,300	−4	159
169	Afghanistan	0.479	60.7	10.1	3.6 [f]	1,871	1	169
170	Malawi	0.476	63.9	10.8	4.4 [f]	1,073	16	170
171	Côte d'Ivoire	0.474	51.9	8.9	5.0 [f]	3,163	−20	172
172	Djibouti	0.473	62.3	6.3	4.1 [k]	3,216	−22	171
173	Gambia	0.452	60.5	8.9	3.3 [f]	1,541	3	173
174	Ethiopia	0.448	64.6	8.4	2.6 [q]	1,523	5	174
175	Mali	0.442	58.5	8.4	2.3	2,218	−9	175
176	Congo (Democratic Republic of the)	0.435	59.1	9.8	6.1	680	15	178
177	Liberia	0.427	61.2	9.9	4.4 [f]	683	13	177
178	Guinea-Bissau	0.424	55.5	9.2 [m]	2.9 [k]	1,369	3	179
179	Eritrea	0.420	64.2	5.0	3.9 [k]	1,490	1	181
179	Sierra Leone	0.420	51.3	9.5	3.3 [f]	1,529	−1	176
181	Mozambique	0.418	55.5	9.1	3.5 [q]	1,098	4	182
181	South Sudan	0.418	56.1	4.9	4.8 [n]	1,882	−12	179
183	Guinea	0.414	59.2	8.8	2.6 [q]	1,058	4	182
184	Burundi	0.404	57.1	10.6	3.0 [c]	691	5	184
185	Burkina Faso	0.402	59.0	7.7	1.4 [q]	1,537	−8	185

HDI rank	Human Development Index (HDI) Value 2015	Life expectancy at birth (years) 2015	Expected years of schooling (years) 2015[a]	Mean years of schooling (years) 2015[a]	Gross national income (GNI) per capita (2011 PPP $) 2015	GNI per capita rank minus HDI rank 2015	HDI rank 2014
186 Chad	0.396	51.9	7.3	2.3 [n]	1,991	−19	186
187 Niger	0.353	61.9	5.4	1.7 [f]	889	1	187
188 Central African Republic	0.352	51.5	7.1	4.2 [n]	587	4	188
OTHER COUNTRIES OR TERRITORIES							
Korea (Democratic People's Rep. of)	..	70.5	12.0	..	..	..	..
Marshall Islands	..	..	..	..	4,412	..	..
Monaco	..	..	..	..	..	..	..
Nauru	..	..	9.7 [k]	..	12,058	..	..
San Marino	..	..	15.1	..	50,063	..	..
Somalia	..	55.7	..	..	294	..	..
Tuvalu	..	..	..	..	5,395	..	..
Human development groups							
Very high human development	0.892	79.4	16.4	12.2	39,605	—	—
High human development	0.746	75.5	13.8	8.1	13,844	—	—
Medium human development	0.631	68.6	11.5	6.6	6,281	—	—
Low human development	0.497	59.3	9.3	4.6	2,649	—	—
Developing countries	0.668	70.0	11.8	7.2	9,257	—	—
Regions							
Arab States	0.687	70.8	11.7	6.8	14,958	—	—
East Asia and the Pacific	0.720	74.2	13.0	7.7	12,125	—	—
Europe and Central Asia	0.756	72.6	13.9	10.3	12,862	—	—
Latin America and the Caribbean	0.751	75.2	14.1	8.3	14,028	—	—
South Asia	0.621	68.7	11.3	6.2	5,799	—	—
Sub-Saharan Africa	0.523	58.9	9.7	5.4	3,383	—	—
Least developed countries	0.508	63.6	9.4	4.4	2,385	—	—
Small island developing states	0.667	70.3	11.5	8.1	7,303	—	—
Organisation for Economic Co-operation and Development	0.887	80.3	15.9	11.9	37,916	—	—
World	**0.717**	**71.6**	**12.3**	**8.3**	**14,447**	**—**	**—**

NOTES

a Data refer to 2015 or the most recent year available.

b In calculating the HDI value, expected years of schooling is capped at 18 years.

c Updated by HDRO using Barro and Lee (2016) estimates.

d Based on data from the national statistical office.

e In calculating the HDI value, GNI per capita is capped at $75,000.

f Based on Barro and Lee (2016).

g Value from UNDESA (2011).

h Calculated as the average of mean years of schooling for Austria and Switzerland.

i Estimated using the purchasing power parity (PPP) rate and projected growth rate of Switzerland.

j Estimated using the PPP rate and projected growth rate of Spain.

k Based on cross-country regression.

l HDRO estimate based on data from World Bank (2016a) and United Nations Statistics Division (2016a).

m Updated by HDRO based on data from UNESCO Institute for Statistics (2016).

n Based on data from United Nations Children's Fund (UNICEF) Multiple Indicator Cluster Surveys for 2006–2015.

o Updated by HDRO based on data from ICF Macro Demographic and Health Surveys for 2006–2015.

p Based on a cross-country regression and the projected growth rate from UNECLAC (2016).

q Based on data from ICF Macro Demographic and Health Surveys for 2006–2015.

r Value from WHO (2016).

s Updated by HDRO based on Syrian Centre for Policy Research (2016).

t Based on projected growth rates from UNESCWA (2016) and World Bank (2016a).

DEFINITIONS

Human Development Index (HDI): A composite index measuring average achievement in three basic dimensions of human development—a long and healthy life, knowledge and a decent standard of living. See *Technical note 1* at http://hdr.undp.org/sites/default/files/hdr2016_technical_notes.pdf for details on how the HDI is calculated.

Life expectancy at birth: Number of years a newborn infant could expect to live if prevailing patterns of age-specific mortality rates at the time of birth stay the same throughout the infant's life.

Expected years of schooling: Number of years of schooling that a child of school entrance age can expect to receive if prevailing patterns of age-specific enrolment rates persist throughout the child's life.

Mean years of schooling: Average number of years of education received by people ages 25 and older, converted from education attainment levels using official durations of each level.

Gross national income (GNI) per capita: Aggregate income of an economy generated by its production and its ownership of factors of production, less the incomes paid for the use of factors of production owned by the rest of the world, converted to international dollars using PPP rates, divided by midyear population.

GNI per capita rank minus HDI rank: Difference in ranking by GNI per capita and by HDI value. A negative value means that the country is better ranked by GNI than by HDI value.

HDI rank for 2014: Ranking by HDI value for 2014, which was calculated using the same most recently revised data available in 2016 that were used to calculate HDI values for 2015.

MAIN DATA SOURCES

Columns 1 and 7: HDRO calculations based on data from UNDESA (2015a), UNESCO Institute for Statistics (2016a), United Nations Statistics Division (2016a), World Bank (2016a), Barro and Lee (2016) and IMF (2016).

Column 2: UNDESA (2015a).

Column 3: UNESCO Institute for Statistics (2016), ICF Macro Demographic and Health Surveys and UNICEF Multiple Indicator Cluster Surveys.

Column 4: UNESCO Institute for Statistics (2016), Barro and Lee (2016), ICF Macro Demographic and Health Surveys and UNICEF Multiple Indicator Cluster Surveys.

Column 5: World Bank (2016a), IMF (2016) and United Nations Statistics Division (2016a).

Column 6: Calculated based on data in columns 1 and 5.

TABLE 1   Human Development Index and its components | 203

TABLE
2

Human Development Index trends, 1990–2015

TABLE
2

	Human Development Index (HDI)								Change in HDI rank	Average annual HDI growth			
	Value									(%)			
HDI rank	1990	2000	2010	2011	2012	2013	2014	2015	2010–2015ª	1990–2000	2000–2010	2010–2015	1990–2015
VERY HIGH HUMAN DEVELOPMENT													
1 Norway	0.849	0.917	0.939	0.941	0.942	0.945	0.948	0.949	0	0.77	0.24	0.21	0.45
2 Australia	0.866	0.899	0.927	0.930	0.933	0.936	0.937	0.939	1	0.38	0.31	0.24	0.32
2 Switzerland	0.831	0.888	0.932	0.932	0.934	0.936	0.938	0.939	0	0.67	0.49	0.16	0.49
4 Germany	0.801	0.860	0.912	0.916	0.919	0.920	0.924	0.926	0	0.71	0.59	0.30	0.58
5 Denmark	0.799	0.862	0.910	0.922	0.924	0.926	0.923	0.925	2	0.76	0.55	0.32	0.59
5 Singapore	0.718	0.820	0.911	0.917	0.920	0.922	0.924	0.925	0	1.34	1.05	0.30	1.02
7 Netherlands	0.830	0.878	0.911	0.921	0.922	0.923	0.923	0.924	−2	0.56	0.37	0.29	0.43
8 Ireland	0.762	0.857	0.909	0.895	0.902	0.910	0.920	0.923	1	1.17	0.60	0.29	0.77
9 Iceland	0.797	0.854	0.894	0.901	0.907	0.915	0.919	0.921	7	0.70	0.46	0.60	0.58
10 Canada	0.849	0.867	0.903	0.907	0.909	0.912	0.919	0.920	1	0.21	0.41	0.38	0.32
10 United States	0.860	0.884	0.910	0.913	0.915	0.916	0.918	0.920	−3	0.28	0.29	0.20	0.27
12 Hong Kong, China (SAR)	0.781	0.825	0.898	0.905	0.907	0.913	0.916	0.917	3	0.55	0.85	0.42	0.64
13 New Zealand	0.818	0.868	0.901	0.904	0.908	0.910	0.913	0.915	0	0.61	0.36	0.32	0.45
14 Sweden	0.815	0.877	0.901	0.903	0.904	0.906	0.909	0.913	−1	0.73	0.28	0.25	0.45
15 Liechtenstein	..	0.862	0.904	0.909	0.908	0.912	0.911	0.912	−5	..	0.48	0.16	..
16 United Kingdom	0.775	0.866	0.902	0.898	0.899	0.904	0.908	0.909	−4	1.13	0.41	0.16	0.64
17 Japan	0.814	0.856	0.884	0.889	0.894	0.899	0.902	0.903	1	0.51	0.32	0.44	0.42
18 Korea (Republic of)	0.731	0.820	0.884	0.889	0.891	0.896	0.899	0.901	0	1.15	0.76	0.37	0.84
19 Israel	0.785	0.850	0.883	0.889	0.891	0.895	0.898	0.899	2	0.81	0.38	0.35	0.54
20 Luxembourg	0.782	0.854	0.894	0.892	0.892	0.892	0.896	0.898	−4	0.88	0.46	0.11	0.56
21 France	0.779	0.849	0.882	0.885	0.887	0.890	0.894	0.897	1	0.86	0.39	0.34	0.57
22 Belgium	0.805	0.873	0.884	0.886	0.889	0.890	0.895	0.896	−4	0.81	0.12	0.27	0.42
23 Finland	0.783	0.856	0.878	0.884	0.887	0.890	0.893	0.895	1	0.90	0.25	0.37	0.53
24 Austria	0.794	0.837	0.880	0.884	0.887	0.892	0.892	0.893	−1	0.53	0.50	0.31	0.47
25 Slovenia	0.767	0.824	0.876	0.877	0.878	0.888	0.888	0.890	0	0.73	0.61	0.33	0.60
26 Italy	0.768	0.828	0.872	0.877	0.876	0.877	0.881	0.887	0	0.76	0.51	0.34	0.58
27 Spain	0.755	0.825	0.867	0.871	0.874	0.877	0.882	0.884	0	0.90	0.49	0.40	0.64
28 Czech Republic	0.761	0.821	0.861	0.864	0.865	0.871	0.875	0.878	0	0.76	0.47	0.39	0.57
29 Greece	0.760	0.801	0.860	0.858	0.860	0.862	0.865	0.866	0	0.52	0.71	0.14	0.52
30 Brunei Darussalam	0.782	0.819	0.846	0.852	0.860	0.863	0.864	0.865	1	0.46	0.33	0.43	0.40
30 Estonia	0.728	0.781	0.838	0.850	0.856	0.860	0.863	0.865	2	0.71	0.70	0.65	0.69
32 Andorra	..	..	0.819	0.819	0.843	0.850	0.857	0.858	9	..	..	0.95	..
33 Cyprus	0.733	0.800	0.847	0.850	0.849	0.850	0.854	0.856	−3	0.88	0.58	0.20	0.62
33 Malta	0.736	0.783	0.826	0.821	0.828	0.847	0.853	0.856	3	0.63	0.53	0.71	0.61
33 Qatar	0.754	0.809	0.827	0.837	0.843	0.854	0.855	0.856	2	0.71	0.22	0.68	0.51
36 Poland	0.712	0.784	0.829	0.834	0.838	0.850	0.852	0.855	−3	0.97	0.56	0.62	0.74
37 Lithuania	0.731	0.757	0.826	0.830	0.834	0.841	0.846	0.848	−1	0.36	0.87	0.53	0.60
38 Chile	0.700	0.761	0.820	0.826	0.831	0.841	0.845	0.847	2	0.84	0.75	0.65	0.76
38 Saudi Arabia	0.698	0.742	0.803	0.818	0.830	0.841	0.845	0.847	9	0.61	0.80	1.05	0.77
40 Slovakia	0.738	0.763	0.829	0.835	0.838	0.841	0.842	0.845	−7	0.34	0.83	0.39	0.54
41 Portugal	0.711	0.782	0.818	0.824	0.827	0.837	0.841	0.843	1	0.97	0.45	0.59	0.68
42 United Arab Emirates	0.726	0.798	0.824	0.826	0.829	0.832	0.836	0.840	−4	0.94	0.32	0.38	0.58
43 Hungary	0.703	0.769	0.821	0.823	0.824	0.834	0.834	0.836	−4	0.89	0.67	0.36	0.70
44 Latvia	0.703	0.728	0.810	0.812	0.814	0.822	0.828	0.830	1	0.35	1.07	0.49	0.67
45 Argentina	0.705	0.771	0.816	0.822	0.823	0.825	0.826	0.827	−2	0.90	0.57	0.28	0.64
45 Croatia	0.669	0.749	0.808	0.815	0.817	0.820	0.823	0.827	1	1.13	0.77	0.47	0.85
47 Bahrain	0.745	0.794	0.812	0.812	0.815	0.820	0.823	0.824	−3	0.63	0.23	0.29	0.40
48 Montenegro	..	..	0.792	0.797	0.799	0.803	0.804	0.807	2	..	..	0.38	..
49 Russian Federation	0.733	0.720	0.785	0.792	0.799	0.803	0.805	0.804	5	−0.18	0.87	0.48	0.37
50 Romania	0.700	0.708	0.798	0.797	0.794	0.797	0.798	0.802	−2	0.11	1.20	0.12	0.55
51 Kuwait	0.713	0.786	0.792	0.794	0.796	0.787	0.799	0.800	−1	0.98	0.07	0.21	0.46
HIGH HUMAN DEVELOPMENT													
52 Belarus	..	0.681	0.787	0.793	0.796	0.796	0.798	0.796	1	..	1.45	0.23	..
52 Oman	..	0.705	0.797	0.797	0.796	0.796	0.795	0.796	−3	..	1.25	−0.04	..
54 Barbados	0.714	0.750	0.780	0.785	0.792	0.793	0.794	0.795	2	0.49	0.39	0.37	0.43
54 Uruguay	0.692	0.742	0.780	0.784	0.788	0.791	0.794	0.795	2	0.70	0.50	0.37	0.55
56 Bulgaria	0.700	0.713	0.775	0.778	0.781	0.787	0.792	0.794	3	0.19	0.83	0.49	0.50
56 Kazakhstan	0.690	0.685	0.766	0.774	0.782	0.789	0.793	0.794	7	−0.07	1.13	0.72	0.56
58 Bahamas	..	0.778	0.788	0.789	0.790	0.789	0.790	0.792	−6	..	0.13	0.08	..
59 Malaysia	0.643	0.725	0.774	0.776	0.779	0.783	0.787	0.789	1	1.20	0.67	0.39	0.83
60 Palau	..	0.741	0.770	0.775	0.779	0.782	0.783	0.788	2	..	0.38	0.47	..
60 Panama	0.662	0.721	0.758	0.765	0.773	0.780	0.785	0.788	4	0.86	0.50	0.76	0.70

	Human Development Index (HDI)								Change in HDI rank	Average annual HDI growth			
	Value									(%)			
HDI rank	1990	2000	2010	2011	2012	2013	2014	2015	2010–2015[a]	1990–2000	2000–2010	2010–2015	1990–2015
62 Antigua and Barbuda	..	..	0.782	0.778	0.781	0.782	0.784	0.786	−7	..	..	0.08	..
63 Seychelles	..	0.714	0.744	0.755	0.762	0.766	0.781	0.782	11	..	0.41	1.02	..
64 Mauritius	0.620	0.673	0.748	0.756	0.765	0.769	0.779	0.781	6	0.83	1.05	0.89	0.93
65 Trinidad and Tobago	0.670	0.715	0.774	0.772	0.773	0.778	0.779	0.780	−5	0.65	0.79	0.16	0.61
66 Costa Rica	0.653	0.708	0.752	0.758	0.762	0.768	0.775	0.776	3	0.82	0.61	0.64	0.70
66 Serbia	0.714	0.709	0.757	0.767	0.766	0.771	0.775	0.776	0	−0.07	0.65	0.50	0.33
68 Cuba	0.676	0.686	0.780	0.778	0.773	0.772	0.772	0.775	−12	0.15	1.28	−0.13	0.55
69 Iran (Islamic Republic of)	0.572	0.666	0.745	0.755	0.769	0.770	0.774	0.774	3	1.53	1.12	0.78	1.22
70 Georgia	..	0.673	0.742	0.749	0.755	0.759	0.768	0.769	5	..	0.99	0.72	..
71 Turkey	0.576	0.653	0.737	0.750	0.754	0.759	0.764	0.767	9	1.26	1.22	0.81	1.15
71 Venezuela (Bolivarian Republic of)	0.634	0.672	0.756	0.767	0.770	0.771	0.769	0.767	−4	0.58	1.18	0.29	0.76
73 Sri Lanka	0.626	0.686	0.746	0.752	0.757	0.760	0.764	0.766	−2	0.92	0.84	0.56	0.82
74 Saint Kitts and Nevis	..	..	0.741	0.746	0.749	0.756	0.762	0.765	2	..	..	0.64	..
75 Albania	0.635	0.662	0.738	0.752	0.759	0.761	0.762	0.764	4	0.41	1.10	0.70	0.74
76 Lebanon	..	..	0.758	0.763	0.766	0.763	0.763	0.763	−12	..	..	0.14	..
77 Mexico	0.648	0.700	0.745	0.748	0.753	0.754	0.758	0.762	−5	0.77	0.63	0.44	0.65
78 Azerbaijan	..	0.642	0.741	0.742	0.745	0.752	0.758	0.759	−2	..	1.43	0.48	..
79 Brazil	0.611	0.685	0.724	0.730	0.734	0.747	0.754	0.754	7	1.15	0.55	0.83	0.85
79 Grenada	..	..	0.741	0.744	0.745	0.749	0.751	0.754	−3	..	..	0.33	..
81 Bosnia and Herzegovina	..	..	0.711	0.728	0.735	0.742	0.747	0.750	14	..	..	1.07	..
82 The former Yugoslav Republic of Macedonia	..	..	0.735	0.739	0.741	0.743	0.746	0.748	0	..	..	0.35	..
83 Algeria	0.577	0.644	0.724	0.732	0.737	0.741	0.743	0.745	3	1.11	1.18	0.56	1.03
84 Armenia	0.634	0.644	0.729	0.732	0.736	0.739	0.741	0.743	1	0.16	1.24	0.39	0.64
84 Ukraine	0.706	0.673	0.734	0.739	0.744	0.746	0.748	0.743	−1	−0.48	0.87	0.25	0.21
86 Jordan	0.620	0.706	0.737	0.735	0.737	0.737	0.741	0.741	−6	1.31	0.43	0.13	0.72
87 Peru	0.613	0.677	0.721	0.725	0.731	0.735	0.737	0.740	3	1.01	0.63	0.53	0.76
87 Thailand	0.574	0.649	0.720	0.729	0.733	0.737	0.738	0.740	4	1.25	1.03	0.56	1.02
89 Ecuador	0.643	0.670	0.710	0.717	0.725	0.737	0.739	0.739	7	0.41	0.58	0.83	0.56
90 China	0.499	0.592	0.700	0.703	0.713	0.723	0.734	0.738	11	1.72	1.70	1.05	1.57
91 Fiji	0.641	0.683	0.709	0.714	0.719	0.727	0.734	0.736	6	0.64	0.37	0.75	0.56
92 Mongolia	0.579	0.588	0.701	0.712	0.720	0.729	0.733	0.735	8	0.17	1.77	0.94	0.96
92 Saint Lucia	..	0.684	0.733	0.735	0.734	0.723	0.735	0.735	−8	..	0.69	0.06	..
94 Jamaica	0.651	0.680	0.722	0.725	0.727	0.727	0.729	0.730	−6	0.44	0.60	0.22	0.46
95 Colombia	0.592	0.653	0.700	0.707	0.712	0.720	0.724	0.727	6	0.99	0.70	0.76	0.83
96 Dominica	..	0.695	0.722	0.722	0.721	0.724	0.724	0.726	−8	..	0.38	0.13	..
97 Suriname	..	..	0.704	0.708	0.719	0.722	0.723	0.725	1	..	..	0.58	..
97 Tunisia	0.569	0.654	0.714	0.717	0.720	0.722	0.723	0.725	−5	1.40	0.88	0.29	0.97
99 Dominican Republic	0.596	0.656	0.703	0.706	0.709	0.712	0.718	0.722	0	0.96	0.69	0.54	0.77
99 Saint Vincent and the Grenadines	..	0.673	0.712	0.713	0.717	0.720	0.720	0.722	−6	..	0.55	0.20	..
101 Tonga	0.648	0.674	0.712	0.717	0.718	0.716	0.718	0.721	−8	0.38	0.56	0.24	0.42
102 Libya	0.681	0.732	0.756	0.706	0.735	0.730	0.719	0.716	−35	0.72	0.32	−1.06	0.20
103 Belize	0.648	0.677	0.700	0.702	0.706	0.705	0.706	0.706	−2	0.43	0.33	0.19	0.34
104 Samoa	0.598	0.645	0.693	0.698	0.700	0.701	0.702	0.704	0	0.75	0.72	0.32	0.65
105 Maldives	..	0.587	0.663	0.675	0.683	0.693	0.701	0.701	10	..	1.24	1.11	..
105 Uzbekistan	..	0.594	0.664	0.673	0.681	0.690	0.697	0.701	6	..	1.12	1.07	..
MEDIUM HUMAN DEVELOPMENT													
107 Moldova (Republic of)	0.652	0.597	0.672	0.679	0.686	0.696	0.701	0.699	0	−0.87	1.18	0.81	0.28
108 Botswana	0.585	0.560	0.678	0.687	0.693	0.697	0.698	0.698	−3	−0.43	1.93	0.56	0.71
109 Gabon	0.620	0.633	0.664	0.669	0.678	0.687	0.694	0.697	5	0.20	0.48	0.97	0.47
110 Paraguay	0.580	0.624	0.675	0.679	0.679	0.688	0.692	0.693	−4	0.73	0.79	0.54	0.71
111 Egypt	0.547	0.612	0.671	0.673	0.681	0.686	0.688	0.691	−3	1.12	0.93	0.60	0.94
111 Turkmenistan	..	..	0.665	0.672	0.678	0.683	0.688	0.691	2	..	..	0.78	..
113 Indonesia	0.528	0.604	0.662	0.669	0.677	0.682	0.686	0.689	3	1.36	0.92	0.78	1.07
114 Palestine, State of	..	..	0.669	0.674	0.684	0.678	0.678	0.684	−5	..	..	0.45	..
115 Viet Nam	0.477	0.576	0.655	0.662	0.668	0.675	0.678	0.683	2	1.92	1.29	0.85	1.45
116 Philippines	0.586	0.622	0.669	0.666	0.671	0.676	0.679	0.682	−7	0.60	0.72	0.39	0.61
117 El Salvador	0.529	0.615	0.666	0.670	0.675	0.676	0.678	0.680	−6	1.52	0.80	0.41	1.01
118 Bolivia (Plurinational State of)	0.535	0.607	0.649	0.655	0.661	0.666	0.671	0.674	0	1.26	0.66	0.77	0.92
119 South Africa	0.621	0.629	0.638	0.644	0.652	0.660	0.665	0.666	2	0.13	0.14	0.89	0.28
120 Kyrgyzstan	0.615	0.593	0.632	0.638	0.647	0.656	0.662	0.664	3	−0.37	0.65	0.98	0.30
121 Iraq	0.572	0.607	0.649	0.656	0.659	0.658	0.649	0.649	−3	0.59	0.67	0.01	0.51
122 Cabo Verde	..	0.562	0.632	0.636	0.643	0.643	0.646	0.648	1	..	1.19	0.50	..
123 Morocco	0.458	0.530	0.612	0.623	0.634	0.640	0.645	0.647	4	1.46	1.47	1.12	1.39

TABLE 2 · TABLE

TABLE 2 Human Development Index trends, 1990–2015 | 205

TABLE 2 HUMAN DEVELOPMENT INDEX TRENDS, 1990–2015

TABLE 2

	Human Development Index (HDI)								Change in HDI rank	Average annual HDI growth (%)			
HDI rank	Value												
	1990	2000	2010	2011	2012	2013	2014	2015	2010–2015[a]	1990–2000	2000–2010	2010–2015	1990–2015
124 Nicaragua	0.495	0.570	0.620	0.625	0.630	0.636	0.642	0.645	2	1.42	0.83	0.82	1.06
125 Guatemala	0.478	0.546	0.609	0.616	0.611	0.614	0.637	0.640	5	1.34	1.09	1.00	1.17
125 Namibia	0.578	0.556	0.612	0.619	0.625	0.632	0.637	0.640	2	−0.39	0.96	0.91	0.41
127 Guyana	0.541	0.606	0.624	0.630	0.633	0.636	0.638	0.638	−2	1.14	0.29	0.45	0.66
127 Micronesia (Federated States of)	..	0.604	0.638	0.640	0.641	0.639	0.637	0.638	−6	..	0.56	−0.01	..
129 Tajikistan	0.616	0.535	0.608	0.613	0.617	0.622	0.625	0.627	2	−1.39	1.28	0.64	0.08
130 Honduras	0.507	0.557	0.611	0.614	0.614	0.618	0.623	0.625	−1	0.94	0.94	0.45	0.84
131 India	0.428	0.494	0.580	0.590	0.599	0.607	0.615	0.624	4	1.45	1.62	1.46	1.52
132 Bhutan	..	..	0.572	0.581	0.589	0.596	0.604	0.607	5	..	..	1.19	..
133 Timor-Leste	..	0.470	0.607	0.618	0.620	0.612	0.603	0.605	−1	..	2.57	−0.03	..
134 Vanuatu	..	..	0.591	0.592	0.591	0.596	0.598	0.597	−1	..	..	0.20	..
135 Congo	0.521	0.487	0.558	0.557	0.576	0.581	0.589	0.592	3	−0.67	1.38	1.20	0.52
135 Equatorial Guinea	..	0.527	0.580	0.582	0.586	0.582	0.582	0.592	0	..	0.96	0.44	..
137 Kiribati	..	..	0.585	0.581	0.589	0.597	0.586	0.588	−3	..	..	0.10	..
138 Lao People's Democratic Republic	0.397	0.463	0.542	0.554	0.563	0.573	0.582	0.586	5	1.54	1.59	1.59	1.57
139 Bangladesh	0.386	0.468	0.545	0.557	0.565	0.570	0.575	0.579	2	1.95	1.54	1.21	1.64
139 Ghana	0.455	0.485	0.554	0.563	0.570	0.576	0.575	0.579	0	0.63	1.34	0.88	0.97
139 Zambia	0.398	0.424	0.543	0.554	0.565	0.570	0.576	0.579	3	0.64	2.50	1.30	1.51
142 Sao Tome and Principe	0.454	0.497	0.546	0.553	0.559	0.562	0.565	0.574	−2	0.91	0.94	1.00	0.94
143 Cambodia	0.357	0.412	0.533	0.540	0.546	0.553	0.558	0.563	1	1.46	2.61	1.09	1.84
144 Nepal	0.378	0.446	0.529	0.538	0.545	0.551	0.555	0.558	2	1.66	1.73	1.07	1.57
145 Myanmar	0.353	0.427	0.526	0.533	0.540	0.547	0.552	0.556	2	1.90	2.12	1.10	1.83
146 Kenya	0.473	0.447	0.530	0.536	0.541	0.546	0.550	0.555	−1	−0.57	1.72	0.90	0.64
147 Pakistan	0.404	0.450	0.525	0.529	0.538	0.542	0.548	0.550	2	1.09	1.55	0.95	1.24
LOW HUMAN DEVELOPMENT													
148 Swaziland	0.548	0.506	0.526	0.534	0.539	0.541	0.541	0.541	−1	−0.78	0.38	0.57	−0.05
149 Syrian Arab Republic	0.556	0.589	0.646	0.645	0.635	0.575	0.553	0.536	−29	0.58	0.94	−3.68	−0.15
150 Angola	..	0.391	0.495	0.508	0.523	0.527	0.531	0.533	4	..	2.38	1.49	..
151 Tanzania (United Republic of)	0.370	0.391	0.498	0.504	0.513	0.512	0.519	0.531	1	0.57	2.45	1.27	1.46
152 Nigeria	..	..	0.500	0.507	0.514	0.521	0.525	0.527	−1	..	..	1.08	..
153 Cameroon	0.444	0.437	0.486	0.496	0.501	0.507	0.514	0.518	5	−0.15	1.06	1.27	0.61
154 Papua New Guinea	0.360	0.422	0.494	0.501	0.506	0.511	0.515	0.516	1	1.60	1.57	0.90	1.45
154 Zimbabwe	0.499	0.427	0.452	0.464	0.488	0.498	0.507	0.516	15	−1.55	0.57	2.67	0.13
156 Solomon Islands	..	0.442	0.497	0.505	0.509	0.512	0.513	0.515	−3	..	1.19	0.71	..
157 Mauritania	0.378	0.444	0.487	0.491	0.501	0.509	0.513	0.513	0	1.62	0.94	1.04	1.23
158 Madagascar	..	0.456	0.504	0.506	0.508	0.509	0.511	0.512	−8	..	1.01	0.33	..
159 Rwanda	0.244	0.332	0.464	0.475	0.485	0.488	0.493	0.498	4	3.14	3.39	1.40	2.89
160 Comoros	..	..	0.479	0.484	0.490	0.497	0.498	0.497	−1	..	..	0.78	..
160 Lesotho	0.493	0.443	0.469	0.479	0.484	0.491	0.495	0.497	2	−1.06	0.56	1.20	0.04
162 Senegal	0.367	0.381	0.455	0.463	0.474	0.483	0.491	0.494	4	0.37	1.80	1.65	1.20
163 Haiti	0.408	0.443	0.470	0.477	0.483	0.487	0.490	0.493	−2	0.82	0.60	0.96	0.76
163 Uganda	0.309	0.396	0.477	0.477	0.478	0.483	0.488	0.493	−3	2.51	1.88	0.66	1.88
165 Sudan	0.331	0.399	0.463	0.468	0.478	0.485	0.488	0.490	−1	1.89	1.49	1.15	1.58
166 Togo	0.404	0.426	0.457	0.464	0.470	0.475	0.484	0.487	−1	0.53	0.69	1.32	0.75
167 Benin	0.345	0.395	0.454	0.458	0.466	0.475	0.481	0.485	0	1.38	1.40	1.32	1.37
168 Yemen	0.405	0.444	0.493	0.494	0.498	0.500	0.499	0.482	−12	0.91	1.06	−0.44	0.70
169 Afghanistan	0.295	0.340	0.454	0.463	0.470	0.476	0.479	0.479	−2	1.43	2.95	1.08	1.97
170 Malawi	0.325	0.387	0.444	0.454	0.459	0.466	0.473	0.476	1	1.74	1.40	1.38	1.53
171 Côte d'Ivoire	0.389	0.395	0.441	0.444	0.452	0.459	0.466	0.474	1	0.16	1.11	1.43	0.79
172 Djibouti	..	0.363	0.451	0.460	0.464	0.467	0.470	0.473	−2	..	2.19	0.98	..
173 Gambia	0.330	0.384	0.441	0.440	0.445	0.449	0.450	0.452	−1	1.54	1.40	0.46	1.27
174 Ethiopia	..	0.283	0.411	0.422	0.427	0.435	0.441	0.448	1	..	3.79	1.71	..
175 Mali	0.222	0.297	0.404	0.411	0.421	0.430	0.438	0.442	4	2.94	3.14	1.82	2.80
176 Congo (Democratic Republic of the)	0.356	0.331	0.398	0.407	0.412	0.419	0.425	0.435	4	−0.73	1.89	1.79	0.81
177 Liberia	..	0.386	0.406	0.416	0.419	0.425	0.427	0.427	0	..	0.51	1.00	..
178 Guinea-Bissau	..	..	0.410	0.416	0.415	0.419	0.421	0.424	−2	..	..	0.67	..
179 Eritrea	..	..	0.405	0.410	0.414	0.416	0.418	0.420	−1	..	..	0.74	..
179 Sierra Leone	0.272	0.302	0.392	0.401	0.413	0.426	0.431	0.420	3	1.04	2.65	1.39	1.75
181 Mozambique	0.209	0.298	0.397	0.400	0.405	0.409	0.414	0.418	0	3.63	2.90	1.03	2.82
181 South Sudan	..	..	0.429	0.419	0.417	0.421	0.421	0.418	−7	..	..	−0.49	..
183 Guinea	0.271	0.322	0.385	0.396	0.406	0.412	0.414	0.414	0	1.74	1.80	1.45	1.71
184 Burundi	0.270	0.268	0.385	0.393	0.398	0.404	0.406	0.404	−1	−0.06	3.67	0.97	1.62
185 Burkina Faso	..	..	0.377	0.384	0.391	0.398	0.399	0.402	0	..	..	1.27	..

HDI rank	Human Development Index (HDI) Value								Change in HDI rank 2010–2015[a]	Average annual HDI growth (%)			
	1990	2000	2010	2011	2012	2013	2014	2015		1990–2000	2000–2010	2010–2015	1990–2015
186 Chad	..	0.300	0.370	0.381	0.387	0.390	0.394	0.396	0	..	2.13	1.37	..
187 Niger	0.212	0.255	0.323	0.331	0.341	0.345	0.351	0.353	1	1.85	2.41	1.76	2.06
188 Central African Republic	0.320	0.314	0.361	0.366	0.370	0.345	0.347	0.352	−1	−0.19	1.41	−0.47	0.39
OTHER COUNTRIES OR TERRITORIES													
Korea (Democratic People's Rep. of)	..	..	..	..	..	..	..	..	..	..	..	..	..
Marshall Islands	..	..	..	..	..	..	..	..	..	..	..	..	..
Monaco	..	..	..	..	..	..	..	..	..	..	..	..	..
Nauru	..	..	..	..	..	..	..	..	..	..	..	..	..
San Marino	..	..	..	..	..	..	..	..	..	..	..	..	..
Somalia	..	..	..	..	..	..	..	..	..	..	..	..	..
Tuvalu	..	..	..	..	..	..	..	..	..	..	..	..	..
Human development groups													
Very high human development	0.791	0.836	0.876	0.881	0.884	0.887	0.890	0.892	—	0.55	0.48	0.35	0.48
High human development	0.574	0.637	0.716	0.721	0.728	0.736	0.744	0.746	—	1.04	1.19	0.83	1.06
Medium human development	0.465	0.525	0.598	0.606	0.613	0.620	0.626	0.631	—	1.23	1.31	1.09	1.23
Low human development	0.356	0.388	0.475	0.481	0.486	0.490	0.494	0.497	—	0.89	2.02	0.92	1.35
Developing countries	0.514	0.569	0.640	0.646	0.653	0.659	0.665	0.668	—	1.02	1.18	0.85	1.05
Regions													
Arab States	0.556	0.611	0.672	0.677	0.684	0.685	0.686	0.687	—	0.96	0.95	0.45	0.85
East Asia and the Pacific	0.516	0.595	0.688	0.692	0.700	0.709	0.717	0.720	—	1.45	1.45	0.92	1.35
Europe and Central Asia	0.652	0.667	0.732	0.741	0.745	0.750	0.754	0.756	—	0.23	0.95	0.63	0.59
Latin America and the Caribbean	0.626	0.685	0.730	0.735	0.739	0.745	0.750	0.751	—	0.92	0.63	0.58	0.74
South Asia	0.438	0.502	0.583	0.592	0.601	0.607	0.614	0.621	—	1.38	1.51	1.25	1.40
Sub-Saharan Africa	0.399	0.421	0.497	0.504	0.510	0.515	0.520	0.523	—	0.54	1.67	1.04	1.09
Least developed countries	0.347	0.399	0.481	0.489	0.495	0.500	0.504	0.508	—	1.40	1.90	1.08	1.54
Small island developing states	0.570	0.604	0.656	0.658	0.661	0.663	0.665	0.667	—	0.59	0.83	0.33	0.63
Organisation for Economic Co-operation and Development	0.785	0.835	0.872	0.876	0.879	0.882	0.885	0.887	—	0.62	0.44	0.33	0.49
World	**0.597**	**0.641**	**0.696**	**0.701**	**0.706**	**0.710**	**0.715**	**0.717**	**—**	**0.71**	**0.82**	**0.61**	**0.74**

TABLE
2

NOTES

a A positive value indicates an improvement in rank.

DEFINITIONS

Human Development Index (HDI): A composite index measuring average achievement in three basic dimensions of human development—a long and healthy life, knowledge and a decent standard of living. See *Technical note 1* at http://hdr.undp.org/sites/default/files/hdr2016_technical_notes.pdf for details on how the HDI is calculated.

Average annual HDI growth: A smoothed annualized growth of the HDI in a given period, calculated as the annual compound growth rate.

MAIN DATA SOURCES

Columns 1–8: HDRO calculations based on data from UNDESA (2015a), UNESCO Institute for Statistics (2016), United Nations Statistics Division (2016a), World Bank (2016a), Barro and Lee (2016) and IMF (2016).

Column 9: Calculated based on data in columns 3 and 8.

Columns 10–13: Calculated based on data in columns 1, 2, 3 and 8.

TABLE 2   Human Development Index trends, 1990–2015 | 207

TABLE 3

Inequality-adjusted Human Development Index

TABLE 3

HDI rank		Human Development Index (HDI) Value	Inequality-adjusted HDI (IHDI) Value	Overall loss (%)	Difference from HDI rank[b]	Coefficient of human inequality	Inequality in life expectancy (%)	Inequality-adjusted life expectancy index Value	Inequality in education[a] (%)	Inequality-adjusted education index Value	Inequality in income[a] (%)	Inequality-adjusted income index Value	Quintile ratio	Palma ratio	Gini coefficient
		2015	2015	2015	2015	2015	2010–2015[c]	2015	2015[d]	2015	2015[d]	2015	2010–2015[e]	2010–2015[e]	2010–2015[e]
VERY HIGH HUMAN DEVELOPMENT															
1	Norway	0.949	0.898	5.4	0	5.4	3.3	0.918	2.4	0.894	10.4	0.882	3.8	0.9	25.9
2	Australia	0.939	0.861	8.2	−1	8.0	4.3	0.921	1.9	0.921	17.7	0.753	6.0	1.4	34.9
2	Switzerland	0.939	0.859	8.6	−4	8.4	3.8	0.934	5.7	0.840	15.7	0.806	4.9	1.2	31.6
4	Germany	0.926	0.859	7.2	−1	7.0	3.7	0.905	2.6	0.891	14.8	0.787	4.6	1.1	30.1
5	Denmark	0.925	0.858	7.2	−2	7.0	3.8	0.894	3.0	0.896	14.3	0.789	4.5	1.0	29.1
5	Singapore	0.925	..	..	..	..	3.0	0.943	..	..	..	..	..	..	..
7	Netherlands	0.924	0.861	6.9	2	6.8	3.7	0.914	4.2	0.859	12.4	0.812	4.2	1.0	28.0
8	Ireland	0.923	0.850	7.9	−2	7.7	3.7	0.905	3.0	0.883	16.3	0.769	5.3	1.3	32.5
9	Iceland	0.921	0.868	5.8	6	5.7	2.9	0.937	2.5	0.884	11.7	0.789	4.0	1.0	26.9
10	Canada	0.920	0.839	8.9	−2	8.7	4.7	0.912	3.9	0.856	17.4	0.755	5.8	1.3	33.7
10	United States	0.920	0.796	13.5	−10	12.9	6.1	0.856	5.6	0.850	27.0	0.692	9.1	2.0	41.1
12	Hong Kong, China (SAR)	0.917	..	..	..	..	2.8	0.959	..	..	..	..	..	..	..
13	New Zealand	0.915	..	..	..	..	4.6	0.910	..	..	..	..	..	..	..
14	Sweden	0.913	0.851	6.7	3	6.6	3.3	0.928	3.4	0.826	13.1	0.806	4.2	0.9	27.3
15	Liechtenstein	0.912	..	..	..	..	..	..	..	..	..	..	..	..	..
16	United Kingdom	0.909	0.836	8.0	−1	7.8	4.5	0.894	2.8	0.871	16.2	0.752	5.3	1.3	32.6
17	Japan	0.903	0.791	12.4	−8	12.2	3.2	0.948	19.8	0.675	13.5	0.774	5.4 [f]	1.2 [f]	32.1 [f]
18	Korea (Republic of)	0.901	0.753	16.4	−19	15.9	3.7	0.920	25.5	0.645	18.4	0.720	..	..	..
19	Israel	0.899	0.778	13.5	−11	12.9	3.9	0.925	8.4	0.796	26.4	0.639	10.3	2.2	42.8
20	Luxembourg	0.898	0.827	8.0	1	7.8	2.6	0.927	5.8	0.738	15.1	0.826	5.9	1.4	34.8
21	France	0.897	0.813	9.4	−1	9.3	4.0	0.921	7.5	0.776	16.3	0.752	5.3	1.3	33.1
22	Belgium	0.896	0.821	8.3	2	8.3	4.0	0.901	8.1	0.773	12.7	0.794	4.2	1.0	27.6
23	Finland	0.895	0.843	5.8	9	5.7	3.4	0.907	2.0	0.830	11.6	0.796	3.9	1.0	27.1
24	Austria	0.893	0.815	8.7	3	8.5	3.7	0.912	4.3	0.785	17.5	0.757	4.9	1.1	30.5
25	Slovenia	0.890	0.838	5.9	9	5.8	3.6	0.898	2.6	0.863	11.3	0.758	3.7	0.9	25.6
26	Italy	0.887	0.784	11.5	−3	11.2	3.0	0.945	9.9	0.734	20.8	0.696	6.7	1.4	35.2
27	Spain	0.884	0.791	10.5	1	10.1	3.5	0.932	5.1	0.777	21.8	0.684	7.3	1.5	35.9
28	Czech Republic	0.878	0.830	5.4	10	5.3	3.5	0.873	1.4	0.866	11.1	0.757	3.8	0.9	26.1
29	Greece	0.866	0.758	12.4	−6	12.2	3.7	0.905	11.7	0.733	21.1	0.657	7.6	1.6	36.7
30	Brunei Darussalam	0.865	..	..	..	..	4.4	0.868	..	..	..	..	..	..	..
30	Estonia	0.865	0.788	8.9	3	8.6	4.8	0.835	2.3	0.856	18.7	0.684	5.7	1.3	33.2
32	Andorra	0.858	..	..	..	..	..	..	..	..	..	..	..	..	..
33	Cyprus	0.856	0.762	10.9	−2	10.8	4.0	0.891	12.4	0.688	15.9	0.722	5.4	1.4	34.3
33	Malta	0.856	0.786	8.1	3	8.0	4.5	0.892	6.0	0.734	13.6	0.742	..	..	..
33	Qatar	0.856	..	..	..	..	6.1	0.843	..	..	..	..	..	..	..
36	Poland	0.855	0.774	9.5	2	9.3	5.2	0.840	5.4	0.806	17.4	0.685	5.0	1.2	32.1
37	Lithuania	0.848	0.759	10.5	0	10.2	5.5	0.778	5.6	0.833	19.6	0.675	6.5	1.4	35.2
38	Chile	0.847	0.692	18.2	−12	17.1	7.6	0.881	8.2	0.719	35.5	0.524	12.2	3.2	50.5
38	Saudi Arabia	0.847	..	..	..	..	11.0	0.745	..	..	..	..	..	..	..
40	Slovakia	0.845	0.793	6.1	12	6.0	5.3	0.822	1.4	0.812	11.4	0.748	4.0	0.9	26.1
41	Portugal	0.843	0.755	10.4	1	10.1	3.9	0.905	5.9	0.712	20.4	0.669	6.7	1.5	36.0
42	United Arab Emirates	0.840	..	..	..	..	5.8	0.828	..	..	..	..	..	..	..
43	Hungary	0.836	0.771	7.8	6	7.6	5.2	0.807	3.1	0.808	14.6	0.704	5.0	1.1	30.6
44	Latvia	0.830	0.742	10.6	−1	10.3	6.7	0.780	3.8	0.803	20.3	0.653	6.7	1.4	35.5
45	Argentina	0.827	0.698	15.6	−6	15.2	10.0	0.782	8.1	0.742	27.4	0.586	10.0	2.1	42.7
45	Croatia	0.827	0.752	9.1	2	8.9	4.5	0.845	4.4	0.763	17.7	0.660	5.7	1.2	32.5
47	Bahrain	0.824	..	..	..	..	6.3	0.818	..	..	..	..	..	..	..
48	Montenegro	0.807	0.736	8.8	1	8.7	5.2	0.823	7.4	0.738	13.6	0.657	4.8	1.2	31.9
49	Russian Federation	0.804	0.725	9.8	1	9.6	8.8	0.705	2.2	0.798	17.7	0.678	8.2	2.0	41.6
50	Romania	0.802	0.714	11.1	0	10.8	8.4	0.773	4.6	0.734	19.5	0.641	4.1	1.0	27.5
51	Kuwait	0.800	..	..	..	..	7.2	0.779	..	..	..	..	..	..	..
HIGH HUMAN DEVELOPMENT															
52	Belarus	0.796	0.745	6.4	6	6.4	5.8	0.746	3.7	0.804	9.7	0.689	3.9	1.0	27.2
52	Oman	0.796	..	..	..	..	7.0	0.815	..	..	..	..	..	..	..
54	Barbados	0.795	..	..	..	..	7.8	0.791	5.5	0.730	..	..	..	..	..
54	Uruguay	0.795	0.670	15.7	−7	15.4	9.5	0.799	10.4	0.642	26.2	0.586	9.1	2.0	41.6
56	Bulgaria	0.794	0.709	10.7	2	10.5	7.8	0.771	5.5	0.735	18.2	0.629	6.9	1.5	36.0
56	Kazakhstan	0.794	0.714	10.1	4	10.1	11.6	0.674	5.9	0.758	12.7	0.712	3.7	0.9	26.3
58	Bahamas	0.792	..	..	..	..	9.4	0.774	..	..	..	..	..	..	..
59	Malaysia	0.789	..	..	..	..	6.7	0.788	..	..	..	..	11.3 [f]	2.6 [f]	46.3 [f]

TABLE 3

HDI rank	Human Development Index (HDI) Value	Inequality-adjusted HDI (IHDI) Value	Overall loss (%)	Difference from HDI rank[b]	Coefficient of human inequality	Inequality in life expectancy (%)	Inequality-adjusted life expectancy index Value	Inequality in education[a] (%)	Inequality-adjusted education index Value	Inequality in income[a] (%)	Inequality-adjusted income index Value	Income inequality Quintile ratio	Palma ratio	Gini coefficient
	2015	2015	2015	2015	2015	2010–2015[c]	2015	2015[d]	2015	2015[d]	2015	2010–2015[e]	2010–2015[e]	2010–2015[e]
60 Palau	0.788	..	..	..	..	..	..	12.0	0.711	23.0	0.573	..	..	..
60 Panama	0.788	0.614	22.0	−19	21.0	11.5	0.786	13.6	0.597	38.0	0.493	16.4	3.4	50.7
62 Antigua and Barbuda	0.786	..	..	..	..	8.4	0.792	..	..	..	..	..	..	..
63 Seychelles	0.782	..	..	..	..	9.0	0.746	..	..	..	..	9.8	2.6	46.8
64 Mauritius	0.781	0.669	14.4	−4	14.3	9.8	0.758	13.2	0.629	19.8	0.628	5.9	1.5	35.8
65 Trinidad and Tobago	0.780	0.661	15.3	−5	15.0	16.6	0.648	6.6	0.670	21.9	0.665	..	..	..
66 Costa Rica	0.776	0.628	19.1	−9	18.2	8.2	0.842	12.4	0.599	34.1	0.492	12.8	3.0	48.5
66 Serbia	0.776	0.689	11.2	3	11.1	7.9	0.780	8.1	0.698	17.4	0.600	4.4	1.1	29.1
68 Cuba	0.775	..	..	..	..	5.5	0.866	10.9	0.694	..	..	..	..	..
69 Iran (Islamic Republic of)	0.774	0.518	33.1	−40	31.5	10.6	0.764	37.3	0.441	46.6	0.412	6.6	1.6	37.4
70 Georgia	0.769	0.672	12.7	3	12.2	10.3	0.759	2.2	0.777	24.1	0.514	8.2	1.9	40.1
71 Turkey	0.767	0.645	15.9	−3	15.8	11.5	0.756	14.2	0.574	21.8	0.618	8.0	1.9	40.2
71 Venezuela (Bolivarian Republic of)	0.767	0.618	19.4	−11	19.1	11.4	0.741	17.6	0.586	28.4	0.543	16.0 [f]	2.8 [f]	46.9 [f]
73 Sri Lanka	0.766	0.678	11.6	8	11.5	8.1	0.778	12.8	0.656	13.7	0.610	6.6	1.8	39.2
74 Saint Kitts and Nevis	0.765	..	..	..	..	..	..	..	..	..	..	..	..	..
75 Albania	0.764	0.661	13.5	4	13.4	9.9	0.804	11.9	0.630	18.3	0.571	4.3	1.0	29.0
76 Lebanon	0.763	0.603	21.0	−10	20.4	7.2	0.850	24.1	0.498	30.0	0.517	..	..	..
77 Mexico	0.762	0.587	22.9	−12	22.4	13.2	0.761	19.7	0.525	34.3	0.506	10.8	2.9	48.2
78 Azerbaijan	0.759	0.659	13.2	5	13.0	21.7	0.613	8.3	0.663	8.9	0.702	4.8 [f]	1.2 [f]	31.8
79 Brazil	0.754	0.561	25.6	−19	25.0	14.4	0.721	22.6	0.527	37.8	0.465	15.5	3.5	51.5
79 Grenada	0.754	..	..	..	..	8.7	0.752	..	..	..	..	..	..	..
81 Bosnia and Herzegovina	0.750	0.650	13.3	6	13.1	6.7	0.813	12.5	0.607	20.2	0.556	5.7	1.3	33.8
82 The former Yugoslav Republic of Macedonia	0.748	0.623	16.7	1	16.1	7.6	0.789	10.6	0.602	30.1	0.509	9.3 [f]	2.3 [f]	44.1 [f]
83 Algeria	0.745	..	..	..	..	18.6	0.689	..	..	..	..	..	..	..
84 Armenia	0.743	0.674	9.3	15	9.2	10.1	0.759	3.7	0.703	13.9	0.573	4.7	1.2	31.5
84 Ukraine	0.743	0.690	7.2	18	7.2	8.7	0.718	3.6	0.774	9.2	0.590	3.3	0.8	24.1
86 Jordan	0.741	0.619	16.5	3	16.4	11.9	0.734	16.9	0.583	20.5	0.554	..	..	..
87 Peru	0.740	0.580	21.6	−8	21.3	14.2	0.724	20.3	0.536	29.5	0.503	10.8	2.3	44.1
87 Thailand	0.740	0.586	20.8	−5	20.2	10.4	0.753	16.1	0.538	34.0	0.496	6.5	1.7	37.9
89 Ecuador	0.739	0.587	20.5	−1	20.2	15.1	0.733	15.5	0.562	30.1	0.492	10.5	2.5	45.4
90 China	0.738	..	..	..	..	8.9	0.784	..	..	29.5	0.521	9.2	2.1	42.2
91 Fiji	0.736	0.624	15.3	9	15.1	12.3	0.677	10.5	0.695	22.6	0.516	8.2 [f]	2.1 [f]	42.8 [f]
92 Mongolia	0.735	0.639	13.0	13	13.0	17.1	0.635	9.4	0.668	12.3	0.616	5.0	1.2	32.0
92 Saint Lucia	0.735	0.618	16.0	7	15.6	10.1	0.763	9.2	0.614	27.4	0.503	..	..	..
94 Jamaica	0.730	0.609	16.6	6	15.9	11.9	0.757	5.6	0.640	30.1	0.467	..	..	..
95 Colombia	0.727	0.548	24.6	−9	23.7	14.4	0.714	17.4	0.520	39.4	0.444	17.3	3.9	53.5
96 Dominica	0.726	..	..	..	..	..	..	..	..	..	..	..	..	..
97 Suriname	0.725	0.551	24.0	−7	23.3	13.6	0.682	19.0	0.510	37.3	0.401	..	..	..
97 Tunisia	0.725	0.562	22.5	−3	21.9	12.2	0.743	34.6	0.421	10.9	0.567	6.4	1.5	35.0
99 Dominican Republic	0.722	0.565	21.7	1	21.6	16.0	0.687	19.9	0.498	29.1	0.527	10.8	2.7	47.1
99 Saint Vincent and the Grenadines	0.722	..	..	..	..	12.7	0.712	..	..	..	..	..	..	..
101 Tonga	0.721	..	..	..	..	13.6	0.704	..	..	..	..	6.9 [f]	1.7 [f]	38.1 [f]
102 Libya	0.716	..	..	..	..	15.8	0.671	..	..	..	..	..	..	..
103 Belize	0.706	0.546	22.7	−6	21.8	11.6	0.681	15.9	0.592	37.9	0.403	..	..	..
104 Samoa	0.704	..	..	..	..	13.3	0.716	..	..	..	..	7.9 [f]	2.2 [f]	42.7 [f]
105 Maldives	0.701	0.529	24.6	−9	23.4	7.1	0.814	40.0	0.337	23.2	0.539	7.1 [f]	1.7 [f]	38.4 [f]
105 Uzbekistan	0.701	0.590	15.8	10	15.3	24.3	0.575	1.4	0.729	20.1	0.489	..	..	..
MEDIUM HUMAN DEVELOPMENT														
107 Moldova (Republic of)	0.699	0.628	10.2	21	10.1	9.0	0.724	7.3	0.672	14.0	0.509	3.8	0.9	26.8
108 Botswana	0.698	0.433	37.9	−23	36.2	20.9	0.542	32.1	0.447	55.5	0.335	22.9 [f]	5.8 [f]	60.5 [f]
109 Gabon	0.697	0.531	23.9	−3	23.8	27.6	0.501	23.5	0.473	20.4	0.631	8.4 [f]	2.1 [f]	42.2 [f]
110 Paraguay	0.693	0.524	24.3	−5	23.5	18.3	0.666	14.0	0.527	38.3	0.410	14.7	3.5	51.7
111 Egypt	0.691	0.491	29.0	−10	28.2	13.4	0.684	35.0	0.390	36.3	0.444	..	..	..
111 Turkmenistan	0.691	..	..	..	..	26.0	0.521	..	..	..	..	..	..	..
113 Indonesia	0.689	0.563	18.2	9	18.2	16.5	0.630	20.8	0.492	17.3	0.576	6.6	1.8	39.5
114 Palestine, State of	0.684	0.581	15.1	13	15.1	13.7	0.705	16.5	0.547	15.0	0.509	5.5 [f]	1.4 [f]	34.5 [f]
115 Viet Nam	0.683	0.562	17.8	9	17.8	14.2	0.738	17.6	0.508	21.4	0.472	6.8	1.6	37.6
116 Philippines	0.682	0.556	18.4	8	18.2	16.2	0.623	11.6	0.563	26.8	0.490	8.4	2.2	43.0
117 El Salvador	0.680	0.529	22.2	3	22.0	13.7	0.707	26.6	0.429	25.7	0.488	8.4	2.0	41.8
118 Bolivia (Plurinational State of)	0.674	0.478	29.0	−6	28.7	29.0	0.532	20.8	0.520	36.4	0.396	14.7	3.0	48.4
119 South Africa	0.666	0.435	34.7	−12	32.0	25.7	0.430	13.8	0.608	56.4	0.316	27.9	7.1	63.4

TABLE 3   Inequality-adjusted Human Development Index | 209

TABLE
3

TABLE 3 INEQUALITY-ADJUSTED HUMAN DEVELOPMENT INDEX

	Human Development Index (HDI)	Inequality-adjusted HDI (IHDI)			Coefficient of human inequality	Inequality in life expectancy	Inequality-adjusted life expectancy index	Inequality in education[a]	Inequality-adjusted education index	Inequality in income[a]	Inequality-adjusted income index	Income inequality		
	Value	Value	Overall loss (%)	Difference from HDI rank[b]		(%)	Value	(%)	Value	(%)	Value	Quintile ratio	Palma ratio	Gini coefficient
HDI rank	2015	2015	2015	2015	2015	2010–2015[c]	2015	2015[d]	2015	2015[d]	2015	2010–2015[e]	2010–2015[e]	2010–2015[e]
120 Kyrgyzstan	0.664	0.582	12.3	20	12.1	13.6	0.675	5.0	0.685	17.7	0.427	3.7	1.0	26.8
121 Iraq	0.649	0.505	22.3	1	22.0	19.3	0.616	30.6	0.347	16.1	0.602	..	..	..
122 Cabo Verde	0.648	0.518	20.1	4	19.9	13.4	0.713	18.2	0.436	28.0	0.446	10.7 [f]	2.7 [f]	47.2 [f]
123 Morocco	0.647	0.456	29.5	−2	28.3	16.0	0.702	45.8	0.273	23.0	0.497	7.4 [f]	1.9 [f]	40.7 [f]
124 Nicaragua	0.645	0.479	25.8	1	25.4	14.6	0.725	29.5	0.382	32.1	0.396	10.9	2.7	47.1
125 Guatemala	0.640	0.450	29.6	−2	29.1	17.0	0.665	36.2	0.324	34.1	0.424	12.1	3.0	48.7
125 Namibia	0.640	0.415	35.2	−13	33.4	21.7	0.543	25.0	0.410	53.6	0.321	20.3 [f]	5.8 [f]	61.0 [f]
127 Guyana	0.638	0.518	18.8	10	18.5	20.7	0.567	10.5	0.508	24.4	0.483	..	..	..
127 Micronesia (Federated States of)	0.638	..	..	..	..	19.8	0.608	..	..	..	..	9.6	2.1	42.5
129 Tajikistan	0.627	0.532	15.2	16	14.9	23.2	0.586	6.5	0.615	15.0	0.418	4.5	1.2	30.8
130 Honduras	0.625	0.443	29.2	0	28.5	19.6	0.660	24.4	0.391	41.5	0.336	15.8	3.4	50.6
131 India	0.624	0.454	27.2	4	26.5	24.0	0.565	39.4	0.324	16.1	0.512	5.3	1.5	35.2
132 Bhutan	0.607	0.428	29.4	−3	28.4	20.7	0.608	44.8	0.250	19.6	0.517	6.8	1.8	38.8
133 Timor-Leste	0.605	0.416	31.2	−5	29.9	24.4	0.564	47.6	0.259	17.8	0.495	4.6 [f]	1.2 [f]	31.6 [f]
134 Vanuatu	0.597	0.494	17.2	12	17.1	15.4	0.678	17.5	0.434	18.5	0.410	6.6	1.6	37.2
135 Congo	0.592	0.446	24.8	6	24.6	31.1	0.455	21.5	0.408	21.2	0.477	12.8	3.1	48.9
135 Equatorial Guinea	0.592	..	..	..	..	38.4	0.359	..	..	..	..	..	..	..
137 Kiribati	0.588	0.394	33.1	−7	32.0	26.1	0.526	21.4	0.464	48.4	0.250	7.2 [f]	1.6 [f]	37.6 [f]
138 Lao People's Democratic Republic	0.586	0.427	27.1	1	26.9	26.2	0.529	34.1	0.313	20.3	0.472	6.3	1.7	37.9
139 Bangladesh	0.579	0.412	28.9	−2	28.6	20.1	0.639	37.3	0.287	28.3	0.380	4.7	1.3	32.1
139 Ghana	0.579	0.391	32.5	−8	32.5	30.8	0.442	34.9	0.358	31.7	0.377	9.3 [f]	2.2 [f]	42.8 [f]
139 Zambia	0.579	0.373	35.6	−11	34.7	33.8	0.416	21.7	0.452	48.6	0.275	16.0	4.3	55.6
142 Sao Tome and Principe	0.574	0.432	24.7	7	24.7	26.9	0.524	21.4	0.400	25.8	0.384	4.7	1.1	30.8
143 Cambodia	0.563	0.436	22.5	11	22.4	19.7	0.603	27.3	0.333	20.3	0.413	4.4	1.2	30.8
144 Nepal	0.558	0.407	27.0	2	25.8	19.6	0.618	43.9	0.267	13.9	0.410	5.0	1.3	32.8
145 Myanmar	0.556	..	..	..	..	26.0	0.525	19.4	0.330	..	..	..	..	..
146 Kenya	0.555	0.391	29.5	−1	29.4	32.1	0.440	22.9	0.400	33.1	0.339	11.6 [f]	2.9 [f]	48.5 [f]
147 Pakistan	0.550	0.380	30.9	−2	29.6	32.8	0.479	44.4	0.220	11.6	0.523	4.4	1.2	30.7
LOW HUMAN DEVELOPMENT														
148 Swaziland	0.541	0.361	33.3	−5	33.1	35.0	0.289	26.8	0.399	37.6	0.408	14.2 [f]	3.5 [f]	51.5 [f]
149 Syrian Arab Republic	0.536	0.419	21.8	10	21.4	14.5	0.653	31.5	0.286	18.3	0.394	..	..	..
150 Angola	0.533	0.336	37.0	−8	36.6	46.2	0.271	34.6	0.316	28.9	0.445	8.9 [f]	2.2 [f]	42.7 [f]
151 Tanzania (United Republic of)	0.531	0.396	25.4	7	25.4	25.0	0.525	28.5	0.315	22.7	0.374	6.2	1.7	37.8
152 Nigeria	0.527	0.328	37.8	−10	37.5	40.8	0.301	43.3	0.270	28.4	0.432	9.1 [f]	2.2 [f]	43.0 [f]
153 Cameroon	0.518	0.348	32.8	−1	32.4	39.4	0.335	34.8	0.322	23.1	0.391	11.4	2.7	46.5
154 Papua New Guinea	0.516	..	..	..	..	26.5	0.484	11.5	0.371	..	..	10.4 [f]	2.3 [f]	43.9 [f]
154 Zimbabwe	0.516	0.369	28.5	2	28.1	31.2	0.415	17.4	0.450	35.8	0.268	8.5	2.2	43.2
156 Solomon Islands	0.515	0.392	23.8	9	23.8	22.3	0.575	22.8	0.343	26.3	0.306	10.5 [f]	2.6 [f]	46.1 [f]
157 Mauritania	0.513	0.347	32.4	1	31.9	33.7	0.441	40.8	0.223	21.2	0.424	5.3	1.2	32.4
158 Madagascar	0.512	0.374	27.0	7	26.8	24.8	0.527	35.0	0.320	20.4	0.310	8.6	2.1	42.7
159 Rwanda	0.498	0.339	31.9	1	31.8	29.8	0.483	29.3	0.301	36.4	0.267	11.0	3.2	50.4
160 Comoros	0.497	0.270	45.8	−18	44.8	30.9	0.463	47.6	0.246	56.0	0.172	..	..	..
160 Lesotho	0.497	0.320	35.6	−6	34.9	33.5	0.308	24.3	0.380	47.0	0.280	20.5	4.3	54.2
162 Senegal	0.494	0.331	33.1	1	32.5	25.0	0.541	44.7	0.196	27.7	0.340	7.7	1.9	40.3
163 Haiti	0.493	0.298	39.6	−7	39.2	30.9	0.458	38.3	0.262	48.4	0.219	32.5	6.5	60.8
163 Uganda	0.493	0.341	30.9	6	30.8	35.7	0.388	29.4	0.330	27.3	0.309	7.6	2.0	41.0
165 Sudan	0.490	..	..	..	..	31.8	0.459	42.7	0.182	..	..	6.2 [f]	1.4 [f]	35.4 [f]
166 Togo	0.487	0.332	31.9	5	31.6	32.4	0.418	38.9	0.299	23.5	0.293	10.7	2.6	46.0
167 Benin	0.485	0.304	37.4	−3	37.1	37.0	0.385	44.8	0.228	29.4	0.318	8.4	2.2	43.4
168 Yemen	0.482	0.320	33.7	0	32.7	29.4	0.478	48.1	0.182	20.6	0.376	..	..	..
169 Afghanistan	0.479	0.327	31.8	3	30.4	35.7	0.403	44.8	0.219	10.8	0.395	..	..	..
170 Malawi	0.476	0.328	31.2	5	31.1	32.7	0.454	28.2	0.320	32.5	0.242	9.6	2.6	46.1
171 Côte d'Ivoire	0.474	0.294	37.8	−2	37.4	39.7	0.296	45.1	0.228	27.4	0.379	9.6 [f]	2.2 [f]	43.2 [f]
172 Djibouti	0.473	0.310	34.6	3	33.7	32.5	0.439	47.0	0.165	21.7	0.410	10.2	2.3	44.1
173 Gambia	0.452	..	..	..	..	31.3	0.428	..	..	26.9	0.302	..	..	..
174 Ethiopia	0.448	0.330	26.3	10	25.5	30.3	0.478	36.6	0.202	9.5	0.372	5.2	1.3	33.2
175 Mali	0.442	0.293	33.7	0	32.7	40.4	0.353	41.6	0.182	16.1	0.393	5.2 [f]	1.3 [f]	33.0 [f]
176 Congo (Democratic Republic of the)	0.435	0.297	31.9	3	31.7	39.1	0.366	27.7	0.343	28.2	0.208	8.7	2.1	42.1
177 Liberia	0.427	0.284	33.4	1	32.9	33.1	0.424	42.9	0.242	22.7	0.224	6.7 [f]	1.6 [f]	36.5 [f]
178 Guinea-Bissau	0.424	0.257	39.3	−5	39.1	44.6	0.302	40.3	0.211	32.5	0.267	12.6	3.3	50.7
179 Eritrea	0.420	..	..	..	..	25.9	0.504	..	..	..	..	..	..	..

	Human Development Index (HDI)	Inequality-adjusted HDI (IHDI)			Coefficient of human inequality	Inequality in life expectancy	Inequality-adjusted life expectancy index	Inequality in education[a]	Inequality-adjusted education index	Inequality in income[a]	Inequality-adjusted income index	Income inequality		
	Value	Value	Overall loss (%)	Difference from HDI rank[b]		(%)	Value	(%)	Value	(%)	Value	Quintile ratio	Palma ratio	Gini coefficient
HDI rank	2015	2015	2015	2015	2015	2010–2015[c]	2015	2015[d]	2015	2015[d]	2015	2010–2015[e]	2010–2015[e]	2010–2015[e]
179 Sierra Leone	0.420	0.262	37.8	−3	36.6	43.4	0.273	47.3	0.197	19.2	0.333	5.4	1.4	34.0
181 Mozambique	0.418	0.280	33.0	3	32.9	36.4	0.347	33.8	0.244	28.4	0.259	9.9 [f]	2.5 [f]	45.6 [f]
181 South Sudan	0.418	..	..	..	..	40.7	0.330	39.6	0.180	..	..	13.1 [f]	2.7 [f]	46.3 [f]
183 Guinea	0.414	0.270	34.8	2	33.6	35.4	0.390	48.3	0.171	17.1	0.296	5.5	1.3	33.7
184 Burundi	0.404	0.276	31.5	4	30.6	40.8	0.338	36.9	0.249	14.1	0.251	4.8 [f]	1.3 [f]	33.4 [f]
185 Burkina Faso	0.402	0.267	33.6	2	33.3	37.1	0.377	38.6	0.161	24.2	0.313	5.3	1.5	35.3
186 Chad	0.396	0.238	39.9	−1	39.6	46.2	0.264	41.9	0.163	30.7	0.313	10.0	2.2	43.3
187 Niger	0.353	0.253	28.3	1	27.5	35.3	0.417	35.0	0.134	12.3	0.290	5.4	1.4	34.0
188 Central African Republic	0.352	0.199	43.5	0	43.1	45.7	0.263	34.5	0.221	49.2	0.136	18.3 [f]	4.5 [f]	56.2 [f]
OTHER COUNTRIES OR TERRITORIES														
Korea (Democratic People's Rep. of)	..	..	..	..	..	15.4	0.658	..	..	..	..	..	..	..
Marshall Islands	..	..	..	..	..	..	..	..	..	..	..	..	..	..
Monaco	..	..	..	..	..	..	..	..	..	..	..	..	..	..
Nauru	..	..	..	..	..	..	..	..	..	..	..	..	..	..
San Marino	..	..	..	..	..	..	..	..	..	..	..	..	..	..
Somalia	..	..	..	..	..	42.1	0.318	43.5	..	..	..	..	..	..
Tuvalu	..	..	..	..	..	..	..	10.5	..	..	..	7.7	1.9	41.1
Human development groups														
Very high human development	0.892	0.793	11.1	—	10.9	5.4	0.865	7.2	0.797	19.9	0.723	—	—	—
High human development	0.746	0.597	20.0	—	19.6	10.5	0.764	18.3	0.535	30.0	0.521	—	—	—
Medium human development	0.631	0.469	25.7	—	25.5	22.6	0.578	33.7	0.357	20.1	0.500	—	—	—
Low human development	0.497	0.337	32.3	—	32.0	35.1	0.392	37.1	0.258	23.9	0.377	—	—	—
Developing countries	0.668	0.499	25.2	—	25.1	19.6	0.619	31.0	0.391	24.7	0.515	—	—	—
Regions														
Arab States	0.687	0.498	27.5	—	27.1	17.9	0.642	37.1	0.347	26.2	0.556	—	—	—
East Asia and the Pacific	0.720	0.581	19.3	—	19.0	11.2	0.740	18.3	0.505	27.4	0.526	—	—	—
Europe and Central Asia	0.756	0.660	12.7	—	12.6	13.2	0.702	7.9	0.670	16.7	0.611	—	—	—
Latin America and the Caribbean	0.751	0.575	23.4	—	22.9	14.0	0.730	19.7	0.537	34.9	0.486	—	—	—
South Asia	0.621	0.449	27.7	—	27.1	23.9	0.670	39.6	0.314	17.8	0.504	—	—	—
Sub-Saharan Africa	0.523	0.355	32.2	—	32.1	34.9	0.389	34.0	0.297	27.4	0.386	—	—	—
Least developed countries	0.508	0.356	30.0	—	29.8	30.5	0.466	35.3	0.264	23.6	0.366	—	—	—
Small island developing states	0.667	0.500	25.1	—	24.7	19.2	0.625	20.7	0.469	34.3	0.426	—	—	—
Organisation for Economic Co-operation and Development	0.887	0.776	12.6	—	12.3	5.9	0.873	9.5	0.758	21.5	0.704	—	—	—
World	**0.717**	**0.557**	**22.3**	—	**22.3**	**17.1**	**0.658**	**25.9**	**0.458**	**23.8**	**0.573**	**—**	**—**	**—**

NOTES

a See http://hdr.undp.org/en/composite/IHDI for the list of surveys used to estimate inequalities.

b Based on countries for which an Inequality-adjusted Human Development Index value is calculated.

c Calculated by HDRO from the 2010–2015 period life tables from UNDESA (2015a).

d Data refer to 2015 or the most recent year available.

e Data refer to the most recent year available during the period specified.

f Data refer to a year earlier than 2010.

DEFINITIONS

Human Development Index (HDI): A composite index measuring average achievement in three basic dimensions of human development—a long and healthy life, knowledge and a decent standard of living. See *Technical note 1* at http://hdr.undp.org/sites/default/files/hdr2016_technical_notes.pdf for details on how the HDI is calculated.

Inequality-adjusted HDI (IHDI): HDI value adjusted for inequalities in the three basic dimensions of human development. See *Technical note 2* at http://hdr.undp.org/sites/default/files/hdr2016_technical_notes.pdf for details on how the IHDI is calculated.

Overall loss: Percentage difference between the IHDI value and the HDI value.

Difference from HDI rank: Difference in ranks on the IHDI and the HDI, calculated only for countries for which an IHDI value is calculated.

Coefficient of human inequality: Average inequality in three basic dimensions of human development.

Inequality in life expectancy: Inequality in distribution of expected length of life based on data from life tables estimated using the Atkinson inequality index.

Inequality-adjusted life expectancy index: HDI life expectancy index value adjusted for inequality in distribution of expected length of life based on data from life tables listed in *Main data sources*.

Inequality in education: Inequality in distribution of years of schooling based on data from household surveys estimated using the Atkinson inequality index.

Inequality-adjusted education index: HDI education index value adjusted for inequality in distribution of years of schooling based on data from household surveys listed in *Main data sources*.

Inequality in income: Inequality in income distribution based on data from household surveys estimated using the Atkinson inequality index.

Inequality-adjusted income index: HDI income index value adjusted for inequality in income distribution based on data from household surveys listed in *Main data sources*.

Quintile ratio: Ratio of the average income of the richest 20 percent of the population to the average income of the poorest 20 percent of the population.

Palma ratio: Ratio of the richest 10 percent of the population's share of gross national income (GNI) divided by the poorest 40 percent's share. It is based on the work of Palma (2011).

Gini coefficient: Measure of the deviation of the distribution of income among individuals or households within a country from a perfectly equal distribution. A value of 0 represents absolute equality, a value of 100 absolute inequality.

MAIN DATA SOURCES

Column 1: HDRO calculations based on data from UNDESA (2015a), UNESCO Institute for Statistics (2016), United Nations Statistics Division (2016a), World Bank (2016a), Barro and Lee (2016) and IMF (2016).

Column 2: Calculated as the geometric mean of the values in inequality-adjusted life expectancy index, inequality-adjusted education index and inequality-adjusted income index using the methodology in *Technical note 2* (available at http://hdr.undp.org/sites/default/files/hdr2016_technical_notes.pdf).

Column 3: Calculated based on data in columns 1 and 2.

Column 4: Calculated based on IHDI values and recalculated HDI ranks for countries for which an IHDI value is calculated.

Column 5: Calculated as the arithmetic mean of the values in inequality in life expectancy, inequality in education and inequality in income using the methodology in *Technical note 2* (available at http://hdr.undp.org/sites/default/files/hdr2016_technical_notes.pdf).

Column 6: Calculated based on abridged life tables from UNDESA (2015a).

Column 7: Calculated based on inequality in life expectancy and the HDI life expectancy index.

Columns 8 and 10: Calculated based on data from the Luxembourg Income Study database, Eurostat's European Union Statistics on Income and Living Conditions, the World Bank's International Income Distribution Database, ICF Macro Demographic and Health Surveys and United Nations Children's Fund Multiple Indicator Cluster Surveys using the methodology in *Technical note 2* (available at http://hdr.undp.org/sites/default/files/hdr2016_technical_notes.pdf).

Column 9: Calculated based on inequality in education and the HDI education index.

Column 11: Calculated based on inequality in income and the HDI income index.

Columns 12 and 13: HDRO calculations based on data from World Bank (2016a).

Column 14: World Bank (2016a).

TABLE
3

TABLE 3   Inequality-adjusted Human Development Index | 211

TABLE 4

Gender Development Index

TABLE 4

HDI rank	Gender Development Index Value 2015	Group[b] 2015	Human Development Index (HDI) Value Female 2015	Male 2015	Life expectancy at birth (years) Female 2015	Male 2015	Expected years of schooling (years) Female 2015[c]	Male 2015[c]	Mean years of schooling (years) Female 2015[c]	Male 2015[c]	Estimated gross national income per capita[a] (2011 PPP $) Female 2015	Male 2015
VERY HIGH HUMAN DEVELOPMENT												
1 Norway	0.993	1	0.944	0.951	83.7	79.7	18.3	17.1	12.8	12.7	59,800	75,314
2 Australia	0.978	1	0.927	0.948	84.6	80.5	20.9[d]	20.0[d]	13.4	13.0	34,271	51,386
2 Switzerland	0.974	2	0.926	0.951	85.1	81.0	16.0	16.1	13.3	13.5	46,798	66,116
4 Germany	0.964	2	0.908	0.942	83.4	78.7	16.9	17.3	12.9[e]	13.6[e]	35,878	54,440
5 Denmark	0.970	2	0.910	0.938	82.3	78.5	20.0[d]	18.4[d]	12.6	12.9	36,857	52,293
5 Singapore	0.985	1	0.913	0.927	86.2	80.1	15.5	15.3	11.1[f]	12.1[f]	60,787	96,001[g]
7 Netherlands	0.946	3	0.895	0.946	83.5	79.9	18.2[d]	18.1[d]	11.6	12.2	30,117	62,773
8 Ireland	0.976	1	0.909	0.931	83.1	79.0	18.6[d]	18.6[d]	12.5	11.9	33,497	54,135
9 Iceland	0.965	2	0.905	0.938	84.2	81.2	20.1[d]	17.9	12.2[e]	12.6[e]	30,530	43,576
10 Canada	0.983	1	0.911	0.926	84.1	80.2	16.8	15.9	13.3[h]	12.9[h]	33,288	52,026
10 United States	0.993	1	0.915	0.922	81.6	76.9	17.3	15.8	13.2	13.2	42,272	64,410
12 Hong Kong, China (SAR)	0.964	2	0.903	0.937	87.0	81.4	15.8	15.5	11.5	12.4	39,525	70,921
13 New Zealand	0.963	2	0.896	0.930	83.7	80.3	20.0[d]	18.5[d]	12.6	12.5	24,413	41,718
14 Sweden	0.997	1	0.909	0.911	84.0	80.6	16.6	15.1	12.4	12.2	40,328	52,181
15 Liechtenstein	..	..	..	..	..	..	13.5	15.9	..	..	..	..
16 United Kingdom	0.964	2	0.890	0.924	82.7	78.9	16.7	15.9	13.2	13.4	26,324	49,872
17 Japan	0.970	2	0.887	0.914	86.9	80.4	15.2	15.5	12.6[e]	12.4[e]	25,385	49,818
18 Korea (Republic of)	0.929	3	0.863	0.929	85.2	78.8	15.8	17.3	11.5	12.9	21,308	47,934
19 Israel	0.973	2	0.884	0.909	84.2	80.8	16.5	15.5	12.8	12.7	23,323	39,239
20 Luxembourg	0.966	2	0.881	0.911	84.1	79.6	14.0	13.7	11.6	12.3	47,539	77,291[g]
21 France	0.988	1	0.892	0.902	85.2	79.4	16.6	15.9	11.5	11.8	31,742	44,776
22 Belgium	0.978	1	0.881	0.901	83.4	78.5	16.7	15.9	11.2[f]	11.6[f]	32,416	50,358
23 Finland	1.000	1	0.895	0.895	83.8	78.2	17.6	16.5	11.5[h]	11.1[h]	32,069	45,882
24 Austria	0.957	2	0.870	0.909	84.0	79.1	16.2	15.6	10.8[e]	11.8[e]	29,829	57,888
25 Slovenia	1.003	1	0.890	0.888	83.5	77.6	18.1	16.7	11.9	12.2	25,654	31,726
26 Italy	0.963	2	0.865	0.899	85.7	80.9	16.7	15.9	10.5	11.0	22,910	44,844
27 Spain	0.974	2	0.870	0.894	85.4	80.0	18.0	17.4	9.6	10.0	24,382	41,500
28 Czech Republic	0.983	1	0.869	0.883	81.6	75.9	17.6	16.1	12.1	12.6	20,997	35,543
29 Greece	0.957	2	0.844	0.883	84.0	78.2	17.1	17.3	10.3	10.8	17,304	32,683
30 Brunei Darussalam	0.986	1	0.854	0.866	80.9	77.2	15.4	14.6	9.0[h]	9.1[h]	55,402	89,256[g]
30 Estonia	1.032	2	0.878	0.851	81.4	72.2	17.3	15.7	13.0[e]	12.2[e]	21,976	31,347
32 Andorra	..	..	..	..	..	..	..	..	10.2	10.3	..	..
33 Cyprus	0.979	1	0.846	0.864	82.6	78.2	14.7	13.8	11.6	11.9	23,450	35,227
33 Malta	0.923	4	0.817	0.885	82.4	79.0	14.3	15.0	10.9	11.6	17,295	41,802
33 Qatar	0.991	1	0.851	0.859	80.1	77.5	13.5	13.3	10.9	9.5	50,324	159,897[g]
36 Poland	1.006	1	0.857	0.852	81.5	73.6	17.2	15.5	11.9	12.0	18,928	29,658
37 Lithuania	1.032	2	0.861	0.834	79.1	67.9	17.1	16.0	12.7	12.7	22,147	30,530
38 Chile	0.966	2	0.829	0.858	84.7	79.0	16.6	16.1	9.8	10.0	14,955	28,556
38 Saudi Arabia	0.882	5	0.779	0.884	75.9	73.2	15.3	17.0	9.0	10.0	19,300	75,923[g]
40 Slovakia	0.991	1	0.838	0.846	80.0	72.7	15.5	14.4	12.0	12.3	20,173	33,770
41 Portugal	0.980	1	0.833	0.850	84.0	78.2	16.5	16.6	8.9	8.9	21,095	31,673
42 United Arab Emirates	0.972	2	0.815	0.838	78.7	76.5	13.9	12.9	10.6[e]	8.7[e]	27,257	80,420[g]
43 Hungary	0.988	1	0.830	0.840	78.8	71.6	16.0	15.2	12.0[f]	12.1[f]	17,787	29,567
44 Latvia	1.025	2	0.840	0.820	79.0	69.3	16.6	15.5	12.0[f,h]	11.6[f,h]	18,824	27,031
45 Argentina	0.982	1	0.813	0.828	80.2	72.6	18.4	16.1	9.7[h]	10.0[h]	12,875	29,367
45 Croatia	0.997	1	0.827	0.830	80.8	74.2	16.0	14.6	11.2	11.6	16,932	23,897
47 Bahrain	0.970	2	0.806	0.831	77.8	75.9	15.1	13.7	9.4[i]	9.4[i]	25,717	44,303
48 Montenegro	0.955	2	0.789	0.827	78.6	74.2	15.7	15.0	10.7[i]	12.0[i]	11,757	19,149
49 Russian Federation	1.016	1	0.809	0.796	75.9	64.6	15.3	14.7	12.0	12.1	17,868	29,531
50 Romania	0.990	1	0.796	0.805	78.4	71.3	15.1	14.4	10.3	11.0	16,272	22,786
51 Kuwait	0.972	2	0.769	0.791	75.9	73.6	13.6	12.4	7.4	6.9	35,164	107,991[g]
HIGH HUMAN DEVELOPMENT												
52 Belarus	1.021	1	0.803	0.786	77.3	65.7	16.1	15.1	11.9	12.1	12,327	19,433
52 Oman	0.927	3	0.755	0.814	79.4	75.3	13.9	13.6	7.7[i]	8.5[i]	15,703	43,894
54 Barbados	1.006	1	0.795	0.791	78.1	73.3	16.7	13.9	10.6[i]	10.3[i]	11,801	18,377
54 Uruguay	1.017	1	0.799	0.786	80.8	73.7	16.6	14.4	8.8	8.3	14,608	24,014
56 Bulgaria	0.984	1	0.789	0.801	77.8	70.9	15.3	14.8	10.8[e]	11.2[e]	12,979	19,736
56 Kazakhstan	1.006	1	0.795	0.790	74.3	64.8	15.4	14.6	11.7[h]	11.7[h]	16,364	28,226
58 Bahamas	..	..	..	..	78.5	72.5	..	..	11.5	10.5	18,070	25,209
59 Malaysia	..	..	..	..	77.3	72.6	..	..	10.0	10.8	17,170	32,208
60 Palau	..	..	..	..	..	..	17.6	13.7	..	..	..	..

TABLE
4

	Gender Development Index		Human Development Index (HDI)		Life expectancy at birth		Expected years of schooling		Mean years of schooling		Estimated gross national income per capita[a]	
			Value		(years)		(years)		(years)		(2011 PPP $)	
	Value	Group[b]	Female	Male	Female	Male	Female	Male	Female	Male	Female	Male
HDI rank	2015	2015	2015	2015	2015	2015	2015[c]	2015[c]	2015[c]	2015[c]	2015	2015
60 Panama	0.997	1	0.783	0.785	80.9	74.8	13.2	12.4	10.3	9.5	14,550	24,365
62 Antigua and Barbuda	..	..	..	..	78.6	73.7	14.6	13.3	..	..	..	..
63 Seychelles	..	..	..	..	78.2	69.1	14.8	13.5	..	..	..	..
64 Mauritius	0.954	2	0.759	0.796	78.2	71.1	15.5	14.8	8.8	9.5	10,540	25,539
65 Trinidad and Tobago	1.004	1	0.786	0.783	74.2	67.1	14.3[k]	12.3[k]	10.8	11.0	21,104	35,179
66 Costa Rica	0.969	2	0.762	0.786	82.1	77.2	14.5	13.8	8.7	8.7	9,955	18,052
66 Serbia	0.969	2	0.763	0.787	77.9	72.2	14.8	13.9	10.3	11.4	9,600	14,932
68 Cuba	0.946	3	0.750	0.792	81.6	77.6	14.4	13.5	11.5[i]	12.0[i]	5,013	9,874
69 Iran (Islamic Republic of)	0.862	5	0.700	0.812	76.7	74.5	14.6	15.0	8.5[h]	9.1[h]	5,132	27,499
70 Georgia	0.970	2	0.754	0.777	78.5	71.3	14.1	13.7	12.3	12.2	6,105	11,871
71 Turkey	0.908	4	0.724	0.797	78.7	72.3	14.0	15.0	7.0	8.8	10,648	27,035
71 Venezuela (Bolivarian Republic of)	1.028	2	0.776	0.754	78.6	70.4	15.4	13.2	9.7	9.0	11,579	18,709
73 Sri Lanka	0.934	3	0.734	0.785	78.4	71.7	14.3	13.6	10.3[h]	11.4[h]	6,067	15,869
74 Saint Kitts and Nevis	..	..	..	..	..	..	13.8	13.5	..	..	..	..
75 Albania	0.959	2	0.747	0.778	80.6	75.6	14.4	14.0	9.5	9.8	7,365	13,186
76 Lebanon	0.893	5	0.709	0.793	81.5	77.9	13.0	13.6	8.3[i]	8.7[i]	5,844	20,712
77 Mexico	0.951	2	0.737	0.775	79.4	74.6	13.5	13.1	8.2	8.6	10,710	22,115
78 Azerbaijan	0.940	3	0.732	0.779	74.1	67.8	12.6	12.7	10.3	12.0	11,029	21,845
79 Brazil	1.005	1	0.754	0.751	78.5	71.0	15.7	14.7	8.1	7.5	10,672	17,736
79 Grenada	..	..	..	..	76.0	71.1	16.2	15.3	..	..	..	..
81 Bosnia and Herzegovina	0.923	4	0.721	0.781	79.2	74.1	14.8	14.0	7.8	10.6	6,950	13,261
82 The former Yugoslav Republic of Macedonia	0.947	3	0.725	0.765	77.9	73.2	13.0	12.8	8.9[i]	9.8[i]	9,050	15,790
83 Algeria	0.854	5	0.665	0.779	77.5	72.7	14.6	14.1	6.6[e]	8.5[e]	4,022	22,926
84 Armenia	0.993	1	0.736	0.741	78.7	71.1	13.8	11.4	11.3	11.3	5,535	11,258
84 Ukraine	1.000	1	0.741	0.741	76.0	66.2	15.5	15.1	11.3[h]	11.3[h]	5,791	9,181
86 Jordan	0.864	5	0.670	0.776	75.9	72.6	13.4	12.9	9.7	10.7	3,203	16,694
87 Peru	0.959	2	0.723	0.754	77.5	72.2	13.5	13.2	8.4	9.5	8,939	13,655
87 Thailand	1.001	1	0.740	0.739	78.0	71.3	14.1	13.1	7.7	8.2	12,938	16,145
89 Ecuador	0.976	1	0.730	0.748	78.9	73.4	14.4	13.9	8.2	8.4	8,278	12,795
90 China	0.954	2	0.718	0.753	77.5	74.5	13.7	13.4	7.2[e]	7.9[e]	10,705	15,830
91 Fiji	..	..	..	..	73.4	67.3	..	..	10.9[h]	10.2[h]	4,695	11,676
92 Mongolia	1.026	2	0.744	0.725	74.2	65.6	15.5	14.2	10.0[i]	9.5[i]	8,809	12,122
92 Saint Lucia	0.986	1	0.729	0.740	78.0	72.5	13.4	12.9	9.4[i]	9.3[i]	8,033	11,617
94 Jamaica	0.975	2	0.719	0.738	78.2	73.5	13.1	12.6	9.7[h]	9.6[h]	6,628	10,086
95 Colombia	1.004	1	0.731	0.728	77.8	70.7	14.5	13.3	7.6[e]	7.5[e]	10,215	15,389
96 Dominica	..	..	..	..	..	..	..	..	..	..	..	..
97 Suriname	0.972	2	0.709	0.730	74.6	68.2	13.0	12.0	8.2[i]	8.5[i]	10,501	21,512
97 Tunisia	0.904	4	0.690	0.752	77.4	72.7	15.1	14.2	6.7[e]	7.8[e]	4,662	15,967
99 Dominican Republic	0.990	1	0.717	0.724	76.9	70.6	13.7	12.7	7.9	7.5	9,281	16,256
99 Saint Vincent and the Grenadines	..	..	..	..	75.2	71.0	13.5[i]	13.1[i]	..	..	7,600	13,095
101 Tonga	0.969	2	0.707	0.730	76.0	70.1	14.6	14.0	11.0	11.1	3,959	6,602
102 Libya	0.950	2	0.691	0.727	74.8	69.0	13.6	13.2	7.7[e]	7.0[e]	7,163	21,364
103 Belize	0.967	2	0.693	0.716	73.1	67.4	13.0	12.5	10.5	10.5	5,360	9,402
104 Samoa	..	..	..	..	77.0	70.7	13.3	12.5	..	..	3,444	7,182
105 Maldives	0.937	3	0.676	0.721	78.0	76.0	12.8[k]	12.7[k]	6.2[f,k]	6.3[f,k]	7,155	13,591
105 Uzbekistan	0.946	3	0.672	0.711	71.9	65.1	11.8	12.2	11.8	12.3	3,891	7,668
MEDIUM HUMAN DEVELOPMENT												
107 Moldova (Republic of)	1.010	1	0.702	0.695	75.9	67.6	12.1	11.6	12.0	11.8	4,461	5,637
108 Botswana	0.984	1	0.693	0.704	66.9	62.2	12.8	12.5	9.2[e]	9.5[e]	13,278	16,050
109 Gabon	0.923	4	0.669	0.725	65.7	64.1	12.5	12.7	7.3[k]	9.0[k]	15,838	22,177
110 Paraguay	0.966	2	0.679	0.703	75.2	70.9	12.6	12.0	8.1	8.2	6,138	10,165
111 Egypt	0.884	5	0.640	0.724	73.6	69.2	13.0	13.2	6.4[h]	7.9[h]	4,750	15,267
111 Turkmenistan	..	..	..	..	70.0	61.6	10.6	11.0	..	..	9,359	18,856
113 Indonesia	0.926	3	0.660	0.712	71.2	67.0	12.9	12.9	7.4	8.5	6,668	13,391
114 Palestine, State of	0.867	5	0.616	0.710	75.1	71.1	13.7	12.1	8.6	9.3	1,766	8,651
115 Viet Nam	1.010	1	0.687	0.681	80.6	71.2	12.9	12.5	7.9[e]	8.2[e]	4,834	5,846
116 Philippines	1.001	1	0.682	0.681	71.9	65.0	12.1	11.4	9.5[f]	9.2[f]	6,845	9,917
117 El Salvador	0.958	2	0.663	0.691	77.7	68.6	13.0	13.3	6.2	6.9	5,386	10,385
118 Bolivia (Plurinational State of)	0.934	3	0.650	0.695	71.3	66.3	13.5	14.1	7.6	8.8	4,695	7,610
119 South Africa	0.962	2	0.651	0.677	59.5	55.5	13.6	12.5	10.2	10.5	8,795	15,489
120 Kyrgyzstan	0.967	2	0.648	0.671	74.8	66.8	13.3	12.7	10.9[e]	10.7[e]	2,123	4,090
121 Iraq	0.804	5	0.569	0.708	71.8	67.4	9.7[k]	11.5[k]	5.4[i]	7.8[i]	3,552	19,467

TABLE 4   Gender Development Index | 213

TABLE 4 GENDER DEVELOPMENT INDEX

	Gender Development Index		Human Development Index (HDI)		Life expectancy at birth		Expected years of schooling		Mean years of schooling		Estimated gross national income per capita[a]	
			Value		(years)		(years)		(years)		(2011 PPP $)	
	Value	Group[b]	Female	Male	Female	Male	Female	Male	Female	Male	Female	Male
HDI rank	2015	2015	2015	2015	2015	2015	2015[c]	2015[c]	2015[c]	2015[c]	2015	2015
122 Cabo Verde	..	..	..	..	75.2	71.6	13.9	13.1	..	..	4,030	8,123
123 Morocco	0.826	5	0.579	0.700	75.3	73.3	11.5	12.6	3.8[h]	6.4[h]	3,388	11,091
124 Nicaragua	0.961	2	0.629	0.654	78.2	72.2	11.9	11.4	6.8[h]	6.4[h]	3,150	6,389
125 Guatemala	0.959	2	0.624	0.651	75.6	68.5	10.5	11.0	6.3	6.3	5,132	9,081
125 Namibia	0.986	1	0.635	0.644	67.5	62.5	11.8	11.5	6.9[h]	6.5[h]	7,971	11,667
127 Guyana	0.943	3	0.615	0.652	68.9	64.2	10.5	10.2	8.5[e]	8.4[e]	4,346	9,397
127 Micronesia (Federated States of)	..	..	..	..	70.3	68.2	..	..	..	..	..	..
129 Tajikistan	0.930	3	0.604	0.650	73.4	66.3	10.6	11.9	9.6[k]	11.2[k]	2,100	3,088
130 Honduras	0.942	3	0.600	0.637	75.9	70.9	11.6	10.9	6.2	6.1	2,680	6,254
131 India	0.819	5	0.549	0.671	69.9	66.9	11.9	11.3	4.8[e]	8.2[e]	2,184	8,897
132 Bhutan	0.900	5	0.573	0.637	70.1	69.6	12.6	12.4	2.1[j]	4.2[j]	5,657	8,308
133 Timor-Leste	0.858	5	0.558	0.651	70.4	66.8	12.1	13.7	3.6[k]	5.3[k]	3,124	7,549
134 Vanuatu	..	..	..	..	74.3	70.2	10.4	11.1	..	..	2,139	3,453
135 Congo	0.932	3	0.568	0.610	64.4	61.4	11.0	11.3	5.5[e]	6.7[e]	4,731	6,274
135 Equatorial Guinea	..	..	..	..	59.4	56.6	..	..	4.0[k]	7.3[k]	17,462	25,375
137 Kiribati	..	..	..	..	69.5	63.0	12.3	11.5	..	..	..	..
138 Lao People's Democratic Republic	0.924	4	0.560	0.607	68.0	65.2	10.4	11.2	4.5[j]	5.6[j]	4,408	5,696
139 Bangladesh	0.927	3	0.556	0.599	73.3	70.7	10.4	9.9	5.0[e]	5.6[e]	2,379	4,285
139 Ghana	0.899	5	0.545	0.606	62.5	60.5	11.1	11.7	5.8[h]	7.9[h]	3,200	4,484
139 Zambia	0.924	4	0.555	0.601	62.9	58.8	12.1	13.0	6.4[h]	7.4[h]	2,803	4,126
142 Sao Tome and Principe	0.907	4	0.542	0.597	68.6	64.5	12.2	11.7	4.7	5.9	2,000	4,149
143 Cambodia	0.892	5	0.529	0.592	70.8	66.7	10.1	11.7	3.7	5.5	2,650	3,563
144 Nepal	0.925	4	0.538	0.582	71.5	68.6	12.7	12.2	3.2[j]	5.0[j]	1,979	2,718
145 Myanmar	..	..	..	..	68.2	64.0	..	..	4.9[h]	4.9[h]	4,182	5,740
146 Kenya	0.919	4	0.531	0.577	64.1	60.3	10.8	11.4	5.7[h]	7.0[h]	2,357	3,405
147 Pakistan	0.742	5	0.452	0.610	67.4	65.4	7.4	8.8	3.7	6.5	1,498	8,376
LOW HUMAN DEVELOPMENT												
148 Swaziland	0.853	5	0.495	0.580	48.1	49.6	11.0	11.8	6.4[j]	7.2[j]	5,078	10,020
149 Syrian Arab Republic	0.851	5	0.475	0.558	76.6	63.9	8.9	9.0	4.6	5.6	835	4,007
150 Angola	..	..	..	..	54.2	51.2	8.7	14.0	..	..	5,073	7,527
151 Tanzania (United Republic of)	0.937	3	0.512	0.546	66.9	64.1	8.3	9.3	5.4	6.2	2,359	2,576
152 Nigeria	0.847	5	0.482	0.569	53.4	52.7	9.2	10.8	4.9[k]	7.1[k]	4,132	6,706
153 Cameroon	0.853	5	0.474	0.555	57.1	54.8	9.6	11.3	4.6[e]	7.4[e]	2,340	3,448
154 Papua New Guinea	..	..	..	..	65.0	60.7	..	..	3.7[h]	5.3[h]	2,362	3,047
154 Zimbabwe	0.927	3	0.496	0.535	60.7	57.7	10.2	10.5	7.3	8.2	1,360	1,822
156 Solomon Islands	..	..	..	..	69.6	66.7	9.1[i]	10.1[i]	..	..	1,061	2,045
157 Mauritania	0.818	5	0.454	0.555	64.7	61.7	8.4	8.5	3.3[h]	5.4[h]	1,608	5,422
158 Madagascar	0.948	3	0.500	0.527	67.0	64.0	10.2	10.5	6.7	6.1	1,091	1,549
159 Rwanda	0.992	1	0.491	0.495	67.4	61.8	11.4	9.3	3.3	4.4	1,428	1,822
160 Comoros	0.817	5	0.437	0.535	65.3	61.9	10.9	11.3	3.7	5.6	715	1,945
160 Lesotho	0.962	2	0.485	0.505	50.0	49.9	11.2	10.3	7.0[f]	5.3[f]	2,631	4,020
162 Senegal	0.886	5	0.464	0.523	68.8	64.9	9.2	9.7	2.1[i]	3.6[i]	1,706	2,814
163 Haiti	..	..	..	..	65.3	61.0	..	..	3.9[e]	6.6[e]	1,370	1,950
163 Uganda	0.878	5	0.459	0.523	61.1	57.3	9.9	10.1	4.5[i]	6.8[i]	1,266	2,075
165 Sudan	0.839	5	0.441	0.526	65.3	62.2	7.0	7.4	3.0	4.1	1,902	5,775
166 Togo	0.841	5	0.444	0.528	60.9	59.4	10.8	13.1	3.2[k]	6.3[k]	1,116	1,412
167 Benin	0.858	5	0.461	0.538	61.2	58.3	10.5	13.7	2.8[e]	4.3[e]	1,673	2,287
168 Yemen	0.737	5	0.400	0.543	65.4	62.7	7.6	10.4	1.9[e]	4.2[e]	1,045	3,530
169 Afghanistan	0.609	5	0.348	0.572	62.0	59.5	8.3[i]	13.1[i]	1.6[h]	5.8[h]	511	3,148
170 Malawi	0.921	4	0.455	0.495	64.8	62.9	10.7	10.8	3.8[h]	5.0[h]	972	1,175
171 Côte d'Ivoire	0.814	5	0.421	0.517	52.8	51.1	7.8	9.8	3.9[h]	6.1[h]	2,136	4,155
172 Djibouti	..	..	..	..	64.0	60.7	5.8	6.8	..	..	1,981	4,441
173 Gambia	0.878	5	0.425	0.484	61.9	59.1	8.7	9.6	2.6[h]	4.2[h]	1,296	1,790
174 Ethiopia	0.842	5	0.408	0.484	66.6	62.7	7.9	8.8	1.5[k]	3.7[k]	1,161	1,886
175 Mali	0.786	5	0.385	0.491	58.3	58.6	7.5	9.4	1.7	3.0	1,349	3,071
176 Congo (Democratic Republic of the)	0.832	5	0.390	0.469	60.5	57.6	8.7	10.0	4.0	8.1	599	761
177 Liberia	0.830	5	0.387	0.466	62.2	60.2	9.3	10.6	3.1	6.0	575	788
178 Guinea-Bissau	..	..	..	..	57.3	53.7	..	..	..	..	1,139	1,603
179 Eritrea	..	..	..	..	66.3	62.0	4.4	5.6	..	..	1,286	1,693
179 Sierra Leone	0.871	5	0.392	0.451	51.9	50.8	9.1	10.0	2.6[h]	4.2[h]	1,354	1,708
181 Mozambique	0.879	5	0.391	0.444	56.8	54.0	8.6	9.5	2.5[k]	4.6[k]	1,016	1,184
181 South Sudan	..	..	..	..	57.1	55.2	3.8	6.3	4.0[j]	5.3[j]	..	..

HDI rank	Gender Development Index Value	Group[b]	Human Development Index (HDI) Value Female	Male	Life expectancy at birth (years) Female	Male	Expected years of schooling (years) Female	Male	Mean years of schooling (years) Female	Male	Estimated gross national income per capita[a] (2011 PPP $) Female	Male
	2015	2015	2015	2015	2015	2015	2015[c]	2015[c]	2015[c]	2015[c]	2015	2015
183 Guinea	0.784	5	0.364	0.464	59.7	58.7	7.5	10.1	1.5[k]	3.9[k]	848	1,267
184 Burundi	0.919	4	0.388	0.422	59.2	55.1	10.2	11.1	2.6[e]	3.6[e]	632	752
185 Burkina Faso	0.874	5	0.375	0.429	60.3	57.6	7.3	8.1	1.0	2.0	1,278	1,800
186 Chad	0.765	5	0.340	0.445	53.0	50.8	5.8	8.8	1.2	3.4	1,581	2,400
187 Niger	0.732	5	0.291	0.397	62.9	61.1	4.7	5.9	1.1[h]	2.3[h]	481	1,292
188 Central African Republic	0.776	5	0.306	0.395	53.4	49.5	5.8	8.4	2.8[i]	5.7[i]	482	696
OTHER COUNTRIES OR TERRITORIES												
Korea (Democratic People's Rep. of)	..	..	..	..	73.9	66.9	11.5	12.5	..	..	..	..
Marshall Islands	..	..	..	..	..	..	..	..	..	..	..	..
Monaco	..	..	..	..	..	..	..	..	..	..	..	..
Nauru	..	..	..	..	..	..	10.2	9.2	..	..	..	..
San Marino	..	..	..	..	..	..	15.6	14.6	..	..	..	..
Somalia	..	..	..	..	57.4	54.1	..	..	..	..	170	418
Tuvalu	..	..	..	..	..	..	..	..	..	..	..	..
Human development groups												
Very high human development	0.980	—	0.881	0.898	82.4	76.6	16.7	16.0	12.1	12.2	29,234	50,284
High human development	0.958	—	0.728	0.760	77.7	73.4	14.1	13.6	7.8	8.3	10,214	17,384
Medium human development	0.871	—	0.582	0.668	70.4	66.8	11.5	11.3	5.6	7.8	3,314	9,131
Low human development	0.849	—	0.455	0.536	60.7	58.0	8.5	10.0	3.6	5.6	1,950	3,365
Developing countries	0.913		0.635	0.695	71.9	68.2	11.8	11.9	6.5	7.9	6,053	12,390
Regions												
Arab States	0.856	—	0.621	0.726	72.8	69.1	11.4	12.1	5.9	7.6	5,455	23,810
East Asia and the Pacific	0.956	—	0.704	0.736	76.2	72.3	13.3	13.0	7.3	8.0	9,569	14,582
Europe and Central Asia	0.951	—	0.733	0.770	76.3	68.7	13.7	14.0	9.9	10.7	8,453	17,547
Latin America and the Caribbean	0.981	—	0.743	0.757	78.4	72.0	14.7	13.8	8.3	8.3	10,053	18,091
South Asia	0.822	—	0.549	0.667	70.2	67.4	11.3	11.1	4.9	7.8	2,278	9,114
Sub-Saharan Africa	0.877	—	0.488	0.557	60.2	57.6	9.1	10.3	4.5	6.3	2,637	4,165
Least developed countries	0.874	—	0.473	0.541	65.1	62.1	8.9	9.9	3.7	5.2	1,792	2,994
Small island developing states	..	—	..	..	72.7	67.9	..	..	..	..	5,223	9,256
Organisation for Economic Co-operation and Development	0.974	—	0.873	0.896	82.9	77.7	16.2	15.7	11.7	12.0	28,441	47,684
World	**0.938**	—	**0.693**	**0.738**	**73.8**	**69.6**	**12.4**	**12.3**	**7.7**	**8.8**	**10,306**	**18,555**

TABLE
4

NOTES

a Because disaggregated income data are not available, data are crudely estimated. See *Definitions* and *Technical note 3* at http://hdr. undp.org/sites/default/files/hdr2016_technical_ notes.pdf for details on how the Gender Development Index is calculated.

b Countries are divided into five groups by absolute deviation from gender parity in HDI values.

c Data refer to 2015 or the most recent year available.

d In calculating the HDI value, expected years of schooling is capped at 18 years.

e Updated by HDRO using Barro and Lee (2016) estimates.

f Updated by HDRO based on data from UNESCO Institute for Statistics (2016) and Barro and Lee (2016).

g In calculating the male HDI value, estimated gross national income per capita is capped at $75,000.

h Based on Barro and Lee (2016).

i Updated by HDRO based on data from UNESCO Institute for Statistics (2016).

j Based on data from United Nations Children's Fund (UNICEF) Multiple Indicator Cluster Surveys for 2006–2015.

k Updated by HDRO based on data from ICF Macro Demographic and Health Surveys for 2006–2015.

DEFINITIONS

Gender Development Index: Ratio of female to male HDI values. See *Technical note 3* at http://hdr.undp.org/sites/default/files/hdr2016_ technical_notes.pdf for details on how the Gender Development Index is calculated.

Gender Development Index groups: Countries are divided into five groups by absolute deviation from gender parity in HDI values. Group 1 comprises countries with high equality in HDI achievements between women and men (absolute deviation of less than 2.5 percent), group 2 comprises countries with medium to high equality in HDI achievements between women and men (absolute deviation of 2.5– 5 percent), group 3 comprises countries with medium equality in HDI achievements between women and men (absolute deviation of 5–7.5 percent), group 4 comprises countries with medium to low equality in HDI achievements between women and men (absolute deviation of 7.5–10 percent) and group 5 comprises countries with low equality in HDI achievements between women and men (absolute deviation from gender parity of more than 10 percent).

Human Development Index (HDI): A composite index measuring average achievement in three basic dimensions of human development—a long and healthy life, knowledge and a decent standard of living. See *Technical note 1* at http://hdr.undp.org/ sites/default/files/hdr2016_technical_notes.pdf for details on how the HDI is calculated.

Life expectancy at birth: Number of years a newborn infant could expect to live if prevailing patterns of age specific mortality rates at the time of birth stay the same throughout the infant's life.

Expected years of schooling: Number of years of schooling that a child of school entrance age can expect to receive if prevailing patterns of age-specific enrolment rates persist throughout the child's life.

Mean years of schooling: Average number of years of education received by people ages 25 and older, converted from educational attainment levels using official durations of each level.

Estimated gross national income per capita: Derived from the ratio of female to male wages, female and male shares of economically active population and gross national income (in 2011 purchasing power parity terms). See *Technical*

note 3 at http://hdr.undp.org/sites/default/files/ hdr2016_technical_notes.pdf for details.

MAIN DATA SOURCES

Column 1: Calculated based on data in columns 3 and 4.

Column 2: Calculated based on data in column 1.

Columns 3 and 4: HDRO calculations based on data from UNDESA (2015a), UNESCO Institute for Statistics (2016), Barro and Lee (2016), World Bank (2016a), ILO (2016a) and IMF (2016).

Columns 5 and 6: UNDESA (2015a).

Columns 7 and 8: UNESCO Institute for Statistics (2016), ICF Macro Demographic and Health Surveys and UNICEF Multiple Indicator Cluster Surveys.

Columns 9 and 10: UNESCO Institute for Statistics (2016), Barro and Lee (2016), ICF Macro Demographic and Health Surveys and UNICEF Multiple Indicator Cluster Surveys.

Columns 11 and 12: HDRO calculations based on ILO (2016a), UNDESA (2015a), World Bank (2016a) and IMF (2016).

TABLE 4 Gender Development Index | 215

TABLE **5**

Gender Inequality Index

TABLE
5

HDI rank	Gender Inequality Index Value 2015	Gender Inequality Index Rank 2015	Maternal mortality ratio (deaths per 100,000 live births) 2015	Adolescent birth rate (births per 1,000 women ages 15–19) 2015[a]	Share of seats in parliament (% held by women) 2015	Population with at least some secondary education (% ages 25 and older) Female 2005–2015[b]	Population with at least some secondary education (% ages 25 and older) Male 2005–2015[b]	Labour force participation rate (% ages 15 and older) Female 2015	Labour force participation rate (% ages 15 and older) Male 2015
VERY HIGH HUMAN DEVELOPMENT									
1 Norway	0.053	6	5	5.9	39.6	96.1	94.6	61.2	68.5
2 Australia	0.120	24	6	14.1	30.5	91.4	91.5	58.6	70.9
2 Switzerland	0.040	1	5	2.9	28.9	96.1	97.4	62.7	74.8
4 Germany	0.066	9	6	6.7	36.9	96.4	97.0	54.5	66.4
5 Denmark	0.041	2	6	4.0	37.4	89.1	98.5	58.0	66.2
5 Singapore	0.068	11	10	3.8	23.9	75.5	81.9	58.2	76.4
7 Netherlands	0.044	3	7	4.0	36.4	86.2	90.3	57.5	70.2
8 Ireland	0.127	26	8	10.4	19.9	86.8	82.2	52.4	67.8
9 Iceland	0.051	5	3	6.1	41.3	100.0	97.2	70.7	77.5
10 Canada	0.098	18	7	9.8	28.3	100.0	100.0	61.0	70.3
10 United States	0.203	43	14	22.6	19.5	95.4	95.1	56.0	68.4
12 Hong Kong, China (SAR)	..	..	..	3.2	..	80.9	74.7	53.4	68.5
13 New Zealand	0.158	34	11	23.6	31.4	98.8	98.7	62.4	73.1
14 Sweden	0.048	4	4	5.7	43.6	87.8	88.3	60.9	68.2
15 Liechtenstein	..	..	..	..	20.0	..	..	..	..
16 United Kingdom	0.131	28	9	14.6	26.7	81.3	84.6	56.9	68.7
17 Japan	0.116	21	5	4.1	11.6	93.0	90.6	49.1	70.2
18 Korea (Republic of)	0.067	10	11	1.6	16.3	88.8	94.6	50.0	71.8
19 Israel	0.103	20	5	9.7	26.7	87.3	90.3	58.9	69.4
20 Luxembourg	0.075	13	10	5.9	28.3	100.6	99.4	52.2	66.1
21 France	0.102	19	8	8.9	25.7	79.7	85.5	50.7	60.1
22 Belgium	0.073	12	7	8.2	42.4	80.1	84.7	48.2	59.3
23 Finland	0.056	8	3	6.5	41.5	100.0	100.0	55.0	62.1
24 Austria	0.078	14	4	7.1	30.3	98.7	99.2	54.7	66.0
25 Slovenia	0.053	6	9	3.8	27.7	96.5	98.3	52.2	63.0
26 Italy	0.085	16	4	6.0	30.1	79.1	83.3	39.3	58.1
27 Spain	0.081	15	5	8.4	38.0	70.9	76.7	52.3	64.8
28 Czech Republic	0.129	27	4	9.9	19.6	99.8	99.8	51.1	68.2
29 Greece	0.119	23	3	7.5	19.7	63.7	71.7	43.9	60.0
30 Brunei Darussalam	..	..	23	21.0	..	67.7[c]	69.6[c]	51.0	75.3
30 Estonia	0.131	28	9	13.1	23.8	100.0	100.0	55.4	69.5
32 Andorra	..	..	..	..	39.3	72.0	73.7	..	..
33 Cyprus	0.116	21	7	5.0	12.5	77.0	82.7	57.5	70.2
33 Malta	0.217	44	9	16.6	12.9	72.7	81.2	38.8	66.0
33 Qatar	0.542	127	13	10.7	0.0[d]	70.9	67.8	53.6	94.2
36 Poland	0.137	30	3	13.4	24.8	81.1	86.9	49.1	65.3
37 Lithuania	0.121	25	10	11.0	23.4	91.1	95.6	53.9	65.5
38 Chile	0.322	65	22	47.8	15.8	76.1	76.9	50.7	74.6
38 Saudi Arabia	0.257	50	12	8.8	19.9	63.3	72.1	20.1	79.1
40 Slovakia	0.179	39	6	20.2	18.7	99.2	99.5	51.4	68.3
41 Portugal	0.091	17	10	9.9	34.8	50.8	52.2	53.6	64.2
42 United Arab Emirates	0.232	46	6	29.7	22.5	77.4	64.5	41.9	91.6
43 Hungary	0.252	49	17	18.0	10.1	95.6	97.9	46.4	62.5
44 Latvia	0.191	41	18	13.6	18.0	99.3	98.8	54.4	67.7
45 Argentina	0.362	77	52	63.8	37.1[e]	63.5	61.4	48.4	74.5
45 Croatia	0.141	31	8	9.5	15.2	92.0	96.0	46.4	58.7
47 Bahrain	0.233	48	15	13.5	15.0	61.6[c]	55.6[c]	39.2	85.4
48 Montenegro	0.156	33	7	12.2	17.3	86.9	96.2	42.0	56.1
49 Russian Federation	0.271	52	25	23.4	14.5	94.6	94.7	56.6	71.7
50 Romania	0.339	72	31	34.6	12.0	86.1	92.2	47.6	64.9
51 Kuwait	0.335	70	4	9.8	1.5	56.8	58.1	48.4	84.5
HIGH HUMAN DEVELOPMENT									
52 Belarus	0.144	32	4	18.2	29.2	87.0	92.2	54.5	68.2
52 Oman	0.281	54	17	8.1	8.2	59.8	57.1	30.0	85.6
54 Barbados	0.291	59	27	40.7	19.6	93.0	90.6	62.4	70.7
54 Uruguay	0.284	55	15	56.1	19.2	55.0	51.6	55.4	76.3
56 Bulgaria	0.223	45	11	37.7	20.4	93.1	95.5	48.6	60.1
56 Kazakhstan	0.202	42	12	27.9	20.1	99.7	100.0	66.1	77.0
58 Bahamas	0.362	77	80	29.6	16.7	87.4	87.6	69.4	79.1
59 Malaysia	0.291	59	40	13.6	13.2	75.4	79.1	49.3	77.6
60 Palau	..	..	..	..	10.3	..	..	..	..

	Gender Inequality Index		Maternal mortality ratio	Adolescent birth rate	Share of seats in parliament	Population with at least some secondary education		Labour force participation rate	
						(% ages 25 and older)		(% ages 15 and older)	
	Value	Rank	(deaths per 100,000 live births)	(births per 1,000 women ages 15–19)	(% held by women)	Female	Male	Female	Male
HDI rank	2015	2015	2015	2015[a]	2015	2005–2015[b]	2005–2015[b]	2015	2015
60 Panama	0.457	100	94	74.5	18.3	70.1	66.1	50.5	80.5
62 Antigua and Barbuda	..	..	..	44.8	25.7	..	..	..	..
63 Seychelles	..	..	..	57.4	43.8	..	..	..	..
64 Mauritius	0.380	82	53	28.5	11.6	57.0	62.0	46.8	74.9
65 Trinidad and Tobago	0.324	67	63	31.5	31.5	70.6	68.4	52.6	73.6
66 Costa Rica	0.308	63	25	56.5	33.3	54.5	53.8	46.8	76.6
66 Serbia	0.185	40	17	19.0	34.0	82.3	91.6	43.4	60.1
68 Cuba	0.304	62	39	45.6	48.9	83.9	86.7	42.6	68.6
69 Iran (Islamic Republic of)	0.509	118	25	26.7	3.1	66.8	70.2	16.2	72.7
70 Georgia	0.361	76	36	39.7	11.3	96.1	97.4	57.3	78.4
71 Turkey	0.328	69	16	27.6	14.9	43.5	64.8	30.4	71.4
71 Venezuela (Bolivarian Republic of)	0.461	101	95	79.4	17.0	72.6	65.0	51.4	78.4
73 Sri Lanka	0.386	87	30	14.8	4.9	80.2	80.6	30.2	75.6
74 Saint Kitts and Nevis	..	..	..	..	13.3	..	..	..	..
75 Albania	0.267	51	29	21.7	20.7	90.2	90.5	40.3	60.7
76 Lebanon	0.381	83	15	12.4	3.1	53.0	55.4	23.5	70.3
77 Mexico	0.345	73	38	62.8	40.6	56.1	59.0	45.4	79.5
78 Azerbaijan	0.326	68	25	59.8	16.9	93.9	97.5	61.9	68.3
79 Brazil	0.414	92	44	67.0	10.8	59.1	55.2	56.3	78.5
79 Grenada	..	..	27	30.5	25.0	..	..	..	..
81 Bosnia and Herzegovina	0.158	34	11	8.6	19.3	69.5	87.5	34.4	58.0
82 The former Yugoslav Republic of Macedonia	0.160	36	8	17.6	33.3	40.2	55.6	43.9	68.1
83 Algeria	0.429	94	140	10.6	25.7	34.1	35.7	16.8	70.4
84 Armenia	0.293	61	25	23.0	10.7	98.5	98.1	54.9	73.6
84 Ukraine	0.284	55	24	24.1	12.1	94.3	96.0	52.2	67.4
86 Jordan	0.478	111	58	23.2	11.6	78.5	82.7	14.2	64.4
87 Peru	0.385	86	68	49.1	22.3	56.2	67.0	65.7	82.6
87 Thailand	0.366	79	20	44.6	6.1	40.9	45.8	62.9	80.2
89 Ecuador	0.391	88	64	75.9	41.6	48.2	49.4	49.0	79.7
90 China	0.164	37	27	7.3	23.6	69.8	79.4	63.6	77.9
91 Fiji	0.358	75	30	44.8	16.0	73.9	66.5	37.0	71.3
92 Mongolia	0.278	53	44	15.7	14.5	89.7	85.8	56.5	68.8
92 Saint Lucia	0.354	74	48	53.9	20.7	48.2	42.0	63.1	76.5
94 Jamaica	0.422	93	89	59.7	16.7	67.1	59.4	57.7	72.2
95 Colombia	0.393	89	64	50.2	20.9	50.3	59.6	57.9	79.8
96 Dominica	..	..	..	..	21.9	..	..	..	..
97 Suriname	0.448	99	155	46.1	25.5	57.7	56.8	40.5	68.6
97 Tunisia	0.289	58	62	6.0	31.3	32.8	46.0	25.1	71.0
99 Dominican Republic	0.470	107	92	97.9	19.1	57.2	55.5	52.3	78.7
99 Saint Vincent and the Grenadines	..	..	45	51.0	13.0	..	..	56.3	77.2
101 Tonga	0.659	152	124	15.2	0.0[d]	91.2	91.1	52.8	74.0
102 Libya	0.167	38	9	6.2	16.0	65.7[c]	44.2[c]	27.8	78.7
103 Belize	0.375	81	28	65.9	13.3	77.9	77.4	56.3	83.6
104 Samoa	0.439	97	51	25.0	6.1	77.8	70.4	23.1	58.0
105 Maldives	0.312	64	68	6.7	5.9	34.3	30.9	57.3	78.8
105 Uzbekistan	0.287	57	36	17.7	16.4	99.9	99.9	48.3	76.2
MEDIUM HUMAN DEVELOPMENT									
107 Moldova (Republic of)	0.232	46	23	22.6	21.8	95.2	97.3	38.8	45.6
108 Botswana	0.435	95	129	32.3	9.5	85.1[c]	86.7[c]	73.4	81.3
109 Gabon	0.542	127	291	99.9	16.0	62.3[c]	45.9[c]	39.9	57.5
110 Paraguay	0.464	104	132	57.4	16.8	46.2	47.0	58.1	84.6
111 Egypt	0.565	135	33	51.9	2.2[f]	54.5[c]	68.2[c]	22.8	76.1
111 Turkmenistan	..	..	42	16.4	25.8	..	..	47.3	77.5
113 Indonesia	0.467	105	126	49.6	17.1	42.9	51.7	50.9	83.9
114 Palestine, State of	..	..	45	58.6	..	56.3	61.2	17.8	69.1
115 Viet Nam	0.337	71	54	38.6	24.3	64.0	76.7	73.8	83.2
116 Philippines	0.436	96	114	61.7	27.1	72.8	70.3	50.5	78.8
117 El Salvador	0.384	85	54	65.2	32.1	39.4	44.8	49.1	79.2
118 Bolivia (Plurinational State of)	0.446	98	206	70.8	51.8	49.6	58.7	63.9	82.5
119 South Africa	0.394	90	138	45.5	41.2[g]	73.7	76.2	46.2	60.2
120 Kyrgyzstan	0.394	90	76	39.6	19.2	100.0	99.9	49.4	77.1
121 Iraq	0.525	123	50	84.0	26.5	35.8[c]	55.5[c]	15.1	69.7

TABLE 5 Gender Inequality Index | 217

TABLE
5

TABLE 5   GENDER INEQUALITY INDEX

HDI rank	Gender Inequality Index Value 2015	Rank 2015	Maternal mortality ratio (deaths per 100,000 live births) 2015	Adolescent birth rate (births per 1,000 women ages 15–19) 2015[a]	Share of seats in parliament (% held by women) 2015	Population with at least some secondary education (% ages 25 and older) Female 2005–2015[b]	Male 2005–2015[b]	Labour force participation rate (% ages 15 and older) Female 2015	Male 2015
122 Cabo Verde	..	..	42	73.4	20.8[h]	..	..	53.2	84.2
123 Morocco	0.494	113	121	31.7	15.7	25.7[c]	33.2[c]	25.3	74.3
124 Nicaragua	0.462	103	150	88.8	41.3	45.7[c]	44.1[c]	49.1	80.3
125 Guatemala	0.494	113	88	80.7	13.9	37.4	36.2	41.3	83.6
125 Namibia	0.474	108	265	76.8	37.7	38.1	39.0	55.7	63.3
127 Guyana	0.508	117	229	88.0	30.4	68.1[c]	53.2[c]	41.8	77.2
127 Micronesia (Federated States of)	..	..	100	15.0	0.0[d]	..	..	..	..
129 Tajikistan	0.322	65	32	38.1	14.7	98.1	88.2	59.4	77.5
130 Honduras	0.461	101	129	65.0	25.8	33.4	31.1	47.2	84.4
131 India	0.530	125	174	24.5	12.2	35.3[c]	61.4[c]	26.8	79.1
132 Bhutan	0.477	110	148	21.4	8.3	5.8	13.4	58.7	72.8
133 Timor-Leste	..	..	215	46.6	38.5	..	..	26.8	55.5
134 Vanuatu	..	..	78	43.1	0.0[d]	..	..	61.6	80.5
135 Congo	0.592	141	442	117.7	11.5	45.0[c]	50.0[c]	67.1	72.6
135 Equatorial Guinea	..	..	342	108.7	19.7	..	..	71.3	92.0
137 Kiribati	..	..	90	17.2	8.7	..	..	..	..
138 Lao People's Democratic Republic	0.468	106	197	64.1	25.0	30.4[c]	42.8[c]	77.7	77.0
139 Bangladesh	0.520	119	176	83.0	20.0	42.0[c]	44.3[c]	43.1	81.0
139 Ghana	0.547	131	319	66.8	10.9	51.8	68.5	75.5	78.5
139 Zambia	0.526	124	224	90.4	12.7	52.3	48.9	69.8	80.9
142 Sao Tome and Principe	0.524	122	156	84.3	18.2	30.8	44.8	45.3	76.2
143 Cambodia	0.479	112	161	51.6	19.0	13.2	26.1	75.5	86.7
144 Nepal	0.497	115	258	71.9	29.5	24.1[c]	41.2[c]	79.7	86.8
145 Myanmar	0.374	80	178	16.5	13.0	27.1[c]	20.0[c]	75.1	81.1
146 Kenya	0.565	135	510	90.9	20.8	27.8	34.1	62.1	72.1
147 Pakistan	0.546	130	178	38.7	20.0	26.5	46.1	24.3	82.2
LOW HUMAN DEVELOPMENT									
148 Swaziland	0.566	137	389	70.4	14.7	27.3[c]	30.5[c]	40.0	64.2
149 Syrian Arab Republic	0.554	133	68	39.4	12.4	34.8	43.4	12.2	70.8
150 Angola	..	..	477	164.3	36.8	..	..	59.9	77.1
151 Tanzania (United Republic of)	0.544	129	398	118.6	36.0	10.1	15.3	74.0	83.3
152 Nigeria	..	..	814	110.6	5.8	..	..	48.4	64.0
153 Cameroon	0.568	138	596	104.6	27.1	31.7	37.9	71.0	81.1
154 Papua New Guinea	0.595	143	215	54.8	2.7	8.8[c]	14.7[c]	69.6	71.0
154 Zimbabwe	0.540	126	443	109.7	35.1	51.9	64.7	77.8	87.3
156 Solomon Islands	..	..	114	48.4	2.0	..	..	61.1	73.5
157 Mauritania	0.626	147	602	78.6	22.2	11.1[c]	23.5[c]	29.1	65.3
158 Madagascar	..	..	353	116.2	20.5	..	..	83.8	89.1
159 Rwanda	0.383	84	290	26.3	57.5	10.5	16.4	86.4	83.2
160 Comoros	..	..	335	68.3	3.0	..	..	35.3	79.4
160 Lesotho	0.549	132	487	92.7	24.8	23.6	22.5	59.2	73.9
162 Senegal	0.521	120	315	78.6	42.7	10.2	19.2	45.0	70.2
163 Haiti	0.593	142	359	39.3	3.5	25.7[c]	38.7[c]	61.5	71.4
163 Uganda	0.522	121	343	111.9	35.0	25.9	32.1	82.3	87.7
165 Sudan	0.575	140	311	74.0	31.0	13.7[c]	18.8[c]	24.3	72.2
166 Togo	0.556	134	368	92.0	17.6	23.1	36.1	81.1	80.6
167 Benin	0.613	144	405	83.2	7.2	15.8	30.8	70.0	73.4
168 Yemen	0.767	159	385	61.5	0.5	15.6[c]	33.2[c]	25.8	73.1
169 Afghanistan	0.667	154	396	74.0	27.4	8.8[c]	35.4[c]	19.1	83.6
170 Malawi	0.614	145	634	136.2	16.7	14.9	24.2	81.2	80.8
171 Côte d'Ivoire	0.672	155	645	135.5	9.2	16.6[c]	32.7[c]	52.4	80.9
172 Djibouti	..	..	229	21.5	12.7	..	..	36.5	68.1
173 Gambia	0.641	148	706	113.0	9.4	25.3[c]	39.1[c]	72.2	82.7
174 Ethiopia	0.499	116	353	58.4	37.3	10.8	20.7	77.0	89.1
175 Mali	0.689	156	587	174.6	8.8	7.3	16.2	50.1	82.3
176 Congo (Democratic Republic of the)	0.663	153	693	122.6	8.2	14.5[c]	35.0[c]	70.5	71.8
177 Liberia	0.649	150	725	108.8	10.7	17.3[c]	39.7[c]	58.0	63.9
178 Guinea-Bissau	..	..	549	89.5	13.7	..	..	67.2	78.3
179 Eritrea	..	..	501	54.3	22.0	..	..	77.7	90.2
179 Sierra Leone	0.650	151	1,360	118.2	12.4	16.8[c]	29.7[c]	65.0	68.6

HDI rank	Gender Inequality Index — Value 2015	Gender Inequality Index — Rank 2015	Maternal mortality ratio (deaths per 100,000 live births) 2015	Adolescent birth rate (births per 1,000 women ages 15–19) 2015[a]	Share of seats in parliament (% held by women) 2015	Population with at least some secondary education (% ages 25 and older) Female 2005–2015[b]	Population with at least some secondary education (% ages 25 and older) Male 2005–2015[b]	Labour force participation rate (% ages 15 and older) Female 2015	Labour force participation rate (% ages 15 and older) Male 2015
181 Mozambique	0.574	139	489	139.7	39.6	2.8[c]	8.0[c]	82.5	75.4
181 South Sudan	..	..	789	65.9	24.3	..	..	71.2	75.3
183 Guinea	..	..	679	140.6	21.9	..	..	79.5	85.1
184 Burundi	0.474	108	712	28.3	37.8	7.1[c]	9.6[c]	84.6	82.7
185 Burkina Faso	0.615	146	371	108.5	9.4	6.0	11.5	76.6	90.7
186 Chad	0.695	157	856	133.5	14.9	1.7	9.9	64.0	79.3
187 Niger	0.695	157	553	202.4	13.3	3.6[c]	8.4[c]	40.2	89.4
188 Central African Republic	0.648	149	882	91.9	12.5[f]	12.3[c]	29.8[c]	71.7	84.6
OTHER COUNTRIES OR TERRITORIES									
Korea (Democratic People's Rep. of)	..	..	82	0.5	16.3	..	..	73.6	85.9
Marshall Islands	..	..	..	..	9.1	91.6	92.5	..	..
Monaco	..	..	..	..	20.8	..	..	..	..
Nauru	..	..	..	..	5.3	..	..	..	..
San Marino	..	..	..	..	16.7	..	..	..	..
Somalia	..	..	732	103.9	13.8	..	..	33.2	75.9
Tuvalu	..	..	..	..	6.7	..	..	..	..
Human development groups									
Very high human development	0.174	—	14	17.0	25.8	88.4	89.3	52.6	68.6
High human development	0.291	—	36	27.4	21.6	66.9	74.0	56.5	77.1
Medium human development	0.491	—	164	40.8	19.9	40.4	57.6	37.2	79.4
Low human development	0.590	—	553	101.8	22.0	14.8	25.9	60.3	77.1
Developing countries	0.469	—	231	48.8	21.0	51.7	63.4	48.7	78.2
Regions									
Arab States	0.535	—	142	47.7	15.5	41.6	52.3	22.3	75.1
East Asia and the Pacific	0.315	—	63	23.1	19.6	64.1	73.0	62.3	79.1
Europe and Central Asia	0.279	—	24	26.6	19.0	78.1	85.7	45.4	70.5
Latin America and the Caribbean	0.390	—	67	64.3	28.1	57.8	58.1	52.8	78.6
South Asia	0.520	—	175	33.7	17.4	36.9	58.6	28.3	79.4
Sub-Saharan Africa	0.572	—	551	103.0	23.3	25.3	33.9	64.9	76.1
Least developed countries	0.555	—	436[T]	91.4	22.3	21.8	29.5	61.5	80.9
Small island developing states	0.463	—	204	59.0	23.4	55.2	58.2	53.4	72.7
Organisation for Economic Co-operation and Development	0.194	—	15	22.4	27.7	84.2	86.9	51.1	68.6
World	**0.443**	**—**	**216**[T]	**44.7**	**22.5**	**60.3**	**69.2**	**49.6**	**76.2**

NOTES

a Data are average of period estimates for 2010–2015 and projections for 2015–2020.

b Data refer to the most recent year available during the period specified.

c Based on Barro and Lee (2016).

d In calculating the Gender Inequality Index, a value of 0.1 percent was used.

e Refers to 2014.

f Refers to 2012.

g Excludes the 36 special rotating delegates appointed on an ad hoc basis.

h Refers to 2013.

T From original data source.

DEFINITIONS

Gender Inequality Index: A composite measure reflecting inequality in achievement between women and men in three dimensions: reproductive health, empowerment and the labour market. See *Technical note 4* at http://hdr.undp.org/sites/default/files/hdr2016_technical_notes.pdf for details on how the Gender Inequality Index is calculated.

Maternal mortality ratio: Number of deaths due to pregnancy-related causes per 100,000 live births.

Adolescent birth rate: Number of births to women ages 15–19 per 1,000 women ages 15–19.

Share of seats in parliament: Proportion of seats held by women in the national parliament expressed as percentage of total seats. For countries with a bicameral legislative system, the share of seats is calculated based on both houses.

Population with at least some secondary education: Percentage of the population ages 25 and older that has reached (but not necessarily completed) a secondary level of education.

Labour force participation rate: Proportion of the working-age population (ages 15 and older) that engages in the labour market, either by working or actively looking for work, expressed as a percentage of the working-age population.

MAIN DATA SOURCES

Column 1: HDRO calculations based on data in columns 3–9.

Column 2: Calculated based on data in column 1.

Column 3: UN Maternal Mortality Estimation Group (2016).

Column 4: UNDESA (2015a).

Column 5: IPU (2016).

Columns 6 and 7: UNESCO Institute for Statistics (2016).

Columns 8 and 9: ILO (2016a).

TABLE **5**

TABLE 5   Gender Inequality Index | 219

TABLE 6

Multidimensional Poverty Index: developing countries

TABLE 6

Country	Multidimensional Poverty Index[a] Year and survey[b] 2005–2015	Index Value	Population in multidimensional poverty[a] Headcount (%)	Headcount (thousands)	Intensity of deprivation (%)	Population near multidimensional poverty[a] (%)	Population in severe multidimensional poverty[a] (%)	Contribution of deprivation in dimension to overall poverty[a] (%) Education	Health	Living standards	Population living below income poverty line (%) National poverty line 2005–2014[c]	PPP $1.90 a day 2005–2014[c]
Afghanistan	2010/2011 M	0.293 [d]	58.8 [d]	16,942 [d]	49.9 [d]	16.0 [d]	29.8 [d]	45.6 [d]	19.2 [d]	35.2 [d]	35.8	..
Albania	2008/2009 D	0.005	1.2	35	38.3	7.2	0.1	22.4	47.1	30.5	14.3	1.1
Argentina	2005 N	0.015 [e]	3.7 [e]	1,457 [e]	39.1 [e]	5.2 [e]	0.5 [e]	38.2 [e]	27.8 [e]	34.0 [e]	..	1.7
Armenia	2010 D	0.002	0.6	18	37.0	3.0	0.1	3.4	87.8	8.7	30.0	2.3
Azerbaijan	2006 D	0.009	2.4	210	38.2	11.5	0.2	20.0	50.7	29.3	6.0	0.5
Bangladesh	2014 D	0.188	40.7	64,816	46.2	19.6	16.0	28.4	26.1	45.5	31.5	18.5
Barbados	2012 M	0.004 [f]	1.2 [f]	3 [f]	33.7 [f]	0.3 [f]	0.0 [f]	1.5 [f]	95.9 [f]	2.6 [f]	..	..
Belarus	2005 M	0.001	0.4	41	34.5	1.1	0.0	2.6	89.7	7.7	5.1	0.0
Belize	2011 M	0.030	7.4	24	41.2	6.4	1.5	36.2	34.8	29.0	..	..
Benin	2011/2012 D	0.343	64.2	6,454	53.3	16.9	37.7	33.1	24.8	42.1	36.2	53.1
Bhutan	2010 M	0.128	29.4	212	43.5	18.0	8.8	40.3	26.3	33.4	12.0	2.2
Bolivia (Plurinational State of)	2008 D	0.097	20.6	1,974	47.0	17.3	7.8	21.9	27.9	50.2	38.6	6.8
Bosnia and Herzegovina	2011/2012 M	0.006 [f]	1.7 [f]	65 [f]	37.3 [f]	3.2 [f]	0.0 [f]	7.8 [f]	79.5 [f]	12.7 [f]	17.9	0.1
Brazil	2014 N	0.010 [d,g]	2.4 [d,g]	4,994 [d,g]	40.0 [d,g]	6.7 [d,g]	0.3 [d,g]	24.9 [d,g]	45.1 [d,g]	30.1 [d,g]	7.4	3.7
Burkina Faso	2010 D	0.508	82.8	12,951	61.3	7.6	63.8	39.0	22.5	38.5	40.1	43.7
Burundi	2010 D	0.442	81.8	7,740	54.0	12.0	48.2	25.0	26.3	48.8	64.6	77.7
Cambodia	2014 D	0.150	33.8	5,180	44.3	21.6	11.4	30.8	26.4	42.8	17.7	2.2
Cameroon	2011 D	0.260	48.2	10,170	54.1	17.8	27.1	24.5	31.3	44.2	37.5	24.0
Central African Republic	2010 M	0.424	76.3	3,392	55.6	15.7	48.5	23.8	26.2	50.0	62.0	66.3
Chad	2010 M	0.545	86.9	10,339	62.7	8.8	67.6	32.3	22.5	45.2	46.7	38.4
China	2012 N	0.023 [g]	5.2 [g]	70,807 [g]	43.3 [g]	22.7 [g]	1.0 [g]	30.0 [g]	36.6 [g]	33.4 [g]	..	1.9
Colombia	2010 D	0.032	7.6	3,494	42.2	10.2	1.8	34.3	24.7	41.0	27.8	5.7
Comoros	2012 D/M	0.165	34.3	252	48.1	23.1	14.9	29.1	25.9	45.0	44.8	13.5
Congo	2011/2012 D	0.192	43.0	1,844	44.7	26.2	12.2	10.6	32.8	56.6	46.5	37.0
Congo (Democratic Republic of the)	2013/2014 D	0.369	72.5	54,314	50.8	18.5	36.7	15.6	31.0	53.4	63.6	77.1
Côte d'Ivoire	2011/2012 D	0.307	59.3	12,521	51.7	17.9	32.4	36.5	25.8	37.7	46.3	29.0
Djibouti	2006 M	0.127	26.9	213	47.3	16.0	11.1	36.1	22.7	41.2	..	22.5
Dominican Republic	2013 D	0.025	6.0	613	41.6	20.6	1.0	28.4	39.6	32.0	32.4	2.3
Ecuador	2013/2014 N	0.015	3.7	585	39.6	8.4	0.5	23.6	42.4	34.0	23.3	3.8
Egypt	2014 D	0.016 [h]	4.2 [h]	3,750 [h]	37.4 [h]	5.6 [h]	0.4 [h]	45.6 [h]	46.7 [h]	7.8 [h]	25.2	..
Ethiopia	2011 D	0.537	88.2	79,298	60.9	6.7	67.0	27.4	25.2	47.4	29.6	33.5
Gabon	2012 D	0.073	16.7	270	43.4	19.9	4.4	15.2	43.8	40.9	32.7	8.0
Gambia	2013 D	0.289	57.2	1,068	50.5	21.3	31.7	32.9	30.9	36.2	48.4	..
Georgia	2005 M	0.008	2.2	99	37.6	4.1	0.1	7.4	67.4	25.2	14.8	9.8
Ghana	2014 D	0.147	32.4	8,688	45.4	20.5	11.1	27.2	31.5	41.2	24.2	25.2
Guinea	2012 D/M	0.425	73.8	8,588	57.6	12.7	49.8	36.6	22.8	40.6	55.2	35.3
Guinea-Bissau	2006 M	0.495	80.4	1,201	61.6	10.5	58.4	30.5	27.9	41.6	69.3	67.1
Guyana	2009 D	0.031	7.8	59	40.0	18.8	1.2	16.8	51.2	32.0	..	..
Haiti	2012 D	0.242	50.2	5,161	48.1	22.2	20.1	24.8	23.4	51.8	58.5	53.9
Honduras	2011/2012 D	0.098 [i]	20.7 [i]	1,601 [i]	47.4 [i]	28.6 [i]	7.2 [i]	36.6 [i]	23.1 [i]	40.3 [i]	62.8	16.0
India	2005/2006 D	0.282	55.3	642,391	51.1	18.2	27.8	22.7	32.5	44.8	21.9	21.2
Indonesia	2012 D	0.024 [d]	5.9 [d]	14,644 [d]	41.3 [d]	8.1 [d]	1.1 [d]	24.7 [d]	35.1 [d]	40.2 [d]	11.3	8.3
Iraq	2011 M	0.052	13.3	4,241	39.4	7.4	2.5	50.1	38.6	11.3	18.9	..
Jamaica	2012 N	0.011 [f,g]	2.7 [f,g]	76 [f,g]	40.5 [f,g]	9.6 [f,g]	0.5 [f,g]	8.8 [f,g]	52.0 [f,g]	39.2 [f,g]	19.9	1.7
Jordan	2012 D	0.004	1.2	85	35.3	1.0	0.1	31.5	65.0	3.5	14.4	..
Kazakhstan	2010/2011 M	0.004	1.1	178	36.4	2.3	0.0	4.3	83.9	11.8	2.7	0.0
Kenya	2014 D	0.166	36.0	16,170	46.1	32.0	10.7	12.3	32.2	55.5	45.9	33.6
Kyrgyzstan	2014 M	0.008	2.2	127	36.3	6.5	0.0	13.0	73.5	13.5	32.1	1.3
Lao People's Democratic Republic	2011/2012 M	0.186	36.8	2,383	50.5	18.5	18.8	37.7	25.4	36.9	23.2	16.7
Lesotho	2009 D	0.227	49.5	984	45.9	20.4	18.2	14.8	33.8	51.4	57.1	59.7
Liberia	2013 D	0.356	70.1	3,010	50.8	21.5	35.4	23.0	25.6	51.4	63.8	68.6
Libya	2007 P	0.005	1.4	82	37.5	6.3	0.1	31.9	47.9	20.2	..	..
Madagascar	2008/2009 D	0.420	77.0	15,774	54.6	11.7	48.0	31.6	24.5	43.9	75.3	77.8
Malawi	2013/2014 M	0.273	56.1	9,369	48.6	27.2	24.3	19.3	27.2	53.5	50.7	70.9
Maldives	2009 D	0.008	2.0	7	37.5	8.5	0.1	27.8	60.2	11.9	15.7	7.3
Mali	2012/2013 D	0.456	78.4	13,009	58.2	10.8	55.9	37.9	22.4	39.7	43.6	49.3
Mauritania	2011 M	0.291	55.6	2,049	52.4	16.8	29.9	34.5	20.3	45.3	42.0	5.9
Mexico	2012 N	0.024	6.0	7,346	39.9	10.1	1.1	31.4	25.6	43.0	53.2	3.0
Moldova (Republic of)	2012 M	0.004	1.1	44	38.4	2.2	0.1	11.0	66.9	22.1	11.4	0.0
Mongolia	2010 M	0.047	11.1	302	42.5	19.3	2.3	18.1	27.7	54.2	21.6	0.2
Montenegro	2013 M	0.002	0.5	3	38.9	2.0	0.0	22.0	59.9	18.1	8.6	0.0

Country	Multidimensional Poverty Index[a] Year and survey[b]	Index	Population in multidimensional poverty[a] Headcount		Intensity of deprivation	Population near multidimensional poverty[a]	Population in severe multidimensional poverty[a]	Contribution of deprivation in dimension to overall poverty[a] (%)			Population living below income poverty line (%)	
	2005–2015	Value	(%)	(thousands)	(%)	(%)	(%)	Education	Health	Living standards	National poverty line 2005–2014[c]	PPP $1.90 a day 2005–2014[c]
Morocco	2011 P	0.069	15.6	5,090	44.3	12.6	4.9	44.8	21.8	33.4	8.9	3.1
Mozambique	2011 D	0.390	70.2	17,552	55.6	14.8	44.1	30.4	22.3	47.3	54.7	68.7
Namibia	2013 D	0.205	44.9	1,054	45.5	19.3	13.4	11.0	39.2	49.8	28.7	22.6
Nepal	2014 M	0.116	26.6	7,493	43.7	14.4	9.3	32.2	25.6	42.2	25.2	15.0
Nicaragua	2011/2012 D	0.088	19.4	1,127	45.6	14.8	6.9	37.8	12.6	49.6	29.6	6.2
Niger	2012 D	0.584	89.8	15,838	65.0	5.9	73.5	35.9	24.0	40.0	48.9	45.7
Nigeria	2013 D	0.279	50.9	88,018	54.8	18.4	30.0	29.8	29.8	40.4	46.0	53.5
Pakistan	2012/2013 D	0.237	45.6	82,612	52.0	14.9	26.5	36.2	32.3	31.6	29.5	6.1
Palestine, State of	2014 M	0.005	1.4	65	38.2	5.4	0.2	20.8	67.8	11.5	25.8	0.1
Peru	2012 D	0.043	10.4	3,150	41.4	12.3	2.1	19.4	29.8	50.8	21.8	3.1
Philippines	2013 D	0.033 [d,j]	6.3 [d,j]	6,169 [d,j]	51.9 [d,j]	8.4 [d,j]	4.2 [d,j]	35.3 [d,j]	30.2 [d,j]	34.5 [d,j]	25.2	13.1
Rwanda	2014/2015 D	0.253	53.9	6,263	47.0	25.0	20.5	28.6	18.4	53.0	44.9	60.4
Saint Lucia	2012 M	0.003 [f]	0.8 [f]	2 [f]	34.5 [f]	0.9 [f]	0.0 [f]	15.8 [f]	65.2 [f]	19.0 [f]	..	..
Sao Tome and Principe	2008/2009 D	0.217	47.5	79	45.5	21.5	16.4	29.1	26.5	44.4	61.7	32.3
Senegal	2014 D	0.278	51.9	7,621	53.5	18.1	30.8	43.6	23.1	33.4	46.7	38.0
Serbia	2014 M	0.002	0.4	38	40.6	2.7	0.1	30.7	40.7	28.7	25.4	0.2
Sierra Leone	2013 D	0.411	77.5	4,791	53.0	14.6	43.9	25.7	28.5	45.9	52.9	52.3
Somalia	2006 M	0.500	81.8	7,104	61.1	8.3	63.6	33.7	18.8	47.5	..	..
South Africa	2012 N	0.041	10.3	5,446	39.6	17.1	1.3	8.4	61.4	30.2	53.8	16.6
South Sudan	2010 M	0.551	89.3	8,980	61.7	8.5	69.6	39.3	14.3	46.3	50.6	42.7
Sudan	2010 M	0.290	53.1	19,161	54.6	17.9	31.9	30.4	20.7	48.9	46.5	14.9
Suriname	2010 M	0.033 [f]	7.6 [f]	39 [f]	43.1 [f]	4.7 [f]	2.0 [f]	31.0 [f]	37.2 [f]	31.8 [f]	..	..
Swaziland	2010 M	0.113	25.9	309	43.5	20.5	7.4	13.7	41.0	45.3	63.0	42.0
Syrian Arab Republic	2009 P	0.028	7.2	1,485	39.1	7.4	1.3	54.7	34.0	11.3	35.2	..
Tajikistan	2012 D	0.031	7.9	623	39.0	23.4	1.2	13.4	52.6	34.0	31.3	19.5
Tanzania (United Republic of)	2010 D	0.335	66.4	30,290	50.4	21.5	32.1	16.9	28.2	54.9	28.2	46.6
Thailand	2005/2006 M	0.004	1.0	667	38.8	4.4	0.1	19.4	51.3	29.4	10.5	0.0
The former Yugoslav Republic of Macedonia	2011 M	0.007 [f]	1.7 [f]	35 [f]	38.4 [f]	2.4 [f]	0.1 [f]	18.5 [f]	57.2 [f]	24.3 [f]	22.1	1.3
Timor-Leste	2009/2010 D	0.322	64.3	680	50.1	21.4	31.5	20.0	30.4	49.6	41.8	46.8
Togo	2013/2014 D	0.242	48.5	3,454	49.9	19.9	23.2	26.4	28.8	44.9	55.1	54.2
Trinidad and Tobago	2006 M	0.007 [d]	1.7 [d]	23 [d]	38.0 [d]	0.5 [d]	0.2 [d]	2.2 [d]	86.1 [d]	11.7 [d]	..	..
Tunisia	2011/2012 M	0.006	1.5	161	39.3	3.2	0.2	33.7	48.2	18.1	15.5	2.0
Turkmenistan	2006 M	0.011	3.0	144	37.0	6.5	0.1	7.4	82.5	10.1	..	..
Uganda	2011 D	0.359	70.3	24,088	51.1	20.6	33.3	18.0	30.2	51.9	19.5	34.6
Ukraine	2012 M	0.001 [d]	0.4 [d]	161 [d]	34.5 [d]	0.0 [d]	0.0 [d]	19.0 [d]	77.5 [d]	3.5 [d]	6.4	0.0
Uzbekistan	2006 M	0.013	3.5	931	36.6	6.2	0.1	3.7	83.4	12.8	14.1	..
Vanuatu	2007 M	0.135	31.2	69	43.1	32.6	7.3	24.4	24.1	51.6	12.7	15.4
Viet Nam	2013/2014 M	0.016 [d]	3.9 [d]	3,646 [d]	39.9 [d]	4.3 [d]	0.6 [d]	39.6 [d]	24.3 [d]	36.1 [d]	13.5	3.1
Yemen	2013 D	0.200	40.0	10,204	50.1	22.4	19.4	29.5	32.2	38.2	34.8	..
Zambia	2013/2014 D	0.264	54.4	8,554	48.6	23.1	22.5	17.9	29.8	52.3	60.5	64.4
Zimbabwe	2014 M	0.128	28.9	4,409	44.1	29.3	7.8	10.8	34.5	54.8	72.3	21.4

TABLE **6**

NOTES

a Not all indicators were available for all countries, so caution should be used in cross-country comparisons. Where an indicator is missing, weights of available indicators are adjusted to total 100 percent. See *Technical note 5* at http://hdr.undp.org/sites/default/files/hdr2016_technical_notes.pdf for details.

b *D* indicates data from Demographic and Health Surveys, *M* from Multiple Indicator Cluster Surveys, *P* from Pan Arab Population and Family Health Survey and *N* from national surveys (see http://hdr.undp.org/en/faq-page/multidimensional-poverty-index-mpi for the list of national surveys).

c Data refer to the most recent year available during the period specified.

d Missing indicators on nutrition.

e Refers to urban areas only

f Missing indicator on child mortality.

g Missing indicator on type of floor.

h Missing indicator on cooking fuel.

i Missing indicator on electricity.

j Missing indicator on school attendance.

DEFINITIONS

Multidimensional Poverty Index: Percentage of the population that is multidimensionally poor adjusted by the intensity of the deprivations. See *Technical note 5* at http://hdr.undp.org/sites/default/files/hdr2016_technical_notes.pdf for details on how the Multidimensional Poverty Index is calculated.

Multidimensional poverty headcount: Percentage of the population with a deprivation score of at least 33 percent. It is also expressed in thousands of the population in the survey year.

Intensity of deprivation of multidimensional poverty: Average deprivation score experienced by people in multidimensional poverty.

Population near multidimensional poverty: Percentage of the population at risk of suffering multiple deprivations—that is, those with a deprivation score of 20–33 percent.

Population in severe multidimensional poverty: Percentage of the population in severe multidimensional poverty—that is, those with a deprivation score of 50 percent or more.

Contribution of deprivation to overall poverty: Percentage of the Multidimensional Poverty Index attributed to deprivations in each dimension.

Population living below national poverty line: Percentage of the population living below the national poverty line, which is the poverty line deemed appropriate for a country by its authorities. National estimates are based on population-weighted subgroup estimates from household surveys.

Population living below PPP$1.90 a day: Percentage of the population living below the international poverty line $1.90 (in purchasing power parity terms) a day.

MAIN DATA SOURCES

Column 1: Refers to the year and the survey whose data were used to calculate the country's multidimensional poverty index and its components.

Columns 2–10: HDRO calculations based on data on household deprivations in education, health and living standards from various household surveys listed in column 1 using a revised methodology described in *Technical note 5* (available *at* at http://hdr.undp.org/sites/default/files/hdr2016_technical_notes.pdf).

Columns 11 and 12: World Bank (2016a).

TABLE 6   Multidimensional Poverty Index: developing countries | 221

Human development indicators

TABLE 7

Population trends

TABLE 7

		Population									Dependency ratio			
		Total		Average annual growth		Urban[a]	Under age 5	Ages 15–64	Ages 65 and older	Median age	(per 100 people ages 15–64)		Total fertility rate	
		(millions)		(%)		(%)		(millions)		(years)	Young age (0–14)	Old age (65 and older)	(births per woman)	
HDI rank		2015	2030[b]	2000/2005	2010/2015	2015	2015	2015	2015	2015	2015	2015	2000/2005	2010/2015
VERY HIGH HUMAN DEVELOPMENT														
1	Norway[c]	5.2	5.9	0.6	1.3	80.5	0.3	3.4	0.9	39.1	27.3	24.9	1.8	1.8
2	Australia[d]	24.0	28.5	1.2	1.6	89.4	1.5	15.9	3.6	37.5	28.2	22.7	1.8	1.9
2	Switzerland	8.3	9.2	0.7	1.2	73.9	0.4	5.6	1.5	42.3	22.0	26.9	1.4	1.5
4	Germany	80.7	79.3	−0.2	0.1	75.3	3.4	53.2	17.1	46.2	19.6	32.2	1.4	1.4
5	Denmark	5.7	6.0	0.3	0.4	87.7	0.3	3.6	1.1	41.6	26.3	29.6	1.8	1.7
5	Singapore	5.6	6.4	2.7	2.0	100.0	0.3	4.1	0.7	40.0	21.4	16.1	1.3	1.2
7	Netherlands	16.9	17.6	0.5	0.4	90.5	0.9	11.0	3.1	42.7	25.3	27.9	1.7	1.8
8	Ireland	4.7	5.2	1.8	0.3	63.2	0.4	3.1	0.6	36.9	33.5	20.2	2.0	2.0
9	Iceland	0.3	0.4	1.1	0.7	94.1	0.0	0.2	0.0	36.0	30.8	20.8	2.0	2.0
10	Canada	35.9	40.4	1.0	1.0	81.8	1.9	..	5.8	40.6	23.5	23.8	1.5	1.6
10	United States	321.8	355.8	0.9	0.8	81.6	19.7	213.2	47.6	38.0	28.6	22.3	2.0	1.9
12	Hong Kong, China (SAR)	7.3	8.0	0.2	0.8	100.0	0.4	5.3	1.1	43.2	16.4	20.6	1.0	1.2
13	New Zealand	4.5	5.1	1.4	0.7	86.3	0.3	2.9	0.7	38.0	31.1	22.9	1.9	2.1
14	Sweden	9.8	10.8	0.4	0.8	85.8	0.6	6.1	1.9	41.0	27.5	31.8	1.7	1.9
15	Liechtenstein	0.0	0.0	0.9	0.7	14.3	..	..	..	..	..	..	..	..
16	United Kingdom	64.7	70.1	0.5	0.6	82.6	4.1	41.7	11.5	40.0	27.6	27.6	1.7	1.9
17	Japan	126.6	120.1	0.2	−0.1	93.5	5.3	77.0	33.3	46.5	21.1	43.3	1.3	1.4
18	Korea (Republic of)	50.3	52.5	0.6	0.5	82.5	2.3	36.7	6.6	40.6	19.2	18.0	1.2	1.3
19	Israel	8.1	10.0	1.9	1.7	92.1	0.8	4.9	0.9	30.3	45.7	18.4	2.9	3.1
20	Luxembourg	0.6	0.7	1.0	2.2	90.2	0.0	0.4	0.1	39.2	23.6	20.1	1.7	1.6
21	France	64.4	68.0	0.6	0.5	79.5	3.9	40.2	12.3	41.2	29.6	30.6	1.9	2.0
22	Belgium	11.3	12.0	0.6	0.7	97.9	0.7	7.3	2.1	41.5	26.1	28.1	1.7	1.8
23	Finland[e]	5.5	5.7	0.3	0.5	84.2	0.3	3.5	1.1	42.5	25.9	32.4	1.8	1.7
24	Austria	8.5	8.8	0.5	0.4	66.0	0.4	5.7	1.6	43.2	21.2	28.0	1.4	1.5
25	Slovenia	2.1	2.1	0.1	0.1	49.7	0.1	1.4	0.4	43.1	22.0	26.7	1.2	1.6
26	Italy	59.8	59.1	0.5	0.1	69.0	2.6	38.2	13.4	45.9	21.5	35.1	1.3	1.4
27	Spain[f]	46.1	45.9	1.5	−0.2	79.6	2.1	30.6	8.7	43.2	22.4	28.3	1.3	1.3
28	Czech Republic	10.5	10.5	−0.1	0.1	73.0	0.5	7.1	1.9	41.5	22.5	27.0	1.2	1.5
29	Greece	11.0	10.5	0.2	−0.4	78.0	0.5	7.0	2.3	43.6	22.8	33.4	1.3	1.3
30	Brunei Darussalam	0.4	0.5	1.8	1.5	77.2	0.0	0.3	0.0	30.6	31.9	6.1	2.1	1.9
30	Estonia	1.3	1.2	−0.6	−0.3	67.5	0.1	0.9	0.2	41.7	24.7	28.8	1.4	1.6
32	Andorra	0.1	0.1	4.3	−3.6	85.1	..	..	..	..	..	..	..	..
33	Cyprus[g]	1.2	1.3	1.8	1.1	66.9	0.1	0.8	0.1	35.9	23.4	18.2	1.6	1.5
33	Malta	0.4	0.4	0.5	0.3	95.4	0.0	0.3	0.1	41.5	21.8	29.0	1.5	1.4
33	Qatar	2.2	2.8	6.9	4.7	99.2	0.1	1.9	0.0	30.7	18.6	1.4	3.0	2.1
36	Poland	38.6	37.2	0.0	0.0	60.5	2.0	26.8	6.0	39.6	21.5	22.3	1.3	1.4
37	Lithuania	2.9	2.7	−0.8	−1.6	66.5	0.2	1.9	0.5	43.1	21.8	28.3	1.3	1.6
38	Chile	17.9	20.2	1.2	1.1	89.5	1.2	12.4	2.0	34.4	29.3	16.0	2.0	1.8
38	Saudi Arabia	31.5	39.1	2.9	2.3	83.1	3.2	21.6	0.9	28.3	41.7	4.2	3.6	2.9
40	Slovakia	5.4	5.4	0.0	0.1	53.6	0.3	3.9	0.8	39.1	21.3	19.5	1.2	1.4
41	Portugal	10.3	9.8	0.4	−0.4	63.5	0.4	6.7	2.2	44.0	21.6	31.9	1.5	1.3
42	United Arab Emirates	9.2	11.0	7.7	1.9	85.5	0.5	7.8	0.1	33.3	16.4	1.3	2.4	1.8
43	Hungary	9.9	9.3	−0.3	−0.3	71.2	0.5	6.7	1.8	41.3	21.5	26.3	1.3	1.3
44	Latvia	2.0	1.8	−1.3	−1.2	67.4	0.1	1.3	0.4	42.9	22.7	29.5	1.3	1.5
45	Argentina	43.4	49.4	1.1	1.0	91.8	3.7	27.7	4.7	30.8	39.4	17.1	2.5	2.3
45	Croatia	4.2	4.0	−0.2	−0.4	59.0	0.2	2.8	0.8	42.8	22.5	28.6	1.4	1.5
47	Bahrain	1.4	1.6	5.3	1.8	88.8	0.1	1.0	0.0	30.3	28.2	3.2	2.7	2.1
48	Montenegro	0.6	0.6	0.1	0.1	64.0	0.0	0.4	0.1	37.6	27.6	20.2	1.9	1.7
49	Russian Federation	143.5	138.7	−0.4	0.0	74.0	9.2	100.3	19.2	38.7	24.0	19.1	1.3	1.7
50	Romania	19.5	17.6	−0.7	−0.8	54.6	0.9	13.1	3.4	42.1	23.1	25.8	1.3	1.5
51	Kuwait	3.9	5.0	3.2	4.8	98.3	0.3	2.9	0.1	31.0	29.5	2.6	2.6	2.2
HIGH HUMAN DEVELOPMENT														
52	Belarus	9.5	9.0	−0.6	0.0	76.7	0.6	6.6	1.3	39.6	23.0	20.0	1.3	1.6
52	Oman	4.5	5.2	2.3	8.4	77.6	0.4	3.5	0.1	29.0	26.7	3.4	3.2	2.9
54	Barbados	0.3	0.3	0.3	0.3	31.5	0.0	0.2	0.0	38.5	29.1	21.3	1.8	1.8
54	Uruguay	3.4	3.6	0.0	0.3	95.3	0.2	2.2	0.5	34.9	33.4	22.5	2.2	2.0
56	Bulgaria	7.1	6.3	−0.8	−0.7	73.9	0.3	4.7	1.4	43.5	21.5	30.4	1.2	1.5
56	Kazakhstan	17.6	20.1	0.7	1.6	53.2	1.9	11.7	1.2	29.3	40.1	10.1	2.0	2.6
58	Bahamas	0.4	0.4	2.0	1.5	82.9	0.0	0.3	0.0	32.4	29.6	11.7	1.9	1.9
59	Malaysia[h]	30.3	36.1	1.9	1.5	74.7	2.5	21.1	1.8	28.5	35.2	8.4	2.5	2.0

	Population									Dependency ratio		Total fertility rate	
	Total		Average annual growth		Urban[a]	Under age 5	Ages 15–64	Ages 65 and older	Median age	(per 100 people ages 15–64)			
										Young age (0–14)	Old age (65 and older)		
	(millions)		(%)		(%)	(millions)			(years)			(births per woman)	
HDI rank	2015	2030[b]	2000/2005	2010/2015	2015	2015	2015	2015	2015	2015	2015	2000/2005	2010/2015
60 Palau	0.0	0.0	0.8	0.8	87.1	..	..	..	..	..	..	..	..
60 Panama	3.9	4.8	1.8	1.6	66.6	0.4	2.6	0.3	28.7	41.7	11.7	2.6	2.5
62 Antigua and Barbuda	0.1	0.1	1.2	1.0	23.8	0.0	0.1	0.0	30.9	35.2	10.4	2.3	2.1
63 Seychelles	0.1	0.1	1.8	0.7	53.9	0.0	0.1	0.0	32.6	33.6	9.9	2.2	2.3
64 Mauritius[i]	1.3	1.3	0.6	0.4	39.7	0.1	0.9	0.1	35.2	27.2	13.4	1.9	1.5
65 Trinidad and Tobago	1.4	1.4	0.5	0.5	8.4	0.1	0.9	0.1	33.8	29.8	13.5	1.8	1.8
66 Costa Rica	4.8	5.4	1.6	1.1	76.8	0.4	3.3	0.4	31.4	32.4	12.9	2.2	1.9
66 Serbia[j]	8.9	8.3	−0.6	−0.5	55.6	0.5	5.9	1.5	40.6	24.5	25.6	1.7	1.6
68 Cuba	11.4	11.2	0.3	0.1	77.1	0.6	7.9	1.6	41.2	23.4	20.0	1.6	1.6
69 Iran (Islamic Republic of)	79.1	88.5	1.3	1.3	73.4	6.9	56.4	4.0	29.5	33.1	7.1	2.0	1.7
70 Georgia[k]	4.0	3.9	−1.2	−1.2	53.6	0.3	2.7	0.6	37.5	25.2	20.4	1.6	1.8
71 Turkey	78.7	87.7	1.4	1.7	73.4	6.8	52.5	5.9	29.8	38.4	11.3	2.4	2.1
71 Venezuela (Bolivarian Republic of)	31.1	36.7	1.8	1.4	89.0	3.0	20.4	2.0	27.4	42.8	9.5	2.7	2.4
73 Sri Lanka	20.7	21.5	0.8	0.5	18.4	1.6	13.7	1.9	32.3	37.2	14.1	2.3	2.1
74 Saint Kitts and Nevis	0.1	0.1	1.5	1.2	32.0	..	..	..	..	..	..	..	..
75 Albania	2.9	3.0	−0.3	0.0	57.4	0.2	2.0	0.4	34.3	26.9	18.0	1.9	1.8
76 Lebanon	5.9	5.3	4.2	6.0	87.8	0.5	4.0	0.5	28.5	35.4	12.0	2.0	1.7
77 Mexico	127.0	148.1	1.3	1.4	79.2	11.6	83.7	8.2	27.4	41.9	9.8	2.6	2.3
78 Azerbaijan[l]	9.8	10.7	1.1	1.4	54.6	0.9	7.1	0.5	30.9	30.3	7.8	2.0	2.3
79 Brazil	207.8	228.7	1.4	0.9	85.7	15.0	143.7	16.3	31.3	33.3	11.3	2.3	1.8
79 Grenada	0.1	0.1	0.3	0.4	35.6	0.0	0.1	0.0	27.2	39.9	10.8	2.4	2.2
81 Bosnia and Herzegovina	3.8	3.6	0.2	−0.1	39.8	0.2	2.7	0.6	41.5	19.0	21.7	1.2	1.3
82 The former Yugoslav Republic of Macedonia	2.1	2.1	0.3	0.2	57.1	0.1	1.5	0.3	37.5	24.0	17.4	1.6	1.5
83 Algeria	39.7	48.3	1.3	1.9	70.7	4.6	26.0	2.4	27.6	43.6	9.1	2.4	2.9
84 Armenia	3.0	3.0	−0.4	0.4	62.7	0.2	2.1	0.3	34.6	26.0	15.3	1.7	1.6
84 Ukraine[m]	44.8	40.9	−0.8	−0.4	69.7	2.5	31.3	6.9	40.3	21.4	21.9	1.1	1.5
86 Jordan	7.6	9.1	2.2	3.1	83.7	1.0	4.6	0.3	22.5	58.5	6.2	3.9	3.5
87 Peru	31.4	36.9	1.3	1.3	78.6	3.0	20.5	2.1	27.5	42.7	10.5	2.8	2.5
87 Thailand	68.0	68.3	1.0	0.4	50.4	3.8	48.8	7.1	38.0	24.7	14.6	1.6	1.5
89 Ecuador	16.1	19.6	1.7	1.6	63.7	1.6	10.4	1.1	26.6	45.1	10.4	2.9	2.6
90 China	1,376.0	1,415.5	0.6	0.5	55.6	83.2	1,000.0	131.4	37.0	23.5	13.0	1.5	1.6
91 Fiji	0.9	0.9	0.3	0.7	53.7	0.1	0.6	0.1	27.6	43.9	8.9	3.0	2.6
92 Mongolia	3.0	3.5	1.0	1.7	72.0	0.3	2.0	0.1	27.3	41.7	6.0	2.1	2.7
92 Saint Lucia	0.2	0.2	1.1	0.8	18.5	0.0	0.1	0.0	31.2	34.1	13.3	2.1	1.9
94 Jamaica	2.8	2.9	0.6	0.4	54.8	0.2	1.9	0.3	29.1	35.0	13.6	2.5	2.1
95 Colombia	48.2	53.2	1.4	1.0	76.4	3.7	33.1	3.4	30.0	35.4	10.2	2.3	1.9
96 Dominica	0.1	0.1	0.2	0.4	69.5	..	..	..	..	..	..	..	..
97 Suriname	0.5	0.6	0.5	0.9	66.0	0.0	0.4	0.0	29.0	40.4	10.4	2.7	2.4
97 Tunisia	11.3	12.7	0.8	1.1	66.8	1.0	7.8	0.9	31.2	33.8	11.0	2.0	2.2
99 Dominican Republic	10.5	12.1	1.5	1.2	79.0	1.1	6.7	0.7	26.1	47.3	10.5	2.8	2.5
99 Saint Vincent and the Grenadines	0.1	0.1	0.2	0.0	50.6	0.0	0.1	0.0	29.8	36.0	10.8	2.2	2.0
101 Tonga	0.1	0.1	0.6	0.4	23.7	0.0	0.1	0.0	21.3	64.1	10.2	4.2	3.8
102 Libya	6.3	7.4	1.7	0.0	78.6	0.6	4.1	0.3	27.5	45.5	6.9	2.8	2.5
103 Belize	0.4	0.5	2.7	2.2	44.0	0.0	0.2	0.0	23.5	50.9	5.9	3.4	2.6
104 Samoa	0.2	0.2	0.6	0.8	19.1	0.0	0.1	0.0	21.2	64.9	9.1	4.4	4.2
105 Maldives	0.4	0.4	1.7	1.8	45.5	0.0	0.2	0.0	26.4	40.5	6.9	2.6	2.2
105 Uzbekistan	29.9	34.4	1.1	1.5	36.4	3.2	20.0	1.4	26.3	42.7	7.0	2.5	2.5
MEDIUM HUMAN DEVELOPMENT													
107 Moldova (Republic of)[n]	4.1	3.8	−0.2	−0.1	45.0	0.2	3.0	0.4	35.6	21.2	13.4	1.2	1.3
108 Botswana	2.3	2.8	1.4	2.0	57.4	0.3	1.5	0.1	24.2	49.7	5.6	3.2	2.9
109 Gabon	1.7	2.3	2.2	2.2	87.2	0.2	1.0	0.1	21.4	64.3	8.8	4.4	4.0
110 Paraguay	6.6	7.8	1.8	1.3	59.7	0.7	4.2	0.4	24.9	47.2	9.4	3.2	2.6
111 Egypt	91.5	117.1	1.8	2.2	43.1	12.1	56.4	4.8	24.7	53.8	8.5	3.2	3.4
111 Turkmenistan	5.4	6.2	1.1	1.3	50.0	0.5	3.6	0.2	26.4	41.7	6.1	2.8	2.3
113 Indonesia	257.6	295.5	1.3	1.3	53.7	24.9	172.9	13.3	28.4	41.2	7.7	2.5	2.5
114 Palestine, State of[o]	4.7	6.8	2.1	2.8	75.3	0.7	2.7	0.1	19.3	70.8	5.2	5.0	4.3
115 Viet Nam	93.4	105.2	1.0	1.1	33.6	7.7	65.6	6.3	30.4	32.9	9.6	1.9	2.0
116 Philippines	100.7	123.6	2.0	1.6	44.4	11.3	63.9	4.6	24.2	50.3	7.2	3.7	3.0
117 El Salvador	6.1	6.4	0.5	0.3	66.7	0.5	4.0	0.5	26.7	41.7	12.6	2.6	2.0
118 Bolivia (Plurinational State of)	10.7	13.2	1.8	1.6	68.5	1.2	6.6	0.7	24.1	53.1	10.6	3.8	3.0
119 South Africa	54.5	60.0	1.5	1.1	64.8	5.4	35.8	2.7	25.7	44.5	7.7	2.8	2.4

TABLE 7 Population trends | 225

TABLE 7 POPULATION TRENDS

	Population								Dependency ratio			
	Total		Average annual growth		Urban[a]	Under age 5	Ages 15–64	Ages 65 and older	Median age	(per 100 people ages 15–64)		Total fertility rate	
	(millions)		(%)		(%)	(millions)			(years)	Young age (0–14)	Old age (65 and older)	(births per woman)	
HDI rank	2015	2030[b]	2000/2005	2010/2015	2015	2015	2015	2015	2015	2015	2015	2000/2005	2010/2015
120 Kyrgyzstan	5.9	7.1	0.6	1.7	35.7	0.8	3.8	0.3	25.1	48.8	6.6	2.5	3.1
121 Iraq	36.4	54.1	2.7	3.3	69.5	5.7	20.4	1.1	19.3	73.2	5.5	4.7	4.6
122 Cabo Verde	0.5	0.6	1.6	1.2	65.5	0.1	0.3	0.0	24.5	45.1	7.0	3.2	2.4
123 Morocco	34.4	39.8	1.0	1.4	60.2	3.4	22.9	2.1	28.0	40.9	9.3	2.5	2.6
124 Nicaragua	6.1	7.0	1.4	1.2	58.8	0.6	3.9	0.3	25.2	46.3	7.8	2.8	2.3
125 Guatemala	16.3	21.4	2.4	2.1	51.6	2.1	9.6	0.8	21.2	62.6	8.3	4.2	3.3
125 Namibia	2.5	3.3	1.3	2.3	46.7	0.3	1.5	0.1	21.2	61.4	5.9	3.8	3.6
127 Guyana	0.8	0.8	0.0	0.4	28.6	0.1	0.5	0.0	24.7	43.5	7.6	2.9	2.6
127 Micronesia (Federated States of)	0.1	0.1	−0.2	0.2	22.4	0.0	0.1	0.0	21.5	55.3	7.1	4.1	3.3
129 Tajikistan	8.5	11.1	1.9	2.2	26.8	1.2	5.3	0.3	22.5	56.0	4.8	3.7	3.6
130 Honduras	8.1	9.7	1.9	1.5	54.7	0.8	5.1	0.4	23.4	50.1	7.7	3.6	2.5
131 India	1,311.1	1,527.7	1.7	1.3	32.7	123.7	860.0	73.6	26.6	43.9	8.6	3.1	2.5
132 Bhutan	0.8	0.9	2.9	1.5	38.6	0.1	0.5	0.0	26.7	39.5	7.4	3.1	2.1
133 Timor-Leste	1.2	1.6	3.1	2.3	32.8	0.2	0.6	0.1	18.5	81.5	10.7	7.0	5.9
134 Vanuatu	0.3	0.4	2.5	2.3	26.1	0.0	0.2	0.0	22.2	61.6	7.1	4.1	3.4
135 Congo	4.6	6.8	2.4	2.6	65.4	0.8	2.5	0.2	18.7	79.4	6.8	5.1	5.0
135 Equatorial Guinea	0.8	1.2	3.3	3.0	39.9	0.1	0.5	0.0	20.5	67.9	5.0	5.6	5.0
137 Kiribati	0.1	0.1	1.8	1.8	44.3	0.0	0.1	0.0	22.4	57.0	6.0	4.0	3.8
138 Lao People's Democratic Republic	6.8	8.5	1.5	1.7	38.6	0.8	4.2	0.3	21.9	56.6	6.2	3.9	3.1
139 Bangladesh	161.0	186.5	1.7	1.2	34.3	15.3	105.6	8.0	25.6	44.9	7.6	2.9	2.2
139 Ghana	27.4	36.9	2.6	2.4	54.0	4.1	15.8	0.9	20.6	67.2	5.9	4.6	4.2
139 Zambia	16.2	25.3	2.6	3.1	40.9	2.9	8.3	0.5	16.9	89.7	5.7	6.1	5.5
142 Sao Tome and Principe	0.2	0.3	2.2	2.2	65.1	0.0	0.1	0.0	18.5	78.5	5.7	5.1	4.7
143 Cambodia	15.6	19.0	1.8	1.6	20.7	1.8	10.0	0.6	23.9	49.2	6.4	3.4	2.7
144 Nepal	28.5	33.1	1.4	1.2	18.6	2.8	17.6	1.6	23.1	52.9	9.0	3.6	2.3
145 Myanmar	53.9	60.2	0.9	0.8	34.1	4.6	36.2	2.9	27.9	41.1	8.0	2.9	2.3
146 Kenya	46.1	65.4	2.6	2.7	25.6	7.2	25.5	1.3	18.9	75.8	5.1	5.0	4.4
147 Pakistan	188.9	244.9	2.1	2.1	38.8	24.7	114.3	8.5	22.5	57.9	7.4	4.2	3.7
LOW HUMAN DEVELOPMENT													
148 Swaziland	1.3	1.5	0.8	1.5	21.3	0.2	0.8	0.0	20.5	63.2	6.1	4.0	3.4
149 Syrian Arab Republic	18.5	28.6	2.1	−2.3	57.7	2.2	10.9	0.8	20.8	63.1	6.9	3.7	3.0
150 Angola	25.0	39.4	3.5	3.3	44.1	4.7	12.5	0.6	16.1	95.2	4.6	6.8	6.2
151 Tanzania (United Republic of)[p]	53.5	82.9	2.8	3.2	31.6	9.4	27.6	1.7	17.3	87.6	6.2	5.7	5.2
152 Nigeria	182.2	262.6	2.6	2.7	47.8	31.1	97.1	5.0	17.9	82.6	5.1	6.1	5.7
153 Cameroon	23.3	32.9	2.6	2.5	54.4	3.7	12.7	0.7	18.5	78.4	5.9	5.5	4.8
154 Papua New Guinea	7.6	10.1	2.5	2.1	13.0	1.0	4.6	0.2	21.2	62.1	5.0	4.4	3.8
154 Zimbabwe	15.6	21.4	0.8	2.2	32.4	2.5	8.7	0.5	18.9	75.0	5.3	4.0	4.0
156 Solomon Islands	0.6	0.8	2.6	2.1	22.3	0.1	0.3	0.0	19.9	69.1	5.9	4.6	4.1
157 Mauritania	4.1	5.7	3.0	2.5	59.9	0.6	2.3	0.1	19.8	70.5	5.7	5.3	4.7
158 Madagascar	24.2	36.0	3.0	2.8	35.1	3.8	13.4	0.7	18.7	75.2	5.1	5.3	4.5
159 Rwanda	11.6	15.8	2.3	2.4	28.8	1.7	6.5	0.3	19.2	73.1	5.0	5.4	4.1
160 Comoros	0.8	1.1	2.4	2.4	28.3	0.1	0.4	0.0	19.7	70.7	4.9	5.2	4.6
160 Lesotho	2.1	2.5	0.7	1.2	27.3	0.3	1.3	0.1	21.0	60.3	6.9	3.8	3.3
162 Senegal	15.1	22.8	2.7	3.1	43.7	2.6	8.1	0.4	18.0	82.1	5.5	5.4	5.2
163 Haiti	10.7	12.6	1.6	1.4	58.6	1.2	6.6	0.5	23.0	54.8	7.5	4.0	3.1
163 Uganda	39.0	61.9	3.3	3.3	16.1	7.3	19.3	1.0	15.9	97.3	5.0	6.7	5.9
165 Sudan	40.2	56.4	2.6	2.2	33.8	6.0	22.6	1.3	19.4	72.1	5.9	5.3	4.5
166 Togo	7.3	10.5	2.7	2.7	40.0	1.2	4.0	0.2	18.7	76.8	5.0	5.3	4.7
167 Benin	10.9	15.6	3.3	2.7	44.0	1.7	6.0	0.3	18.6	76.7	5.3	5.8	4.9
168 Yemen	26.8	36.3	2.8	2.6	34.6	3.9	15.3	0.7	19.3	70.7	4.9	6.0	4.4
169 Afghanistan	32.5	43.9	4.3	3.0	26.7	5.0	17.4	0.8	17.5	82.3	4.6	7.2	5.1
170 Malawi	17.2	26.6	2.6	3.1	16.3	3.0	8.8	0.6	17.2	87.9	6.7	6.1	5.3
171 Côte d'Ivoire	22.7	32.1	1.9	2.4	54.2	3.7	12.4	0.7	18.4	77.9	5.6	5.7	5.1
172 Djibouti	0.9	1.1	1.5	1.3	77.3	0.1	0.6	0.0	23.6	51.9	6.6	4.2	3.3
173 Gambia	2.0	3.1	3.2	3.2	59.6	0.4	1.0	0.0	16.8	89.7	4.5	5.9	5.8
174 Ethiopia	99.4	138.3	2.8	2.5	19.5	14.6	54.7	3.5	18.6	75.2	6.3	6.1	4.6
175 Mali	17.6	27.4	3.1	3.0	39.9	3.3	8.8	0.4	16.2	95.1	5.0	6.9	6.4
176 Congo (Democratic Republic of the)	77.3	120.3	3.1	3.2	42.5	13.9	39.4	2.3	16.9	90.1	5.8	7.0	6.2
177 Liberia	4.5	6.4	2.5	2.6	49.7	0.7	2.5	0.1	18.6	77.4	5.5	5.7	4.8
178 Guinea-Bissau	1.8	2.5	2.1	2.4	49.3	0.3	1.0	0.1	19.4	72.8	5.7	5.6	5.0
179 Eritrea	5.2	7.3	3.4	2.2	22.6	0.8	2.9	0.1	18.6	78.4	4.8	5.1	4.4

TABLE 7

HDI rank	Total (millions) 2015	Total (millions) 2030[b]	Average annual growth (%) 2000/2005	Average annual growth (%) 2010/2015	Urban[a] (%) 2015	Under age 5 (millions) 2015	Ages 15–64 (millions) 2015	Ages 65 and older (millions) 2015	Median age (years) 2015	Dependency ratio (per 100 people ages 15–64) Young age (0–14) 2015	Dependency ratio (per 100 people ages 15–64) Old age (65 and older) 2015	Total fertility rate (births per woman) 2000/2005	Total fertility rate (births per woman) 2010/2015
179 Sierra Leone	6.5	8.6	4.4	2.2	39.9	1.0	3.5	0.2	18.5	77.1	4.9	6.0	4.8
181 Mozambique	28.0	41.4	2.9	2.8	32.2	4.8	14.4	0.9	17.1	88.2	6.5	5.8	5.5
181 South Sudan	12.3	17.8	3.8	4.1	18.8	2.0	6.7	0.4	18.6	77.3	6.4	6.0	5.2
183 Guinea	12.6	18.3	1.9	2.7	37.2	2.0	6.9	0.4	18.5	78.2	5.6	5.9	5.1
184 Burundi	11.2	17.4	3.2	3.3	12.1	2.1	5.9	0.3	17.6	85.0	4.7	6.9	6.1
185 Burkina Faso	18.1	27.2	2.9	2.9	29.9	3.1	9.4	0.4	17.0	87.6	4.6	6.4	5.6
186 Chad	14.0	21.9	3.8	3.3	22.5	2.6	7.0	0.3	16.0	95.8	4.9	7.2	6.3
187 Niger	19.9	36.0	3.7	4.0	18.7	4.1	9.3	0.5	14.8	107.5	5.5	7.7	7.6
188 Central African Republic	4.9	6.5	1.7	2.0	40.0	0.7	2.8	0.2	20.0	68.4	6.8	5.3	4.4
OTHER COUNTRIES OR TERRITORIES													
Korea (Democratic People's Rep. of)	25.2	26.7	0.8	0.5	60.9	1.7	17.4	2.4	33.9	30.5	13.8	2.0	2.0
Marshall Islands	0.1	0.1	0.0	0.2	72.7	..	..	..	..	..	..	..	..
Monaco	0.0	0.0	1.0	0.5	100.0	..	..	..	..	..	..	..	..
Nauru	0.0	0.0	0.1	0.4	100.0	..	..	..	..	..	..	..	..
San Marino	0.0	0.0	1.3	0.7	94.2	..	..	..	..	..	..	..	..
Somalia	10.8	16.5	2.7	2.4	39.6	2.0	5.4	0.3	16.5	92.5	5.6	7.4	6.6
Tuvalu	0.0	0.0	0.6	0.2	59.7	..	..	..	..	..	..	..	..
Human development groups													
Very high human development	1,350.1	1,414.3	0.6	0.5	80.4	77.1	870.8	225.3	40.2	25.7	25.2	1.6	1.7
High human development	2,379.4	2,524.4	0.8	0.8	62.7	165.3	1,683.6	210.4	34.4	28.3	12.4	1.8	1.8
Medium human development	2,622.3	3,124.5	1.7	1.4	38.5	269.0	1,696.4	138.2	25.9	46.4	8.1	3.2	2.7
Low human development	929.2	1,361.4	2.8	2.7	35.8	153.3	496.3	27.7	17.9	81.7	5.6	6.0	5.2
Developing countries	6,071.2	7,178.3	1.5	1.4	48.5	601.1	3,971.0	385.6	28.1	42.9	9.7	2.9	2.7
Regions													
Arab States	387.6	504.2	2.2	2.1	57.9	48.4	242.3	16.8	24.3	53.0	7.0	3.6	3.4
East Asia and the Pacific	2,041.6	2,176.5	0.8	0.7	52.9	144.1	1,448.7	171.3	34.3	28.5	11.0	1.0	1.0
Europe and Central Asia	239.4	255.4	0.5	1.0	60.3	20.1	162.4	22.1	32.3	33.9	13.6	2.0	2.1
Latin America and the Caribbean	629.0	715.5	1.4	1.1	79.8	53.1	419.3	47.5	29.3	38.7	11.3	2.5	2.2
South Asia	1,823.0	2,147.4	1.7	1.4	34.8	180.1	1,185.8	98.5	26.1	45.4	8.3	3.2	2.6
Sub-Saharan Africa	949.5	1,378.0	2.7	2.7	37.9	155.2	511.8	29.3	18.3	79.8	5.7	5.7	5.1
Least developed countries	954.4	1,325.9	2.5	2.4	31.5	139.6	538.7	34.1	19.9	70.8	6.3	5.1	4.3
Small island developing states	55.7	63.9	1.3	1.2	55.5	5.5	35.5	4.0	27.9	45.2	11.3	3.1	2.8
Organisation for Economic Co-operation and Development	1,276.4	1,359.2	0.7	0.6	80.3	76.3	813.5	207.1	39.1	27.7	24.8	1.8	1.8
World	7,349.5[T]	8,500.8[T]	1.2[T]	1.2[T]	54.0[T]	670.9[T]	4,825.5[T]	608.2[T]	29.6[T]	39.7[T]	12.6[T]	2.6[T]	2.5[T]

TABLE **7**

NOTES

a Because data are based on national definitions of what constitutes a city or metropolitan area, cross-country comparison should be made with caution.

b Projections based on medium-fertility variant.

c Includes Svalbard and Jan Mayen Islands.

d Includes Christmas Island, Cocos (Keeling) Islands and Norfolk Island.

e Includes Åland Islands.

f Includes Canary Islands, Ceuta and Melilla.

g Includes Northern Cyprus.

h Includes Sabah and Sarawak.

i Includes Agalega, Rodrigues and Saint Brandon.

j Includes Kosovo.

k Includes Abkhazia and South Ossetia.

l Includes Nagorno-Karabakh.

m Includes Crimea.

n Includes Transnistria.

o Includes East Jerusalem.

p Includes Zanzibar.

T From original data source.

DEFINITIONS

Total population: De facto population in a country, area or region as of 1 July.

Population average annual growth: Average annual exponential growth rate for the period specified.

Urban population: De facto population living in areas classified as urban according to the criteria used by each country or area as of 1 July.

Population under age 5: De facto population in a country, area or region under age 5 as of 1 July.

Population ages 15–64: De facto population in a country, area or region ages 15–64 as of 1 July.

Population ages 65 and older: De facto population in a country, area or region ages 65 and older as of 1 July.

Median age: Age that divides the population distribution into two equal parts—that is, 50 percent of the population is above that age and 50 percent is below it.

Young age dependency ratio: Ratio of the population ages 0–14 to the population ages 15–64, expressed as the number of dependants per 100 people of working age (ages 15–64).

Old-age dependency ratio: Ratio of the population ages 65 and older to the population ages 15–64, expressed as the number of dependants per 100 people of working age (ages 15–64).

Total fertility rate: Number of children who would be born to a woman if she were to live to the end of her child-bearing years and bear children at each age in accordance with prevailing age-specific fertility rates.

MAIN DATA SOURCES

Columns 1–4 and 6–13: UNDESA (2015a).

Column 5: UNDESA (2014).

TABLE 7 Population trends | 227

TABLE 8

Health outcomes

HDI rank	Infants exclusively breastfed (% ages 0–5 months) 2010–2015[a]	Infants lacking immunization DTP (% of one-year-olds) 2014	Infants lacking immunization Measles 2014	Child malnutrition Stunting (moderate or severe) (% under age 5) 2010–2015[a]	Mortality rate Infant (per 1,000 live births) 2015	Mortality rate Under-five 2015	Mortality rate Female Adult (per 1,000 people) 2014	Mortality rate Male Adult (per 1,000 people) 2014	Deaths due to Malaria (per 100,000 people) 2012	Deaths due to Tuberculosis 2014	HIV prevalence, adult (% ages 15–49) 2015	Life expectancy at age 60 (years) 2010/2015[b]	Physicians (per 10,000 people) 2001–2014[a]	Public health expenditure (% of GDP) 2014
VERY HIGH HUMAN DEVELOPMENT														
1 Norway	..	1	6	..	2.0	2.6	44	69	..	0.2	..	23.9	42.8	8.3
2 Australia	..	8	7	2.0 [c]	3.0	3.8	..	..	..	0.2	0.2	24.9	32.7	6.3
2 Switzerland	..	2	7	..	3.4	3.9	..	..	..	0.1	..	25.0	40.5	7.7
4 Germany	..	2	3	1.3 [c]	3.1	3.7	..	..	..	0.4	..	23.5	38.9	8.7
5 Denmark	..	4	10	..	2.9	3.5	..	..	..	0.4	..	22.8	34.9	9.2
5 Singapore	..	2	5	4.4 [c]	2.1	2.7	39	71	..	1.0	..	25.1	19.5	2.1
7 Netherlands	..	2	4	..	3.2	3.8	..	..	..	0.1	..	23.8	28.6	9.5
8 Ireland	..	2	7	..	3.0	3.6	..	..	..	0.4	..	23.4	26.7	5.1
9 Iceland	..	4	10	..	1.6	2.0	39 [d]	67 [d]	..	0.3	..	24.5	34.8	7.2
10 Canada	..	2	5	..	4.3	4.9	..	..	..	0.2	..	24.7	20.7	7.4
10 United States	..	2	9	2.1	5.6	6.5	78 [d]	131 [d]	..	0.1	..	23.3	24.5	8.3
12 Hong Kong, China (SAR)	..	..	..	..	..	..	32	64	..	2.5	..	25.8	..	..
13 New Zealand	..	7	7	..	4.7	5.7	52 [d]	81 [d]	..	0.1	..	24.5	27.4	9.1
14 Sweden	..	1	3	..	2.4	3.0	43	66	..	0.3	..	24.3	39.3	10.0
15 Liechtenstein	..	..	..	..	..	..	..	..	..	..	..	..	..	..
16 United Kingdom	..	2	7	..	3.5	4.2	54 [d]	85 [d]	..	0.5	..	23.5	28.1	7.6
17 Japan	..	1	2	7.1	2.0	2.7	..	..	..	1.8	..	25.8	23.0	8.6
18 Korea (Republic of)	..	1	1	2.5	2.9	3.4	37	90	0.0	3.8	..	24.3	21.4	4.0
19 Israel	..	5	4	..	3.2	4.0	..	..	..	0.2	..	24.6	33.4	4.8
20 Luxembourg	..	1	1	..	1.5	1.9	..	..	..	0.2	..	23.9	29.0	5.8
21 France	..	1	10	..	3.5	4.3	51 [d]	105 [d]	..	0.6	..	25.2	31.9	9.0
22 Belgium	..	1	4	..	3.3	4.1	..	..	..	0.3	..	23.7	48.9	8.2
23 Finland	..	1	3	..	1.9	2.3	..	..	..	0.2	..	23.7	29.1	7.3
24 Austria	..	7	24	..	2.9	3.5	46	86	..	0.7	..	23.8	48.3	8.7
25 Slovenia	..	2	6	..	2.1	2.6	..	..	..	0.8	..	23.1	25.2	6.6
26 Italy	..	2	14	..	2.9	3.5	..	..	..	0.4	0.4	25.1	37.6	7.0
27 Spain	..	1	4	..	3.5	4.1	..	..	..	0.5	0.4	24.8	49.5	6.4
28 Czech Republic	..	1	1	2.6 [c]	2.8	3.4	53	115	..	0.6	..	21.5	36.2	6.3
29 Greece	..	1	3	..	3.6	4.6	45	101	..	1.0	0.3	23.6	61.7	5.0
30 Brunei Darussalam	..	1	3	19.7 [c]	8.6	10.2	52	85	..	3.6	..	21.4	14.4	2.5
30 Estonia	..	5	7	..	2.3	2.9	..	..	..	2.1	..	21.3	32.4	5.0
32 Andorra	..	1	4	..	2.1	2.8	..	..	..	0.8	..	..	40.0	6.3
33 Cyprus	..	1	14	..	2.5	2.7	35	70	..	0.4	..	22.1	23.3	3.3
33 Malta	..	1	2	..	5.1	6.4	41	70	..	0.3	..	22.8	34.9	6.7
33 Qatar	29.3	1	1	..	6.8	8.0	47	76	..	0.2	..	21.0	77.4	1.9
36 Poland	..	1	2	..	4.5	5.2	..	..	..	1.4	..	21.5	22.2	4.5
37 Lithuania	..	3	7	..	3.3	5.2	92 [d]	266 [d]	..	7.7	..	19.2	41.2	4.4
38 Chile	..	4	6	1.8	7.0	8.1	44	96	..	1.6	0.3	25.2	10.3	3.9
38 Saudi Arabia	..	1	2	9.3 [c]	12.5	14.5	80	94	0.0	2.1	..	18.5	24.9	3.5
40 Slovakia	..	1	3	..	5.8	7.3	..	..	..	0.5	..	20.3	33.2	5.8
41 Portugal	..	1	2	..	3.0	3.6	..	..	..	1.2	..	23.7	41.0	6.2
42 United Arab Emirates	34.0 [c]	6	6	..	5.9	6.8	57	81	..	0.3	..	19.8	25.3	2.6
43 Hungary	..	1	1	..	5.3	5.9	..	..	..	0.7	..	20.1	30.8	4.9
44 Latvia	..	7	5	..	6.9	7.9	94 [d]	243 [d]	..	2.7	0.7	19.8	35.8	3.7
45 Argentina	32.7	2	5	8.2 [c]	11.1	12.5	75	154	..	1.4	0.4	21.4	38.6	2.7
45 Croatia	23.3 [c]	2	6	..	3.6	4.3	57	134	..	1.1	..	20.6	30.0	6.4
47 Bahrain	33.8 [c]	1	1	..	5.3	6.2	60	75	..	0.4	..	19.4	9.2	3.2
48 Montenegro	16.8	3	12	9.4	4.3	4.7	73	130	..	0.6	..	19.8	21.1	3.7
49 Russian Federation	..	3	2	..	8.2	9.6	..	..	..	11.0	..	18.4	43.1	3.7
50 Romania	15.8 [c]	2	11	12.8 [c]	9.7	11.1	79	195	..	5.5	..	19.8	24.5	4.5
51 Kuwait	11.9 [c]	3	6	5.8	7.3	8.6	58	98	..	0.2	..	17.7	27.0	2.6
HIGH HUMAN DEVELOPMENT														
52 Belarus	19.0	3	1	4.5 [c]	3.4	4.6	90	261	..	7.7	0.6	18.1	39.3	3.7
52 Oman	32.8	1	1	14.1	9.9	11.6	70	111	..	0.6	..	20.6	24.3	3.2
54 Barbados	19.7 [e]	2	5	7.7	12.0	13.0	75	125	..	0.0	1.6	19.5	18.1	4.7
54 Uruguay	..	1	4	10.7	8.7	10.1	77	136	..	1.7	0.5	22.0	37.4	6.1
56 Bulgaria	..	10	7	8.8 [c]	9.3	10.4	..	..	..	2.1	..	19.2	38.7	4.6
56 Kazakhstan	31.8	4	1	13.1	12.6	14.1	124	302	..	8.6	0.2	17.1	36.2	2.4

		Infants exclusively breastfed	Infants lacking immunization		Child malnutrition	Mortality rate				Deaths due to		HIV prevalence, adult	Life expectancy at age 60	Physicians	Public health expenditure
			DTP	Measles	Stunting (moderate or severe)	Infant	Under-five	Female	Male	Malaria	Tuberculosis				
		(% ages 0–5 months)	(% of one-year-olds)		(% under age 5)	(per 1,000 live births)		Adult (per 1,000 people)		(per 100,000 people)		(% ages 15–49)	(years)	(per 10,000 people)	(% of GDP)
HDI rank		2010–2015[a]	2014	2014	2010–2015[a]	2015	2015	2014	2014	2012	2014	2015	2010/2015[b]	2001–2014[a]	2014
58	Bahamas	..	4	8	..	9.9	12.1	120	200	..	0.6	3.2	22.3	28.2	3.6
59	Malaysia	29.0 [c]	1	6	17.2 [c]	6.0	7.0	80	167	1.0	8.0	0.4	19.3	12.0	2.3
60	Palau	..	1	17	..	14.2	16.4	..	..	..	1.2	..	..	13.8	6.5
60	Panama	21.5	4	10	19.1 [c]	14.6	17.0	81	153	0.0	5.5	0.7	23.9	16.5	5.9
62	Antigua and Barbuda	..	1	2	..	5.8	8.1	108	154	..	3.8	..	21.5	..	3.8
63	Seychelles	..	1	1	..	11.7	13.6	92	238	..	0.0	..	19.4	10.7	3.1
64	Mauritius	21.0 [c]	3	2	..	11.8	13.5	95	194	..	1.3	0.9	20.2	10.6	2.4
65	Trinidad and Tobago	12.8 [c]	7	4	5.3 [c]	18.2	20.4	124	217	..	2.0	1.2	18.2	11.8	3.2
66	Costa Rica	32.5	9	5	5.6 [c]	8.5	9.7	61	114	0.0	0.8	0.3	23.6	11.1	6.8
66	Serbia	12.8	3	14	6.0	5.9	6.7	79	152	..	1.4	..	19.1	21.1	6.4
68	Cuba	33.2	2	1	7.0 [c]	4.0	5.5	72	109	..	0.3	0.3	23.1	67.2	10.6
69	Iran (Islamic Republic of)	53.1	1	1	6.8	13.4	15.5	64	105	0.0	3.5	0.1	19.4	8.9	2.8
70	Georgia	54.8 [c]	1	8	11.3 [c]	10.6	11.9	64	171	0.0	6.6	0.4	19.8	42.7	1.6
71	Turkey	30.1	3	6	9.5	11.6	13.5	73	142	0.0	0.6	..	20.8	17.1	4.2
71	Venezuela (Bolivarian Republic of)	7.1 [c]	12	11	13.4 [c]	12.9	14.9	91	195	2.2	1.8	0.5	20.7	19.4	1.5
73	Sri Lanka	75.0 [f]	1	1	14.7	8.4	9.8	75	201	0.0	6.1	0.1 [f]	20.4	6.8	2.0
74	Saint Kitts and Nevis	..	1	7	..	8.4	10.5	..	..	..	2.7	..	..	11.7	2.1
75	Albania	38.6 [c]	1	2	23.1 [c]	12.5	14.0	50	85	..	0.6	..	21.2	11.5	2.9
76	Lebanon	26.6 [c]	16	21	16.5 [c]	7.1	8.3	50	71	..	1.6	0.1 [f]	22.0	32.0	3.0
77	Mexico	14.4	10	3	13.6	11.3	13.2	81	143	0.0	1.7	0.2	22.7	21.0	3.3
78	Azerbaijan	12.1	4	2	18.0	27.9	31.7	86	178	0.1	0.4	0.2	18.3	34.0	1.2
79	Brazil	38.6 [c]	1	3	7.1 [c]	14.6	16.4	93	194	0.6	2.6	0.6	21.3	18.9	3.8
79	Grenada	39.0 [c]	3	6	..	10.8	11.8	98	186	..	0.4	..	18.8	6.6	2.8
81	Bosnia and Herzegovina	18.5	8	11	8.9	5.1	5.4	66	130	..	3.8	..	20.2	19.3	6.8
82	The former Yugoslav Republic of Macedonia	23.0	2	7	4.9	4.8	5.5	71	134	..	2.3	..	19.1	26.3	4.1
83	Algeria	25.7	1	5	11.7	21.9	25.5	84	135	0.0	11.0	0.1 [f]	21.6	12.1	5.2
84	Armenia	34.6	3	3	20.8	12.6	14.1	70	170	..	4.7	0.2	19.6	27.0	1.9
84	Ukraine	19.7	10	21	3.7 [c]	7.7	9.0	111 [d]	292 [d]	..	13.0	0.9	18.1	35.4	3.6
86	Jordan	22.7	2	2	7.8	15.4	17.9	94	128	..	0.3	..	19.0	25.6	5.2
87	Peru	68.4	2	11	14.6	13.1	16.9	96	154	0.7	7.2	0.3	21.3	11.3	3.3
87	Thailand	12.3	1	1	16.3	10.5	12.3	105	207	0.9	11.0	1.1	21.4	3.9	5.6
89	Ecuador	40.0 [c]	16	15	25.2	18.4	21.6	87	164	0.0	2.9	0.3	22.9	17.2	4.5
90	China	27.6 [c]	1	1	9.4	9.2	10.7	72	98	0.0	2.9	..	19.4	19.4	3.1
91	Fiji	39.8 [c]	1	6	7.5 [c]	19.1	22.4	139	236	..	4.7	..	17.0	4.3	3.0
92	Mongolia	47.1	1	2	10.8	19.0	22.4	132	300	..	2.2	0.1 [f]	18.0	28.4	2.6
92	Saint Lucia	..	1	1	2.5	12.7	14.3	110	188	..	2.4	..	21.1	1.1	3.8
94	Jamaica	23.8	3	8	5.7	13.5	15.7	101	166	..	0.3	1.6	22.2	4.1	2.8
95	Colombia	42.8	9	9	12.7	13.8	15.9	90	192	0.9	1.5	0.5	21.4	14.7	5.4
96	Dominica	..	1	6	..	19.6	21.2	..	..	..	2.7	..	..	15.9	3.8
97	Suriname	2.8	9	15	8.8	19.0	21.3	121	222	1.2	2.1	1.1	18.5	9.1	2.9
97	Tunisia	8.5	2	2	10.1	12.1	14.0	73	126	..	2.0	0.1 [f]	19.5	12.2	4.0
99	Dominican Republic	4.7	9	12	7.1	25.7	30.9	121	205	0.1	3.9	1.0	21.7	14.9	2.9
99	Saint Vincent and the Grenadines	..	1	1	..	16.6	18.3	130	182	..	1.0	..	19.9	5.3	4.4
101	Tonga	52.2	14	33	8.1	14.4	16.7	102	167	..	2.1	..	18.6	5.6	4.3
102	Libya	..	4	7	21.0 [c]	11.4	13.4	99	173	..	9.7	..	18.2	19.0	3.7
103	Belize	14.7	4	5	19.3	14.2	16.5	132	224	0.0	1.8	1.5	17.0	8.3	3.9
104	Samoa	51.3 [c]	1	9	..	15.0	17.5	93	159	..	3.4	..	18.9	4.8	6.5
105	Maldives	47.8 [c]	1	1	20.3 [c]	7.4	8.6	59	83	..	2.3	..	19.5	14.2	10.8
105	Uzbekistan	26.4 [c]	1	1	19.6 [c]	33.9	39.1	133	238	..	9.1	0.2	18.3	25.3	3.1
MEDIUM HUMAN DEVELOPMENT															
107	Moldova (Republic of)	36.4	6	10	6.4	13.6	15.8	101	244	..	7.8	0.6	17.3	29.8	5.3
108	Botswana	20.3 [c]	2	3	31.4 [c]	34.8	43.6	262	346	0.4	28.0	22.2	17.1	3.4	3.2
109	Gabon	6.0	23	39	17.5	36.1	50.8	246	245	67.4	55.0	3.8	18.3	2.9	2.4
110	Paraguay	24.4 [c]	2	10	10.9	17.5	20.5	126	166	0.0	2.9	0.4	21.0	12.3	4.5
111	Egypt	39.7	4	7	22.3	20.3	24.0	113	189	..	0.3	0.1 [f]	17.3	28.3	2.2
111	Turkmenistan	10.9 [c]	1	1	18.9 [c]	43.7	51.4	153	297	..	3.4	..	17.0	23.9	1.3
113	Indonesia	41.5	6	23	36.4	22.8	27.2	147	205	9.8	41.0	0.5	16.5	2.0	1.1
114	Palestine, State of	38.6	1	1	7.4	18.0	21.1	98	143	..	0.2	..	18.5	8.4	..
115	Viet Nam	24.3	5	3	19.4	17.3	21.7	68	186	0.2	18.0	0.5	22.4	11.9	3.8

TABLE 8   Health outcomes | 229

TABLE 8 HEALTH OUTCOMES

	Infants exclusively breastfed	Infants lacking immunization		Child malnutrition	Mortality rate				Deaths due to		HIV prevalence, adult	Life expectancy at age 60	Physicians	Public health expenditure
		DTP	Measles	Stunting (moderate or severe)	Infant	Under-five	Female	Male	Malaria	Tuberculosis				
	(% ages 0–5 months)	(% of one-year-olds)		(% under age 5)	(per 1,000 live births)		Adult (per 1,000 people)		(per 100,000 people)		(% ages 15–49)	(years)	(per 10,000 people)	(% of GDP)
HDI rank	2010–2015[a]	2014	2014	2010–2015[a]	2015	2015	2014	2014	2012	2014	2015	2010/2015[b]	2001–2014[a]	2014
116 Philippines	34.0[c]	14	12	30.3	22.2	28.0	144	272	0.1	10.0	0.1[f]	16.8	11.5	1.6
117 El Salvador	47.0	4	6	14.0	14.4	16.8	105	265	0.0	1.9	0.5	21.5	16.0	4.5
118 Bolivia (Plurinational State of)	64.3	2	5	18.1	30.6	38.4	156	219	0.1	3.1	0.3	21.1	4.7	4.6
119 South Africa	8.3[c]	27	30	23.9[c]	33.6	40.5	419	464	2.2	44.0	19.2	16.1	7.8	4.2
120 Kyrgyzstan	41.1	4	4	12.9	19.0	21.3	111	251	0.0	11.0	0.2	17.7	19.7	3.6
121 Iraq	19.6	23	43	22.6	26.5	32.0	132	198	..	2.2	..	17.5	6.1	3.3
122 Cabo Verde	59.6[c]	1	7	..	20.7	24.5	97	137	0.0	31.0	1.0	18.6	3.1	3.6
123 Morocco	27.8	1	1	14.9	23.7	27.6	87	106	..	7.9	0.1	19.1	6.2	2.0
124 Nicaragua	31.7	1	1	23.0[c]	18.8	22.1	106	194	0.1	3.4	0.3	22.3	9.0	5.1
125 Guatemala	53.2	11	33	46.5	24.3	29.1	129	236	0.0	1.6	0.6	21.3	9.3	2.3
125 Namibia	48.5	8	17	23.1	32.8	45.4	249	325	0.1	63.0	13.3	17.3	3.7	5.4
127 Guyana	23.3	2	1	12.0	32.0	39.4	173	250	23.6	21.0	1.5	16.0	2.1	3.1
127 Micronesia (Federated States of)	60.0[c]	2	9	..	28.6	34.7	150	178	..	16.0	..	17.3	1.8	12.4
129 Tajikistan	34.3	2	2	26.8	38.5	44.8	118	207	0.0	3.3	0.3	18.3	19.2	2.0
130 Honduras	31.2	14	12	22.7	17.4	20.4	122	174	0.1	1.0	0.4	22.1	3.7	4.4
131 India	46.4[c]	10	17	38.7	37.9	47.7	145	217	4.1	17.0	..	17.7	7.0	1.4
132 Bhutan	51.4	1	3	33.6	27.2	32.9	216	210	0.0	9.5	..	20.2	2.6	2.6
133 Timor-Leste	62.3	19	26	50.2	44.7	52.6	128	174	16.2	94.0	..	16.9	0.7	1.3
134 Vanuatu	72.6	25	47	28.5	23.1	27.5	108	156	3.7	7.9	..	18.0	1.2	4.5
135 Congo	32.9	5	20	21.2	33.2	45.0	247	286	103.8	46.0	..	17.9	1.0	4.2
135 Equatorial Guinea	7.4	35	56	26.2	68.2	94.1	286	326	69.3	6.6	4.9	16.8	3.0	2.9
137 Kiribati	69.0[c]	17	9	..	43.6	55.9	159	240	..	49.0	..	16.8	3.8	8.3
138 Lao People's Democratic Republic	40.4	6	13	43.8	50.7	66.7	176	217	9.5	55.0	..	16.6	1.8	0.9
139 Bangladesh	55.3	3	11	36.1	30.7	37.6	107	152	13.9	51.0	0.1[f]	18.7	3.6	0.8
139 Ghana	52.3	1	8	18.8	42.8	61.6	231	270	67.0	36.0	1.6	15.6	1.0	2.1
139 Zambia	72.5	4	15	40.0	43.3	64.0	270	331	79.2	32.0	12.9	17.7	1.7	2.8
142 Sao Tome and Principe	73.8	2	8	17.2	34.6	47.3	165	219	42.5	7.3	..	18.2	4.9	3.6
143 Cambodia	65.2	1	6	32.4	24.6	28.7	145	210	3.7	58.0	0.6	17.1	1.7	1.3
144 Nepal	56.9	6	12	37.4	29.4	35.8	139	177	0.2	17.0	0.2	17.3	2.1	2.3
145 Myanmar	23.6	10	14	35.1	39.5	50.0	173	229	11.3	53.0	0.8	16.7	6.1	1.0
146 Kenya	61.4	12	21	26.0	35.5	49.4	251	296	49.6	21.0	5.9	17.8	2.0	3.5
147 Pakistan	37.7	21	37	45.0	65.8	81.1	143	179	1.8	26.0	0.1[f]	17.8	8.3	0.9
LOW HUMAN DEVELOPMENT														
148 Swaziland	63.8	1	14	25.5	44.5	60.7	612	576	1.2	51.0	28.8	16.3	1.7	7.0
149 Syrian Arab Republic	42.6[c]	35	46	27.5[c]	11.1	12.9	86	283	..	0.1	..	18.7	14.6	1.5
150 Angola	..	1	15	29.2[c]	96.0	156.9	321	369	100.9	52.0	2.2	15.7	1.7	2.1
151 Tanzania (United Republic of)	41.1	1	1	34.7	35.2	48.7	243	281	50.5	58.0	4.7	18.5	0.3	2.6
152 Nigeria	17.4	25	49	32.9	69.4	108.8	346	379	106.6	97.0	3.1	13.7	4.0	0.9
153 Cameroon	28.2	7	20	31.7	57.1	87.9	345	370	64.7	31.0	4.5	16.5	0.8	0.9
154 Papua New Guinea	56.1[c]	13	35	49.5	44.5	57.3	237	313	40.3	40.0	0.8	14.9	0.6	3.5
154 Zimbabwe	41.0	2	8	27.6	46.6	70.7	382	413	18.4	15.0	14.7	17.5	0.8	2.5
156 Solomon Islands	73.7[c]	5	7	32.8[c]	23.6	28.1	157	198	5.5	13.0	..	16.9	2.2	4.6
157 Mauritania	26.9	12	16	22.0	65.1	84.7	183	228	67.2	22.0	0.6	16.5	0.7	1.9
158 Madagascar	41.9	17	36	49.2[c]	35.9	49.6	199	248	41.4	51.0	0.4	16.9	1.6	1.5
159 Rwanda	87.3	1	2	37.9	31.1	41.7	178	296	33.2	6.4	2.9	17.9	0.6	2.9
160 Comoros	12.1	17	20	32.1	55.1	73.5	204	254	70.4	7.5	..	16.2	1.5	2.2
160 Lesotho	66.9	3	8	33.2	69.2	90.2	599	581	..	64.0	22.7	15.5	0.5	8.1
162 Senegal	33.0	6	20	19.4	41.7	47.2	160	227	59.5	21.0	0.5	16.6	0.6	2.4
163 Haiti	39.7	28	47	21.9	52.2	69.0	215	277	5.1	20.0	1.7	17.8	..	1.6
163 Uganda	63.2	11	18	34.2	37.7	54.6	283	346	57.9	12.0	7.1	17.3	1.2	1.8
165 Sudan	55.4	1	14	38.2	47.6	70.1	197	254	16.5	21.0	0.3	17.8	2.8	1.8
166 Togo	57.5	9	18	27.5	52.3	78.4	256	289	82.8	8.8	2.4	15.1	0.5	2.0
167 Benin	41.4	16	37	34.0	64.2	99.5	223	270	79.6	9.8	1.1	15.6	0.6	2.3
168 Yemen	10.3	6	25	46.5	33.8	41.9	201	245	10.0	4.4	0.1[f]	16.3	2.0	1.3
169 Afghanistan	..	18	34	40.9	66.3	91.1	238	281	0.2	44.0	0.1[f]	15.7	2.7	2.9
170 Malawi	70.2	3	15	42.4	43.4	64.0	262	279	62.9	17.0	9.1	18.8	0.2	6.0
171 Côte d'Ivoire	12.1	22	37	29.6	66.6	92.6	388	424	70.6	..	3.2	14.1	1.4	1.7
172 Djibouti	1.3[c]	7	29	33.5	54.2	65.3	230	277	27.9	120.0	1.6	17.5	2.3	6.8
173 Gambia	46.8	2	4	24.5	47.9	68.9	237	291	83.7	18.0	1.8	15.2	0.4	5.0

TABLE 8

HDI rank	Infants exclusively breastfed (% ages 0–5 months) 2010–2015[a]	Infants lacking immunization (% of one-year-olds) DTP 2014	Infants lacking immunization Measles 2014	Child malnutrition Stunting (moderate or severe) (% under age 5) 2010–2015[a]	Mortality rate Infant (per 1,000 live births) 2015	Mortality rate Under-five 2015	Mortality rate Female Adult (per 1,000 people) 2014	Mortality rate Male Adult 2014	Deaths due to Malaria (per 100,000 people) 2012	Deaths due to Tuberculosis 2014	HIV prevalence, adult (% ages 15–49) 2015	Life expectancy at age 60 (years) 2010/2015[b]	Physicians (per 10,000 people) 2001–2014[a]	Public health expenditure (% of GDP) 2014
174 Ethiopia	52.0	14	30	40.4	41.4	59.2	203	255	48.1	33.0	..	17.8	0.2	2.9
175 Mali	37.8 [c]	20	20	38.5 [c]	74.5	114.7	263	258	92.1	11.0	1.3	15.2	0.8	1.6
176 Congo (Democratic Republic of the)	47.6	19	23	42.6	74.5	98.3	241	290	106.6	69.0	0.8	16.6	1.1	1.6
177 Liberia	55.2	26	42	32.1	52.8	69.9	231	269	69.2	68.0	1.1	15.4	0.1	3.2
178 Guinea-Bissau	52.5	8	31	27.6	60.3	92.5	252	306	96.2	63.0	..	15.0	0.5	1.1
179 Eritrea	68.7	3	4	50.3	34.1	46.5	228	295	3.6	14.0	0.6	15.4	0.5	1.5
179 Sierra Leone	32.0	12	22	37.9	87.1	120.4	399	407	108.7	45.0	1.3	13.0	0.2	1.9
181 Mozambique	41.0	7	15	43.1	56.7	78.5	382	425	71.4	67.0	10.5	17.0	0.4	3.9
181 South Sudan	45.1	51	78	31.1	60.3	92.6	321	348	55.4	29.0	2.5	16.4	..	1.1
183 Guinea	20.5	40	48	31.3	61.0	93.7	260	285	104.8	29.0	1.6	15.0	1.0	2.7
184 Burundi	69.3	2	6	57.5	54.1	81.7	267	327	63.7	23.0	1.0	16.4	0.3	4.0
185 Burkina Faso	50.1	5	12	32.9	60.9	88.6	250	279	103.3	9.1	0.8	15.1	0.5	2.6
186 Chad	0.3	40	46	39.9	85.0	138.7	346	388	152.6	23.0	2.0	15.7	0.4	2.0
187 Niger	23.3	11	28	43.0	57.1	95.5	203	239	131.1	18.0	0.5	16.0	0.2	3.2
188 Central African Republic	34.3	31	51	40.7	91.5	130.1	382	423	114.9	48.0	3.7	15.8	0.5	2.1
OTHER COUNTRIES OR TERRITORIES														
Korea (Democratic People's Rep. of)	68.9	6	1	27.9	19.7	24.9	106	176	0.0	20.0	..	16.8	32.9	..
Marshall Islands	31.3 [c]	3	21	..	29.6	36.0	..	..	..	38.0	..	..	4.4	14.4
Monaco	..	1	1	..	2.8	3.5	..	..	..	0.2	..	..	71.7	3.8
Nauru	67.2 [c]	1	2	24.0 [c]	29.1	35.4	..	..	..	6.0	..	..	7.1	2.9
San Marino	..	18	43	..	2.6	2.9	..	..	..	0.0	..	..	51.0	5.7
Somalia	5.3 [c]	48	54	25.9 [c]	85.0	136.8	285	346	33.5	67.0	0.5	16.1	0.4	..
Tuvalu	34.7 [c]	1	4	10.0 [c]	22.8	27.1	..	..	..	14.0	..	..	10.9	16.4
Human development groups														
Very high human development	..	2	6	..	5.4	6.3	..	..	..	2.0	0.4	23.4	30.9	7.5
High human development	29.3	3	3	10.4	11.6	13.4	79	129	..	3.5	0.4	19.9	19.0	3.4
Medium human development	43.0	10	18	35.0	35.5	44.6	147	215	7.1	22.7	1.6	17.8	7.3	1.8
Low human development	37.8	15	29	36.7	57.3	84.0	269	316	71.0	46.8	3.0	16.3	1.8	1.7
Developing countries	37.7	9	17	28.3	34.4	45.8	133	190	14.2	18.4	1.6	18.9	11.5	3.0
Regions														
Arab States	31.4	8	16	23.3	26.8	34.9	118	169	..	7.1	0.1	18.6	15.6	3.0
East Asia and the Pacific	31.4	4	7	18.4	14.9	17.9	90	134	1.8	11.3	0.5	19.2	15.4	3.0
Europe and Central Asia	27.4	4	6	12.5	18.2	20.5	97	210	..	5.7	0.5	19.0	25.8	3.7
Latin America and the Caribbean	32.9	6	8	13.0	15.1	17.8	92	176	..	2.7	0.5	21.8	19.6	3.6
South Asia	46.6	11	19	37.9	40.7	50.8	137	202	4.4	20.7	0.1	17.9	6.8	1.6
Sub-Saharan Africa	38.7	15	28	34.9	56.1	82.2	288	331	73.2	48.4	5.1	16.2	1.9	2.4
Least developed countries	46.1	11	21	37.9	51.0	72.0	208	254	47.9	39.5	1.9	17.3	1.8	1.8
Small island developing states	35.7	13	24	22.8	34.9	44.9	148	212	..	15.4	1.0	20.7	22.5	5.3
Organisation for Economic Co-operation and Development	..	3	6	..	5.9	6.9	..	..	..	0.8	0.3	24.0	27.7	7.7
World	**37.7**	**9**	**16**	**26.9**	**31.6**	**41.7**	**127**	**183**	**..**	**15.5**	**1.5**	**20.4**	**14.9**	**6.0**

TABLE 8

NOTES

a Data refer to the most recent year available during the period specified.

b Data are annual average of projected values for 2010–2015.

c Refers to a year earlier than that specified.

d Refers to 2013.

e Based on small denominators (typically 25–49 unweighted cases).

f 0.1 or less.

DEFINITIONS

Infants exclusively breastfed: Percentage of children ages 0–5 months who are fed exclusively with breast milk in the 24 hours prior to the survey.

Infants lacking immunization against DPT: Percentage of surviving infants who have not received their first dose of diphtheria, pertussis and tetanus vaccine.

Infants lacking immunization against measles: Percentage of surviving infants who have not received the first dose of measles vaccine.

Child malnutrition (stunting moderate or severe): Percentage of children ages 0–59 months who are more than two standard deviations below the median height-for-age of the World Health Organization Child Growth Standards.

Infant mortality rate: Probability of dying between birth and exactly age 1, expressed per 1,000 live births.

Under-five mortality rate: Probability of dying between birth and exactly age 5, expressed per 1,000 live births.

Adult mortality rate: Probability that a 15-year-old will die before reaching age 60, expressed per 1,000 people.

Deaths due to malaria: Number of deaths due to malaria from confirmed and probable cases, expressed per 100,000 people.

Deaths due to tuberculosis: Number of deaths due to tuberculosis from confirmed and probable cases, expressed per 100,000 people.

HIV prevalence, adult: Percentage of the population ages 15–49 that is living with HIV.

Life expectancy at age 60: Additional number of years that a 60-year-old could expect to live if prevailing patterns of age-specific mortality rates stay the same throughout the rest of his or her life.

Physicians: Number of medical doctors (physicians), both generalists and specialists, expressed per 10,000 people.

Public health expenditure: Current and capital spending on health from government (central and local) budgets, external borrowing and grants (including donations from international agencies and nongovernmental organizations) and social (or compulsory) health insurance funds, expressed as a percentage of GDP.

MAIN DATA SOURCES

Columns 1 and 4: UNICEF (2016).

Columns 2 and 3: WHO and UNICEF (2016).

Columns 5 and 6: UN Inter-agency Group for Child Mortality Estimation (2015).

Columns 7, 8, 11, 13 and 14: World Bank (2016a).

Column 9: United Nations Statistics Division (2016b).

Column 10: United Nations Statistics Division (2016c).

Column 12: UNDESA (2015a).

TABLE 8   Health outcomes | 231

TABLE 9

Education achievements

HDI rank	Literacy rate Adult (% ages 15 and older) 2005–2015[a]	Literacy rate Youth (% ages 15–24) Female 2005–2015[a]	Literacy rate Youth (% ages 15–24) Male 2005–2015[a]	Population with at least some secondary education (% ages 25 and older) 2005–2015[a]	Gross enrolment ratio Pre-primary (% of preschool-age children) 2010–2015[a]	Gross enrolment ratio Primary (% of primary school-age population) 2010–2015[a]	Gross enrolment ratio Secondary (% of secondary school-age population) 2010–2015[a]	Gross enrolment ratio Tertiary (% of tertiary school-age population) 2010–2015[a]	Primary school dropout rate (% of primary school cohort) 2005–2015[a]	Primary school teachers trained to teach (%) 2005–2015[a]	Pupil–teacher ratio, primary school (number of pupils per teacher) 2010–2015[a]	Government expenditure on education (% of GDP) 2010–2014[a]
VERY HIGH HUMAN DEVELOPMENT												
1 Norway	..	..	..	95.3	98	100	113	77	0.4	..	9	7.4
2 Australia	..	..	..	91.5	109	107	138	87	..	..	..	5.3
2 Switzerland	..	..	..	96.7	105	103	100	57	..	..	10	5.1
4 Germany	..	..	..	96.7 [b]	111	103	102	65	3.5	..	12	4.9
5 Denmark	..	..	..	89.5	96	101	130	82	0.5	..	..	8.5
5 Singapore	96.8	99.9	99.9	78.6	..	..	..	..	1.3	94	..	2.9
7 Netherlands	..	..	..	88.2	95	104	132	79	..	..	12	5.6
8 Ireland	..	..	..	85.5	108	103	126	73	..	..	16	5.8
9 Iceland	..	..	..	98.6	97	99	111	82	2.1	..	10	7.0
10 Canada	..	..	..	100.0	74	101	110	..	..	..	..	5.3
10 United States	..	..	..	95.3	71	100	98	87	..	..	15	5.2
12 Hong Kong, China (SAR)	..	..	..	77.4	109	111	101	69	1.6	96	14	3.6
13 New Zealand	..	..	..	98.7	92	99	117	81	..	..	14	6.4
14 Sweden	..	..	..	88.0	96	121	133	62	0.4	..	10	7.7
15 Liechtenstein	..	..	..	..	106	103	116	37	20.6	..	7	2.6
16 United Kingdom	..	..	..	82.9	88	108	128	56	..	..	17	5.7
17 Japan	..	..	..	91.8	90	102	102	62	0.2	..	17	3.8
18 Korea (Republic of)	..	..	..	91.4	92	99	98	95	0.4	..	17	4.6
19 Israel	..	..	..	88.8	111	104	102	66	0.8	..	13	5.9
20 Luxembourg	..	..	..	100.0	93	97	102	19	15.2	..	8	..
21 France	..	..	..	82.5	109	105	111	64	..	..	18	5.5
22 Belgium	..	..	..	82.3	118	105	165	73	7.8	..	11	6.4
23 Finland	..	..	..	100.0	80	101	145	89	0.4	..	13	7.2
24 Austria	..	..	..	98.9	102	102	99	80	0.5	..	11	5.6
25 Slovenia	99.7	99.9	99.8	97.3	93	99	111	83	1.0	..	17	5.7
26 Italy	99.2	99.9	99.9	82.3	100	102	102	63	1.1	..	12	4.1
27 Spain	98.1	99.8	99.7	73.7	98	105	130	89	3.7	..	13	4.3
28 Czech Republic	..	..	..	99.8	105	99	105	66	0.7	..	19	4.3
29 Greece	97.7	99.4	99.5	67.5	76	99	108	110	9.3	..	9	..
30 Brunei Darussalam	96.4	99.7	99.5	68.6 [b]	74	107	99	32	3.6	87	10	3.8
30 Estonia	99.8	100.0	100.0	100.0	88	101	109	73	3.4	..	11	4.7
32 Andorra	..	..	..	72.8	..	..	..	..	29.3	100	10	3.1
33 Cyprus	99.1	99.9	99.8	79.0	77	99	99	53	9.2	..	13	6.6
33 Malta	94.1	99.5	98.8	76.9	115	97	85	45	3.1	..	11	6.8
33 Qatar	97.8	99.7	98.3	68.4	58	101	109	16	2.3	49	11	3.5
36 Poland	99.8	100.0	100.0	83.9	77	101	109	71	1.5	..	10	4.8
37 Lithuania	99.8	99.9	99.9	93.1	88	102	107	69	2.8	..	13	4.8
38 Chile	97.3	99.7	99.0	76.5	128	101	100	87	0.5	..	20	4.6
38 Saudi Arabia	94.7	99.3	99.4	66.5	16	109	108	61	1.3	100	11	..
40 Slovakia	99.6	99.5	99.4	99.3	92	101	92	53	2.1	..	15	4.1
41 Portugal	95.7	99.6	99.5	51.4	92	109	116	66	..	..	13	5.1
42 United Arab Emirates	93.8	99.1	99.6	67.7	92	107	..	22	8.0	100	19	..
43 Hungary	99.1	99.0	98.7	96.6	84	102	107	53	1.7	..	11	4.6
44 Latvia	99.9	99.9	99.8	99.1	91	100	115	67	6.5	..	11	4.9
45 Argentina	98.1	99.5	99.1	62.4	72	111	106	80	5.4	..	..	5.3
45 Croatia	99.3	99.8	99.7	95.8	61	99	99	70	0.6	..	14	4.2
47 Bahrain	95.7	99.7	99.8	57.9 [b]	55	..	..	37	2.2	83	12	2.6
48 Montenegro	98.7	99.0	99.3	89.2	55	94	90	55	19.5	..	..	..
49 Russian Federation	99.7	99.8	99.7	94.6	84	99	101	79	3.6	..	20	4.2
50 Romania	98.8	99.3	99.3	89.1	90	96	95	53	6.0	..	18	2.9
51 Kuwait	96.2	99.5	99.6	57.4	81	103	94	27	4.3	79	9	..
HIGH HUMAN DEVELOPMENT												
52 Belarus	99.7	99.9	99.8	89.3	105	99	107	89	1.7	99	16	5.0
52 Oman	94.8	99.1	99.1	58.8	54	110	102	29	1.3	..	..	5.0
54 Barbados	..	..	..	92.6	84	94	109	65	6.6	100	18	6.7
54 Uruguay	98.4	99.3	98.5	53.4	70	110	94	63	5.3	..	14	4.4
56 Bulgaria	98.4	97.8	98.2	94.2	83	99	101	71	2.2	..	18	3.5
56 Kazakhstan	99.8	99.9	99.8	100.0	60	111	109	46	1.2	100	16	..

		Literacy rate				Gross enrolment ratio					Education quality		
		Adult (% ages 15 and older)	Youth (% ages 15–24)		Population with at least some secondary education	Pre-primary	Primary	Secondary	Tertiary	Primary school dropout rate	Primary school teachers trained to teach	Pupil–teacher ratio, primary school	Government expenditure on education
			Female	Male	(% ages 25 and older)	(% of preschool-age children)	(% of primary school-age population)	(% of secondary school-age population)	(% of tertiary school-age population)	(% of primary school cohort)	(%)	(number of pupils per teacher)	(% of GDP)
HDI rank		2005–2015ᵃ	2005–2015ᵃ	2005–2015ᵃ	2005–2015ᵃ	2010–2015ᵃ	2010–2015ᵃ	2010–2015ᵃ	2010–2015ᵃ	2005–2015ᵃ	2005–2015ᵃ	2010–2015ᵃ	2010–2014ᵃ
58	Bahamas	..	..	..	87.5	..	108	93	..	10.5	92	14	..
59	Malaysia	94.6	98.5	98.3	77.1	99	107	79	30	5.8	99	11	6.1
60	Palau	99.5	99.8	99.8	..	74	114	114	62	..	..	..	..
60	Panama	95.0	98.0	98.3	68.6	71	105	75	39	6.8	90	25	3.3
62	Antigua and Barbuda	99.0	..	..	..	75	97	102	23	8.7	70	14	..
63	Seychelles	95.2	99.6	98.6	..	93	104	75	6	..	87	13	3.6
64	Mauritius	90.6	99.1	98.4	59.7	102	103	98	39	1.8	100	19	5.0
65	Trinidad and Tobago	99.0	99.6	99.6	69.8	..	106	..	..	10.6	88	..	..
66	Costa Rica	97.8	99.4	99.2	54.2	53	111	120	53	9.6	94	13	7.0
66	Serbia	98.1	98.4	98.6	86.7	59	101	94	58	1.7	56	16	4.4
68	Cuba	99.7	99.9	99.9	84.8	98	98	100	41	3.5	100	9	12.8
69	Iran (Islamic Republic of)	86.8	98.2	98.5	67.7	42	109	88	66	3.8	100	26	3.0
70	Georgia	99.8	99.8	99.7	96.7	..	117	99	39	1.3	95	9	2.0
71	Turkey	95.0	98.8	99.7	54.0	28	107	100	79	10.0	..	20	..
71	Venezuela (Bolivarian Republic of)	95.4	98.3	97.1	68.9	73	101	92	..	12.9			
73	Sri Lanka	92.6	99.2	98.4	80.5	95	101	100	21	1.8	80	24	1.6
74	Saint Kitts and Nevis	..	..	..	..	94	84	92	79	7.2	68	14	..
75	Albania	97.6	99.1	99.0	90.3	89	112	96	63	1.3	..	19	3.5
76	Lebanon	93.9	99.3	98.8	54.2	84	97	68	43	6.7	97	12	2.6
77	Mexico	94.4	98.8	98.7	57.4	69	103	91	30	4.3	96	27	5.2
78	Azerbaijan	99.8	99.9	100.0	95.6	23	106	103	23	2.7	100	13	2.5
79	Brazil	92.6	99.2	98.6	57.5	86	110	102	46	..	..	21	5.9
79	Grenada	..	..	..	..	91	103	101	..	..	63	14	..
81	Bosnia and Herzegovina	98.5	99.6	99.7	78.0	15	100	89	48	13.5	..	17	..
82	The former Yugoslav Republic of Macedonia	97.8	98.5	98.7	47.8	29	86	82	39	2.5	..	15	..
83	Algeria	80.2	95.5	95.6	34.9	79	119	100	35	6.6	95	24	..
84	Armenia	99.8	99.9	99.8	98.3	52	..	..	44	9.0	77	..	2.2
84	Ukraine	99.8	99.8	99.7	95.1	104	104	99	82	1.5	100	17	6.7
86	Jordan	96.7	99.4	99.0	81.3	32	89	84	48	2.1	..	..	..
87	Peru	94.5	99.0	98.9	61.5	88	101	96	41	9.5	..	18	3.7
87	Thailand	96.7	98.2	98.3	43.3	73	104	86	53	6.5	100	15	4.1
89	Ecuador	94.5	98.8	98.8	48.8	62	113	104	40	11.1	82	24	4.2
90	China	96.4	99.7	99.7	75.0	82	104	94	39	..	..	16	..
91	Fiji	..	..	..	72.9	..	106	89	..	2.8	100	28	3.9
92	Mongolia	98.4	98.0	98.1	87.8	86	102	91	64	..	100	27	4.6
92	Saint Lucia	..	..	..	45.2	65	..	86	17	9.9	79	14	4.8
94	Jamaica	88.7	98.9	94.2	63.4	105	..	69	28	5.1	96	22	6.0
95	Colombia	94.7	99.1	98.2	54.9	55	114	99	51	16.5	98	24	4.7
96	Dominica	..	..	..	..	85	118	97	..	15.0	65	14	..
97	Suriname	95.6	99.7	98.4	57.6	94	120	78	..	14.1	6	14	..
97	Tunisia	81.8	97.8	98.3	43.9	43	113	88	35	6.0	100	17	6.2
99	Dominican Republic	91.8	98.6	97.3	56.4	44	101	78	48	21.4	85	21	..
99	Saint Vincent and the Grenadines	..	..	..	..	69	105	105	..	31.4	76	16	5.1
101	Tonga	99.4	99.5	99.4	91.2	39	108	90	..	9.6	97	22	..
102	Libya	91.0	99.9	100.0	55.1 ᵇ	..	..	..	..	..	..	..	..
103	Belize	82.7	89.9	87.3	77.6	50	112	80	24	5.3	61	22	6.2
104	Samoa	99.0	99.4	98.9	74.5	37	106	87	..	10.0	..	30	..
105	Maldives	99.3	99.5	100.0	32.6	..	..	..	..	17.8	86	12	5.2
105	Uzbekistan	99.6	100.0	99.9	99.9	25	97	95	9	1.9	100	16	..
MEDIUM HUMAN DEVELOPMENT													
107	Moldova (Republic of)	99.4	100.0	100.0	96.2	84	93	87	41	4.9	94	17	7.5
108	Botswana	88.5	99.6	96.1	85.9 ᵇ	18	109	84	28	6.0	99	23	..
109	Gabon	83.2	90.5	87.8	54.1 ᵇ	37	142	..	..	..	..	25	..
110	Paraguay	95.6	99.5	98.6	46.6	38	106	77	35	15.9	92	24	5.0
111	Egypt	75.2	92.1	94.5	61.4 ᵇ	30	104	86	32	3.9	73	23	..
111	Turkmenistan	99.7	99.9	99.8	..	63	89	85	8	..	..	..	3.0
113	Indonesia	93.9	99.1	98.9	47.3	58	106	82	31	18.1	..	17	3.3
114	Palestine, State of	96.7	99.3	99.4	58.8	51	95	82	44	2.5	100	24	..
115	Viet Nam	94.5	98.0	98.2	71.7	81	109	..	30	10.4	100	19	6.3

TABLE 9   Education achievements | 233

TABLE
9

TABLE 9 EDUCATION ACHIEVEMENTS

	Literacy rate			Population with at least some secondary education	Gross enrolment ratio				Primary school dropout rate	Education quality		Government expenditure on education
	Adult (% ages 15 and older)	Youth (% ages 15–24)			Pre-primary	Primary	Secondary	Tertiary		Primary school teachers trained to teach	Pupil–teacher ratio, primary school	
		Female	Male	(% ages 25 and older)	(% of preschool-age children)	(% of primary school–age population)	(% of secondary school–age population)	(% of tertiary school–age population)	(% of primary school cohort)	(%)	(number of pupils per teacher)	(% of GDP)
HDI rank	2005–2015[a]	2005–2015[a]	2005–2015[a]	2005–2015[a]	2010–2015[a]	2010–2015[a]	2010–2015[a]	2010–2015[a]	2005–2015[a]	2005–2015[a]	2010–2015[a]	2010–2014[a]
116 Philippines	96.3	98.9	97.0	71.6	..	117	88	36	24.2	100	31	3.4
117 El Salvador	88.4	97.9	97.5	41.0	72	112	81	29	17.4	96	24	3.4
118 Bolivia (Plurinational State of)	95.7	98.9	99.2	54.2	63	..	85	..	3.3	..	..	7.3
119 South Africa	94.3	99.4	98.6	74.9	76	100	94	20	..	..	32	6.1
120 Kyrgyzstan	99.5	99.8	99.7	100.0	25	108	91	46	1.2	72	25	6.8
121 Iraq	79.7	80.6	82.4	45.6 [b]	..	..	..	..	..	..	..	..
122 Cabo Verde	87.6	98.6	98.1	..	70	113	93	23	9.4	96	23	5.0
123 Morocco	72.4	93.5	96.6	29.4 [b]	60	116	69	25	10.7	100	26	..
124 Nicaragua	82.8	93.6	89.7	45.0 [b]	58	123	74	..	51.6	75	30	4.5
125 Guatemala	79.3	91.0	95.5	36.8	66	104	64	18	28.2	..	23	2.8
125 Namibia	81.9	93.3	86.5	38.5	21	111	..	..	9.4	96	30	8.3
127 Guyana	88.5	94.8	94.1	60.9 [b]	94	85	89	12	7.8	70	23	3.2
127 Micronesia (Federated States of)	..	..	..	..	..	98	..	..	..	..	..	..
129 Tajikistan	99.8	99.9	99.9	93.3	11	98	88	26	1.4	100	22	4.0
130 Honduras	88.5	98.1	96.2	32.3	47	109	68	21	24.6	..	14	5.9
131 India	72.1	87.2	91.8	48.7 [b]	10	111	69	24	..	..	32	3.8
132 Bhutan	64.9	87.3	89.9	9.6	17	102	84	11	21.1	91	27	5.9
133 Timor-Leste	67.5	82.9	81.9	..	17	137	73	18	18.8	..	31	7.7
134 Vanuatu	85.2	96.0	95.5	..	97	124	60	..	28.5	100	23	4.9
135 Congo	79.3	76.9	85.7	47.4	14	111	55	10	29.7	80	44	6.2
135 Equatorial Guinea	95.3	98.8	97.7	..	68	84	..	..	27.9	49	26	..
137 Kiribati	..	..	..	..	..	113	..	..	..	85	26	..
138 Lao People's Democratic Republic	79.9	87.3	93.1	36.4 [b]	30	116	57	17	22.4	98	25	4.2
139 Bangladesh	61.5	85.8	80.6	43.1 [b]	32	112	58	13	33.8	58	40	2.0
139 Ghana	76.6	89.9	91.3	59.8	121	110	71	16	16.3	55	31	6.0
139 Zambia	63.4	62.1	69.4	51.8	..	104	..	..	44.5	93	48	..
142 Sao Tome and Principe	74.9	82.3	84.0	37.7	51	114	85	13	20.5	34	39	3.9
143 Cambodia	77.2	91.9	91.1	19.6	18	116	..	16	53.1	100	45	2.0
144 Nepal	64.7	87.4	92.6	32.0 [b]	85	135	67	16	29.9	94	23	4.7
145 Myanmar	93.1	96.3	96.3	23.8 [b]	23	100	51	14	25.2	100	28	..
146 Kenya	78.0	86.6	85.2	32.0	74	111	68	..	..	97	57	5.5
147 Pakistan	58.7	69.3	81.5	35.4	70	94	42	10	20.4	84	47	2.5
LOW HUMAN DEVELOPMENT												
148 Swaziland	87.5	96.0	93.5	28.8 [b]	25	113	63	5	25.3	79	28	8.6
149 Syrian Arab Republic	86.4	95.6	97.1	38.9	6	80	50	33	83.9	..	..	..
150 Angola	71.1	67.3	78.6	..	79	129	29	10	68.1	47	43	3.4
151 Tanzania (United Republic of)	80.3	87.2	87.4	12.6	32	87	32	4	33.3	99	43	3.5
152 Nigeria	59.6	65.3	79.9	..	13	85	44	..	20.7	66	38	..
153 Cameroon	75.0	80.4	87.1	31.8	34	114	56	12	30.2	79	44	3.0
154 Papua New Guinea	64.2	78.8	66.3	11.7 [b]	..	115	40	..	..	..	..	..
154 Zimbabwe	86.5	93.5	90.0	57.7	42	100	48	6	23.1	86	36	2.0
156 Solomon Islands	..	..	..	..	98	114	48	..	28.5	65	20	10.0
157 Mauritania	52.1	55.0	70.0	17.3 [b]	3	98	30	6	35.9	91	34	3.3
158 Madagascar	64.7	64.8	65.4	..	14	147	38	4	59.9	17	42	2.1
159 Rwanda	70.5	82.2	78.5	13.2	14	134	39	8	65.3	95	58	5.0
160 Comoros	77.8	88.2	86.9	..	23	105	59	9	..	75	28	5.1
160 Lesotho	79.4	93.4	77.0	23.0	31	107	52	10	32.6	76	33	..
162 Senegal	55.7	63.6	75.9	13.9	15	81	40	7	38.6	70	32	5.6
163 Haiti	60.7	81.6	82.6	32.0 [b]	..	..	..	..	..	..	..	..
163 Uganda	73.9	86.6	87.4	30.8	11	110	28	4	75.2	95	46	2.2
165 Sudan	75.9	87.8	91.3	16.3 [b]	34	70	43	17	20.6	60	25	..
166 Togo	66.5	81.4	88.9	33.3	15	125	55	10	47.2	76	41	4.8
167 Benin	38.4	42.5	62.6	23.3	21	126	54	15	46.6	68	46	4.4
168 Yemen	70.1	82.7	97.6	24.4 [b]	1	97	49	10	30.5	..	30	..
169 Afghanistan	38.2	46.3	69.6	22.2 [b]	..	112	56	9	..	..	46	4.8
170 Malawi	65.8	75.2	74.9	19.6	..	147	39	1	50.9	91	61	6.9
171 Côte d'Ivoire	43.1	40.7	59.6	24.9 [b]	7	90	40	9	26.0	85	43	4.7
172 Djibouti	..	..	..	..	5	66	47	5	15.6	100	33	4.5
173 Gambia	55.5	70.8	75.6	31.9 [b]	34	86	57	3	22.7	84	37	2.8

TABLE 9

	Literacy rate			Population with at least some secondary education	Gross enrolment ratio				Primary school dropout rate	Education quality		Government expenditure on education
	Adult (% ages 15 and older)	Youth (% ages 15–24)			Pre-primary	Primary	Secondary	Tertiary		Primary school teachers trained to teach	Pupil–teacher ratio, primary school	
		Female	Male	(% ages 25 and older)	(% of preschool-age children)	(% of primary school–age population)	(% of secondary school–age population)	(% of tertiary school–age population)	(% of primary school cohort)	(%)	(number of pupils per teacher)	(% of GDP)
HDI rank	2005–2015[a]	2005–2015[a]	2005–2015[a]	2005–2015[a]	2010–2015[a]	2010–2015[a]	2010–2015[a]	2010–2015[a]	2005–2015[a]	2005–2015[a]	2010–2015[a]	2010–2014[a]
174 Ethiopia	49.1	67.8	71.1	15.8	25	100	36	8	63.4	95	64	4.5
175 Mali	38.7	46.4	61.5	11.5	4	77	44	7	38.4	52	42	4.3
176 Congo (Democratic Republic of the)	77.3	80.5	91.6	24.6 [b]	4	107	44	7	44.6	95	35	2.2
177 Liberia	47.6	44.0	64.7	28.3 [b]	..	96	38	12	32.2	56	26	2.8
178 Guinea-Bissau	59.9	73.7	80.8	..	6	114	..	..	..	39	52	2.4
179 Eritrea	73.8	91.9	94.5	..	15	51	36	3	22.4	80	40	..
179 Sierra Leone	48.1	59.3	75.8	23.1 [b]	10	130	43	..	52.2	57	35	2.8
181 Mozambique	58.8	69.7	83.7	5.2 [b]	..	104	25	6	69.3	90	54	6.5
181 South Sudan	31.9	41.7	46.9	..	6	84	..	..	..	44	50	0.8
183 Guinea	30.4	47.5	43.0	..	15	91	39	11	34.1	75	46	3.5
184 Burundi	85.6	87.8	87.4	8.7 [b]	7	128	38	4	47.4	92	44	5.4
185 Burkina Faso	36.0	43.2	47.6	8.5	4	87	30	5	30.5	86	44	4.5
186 Chad	40.2	50.2	55.3	5.5	1	101	22	3	49.0	65	62	2.9
187 Niger	19.1	17.1	36.4	6.1 [b]	7	71	19	2	35.6	50	36	6.8
188 Central African Republic	36.8	27.0	48.9	20.9 [b]	6	93	17	3	53.4	58	80	1.2
OTHER COUNTRIES OR TERRITORIES												
Korea (Democratic People's Rep. of)	100.0	100.0	100.0	..	..	..	..	30	..	..	..	..
Marshall Islands	..	..	..	92.1	48	105	..	43	16.5	..	..	..
Monaco	..	..	..	..	..	..	..	..	..	..	..	1.0
Nauru	..	..	..	..	90	105	83	..	..	74	39	..
San Marino	..	..	..	..	107	93	95	60	3.8	..	6	2.4
Somalia	..	..	..	..	..	..	..	..	..	..	..	..
Tuvalu	..	..	..	..	93	101	81	..	..	..	..	..
Human development groups												
Very high human development	..	..	..	88.8	84	102	106	75	..	..	14	5.1
High human development	95.3	99.3	99.2	70.6	74	105	95	43	..	..	18	..
Medium human development	76.4	88.5	91.5	49.1	34	109	68	23	..	..	29	3.9
Low human development	60.9	69.1	77.5	20.3	18	98	40	8	42.2	78	42	3.8
Developing countries	83.3	88.7	91.8	57.7	42	105	71	29	..	..	26	..
Regions												
Arab States	80.7	91.6	94.6	47.0	37	98	76	30	16.1	85	21	..
East Asia and the Pacific	95.7	99.0	98.9	68.9	74	106	88	37	..	..	17	..
Europe and Central Asia	98.1	99.4	99.7	81.7	44	104	98	55	5.2	..	18	..
Latin America and the Caribbean	93.2	98.4	98.0	58.1	74	107	95	44	..	..	22	5.4
South Asia	70.3	84.8	80.6	47.0	23	100	66	23	..	..	33	3.4
Sub-Saharan Africa	64.3	71.1	78.3	29.6	26	100	43	8	41.7	78	43	4.8
Least developed countries	63.3	74.3	78.9	25.7	22	104	44	9	45.4	78	41	3.3
Small island developing states	82.8	90.0	87.8	56.6	..	107	73	..	..	..	..	..
Organisation for Economic Co-operation and Development	..	..	..	85.5	80	103	104	70	..	..	16	5.1
World	**84.3**	**89.1**	**92.1**	**64.9**	**47**	**105**	**76**	**35**	**..**	**..**	**24**	**5.0**

TABLE 9

NOTES

a Data refer to the most recent year available during the period specified.

b Based on Barro and Lee (2016).

DEFINITIONS

Adult literacy rate: Percentage of the population ages 15 and older that can, with understanding, both read and write a short simple statement on everyday life.

Youth literacy rate: Percentage of the population ages 15–24 that can, with understanding, both read and write a short simple statement on everyday life.

Population with at least some secondary education: Percentage of the population ages 25 and older that has reached (but not necessarily completed) a secondary level of education.

Gross enrolment ratio: Total enrolment in a given level of education (pre-primary, primary, secondary or tertiary), regardless of age, expressed as a percentage of the official school-age population for the same level of education.

Primary school dropout rate: Percentage of students from a given cohort who have enrolled in primary school but who drop out before reaching the last grade of primary education. It is calculated as 100 minus the survival rate to the last grade of primary education and assumes that observed flow rates remain unchanged throughout the cohort life and that dropouts do not re-enter school.

Primary school teachers trained to teach: Percentage of primary school teachers who have received the minimum organized teacher training (pre-service or in-service) required for teaching at the primary level.

Pupil–teacher ratio, primary school: Average number of pupils per teacher in primary education in a given school year.

Government expenditure on education: Current, capital and transfer spending on education, expressed as a percentage of GDP.

MAIN DATA SOURCES

Columns 1–11: UNESCO Institute for Statistics (2016).

Column 12: World Bank (2016a).

TABLE 9   Education achievements | 235

TABLE **10**

National income and composition of resources

		Gross domestic product (GDP)		Gross fixed capital formation	General government final consumption expenditure		Total tax revenue	Taxes on income, profits and capital gains	Debts — Domestic credit provided by financial sector	Total debt service	Prices — Consumer price index	Domestic food price level	
		Total (2011 PPP $ billions)	Per capita (2011 PPP $)	(% of GDP)	Total (% of GDP)	Average annual growth (%)	(% of GDP)	(% of total tax revenue)	(% of GDP)	(% of GNI)	(2010=100)	Index	Volatility index
HDI rank		2015	2015	2010–2015[a]	2010–2015[a]	2010–2015[a]	2005–2014[a]	2005–2014[a]	2010–2015[a]	2014	2015	2010–2014[a]	2010–2014[a]
VERY HIGH HUMAN DEVELOPMENT													
1	Norway	334.9	64,451	23.3	23.2	1.9	23.8	26.2	..	..	109	1.5	11.3
2	Australia	1,038.2	43,655	26.5	18.0	1.3	22.2	63.6	177.2	..	112	1.4	..
2	Switzerland	456.7	55,112	23.7	11.3	2.4	9.6	20.9	178.8	..	98	1.4	6.6
4	Germany	3,586.5	44,053	20.0	19.4	2.5	11.5	16.5	135.1	..	107	1.5	5.6
5	Denmark	246.4	43,415	19.1	26.2	0.6	34.8	44.0	219.0	..	107	1.3	6.0
5	Singapore	443.9	80,192	25.5	10.4	0.1	13.9	34.7	121.1	..	113	1.0	4.0
7	Netherlands	785.4	46,374	19.5	25.3	0.3	20.9	24.1	218.9	..	109	1.4	5.6
8	Ireland	240.8	51,899	22.0	17.2	−0.8	23.8	37.6	130.5	..	105	1.2	3.3
9	Iceland	14.0	42,449	19.2	23.8	1.8	25.7	29.8	108.0	..	118	1.8	5.4
10	Canada	1,537.7	42,891	23.3	21.2	1.7	11.8	52.9	..	..	109	1.3	7.1
10	United States	16,890.2	52,549	19.6	14.3	0.4	10.9	52.8	238.3	..	109	1.0	0.0
12	Hong Kong, China (SAR)	390.0	53,380	22.6	9.6	3.4	12.5	36.2	211.5	..	123	..	..
13	New Zealand	159.8	34,762	22.4	18.6	2.3	26.7	50.8	150.7	..	108	2.0	..
14	Sweden	443.9	45,296	24.2	26.1	2.5	26.4	14.3	152.4	..	104	1.5	6.7
15	Liechtenstein	..	..	..	..	..	..	..	..	..	..	..	..
16	United Kingdom	2,518.1	38,658	17.3	19.4	1.5	25.0	32.6	163.2	..	112	1.2	5.0
17	Japan	4,545.7	35,804	21.7	20.4	1.2	10.9	47.6	376.6	..	104	1.9	5.6
18	Korea (Republic of)	1,740.5	34,387	29.1	15.2	3.4	14.4	30.3	166.5	..	110	1.9	9.1
19	Israel	265.4	31,671	18.6	22.3	2.9	23.5	28.9	83.2	..	107	2.2	5.9
20	Luxembourg	53.3	93,553	17.4	16.6	2.7	25.9	29.1	191.2	..	109	1.3	8.9
21	France	2,492.3	37,306	21.5	23.9	1.4	23.3	25.4	148.4	..	106	1.7	6.0
22	Belgium	464.3	41,138	23.3	24.2	0.2	26.1	36.5	148.3	..	109	1.7	6.0
23	Finland	211.8	38,643	20.3	24.6	−0.9	20.8	14.8	158.6	..	109	1.6	6.2
24	Austria	378.0	43,893	22.1	20.1	1.4	26.4	28.1	126.1	..	111	1.4	5.9
25	Slovenia	59.7	28,942	19.4	18.5	0.7	17.6	10.4	71.3	..	106	2.2	9.4
26	Italy	2,042.2	33,587	16.5	19.0	−0.7	23.6	31.6	171.4	..	107	2.0	5.0
27	Spain	1,523.2	32,814	20.4	19.3	2.7	12.2	28.2	193.6	..	107	2.0	8.4
28	Czech Republic	314.5	29,805	25.8	19.3	2.8	13.5	14.5	70.8	..	108	2.3	10.7
29	Greece	266.4	24,617	11.7	20.0	0.0	24.6	18.8	135.4	..	101	2.6	11.2
30	Brunei Darussalam	28.2	66,647	27.3	21.6	1.1	..	..	33.4	..	102	3.0	4.7
30	Estonia	35.3	26,930	24.2	19.9	2.1	1.0	10.4	76.5	..	111	2.8	7.4
32	Andorra	..	..	..	..	..	..	..	..	..	..	..	..
33	Cyprus	25.5	30,310	10.8	15.7	−8.7	24.5	23.3	314.2	..	102	2.0	12.7
33	Malta	12.2 [b]	28,822 [b]	14.3	20.2	0.9	28.0	32.6	151.5	..	108	2.6	8.6
33	Qatar	302.5	135,322	..	19.4	8.3	14.7	40.2	120.2	..	112	1.8	6.3
36	Poland	943.8	24,836	20.1	18.0	3.4	15.5	19.1	73.6	..	108	2.7	7.0
37	Lithuania	76.8	26,397	18.9	16.9	1.3	4.6	15.1	47.5	..	108	3.5	5.5
38	Chile	397.5	22,145	22.7	13.4	5.8	17.1	28.9	123.6	..	118	2.6	7.4
38	Saudi Arabia	1,586.0	50,284	28.8	29.6	12.0	..	..	20.8	..	118	2.9	3.8
40	Slovakia	148.6	27,394	23.0	19.0	3.4	16.1	28.3	74.4	..	109	2.6	9.2
41	Portugal	276.2	26,690	15.0	18.1	0.6	22.7	25.1	167.0	..	107	2.5	9.0
42	United Arab Emirates	605.3	66,102	23.7	7.5	3.7	0.4	..	100.1	..	109	..	..
43	Hungary	240.9	24,474	21.7	20.2	2.9	23.0	15.0	59.4	..	111	2.4	5.8
44	Latvia	44.8	22,628	22.9	17.6	4.9	14.0	8.7	58.0	..	108	2.9	7.9
45	Argentina	..	..	15.6	18.3	6.7	..	..	41.2	..	106 [c]	..	..
45	Croatia	86.3	20,430	19.1	19.7	0.6	19.6	7.9	88.7	..	107	3.2	2.7
47	Bahrain	60.8	44,182	15.3	15.7	2.9	1.1	0.5	87.8	..	111	2.2	18.5
48	Montenegro	9.3	15,010	22.9	17.6	−3.0	..	..	59.9	5.8	111	5.6	9.1
49	Russian Federation	3,498.4	23,895	21.9	19.1	−1.8	13.4	1.9	54.5	..	152	4.3	5.2
50	Romania	395.2	19,926	24.7	13.5	1.8	18.0	18.7	37.5	12.5	114	3.7	4.3
51	Kuwait	261.2	67,113	..	19.4	8.8	..	..	88.0	..	118	2.6	3.7
HIGH HUMAN DEVELOPMENT													
52	Belarus	158.1	16,621	28.6	14.9	−0.4	15.1	3.5	51.5	7.2	..	5.3	6.0
52	Oman	161.6	35,983	28.0	25.0	3.9	2.6	2.6	64.2	..	110	3.3	9.2
54	Barbados	4.4	15,426	13.0	20.6	31.3	25.2	27.6	..	..	117	2.4	5.4
54	Uruguay	68.5	19,952	19.9	13.9	2.6	18.8	18.4	36.3	..	150	3.1	6.4
56	Bulgaria	121.7	16,956	21.2	16.3	0.3	18.6	14.6	61.8	10.4	107	3.2	5.9
56	Kazakhstan	427.2	24,353	19.9	10.3	10.3	..	..	44.9	15.2	137	..	..

		Gross domestic product (GDP)		Gross fixed capital formation	General government final consumption expenditure		Total tax revenue	Taxes on income, profits and capital gains	Debts — Domestic credit provided by financial sector	Total debt service	Prices — Consumer price index	Domestic food price level	
		Total (2011 PPP $ billions)	Per capita (2011 PPP $)	(% of GDP)	Total (% of GDP)	Average annual growth (%)	(% of GDP)	(% of total tax revenue)	(% of GDP)	(% of GNI)	(2010=100)	Index	Volatility index
HDI rank		2015	2015	2010–2015[a]	2010–2015[a]	2010–2015[a]	2005–2014[a]	2005–2014[a]	2010–2015[a]	2014	2015	2010–2014[a]	2010–2014[a]
58	Bahamas	8.7	22,394	20.6	15.7	4.4	..	..	99.4	..	109	1.6	5.4
59	Malaysia	767.6	25,308	26.2	13.2	4.3	15.6	52.0	144.8	4.0	113	2.9	4.3
60	Palau	0.3	14,386	..	..	..	..	..	..	..	..	..	..
60	Panama	82.1	20,885	43.3	9.9	3.0	..	..	82.4	3.1	120	3.0	2.1
62	Antigua and Barbuda	2.0	21,615	25.0	23.0	41.5	18.6	12.0	68.0	..	110	2.6	..
63	Seychelles	2.4	25,668	33.7	26.3	..	28.4	27.9	33.7	..	121	6.7	7.2
64	Mauritius	23.1	18,333	17.7	14.4	4.3	18.7	19.9	118.1	28.2	120	4.9	11.7
65	Trinidad and Tobago	41.7	30,677	13.8	15.5	8.3	27.6	49.6	33.5	..	134	4.0	16.5
66	Costa Rica	69.6	14,472	21.8	17.8	3.5	13.7	15.6	69.9	7.2	122	3.2	7.6
66	Serbia	91.3	12,863	18.1	16.9	−1.2	19.7	7.6	55.5	19.6	133	4.0	8.5
68	Cuba	226.7[b]	19,950[b]	10.4	33.3	2.2	..	..	..	..	..	..	..
69	Iran (Islamic Republic of)	1,289.9[c]	16,507[c]	26.2	10.7	2.7	7.7	19.3	..	0.1	285	4.5	13.0
70	Georgia	33.5	9,109	28.5	16.5	6.6	24.1	35.2	52.6	11.4	115	..	..
71	Turkey	1,491.4	18,959	20.3	15.7	6.7	21.1	17.4	92.8	7.1	146	3.8	12.9
71	Venezuela (Bolivarian Republic of)	485.4	15,603	22.2	12.4	0.6	15.5	21.5	61.9	..	730	4.5	12.8
73	Sri Lanka	231.6	11,048	26.5	8.8	10.3	10.4	16.2	66.9	3.2	128	6.9	8.3
74	Saint Kitts and Nevis	1.3	22,934	29.0	22.6	..	20.2	9.8	79.0	..	106	2.9	..
75	Albania	30.0	10,397	27.3	10.9	−2.8	..	..	62.6	2.5	111	6.4	10.3
76	Lebanon	76.7	13,117	27.6	13.8	−0.3	14.8	19.3	206.0	7.2	115	..	..
77	Mexico	2,096.0	16,502	22.2	12.3	2.3	..	..	53.7	4.1	119	3.7	4.7
78	Azerbaijan	161.1	16,695	28.6	12.5	2.2	13.0	13.6	35.4	2.5	..	..	..
79	Brazil	3,004.4	14,455	18.2	20.2	−1.0	14.1	26.5	108.7	2.5	138	2.6	4.4
79	Grenada	1.3	12,203	15.0	15.0	..	18.7	16.9	58.0	2.9	104	3.4	..
81	Bosnia and Herzegovina	38.2	10,024	18.9	22.3	0.9	19.8	6.5	58.5	4.4	104	4.8	6.3
82	The former Yugoslav Republic of Macedonia	26.4	12,725	25.0	16.7	4.6	16.4	10.7	59.6	8.8	110	5.1	7.9
83	Algeria	548.3	13,823	36.7	19.4	1.1	37.2	60.2	39.8	0.1	127	5.1	5.5
84	Armenia	23.8	7,899	20.4	13.8	3.1	17.5	21.3	48.7	11.8	125	8.9	11.9
84	Ukraine	319.2	7,450	13.3	19.0	−15.0	10.3	11.0	85.6	13.7	181	5.2	3.0
86	Jordan	77.8	10,240	22.1	18.9	−1.1	15.3	13.6	105.5	3.9	116	4.5	6.1
87	Peru	366.2	11,672	24.3	13.0	9.5	16.5	34.0	27.6	2.6	118	3.9	3.4
87	Thailand	1,042.9	15,345	24.7	17.1	1.7	16.0	34.6	173.4	3.9	110	4.5	2.8
89	Ecuador	173.0	10,718	27.0	14.6	1.1	..	..	30.9	4.0	121	3.4	5.7
90	China	18,374.7	13,400	44.3	13.6	3.1	10.4	24.9	196.9	0.5	115	3.3	8.1
91	Fiji	7.7	8,620	17.1	15.2	..	23.2	32.5	119.9	1.2	116	5.1	8.3
92	Mongolia	33.9	11,471	18.2	11.8	−7.8	15.3	11.6	69.3	12.1	163	4.8	16.7
92	Saint Lucia	1.9	10,344	20.8	19.3	..	22.9	27.1	97.4	2.7	111	3.4	12.3
94	Jamaica	23.2	8,529	22.0	14.8	−1.0	26.6	29.0	50.4	11.3	141	5.0	7.0
95	Colombia	626.4	12,988	26.7	18.2	2.8	14.7	19.4	52.6	3.6	118	2.7	4.5
96	Dominica	0.8	10,614	12.3	21.3	..	23.1	16.2	51.6	3.8	104	..	..
97	Suriname	8.7	15,970	50.1	17.0	34.0	19.5	31.9	53.4	..	139	6.2	9.7
97	Tunisia	119.1	10,726	19.6	19.7	10.3	21.1	26.7	90.2	4.2	127	3.9	4.7
99	Dominican Republic	140.8	13,375	21.3	11.8	8.8	13.8	27.2	54.8	5.3	122	4.1	5.2
99	Saint Vincent and the Grenadines	1.1	10,379	23.4	16.6	..	..	..	58.4	4.3	105	3.4	4.8
101	Tonga	0.5[c]	4,972[c]	33.6	19.2	..	..	..	29.5	1.5	110	..	..
102	Libya	83.6	13,321	..	..	..	..	..	2.7	..	126[b]	..	..
103	Belize	2.9	8,025	19.7	15.0	5.5	22.6	28.7	66.6	5.8	98	3.0	27.9
104	Samoa	1.1	5,574	..	..	..	0.0	20.3	76.1	2.5	108	..	..
105	Maldives	4.9	11,892	..	..	..	13.7	2.8	80.1	2.9	133	3.5	14.2
105	Uzbekistan	176.6	5,643	23.8	15.8	..	..	..	..	1.4	..	..	..
MEDIUM HUMAN DEVELOPMENT													
107	Moldova (Republic of)	16.9	4,742	24.2	20.4	0.0	18.6	2.7	37.2	6.7	136	4.8	5.7
108	Botswana	33.7	14,876	29.5	17.4	8.7	26.9	23.9	12.4	0.4	133	2.9	3.6
109	Gabon	32.5	18,832	29.3	15.0	−7.3	..	..	16.9	2.4	110	5.2	21.0
110	Paraguay	57.4	8,644	17.1	12.9	6.0	12.8	11.6	48.7	9.3	125	4.3	11.2
111	Egypt	938.0	10,250	13.7	11.8	7.0	12.5	26.2	95.8	2.0	157	7.5	9.8
111	Turkmenistan	83.4	15,527	47.2	8.9	..	..	..	..	0.1	..	..	..
113	Indonesia	2,674.9	10,385	33.2	9.8	5.4	11.4	34.8	46.7	5.4	132	6.7	10.7
114	Palestine, State of	20.9	4,715	23.8	26.6	11.8	5.7	3.5	11.2	..	111	..	..
115	Viet Nam	519.8	5,668	24.7	6.3	7.0	..	..	128.3	3.8	145	..	..

TABLE
10

TABLE 10   National income and composition of resources | 237

TABLE 10 NATIONAL INCOME AND COMPOSITION OF RESOURCES

		Gross domestic product (GDP)		Gross fixed capital formation	General government final consumption expenditure		Total tax revenue	Taxes on income, profits and capital gains	Debts		Prices		
									Domestic credit provided by financial sector	Total debt service	Consumer price index	Domestic food price level	
		Total (2011 PPP $ billions)	Per capita (2011 PPP $)	(% of GDP)	Total (% of GDP)	Average annual growth (%)	(% of GDP)	(% of total tax revenue)	(% of GDP)	(% of GNI)	(2010=100)	Index	Volatility index
HDI rank		2015	2015	2010–2015[a]	2010–2015[a]	2010–2015[a]	2005–2014[a]	2005–2014[a]	2010–2015[a]	2014	2015	2010–2014[a]	2010–2014[a]
116	Philippines	697.4[c]	6,926	21.7	11.0	9.4	12.9	42.1	59.2	1.8	117	6.8	2.6
117	El Salvador	49.6	8,096	14.0	11.9	4.7	15.4	25.8	77.8	5.2	108	4.3	3.0
118	Bolivia (Plurinational State of)	69.5	6,476	21.0	14.7	6.7	17.0	9.6	66.7	3.2	134	5.9	12.2
119	South Africa	680.9	12,390	20.0	20.3	0.3	26.6	48.4	180.1	2.9	130	3.0	6.2
120	Kyrgyzstan	19.2	3,225	32.8	17.5	−0.5	18.1	19.1	19.0	5.6	146	..	..
121	Iraq	510.6	14,018	23.5	22.4	..	..	..	9.3	..	116	5.1	16.4
122	Cabo Verde	3.3	6,296	46.7	18.5	3.4	18.4	18.2	82.8	2.5	109	5.7	5.4
123	Morocco	257.3	7,361	29.4	19.9	−0.5	23.3	25.4	107.4	4.5	106	5.7	4.9
124	Nicaragua	29.7	4,884	30.3	7.2	4.1	15.1	30.0	48.2	6.5	137	4.5	6.4
125	Guatemala	118.5	7,253	13.2	10.4	−0.1	10.8	29.4	42.8	3.6	122	7.1	5.5
125	Namibia	24.1	9,801	33.4	26.9	9.4	23.1	32.6	56.6	..	129	3.5	7.2
127	Guyana	5.4	7,064	25.2	17.0	..	..	..	56.8	2.2	109	..	..
127	Micronesia (Federated States of)	0.3[c]	3,177[c]	..	..	..	..	..	−26.2	..	..	..	..
129	Tajikistan	22.2	2,616	14.1	11.7	1.1	..	..	20.2	3.7	..	..	..
130	Honduras	38.6	4,785	23.1	15.2	1.6	16.7	21.5	59.7	3.9	129	4.8	4.8
131	India	7,512.5	5,730	30.8	10.9	12.8	10.8	44.8	76.8	4.6	148	4.7	8.4
132	Bhutan	5.9	7,601	56.8	17.7	2.4	9.2	15.9	54.3	4.5	146	5.1	6.4
133	Timor-Leste	2.6	2,126	37.9	67.2	−24.0	..	..	−9.0	..	143	..	..
134	Vanuatu	0.7[c]	2,891[c]	25.9	14.9	−1.1	16.0	..	72.1	1.0	107	..	..
135	Congo	27.7	5,993	40.9	18.1	−6.5	7.6	4.6	21.5	2.6	117	6.3	18.8
135	Equatorial Guinea	23.9	28,272	54.6	9.3	−2.8	18.8	35.7	16.9	..	123	..	..
137	Kiribati	0.2	1,749	..	..	..	..	..	..	..	..	..	..
138	Lao People's Democratic Republic	36.3	5,341	32.9	14.2	..	14.8	17.6	26.5	3.2	126	8.6	3.6
139	Bangladesh	505.0	3,137	28.9	5.4	8.8	8.7	22.4	59.7	0.9	144	8.0	4.5
139	Ghana	108.4	3,953	23.6	19.0	4.3	14.9	24.7	35.1	2.1	179	5.4	18.3
139	Zambia	58.8	3,626	25.9	2.8	..	16.1	48.0	29.4	1.6	144	10.1	3.2
142	Sao Tome and Principe	0.6[c]	3,030[c]	..	..	..	13.9	12.8	26.2	4.1	154	9.1	50.5
143	Cambodia	51.1	3,278	21.2	5.3	4.0	14.6	15.2	53.9	1.0	117	7.8	4.7
144	Nepal	66.0[c]	2,313	23.0	11.1	18.0	15.3	18.7	75.1	1.1	152	9.5	10.2
145	Myanmar	..	..	..	..	..	..	25.2	32.1	0.1	131	8.5	8.1
146	Kenya	133.6	2,901	21.5	14.5	15.4	15.9	40.9	45.2	2.0	150	5.8	6.0
147	Pakistan	896.4	4,745	13.5	11.8	16.0	11.2	27.9	48.8	2.3	145	7.1	13.2
LOW HUMAN DEVELOPMENT													
148	Swaziland	10.2	7,930	14.3	16.5	−5.8	..	..	16.8	0.7	135	..	..
149	Syrian Arab Republic	..	..	..	..	..	14.2	30.2	..	1.7[d]	143[e]	..	..
150	Angola	173.6	6,937	10.3	17.9	..	18.8	31.9	31.0	6.4	161	7.2	13.7
151	Tanzania (United Republic of)	130.3	2,510	31.3	14.3	10.0	11.7	21.9	22.8	0.5	158	11.5	4.8
152	Nigeria	1,027.4	5,639	15.1	7.4	5.6	1.6	28.3	21.8	0.1	159	6.3	4.0
153	Cameroon	68.6	2,939	21.0	11.4	54.8	..	..	14.8	1.4	113	7.8	10.0
154	Papua New Guinea	20.3[c]	2,723[c]	..	..	..	..	..	51.0	7.1	128	..	..
154	Zimbabwe	26.3	1,688	13.2	25.1	4.5	..	..	..	25.3	106	..	..
156	Solomon Islands	1.2	2,058	..	..	..	..	..	24.3	1.6	125	..	..
157	Mauritania	14.7[c]	3,694[c]	42.9	21.3	2.3	..	..	29.6	4.3	120	10.1	3.1
158	Madagascar	33.3	1,373	14.8	13.1	3.5	10.1	21.2	18.0	0.9	140	7.1	3.5
159	Rwanda	19.2	1,655	25.7	12.3	−14.7	13.4	25.7	..	0.7	122	8.6	10.5
160	Comoros	1.0[c]	1,364[c]	20.4	16.7	1.4	..	..	29.2	0.1	98	..	..
160	Lesotho	5.3[c]	2,517[c]	35.2	35.1	−0.9	58.7	17.4	0.7	1.6	127	4.4	6.4
162	Senegal	34.6	2,288	27.0	15.4	4.6	19.2	23.1	36.0	2.3	105	8.4	8.7
163	Haiti	17.8	1,658	..	..	..	..	..	31.6	0.3	139	9.7	3.4
163	Uganda	67.1	1,718	24.9	9.6	17.6	11.0	30.6	17.9	0.4	157	5.2	21.8
165	Sudan	158.0	3,927	17.9	7.0	4.1	..	..	20.9	0.4	349	..	..
166	Togo	10.0	1,374	21.3	14.6	3.6	20.0	11.1	42.0	1.5	110	6.8	15.5
167	Benin	21.6	1,986	26.0	15.1	4.6	15.5	16.7	19.6	1.1	110	8.1	21.8
168	Yemen	93.5[b]	3,663[b]	..	..	..	..	..	33.9	0.8[b]	158[c]	7.6	11.0
169	Afghanistan	59.2	1,820	21.2	13.6	..	7.5	3.7	0.4	0.2	131	..	..
170	Malawi	19.2	1,113	12.8	13.6	11.7	..	..	15.1	1.1	251	7.6	23.6
171	Côte d'Ivoire	74.7	3,290	16.1	14.9	−20.9	14.4	22.1	31.5	5.1	111	6.7	8.8
172	Djibouti	2.7[c]	3,120[c]	..	..	..	..	..	33.2	2.3[f]	115[c]	..	..
173	Gambia	3.0[c]	1,556[c]	21.2	9.3	0.7	..	..	53.7	5.3	122[c]	7.3	2.7

TABLE 10

		Gross domestic product (GDP)		Gross fixed capital formation	General government final consumption expenditure		Total tax revenue	Taxes on income, profits and capital gains	Debts — Domestic credit provided by financial sector	Total debt service	Prices — Consumer price index	Domestic food price level	
		Total (2011 PPP $ billions)	Per capita (2011 PPP $)	(% of GDP)	Total (% of GDP)	Average annual growth (%)	(% of GDP)	(% of total tax revenue)	(% of GDP)	(% of GNI)	(2010=100)	Index	Volatility index
HDI rank		2015	2015	2010–2015[a]	2010–2015[a]	2010–2015[a]	2005–2014[a]	2005–2014[a]	2010–2015[a]	2014	2015	2010–2014[a]	2010–2014[a]
174	Ethiopia	152.1	1,530	39.3	9.0	5.5	9.2	16.0	..	1.4	209	6.3	9.0
175	Mali	40.2	2,285	16.7	16.2	12.4	13.0	21.9	21.9	0.6	110	7.7	9.4
176	Congo (Democratic Republic of the)	56.9	737	16.1	15.0	2.6	8.8	11.9	9.7	1.4	129 [b]	..	..
177	Liberia	3.5	787	20.0	16.7	5.2	..	..	36.2	1.0	137 [c]	..	..
178	Guinea-Bissau	2.5	1,367	6.4	8.5	..	..	..	19.9	0.2	108	..	..
179	Eritrea	6.8 [g]	1,411 [g]	10.0	21.1	−9.5	..	..	104.0	0.9 [g]	..	..	..
179	Sierra Leone	9.7	1,497	13.3	11.1	3.6	..	..	17.2	0.7	168	6.8	3.3
181	Mozambique	31.2	1,116	38.1	25.8	6.3	20.4	29.5	43.5	1.1	125	8.6	6.7
181	South Sudan	21.5	1,741	11.2	35.8	0.4	..	..	39.5	..	331	..	..
183	Guinea	14.3	1,135	13.2	8.6	2.5	..	..	34.3	1.2	186	9.9	7.3
184	Burundi	7.7	693	21.7	21.9	−0.4	..	..	28.5	0.9	154	7.0	8.3
185	Burkina Faso	28.3	1,562	31.2	20.7	0.3	15.2	19.9	29.3	0.8	108	8.4	11.8
186	Chad	28.7	2,044	28.0	5.2	−55.3	..	..	17.8	0.9	116	8.0	11.7
187	Niger	17.9	897	38.8	16.7	15.4	..	..	16.3	0.7	106	7.2	9.4
188	Central African Republic	2.8	562	11.4	13.8	..	9.4	6.9	34.8	0.9	187	..	..
OTHER COUNTRIES OR TERRITORIES													
	Korea (Democratic People's Rep. of)	..	..	..	..	..	..	..	..	..	..	..	..
	Marshall Islands	0.2 [c]	3,628 [c]	..	..	..	..	..	..	..	..	..	..
	Monaco	..	..	..	..	..	..	..	..	..	..	..	..
	Nauru	..	..	..	..	..	..	..	..	..	..	..	..
	San Marino	..	..	..	..	..	22.3	15.5	..	..	108	..	..
	Somalia	..	..	8.0	6.9	..	..	..	..	0.0	..	..	..
	Tuvalu	0.0 [c]	3,592 [c]						..	..	..	..	..
Human development groups													
	Very high human development	52,478.7	39,989	20.7	17.7	1.3	14.9	36.5	200.0	..	—	—	—
	High human development	33,383.7	14,079	35.5	14.5	2.8	12.2	26.3	154.6	1.9	—	—	—
	Medium human development	16,333.5	6,361	27.0	11.8	9.1	12.7	38.5	73.1	3.8	—	—	—
	Low human development	2,516.0	2,775	18.7	11.1	5.5	..	..	23.8	1.6	—	—	—
Developing countries		55,360.8	9,376	32.2	14.2	4.5	12.0	29.3	125.3	2.3	—	—	—
Regions													
	Arab States	5,863.9	16,377	24.7	19.1	6.8	..	..	64.9	2.2	—	—	—
	East Asia and the Pacific	24,233.9	12,386	41.7	13.3	..	..	..	179.4	1.1	—	—	—
	Europe and Central Asia	3,128.1	13,226	21.5	14.9	4.5	20.0	15.6	76.5	8.3	—	—	—
	Latin America and the Caribbean	8,221.0	14,041	20.4	16.5	2.2	..	..	73.8	3.4	—	—	—
	South Asia	10,571.4	5,806	28.3	10.6	11.4	10.3	38.2	71.8	3.4	—	—	—
	Sub-Saharan Africa	3,317.0	3,493	20.1	13.7	4.6	13.0	38.4	60.7	2.1	—	—	—
Least developed countries		2,041.5	2,306	24.5	11.3	5.7	12.5	25.6	35.5	1.5	—	—	—
Small island developing states		557.4	10,032	..	..	..	..	..	57.5	7.2	—	—	—
Organisation for Economic Co-operation and Development		48,239.7	37,660	20.6	17.5	1.2	15.1	37.5	206.6	..	—	—	—
World		**104,713.0**	**14,600**	**24.8**	**16.4**	**2.3**	**14.0**	**34.7**	**176.4**	**2.4**	**—**	**—**	**—**

TABLE
10

NOTES

a Data refer to the most recent year available during the period specified.

b Refers to 2013.

c Refers to 2014.

d Refers to 2007.

e Refers to 2012.

f Refers to 2005.

g Refers to 2011.

DEFINITIONS

Gross domestic product (GDP): Sum of gross value added by all resident producers in the economy plus any product taxes and minus any subsidies not included in the value of the products, expressed in 2011 international dollars using purchasing power parity (PPP) rates.

GDP per capita: GDP in a particular period divided by the total population in the same period.

Gross fixed capital formation: Value of acquisitions of new or existing fixed assets by the business sector, governments and households (excluding their unincorporated enterprises) less disposals of fixed assets, expressed as a percentage of GDP. No adjustment is made for depreciation of fixed assets.

General government final consumption expenditure: All government current expenditures for purchases of goods and services (including compensation of employees and most expenditures on national defence and security but excluding government military expenditures that are part of government capital formation), expressed as a percentage of GDP.

Total tax revenue: Compulsory transfers to the central government for public purposes, expressed as a percentage of GDP.

Taxes on income, profits and capital gains: Taxes levied on the actual or presumptive net income of individuals, on the profits of corporations and enterprises and on capital gains, whether realized or not, on land, securities and other assets.

Domestic credit provided by financial sector: Credit to various sectors on a gross basis (except credit to the central government, which is net), expressed as a percentage of GDP.

Total debt service: Sum of principal repayments and interest actually paid in foreign currency, goods or services on long-term debt; interest paid on short-term debt; and repayments (repurchases and charges) to the International Monetary Fund, expressed as a percentage of gross national income (GNI).

Consumer price index: Index that reflects changes in the cost to the average consumer of acquiring a basket of goods and services that may be fixed or changed at specified intervals, such as yearly.

Domestic food price level index: Food PPP rate divided by the general PPP rate. The index shows the price of food in a country relative to the price of the generic consumption basket in the country.

Domestic food price level volatility index: Measure of variation of the domestic food price level index, computed as the standard deviation of the deviations from the trend over the previous eight months.

MAIN DATA SOURCES

Columns 1–10: World Bank (2016a).

Columns 11 and 12: FAO (2016a).

TABLE 10   National income and composition of resources | 239

TABLE 11

Work and employment

		Employment				Unemployment			Work that is a risk to human development			Employment-related social security	
		Employment to population ratio[a]	Labour force participation rate[a]	Employment in agriculture	Employment in services	Total	Youth	Youth not in school or employment	Vulnerable employment	Child labour	Working poor at PPP$3.10 a day	Mandatory paid maternity leave	Old-age pension recipients
		(% ages 15 and older)		(% of total employment)		(% of labour force)	(% ages 15–24)		(% of total employment)	(% ages 5–14)	(% of total employment)	(days)	(% of statutory pension age population)
HDI rank		2015	2015	2010–2014[b]	2010–2014[b]	2015	2015	2010–2014[b]	2005–2014[b]	2009–2015[b]	2004–2013[b]	2015	2004–2013[b,c]
VERY HIGH HUMAN DEVELOPMENT													
1	Norway	62.2	64.9	2.1	77.0	4.1	10.1	5.5	5.3	..	..	..	100.0
2	Australia	60.7	64.7	2.6	69.5	6.3	13.5	9.8	..	..	..	..	83.0
2	Switzerland	65.7	68.7	3.2	73.9	4.3	7.0	7.3	9.1	..	..	98	100.0
4	Germany	57.6	60.3	1.3	70.4	4.6	7.1	6.4	6.3	..	..	98	100.0
5	Denmark	58.1	62.0	2.3	78.0	6.3	10.8	5.8	5.4	..	..	126	100.0
5	Singapore	65.0	67.2	..	70.6	3.3	7.3	18.9	8.7	..	..	105	0.0
7	Netherlands	59.9	63.8	2.0	75.3	6.1	8.8	5.0	12.8	..	..	112	100.0
8	Ireland	54.3	60.0	6.1	75.2	9.5	20.9	15.2	12.7	..	..	182	90.5
9	Iceland	70.8	74.1	4.2	77.1	4.4	8.7	5.8	8.5	..	..	90	100.0
10	Canada	61.0	65.6	2.1	78.2	6.9	13.2	13.3	..	..	..	105	97.7
10	United States	58.8	62.1	1.6	81.2	5.3	11.8	16.5[d]	..	..	..	..	92.5
12	Hong Kong, China (SAR)	58.3	60.3	..	79.9	3.3	9.5	6.6	6.9	..	..	70	72.9
13	New Zealand	63.6	67.6	6.4	73.0	5.9	14.4	11.9	..	..	..	112	98.0
14	Sweden	59.8	64.5	1.7	79.0	7.4	20.8	7.2	6.7	..	..	..	100.0
15	Liechtenstein	..	..	..	..	..	..	..	..	..	..	..	..
16	United Kingdom	59.3	62.7	1.1	79.1	5.5	15.1	11.9	12.7	..	..	14	99.5
17	Japan	57.3	59.3	3.7	69.1	3.3	5.3	3.9	..	..	..	98	80.3
18	Korea (Republic of)	58.6	60.8	6.1	69.5	3.7	10.4	18.8[e]	..	..	..	90	77.6
19	Israel	60.8	64.0	1.1	79.7	5.0	8.1	15.7	..	..	..	98	73.6
20	Luxembourg	55.7	59.1	1.3	85.7	5.9	18.6	6.3	6.3	..	..	112	90.0
21	France	49.4	55.2	2.8	75.8	10.6	24.7	10.7	7.2	..	..	112	100.0
22	Belgium	48.9	53.6	1.1	77.4	8.7	21.8	12.1	10.5	..	..	105	84.6
23	Finland	52.9	58.5	3.9	73.7	9.6	23.3	10.2	9.8	..	..	147	100.0
24	Austria	56.8	60.2	4.3	69.7	5.7	10.2	7.7	8.6	..	..	112	100.0
25	Slovenia	52.1	57.5	7.7	60.2	9.3	16.7	9.4	15.1	..	..	105	95.1
26	Italy	42.5	48.4	3.5	69.5	12.1	42.1	22.0	18.1	..	..	150	81.1
27	Spain	45.3	58.4	4.2	76.3	22.4	49.4	17.1	12.5	..	..	112	68.2
28	Czech Republic	56.4	59.4	2.7	58.9	5.2	13.0	8.1	14.5	..	..	196	100.0
29	Greece	38.8	51.7	13.0	71.8	24.9	49.2	19.1	29.6	..	..	119	77.4
30	Brunei Darussalam	62.3	63.5	0.6	80.8	1.9	5.7	..	..	..	..	91	81.7
30	Estonia	58.2	61.9	3.9	65.5	5.9	11.3	11.7	5.7	..	..	140	98.0
32	Andorra	..	..	..	..	..	..	..	..	..	..	..	..
33	Cyprus	53.9	63.9	3.9	79.6	15.6	32.3	17.0	14.2	..	..	126	85.2
33	Malta	49.5	52.3	1.2	77.1	5.4	12.3	11.4	9.4	..	..	126	60.5
33	Qatar	84.4	84.6	1.4	46.8	0.2	0.8	..	0.2	..	..	50	7.9
36	Poland	52.7	56.9	11.2	57.9	7.4	19.9	12.0	17.2	..	..	182	96.5
37	Lithuania	53.5	59.1	9.0	65.8	9.5	17.6	9.9	9.8	..	..	126	100.0
38	Chile	58.4	62.4	9.2	67.1	6.4	16.4	11.8	..	7.0[f]	4.9	126	74.5
38	Saudi Arabia	51.6	54.8	4.9	70.9	5.8	31.0	18.4	..	..	..	70	..
40	Slovakia	52.8	59.5	3.5	60.9	11.3	25.2	12.8	12.2	..	..	238	100.0
41	Portugal	51.4	58.5	5.5	69.5	12.1	30.1	12.3	14.5	3.0[f,g]	..	..	100.0
42	United Arab Emirates	77.1	80.1	..	..	3.7	11.1	..	1.0	..	..	45	..
43	Hungary	50.2	54.0	4.6	64.5	7.0	18.2	13.6	5.8	..	..	168	91.4
44	Latvia	54.4	60.4	7.3	68.6	9.8	14.8	12.0	7.6	..	..	112	100.0
45	Argentina	56.9	61.0	0.5	74.7	6.7	19.1	18.6	20.5	4.0	5.1	90	90.7
45	Croatia	43.9	52.3	8.7	63.9	16.1	43.8	19.3	10.4	..	..	208	57.6
47	Bahrain	68.3	69.2	1.1	62.4	1.2	5.4	..	2.0	5.0[g]	..	60	40.1
48	Montenegro	40.0	48.9	5.7	73.0	18.2	37.5	..	..	13.0[f]	1.8	45	52.3
49	Russian Federation	59.8	63.5	6.7	65.8	5.8	15.0	12.0	6.0	..	3.9	140	100.0
50	Romania	52.0	55.9	25.4	44.5	6.9	23.1	17.0	30.9	1.0[g]	..	126	98.0
51	Kuwait	66.7	69.2	1.2	58.6	3.5	17.3	..	2.2	..	..	70	27.3
HIGH HUMAN DEVELOPMENT													
52	Belarus	57.0	60.8	9.6	57.2	6.1	12.9	..	2.1	1.0	3.1	126	93.6
52	Oman	64.8	69.1	5.2	57.9	6.3	19.3	..	..	..	..	50	24.7
54	Barbados	58.2	66.3	2.7	78.4	12.3	30.4	..	..	2.0	..	84	68.3
54	Uruguay	60.6	65.3	9.3	69.1	7.3	20.3	20.5[h]	22.5	8.0[f,g]	5.3	98	76.5
56	Bulgaria	48.9	54.2	6.9	62.8	9.8	22.2	20.2	8.7	..	..	410	96.9
56	Kazakhstan	67.2	71.2	24.2	56.0	5.6	5.1	..	28.6	2.0[g]	3.4	126	95.9
58	Bahamas	63.5	74.1	3.7	83.0	14.4	28.4	..	..	..	..	91	84.2

		Employment				Unemployment			Work that is a risk to human development			Employment-related social security	
		Employment to population ratio[a]	Labour force participation rate[a]	Employment in agriculture	Employment in services	Total	Youth	Youth not in school or employment	Vulnerable employment	Child labour	Working poor at PPP$3.10 a day	Mandatory paid maternity leave	Old-age pension recipients
		(% ages 15 and older)		(% of total employment)		(% of labour force)	(% ages 15–24)		(% of total employment)	(% ages 5–14)	(% of total employment)	(days)	(% of statutory pension age population)
HDI rank		2015	2015	2010–2014[b]	2010–2014[b]	2015	2015	2010–2014[b]	2005–2014[b]	2009–2015[b]	2004–2013[b]	2015	2004–2013[b,c]
59	Malaysia	61.5	63.3	12.2	60.3	2.9	10.4	1.2	21.1	..	6.9	60	19.8
60	Palau	..	..	..	..	..	..	..	..	..	..	..	48.0
60	Panama	62.0	65.4	16.7	65.0	5.2	13.7	17.6	29.9	6.0[f]	10.4	98	37.3
62	Antigua and Barbuda	..	..	..	..	..	..	..	..	..	..	91	69.7
63	Seychelles	..	..	3.6	78.2	..	..	20.0	10.4	..	..	98	100.0
64	Mauritius	55.8	60.5	8.0	63.5	7.9	17.5	..	17.1	..	6.1	84	100.0
65	Trinidad and Tobago	60.5	62.9	..	..	3.8	9.6	52.5	15.6	1.0[g]	..	98	98.7
66	Costa Rica	56.3	61.6	12.7	68.2	8.6	21.1	17.8	20.7	4.0	1.7	120	55.8
66	Serbia	41.7	51.5	21.3	52.9	19.0	45.2	19.5	28.6	10.0[f]	0.4	135	46.1
68	Cuba	53.9	55.6	18.6	64.2	3.0	6.5	..	..	..	5.6	..	..
69	Iran (Islamic Republic of)	39.9	44.5	17.9	48.3	10.5	24.1	34.3	40.5	11.0[f]	3.7	270	26.4
70	Georgia	58.9	67.1	..	..	12.3	29.8	..	59.8	18.0[g]	15.2	183	89.8
71	Turkey	45.1	50.3	19.7	51.9	10.3	16.4	24.8	29.4	6.0[f]	4.0	112	88.1
71	Venezuela (Bolivarian Republic of)	59.5	64.7	7.4	71.1	8.0	16.7	19.2	30.3	8.0[g]	9.2	182	59.4
73	Sri Lanka	49.3	51.8	30.4	43.4	4.7	20.2	0.5[f]	43.1	3.0[f]	12.2	84	17.1
74	Saint Kitts and Nevis	..	..	..	..	..	..	..	..	..	..	91	44.7
75	Albania	41.6	50.3	..	..	17.3	32.7	30.5	58.1	5.0[f]	2.0	365	77.0
76	Lebanon	43.7	47.0	..	..	7.1	21.6	..	27.8	2.0	..	70	0.0
77	Mexico	59.5	62.2	13.4	62.4	4.3	8.8	20.0	..	4.0	9.0	84	25.2
78	Azerbaijan	61.9	65.0	36.8	48.9	4.7	14.3	..	56.4	7.0[f,g]	1.7	126	81.7
79	Brazil	62.3	67.1	14.5	70.6	7.2	16.8	19.6	23.1	8.0[f]	5.1	120	86.3
79	Grenada	..	..	..	..	..	..	..	..	..	..	90	34.0
81	Bosnia and Herzegovina	32.2	46.1	..	..	30.3	66.9	..	25.3	5.0[g]	1.5	365	29.6
82	The former Yugoslav Republic of Macedonia	40.9	55.9	18.0	51.4	26.9	49.4	25.1	22.8	13.0	3.0	270	52.2
83	Algeria	39.1	43.7	10.8	58.4	10.5	28.6	22.8	26.9	5.0	..	98	63.6
84	Armenia	53.0	63.3	36.3	46.7	16.3	37.2	40.9	42.4	4.0	13.6	140	80.0
84	Ukraine	53.2	59.1	14.8	59.1	9.9	23.1	20.0	18.1	2.0	1.9	126	95.0
86	Jordan	34.8	40.0	1.8	79.6	12.8	33.4	24.6	9.7	2.0[f,g]	12.7	70	42.2
87	Peru	71.5	74.1	..	75.9	3.5	9.3	15.3[h]	46.3	34.0[f,g]	12.1	90	33.2
87	Thailand	70.6	71.4	41.9	37.5	1.1	4.7	13.8	55.9	8.0[g]	1.5	90	81.7
89	Ecuador	61.4	64.2	25.3	54.3	4.3	10.9	3.8	39.0	3.0[f]	11.2	84	53.0
90	China	67.6	70.9	2.5	47.0	4.6	12.1	..	..	..	14.8	128	74.4
91	Fiji	50.2	54.3	..	..	7.7	18.2	..	38.8	..	13.2	84	10.6
92	Mongolia	58.1	62.5	35.0	46.8	7.1	14.7	1.5	51.4	15.0[f]	6.8	120	100.0
92	Saint Lucia	55.6	69.6	..	..	20.1	47.2	..	..	4.0	..	91	26.5
94	Jamaica	56.0	64.0	18.2	66.5	13.7	32.7	20.0	37.5	3.0	7.0	56	65.6
95	Colombia	61.7	68.6	16.3	64.1	10.0	20.5	22.0[i]	47.9	10.0[f]	9.2	98	23.0
96	Dominica	..	..	..	..	..	..	..	..	..	..	84	38.5
97	Suriname	50.2	54.5	3.2	72.9	7.8	18.6	..	12.9	4.0	..	0	..
97	Tunisia	40.6	47.7	14.8	51.5	14.8	34.5	25.4	21.6	2.0	4.6	30	68.8
99	Dominican Republic	55.9	65.3	14.5	41.9	14.4	29.8	21.3	41.7	13.0[f]	7.8	84	11.1
99	Saint Vincent and the Grenadines	53.5	66.8	..	..	20.0	39.6	..	8.0	..	..	91	76.6
101	Tonga	60.0	63.2	..	..	5.2	11.7	..	..	..	..	0	1.0
102	Libya	42.2	53.2	..	..	20.6	50.0	..	..	..	..	98	43.3
103	Belize	61.6	69.8	..	..	11.8	22.0	27.9	23.5	3.0[f]	..	98	64.6
104	Samoa	38.7	41.1	5.4	79.9	5.8	14.1	38.2	30.9	..	..	28	49.5
105	Maldives	59.9	68.0	14.6	67.0	11.8	27.9	56.4[k]	18.8	..	13.0	60	99.7
105	Uzbekistan	55.6	61.8	..	..	10.1	19.8	..	..	..	..	126	98.1
MEDIUM HUMAN DEVELOPMENT													
107	Moldova (Republic of)	39.9	42.0	28.8	53.5	5.0	15.6	28.6	32.0	16.0	1.2	126	72.8
108	Botswana	63.0	77.4	26.4	56.1	18.6	29.4	..	12.9	9.0[f,g]	26.3	84	100.0
109	Gabon	38.8	48.8	..	..	20.5	36.3	..	31.3	13.0	17.7	98	38.8
110	Paraguay	68.0	71.5	22.8	58.2	4.9	12.3	12.3[i]	38.1	28.0[f]	6.0	63	22.2
111	Egypt	43.5	49.4	28.0	47.9	12.1	35.5	27.9	26.4	7.0[f]	48.2	90	32.7
111	Turkmenistan	55.8	62.0	..	..	10.0	19.5	..	..	..	..	..	..
113	Indonesia	63.4	67.4	34.3	44.8	5.8	19.3	24.1	33.0	7.0	38.7	90	8.1
114	Palestine, State of	32.4	43.7	10.5	61.1	25.9	39.8	31.0	25.6	6.0	2.6	70	8.0
115	Viet Nam	76.7	78.3	46.8	32.0	2.1	5.3	9.3	62.6	16.0[f]	14.6	180	34.5
116	Philippines	60.4	64.7	30.4	53.6	6.7	15.7	24.8	38.4	11.0[f]	32.0	60	28.5
117	El Salvador	58.7	62.8	19.6	60.1	6.4	13.0	5.7[d]	37.6	19.0[f]	9.4	84	18.1

TABLE 11 Work and employment | 241

TABLE 11

TABLE 11 WORK AND EMPLOYMENT

		Employment				Unemployment			Work that is a risk to human development			Employment-related social security	
		Employment to population ratio[a]	Labour force participation rate[a]	Employment in agriculture	Employment in services	Total	Youth	Youth not in school or employment	Vulnerable employment	Child labour	Working poor at PPP$3.10 a day	Mandatory paid maternity leave	Old-age pension recipients
		(% ages 15 and older)		(% of total employment)		(% of labour force)	(% ages 15–24)		(% of total employment)	(% ages 5–14)	(% of total employment)	(days)	(% of statutory pension age population)
HDI rank		2015	2015	2010–2014[b]	2010–2014[b]	2015	2015	2010–2014[b]	2005–2014[b]	2009–2015[b]	2004–2013[b]	2015	2004–2013[b,c]
118	Bolivia (Plurinational State of)	70.5	73.1	..	..	3.6	7.1	..	54.3	26.0 [f,g]	12.7	90	100.0
119	South Africa	39.7	53.0	4.6	71.9	25.1	50.0	31.3	9.3	..	16.6	120	92.6
120	Kyrgyzstan	57.7	62.9	31.7	48.1	8.2	14.6	21.2	41.6	26.0 [f]	15.4	126	100.0
121	Iraq	35.3	42.4	..	..	16.9	35.1	..	..	5.0	29.7	72	56.0
122	Cabo Verde	60.9	68.3	..	..	10.8	17.5	..	..	6.0 [f]	48.7	60	55.7
123	Morocco	44.5	49.2	39.2	39.4	9.6	19.3	..	50.7	8.0 [g]	13.1	98	39.8
124	Nicaragua	60.4	64.2	32.2	51.3	6.0	9.7	..	47.1	15.0 [g]	20.2	84	23.7
125	Guatemala	59.8	61.5	32.7	50.2	2.7	6.2	29.8	44.5	26.0 [f]	14.4	84	14.1
125	Namibia	44.2	59.3	31.4	54.2	25.5	49.6	32.0	7.8	..	31.2	84	98.4
127	Guyana	52.9	59.5	..	..	11.2	25.1	..	..	18.0 [f]	..	91	100.0
127	Micronesia (Federated States of)	..	..	..	..	..	..	..	..	..	..	..	..
129	Tajikistan	61.0	68.5	..	..	10.9	16.8	..	47.1	10.0 [g]	21.6	140	80.2
130	Honduras	63.1	65.6	35.8	45.4	3.9	7.1	41.4 [l]	53.3	15.0 [f]	28.2	84	8.4
131	India	51.9	53.7	49.7	28.7	3.5	9.7	27.2	80.8	12.0 [g]	52.9	84	24.1
132	Bhutan	64.7	66.4	56.3	32.7	2.6	9.2	..	53.1	3.0	10.9	56	3.2
133	Timor-Leste	39.3	41.3	50.6	39.8	5.0	15.7	..	69.6	4.0 [g]	77.7	84	100.0
134	Vanuatu	68.0	71.0	..	..	4.3	8.8	..	70.0	15.0 [f]	..	84	3.5
135	Congo	64.8	69.8	..	..	7.2	12.2	..	75.1	23.0 [f]	46.3	105	22.1
135	Equatorial Guinea	74.3	82.0	..	..	9.4	15.3	..	..	28.0 [g]	20.4	84	..
137	Kiribati	..	..	22.1	61.8	..	..	..	53.3	..	..	84	..
138	Lao People's Democratic Republic	76.1	77.4	71.3	20.2	1.6	4.0	..	83.9	10.0 [f]	84.1	105	5.6
139	Bangladesh	59.4	62.2	47.5	35.3	4.4	11.6	40.3	57.8	4.0 [f]	86.1	112	39.5
139	Ghana	72.1	77.0	44.7	40.9	6.3	12.2	..	76.8	22.0 [f]	44.1	84	7.6
139	Zambia	67.3	75.3	52.2	38.3	10.7	19.7	28.3 [e]	79.0	41.0 [f,g]	78.4	84	7.7
142	Sao Tome and Principe	52.1	60.5	26.1	46.9	14.0	21.8	..	..	26.0 [f]	..	90	41.8
143	Cambodia	80.5	80.9	54.1	29.6	0.5	0.8	7.8	64.1	19.0 [f]	71.8	90	5.0
144	Nepal	80.5	83.0	66.5	22.4	3.1	5.1	9.2	..	37.0 [f]	43.9	52	62.5
145	Myanmar	74.3	78.0	..	..	4.7	12.1	..	..	..	82.6	98	..
146	Kenya	60.9	67.1	..	..	9.2	17.6	..	..	26.0 [g]	..	90	7.9
147	Pakistan	51.0	53.9	43.5	34.0	5.4	10.7	..	63.1	..	37.1	84	2.3
LOW HUMAN DEVELOPMENT													
148	Swaziland	38.6	51.8	..	..	25.6	53.0	..	..	7.0	22.9	14	86.0
149	Syrian Arab Republic	36.5	41.7	13.2	55.3	12.3	28.5	..	32.9	4.0 [g]	34.8	120	16.7
150	Angola	63.2	68.4	..	..	7.6	12.0	..	..	24.0 [g]	49.9	90	14.5
151	Tanzania (United Republic of)	76.0	78.6	66.9	26.6	3.2	6.3	31.8	74.0	29.0 [f]	72.6	84	3.2
152	Nigeria	53.1	56.3	..	..	5.8	8.6	..	..	25.0	72.3	84	..
153	Cameroon	72.5	76.0	..	..	4.6	7.0	10.8	73.6	47.0 [f]	48.1	98	12.5
154	Papua New Guinea	68.1	70.3	..	..	3.1	6.7	..	..	..	66.5	0	0.9
154	Zimbabwe	74.7	82.4	65.8	25.0	9.3	15.4	..	65.5	..	82.9	98	6.2
156	Solomon Islands	43.9	67.4	..	..	34.8	51.5	..	..	..	52.6	84	13.1
157	Mauritania	32.5	47.2	..	..	31.1	47.3	..	..	15.0	17.6	98	9.3 [m]
158	Madagascar	84.6	86.4	75.3	16.9	2.2	3.6	5.0	86.0	23.0 [f]	90.0	98	4.6
159	Rwanda	82.9	84.9	75.3	16.2	2.4	3.0	..	77.7	29.0	82.1	84	4.7
160	Comoros	46.2	57.4	..	..	19.6	37.7	..	..	22.0	25.3	98	..
160	Lesotho	48.1	66.4	..	..	27.5	37.6	..	17.4	23.0 [g]	64.6	84	100.0
162	Senegal	51.7	57.1	46.1	22.4	9.3	13.1	..	58.0	15.0	63.8	98	23.5
163	Haiti	61.7	66.3	..	..	6.9	17.4	..	..	24.0	60.5	42	1.0 [n]
163	Uganda	81.9	85.0	71.9	20.2	3.6	6.0	5.9 [h]	78.9	16.0 [f]	60.6	84	6.6
165	Sudan	41.6	48.1	44.6	40.1	13.6	22.5	..	..	25.0 [f]	27.6	56	4.6
166	Togo	74.6	80.9	..	..	7.7	12.2	9.0	89.1	28.0 [f]	65.7	98	10.9
167	Benin	70.9	71.7	45.1	44.0	1.1	2.3	20.0	87.7	15.0	65.7	98	9.7
168	Yemen	41.7	49.6	24.7	56.2	15.9	30.1	48.1	29.6	23.0 [g]	50.5	70	8.5
169	Afghanistan	47.5	52.5	..	..	9.6	19.9	..	..	29.0 [f]	89.8	90	10.7
170	Malawi	75.5	81.0	64.1	28.5	6.7	8.9	16.7	..	39.0 [f]	87.6	56	4.1
171	Côte d'Ivoire	60.6	67.0	..	..	9.5	13.7	..	79.0	26.0	53.9	98	7.7
172	Djibouti	24.1	52.3	..	..	53.9	..	..	..	8.0 [g]	..	98	12.0 [m]
173	Gambia	54.0	77.3	31.5	54.6	30.1	44.4	..	60.5	19.0	..	180	10.8
174	Ethiopia	78.4	83.0	72.7	19.9	5.5	7.6	1.1 [i]	88.8	27.0	75.3	90	9.0
175	Mali	60.6	66.2	..	..	8.5	10.7	13.5	82.9	21.0	80.0	98	5.7
176	Congo (Democratic Republic of the)	68.4	71.1	..	..	3.8	6.2	..	..	38.0 [f]	85.3	98	15.0

TABLE 11

		Employment				Unemployment			Work that is a risk to human development			Employment-related social security	
		Employment to population ratio[a]	Labour force participation rate[a]	Employment in agriculture	Employment in services	Total	Youth	Youth not in school or employment	Vulnerable employment	Child labour	Working poor at PPP$3.10 a day	Mandatory paid maternity leave	Old-age pension recipients
		(% ages 15 and older)		(% of total employment)		(% of labour force)	(% ages 15–24)		(% of total employment)	(% ages 5–14)	(% of total employment)	(days)	(% of statutory pension age population)
HDI rank		2015	2015	2010–2014[b]	2010–2014[b]	2015	2015	2010–2014[b]	2005–2014[b]	2009–2015[b]	2004–2013[b]	2015	2004–2013[b,c]
177	Liberia	58.4	60.9	46.5	41.2	4.2	4.9	14.5	78.7	21.0[g]	89.0	90	..
178	Guinea-Bissau	67.2	72.7	..	..	7.6	12.4	..	..	38.0	79.4	60	6.2
179	Eritrea	76.9	83.9	..	..	8.4	13.0	..	..	..	69.0	60	..
179	Sierra Leone	64.5	66.8	..	..	3.4	5.3	..	..	37.0	81.4	84	0.9
181	Mozambique	61.5	79.1	..	..	22.3	37.8	10.1	..	22.0[g]	90.9	60	17.3
181	South Sudan	..	73.2	..	..	..	..	..	..	..	..	56	..
183	Guinea	80.9	82.3	74.8	19.3	1.8	1.2	..	89.8	28.0	72.5	98	8.8
184	Burundi	82.4	83.7	..	..	1.5	2.9	..	93.7	26.0	93.5	84	4.0
185	Burkina Faso	81.1	83.5	..	..	2.9	4.7	..	89.6	39.0	80.5	98	3.2
186	Chad	67.6	71.6	..	..	5.6	8.3	..	..	26.0	67.0	98	1.6
187	Niger	62.9	64.7	..	..	2.8	3.9	..	84.8	31.0	85.1	98	6.1
188	Central African Republic	72.1	78.0	..	..	7.6	12.3	..	..	29.0	81.3	98	..
OTHER COUNTRIES OR TERRITORIES													
	Korea (Democratic People's Rep. of)	74.2	79.5	..	..	6.7	12.8	..	..	..	81.4	..	..
	Marshall Islands	..	..	11.0	79.6	..	..	..	..	..	..	..	64.2
	Monaco	..	..	..	..	..	..	..	..	..	..	..	..
	Nauru	..	..	..	..	..	..	..	..	..	..	..	56.5
	San Marino	..	..	0.3	65.4	..	..	..	..	..	..	150	..
	Somalia	50.2	54.3	..	..	7.5	11.7	..	..	49.0[g]	76.7	..	..
	Tuvalu	..	..	..	..	..	..	..	..	..	..	..	19.5
Human development groups													
	Very high human development	56.4	60.4	3.8	72.7	6.8	16.3	13.4	..	..	..	114	90.4
	High human development	63.1	66.8	14.0	53.8	5.8	14.4	..	..	..	11.8	116	70.9
	Medium human development	55.5	58.6	43.7	35.6	5.2	13.4	..	63.0	12.1	47.9	91	25.6
	Low human development	64.0	68.6	..	..	7.0	11.4	..	..	26.8	71.9	85	9.4
Developing countries		60.0	63.6	35.1	41.4	5.7	13.5	..	..	15.6	33.3	95	50.9
Regions													
	Arab States	44.2	49.8	22.8	51.9	11.7	29.0	..	..	12.1	34.9	73	36.6
	East Asia and the Pacific	67.6	70.8	25.1	44.1	4.6	12.6	..	..	..	20.7	82	65.5
	Europe and Central Asia	51.5	57.4	20.3	54.4	10.4	19.3	..	28.5	6.4	4.3	165	86.1
	Latin America and the Caribbean	61.2	65.4	14.8	65.0	6.4	14.3	19.5	31.3	10.2	8.6	89	59.6
	South Asia	52.2	54.5	47.3	30.9	4.2	10.7	28.2	74.8	12.1	52.5	99	23.9
	Sub-Saharan Africa	65.2	70.4	..	..	7.8	12.5	..	..	27.4	70.0	89	20.5
Least developed countries		66.9	71.1	..	..	6.2	11.4	..	..	24.5	75.7	85	19.5
Small island developing states		57.9	63.0	..	..	7.9	18.2	..	..	..	..	..	29.0
Organisation for Economic Co-operation and Development		55.6	59.6	4.8	72.3	6.9	14.7	15.0	..	..	..	122	87.0
World		**59.3**	**62.9**	**26.2**	**50.4**	**5.9**	**13.8**	**..**	**46.3[T]**	**..**	**32.5**	**103**	**64.4**

NOTES

a Modeled International Labour Organization estimates.

b Data refer to the most recent year available during the period specified.

c Because statutory pension ages differ by country, cross-country comparisons should be made with caution.

d Refers to population ages 16–24.

e Refers to population ages 15–29.

f Differs from standard definition or refers to only part of the country.

g Refers to years or periods other than those specified.

h Refers to population ages 14–24.

i Refers to population ages 10–24.

j Refers to population ages 14–28.

k Refers to population ages 18–35.

l Refers to population ages 12–30.

m Refers to 2002.

n Refers to 2001.

T From original data source.

DEFINITIONS

Employment to population ratio: Percentage of the population ages 15 years and older that is employed.

Labour force participation rate: Percentage of a country's working-age population that engages actively in the labour market, either by working or looking for work. It provides an indication of the relative size of the supply of labour available to engage in the production of goods and services.

Employment in agriculture: Share of total employment that is employed in agriculture.

Employment in services: Share of total employment that is employed in services.

Total unemployment rate: Percentage of the labour force population ages 15 and older that is not in paid employment or self-employed but is available for work and has taken steps to seek paid employment or self-employment.

Youth unemployment rate: Percentage of the labour force population ages 15–24 that is not in paid employment or self-employed but is available for work and has taken steps to seek paid employment or self-employment.

Youth not in school or employment: Percentage of people ages 15–24 who are not in employment or in education or training.

Vulnerable employment: Percentage of employed people engaged as unpaid family workers and own-account workers.

Child labour: Percentage of children ages 5–11 who, during the reference week, engaged in at least one hour of economic activity or at least 28 hours of household chores, or children ages 12–14 who, during the reference week, engaged in at least 14 hours of economic activity or at least 28 hours of household chores.

Working poor at PPP$3.10 a day: Proportion of employed people who live on less than $3.10 (in purchasing power parity terms) a day, expressed as a percentage of the total employed population ages 15 and older.

Mandatory paid maternity leave: Number of days of paid time off work to which a female employee is entitled to take care of a newborn child.

Old-age pension recipients: Proportion of people older than the statutory pensionable age receiving an old-age pension (contributory, noncontributory or both), expressed as a percentage of the eligible population.

MAIN DATA SOURCES

Columns 1–8 and 10: ILO (2016a).

Column 9: UNICEF (2016).

Column 11: World Bank (2016b).

Column 12: ILO (2016c).

TABLE **11**

TABLE 11 Work and employment | 243

TABLE 12

Human security

HDI rank		Birth registration (% under age 5) 2010–2015[b]	Refugees by country of origin (thousands) 2015[c]	Internally displaced persons (thousands) 2015	Homeless people due to natural disaster (average annual per million people) 2005/2015	Orphaned children (thousands) 2014	Prison population (per 100,000 people) 2004–2015[b]	Homicide rate (per 100,000 people) 2010–2014[b]	Suicide rate (per 100,000 people) Female 2012	Suicide rate (per 100,000 people) Male 2012	Justification of wife beating (% ages 15–49) Female 2010–2015[b]	Justification of wife beating (% ages 15–49) Male 2010–2015[b]	Violence against women ever experienced[a] Intimate partner (%) 2005–2015[b]	Violence against women ever experienced[a] Nonintimate partner (%) 2005–2015[b]	Depth of food deficit (kilocalories per person per day) 2013/2015
VERY HIGH HUMAN DEVELOPMENT															
1	Norway	100	0.0	..	0	..	71	0.6	5.2	13.0	..	..	27.0	..	..
2	Australia	100	0.0	..	57	..	151	1.0	5.2	16.1	..	..	16.9	..	..
2	Switzerland	100	0.0	..	0	..	84	0.5	5.1	13.6	..	..	..	..	..
4	Germany	100	0.2	..	0	..	78	0.9	4.1	14.5	..	..	22.0	7.0	..
5	Denmark	100	0.0	..	0	..	61	1.0	4.1	13.6	..	..	32.0	11.0	..
5	Singapore	..	0.1	..	0	..	227	0.3	5.3	9.8	..	..	6.1	..	..
7	Netherlands	100	0.1	..	0	..	69	0.7	4.8	11.7	..	..	25.0	12.0	..
8	Ireland	100	0.0	..	0	..	80	1.1	5.2	16.9	..	..	15.0	5.0	..
9	Iceland	100	..	..	0	..	45	0.3	6.7	21.0	..	..	22.4	..	..
10	Canada	100	0.1	..	19	..	106	1.4	4.8	14.9	..	..	..	..	..
10	United States	100	4.8	..	16	..	698	3.9	5.2	19.4	..	..	..	..	..
12	Hong Kong, China (SAR)	..	0.0	..	0	..	114	0.9	..	..	..	..	..	..	..
13	New Zealand	100	0.0	..	15	..	194	0.9	5.0	14.4	..	..	..	..	..
14	Sweden	100	0.0	..	0	..	55	0.9	6.1	16.2	..	..	28.0	12.0	..
15	Liechtenstein	100	..	..	..	..	21[d]	2.7	..	..	..	..	..	..	..
16	United Kingdom	100	0.1	..	44	..	146[e]	0.9	2.6	9.8	..	..	29.0	7.0	..
17	Japan	100	0.1	..	29	..	48	0.3	10.1	26.9	..	..	..	..	..
18	Korea (Republic of)	..	0.4	..	8	..	101	0.7	18.0	41.7	..	..	..	..	4
19	Israel	100	0.8	..	0	..	256	1.7	2.3	9.8	..	..	..	..	..
20	Luxembourg	100	0.0	..	0	..	112	0.7	4.4	13.0	..	..	22.0	8.0	..
21	France	100	0.1	..	1	..	95[d]	1.2	6.0	19.3	..	..	26.0	9.0	..
22	Belgium	100	0.1	..	0	..	105	1.8	7.7	21.0	..	..	24.0	8.0	..
23	Finland	100	0.0	..	0	..	57	1.6	7.5	22.2	..	..	30.0	11.0	..
24	Austria	100	0.0	..	0	..	95	0.5	5.4	18.2	..	..	13.0	4.0	..
25	Slovenia	100	0.0	..	47	..	73	0.7	4.4	20.8	..	..	13.0	4.0	..
26	Italy	100	0.1	..	116	..	86	0.8	1.9	7.6	..	..	19.0	5.0	..
27	Spain	100	0.1	..	30	..	136	0.7	2.2	8.2	..	..	13.0	3.0	..
28	Czech Republic	100	1.3	..	0	..	195	0.7	3.9	21.5	..	..	21.0	4.0	..
29	Greece	100	0.1	..	33	..	109	0.1	1.3	6.3	..	..	19.0	1.0	..
30	Brunei Darussalam	..	..	..	0	..	132	0.5	5.2	7.7	..	..	..	..	13
30	Estonia	100	0.3	..	0	..	216	3.1	3.8	24.9	..	..	20.0	9.0	..
32	Andorra	100	0.0	..	..	..	72	0.0	..	..	..	..	..	..	..
33	Cyprus	100	0.0	272.0	0	..	94[d]	0.1	1.5	7.7	..	..	15.0	2.0	..
33	Malta	100	0.0	..	0	..	135	1.4	0.7	11.1	..	..	15.0	5.0	..
33	Qatar	..	0.0	..	0	..	53	7.2	1.2	5.7	7.0	16.0	..	..	..
36	Poland	100	1.3	..	0	..	191	0.7	3.8	30.5	..	..	13.0	2.0	..
37	Lithuania	100	0.1	..	0	..	268	5.5	8.4	51.0	..	..	24.0	5.0	..
38	Chile	99[f]	0.6	..	4,573	..	247	3.6	5.8	19.0	..	..	..	..	22
38	Saudi Arabia	..	0.7	..	32	..	161	6.2	0.2	0.6	..	..	..	..	10
40	Slovakia	100	0.3	..	0	..	184	1.1	2.5	18.5	..	..	23.0	4.0	..
41	Portugal	100	0.0	..	1	..	138	0.9	3.5	13.6	..	..	19.0	1.0	..
42	United Arab Emirates	100[f]	0.1	..	..	..	229	0.7	1.7	3.9	..	..	..	..	22
43	Hungary	100	1.4	..	0	..	187	1.5	7.4	32.4	..	..	21.0	3.0	..
44	Latvia	100	0.2	..	0	..	239	3.9	4.3	30.7	..	..	32.0	7.0	..
45	Argentina	100[f]	0.2	..	16	..	160	7.6	4.1	17.2	2.0	..	..	..	3
45	Croatia	..	33.5	..	0	..	89	0.8	4.5	19.8	..	..	13.0	3.0	..
47	Bahrain	..	0.4	..	0	..	301	0.5	2.9	11.6	..	..	..	..	..
48	Montenegro	99	0.7	..	0	..	174	3.2	6.4	24.7	3.0	5.0	..	..	..
49	Russian Federation	100	67.1	27.0	9	..	445	9.5	6.2	35.1	..	..	..	..	..
50	Romania	..	1.7	..	26	..	143	1.5	2.9	18.4	..	..	24.0	2.0	..
51	Kuwait	..	1.1	..	0	..	92	1.8	0.8	1.0	..	..	..	..	20
HIGH HUMAN DEVELOPMENT															
52	Belarus	100[f]	4.1	..	..	..	306	3.6	6.4	32.7	4.0	4.0	..	..	..
52	Oman	..	0.0	..	0	..	36	1.1	0.6	1.2	8.0	..	..	..	36
54	Barbados	99	0.1	..	0	..	322	8.8	0.6	4.1	3.0	..	..	..	23
54	Uruguay	100	0.1	..	269	..	291	7.8	5.2	20.0	2.0	..	..	..	25
56	Bulgaria	100	1.3	..	15	..	125	1.6	5.3	16.6	..	..	23.0	6.0	..
56	Kazakhstan	100	2.3	..	49	..	234	7.4	9.3	40.6	12.0	17.0	..	..	19
58	Bahamas	..	0.2	..	0	..	363	29.8	1.3	3.6	..	..	..	..	..
59	Malaysia	..	0.4	..	94	..	171	1.9	1.5	4.7	..	..	..	..	17

HDI rank		Birth registration (% under age 5)	Refugees by country of origin (thousands)	Internally displaced persons (thousands)	Homeless people due to natural disaster (average annual per million people)	Orphaned children (thousands)	Prison population (per 100,000 people)	Homicide rate (per 100,000 people)	Suicide rate (per 100,000 people)		Justification of wife beating (% ages 15–49)		Violence against women ever experienced[a]		Depth of food deficit (kilocalories per person per day)
									Female	Male	Female	Male	Intimate partner (%)	Nonintimate partner (%)	
		2010–2015[b]	2015[c]	2015	2005/2015	2014	2004–2015[b]	2010–2014[b]	2012	2012	2010–2015[b]	2010–2015[b]	2005–2015[b]	2005–2015[b]	2013/2015
60	Palau	..	0.0	..	0	..	343	3.1	..	..	..	..	25.3	15.1	..
60	Panama	96	0.1	..	32	..	392	17.4	1.3	8.1	6.0	..	..	..	69
62	Antigua and Barbuda	..	0.1	..	0	..	373	11.2	..	..	..	..	..	..	..
63	Seychelles	..	0.0	..	0	..	799	2.1	..	..	..	..	..	..	..
64	Mauritius	..	0.1	..	0	..	155	2.7	2.9	13.2	..	..	..	..	36
65	Trinidad and Tobago	97[g]	0.4	..	0	..	258	25.9	6.2	20.4	8.0[g]	..	..	..	59
66	Costa Rica	100[f]	0.4	..	0	..	352	10.0	2.2	11.2	4.0	..	..	..	39
66	Serbia	99	..	..	15	..	148	1.3	5.8	19.9	4.0	..	..	..	..
68	Cuba	100	5.9	..	1,307	..	510	4.7	4.5	18.5	4.0[f]	7.0[f]	..	..	8
69	Iran (Islamic Republic of)	99[f]	84.9	..	25	..	287	4.8	3.6	6.7	..	..	..	..	36
70	Georgia	100	6.5	239.0	129	..	274[d]	2.7	1.0	5.7	7.0[g]	..	9.0	0.2	60
71	Turkey	99[f]	59.6	954.0	43	..	220	4.3	4.2	11.8	13.0	..	38.0	..	1
71	Venezuela (Bolivarian Republic of)	81[f]	7.5	..	12	..	178	62.0	1.0	4.3	..	..	..	..	10
73	Sri Lanka	97[g]	121.4	44.0	5,380	..	92	2.9	12.8	46.4	53.0[f,g]	..	..	..	200
74	Saint Kitts and Nevis	..	0.0	..	0	..	607	33.6	..	..	..	..	..	..	..
75	Albania	99[g]	10.4	..	7	..	189	4.0	5.2	6.6	30.0[g]	36.0[g]	24.6	..	..
76	Lebanon	100[g]	4.4	12.0	0	..	120	4.3	0.6	1.2	10.0[f,g]	..	..	..	33
77	Mexico	93	11.3	287.0	288	..	212	15.7	1.7	7.1	..	..	14.1	..	30
78	Azerbaijan	94[g]	9.7	564.0	69	..	236	2.5	1.0	2.4	28.0	..	13.5	..	13
79	Brazil	96	0.9	..	82	..	301	24.6	2.5	9.4	..	..	..	..	11
79	Grenada	..	0.3	..	0	..	398	7.5	..	..	..	..	..	..	..
81	Bosnia and Herzegovina	100[g]	18.7	98.0	0	..	73[e]	1.3	4.1	18.0	5.0	6.0	..	..	..
82	The former Yugoslav Republic of Macedonia	100	1.8	0.2	0	..	147	1.6	3.2	7.3	15.0	..	..	..	..
83	Algeria	100[g]	3.5	..	11	..	162	1.5	1.5	2.3	50.0[f]	..	..	..	21
84	Armenia	100	11.2	8.4	0	..	130	2.0	0.9	5.0	9.0	20.0	9.5	..	45
84	Ukraine	100	321.0	1,679.0	6	..	195[d]	4.4	5.3	30.3	3.0	9.0	13.2	1.3	..
86	Jordan	99	1.8	..	0	..	150	2.3	1.9	2.2	70.0[f]	..	23.6	..	13
87	Peru	97[f]	3.0	60.0	193	..	242	6.7	2.1	4.4	..	..	36.4	..	54
87	Thailand	99[f]	0.2	35.0	25	..	461	3.9	4.5	19.1	13.0	..	..	..	57
89	Ecuador	82	1.0	..	89	..	162	8.2	5.3	13.2	..	..	37.5	..	72
90	China	..	212.9	..	203	..	119[d]	0.8	8.7	7.1	..	..	..	..	78
91	Fiji	..	0.9	..	0	..	174	3.0	4.1	10.6	..	..	64.0	9.0	30
92	Mongolia	99	2.2	..	0	..	266	7.5	3.7	16.3	10.0	9.0[f]	..	..	165
92	Saint Lucia	92	1.0	..	0	..	349	21.6	..	..	7.0	..	..	..	..
94	Jamaica	100	1.9	..	39	..	145	36.1	0.7	1.8	5.0	..	35.0	..	62
95	Colombia	97	90.8	6,270.0	26	..	244	27.9	1.9	8.1	..	..	37.4	..	67
96	Dominica	..	0.0	..	853	..	300	8.4	..	..	..	..	..	..	..
97	Suriname	99	0.0	..	0	..	183	9.5	11.9	44.5	13.0	..	..	..	58
97	Tunisia	99	1.6	..	0	..	212	3.1	1.4	3.4	30.0	..	..	..	4
99	Dominican Republic	88	0.4	..	128	..	233	17.4	2.1	6.1	2.0	..	22.4	..	88
99	Saint Vincent and the Grenadines	..	1.8	..	499	..	378	25.6	..	..	..	..	..	..	46
101	Tonga	93	0.0	..	0	..	166	0.1	..	..	29.0	21.0	39.6	..	..
102	Libya	..	6.1	500.0	0	..	99	2.5	1.4	2.2	..	..	..	..	..
103	Belize	95	0.1	..	0	..	449	34.4	0.5	4.9	9.0	..	..	..	41
104	Samoa	59	0.0	..	0	..	250	3.2	..	..	37.0	30.0	46.1	11.0	22
105	Maldives	93[g]	0.0	..	0	..	341	0.9	4.9	7.8	31.0[f,g]	14.0[f,g]	19.5	6.2	39
105	Uzbekistan	100[g]	4.2	..	0	..	150	3.2	4.1	13.2	70.0[g]	61.0[g]	..	..	31
MEDIUM HUMAN DEVELOPMENT															
107	Moldova (Republic of)	100	2.3	..	0	..	215[d]	3.2	4.8	24.1	11.0	13.0	45.5	..	..
108	Botswana	72[g]	0.3	..	0	100	188	14.8	2.0	5.7	..	..	..	..	183
109	Gabon	90	0.2	..	47	68	210	9.4	4.5	12.1	50.0	40.0	48.6	5.0	19
110	Paraguay	85[f]	0.1	..	29	..	158	8.8	3.2	9.1	..	..	..	..	76
111	Egypt	99	17.9	78.0	1	..	76	3.2	1.2	2.4	36.0[f]	..	26.0	..	12
111	Turkmenistan	96[g]	0.5	..	0	..	583	4.3	7.5	32.5	38.0[f,g]	..	..	..	24
113	Indonesia	69[f]	9.3	6.1	296	..	64	0.5	4.9	3.7	35.0	18.0[f]	..	..	51
114	Palestine, State of	99	98.0[h]	221.0	11	..	..	0.6	..	..	..	..	..	..	..
115	Viet Nam	96	313.2	..	863	..	154	1.5	2.4	8.0	28.0	..	34.4	..	89
116	Philippines	90	0.6	62.0	91	..	121	9.9	1.2	4.8	13.0	..	14.6	1.6	96
117	El Salvador	99	14.8	289.0	268	..	492	64.2	5.7	23.5	8.0	..	26.3	..	86
118	Bolivia (Plurinational State of)	76[f,g]	0.6	..	47	..	122	12.4	8.5	16.2	16.0[g]	..	..	4.0	109

TABLE 12

TABLE 12   Human security | 245

TABLE 12 HUMAN SECURITY

HDI rank		Birth registration (% under age 5) 2010–2015[b]	Refugees by country of origin (thousands) 2015[c]	Internally displaced persons (thousands) 2015	Homeless people due to natural disaster (average annual per million people) 2005/2015	Orphaned children (thousands) 2014	Prison population (per 100,000 people) 2004–2015[b]	Homicide rate (per 100,000 people) 2010–2014[b]	Suicide rate (per 100,000 people) Female 2012	Suicide rate (per 100,000 people) Male 2012	Justification of wife beating (% ages 15–49) Female 2010–2015[b]	Justification of wife beating (% ages 15–49) Male 2010–2015[b]	Violence against women ever experienced[a] Intimate partner (%) 2005–2015[b]	Violence against women ever experienced[a] Nonintimate partner (%) 2005–2015[b]	Depth of food deficit (kilocalories per person per day) 2013/2015
119	South Africa	85[f]	0.4	..	15	2,800	292	33.0	1.1	5.5	..	..	..	..	14
120	Kyrgyzstan	98	2.5	..	140	..	166	3.7	4.5	14.2	33.0	..	25.4	0.1	41
121	Iraq	99	261.1	3,290.0	8	..	123	7.9	2.1	1.2	51.0	..	..	..	188
122	Cabo Verde	91	0.0	..	0	..	286	10.6	1.6	9.1	17.0[f,g]	16.0[f,g]	12.6	..	72
123	Morocco	94[f]	1.8	..	0	..	222	1.0	1.2	9.9	64.0[g]	..	..	..	33
124	Nicaragua	85	1.5	..	91	..	171	11.5	4.9	15.4	14.0[f,g]	..	29.3	..	126
125	Guatemala	97[g]	10.3	251.0	379	..	121	31.2	4.3	13.7	..	..	27.6	..	101
125	Namibia	87[f]	1.5	..	0	100	144	16.9	1.4	4.4	28.0	22.0	..	..	323
127	Guyana	89	0.5	..	0	..	259	20.4	22.1	70.8	10.0	10.0	..	..	77
127	Micronesia (Federated States of)	..	..	..	0	..	127	4.8	..	..	..	..	32.8	8.0	..
129	Tajikistan	88	0.8	..	29	..	121	1.4	2.8	5.7	60.0	..	20.3	..	258
130	Honduras	94	6.8	174.0	129	..	196	74.6	2.8	8.3	12.0	10.0	..	..	85
131	India	72	9.9	612.0	662	29,600	33	3.2	16.4	25.8	47.0[g]	42.0[g]	37.2	0.3	110
132	Bhutan	100	17.7	..	0	..	145	2.7	11.2	23.1	68.0	..	..	..	..
133	Timor-Leste	55	0.0	..	0	..	50	3.7	5.8	10.2	86.0	81.0	34.6	0.4	190
134	Vanuatu	43[f]	0.0	..	0	..	87	2.9	..	..	60.0	60.0	60.0	33.0	41
135	Congo	96	14.8	7.8	437	210	27	10.5	4.6	14.7	54.0	40.0	..	..	196
135	Equatorial Guinea	54	0.2	..	0	43	129	3.4	8.6	24.1	53.0	52.0	56.9	..	..
137	Kiribati	94[g]	0.0	..	75	..	136	7.5	..	..	76.0[g]	60.0[g]	67.6	10.0	23
138	Lao People's Democratic Republic	75	7.4	..	1	..	71	7.3	6.6	11.2	58.0	49.0	15.0	5.0	131
139	Bangladesh	37	12.2	426.0	71	..	43	2.8	8.7	6.8	33.0[f]	..	67.2	..	120
139	Ghana	71	23.0	..	19	950	53	1.7	2.2	4.2	28.0	13.0	22.9	4.2	22
139	Zambia	11	0.3	..	131	950	125	5.8	10.8	20.8	47.0	32.0	49.5	2.9	411
142	Sao Tome and Principe	95	0.0	..	0	..	101	3.4	..	..	19.0	14.0	27.9	..	38
143	Cambodia	73	12.8	..	366	..	105	1.8	6.5	12.6	50.0[f]	27.0[f]	21.0	4.0	102
144	Nepal	58	8.9	50.0	284	..	59	2.9	20.0	30.1	43.0	..	28.2	0.4	49
145	Myanmar	72	198.7	644.0	15	..	113	2.5	10.3	16.5	..	..	..	..	108
146	Kenya	67	7.9	309.0	11	2,000	118	5.9	8.4	24.4	42.0	36.0	41.2	3.5	136
147	Pakistan	34	277.3	1,459.0	2,742	..	43	7.8	9.6	9.1	42.0[f]	32.0[f]	..	..	171
LOW HUMAN DEVELOPMENT															
148	Swaziland	54	0.2	..	20	87	289	17.4	4.1	8.6	20.0	17.0	..	..	190
149	Syrian Arab Republic	96[g]	4,850.8	6,600.0	0	..	60	2.2	0.2	0.7	..	..	..	..	..
150	Angola	36	11.9	..	436	1,300	106	9.8	7.3	20.7	..	..	..	..	96
151	Tanzania (United Republic of)	15[f]	6.2	..	70	2,600	69	7.9	18.3	31.6	54.0	38.0	43.6	2.9	237
152	Nigeria	30[f]	152.1	2,096.0	8	9,900	31	10.1	2.9	10.3	35.0	25.0	16.2	1.5	40
153	Cameroon	66	10.6	124.0	204	1,200	115	2.7	3.4	10.9	36.0	39.0	51.1	5.0	64
154	Papua New Guinea	..	0.3	6.3	295	300	61	10.4	9.1	15.9	..	..	..	..	..
154	Zimbabwe	32	21.3	..	3	810	145	6.7	9.7	27.2	37.0	24.0	42.3	1.2	264
156	Solomon Islands	..	0.1	..	171	..	56	..	7.2	13.9	69.0[g]	65.0[g]	63.5	..	67
157	Mauritania	59	34.7	..	326	..	44	11.4	1.5	4.5	38.0	..	..	..	37
158	Madagascar	83	0.3	..	1,967	..	83	0.6	6.9	15.2	45.0	46.0[f]	..	..	227
159	Rwanda	63	286.4	..	52	500	434	4.9	7.2	17.1	56.0	25.0	56.4	..	240
160	Comoros	87	0.6	..	0	..	31	7.8	10.3	24.0	39.0	17.0	6.4	1.5	..
160	Lesotho	45[g]	0.0	..	117	120	92	38.0	3.4	9.2	37.0[g]	48.0[g]	..	..	76
162	Senegal	73	21.3	24.0	0	..	62	7.9	2.8	8.6	57.0	27.0	..	..	66
163	Haiti	80	34.8	..	867	300	97	10.0	2.4	3.3	17.0	15.0	20.8	2.0	530
163	Uganda	30	6.3	30.0	782	1,900	115	11.8	12.3	26.9	58.0	44.0	50.5	3.7	170
165	Sudan	67	622.5[i]	3,182.0	556	..	50	6.5	11.5	23.0	34.0	..	..	..	176[j]
166	Togo	78	8.8	3.0	190	330	64	9.2	2.8	8.5	29.0	18.0	..	..	85
167	Benin	85	0.4	..	1,468	440	77	6.3	3.1	8.8	36.0	17.0	..	..	52
168	Yemen	31	15.9	2,509.0	15	..	53	6.7	3.0	4.3	49.0	..	..	..	180
169	Afghanistan	37	2,663.0	1,174.0	281	..	74	6.6	5.3	6.2	90.0	..	..	..	166
170	Malawi	6[f]	0.4	..	514	990	73	1.8	8.9	23.9	13.0	8.0	31.0	1.7	139
171	Côte d'Ivoire	65	71.1	303.0	45	1,200	52	11.4	4.1	10.6	48.0	42.0	25.5	..	94
172	Djibouti	92[g]	1.1	..	0	32	68	7.0	9.5	20.9	..	..	..	..	130
173	Gambia	72	8.5	..	21	87	58	9.4	2.6	7.6	58.0	33.0	..	..	33
174	Ethiopia	7[g]	85.8	450.0	1	3,500	128	8.0	6.7	16.5	68.0	45.0	..	..	244
175	Mali	81	154.2	50.0	308	810	33	10.2	2.7	7.2	87.0	..	34.6	..	23
176	Congo (Democratic Republic of the)	25	541.3	1,500.0	32	4,000	32	12.5	4.8	15.8	75.0	61.0	64.1	2.7	..
177	Liberia	25[f]	10.0	..	89	190	39	3.2	2.0	6.8	43.0	24.0	38.6	2.6	261
178	Guinea-Bissau	24	1.5	..	42	120	..	9.9	2.4	7.2	42.0	29.0	..	..	152

TABLE 12

HDI rank		Birth registration (% under age 5) 2010–2015[b]	Refugees by country of origin (thousands) 2015[c]	Internally displaced persons (thousands) 2015	Homeless people due to natural disaster (average annual per million people) 2005/2015	Orphaned children (thousands) 2014	Prison population (per 100,000 people) 2004–2015[b]	Homicide rate (per 100,000 people) 2010–2014[b]	Suicide rate (per 100,000 people) Female 2012	Suicide rate (per 100,000 people) Male 2012	Justification of wife beating (% ages 15–49) Female 2010–2015[b]	Justification of wife beating (% ages 15–49) Male 2010–2015[b]	Violence against women ever experienced[a] Intimate partner (%) 2005–2015[b]	Violence against women ever experienced[a] Nonintimate partner (%) 2005–2015[b]	Depth of food deficit (kilocalories per person per day) 2013/2015
179	Eritrea	..	379.8	..	0	140	..	9.7	8.7	25.8	51.0	45.0	..	..	..
179	Sierra Leone	77	4.9	..	36	310	55	1.9	4.5	11.0	63.0	34.0	45.3	..	162
181	Mozambique	48	0.1	..	292	1,800	61	3.6	21.1	34.2	23.0	20.0	33.1	..	188
181	South Sudan	35	778.6[k]	1,697.0	0	570	65	13.9	12.8	27.1	79.0	..	..	..	..
183	Guinea	58	17.0	..	33	..	26	8.7	2.4	7.1	92.0	66.0	..	..	118
184	Burundi	75	292.8	99.0	519	580	93	4.0	12.5	34.1	73.0	44.0	..	..	..
185	Burkina Faso	77	2.1	..	367	830	34	0.7	2.8	7.3	44.0	34.0	11.5	..	167
186	Chad	12	14.9	107.0	93	970	39	9.2	2.3	7.4	62.0	..	..	..	276
187	Niger	64	1.4	153.0	449	..	39	4.5	1.9	5.3	60.0	27.0	..	..	58
188	Central African Republic	61	471.1	452.0	920	300	16	13.2	5.3	14.1	80.0	75.0	29.8	..	349
OTHER COUNTRIES OR TERRITORIES															
	Korea (Democratic People's Rep. of)	100[g]	1.1	..	1,315	..	..	4.7	..	..	..	..	..	..	344
	Marshall Islands	96[g]	0.0	..	0	..	..	4.7	..	..	56.0[g]	58.0[g]	51.0	13.0	..
	Monaco	100	0.0	..	..	..	74[d]	..	..	..	..	..	..	..	..
	Nauru	83[g]	..	..	..	..	140	1.3	..	..	..	..	48.1	47.0	..
	San Marino	100	0.0	..	..	..	..	0.0	..	..	..	..	..	..	..
	Somalia	3[g]	1,123.0	1,223.0	234	630	..	5.6	6.8	18.1	76.0[f,g]	..	..	..	..
	Tuvalu	50[g]	0.0	..	0	..	110	20.3	..	..	70.0[g]	73.0[g]	36.8	..	..
Human development groups															
	Very high human development	100	118.2[l]	299.0[l]	81	..	289	2.9	5.6	19.9	..	..	..	..	..
	High human development	..	1,019.2[l]	10,750.6[l]	203	..	174	6.0	6.4	8.9	..	..	..	..	60
	Medium human development	70	1,335.9[l]	7,878.9[l]	609	..	66	4.8	11.0	17.3	41.3	..	37.3	..	104
	Low human development	39	11,584.9[l]	20,559.3[l]	233	3,982	70	8.2	6.6	15.2	51.8	36.1	..	..	147
Developing countries		65	15,066.6[l]	40,683.8[l]	399	..	111	5.8	8.3	13.5	..	..	..	..	92
Regions															
	Arab States	84	7,011.7[l]	17,615.0[l]	72	..	116	4.0	2.6	5.5	45.8	..	..	..	67
	East Asia and the Pacific	..	760.1[l]	753.4[l]	241	..	126	1.5	7.3	7.3	..	..	..	..	79
	Europe and Central Asia	98	456.2[l]	3,542.6[l]	29	..	209	3.9	4.8	18.6	21.5	..	26.2	..	27
	Latin America and the Caribbean	94	197.8[l]	7,331.0[l]	290	..	244	21.0	2.0	9.9	..	..	..	..	41
	South Asia	64	3,195.4[l]	3,765.0[l]	838	..	48	3.8	14.3	21.6	45.8	..	..	..	115
	Sub-Saharan Africa	41	3,445.3[l]	7,404.8[l]	189	3,702	88	9.5	6.3	15.5	50.3	35.5	..	..	131
Least developed countries		40	7,859.6[l]	13,773.0[l]	249	..	75	6.4	8.5	15.8	51.9	..	..	..	105
Small island developing states		82	50.9[l]	6.3[l]	506	..	229	12.0	4.3	11.8	13.2	..	..	..	169
Organisation for Economic Co-operation and Development		99	83.3[l]	1,241.0[l]	114	..	274	3.3	5.3	17.4	..	..	..	..	..
World		69	15,182.3[l]	40,710.8[l]	334	..	143	5.2	7.9	14.7	..	..	..	..	91

NOTES

a Data collection methods, age ranges, sampled women (ever-partnered, ever-married or all women) and definitions of the forms of violence and of perpetrators vary by survey. Thus data are not necessarily comparable across countries.

b Data refer to the most recent year available during the period specified.

c Data refer to people recognized as refugees under the 1951 UN Convention, the 1967 UN Protocol and the 1969 Organization of African Unity Convention. In the absence of government figures, the Office of the UN High Commissioner for Refugees (UNHCR) has estimated the refugee population in many industrial countries based on 10 years of individual asylum-seeker recognition.

d For more detailed country notes, see www.prisonstudies.org.

e HDRO calculations based on data from ICPS (2016).

f Differs from standard definition or refers to only part of the country.

g Refers to years or periods other than those specified.

h Refers to Palestinian refugees under the UNHCR mandate only. Another 5,589,488 Palestinian refugees are under the responsibility of United Nations Relief and Works Agency for Palestinian Refugees in the Near East.

i May include citizens of South Sudan.

j Refers to the average for 2009–2011, prior to South Sudan's independence.

k An unknown number of refugees and asylum-seekers from South Sudan may be included under data for Sudan.

l Unweighted sum of national estimates.

DEFINITIONS

Birth registration: Percentage of children under age 5 who were registered at the moment of the survey. It includes children whose birth certificate was seen by the interviewer and children whose mother or caretaker says the birth has been registered.

Refugees by country of origin: Number of people who have fled their country of origin because of a well founded fear of persecution due to their race, religion, nationality, political opinion or membership in a particular social group and who cannot or do not want to return to their country of origin.

Internally displaced persons: Number of people who have been forced to leave their homes or places of habitual residence—in particular, as a result of or to avoid the effects of armed conflict, situations of generalized violence, violations of human rights or natural or human-made disasters—and who have not crossed an internationally recognized state border.

Homeless people due to natural disaster: Average annual number of people who lack a shelter for living quarters as a result of natural disasters, who carry their few possessions with them and who sleep in the streets, in doorways or on piers, or in any other space, on a more or less random basis, expressed per million people.

Orphaned children: Number of children (ages 0–17) who have lost one or both parents due to any cause.

Prison population: Number of adult and juvenile prisoners—including pretrial detainees, unless otherwise noted—expressed per 100,000 people.

Homicide rate: Number of unlawful deaths purposefully inflicted on a person by another person, expressed per 100,000 people.

Suicide rate: Number of deaths from purposely self-inflicted injuries, expressed per 100,000 people in the reference population.

Justification of wife beating: Percentage of women and men ages 15–49 who consider a husband to be justified in hitting or beating his wife for at least one of the following reasons: if his wife burns the food, argues with him, goes out without telling him, neglects the children or refuses sexual relations.

Violence against women ever experienced, intimate partner: Percentage of the female population, ages 15 and older, that has ever experienced physical or sexual violence from an intimate partner.

Violence against women ever experienced, nonintimate partner: Percentage of the female population, ages 15 and older, that has ever experienced sexual violence from a nonintimate partner.

Depth of the food deficit: Number of kilocalories needed to lift the undernourished from their status, holding all other factors constant.

MAIN DATA SOURCES

Columns 1, 5, 10 and 11: UNICEF (2016).

Column 2: UNHCR (2016).

Column 3: IDMC (2016).

Column 4: CRED EM-DAT (2016) and UNDESA (2015a).

Column 6: ICPS (2016).

Column 7: UNODC (2016).

Columns 8 and 9: WHO (2016).

Columns 12 and 13: UN Women (2016).

Column 14: FAO (2016a).

TABLE **12**

TABLE 12 Human security | 247

TABLE **13**

International integration

	Trade	Financial flows				Human mobility				Communication		
	Exports and imports	Foreign direct investment, net inflows	Private capital flows	Net official development assistance received[a]	Remittances, inflows	Net migration rate	Stock of immigrants	International student mobility	International inbound tourists	Internet users	Mobile phone subscriptions	
	(% of GDP)	(% of GDP)	(% of GDP)	(% of GNI)	(% of GDP)	(per 1,000 people)	(% of population)	(% of total tertiary enrolment)	(thousands)	(% of population)	(per 100 people)	(% change)
HDI rank	2015[b]	2015[b]	2015[b]	2014[c]	2015[b]	2010/2015[d]	2015	2013[e]	2014[c]	2015	2015	2010–2015
VERY HIGH HUMAN DEVELOPMENT												
1 Norway	68.5	−1.5	14.6	..	0.16	9.3[f]	14.2[f]	−3.4	4,855	96.8	113.6	−0.8
2 Australia	41.0	2.8	−7.2	..	0.16	8.9[g]	28.2[g]	17.1	6,868	84.6	132.8	32.2
2 Switzerland	114.6	18.0	8.5	..	0.34	9.5	29.4	12.6	9,158	88.0	142.0	15.3
4 Germany	86.0	1.4	8.4	..	0.46	3.1	14.9	2.8	32,999	87.6	116.7	9.6
5 Denmark	100.2	0.6	−2.1	..	0.42	3.5	10.1	8.3	10,267	96.3	128.3	11.0
5 Singapore	326.1	22.3	8.5	..	..	14.9	45.4	10.3	11,864	82.1	146.1	0.5
7 Netherlands	154.3	9.0	4.5	..	0.18	1.3	11.7	5.4	13,925	93.1	123.5	7.0
8 Ireland	222.0	85.5	−64.8	..	0.25	−6.0	15.9	−3.9	8,813	80.1	103.7	−1.5
9 Iceland	100.4	2.3	20.5	..	1.15	−0.2	11.4	−8.2	998	98.2	114.0	6.3
10 Canada	65.4	3.6	−0.1	..	0.09	6.7	21.8	..	16,537	88.5	81.9	8.3
10 United States	28.1	2.1	−0.7	..	0.04	3.2	14.5	3.6	75,011	74.6	117.6	28.8
12 Hong Kong, China (SAR)	400.0	58.4	6.9	..	0.12	4.2	39.0	−1.7	27,770	84.9	228.8	16.9
13 New Zealand	55.2	−0.3	−0.3	..	0.24	0.3	23.0	14.0	2,772	88.2	121.8	13.0
14 Sweden	86.1	3.2	−0.1	..	0.66	5.7	16.8	1.8	5,660	90.6	130.4	11.3
15 Liechtenstein	..	..	..	..	..	..	62.6	−16.8	54	96.6	108.8	10.7
16 United Kingdom	56.8	1.8	−18.2	..	0.18	2.8	13.2	16.3	32,613	92.0	125.8	1.7
17 Japan	36.8	0.0	6.4	..	0.09	0.6	1.6	3.0	13,413	93.3	125.1	29.2
18 Korea (Republic of)	84.8	0.4	5.2	..	0.47	1.2	2.6	−1.7	14,202	89.9	118.5	13.1
19 Israel	59.4	3.9	1.7	..	0.29	0.5	24.9	−2.6	2,927	78.9	133.5	8.7
20 Luxembourg	391.5	42.6	−98.4	..	2.79	18.1	44.0	−85.9	1,038	97.3	148.5	3.8
21 France	61.4	1.8	1.4	..	0.96	1.0	12.1	6.6	83,767	84.7	102.6	12.3
22 Belgium	167.1	−4.6	−2.7	..	2.19	4.9	12.3	6.6	7,887	85.1	115.7	4.1
23 Finland	74.3	8.1	−7.9	..	0.35	4.0[h]	5.7[h]	4.4	4,226	92.7	135.5	−13.3
24 Austria	102.4	1.5	6.7	..	0.75	3.5	17.5	13.1	25,291	83.9	157.4	8.0
25 Slovenia	146.3	3.9	4.3	..	1.70	0.4	11.4	−0.1	2,411	73.1	113.2	9.6
26 Italy	57.3	0.4	6.3	..	0.52	1.8	9.7	1.6	48,576	65.6	151.3	−2.2
27 Spain	63.8	1.9	3.8	..	0.22	−2.6[i]	12.7[i]	1.4	64,995	78.7	107.9	−3.0
28 Czech Republic	162.5	1.4	−3.1	..	1.48	0.6	3.8	6.5	10,617	81.3	129.2	5.4
29 Greece	60.4	−0.1	4.9	..	0.22	−2.5	11.3	−0.8	22,033	66.8	114.0	3.0
30 Brunei Darussalam	106.6	1.1	6.8	..	..	1.0	24.3	−38.3	201	71.2	108.1	−0.5
30 Estonia	155.4	−0.8	3.0	..	1.96	−1.8	15.4	−3.5	2,918	88.4	148.7	16.8
32 Andorra	..	..	..	..	..	..	59.7	−182.3	2,363	96.9	88.1	4.8
33 Cyprus	108.1	27.1	13.9	..	1.29	6.2[j]	16.8[j]	−61.0	2,441	71.7	95.4	1.8
33 Malta	182.5	5.7	−45.9	..	2.09	3.0	9.9	−6.3	1,690	76.2	129.3	20.5
33 Qatar	90.9	0.6	11.7	..	0.26	36.3	75.5	16.6	2,826	92.9	153.6	22.9
36 Poland	95.9	1.5	−0.3	..	1.43	−0.4	1.6	0.2	16,000	68.0	148.7	21.0
37 Lithuania	154.7	1.5	−2.6	..	3.33	−11.3	4.7	−5.0	2,063	71.4	139.5	−12.5
38 Chile	60.4	8.5	−3.0	0.1	0.05	2.3	2.6	−0.5	3,674	64.3	129.5	11.9
38 Saudi Arabia	72.5	1.3	1.1	..	0.05	5.7	32.3	−0.8	18,259	69.6	176.6	−6.7
40 Slovakia	185.2	2.5	0.1	..	2.47	0.0	3.3	−10.9	6,235	85.0	122.3	12.2
41 Portugal	79.9	−0.7	−0.3	..	0.18	−2.7	8.1	1.4	9,092	68.6	110.4	−4.2
42 United Arab Emirates	175.9	3.0	..	..	..	9.3	88.4	38.2	..	91.2	187.3	44.7
43 Hungary	171.2	−0.8	4.9	..	3.33	0.6	4.6	3.4	12,140	72.8	118.9	−0.9
44 Latvia	118.9	2.7	6.2	..	5.24	−7.2	13.4	−2.9	1,843	79.2	127.0	15.1
45 Argentina	22.9	2.1	−1.8	0.0	0.08	0.1	4.8	..	5,931	69.4	143.9	1.8
45 Croatia	96.0	0.3	−0.5	0.2	4.32	−0.9	13.6	−5.2	11,623	69.8	103.8	−8.7
47 Bahrain	115.3	−4.5	88.7	..	..	4.5	51.1	−4.7	10,452	93.5	185.3	48.0
48 Montenegro	104.4	17.5	−20.5	2.2	9.55	−0.8	13.2	..	1,350	64.6	162.2	−14.1
49 Russian Federation	50.7	0.5	3.2	..	0.52	1.6	8.1	1.2	32,421	73.4	160.0	−3.4
50 Romania	82.7	2.2	−1.2	..	1.65	−4.4	1.2	−1.4	8,442	55.8	107.1	−3.8
51 Kuwait	99.1	0.3	33.5	..	0.03	29.8	73.6	..	307	82.1	231.8	74.2
HIGH HUMAN DEVELOPMENT												
52 Belarus	119.2	2.9	−0.9	0.2	1.27	2.5	11.4	−4.0	137	62.2	123.6	13.6
52 Oman	115.4	1.2	1.9	0.0	0.06	65.2	41.1	−11.8	1,519	74.2	159.9	−2.7
54 Barbados	81.2	5.7	0.9	0.4	2.43	1.5	12.1	3.9	521	76.1	116.5	−6.7
54 Uruguay	44.9	3.3	−2.5	0.2	0.22	−1.8	2.1	..	2,682	64.6	160.2	21.8
56 Bulgaria	131.5	3.6	−5.5	..	2.95	−1.4	1.4	−4.6	7,311	56.7	129.3	−6.4
56 Kazakhstan	53.3	2.2	−2.8	0.0	0.10	1.9	20.1	−5.1	4,560	72.9	187.2	53.6
58 Bahamas	93.4	0.9	−0.7	..	..	5.2	15.3	..	1,427	78.0	80.3	−32.4

TABLE
13

	Trade	Financial flows				Human mobility				Communication		
	Exports and imports	Foreign direct investment, net inflows	Private capital flows	Net official development assistance received[a]	Remittances, inflows	Net migration rate	Stock of immigrants	International student mobility	International inbound tourists	Internet users	Mobile phone subscriptions	
	(% of GDP)	(% of GDP)	(% of GDP)	(% of GNI)	(% of GDP)	(per 1,000 people)	(% of population)	(% of total tertiary enrolment)	(thousands)	(% of population)	(per 100 people)	(% change)
HDI rank	2015[b]	2015[b]	2015[b]	2014[c]	2015[b]	2010/2015[d]	2015	2013[e]	2014[c]	2015	2015	2010–2015
59 Malaysia	134.4	3.7	2.2	0.0	0.55	3.1[k]	8.3[k]	−0.2	27,437	71.1	143.9	20.2
60 Palau	134.5	−3.1	−16.3	9.8	0.79	..	26.6	..	141	..	111.5	57.3
60 Panama	115.0	11.0	−6.8	−0.4	1.07	1.5	4.7	..	1,745	51.2	174.2	−3.6
62 Antigua and Barbuda	97.8	11.9	−10.8	0.2	1.68	−0.1	30.6	−19.0	249	65.2	137.2	−28.7
63 Seychelles	181.3	7.4	−15.9	0.7	1.14	−3.3	13.3	−198.3	233	58.1	158.1	22.6
64 Mauritius	109.4	1.8	−0.6	0.4	0.01	0.0[l]	2.2[l]	−11.6	1,039	50.1	140.6	45.3
65 Trinidad and Tobago	59.9	5.8	..	0.0	0.45	−0.7	3.7	..	412	69.2	157.7	10.5
66 Costa Rica	72.3	5.9	−5.9	0.1	1.08	0.8	8.8	..	2,527	59.8	150.7	124.9
66 Serbia	105.1	6.4	−4.6	0.9	9.23	−2.2[m]	9.1[m]	−1.2	1,029	65.3	120.5	−3.8
68 Cuba	44.3	..	..	0.1	..	−1.4	0.1	4.1	2,970	31.1	29.7	233.5
69 Iran (Islamic Republic of)	43.1	0.5	..	0.0	0.31	−0.8	3.4	−1.0	4,967	44.1	93.4	28.6
70 Georgia	110.0	9.6	−7.5	3.4	10.45	−14.4[n]	4.2[n]	−5.8	5,516	45.2	129.0	42.3
71 Turkey	58.8	2.4	0.5	0.4	0.19	5.3	3.8	0.2	39,811	53.7	96.0	12.1
71 Venezuela (Bolivarian Republic of)	54.3	0.6	0.1	0.0	0.03	−0.5	4.5	−0.5	857	61.9	93.0	−3.1
73 Sri Lanka	48.5	0.8	−1.6	0.6	8.50	−4.7	0.2	−5.1	1,527	30.0	112.8	34.9
74 Saint Kitts and Nevis	79.0	8.5	−13.1	3.8	5.61	..	13.4	−57.9	113	75.7	131.8	−13.7
75 Albania	71.4	8.6	−11.5	2.1	9.14	−6.3	2.0	−12.1	3,341	63.3	106.4	24.5
76 Lebanon	121.9	5.0	−5.3	1.0	15.00	49.1	34.1	6.9	1,355	74.0	87.1	32.0
77 Mexico	72.8	2.6	−3.5	0.1	2.29	−0.9	0.9	−0.6	29,346	57.4	85.3	10.0
78 Azerbaijan	72.6	7.6	−3.6	0.3	2.39	−0.3[o]	2.7[o]	−6.6	2,160	77.0	111.3	11.2
79 Brazil	27.4	4.2	−4.7	0.0	0.16	0.0	0.3	−0.2	6,430	59.1	126.6	25.5
79 Grenada	68.7	6.2	−9.1	4.5	3.03	−8.1	6.6	54.1	134	53.8	112.3	−3.6
81 Bosnia and Herzegovina	90.8	1.7	−1.1	3.4	11.08	−0.1	0.9	−3.2	536	65.1	90.2	11.5
82 The former Yugoslav Republic of Macedonia	113.3	1.9	−2.5	1.9	3.04	−0.5	6.3	−5.2	425	70.4	105.4	2.9
83 Algeria	62.5	−0.2	0.3	0.1	0.16	−0.8	0.6	−1.1	2,301	38.2	113.0	27.8
84 Armenia	71.0	1.7	−4.0	2.2	14.12	−0.7	6.3	−2.6	1,204	58.2	115.1	−11.7
84 Ukraine	107.5	3.4	−3.7	1.1	6.45	0.9[p]	10.8	0.5	12,712	49.3	144.0	23.0
86 Jordan	97.9	3.4	6.8	7.6	14.26	6.5	41.0	3.7	3,990	53.4	179.4	74.9
87 Peru	44.6	3.6	−5.1	0.2	1.42	−1.6	0.3	..	3,215	40.9	109.9	10.4
87 Thailand	131.9	1.8	5.4	0.1	1.32	0.3	5.8	−0.2	24,810	39.3	125.8	16.5
89 Ecuador	45.1	1.1	−2.5	0.2	2.37	−0.5	2.4	−1.3	1,557	48.9	79.4	−19.4
90 China	41.2	2.3	0.0	0.0	0.41	−0.3	0.1	−1.8	55,622	50.3	93.2	47.5
91 Fiji	137.0	7.6	−5.7	2.1	5.07	−6.6	1.5	..	693	46.3	108.2	33.4
92 Mongolia	87.0	1.7	−3.8	2.8	2.26	−1.1	0.6	−3.9	393	21.4	105.0	13.4
92 Saint Lucia	95.3	6.6	−12.4	1.3	2.10	0.0	6.9	−31.5	338	52.4	101.5	−9.1
94 Jamaica	77.1	5.7	−15.1	0.7	10.00	7.0	0.0	..	2,000	43.2	111.6	3.0
95 Colombia	39.0	4.1	−5.9	0.3	1.60	−0.6	0.3	..	2,565	55.9	115.7	20.9
96 Dominica	80.7	6.7	−0.3	3.1	4.38	..	9.2	..	81	67.6	106.3	−28.3
97 Suriname	91.1	4.0	−5.5	0.2	0.14	−1.9	8.6	..	252	42.8	180.7	82.0
97 Tunisia	102.1	2.3	−2.5	2.0	5.46	−0.6	0.5	−3.2	6,069	48.5	129.9	24.3
99 Dominican Republic	53.6	3.3	−8.3	0.3	7.74	−3.0	3.9	2.7	5,141	51.9	82.6	−7.0
99 Saint Vincent and the Grenadines	78.1	16.1	−18.8	1.3	4.20	−9.1	4.2	..	71	51.8	103.7	−14.0
101 Tonga	71.3	12.9	..	18.2	27.08	−15.4	5.4	..	50	45.0	65.6	25.8
102 Libya	137.0	2.5	8.8	0.5	..	−16.0	12.3	..	..	19.0	157.0	−13.0
103 Belize	125.6	3.4	−3.3	2.3	4.81	4.5	15.0	..	321	41.6	48.9	−22.3
104 Samoa	77.7	2.1	−1.8	12.0	20.27	−13.4	2.6	..	120	25.4	58.5	21.0
105 Maldives	200.7	10.3	−10.1	0.9	0.12	0.0	25.9	..	1,205	54.5	206.7	36.2
105 Uzbekistan	42.8	1.6	..	0.5	4.65	−1.4	3.9	−8.3	1,969	42.8	73.3	−2.8
MEDIUM HUMAN DEVELOPMENT												
107 Moldova (Republic of)	117.2	4.1	−4.1	5.9	23.41	−0.5[q]	3.5[q]	−12.3	11	49.8	108.0	51.3
108 Botswana	99.2	2.7	4.0	0.6	0.21	1.9	7.1	−5.4	1,544	27.5	169.0	40.8
109 Gabon	74.0	4.4	..	0.6	..	0.6	15.6	..	..	23.5	168.9	63.3
110 Paraguay	82.1	1.1	−1.9	0.2	2.00	−2.7	2.4	..	649	44.4	105.4	15.0
111 Egypt	34.9	2.1	−0.7	1.2	5.96	−0.5	0.5	1.0	9,628	35.9	111.0	22.6
111 Turkmenistan	117.7	11.4	..	0.1	0.04	−1.0	3.7	..	..	15.0	145.9	130.1
113 Indonesia	41.9	1.8	−4.9	0.0	1.12	−0.6	0.1	−0.5	9,435	22.0	132.3	50.8
114 Palestine, State of	77.5	0.9	−0.8	17.5	17.40	−2.0[r]	5.5[s]	−9.8	556	57.4	77.6	19.6
115 Viet Nam	178.8	6.1	−5.5	2.4	6.82	−0.4	0.1	−2.2	7,874	52.7	130.6	4.3
116 Philippines	60.8	2.0	1.6	0.2	10.27	−1.4	0.2	−0.2	4,833	40.7	118.1	32.7
117 El Salvador	68.0	2.0	−1.7	0.4	16.58	−7.9	0.7	−1.3	1,345	26.9	145.3	17.3

TABLE 13

TABLE 13   International integration | 249

TABLE 13 INTERNATIONAL INTEGRATION

	Trade	Financial flows				Human mobility				Communication		
	Exports and imports	Foreign direct investment, net inflows	Private capital flows	Net official development assistance received[a]	Remittances, inflows	Net migration rate	Stock of immigrants	International student mobility	International inbound tourists	Internet users	Mobile phone subscriptions	
	(% of GDP)	(% of GDP)	(% of GDP)	(% of GNI)	(% of GDP)	(per 1,000 people)	(% of population)	(% of total tertiary enrolment)	(thousands)	(% of population)	(per 100 people)	(% change)
HDI rank	2015[b]	2015[b]	2015[b]	2014[c]	2015[b]	2010/2015[d]	2015	2013[e]	2014[c]	2015	2015	2010–2015
118 Bolivia (Plurinational State of)	85.3	1.5	1.5	2.1	3.62	−1.2	1.3	..	871	45.1	92.2	30.4
119 South Africa	62.8	0.5	−0.4	0.3	0.26	2.3	5.8	3.6	9,549	51.9	159.3	62.7
120 Kyrgyzstan	125.1	11.6	−10.8	8.6	25.68	−4.0	3.4	1.9	2,849	30.2	132.8	34.3
121 Iraq	50.4	2.1	1.6	0.6	0.16	3.3	1.0	..	892	17.2	93.8	24.9
122 Cabo Verde	91.8	4.6	−4.3	12.9	12.32	−4.4	2.9	−34.5	494	43.0	127.2	66.7
123 Morocco	80.9	3.1	−3.8	2.1	7.04	−1.9	0.3	−7.7	10,283	57.1	126.9	25.5
124 Nicaragua	93.0	6.6	−6.1	3.7	9.43	−4.6	0.7	..	1,330	19.7	116.1	70.6
125 Guatemala	51.3	1.8	−1.7	0.5	10.33	−1.5	0.5	..	1,455	27.1	111.5	−11.5
125 Namibia	111.5	9.2	−18.3	1.8	0.08	−0.1	3.8	−32.7	1,176	22.3	102.1	14.1
127 Guyana	120.5	3.7	−1.9	5.2	9.27	−7.2	2.0	−16.9	206	38.2	67.2	−5.8
127 Micronesia (Federated States of)	..	6.4	−4.6	33.9	7.34	−15.7	2.6	..	35	31.5	..	−100.0
129 Tajikistan	87.5	5.0	−5.0	3.1	28.76	−2.9	3.2	−4.2	213	19.0	98.6	26.6
130 Honduras	109.1	6.5	−5.5	3.3	18.19	−2.1	0.3	−0.9	868	20.4	95.5	−23.4
131 India	48.8	2.1	−3.0	0.1	3.32	−0.4	0.4	−0.6	7,679	26.0	78.8	26.4
132 Bhutan	116.0	1.7	..	7.1	1.00	2.7	6.6	−29.9	134	39.8	87.1	58.4
133 Timor-Leste	110.9	3.0	−12.8	7.7	4.36	−8.9	0.9	..	60	13.4	117.4	167.9
134 Vanuatu	97.4	1.6	−2.8	12.1	3.45	0.5	1.2	..	109	22.4	66.2	−7.9
135 Congo	165.6	17.4	..	0.9	..	−2.8	8.5	−20.9	373	7.6	111.7	23.5
135 Equatorial Guinea	178.3	3.4	..	0.0	..	5.1	1.3	..	..	21.3	66.7	16.3
137 Kiribati	104.3	1.2	6.1	24.3	11.01	−4.0	2.8	..	6	13.0	38.8	258.3
138 Lao People's Democratic Republic	79.0	8.8	−13.1	4.2	0.75	−3.6	0.3	−3.4	3,164	18.2	53.1	−15.2
139 Bangladesh	42.1	1.7	−1.9	1.3	7.89	−2.8	0.9	−1.1	125	14.4	83.4	85.5
139 Ghana	98.8	8.4	−10.2	3.1	13.16	−0.4	1.5	0.5	1,093	23.5	129.7	80.5
139 Zambia	67.9	7.8	−17.4	3.8	0.27	−0.5	0.8	..	947	21.0	74.5	80.7
142 Sao Tome and Principe	..	8.0	−7.6	11.5	7.95	−6.2	1.3	..	12	25.8	65.1	12.9
143 Cambodia	141.7	9.4	−9.3	5.1	2.20	−2.0	0.5	−2.7	4,503	19.0	133.0	134.4
144 Nepal	53.2	0.1	..	4.4	32.23	−2.7	1.8	−7.6	790	17.6	96.7	182.5
145 Myanmar	..	4.8	..	2.2	4.99	−1.8	0.1	−1.0	3,081	21.8	76.7	6,603.2
146 Kenya	44.8	2.3	−7.1	4.4	2.46	−0.2	2.4	..	1,261	45.6	80.7	32.2
147 Pakistan	28.1	0.4	−0.7	1.4	7.15	−1.2	1.9	..	966	18.0	66.9	16.8
LOW HUMAN DEVELOPMENT												
148 Swaziland	101.2	−3.0	−0.6	2.0	0.60	−1.0	2.5	−32.8	968	30.4	73.2	20.3
149 Syrian Arab Republic	..	..	..	..	..	−41.1	4.7	..	5,070	30.0	62.4	15.0
150 Angola	75.1	8.5	2.3	0.2	0.01	0.9	0.4	..	595	12.4	60.8	26.5
151 Tanzania (United Republic of)	49.5	4.4	−4.4	5.6	0.87	−0.8[t]	0.5[t]	..	1,113	5.4	75.9	62.6
152 Nigeria	30.9	0.6	−1.0	0.5	4.29	−0.4	0.7	..	600	47.4	82.2	50.4
153 Cameroon	42.8	2.1	−2.2	2.7	0.84	−0.5	1.6	−8.0	912	20.7	71.8	71.6
154 Papua New Guinea	..	−0.2	−2.0	3.5	0.06	0.0	0.3	..	182	7.9	46.6	67.6
154 Zimbabwe	75.0	3.0	..	5.8	..	−3.0	2.6	−16.7	1,905	16.4	84.8	44.0
156 Solomon Islands	98.2	1.9	−1.4	18.1	1.60	−4.3	0.4	..	20	10.0	72.7	231.2
157 Mauritania	103.7	9.2	..	5.0	..	−1.0	3.4	..	..	15.2	89.3	16.1
158 Madagascar	69.7	5.2	−5.5	5.4	4.28	0.0	0.1	−2.6	222	4.2	46.0	25.8
159 Rwanda	45.3	4.0	−4.0	13.3	1.99	−1.4	3.8	−5.7	926	18.0	70.5	115.2
160 Comoros	79.9	0.8	−1.7	11.9	20.19	−2.7	1.6	−70.5	19	7.5	54.8	126.5
160 Lesotho	141.6	4.3	−5.1	4.0	17.43	−1.9	0.3	−11.7	1,079	16.1	105.5	114.7
162 Senegal	73.6	2.5	−8.5	7.2	11.71	−1.4	1.7	..	836	21.7	99.9	55.1
163 Haiti	69.5	1.2	..	12.3	24.73	−2.9	0.4	..	465	12.2	69.9	72.9
163 Uganda	46.9	4.0	−3.1	6.2	3.98	−0.8	1.9	7.2	1,266	19.2	50.4	33.5
165 Sudan	19.0	2.1	−2.1	1.2	0.18	−4.2	1.3	..	684	26.6	70.5	69.8
166 Togo	106.6	1.3	12.2	5.2	9.93	−0.3	3.8	−9.4	282	7.1	64.9	57.4
167 Benin	62.8	2.7	−3.6	6.3	3.59	−0.2	2.3	4.3	242	6.8	85.6	15.1
168 Yemen	..	−0.4	1.3	3.0	9.30	−0.4	1.3	−0.8	990	25.1	68.0	39.6
169 Afghanistan	53.2	0.9	−0.4	23.3	1.57	3.1	1.2	−5.8	..	8.3	61.6	71.2
170 Malawi	61.9	2.2	−11.0	15.8	0.59	−0.4	1.3	−20.1	795	9.3	35.3	70.2
171 Côte d'Ivoire	87.8	1.4	−1.9	2.8	1.21	0.5	9.6	0.2	471	21.0	119.3	45.1
172 Djibouti	..	9.6	..	..	2.24	−3.7	12.7	−39.3	63	11.9	34.7	74.6
173 Gambia	70.1	3.3	..	12.1	21.24	−1.5	9.7	..	156	17.1	131.3	49.2
174 Ethiopia	37.2	3.5	..	6.5	1.01	−0.1	1.1	..	770	11.6	42.8	443.4
175 Mali	50.7	1.2	−1.5	8.8	6.83	−3.7	2.1	−5.3	168	10.3	139.6	162.4
176 Congo (Democratic Republic of the)	64.5	−1.4	−3.0	8.1	0.01	−0.3	0.7	−0.1	191	3.8	53.0	178.8

TABLE
13

	Trade	Financial flows				Human mobility				Communication		
	Exports and imports	Foreign direct investment, net inflows	Private capital flows	Net official development assistance received[a]	Remittances, inflows	Net migration rate	Stock of immigrants	International student mobility	International inbound tourists	Internet users	Mobile phone subscriptions	
	(% of GDP)	(% of GDP)	(% of GDP)	(% of GNI)	(% of GDP)	(per 1,000 people)	(% of population)	(% of total tertiary enrolment)	(thousands)	(% of population)	(per 100 people)	(% change)
HDI rank	2015[b]	2015[b]	2015[b]	2014[c]	2015[b]	2010/2015[d]	2015	2013[e]	2014[c]	2015	2015	2010–2015
177 Liberia	112.4	35.1	..	44.3	31.21	−0.9	2.5	..	..	5.9	81.1	104.3
178 Guinea-Bissau	36.8	1.7	−0.3	9.8	6.04	−1.2	1.2	..	..	3.5	69.3	62.3
179 Eritrea	37.5	1.5	..	5.1	..	−6.5	0.3	..	107	1.1	7.0	118.5
179 Sierra Leone	59.2	11.6	−9.1	18.9	1.48	−0.7	1.4	..	44	2.5	89.5	157.5
181 Mozambique	91.6	25.3	−24.8	12.6	1.33	−0.2	0.8	−1.1	1,661	9.0	74.2	146.3
181 South Sudan	67.4	−3.1	..	16.6	0.01	15.4	6.7	..	..	17.9	23.9	65.1
183 Guinea	78.1	1.3	−2.0	9.1	1.39	−0.2	1.8	−5.1	33	4.7	87.2	137.0
184 Burundi	40.0	0.2	..	16.2	1.58	0.8	2.6	−3.5	142	4.9	46.2	154.3
185 Burkina Faso	68.7	1.5	−1.9	9.2	3.57	−1.5	3.9	−2.0	191	11.4	80.6	119.6
186 Chad	67.2	5.5	..	2.9	..	1.5	3.7	−11.9	122	2.7	40.2	63.8
187 Niger	56.6	7.3	−8.4	11.3	2.04	−0.3	1.0	−5.1	135	2.2	46.5	101.4
188 Central African Republic	39.5	0.2	..	35.9	..	0.4	1.7	6.2	71	4.6	20.4	−9.2
OTHER COUNTRIES OR TERRITORIES												
Korea (Democratic People's Rep. of)	..	..	..	..	..	0.0	0.2	..	..	..	12.9	630.6
Marshall Islands	..	4.8	−8.1	24.2	13.97	..	6.2	−18.0	5	19.3	29.2	..
Monaco	..	..	..	..	..	..	55.8	..	329	93.4	88.8	39.7
Nauru	..	..	..	..	..	..	31.1	..	..	..	..	−100.0
San Marino	..	..	..	..	..	..	14.8	..	75	..	115.2	16.2
Somalia	75.8	8.7	..	21.1	..	−7.9	0.2	..	..	1.8	52.5	680.0
Tuvalu	..	1.7	2.0	63.3	10.72	..	1.4	..	1	42.7	40.3	147.8
Human development groups												
Very high human development	59.7	2.9	0.4	..	0.29	2.3	12.5	3.4	713,818	79.4	128.5	11.3
High human development	49.5	2.6	−0.9	0.1	0.82	0.1	1.6	−1.3	279,216	51.4	101.2	19.4
Medium human development	55.7	2.3	−2.7	0.7	4.27	−0.7	0.8	−0.8	90,399	27.2	92.7	170.7
Low human development	45.5	2.5	−1.7	3.5	3.20	−1.1	1.6	−3.2	23,496	19.0	67.4	87.8
Developing countries	52.9	2.5	−0.9	0.4	1.57	−0.4	1.6	−1.1	431,046	36.2	92.9	78.5
Regions												
Arab States	86.4	1.7	4.2	1.6	2.42	−0.2	8.9	−0.3	75,244	40.0	111.0	46.1
East Asia and the Pacific	48.9	2.4	−0.2	0.1	0.83	−0.4	0.4	−1.5	142,574	44.9	101.5	335.8
Europe and Central Asia	69.0	3.2	−1.2	0.6	2.09	1.3	6.7	−1.3	77,823	52.3	114.9	26.5
Latin America and the Caribbean	46.2	3.5	−3.7	0.1	1.33	−0.6	1.3	−0.2	81,828	54.4	110.6	14.1
South Asia	46.0	1.7	−2.6	0.5	3.85	−0.7	0.8	−0.8	17,393	24.5	79.0	50.1
Sub-Saharan Africa	55.6	2.6	−2.3	2.5	2.63	−0.1	1.9	−1.3	33,743	22.2	76.4	71.4
Least developed countries	56.5	3.9	−3.0	4.7	4.57	−1.0	1.3	−2.2	26,440	12.6	68.3	254.2
Small island developing states	65.4	3.7	..	1.6	6.43	−2.5	1.9	0.5	18,684	29.7	71.0	38.4
Organisation for Economic Co-operation and Development	55.1	2.6	−0.1	..	0.32	2.1	10.0	3.3	641,075	77.2	115.9	9.0
World	**56.7**	**2.8**	**−0.2**	**0.4**	**0.76**	**0.0**	**3.3**	**0.3**	**1,107,339**	**43.7**	**98.5**	**59.1**

NOTES

a A negative value refers to net official development assistance disbursed by donor countries.

b Data refer to 2015 or the most recent year available.

c Data refer to 2014 or the most recent year available.

d Data are average annual estimates for 2010–2015.

e Data refer to 2013 or the most recent year available.

f Includes Svalbard and Jan Mayen Islands.

g Includes Christmas Island, Cocos (Keeling) Islands and Norfolk Island.

h Includes Åland Islands.

i Includes Canary Islands, Ceuta and Melilla.

j Includes Northern Cyprus.

k Includes Sabah and Sarawak.

l Includes Agalega, Rodrigues and Saint Brandon.

m Includes Kosovo.

n Includes Abkhazia and South Ossetia.

o Includes Nagorno-Karabakh.

p Includes Crimea.

q Includes Transnistria.

r Includes East Jerusalem.

s Includes East Jerusalem. Refugees are not part of the foreign-born migrant stock in the State of Palestine.

t Includes Zanzibar.

DEFINITIONS

Exports and imports: Sum of exports and imports of goods and services, expressed as a percentage of gross domestic product (GDP). It is a basic indicator of openness to foreign trade and economic integration and indicates the dependence of domestic producers on foreign demand (exports) and of domestic consumers and producers on foreign supply (imports), relative to the country's economic size (GDP).

Foreign direct investment, net inflows: Sum of equity capital, reinvestment of earnings, other long-term capital and short-term capital, expressed as a percentage of GDP.

Private capital flows: Net foreign direct investment and portfolio investment, expressed as a percentage of GDP.

Net official development assistance received: Disbursements of loans made on concessional terms (net of repayments of principal) and grants by official agencies to promote economic development and welfare in countries and territories on the Development Assistance Committee list of aid recipients, expressed as a percentage of the recipient country's gross national income (GNI).

Remittances, inflows: Earnings and material resources transferred by international migrants or refugees to recipients in their country of origin or countries in which the migrant formerly resided.

Net migration rate: Ratio of the difference between the number of in-migrants and out-migrants from a country to the average population, expressed per 1,000 people.

Stock of immigrants: Ratio of the stock of immigrants into a country, expressed as a percentage of the country's population. The definition of immigrant varies across countries but generally includes the stock of foreign-born people, the stock of foreign people (according to citizenship) or a combination of the two.

International student mobility: Total number of tertiary students from abroad (inbound students) studying in a given country minus the number of students at the same level of education from that country studying abroad (outbound students), expressed as a percentage of total tertiary enrolment in the country.

International inbound tourists: Arrivals of nonresident visitors (overnight visitors, tourists, same-day visitors and excursionists) at national borders.

Internet users: People with access to the worldwide network.

Mobile phone subscriptions: Number of subscriptions for the mobile phone service, expressed per 100 people.

MAIN DATA SOURCES

Columns 1, 2, 4, 5 and 9: World Bank (2016a).

Column 3: HDRO calculations based on data from World Bank (2016a).

Columns 6 and 7: UNDESA (2015b).

Column 8: UNESCO Institute for Statistics (2016).

Columns 10 and 11: ITU (2016).

Column 12: HDRO calculations based on data from ITU (2016).

TABLE **13**

TABLE 13 International integration | 251

TABLE 14

Supplementary indicators: perceptions of well-being

HDI rank	Education quality (% satisfied)	Health care quality (% satisfied)	Standard of living (% satisfied)	Ideal job (% answering yes)	Feeling safe (% answering yes)	Freedom of choice (% satisfied) Female	Freedom of choice (% satisfied) Male	Overall life satisfaction, index (0, least satisfied, to 10, most satisfied)	Local labour market (% answering good)	Volunteered time (% answering yes)	Community (% answering yes)	Confidence in judicial system (% answering yes)	Actions to preserve the environment (% satisfied)	Trust in national government (% answering yes)
	2014–2015[a]	2014–2015[a]	2014–2015[a]	2014–2015[a]	2014–2015[a]	2014–2015[a]	2014–2015[a]	2014–2015[a]	2014–2015[a]	2014–2015[a]	2014–2015[a]	2014–2015[a]	2014–2015[a]	2014–2015[a]
VERY HIGH HUMAN DEVELOPMENT														
1 Norway	84	85	93	85	90	95	92	7.6	42	31	94	82	56	59
2 Australia	73	87	86	70	63	92	91	7.3	26	40	91	55	59	48
2 Switzerland	83	93	94	84	87	93	92	7.6	47	31	95	82	84	79
4 Germany	62	89	90	80	75	87	90	7.0	61	27	94	71	64	63
5 Denmark	75	88	91	79	85	94	94	7.5	45	23	93	84	71	58
5 Singapore	83	88	84	71	92	89	83	6.6	45	23	94	86	87	91
7 Netherlands	82	86	87	60	81	91	89	7.3	28	33	90	64	73	58
8 Ireland	85	67	78	68	77	89	90	6.8	45	40	91	66	72	57
9 Iceland	83[b]	73[b]	81[b]	66	78[b]	92[b]	90[b]	7.5[b]	42[b]	29[b]	86[b]	63[b]	64[b]	46[b]
10 Canada	73	77	79	71	80	94	94	7.3	50	44	88	67	59	52
10 United States	68	77	74	65	73	87	86	7.2	51	44	81	59	60	35
12 Hong Kong, China (SAR)	51	62	75	60	91	84	83	5.5	46	15	88	76	51	46
13 New Zealand	78	85	90	66	64	92	94	7.4	39	44	92	66	67	62
14 Sweden	63	81	87	79	77	94	92	7.3	39	15	94	70	69	50
15 Liechtenstein	..	..	..	..	..	..	..	..	..	..	..	..	..	..
16 United Kingdom	70	77	84	71	78	88	78	6.5	46	33	86	62	67	46
17 Japan	60	71	61	69	68	79	75	5.9	30	26	82	64	51	38
18 Korea (Republic of)	49	62	63	51	61	55	61	5.8	19	21	73	19	34	28
19 Israel	67	72	67	57	77	68	69	7.4	36	21	81	60	45	44
20 Luxembourg	79	87	89	58	71	91	96	6.7	25	31	93	76	78	69
21 France	71	77	78	74	71	81	83	6.4	13	29	86	51	63	33
22 Belgium	80	89	85	73	70	89	85	6.9	26	28	85	53	62	46
23 Finland	81	71	80	71	86	94	91	7.4	16	31	90	72	63	56
24 Austria	78	88	88	84	81	90	89	7.1	32	26	92	66	72	45
25 Slovenia	73	80	67	65	84	89	88	5.7	15	34	87	24	71	20
26 Italy	55	49	68	66	59	56	58	5.8	3	15	62	29	25	26
27 Spain	57	66	75	62	82	71	75	6.4	17	17	80	36	46	28
28 Czech Republic	74	74	75	70	70	80	77	6.6	39	14	89	45	67	44
29 Greece	52	36	49	59	63	50	54	5.6	8	8	78	52	36	44
30 Brunei Darussalam	..	..	..	..	..	..	..	..	..	..	..	..	..	..
30 Estonia	58	48	49	50	67	75	81	5.6	25	13	88	56	65	34
32 Andorra	..	..	..	..	..	..	..	..	..	..	..	..	..	..
33 Cyprus	57	52	66	67	70	58	64	5.4	17	25	85	27	40	20
33 Malta	80	83	83	80	77	92	89	6.6	55	28	87	51	64	73
33 Qatar	72[c]	90[d]	86	73	92[c]	89[c]	91[c]	6.4	66[c]	19[c]	92[c]	..	91[c]	..
36 Poland	67	47	68	44	66	73	73	6.0	25	9	86	42	51	21
37 Lithuania	59	53	34	50	53	57	59	5.7	16	11	85	38	55	37
38 Chile	41	34	81	74	55	69	74	6.8	41	16	84	23	40	40
38 Saudi Arabia	70	74	81	61	..	79	84	6.3	64	15	85	..	71	..
40 Slovakia	66	52	59	61	62	54	47	6.2	12	11	81	26	38	28
41 Portugal	70	57	54	71	69	78	80	5.1	21	17	87	35	55	22
42 United Arab Emirates	70	84	81	70	90[e]	94	91	6.6	59	22	89	..	93	..
43 Hungary	55	53	56	71	53	52	50	5.3	23	9	80	42	46	28
44 Latvia	62	52	47	41	62	63	59	5.9	20	11	86	37	54	30
45 Argentina	62	57	79	69	43	86	87	6.7	32	20	77	33	50	38
45 Croatia	63	56	51	42	69	64	68	5.2	20	10	73	46	46	36
47 Bahrain	70	82	75	69	60[d]	85	86	5.8	41	15[d]	88	..	69	..
48 Montenegro	65	47	41	50	77	60	56	5.1	16	8	64	44	37	40
49 Russian Federation	51	34	49	48	53	63	60	6.0	18	12	78	36	27	65
50 Romania	64	65	49	41	55	74	80	5.8	22	7	80	40	28	25
51 Kuwait	53	75	81	69	..	82	78	6.2	47	15	84	..	66	..
HIGH HUMAN DEVELOPMENT														
52 Belarus	55	40	47	46	58	58	55	5.7	11	22	78	46	51	52
52 Oman	70[d]	78[d]	87[d]	..	..	92[d]	90[d]	6.9[d]	69[d]	22[d]	90[d]	..	..	..
54 Barbados	..	..	..	..	..	..	..	..	..	..	..	..	..	..
54 Uruguay	55	69	77	63	46	90	88	6.6	17	21	77	50	63	55
56 Bulgaria	42	38	37	51	54	53	53	4.4	13	4	77	19	22	14
56 Kazakhstan	65	48	69	48	63	68	74	5.9	38	14	77	57	45	82
58 Bahamas	..	..	..	..	..	..	..	..	..	..	..	..	..	..

		Perceptions of individual well-being								Perceptions about community			Perceptions about government		
		Education quality	Health care quality	Standard of living	Ideal job	Feeling safe	Freedom of choice		Overall life satisfaction, index	Local labour market	Volunteered time	Community	Confidence in judicial system	Actions to preserve the environment	Trust in national government
							(% satisfied)		(0, least satisfied, to 10, most satisfied)						
		(% satisfied)	(% satisfied)	(% satisfied)	(% answering yes)	(% answering yes)	Female	Male		(% answering good)	(% answering yes)	(% answering yes)	(% answering yes)	(% satisfied)	(% answering yes)
HDI rank		2014–2015[a]	2014–2015[a]	2014–2015[a]	2014–2015[a]	2014–2015[a]	2014–2015[a]	2014–2015[a]	2014–2015[a]	2014–2015[a]	2014–2015[a]	2014–2015[a]	2014–2015[a]	2014–2015[a]	2014–2015[a]
59	Malaysia	75	78	75	76	44	62	71	6.3	54	33	78	55	62	44
60	Palau	..	..	..	..	..	..	..	..	..	..	..	..	..	..
60	Panama	66	53	75	76	50	80	84	6.6	47	32	80	38	46	38
62	Antigua and Barbuda	..	..	..	..	..	..	..	..	..	..	..	..	..	..
63	Seychelles	..	..	..	..	..	..	..	..	..	..	..	..	..	..
64	Mauritius	81	78	71	74	64	81	80	5.6	31	34	90	61	75	56
65	Trinidad and Tobago	64[b]	54[b]	54[b]	56	57[b]	82[b]	83[b]	6.2[b]	43[b]	37[b]	75[b]	33[b]	34[b]	38[b]
66	Costa Rica	80	65	81	80	48	90	89	6.9	20	23	78	40	55	26
66	Serbia	58	49	37	45	68	48	51	5.3	7	5	67	36	28	39
68	Cuba	..	..	..	..	..	..	..	..	..	..	..	..	..	..
69	Iran (Islamic Republic of)	56	44	62	72	..	..	..	4.7	18	21	69	..	58	75
70	Georgia	66	59	24	33	73	56	61	4.1	5	18	74	37	30	25
71	Turkey	51	71	65	61	60	60	67	5.5	31	5[b]	75	43	44	49
71	Venezuela (Bolivarian Republic of)	61	40	54	78	22	56	57	6.1	22	11	73	22	27	20
73	Sri Lanka	79	81	73	73	74	87	88	4.6	59	49	90	77	75	74
74	Saint Kitts and Nevis	..	..	..	..	..	..	..	..	..	..	..	..	..	..
75	Albania	60	54	43	32	61	66	72	4.6	18	11	63	28	36	51
76	Lebanon	72	54	55	64	60	57	60	5.2	20	10	76	29	24	19
77	Mexico	55	43	65	72	40	72	69	6.2	41	13	72	29	44	26
78	Azerbaijan	54	38	53	45	76	72	65	5.1	32	17	76	42	54	79
79	Brazil	46	33	75	76	36	70	71	7.0	44	13	66	41	41	36
79	Grenada	..	..	..	..	..	..	..	..	..	..	..	..	..	..
81	Bosnia and Herzegovina	59	53	49	47	72	57	60	5.1	11	4	67	33	24	19
82	The former Yugoslav Republic of Macedonia	53	57	47	56	65	60	63	5.0	22	7	68	30	42	37
83	Algeria	70	47	72	51	53[c]	57[c]	56[c]	6.4	43	8[c]	83[c]	..	48[c]	..
84	Armenia	52	39	27	30	84	53	47	4.3	12	6	56	27	30	17
84	Ukraine	50	22	17	39	44	34	43	4.0	9	16	76	4	13	8
86	Jordan	54	72	67	62	80	77	74	5.4	32	11	73	..	62	..
87	Peru	54	37	68	67	40	76	81	5.6	42	26	89	15	54	18
87	Thailand	90	89	83	80	69	88	85	6.2	57	17	92	64	86	66
89	Ecuador	74	59	78	77	52	79	79	6.0	32	16	82	42	70	52
90	China	64[b]	65[b]	74	51	75[b]	76[b]	77[b]	5.3	38[b]	4	78[b]	..	63[h]	..
91	Fiji	..	..	..	..	..	..	..	..	..	..	..	..	..	..
92	Mongolia	54	47	58	74	52	60	68	5.0	9	39	77	33	30	23
92	Saint Lucia	..	..	..	..	..	..	..	..	..	..	..	..	..	..
94	Jamaica	65	53	42	50	65	82	79	5.9	22	30	59	29	35	20
95	Colombia	62	43	70	69	47	80	77	6.4	36	19	77	22	45	27
96	Dominica	..	..	..	..	..	..	..	..	..	..	..	..	..	..
97	Suriname	82[c]	78[c]	64[c]	70	60[c]	85[c]	88[c]	6.3[c]	34[c]	22[c]	90[c]	71[c]	65[c]	72[c]
97	Tunisia	30	38	61	55	62	65	71	5.1	19	11	67	56	30	48
99	Dominican Republic	84	57	70	56	38	89	91	5.4	31	35	74	31	61	56
99	Saint Vincent and the Grenadines	..	..	..	..	..	..	..	..	..	..	..	..	..	..
101	Tonga	..	..	..	..	..	..	..	..	..	..	..	..	..	..
102	Libya	33[c]	..	..	62	..	67[c]	70[c]	5.8[c]	49[c]	37[c]	72[c]	..	37[c]	..
103	Belize	62	50	66	..	50	88	84	6.0	40	26	74	37	62	38
104	Samoa	..	..	..	..	..	..	..	..	..	..	..	..	..	..
105	Maldives	..	..	..	..	..	..	..	..	..	..	..	..	..	..
105	Uzbekistan	90	92	78	66	83	97	98	6.0	75	27	96	..	92	..
MEDIUM HUMAN DEVELOPMENT															
107	Moldova (Republic of)	55	40	44	32	45	55	53	6.0	9	17	71	22	24	17
108	Botswana	63	62	26	48	40	86	84	3.8	28	21	58	83	79	82
109	Gabon	34	25	39	46	35	65	68	4.7	37	12	47	49	49	37
110	Paraguay	64	43	75	79	42	81	76	5.6	28	19	90	16	31	18
111	Egypt	52	43	78	58	84	65	65	4.8	33	4	76	76	44	77
111	Turkmenistan	77[d]	64[d]	81	76	73	55	47	5.8	77	60	88	..	80	..
113	Indonesia	81	76	68	76	79	74	74	5.0	49	50	85	53	56	65
114	Palestine, State of	73	60	54	56	64	52	58	4.7	13	9	75	45	37	45
115	Viet Nam	83	69	78	65	61	80[b]	82[b]	5.1	42	19	83	66[b]	60	81[b]
116	Philippines	81	84	78	87	62	91	92	5.5	71	42	87	58	86	67
117	El Salvador	70	59	72	78	36	71	74	6.0	27	28	76	31	40	31

TABLE 14   Supplementary indicators: perceptions of well-being | 253

TABLE
14

TABLE 14 SUPPLEMENTARY INDICATORS: PERCEPTIONS OF WELL-BEING

	Perceptions of individual well-being								Perceptions about community			Perceptions about government		
	Education quality	Health care quality	Standard of living	Ideal job	Feeling safe	Freedom of choice		Overall life satisfaction, index	Local labour market	Volunteered time	Community	Confidence in judicial system	Actions to preserve the environment	Trust in national government
						(% satisfied)		(0, least satisfied, to 10, most satisfied)						
	(% satisfied)	(% satisfied)	(% satisfied)	(% answering yes)	(% answering yes)	Female	Male		(% answering good)	(% answering yes)	(% answering yes)	(% answering yes)	(% satisfied)	(% answering yes)
HDI rank	2014–2015ᵃ	2014–2015ᵃ	2014–2015ᵃ	2014–2015ᵃ	2014–2015ᵃ	2014–2015ᵃ	2014–2015ᵃ	2014–2015ᵃ	2014–2015ᵃ	2014–2015ᵃ	2014–2015ᵃ	2014–2015ᵃ	2014–2015ᵃ	2014–2015ᵃ
118 Bolivia (Plurinational State of)	66	39	74	76	44	87	87	5.8	50	21	82	23	63	49
119 South Africa	74	59	42	51	40	83	88	4.9	36	28	53	69	53	58
120 Kyrgyzstan	62	65	78	55	51	78	80	4.9	47	29	88	40	52	58
121 Iraq	42	44	66	64	61	60	58	4.5	26	17	63	40	40	44
122 Cabo Verde	..	..	..	..	..	..	..	..	..	..	..	..	..	..
123 Morocco	34	27	76	40	66	58	65	5.2	18	5	75	28	45	38ᵇ
124 Nicaragua	84	55	72	76	56	80	81	5.9	44	23	84	46	65	60
125 Guatemala	70	49	70	77	51	85	84	6.5	32	36	84	41	56	27
125 Namibia	71	58	43	..	44	85	85	4.6	46	21	67	68	64	78
127 Guyana	..	..	..	..	..	..	..	..	..	..	..	..	..	..
127 Micronesia (Federated States of)	..	..	..	..	..	..	..	..	..	..	..	..	..	..
129 Tajikistan	76	65	81	67	84	79	80	5.1	47	19	93		62	..
130 Honduras	67	47	69	78	48	49	57	4.8	25	41	86	30	53	30
131 India	76	62	63	80	69	72	78	4.3	39	21	78	74	56	69
132 Bhutan	93	86	89	88	63	83	79	5.1	51	39	93	97	99	95
133 Timor-Leste	..	..	..	..	..	..	..	..	..	..	..	..	..	..
134 Vanuatu	..	..	..	..	..	..	..	..	..	..	..	..	..	..
135 Congo	51	33	45	55	52	85	82	4.7	43	15	62	56	52	50
135 Equatorial Guinea	..	..	..	..	..	..	..	..	..	..	..	..	..	..
137 Kiribati														
138 Lao People's Democratic Republic	73ᶜ	66ᶜ	73ᶜ	80	75ᶜ	87ᵈ	87ᵈ	4.9ᶜ	66ᶜ	20ᶜ	94ᵈ	..	90ᵈ	
139 Bangladesh	85	61	80	85	80	74	75	4.6	42	14	90	76	59	76
139 Ghana	61	48	34	59	78	82	83	4.0	22	26	52	62	39	44
139 Zambia	62	45	30	53	36	79	82	4.3	39	29	47	59	44	61
142 Sao Tome and Principe	..	..	..	..	..	..	..	..	..	..	..	..	..	..
143 Cambodia	88	81	80	80	45	96	95	4.2	73	15	89		92	
144 Nepal	72	56	65	87	60	77	69	4.8	50	36	86	58	61	47
145 Myanmar	73	65	64	52	79	82	77	4.2	53	55	91		64	..
146 Kenya	69	56	47	63	54	76	82	4.4	47	41	64	66	65	75
147 Pakistan	65	41	63	74	58	59	58	4.8	26	11	84	59	44	46
LOW HUMAN DEVELOPMENT														
148 Swaziland	77ᵈ	58ᵈ	45ᵈ	56	42ᵈ	62ᵈ	60ᵈ	4.9ᵈ	25ᵈ	27ᵈ	62ᵈ	56ᵈ	56ᵈ	35ᵈ
149 Syrian Arab Republic	24	38	20	28	32	32	45	3.5	17	20	36	..	38	..
150 Angola	46	29	35	60	46	30	37	3.8	43	17	50	44	37	57
151 Tanzania (United Republic of)	42	27	27	60	64	72	79	3.7	47	15	64	64	47	68
152 Nigeria	55	48	36	48	61	71	65	4.9	39	25	62	56	33	41
153 Cameroon	58	44	53	56	50	77	78	5.0	46	24	65	52	56	61
154 Papua New Guinea	..	..	..	..	..	..	..	..	..	..	..	..	..	..
154 Zimbabwe	71	59	39	52	57	67	64	3.7	17	17	61	67	49	59
156 Solomon Islands	..	..	..	..	..	..	..	..	..	..	..	..	..	..
157 Mauritania	37	26	63	52	45	50	36	3.9	42	22	69	30	31	29
158 Madagascar	51	34	25	56	46	52	57	3.6	41	22	75	48	36	48
159 Rwanda	77	70	35	63	82	90	91	3.5	38	14	61	..	93	..
160 Comoros	49ᶜ	24ᶜ	38ᶜ	64	72ᶜ	50ᶜ	57ᶜ	4.0ᶜ	30ᶜ	18ᶜ	75ᶜ	34ᶜ	39ᶜ	46ᶜ
160 Lesotho	40ᵈ	21ᵈ	27ᵈ	41	38ᵈ	61ᵈ	62ᵈ	4.9ᵈ	21ᵈ	16ᵈ	52ᵈ	64ᵈ	23ᵈ	40ᵈ
162 Senegal	36	32	30	43	52	69	75	4.6	34	13	59	77	34	62
163 Haiti	37	20	23	31	49	38	40	3.6	20	26	42	20	29	30
163 Uganda	47	38	35	53	46	83	81	3.8	31	24	52	36	52	58
165 Sudan	28	22	52	51	71	25	29	4.1	18	23	50	65ᵈ	11	..
166 Togo	35	22	28	43	56	74	72	3.8	38	19	46	50	46	50
167 Benin	38	34	32	51	45	73	70	3.6	41	18	52	55	46	51
168 Yemen	44	21	51	47	57	60	63	4.0	14	3	78	29	27	34
169 Afghanistan	52	32	32	87	34	45	51	3.1	19	9	78	27	41	41
170 Malawi	56	47	39	48	39	81	79	3.9	44	32	69	54	63	57
171 Côte d'Ivoire	55	38	31	50	58	81	76	4.4	52	7	59	58	56	64
172 Djibouti	67ᵈ	49ᵈ	63ᵈ	59	72ᵈ	76ᵈ	70ᵈ	4.4ᵈ	55ᵈ	8ᵈ	75ᵈ	57ᵈ	58ᵈ	68ᵈ
173 Gambia	..	..	..	..	..	..	..	..	..	..	..	..	..	..
174 Ethiopia	80	59	61	65	67	76	79	4.6	52	18	71	72	76	83
175 Mali	34	30	35	62	64	62	68	4.0	58	5	62	45	32	62
176 Congo (Democratic Republic of the)	40	29	26	49	43	49	59	3.9	26	12	43	37	33	27

TABLE 14

	Perceptions of individual well-being								Perceptions about community			Perceptions about government		
	Education quality	Health care quality	Standard of living	Ideal job	Feeling safe	Freedom of choice		Overall life satisfaction, index	Local labour market	Volunteered time	Community	Confidence in judicial system	Actions to preserve the environment	Trust in national government
						(% satisfied)		(0, least satisfied, to 10, most satisfied)						
	(% satisfied)	(% satisfied)	(% satisfied)	(% answering yes)	(% answering yes)	Female	Male		(% answering good)	(% answering yes)	(% answering yes)	(% answering yes)	(% satisfied)	(% answering yes)
HDI rank	2014–2015[a]	2014–2015[a]	2014–2015[a]	2014–2015[a]	2014–2015[a]	2014–2015[a]	2014–2015[a]	2014–2015[a]	2014–2015[a]	2014–2015[a]	2014–2015[a]	2014–2015[a]	2014–2015[a]	2014–2015[a]
177 Liberia	36	40	29	31	48	58	65	2.7	39	34	48	47	21	47
178 Guinea-Bissau	..	..	..	..	..	..	..	..	..	..	..	..	..	..
179 Eritrea	..	..	..	..	..	..	..	..	..	..	..	..	..	..
179 Sierra Leone	40	37	46	49	55	59	60	4.9	33	28	69	54	38	65
181 Mozambique	65[d]	47[d]	38[d]	59	42[d]	63[d]	64[d]	5.0[d]	45[d]	17[d]	83[d]	62[d]	55[d]	63[d]
181 South Sudan	33	21	25	..	44	51	55	3.8	23	24	48	43	30	45
183 Guinea	37	29	38	53	50	62	63	3.5	45	20	64	47	36	61
184 Burundi	54	37	26	60	43	47	39	2.9	10	10	47	..	41	..
185 Burkina Faso	54	33	31	50	57	61	68	4.4	49	19	60	59	49	67
186 Chad	49	26	43	70	51	57	55	3.5	38	9	62	30	53	37
187 Niger	54	33	55	62	83	71	72	3.7	52	14	63	72	54	58
188 Central African Republic	39[d]	23[d]	34[d]	62	60[d]	75[d]	80[d]	3.7[d]	36[d]	15[d]	76[d]	67[d]	69[d]	78[d]
OTHER COUNTRIES OR TERRITORIES														
Korea (Democratic People's Rep. of)	..	..	..	..	..	..	..	..	..	..	..	..	..	..
Marshall Islands	..	..	..	..	..	..	..	..	..	..	..	..	..	..
Monaco	..	..	..	..	..	..	..	..	..	..	..	..	..	..
Nauru	..	..	..	..	..	..	..	..	..	..	..	..	..	..
San Marino	..	..	..	..	..	..	..	..	..	..	..	..	..	..
Somalia	70	47	68	..	85	96	96	5.4	39	21	93	58	92	78
Tuvalu	..	..	..	..	..	..	..	..	..	..	..	..	..	..
Human development groups														
Very high human development	64	68	71	64	68	79	78	6.5	35	27	82	52	53	42
High human development	62	59	71	62	65	73	75	5.6	38	9	77	..	57	..
Medium human development	74	61	66	76	68	73	76	4.6	40	24	79	67	56	66
Low human development	51	39	38	57	55	63	65	4.2	37	18	61	53	44	53
Developing countries	66	57	64	70	65	72	74	5.0	39	17	76	58	55	58
Regions														
Arab States	49	44	67	52	68	80	83	5.1	32	12	72	55	44	..
East Asia and the Pacific	..	..	..	..	..	..	..	..	..	..	..	..	..	..
Europe and Central Asia	60	57	55	50	62	61	66	5.2	32	14	78	34	45	42
Latin America and the Caribbean	55	41	70	73	40	73	73	6.4	38	17	72	32	45	32
South Asia	74	59	64	79	68	71	75	4.4	37	20	80	71	55	67
Sub-Saharan Africa	56	43	38	58	55	69	71	4.3	40	21	60	57	48	56
Least developed countries	59	44	49	68	61	66	68	4.2	40	19	70	57	51	60
Small island developing states	..	..	..	..	..	..	..	..	..	..	..	..	..	..
Organisation for Economic Co-operation and Development	63	69	73	67	68	78	78	6.5	37	27	81	51	54	38
World	**65**	**59**	**65**	**68**	**66**	**73**	**75**	**5.2**	**38**	**19**	**77**	**57**	**54**	**54**

NOTES

a Data refer to the most recent year available during the period specified.

b Refers to 2013.

c Refers to 2012.

d Refers to 2011.

e Refers to 2010.

DEFINITIONS

Satisfaction with education quality: Percentage of respondents answering "satisfied" to the Gallup World Poll question, "Are you satisfied or dissatisfied with the education system or the schools?"

Satisfaction with health care quality: Percentage of respondents answering "satisfied" to the Gallup World Poll question, "Are you satisfied or dissatisfied with the availability of quality healthcare?"

Satisfaction with standard of living: Percentage of respondents answering "satisfied" to the Gallup World Poll question, "Are you satisfied or dissatisfied with your standard of living, all the things you can buy and do?"

Ideal job: Percentage of employed respondents answering "yes" to the Gallup World Poll question, "Would you say that your job is the ideal job for you, or not?"

Feeling safe: Percentage of respondents answering "yes" to the Gallup World Poll question, "Do you feel safe walking alone at night in the city or area where you live?"

Satisfaction with freedom of choice: Percentage of respondents answering "satisfied" to the Gallup World Poll question, "In this country, are you satisfied or dissatisfied with your freedom to choose what you do with your life?"

Overall life satisfaction, index: Average response to the Gallup World Poll question, "Please imagine a ladder, with steps numbered from zero at the bottom to ten at the top. Suppose we say that the top of the ladder represents the best possible life for you, and the bottom of the ladder represents the worst possible life for you. On which step of the ladder would you say you personally feel you stand at this time, assuming that the higher the step the better you feel about your life, and the lower the step the worse you feel about it? Which step comes closest to the way you feel?"

Perception of local labour market: Percentage of respondents answering "good" to the Gallup World Poll question, "Thinking about the job situation in the city or area where you live today, would you say that it is now a good time or a bad time to find a job?"

Volunteered time: Percentage of respondents answering "yes" to the Gallup World Poll question, "In the past month have you volunteered your time to an organization?"

Satisfaction with community: Percentage of respondents answering "yes" to the Gallup World Poll question, "Are you satisfied or dissatisfied with the city or area where you live?"

Confidence in judicial system: Percentage of respondents answering "yes" to the Gallup World Poll question, "In this country, do you have confidence in the judicial system and courts?"

Satisfaction with actions to preserve the environment: Percentage of respondents answering "satisfied" to Gallup World Poll question, "In this country, are you satisfied or dissatisfied with the efforts to preserve the environment?"

Trust in national government: Percentage of respondents answering "yes" to the Gallup World Poll question, "In this country, do you have confidence in the national government?"

MAIN DATA SOURCES

Columns 1–14: Gallup (2016).

TABLE
14

TABLE 14 Supplementary indicators: perceptions of well-being | 255

TABLE 15

Status of fundamental human rights treaties

Country	ICERD: International Convention on the Elimination of All Forms of Racial Discrimination, 1965 — Entry into force: 4 January 1969 — Year of ratification	ICCPR: International Covenant on Civil and Political Rights, 1966 — Entry into force: 23 March 1969 — Year of ratification	ICESCR: International Covenant on Economic, Social and Cultural Rights, 1966 — Entry into force: 3 January 1976 — Year of ratification	CEDAW: Convention on the Elimination of All Forms of Discrimination against Women, 1979 — Entry into force: 3 September 1981 — Year of ratification	CAT: Convention against Torture and Other Cruel, Inhuman or Degrading Treatment or Punishment, 1984 — Entry into force: 26 June 1987 — Year of ratification	CRC: Convention on the Rights of the Child, 1989 — Entry into force: 2 September 1990 — Year of ratification	ICMW: International Convention on the Protection of the Rights of All Migrant Workers and Members of Their Families, 1990 — Entry into force: 1 July 2003 — Year of ratification	CRC-AC: Optional Protocol to the Convention on the Rights of the Child on the involvement of children in armed conflict, 2000 — Entry into force: 12 February 2002 — Year of ratification	CRC-SC: Optional Protocol to the Convention on the Rights of the Child on the sale of children, child prostitution and child pornography, 2000 — Entry into force: 18 January 2002 — Year of ratification	ICPED: International Convention for the Protection of All Persons from Enforced Disappearance, 2006 — Entry into force: 23 December 2010 — Year of ratification	CRPD: Convention on the Rights of Persons with Disabilities, 2006 — Entry into force: 3 May 2008 — Year of ratification
Afghanistan	1983	1983	1983	2003	1987	1994		2003	2002		2012
Albania	1994	1991	1991	1994	1994	1992	2007	2008	2008	2007	2013
Algeria	1972	1989	1989	1996	1989	1993	2005	2009	2006		2009
Andorra	2006	2006		1997	2006	1996		2001	2001		2014
Angola		1992	1992	1986		1990		2007	2005		2014
Antigua and Barbuda	1988			1989	1993	1993			2002		
Argentina	1968	1986	1986	1985	1986	1990	2007	2002	2003	2007	2008
Armenia	1993	1993	1993	1993	1993	1993		2005	2005	2011	2010
Australia	1975	1980	1975	1983	1989	1990		2006	2007		2008
Austria	1972	1978	1978	1982	1987	1992		2002	2004	2012	2008
Azerbaijan	1996	1992	1992	1995	1996	1992	1999	2002	2002		2009
Bahamas	1975	2008	2008	1993		1991		2015	2015		2015
Bahrain	1990	2006	2007	2002	1998	1992		2004	2004		2011
Bangladesh	1979	2000	1998	1984	1998	1990	2011	2000	2000		2007
Barbados	1972	1973	1973	1980		1990					2013
Belarus	1969	1973	1973	1981	1987	1990		2006	2002		
Belgium	1975	1983	1983	1985	1999	1991		2002	2006	2011	2009
Belize	2001	1996	2015	1990	1986	1990	2001	2003	2003	2015	2011
Benin	2001	1992	1992	1992	1992	1990		2005	2005		2012
Bhutan				1981		1990		2009	2009		
Bolivia (Plurinational State of)	1970	1982	1982	1990	1999	1990	2000	2004	2003	2008	2009
Bosnia and Herzegovina	1993	1993	1993	1993	1993	1993	1996	2003	2002	2012	2010
Botswana	1974	2000		1996	2000	1995		2004	2003		
Brazil	1968	1992	1992	1984	1989	1990		2004	2004	2010	2008
Brunei Darussalam				2006		1995			2006		
Bulgaria	1966	1970	1970	1982	1986	1991		2002	2002		2012
Burkina Faso	1974	1999	1999	1987	1999	1990	2003	2007	2006	2009	2009
Burundi	1977	1990	1990	1992	1993	1990		2008	2007		2014
Cabo Verde	1979	1993	1993	1980	1992	1992	1997	2002	2002		2011
Cambodia	1983	1992	1992	1992	1992	1992		2004	2002	2013	2012
Cameroon	1971	1984	1984	1994	1986	1993		2013			
Canada	1970	1976	1976	1981	1987	1991		2000	2005		2010
Central African Republic	1971	1981	1981	1991		1992			2012		
Chad	1977	1995	1995	1995	1995	1990		2002	2002		
Chile	1971	1972	1972	1989	1988	1990	2005	2003	2003	2009	2008
China	1981		2001	1980	1988	1992		2008	2002		2008
Colombia	1981	1969	1969	1982	1987	1991	1995	2005	2003	2012	2011
Comoros	2004			1994		1993			2007		
Congo	1988	1983	1983	1982	2003	1993		2010	2009		2014
Congo (Democratic Republic of the)	1976	1976	1976	1986	1996	1990		2001	2001		2015
Costa Rica	1967	1968	1968	1986	1993	1990		2003	2002	2012	2008
Côte d'Ivoire	1973	1992	1992	1995	1995	1991		2012	2011		2014
Croatia	1992	1992	1992	1992	1992	1992		2002	2002		2007
Cuba	1972			1980	1995	1991		2007	2001	2009	2007
Cyprus	1967	1969	1969	1985	1991	1991		2010	2006		2011
Czech Republic	1993	1993	1993	1993	1993	1993		2001	2013		2009
Denmark	1971	1972	1972	1983	1987	1991		2002	2003		2009
Djibouti	2011	2002	2002	1998	2002	1990		2011	2011		2012
Dominica		1993	1993	1980		1991		2002	2002		2012
Dominican Republic	1983	1978	1978	1982	2012	1991		2014	2006		2009
Ecuador	1966	1969	1969	1981	1988	1990	2002	2004	2004	2009	2008
Egypt	1967	1982	1982	1981	1986	1990	1993	2007	2002		2008
El Salvador	1979	1979	1979	1981	1996	1990	2003	2002	2004		2007
Equatorial Guinea	2002	1987	1987	1984	2002	1992			2003		
Eritrea	2001	2002	2001	1995	2014	1994		2005	2005		
Estonia	1991	1991	1991	1991	1991	1991		2014	2004		2012

Country	ICERD: International Convention on the Elimination of All Forms of Racial Discrimination, 1965 — Entry into force: 4 January 1969 — Year of ratification	ICCPR: International Covenant on Civil and Political Rights, 1966 — Entry into force: 23 March 1969 — Year of ratification	ICESCR: International Covenant on Economic, Social and Cultural Rights, 1966 — Entry into force: 3 January 1976 — Year of ratification	CEDAW: Convention on the Elimination of All Forms of Discrimination against Women, 1979 — Entry into force: 3 September 1981 — Year of ratification	CAT: Convention against Torture and Other Cruel, Inhuman or Degrading Treatment or Punishment, 1984 — Entry into force: 26 June 1987 — Year of ratification	CRC: Convention on the Rights of the Child, 1989 — Entry into force: 2 September 1990 — Year of ratification	ICMW: International Convention on the Protection of the Rights of All Migrant Workers and Members of Their Families, 1990 — Entry into force: 1 July 2003 — Year of ratification	CRC-AC: Optional Protocol to the Convention on the Rights of the Child on the involvement of children in armed conflict, 2000 — Entry into force: 12 February 2002 — Year of ratification	CRC-SC: Optional Protocol to the Convention on the Rights of the Child on the sale of children, child prostitution and child, pornography, 2000 — Entry into force: 18 January 2002 — Year of ratification	ICPED: International Convention for the Protection of All Persons from Enforced Disappearance, 2006 — Entry into force: 23 December 2010 — Year of ratification	CRPD: Convention on the Rights of Persons with Disabilities, 2006 — Entry into force: 3 May 2008 — Year of ratification
Ethiopia	1976	1993	1993	1981	1994	1991		2014	2014		2010
Fiji	1973			1995		1993					
Finland	1970	1975	1975	1986	1989	1991		2002	2012		
France	1971	1980	1980	1983	1986	1990		2003	2003	2008	2010
Gabon	1980	1983	1983	1983	2000	1994		2010	2007	2011	2007
Gambia	1978	1979	1978	1993		1990			2010		2015
Georgia	1999	1994	1994	1994	1994	1994		2010	2005		2014
Germany	1969	1973	1973	1985	1990	1992		2004	2009	2009	2009
Ghana	1966	2000	2000	1986	2000	1990	2000	2014			2012
Greece	1970	1997	1985	1983	1988	1993		2003	2008	2015	2012
Grenada	2013	1991	1991	1990		1990		2012	2012		2014
Guatemala	1983	1992	1988	1982	1990	1990	2003	2002	2002		2009
Guinea	1977	1978	1978	1982	1989	1990	2000		2011		2008
Guinea-Bissau	2010	2010	1992	1985	2013	1990		2014	2010		2014
Guyana	1977	1977	1977	1980	1988	1991	2010	2010	2010		2014
Haiti	1972	1991	2013	1981		1995			2014		2009
Holy See	1969				2002	1990		2001	2001		
Honduras	2002	1997	1981	1983	1996	1990	2005	2002	2002	2008	2008
Hungary	1967	1974	1974	1980	1987	1991		2010	2010		2007
Iceland	1967	1979	1979	1985	1996	1992		2001	2001		
India	1968	1979	1979	1993		1992		2005	2005		2007
Indonesia	1999	2006	2006	1984	1998	1990	2012	2012	2012		2011
Iran (Islamic Republic of)	1968	1975	1975			1994			2007		2009
Iraq	1970	1971	1971	1986	2011	1994		2008	2008	2010	2013
Ireland	2000	1989	1989	1985	2002	1992		2002			
Israel	1979	1991	1991	1991	1991	1991		2005	2008		2012
Italy	1976	1978	1978	1985	1989	1991		2002	2002	2015	2009
Jamaica	1971	1975	1975	1984		1991	2008	2002	2011		2007
Japan	1995	1979	1979	1985	1999	1994		2004	2005	2009	2014
Jordan	1974	1975	1975	1992	1991	1991		2007	2006		2008
Kazakhstan	1998	2006	2006	1998	1998	1994		2003	2001	2009	2015
Kenya	2001	1972	1972	1984	1997	1990		2002			2008
Kiribati				2004		1995		2015	2015		2013
Korea (Democratic People's Rep. of)		1981	1981	2001		1990			2014		
Korea (Republic of)	1978	1990	1990	1984	1995	1991		2004	2004		2008
Kuwait	1968	1996	1996	1994	1996	1991		2004	2004		2013
Kyrgyzstan	1997	1994	1994	1997	1997	1994	2003	2003	2003		
Lao People's Democratic Republic	1974	2009	2007	1981	2012	1991		2006	2006		2009
Latvia	1992	1992	1992	1992	1992	1992		2005	2006		2010
Lebanon	1971	1972	1972	1997	2000	1991			2004		
Lesotho	1971	1992	1992	1995	2001	1992	2005	2003	2003	2013	2008
Liberia	1976	2004	2004	1984	2004	1993					2012
Libya	1968	1970	1970	1989	1989	1993	2004	2004	2004		
Liechtenstein	2000	1998	1998	1995	1990	1995		2005	2013		
Lithuania	1998	1991	1991	1994	1996	1992		2003	2004	2013	2010
Luxembourg	1978	1983	1983	1989	1987	1994		2004	2011		2011
Madagascar	1969	1971	1971	1989	2005	1991	2015	2004	2004		2015
Malawi	1996	1993	1993	1987	1996	1991		2010	2009		2009
Malaysia				1995		1995		2012	2012		2010
Maldives	1984	2006	2006	1993	2004	1991		2004	2002		2010
Mali	1974	1974	1974	1985	1999	1990	2003	2002	2002	2009	2008
Malta	1971	1990	1990	1991	1990	1990		2002	2010	2015	2012
Marshall Islands				2006		1993					2015
Mauritania	1988	2004	2004	2001	2004	1991	2007		2007	2012	2012
Mauritius	1972	1973	1973	1984	1992	1990		2009	2011		2010
Mexico	1975	1981	1981	1981	1986	1990	1999	2002	2002	2008	2007

TABLE 15

TABLE 15   Status of fundamental human rights treaties | 257

TABLE 15   STATUS OF FUNDAMENTAL HUMAN RIGHTS TREATIES

Country	ICERD: International Convention on the Elimination of All Forms of Racial Discrimination, 1965 — Entry into force: 4 January 1969 — Year of ratification	ICCPR: International Covenant on Civil and Political Rights, 1966 — Entry into force: 23 March 1969 — Year of ratification	ICESCR: International Covenant on Economic, Social and Cultural Rights, 1966 — Entry into force: 3 January 1976 — Year of ratification	CEDAW: Convention on the Elimination of All Forms of Discrimination against Women, 1979 — Entry into force: 3 September 1981 — Year of ratification	CAT: Convention against Torture and Other Cruel, Inhuman or Degrading Treatment or Punishment, 1984 — Entry into force: 26 June 1987 — Year of ratification	CRC: Convention on the Rights of the Child, 1989 — Entry into force: 2 September 1990 — Year of ratification	ICMW: International Convention on the Protection of the Rights of All Migrant Workers and Members of Their Families, 1990 — Entry into force: 1 July 2003 — Year of ratification	CRC-AC: Optional Protocol to the Convention on the Rights of the Child on the involvement of children in armed conflict, 2000 — Entry into force: 12 February 2002 — Year of ratification	CRC-SC: Optional Protocol to the Convention on the Rights of the Child on the sale of children, child prostitution and child, pornography, 2000 — Entry into force: 18 January 2002 — Year of ratification	ICPED: International Convention for the Protection of All Persons from Enforced Disappearance, 2006 — Entry into force: 23 December 2010 — Year of ratification	CRPD: Convention on the Rights of Persons with Disabilities, 2006 — Entry into force: 3 May 2008 — Year of ratification
Micronesia (Federated States of)				2004		1993		2015	2012		
Moldova (Republic of)	1993	1993	1993	1994	1995	1993		2004	2007		2010
Monaco	1995	1997	1997	2005	1991	1993		2001	2008		
Mongolia	1969	1974	1974	1981	2002	1990		2004	2003	2015	2009
Montenegro	2006	2006	2006	2006	2006	2006		2007	2006	2011	2009
Morocco	1970	1979	1979	1993	1993	1993	1993	2002	2001	2013	2009
Mozambique	1983	1993		1997	1999	1994	2013	2004	2003		2012
Myanmar				1997		1991			2012		2011
Namibia	1982	1994	1994	1992	1994	1990		2002	2002		2007
Nauru				2011	2012	1994					2012
Nepal	1971	1991	1991	1991	1991	1990		2007	2006		2010
Netherlands	1971	1978	1978	1991	1988	1995		2009	2005	2011	
New Zealand	1972	1978	1978	1985	1989	1993		2001	2011		2008
Nicaragua	1978	1980	1980	1981	2005	1990	2005	2005	2004		2007
Niger	1967	1986	1986	1999	1998	1990	2009	2012	2004	2015	2008
Nigeria	1967	1993	1993	1985	2001	1991	2009	2012	2010	2009	2010
Norway	1970	1972	1972	1981	1986	1991		2003	2001		2013
Oman	2003			2006		1996		2004	2004		2009
Pakistan	1966	2010	2008	1996	2010	1990			2011		2011
Palau						1995					2013
Palestine, State of	2014	2014	2014	2014	2014	2014		2014			2014
Panama	1967	1977	1977	1981	1987	1990		2001	2001	2011	2007
Papua New Guinea	1982	2008	2008	1995		1993					2013
Paraguay	2003	1992	1992	1987	1990	1990	2008	2002	2003	2010	2008
Peru	1971	1978	1978	1982	1988	1990	2005	2002	2002	2012	2008
Philippines	1967	1986	1974	1981	1986	1990	1995	2003	2002		2008
Poland	1968	1977	1977	1980	1989	1991		2005	2005		2012
Portugal	1982	1978	1978	1980	1989	1990		2003	2003	2014	2009
Qatar	1976			2009	2000	1995		2002	2001		2008
Romania	1970	1974	1974	1982	1990	1990		2001	2001		2011
Russian Federation	1969	1973	1973	1981	1987	1990		2008	2013		2012
Rwanda	1975	1975	1975	1981	2008	1991	2008	2002	2002		2008
Saint Kitts and Nevis	2006			1985		1990					
Saint Lucia	1990			1982		1993		2014	2013		
Saint Vincent and the Grenadines	1981	1981	1981	1981	2001	1993	2005	2011	2005		2010
Samoa		2008		1992		1994				2012	
San Marino	2002	1985	1985	2003	2006	1991		2011	2011		2008
Sao Tome and Principe				2003		1991					2015
Saudi Arabia	1997			2000	1997	1996		2011	2010		2008
Senegal	1972	1978	1978	1985	1986	1990	1999	2004	2003	2008	2010
Serbia	2001	2001	2001	2001	2001	2001		2003	2002	2011	2009
Seychelles	1978	1992	1992	1992	1992	1990	1994	2010	2012		2009
Sierra Leone	1967	1996	1996	1988	2001	1990		2002	2001		2010
Singapore				1995		1995		2008			2013
Slovakia	1993	1993	1993	1993	1993	1993		2006	2004	2014	2010
Slovenia	1992	1992	1992	1992	1993	1992		2004	2004		2008
Solomon Islands	1982		1982	2002		1995					
Somalia	1975	1990	1990		1990	2015					
South Africa	1998	1998	2015	1995	1998	1995		2009	2003		2007
South Sudan				2015	2015	2015					
Spain	1968	1977	1977	1984	1987	1990		2002	2001	2009	2007
Sri Lanka	1982	1980	1980	1981	1994	1991	1996	2000	2006		
Sudan	1977	1986	1986			1990		2005	2004		2009
Suriname	1984	1976	1976	1993		1993			2012		
Swaziland	1969	2004	2004	2004	2004	1995		2012	2012		2012
Sweden	1971	1971	1971	1980	1986	1990		2003	2007		2008

TABLE 15

Country	ICERD: International Convention on the Elimination of All Forms of Racial Discrimination, 1965 — Entry into force: 4 January 1969 — Year of ratification	ICCPR: International Covenant on Civil and Political Rights, 1966 — Entry into force: 23 March 1969 — Year of ratification	ICESCR: International Covenant on Economic, Social and Cultural Rights, 1966 — Entry into force: 3 January 1976 — Year of ratification	CEDAW: Convention on the Elimination of All Forms of Discrimination against Women, 1979 — Entry into force: 3 September 1981 — Year of ratification	CAT: Convention against Torture and Other Cruel, Inhuman or Degrading Treatment or Punishment, 1984 — Entry into force: 26 June 1987 — Year of ratification	CRC: Convention on the Rights of the Child, 1989 — Entry into force: 2 September 1990 — Year of ratification	ICMW: International Convention on the Protection of the Rights of All Migrant Workers and Members of Their Families, 1990 — Entry into force: 1 July 2003 — Year of ratification	CRC-AC: Optional Protocol to the Convention on the Rights of the Child on the involvement of children in armed conflict, 2000 — Entry into force: 12 February 2002 — Year of ratification	CRC-SC: Optional Protocol to the Convention on the Rights of the Child on the sale of children, child prostitution and child pornography, 2000 — Entry into force: 18 January 2002 — Year of ratification	ICPED: International Convention for the Protection of All Persons from Enforced Disappearance, 2006 — Entry into force: 23 December 2010 — Year of ratification	CRPD: Convention on the Rights of Persons with Disabilities, 2006 — Entry into force: 3 May 2008 — Year of ratification
Switzerland	1994	1992	1992	1997	1986	1997		2002	2006		2014
Syrian Arab Republic	1969	1969	1969	2003	2004	1993	2005	2003	2003		2009
Tajikistan	1995	1999	1999	1993	1995	1993	2002	2002	2002		
Tanzania (United Republic of)	1972	1976	1976	1985		1991		2004	2003		2009
Thailand	2003	1996	1999	1985	2007	1992		2006	2006		2008
The former Yugoslav Republic of Macedonia	1994	1994	1994	1994	1994	1993		2004	2003		2011
Timor-Leste	2003	2003	2003	2003	2003	2003	2004	2004	2003		
Togo	1972	1984	1984	1983	1987	1990		2005	2004	2014	2011
Tonga	1972					1995					
Trinidad and Tobago	1973	1978	1978	1990		1991					2015
Tunisia	1967	1969	1969	1985	1988	1992		2003	2002	2011	2008
Turkey	2002	2003	2003	1985	1988	1995	2004	2004	2002		2009
Turkmenistan	1994	1997	1997	1997	1999	1993		2005	2005		2008
Tuvalu				1999		1995					2013
Uganda	1980	1995	1987	1985	1986	1990	1995	2002	2001		2008
Ukraine	1969	1973	1973	1981	1987	1991		2005	2003	2015	2010
United Arab Emirates	1974			2004	2012	1997					2010
United Kingdom	1969	1976	1976	1986	1988	1991		2003	2009		2009
United States	1994	1992			1994			2002	2002		
Uruguay	1968	1970	1970	1981	1986	1990	2001	2003	2003	2009	2009
Uzbekistan	1995	1995	1995	1995	1995	1994		2008	2008		
Vanuatu		2008		1995	2011	1993		2007	2007		2008
Venezuela (Bolivarian Republic of)	1967	1978	1978	1983	1991	1990		2003	2002		2013
Viet Nam	1982	1982	1982	1982	2015	1990		2001	2001		2015
Yemen	1972	1987	1987	1984	1991	1991		2007	2004		2009
Zambia	1972	1984	1984	1985	1998	1991				2011	2010
Zimbabwe	1991	1991	1991	1991		1990		2013	2012		2013

DEFINITIONS

ICERD: International Convention on the Elimination of All Forms of Racial Discrimination, 1965: Prohibits all forms of racial discrimination— defined as any distinction, exclusion, restriction or preference based on race, colour, descent, or national or ethnic origin which has the purpose or effect of nullifying or impairing the equal recognition, enjoyment or exercise of human rights and fundamental freedoms and sets out the obligations of the state to combat this phenomenon. The Convention also requires a state to take appropriate measures against racial discrimination, including the propagation of racist ideas advocated by groups and organizations.

ICCPR: International Covenant on Civil and Political Rights, 1966: Says that all individuals possess civil and political rights, starting with the right to self-determination and including the right to life, the right to liberty and freedom of movement, the freedom of religion, of speech and of assembly, the right to equality between men and women, the right to equality before the law and the right to effective legal recourse. Some of these rights, such as the right not to be arbitrarily deprived of one's life, freedom from torture and other forms of cruel, inhuman and degrading treatment, may not be suspended or derogated even in a state of emergency. The ICCPR, its optional protocols, the ICESCR and the Universal Declaration of Human Rights together form the International Bill of Human Rights.

ICESCR: International Covenant on Economic, Social and Cultural Rights, 1966: Establishes economic, social and cultural rights, including the right to work in just and favourable conditions, to social protection, to an adequate standard of living, to the highest attainable standards of physical and mental health, to education, to participate in cultural life, and to enjoy the benefits of scientific progress. The ICESCR is part of the International Bill of Human Rights.

CEDAW: Convention on the Elimination of All Forms of Discrimination against Women, 1979: Is the first global and comprehensive legally binding international treaty aimed at the elimination of all forms of sex-based discrimination against women. It requires states to incorporate the principle of gender equality in their national constitutions or other appropriate legislation and to ensure the practical realisation of that principle. Discrimination against women is defined as any distinction, exclusion or restriction made on the basis of sex which has the effect or purpose of impairing or nullifying the recognition, enjoyment or exercise by women, irrespective of their marital status, on a basis of equality of men and women, of human rights and fundamental freedoms in the political, economic, social, cultural, civil or any other field.

CAT: Convention against Torture and Other Cruel, Inhuman or Degrading Treatment or Punishment, 1984: Defines and outlaws torture and other forms of ill-treatment under all circumstances, requires states to criminalize it under domestic law, to prevent its occurrence, to properly educate their law enforcement and other personnel about the prohibition of torture, to impartially investigate allegations of torture and to offer fair and adequate compensation to any victim. The Convention clearly states that no circumstances of any kind, including orders from a superior, a state of war or a state of emergency, can justify an act of torture – the ban is absolute. States commit to not extradite, deport or refoule a person if they are at risk of being tortured in the territory to which they would return, and to the universal obligation to prosecute or extradite any individual accused of having committed torture.

CRC: Convention on the Rights of the Child, 1989: Defines a child as a person under the age of 18, unless national law sets a lower age of majority, and sets standards for health, education, legal, civil, and social services for children in accordance with four general principles: non-discrimination between children; the best interest of the child; the right to life, survival and development of the child; and respect for the views of the child.

ICMW: International Convention on the Protection of the Rights of All Migrant Workers and Members of Their Families, 1990: Establishes minimum standards that states should apply to migrant workers and members of their families, regardless of their migratory status. Such standards apply to the entire migration process, from preparation for migration, departure and transit to the total period of stay and remunerated activity in the state of employment and the return to the state of origin or of habitual residence.

CRC-AC: Optional Protocol to the Convention on the Rights of the Child on the involvement of children in armed conflict, 2000: Requires states to take all feasible measures to ensure that members of their armed forces under the age of 18 do not take a direct part in hostilities, to ban compulsory recruitment below the age of 18, to ensure any voluntary member of the armed forces under the age of 18 does not take direct part in hostilities and to take legal measures to prohibit independent armed groups from recruiting and using children under the age of 18 in conflicts.

CRC-SC: Optional Protocol to the Convention on the Rights of the Child on the sale of children, child prostitution and child pornography, 2000: Prohibits the sale of children for sexual and non-sexual purposes, child prostitution and child pornography and provides states with detailed requirements to end the exploitation and abuse of children. It requires ratifying states to provide legal and other support to child victims and to criminalise and punish the activities related to these offences not only for those offering or delivering children for any of the purposes, but also for anyone accepting the child for these activities.

ICPED: International Convention for the Protection of All Persons from Enforced Disappearance, 2006: Prohibits enforced disappearance, defined as the abduction or deprivation of liberty of a person by state authorities, followed by the denial of those authorities to disclose the whereabouts or fate of the person, and establishes minimum legal standards on its prevention, combating impunity, effective law enforcement and upholding the rights of victims. The convention also enshrines the right of victims to the truth and to reparations.

CRPD: Convention on the Rights of Persons with Disabilities, 2006: Guarantees the full and equal enjoyment of all human rights and fundamental freedoms to persons with disabilities and promotes respect for their inherent dignity. It considers disability as the result of an interaction between an individual's condition and an inaccessible society. The barriers that can make society inaccessible are manifold and the Convention identifies these barriers as discriminatory and requires their removal. In adopting a rights-based approach to disability, the Convention moves away from viewing disability as a sickness inherent in the individual requiring either a medical intervention (medical approach) to fix the person, or a charitable intervention (charity approach) based on voluntary assistance rather than individual right.

MAIN DATA SOURCE

Columns 1–11: UNOHCHR (2016).

TABLE
15

TABLE 15 Status of fundamental human rights treaties | 259

Human development dashboards

Life-course gender gap

Country groupings (terciles)

Top third	Middle third	Bottom third

Three-colour coding is used to visualize partial grouping of countries by indicator. For each indicator countries are divided into three groups of approximately equal size (terciles): the top third, the middle third and the bottom third. See *Notes* after the table.

			Childhood and youth					Adulthood					Older age	
			Gross enrolment ratio, female							Share of paid employment in non-agriculture, female	Female legislators, senior officials and managers	Share of seats in parliament	Life expectancy at age 50, female	Old-age pension recipients
	Sex ratio at birth[a]	Adolescent birth rate	Pre-primary	Primary	Secondary	Youth unemployment rate	Maternal mortality ratio	Population with at least some secondary education	Total unemployment rate					
	(male to female births)	(births per 1,000 women ages 15–19)	(% of preschool-age female population)	(% of primary school–age female population)	(% of secondary school–age female population)	(female to male ratio)	(deaths per 100,000 live births)	(female to male ratio)	(female to male ratio)	(% of total paid employment in non-agriculture)	(% of total)	(% held by women)	(years)	(female to male ratio)
HDI rank	2015[b]	2015[b]	2015[c]	2015[c]	2015[c]	2015	2015	2005–2015[d]	2015	2015[c]	2014[e]	2015	2015[b]	2006–2013[d]
VERY HIGH HUMAN DEVELOPMENT														
1 Norway	1.06	5.9	98	100	111	0.87	5	1.02	0.84	48.7	31.5	39.6	34.5	1.00
2 Australia	1.06	14.1	108	106	134	0.94	6	1.00	0.99	47.4	36.7	30.5	35.7	1.13
2 Switzerland	1.05	2.9	104	103	98	0.96	5	0.99	1.06	47.6	33.0	28.9	35.9	1.00
4 Germany	1.06	6.7	110	103	100	0.92	6	0.99	0.83	48.3	30.3	36.9	34.3	1.00
5 Denmark	1.06	4.0	97	101	132	0.95	6	0.90	1.04	49.1	27.8	37.4	33.1	1.00
5 Singapore	1.07	3.8	..	..	..	1.32	10	0.92	1.13	48.2	33.9	23.9	36.7	..
7 Netherlands	1.05	4.0	95	104	130	1.07	7	0.95	0.91	48.3	29.6	36.4	34.4	1.00
8 Ireland	1.07	10.4	110	103	127	0.90	8	1.06	0.76	51.0	33.3	19.9	34.0	0.66
9 Iceland	1.04	6.1	97	99	111	0.82	3	1.03	1.10	51.5	40.0	41.3	34.8	1.00
10 Canada	1.06	9.8	73	101	110	0.88	7	1.00	0.84	49.5	35.8	28.3	35.2	..
10 United States	1.05	22.6	72	99	98	0.92	14	1.00	0.96	47.7	43.4	19.5	33.4	0.96
12 Hong Kong, China (SAR)	1.07	3.2	108	110	99	0.89	..	1.08	0.83	46.7	31.8	..	37.5	..
13 New Zealand	1.05	23.6	93	98	121	1.02	11	1.00	1.27	50.0	40.0	31.4	34.9	0.97
14 Sweden	1.06	5.7	95	124	142	0.94	4	0.99	0.97	50.0	34.8	43.6	34.8	1.00
15 Liechtenstein	..	..	102	102	103	..	..	..	..	..	..	20.0	..	..
16 United Kingdom	1.05	14.6	88	108	130	0.90	9	0.96	0.93	49.4	34.3	26.7	33.9	0.99
17 Japan	1.06	4.1	..	101	102	0.99	5	1.03	0.89	43.9	..	11.6	37.7	..
18 Korea (Republic of)	1.07	1.6	92	99	97	0.92	11	0.94	0.94	43.5	9.6	16.3	35.9	..
19 Israel	1.05	9.7	111	104	103	1.05	5	0.97	1.01	49.4	32.1	26.7	35.0	..
20 Luxembourg	1.05	5.9	94	97	104	0.85	10	1.01	1.29	45.9	24.2	28.3	34.6	0.56
21 France	1.05	8.9	109	105	111	0.98	8	0.93	0.93	50.5	39.4	25.7	36.2	1.00
22 Belgium	1.05	8.2	118	105	175	0.96	7	0.95	0.85	48.8	29.9	42.4	34.4	0.68
23 Finland	1.05	6.5	79	101	152	0.87	3	1.00	0.86	51.8	32.0	41.5	34.7	1.00
24 Austria	1.06	7.1	101	102	97	0.96	4	0.99	0.89	48.6	27.2	30.3	34.7	1.21
25 Slovenia	1.05	3.8	92	99	111	0.90	9	0.98	1.25	47.3	38.5	27.7	34.3	0.86
26 Italy	1.06	6.0	99	101	101	1.07	4	0.95	1.12	45.6	25.0	30.1	36.2	0.69
27 Spain	1.06	8.4	98	105	130	0.99	5	0.92	1.15	48.6	29.8	38.0	36.1	0.48
28 Czech Republic	1.06	9.9	104	99	105	1.09	4	1.00	1.41	46.7	25.8	19.6	32.4	1.00
29 Greece	1.06	7.5	76	98	106	1.11	3	0.89	1.36	46.2	23.0	19.7	34.8	0.55
30 Brunei Darussalam	1.06	21.0	74	108	99	1.09	23	0.97	1.13	..	33.7	..	31.8	..
30 Estonia	1.06	13.1	87	100	108	0.95	9	1.00	0.97	50.9	36.2	23.8	32.7	0.99
32 Andorra	..	..	..	..	..	..	..	0.98	..	49.3	..	39.3	..	..
33 Cyprus	1.07	5.0	77	100	99	0.91	7	0.93	0.89	51.3	13.6	12.5	33.1	0.57
33 Malta	1.06	16.6	119	95	81	0.85	9	0.90	0.98	42.0	23.4	12.9	33.1	0.33
33 Qatar	1.05	10.7	58	99	103	2.13	13	1.05	13.26	13.4	12.2	0.0	31.1	..
36 Poland	1.06	13.4	77	101	107	1.07	3	0.93	1.06	47.3	38.4	24.8	32.6	0.95
37 Lithuania	1.05	11.0	88	103	105	1.02	10	0.95	0.77	..	38.5	23.4	30.9	1.00
38 Chile	1.04	47.8	126	99	101	1.19	22	0.99	1.29	40.1	..	15.8	36.0	0.96
38 Saudi Arabia	1.03	8.8	18	108	94	1.36	12	0.88	6.89	15.0	6.8	19.9	28.5	..
40 Slovakia	1.05	20.2	91	100	92	0.98	6	1.00	1.26	47.6	31.0	18.7	31.3	1.00
41 Portugal	1.06	9.9	90	106	115	1.12	10	0.97	1.12	51.8	32.7	34.8	34.8	1.00
42 United Arab Emirates	1.05	29.7	92	107	..	1.21	6	1.20	3.13	..	9.9	22.5	29.6	..
43 Hungary	1.06	18.0	83	101	107	0.95	17	0.98	1.10	48.1	40.4	10.1	30.4	0.90
44 Latvia	1.05	13.6	90	100	114	1.01	18	1.00	0.79	53.3	45.0	18.0	30.8	1.00
45 Argentina	1.04	63.8	72	110	110	1.13	52	1.03	1.46	44.8	23.1	37.1[f]	32.6	1.07
45 Croatia	1.06	9.5	61	99	101	0.99	8	0.96	1.01	48.8	24.8	15.2	31.8	0.52
47 Bahrain	1.04	13.5	55	..	..	2.01	15	1.11	8.28	..	..	15.0	29.0	..
48 Montenegro	1.07	12.2	54	93	90	1.00	7	0.90	1.11	47.8	30.3	17.3	29.9	..
49 Russian Federation	1.06	23.4	83	99	100	1.05	25	1.00	0.88	50.1	38.4	14.5	29.0	1.00

		Childhood and youth					Adulthood						Older age	
			Gross enrolment ratio, female											
	Sex ratio at birth[a]	Adolescent birth rate	Pre-primary	Primary	Secondary	Youth unemployment rate	Maternal mortality ratio	Population with at least some secondary education	Total unemployment rate	Share of paid employment in non-agriculture, female	Female legislators, senior officials and managers	Share of seats in parliament	Life expectancy at age 50, female	Old-age pension recipients
	(male to female births)	(births per 1,000 women ages 15–19)	(% of preschool-age female population)	(% of primary school–age female population)	(% of secondary school–age female population)	(female to male ratio)	(deaths per 100,000 live births)	(female to male ratio)	(female to male ratio)	(% of total paid employment in non-agriculture)	(% of total)	(% held by women)	(years)	(female to male ratio)
HDI rank	2015[b]	2015[b]	2015[c]	2015[c]	2015[c]	2015	2015	2005–2015[d]	2015	2015[c]	2014[e]	2015	2015[b]	2006–2013[d]
50 Romania	1.06	34.6	91	95	94	1.02	31	0.93	0.74	44.6	31.2	12.0	30.3	0.88
51 Kuwait	1.04	9.8	80	103	99	0.91	4	0.98	0.77	..	13.9	1.5	27.3	..
HIGH HUMAN DEVELOPMENT														
52 Belarus	1.06	18.2	103	99	106	1.03	4	0.94	0.58	..	46.3	29.2	29.3	..
52 Oman	1.05	8.1	55	115	98	1.22	17	1.05	2.78	17.6	..	8.2	30.8	..
54 Barbados	1.04	40.7	86	94	111	1.09	27	1.03	1.06	..	48.2	19.6	30.0	..
54 Uruguay	1.05	56.1	70	108	100	1.10	15	1.07	1.52	48.7	43.9	19.2	33.2	1.04
56 Bulgaria	1.06	37.7	83	99	99	1.03	11	0.97	0.82	49.7	36.9	20.4	29.9	0.96
56 Kazakhstan	1.06	27.9	64	111	111	1.16	12	1.00	1.34	50.6	38.4	20.1	27.5	..
58 Bahamas	1.06	29.6	..	109	95	1.16	80	1.00	1.08	..	51.6	16.7	32.2	..
59 Malaysia	1.06	13.6	..	..	..	1.09	40	0.95	1.17	39.3	25.0	13.2	28.8	..
60 Palau	..	..	77	112	117	..	..	..	..	..	..	10.3	..	..
60 Panama	1.05	74.5	72	104	78	1.14	94	1.06	1.56	44.6	46.0	18.3	34.1	0.59
62 Antigua and Barbuda	1.03	44.8	72	93	103	..	..	..	..	..	..	25.7	31.1	..
63 Seychelles	1.06	57.4	93	105	75	..	..	..	..	55.1	..	43.8	30.5	1.00
64 Mauritius	1.04	28.5	104	104	99	1.21	53	0.92	2.30	41.2	23.1	11.6	30.6	1.00
65 Trinidad and Tobago	1.04	31.5	..	104	..	1.26	63	1.03	1.41	..	43.5	31.5	28.5	..
66 Costa Rica	1.05	56.5	53	110	124	1.15	25	1.01	1.44	43.0	35.2	33.3	33.9	0.75
66 Serbia	1.05	19.0	59	101	95	1.04	17	0.90	1.12	47.0	32.7	34.0	29.5	0.93
68 Cuba	1.06	45.6	99	96	101	1.03	39	0.97	1.28	44.8	..	48.9	33.3	..
69 Iran (Islamic Republic of)	1.05	26.7	42	112	88	1.17	25	0.95	2.04	16.0	13.3	3.1	28.8	..
70 Georgia	1.10	39.7	..	118	100	1.04	36	0.99	0.76	47.3	34.0	11.3	30.6	..
71 Turkey	1.05	27.6	27	107	99	1.13	16	0.67	1.33	27.5	10.0	14.9	31.7	..
71 Venezuela (Bolivarian Republic of)	1.05	79.4	73	100	95	1.16	95	1.12	1.20	43.7	..	17.0	31.1	0.72
73 Sri Lanka	1.04	14.8	95	100	102	1.32	30	1.00	2.37	27.1	28.4	4.9	30.5	..
74 Saint Kitts and Nevis	..	..	92	84	93	..	..	..	..	..	..	13.3	..	0.77
75 Albania	1.08	21.7	87	111	93	0.93	29	1.00	0.84	44.7	22.5	20.7	32.5	0.61
76 Lebanon	1.05	12.4	82	93	68	1.07	15	0.96	1.94	..	8.4	3.1	32.9	..
77 Mexico	1.05	62.8	70	103	93	1.07	38	0.95	1.06	40.1	30.7	40.6	32.3	0.50
78 Azerbaijan	1.14	59.8	24	105	102	1.11	25	0.96	1.39	42.7	7.1	16.9	28.5	0.96
79 Brazil	1.05	67.0	86	107	106	1.26	44	1.07	1.65	47.7	37.5	10.8	31.4	0.92
79 Grenada	1.05	30.5	88	102	101	..	27	..	..	..	..	25.0	28.5	..
81 Bosnia and Herzegovina	1.06	8.6	14	100	90	1.01	11	0.79	1.12	36.2	..	19.3	30.6	..
82 The former Yugoslav Republic of Macedonia	1.05	17.6	29	85	81	0.96	8	0.72	0.93	43.0	27.9	33.3	29.2	..
83 Algeria	1.05	10.6	79	115	102	1.15	140	0.96	1.95	19.2	10.6	25.7	31.1	..
84 Armenia	1.13	23.0	60	..	..	1.15	25	1.00	1.26	47.5	21.5	10.7	30.8	..
84 Ukraine	1.06	24.1	103	105	98	0.95	24	0.98	0.71	50.8	37.8	12.1	28.7	..
86 Jordan	1.05	23.2	31	88	86	1.19	58	0.95	2.13	..	..	11.6	28.8	0.14
87 Peru	1.05	49.1	88	101	96	1.04	68	0.84	1.25	37.1	29.7	22.3	31.2	0.63
87 Thailand	1.06	44.6	73	104	89	1.12	20	0.89	0.91	45.6	25.1	6.1	31.1	1.09
89 Ecuador	1.05	75.9	62	113	106	1.31	64	0.98	1.61	38.5	39.7	41.6	32.6	0.92
90 China	1.16	7.3	82	104	95	0.94	27	0.88	0.79	37.7	16.8	23.6	29.5	..
91 Fiji	1.06	44.8	..	106	93	1.23	30	1.11	1.78	..	23.8	16.0	26.8	..
92 Mongolia	1.03	15.7	86	101	92	1.06	44	1.04	1.04	50.2	47.4	14.5	27.9	1.00
92 Saint Lucia	1.03	53.9	67	..	86	1.39	48	1.15	1.77	..	46.1	20.7	31.3	0.81
94 Jamaica	1.05	59.7	108	..	72	1.28	89	1.13	1.80	..	..	16.7	32.1	..
95 Colombia	1.05	50.2	55	112	103	1.28	64	0.84	1.72	46.5	53.1	20.9	31.1	0.65
96 Dominica	..	..	82	118	100	..	..	..	..	..	..	21.9	..	..
97 Suriname	1.07	46.1	96	118	89	1.61	155	1.02	2.79	..	35.8	25.5	28.5	..
97 Tunisia	1.05	6.8	43	111	94	1.02	62	0.75	1.52	..	..	31.3	30.1	..
99 Dominican Republic	1.05	97.9	45	96	82	1.43	92	1.03	2.46	48.6	37.0	19.1	31.4	0.38
99 Saint Vincent and the Grenadines	1.03	51.0	70	103	103	1.13	45	..	0.94	..	..	13.0	29.1	..
101 Tonga	1.05	15.2	38	107	94	1.20	124	1.00	2.07	..	..	0.0	29.3	..
102 Libya	1.06	6.2	..	..	..	1.20	9	1.48	1.73	..	..	16.0	28.3	..
103 Belize	1.03	65.9	51	109	82	1.55	28	1.01	2.61	43.4	41.3	13.3	26.7	..
104 Samoa	1.08	25.0	39	106	92	1.14	51	1.11	1.30	37.6	36.3	6.1	29.9	..

HDI rank		Childhood and youth							Adulthood				Older age		
			Gross enrolment ratio, female												
	Sex ratio at birth[a]	Adolescent birth rate	Pre-primary	Primary	Secondary	Youth unemployment rate	Maternal mortality ratio	Population with at least some secondary education	Total unemployment rate	Share of paid employment in non-agriculture, female	Female legislators, senior officials and managers	Share of seats in parliament	Life expectancy at age 50, female	Old-age pension recipients
	(male to female births)	(births per 1,000 women ages 15–19)	(% of preschool-age female population)	(% of primary school–age female population)	(% of secondary school–age female population)	(female to male ratio)	(deaths per 100,000 live births)	(female to male ratio)	(female to male ratio)	(% of total paid employment in non-agriculture)	(% of total)	(% held by women)	(years)	(female to male ratio)
	2015[b]	2015[b]	2015[c]	2015[c]	2015[c]	2015	2015	2005–2015[d]	2015	2015[c]	2014[e]	2015	2015[b]	2006–2013[d]
105 Maldives	1.09	6.7	..	..	..	0.93	68	1.11	1.43	40.4	14.3	5.9	29.0	..
105 Uzbekistan	1.06	17.7	25	96	95	1.05	36	1.00	1.00	..	..	16.4	28.0	
MEDIUM HUMAN DEVELOPMENT														
107 Moldova (Republic of)	1.06	22.6	83	93	88	0.83	23	0.98	0.67	56.1	44.1	21.8	27.9	1.21
108 Botswana	1.03	32.3	18	107	86	1.16	129	0.98	1.34	..	38.6	9.5	25.7	1.00
109 Gabon	1.03	99.9	38	140	..	1.16	291	1.36	2.00	..	..	16.0	26.9	..
110 Paraguay	1.05	57.4	38	104	79	1.27	132	0.98	1.62	42.8	33.8	16.8	30.4	0.80
111 Egypt	1.06	51.9	30	104	86	1.30	33	0.80	3.03	18.2	7.1	2.2[g]	26.7	0.13
111 Turkmenistan	1.05	16.4	62	89	84	1.04	42	..	0.99	..	..	25.8	26.8	..
113 Indonesia	1.05	49.6	59	104	82	1.06	126	0.83	1.22	35.8	23.2	17.1	26.0	..
114 Palestine, State of	1.05	58.6	51	95	86	1.07	45	0.92	1.22	16.9	9.9	..	28.3	..
115 Viet Nam	1.11	38.6	80	109	..	1.10	54	0.83	1.07	43.1	..	24.3	33.6	..
116 Philippines	1.06	61.7	..	117	93	1.07	114	1.04	0.92	41.3	54.8	27.1	26.4	..
117 El Salvador	1.05	65.2	73	110	81	0.98	54	0.88	0.58	37.0	37.1	32.1	31.1	0.33
118 Bolivia (Plurinational State of)	1.05	70.8	63	..	84	1.20	206	0.84	1.55	..	35.1	51.8	30.0	1.00
119 South Africa	1.03	45.5	76	97	104	1.07	138	0.97	1.18	45.7	31.3	41.2[h]	24.5	..
120 Kyrgyzstan	1.06	39.6	25	107	91	1.14	76	1.00	1.30	42.3	35.2	19.2	28.0	1.00
121 Iraq	1.07	84.0	..	..	..	1.14	50	0.65	1.81	15.4	..	26.5	26.9	..
122 Cabo Verde	1.03	73.4	70	110	99	1.33	42	..	1.36	..	..	20.8[i]	28.3	0.88
123 Morocco	1.06	31.7	53	113	64	0.98	121	0.77	1.05	21.5	12.8	15.7	28.4	..
124 Nicaragua	1.05	88.8	59	123	79	1.14	150	1.04	1.04	..	41.0	41.3	31.8	0.38
125 Guatemala	1.05	80.7	66	102	62	1.20	88	1.03	1.26	38.6	..	13.9	30.7	0.57
125 Namibia	1.03	76.8	22	110	..	1.11	265	0.98	1.22	..	42.8	37.7	26.1	..
127 Guyana	1.05	88.0	93	84	89	1.22	229	1.28	1.70	..	..	30.4	24.4	1.00
127 Micronesia (Federated States of)	1.07	15.0	..	97	..	..	100	..	..	..	..	0.0	26.1	..
129 Tajikistan	1.05	38.1	10	98	83	0.90	32	1.11	0.05	..	..	14.7	29.1	0.75
130 Honduras	1.05	65.0	48	108	74	1.30	129	1.07	1.40	41.7	..	25.8	31.8	0.42
131 India	1.11	24.5	9	117	69	1.01	174	0.58	1.14	..	13.8	12.2	26.6	..
132 Bhutan	1.04	21.4	18	103	87	1.08	148	0.43	1.60	26.3	17.0	8.3	27.3	..
133 Timor-Leste	1.05	46.6	17	136	76	1.28	215	..	1.61	..	10.3	38.5	26.0	1.00
134 Vanuatu	1.07	43.1	97	122	59	1.06	78	..	1.31	..	28.5	0.0	27.7	..
135 Congo	1.03	117.7	14	115	51	1.08	442	0.90	1.20	..	..	11.5	26.4	0.11
136 Equatorial Guinea	1.03	108.7	08	84	..	1.10	342	1.11	..	..	..	19.7	25.1	..
137 Kiribati	1.07	17.2	..	115	..	..	90	..	..	..	36.5	8.7	25.9	..
138 Lao People's Democratic Republic	1.05	64.1	31	113	55	0.78	197	0.71	0.75	..	..	25.0	25.3	..
139 Bangladesh	1.05	83.0	32	115	61	1.03	176	0.95	1.15	..	5.4	20.0	27.6	..
139 Ghana	1.05	66.8	122	110	69	1.12	319	0.76	1.14	..	..	10.9	23.9	..
139 Zambia	1.03	90.4	..	104	..	0.96	224	1.07	1.02	..	..	12.7	26.1	..
142 Sao Tome and Principe	1.03	84.3	54	111	89	1.13	156	0.69	1.35	..	24.4	18.2	27.0	..
143 Cambodia	1.05	51.6	18	113	..	0.79	161	0.50	0.63	38.7	21.0	19.0	26.0	..
144 Nepal	1.07	71.9	84	141	70	0.81	258	0.58	0.81	..	18.3	29.5	26.3	..
145 Myanmar	1.03	16.5	24	98	52	1.10	178	1.36	1.17	..	..	13.0	25.5	..
146 Kenya	1.03	90.9	73	112	65	1.03	510	0.82	1.35	35.7	..	20.8	26.3	..
147 Pakistan	1.09	38.7	66	86	37	1.12	178	0.57	2.16	11.1	3.0	20.0	26.2	..
LOW HUMAN DEVELOPMENT														
148 Swaziland	1.03	70.4	26	108	62	1.02	389	0.90	1.16	..	..	14.7	24.1	..
149 Syrian Arab Republic	1.05	39.4	6	79	51	1.25	68	0.80	3.27	16.3	9.2	12.4	29.7	..
150 Angola	1.03	164.3	94	100	23	1.08	477	..	1.21	..	..	36.8	23.5	..
151 Tanzania (United Republic of)	1.03	118.6	33	87	31	1.22	398	0.66	1.88	36.4	16.5	36.0	26.9	..
152 Nigeria	1.06	110.6	13	81	41	1.27	814	..	1.25	..	..	5.8	21.2	..
153 Cameroon	1.03	104.6	35	107	52	1.20	596	0.83	1.42	..	..	27.1	24.1	0.29
154 Papua New Guinea	1.08	54.8	..	109	35	1.08	215	0.60	1.30	..	..	2.7	23.7	..
154 Zimbabwe	1.02	109.7	43	99	47	1.12	443	0.80	1.37	36.6	..	35.1	24.7	..
156 Solomon Islands	1.07	48.4	98	112	47	1.00	114	..	1.03	..	..	2.0	25.9	..
157 Mauritania	1.05	78.6	4	101	29	1.19	602	0.47	1.22	..	..	22.2	25.2	..
158 Madagascar	1.03	116.2	14	147	38	1.13	353	..	1.67	37.3	25.1	20.5	25.4	..

DASHBOARD **1**

		Childhood and youth					Adulthood						Older age	
			Gross enrolment ratio, female					Population with at least some secondary education		Share of paid employment in non-agriculture, female	Female legislators, senior officials and managers	Share of seats in parliament	Life expectancy at age 50, female	Old-age pension recipients
	Sex ratio at birth[a]	Adolescent birth rate	Pre-primary	Primary	Secondary	Youth unemployment rate	Maternal mortality ratio		Total unemployment rate					
	(male to female births)	(births per 1,000 women ages 15–19)	(% of preschool-age female population)	(% of primary school-age female population)	(% of secondary school-age female population)	(female to male ratio)	(deaths per 100,000 live births)	(female to male ratio)	(female to male ratio)	(% of total paid employment in non-agriculture)	(% of total)	(% held by women)	(years)	(female to male ratio)
HDI rank	2015[b]	2015[b]	2015[c]	2015[c]	2015[c]	2015	2015	2005–2015[d]	2015	2015[c]	2014[e]	2015	2015[b]	2006–2013[d]
159 Rwanda	1.02	26.3	15	135	41	1.07	290	0.64	1.06	..	..	57.5	26.5	..
160 Comoros	1.05	68.3	24	102	60	1.02	335	..	1.34	..	..	3.0	24.8	..
160 Lesotho	1.03	92.7	32	106	60	1.20	487	1.05	1.31	..	36.1	24.8	21.6	1.00
162 Senegal	1.04	78.6	16	84	38	1.35	315	0.53	1.73	..	..	42.7	25.7	..
163 Haiti	1.05	39.3	..	..	..	1.18	359	0.66	1.33	..	..	3.5	26.5	..
163 Uganda	1.03	111.9	11	111	26	1.04	343	0.81	1.31	29.8	..	35.0	25.5	..
165 Sudan	1.04	74.0	35	67	41	1.20	311	0.73	1.70	..	..	31.0	26.2	..
166 Togo	1.02	92.0	15	121	..	1.10	368	0.64	1.21	..	..	17.6	23.1	..
167 Benin	1.04	83.2	21	120	44	1.56	405	0.51	1.33	26.0	..	7.2	24.0	..
168 Yemen	1.05	61.5	1	89	40	1.17	385	0.47	2.07	..	5.2	0.5	24.9	..
169 Afghanistan	1.06	74.0	..	92	40	1.01	396	0.25	1.50	..	..	27.4	24.0	..
170 Malawi	1.03	136.2	..	148	38	0.95	634	0.62	1.11	..	..	16.7	28.3	..
171 Côte d'Ivoire	1.03	135.5	7	84	33	1.24	645	0.51	1.27	..	..	9.2	21.2	..
172 Djibouti	1.04	21.5	4	62	42	..	229	..	..	..	..	12.7	25.8	..
173 Gambia	1.03	113.0	35	88	56	1.15	706	0.65	1.77	..	..	9.4	23.7	..
174 Ethiopia	1.04	58.4	24	96	35	1.61	353	0.52	2.71	38.8	22.1	37.3	26.3	..
175 Mali	1.05	174.6	4	73	37	1.35	587	0.45	1.86	..	..	8.8	23.0	0.44
176 Congo (Democratic Republic of the)	1.03	122.6	4	102	33	1.23	693	0.41	1.46	..	..	8.2	24.8	..
177 Liberia	1.05	108.8	..	92	33	1.22	725	0.44	0.98	..	..	10.7	23.7	..
178 Guinea-Bissau	1.03	89.5	7	110	..	1.08	549	..	1.20	..	..	13.7	23.2	..
179 Eritrea	1.05	54.3	15	47	32	1.09	501	..	1.21	..	..	22.0	24.3	..
179 Sierra Leone	1.02	118.2	10	130	40	0.70	1,360	0.57	0.47	..	..	12.4	19.6	..
181 Mozambique	1.03	139.7	..	100	24	0.98	489	0.34	1.18	33.5	..	39.6	25.1	0.80
181 South Sudan	1.04	65.9	6	67	..	..	789	..	..	..	..	24.3	24.1	..
183 Guinea	1.02	140.6	15	84	31	0.69	679	..	0.34	18.3	..	21.9	23.0	..
184 Burundi	1.03	28.3	7	128	35	1.07	712	0.74	1.50	..	..	37.8	24.6	0.29
185 Burkina Faso	1.05	108.5	4	85	28	0.83	371	0.52	0.57	..	31.0	9.4	23.2	0.07
186 Chad	1.03	133.5	1	88	14	1.21	856	0.17	1.48	..	..	14.9	23.5	..
187 Niger	1.05	202.4	7	65	16	0.80	553	0.43	0.71	..	..	13.3	24.5	..
188 Central African Republic	1.03	91.9	6	80	12	1.06	882	0.41	1.13	..	..	12.5[g]	23.7	..
OTHER COUNTRIES OR TERRITORIES														
Korea (Democratic People's Rep. of)	1.05	0.5	..	..	..	1.01	82	..	1.02	..	..	16.3	27.9	..
Marshall Islands	..	..	49	105	..	..	..	0.99	..	..	..	9.1	..	..
Monaco	..	..	..	..	..	..	..	..	..	..	..	20.8	..	..
Nauru	..	..	96	100	83	..	..	..	..	..	..	5.3	..	..
San Marino	..	..	108	93	96	..	..	..	..	43.4	17.8	16.7	..	..
Somalia	1.03	103.9	..	..	..	1.06	732	..	1.21	..	..	13.8	24.0	..
Tuvalu	..	..	93	102	90	..	..	..	..	..	..	6.7	..	..
Human development groups														
Very high human development	1.05	17.0	83	102	106	1.01	14	0.99	1.06	46.9	35.3	25.8	34.0	0.93
High human development	1.11	27.4	74	105	97	1.05	36	0.90	1.10	38.9	32.3	21.6	30.0	..
Medium human development	1.08	40.8	33	111	68	1.06	164	0.70	1.35	..	16.4	19.9	26.9	..
Low human development	1.04	101.8	18	94	36	1.16	553	0.57	1.54	..	..	22.0	24.4	..
Developing countries	1.08	48.8	41	105	71	1.07	231	0.82	1.28	..	23.0	21.0	28.4	..
Regions														
Arab States	1.05	47.7	36	96	73	1.20	142	0.80	2.31	..	8.6	15.5	28.0	..
East Asia and the Pacific	1.12	23.1	73	105	90	0.99	63	0.88	0.87	..	23.8	19.6	29.2	..
Europe and Central Asia	1.06	26.6	44	104	97	1.04	24	0.91	1.03	40.6	28.7	19.0	29.6	..
Latin America and the Caribbean	1.05	64.3	75	105	99	1.20	67	0.99	1.48	42.9	36.5	28.1	31.8	0.88
South Asia	1.10	33.7	23	112	65	1.04	175	0.63	1.37	..	12.5	17.4	26.8	..
Sub-Saharan Africa	1.04	103.0	26	97	40	1.12	551	0.74	1.34	..	..	23.3	24.3	..
Least developed countries	1.04	91.4	23	100	41	1.10	432	0.74	1.42	..	..	22.3	25.8	..
Small island developing states	1.06	59.0	..	104	74	1.24	204	0.95	1.73	..	..	23.4	30.1	..
Organisation for Economic Co-operation and Development	1.05	22.4	79	102	104	0.99	15	0.97	1.04	45.7	34.0	27.7	34.6	0.91
World	**1.07**	**44.7**	**46**	**104**	**75**	**1.06**	**210**	**0.87**	**1.21**	**40.4**	**28.0**	**22.5**	**30.1**	**..**

DASH BOARD 1

NOTES

Three-colour coding is used to visualize partial grouping of countries by indicator. For each indicator countries are divided into three groups of approximately equal size (terciles): the top third, the middle third and the bottom third. Sex ratio at birth is an exception—countries are divided into two groups: the natural group (countries with a value between 1.04–1.07, inclusive), which uses darker shading, and the gender-biased group (all other countries), which uses lighter shading. See *Technical note 6* at http://hdr.undp.org/sites/default/files/hdr2016_technical_notes.pdf for details about partial grouping in this table.

a The natural sex ratio at birth is commonly assumed and empirically confirmed to be 1.05 male births to 1 female birth.

b Data are the average of period estimates for 2010–2015 and projections for 2015–2020.

c Data refer to 2015 or the most recent year available.

d Data refer to the most recent year available during the period specified.

e Data refer to 2014 or the most recent year available.

f Refers to 2014.

g Refers to 2012.

h Excludes the 36 special rotating delegates appointed on an ad hoc basis.

i Refers to 2013.

DEFINITIONS

Sex ratio at birth: Number of male births per female birth.

Adolescent birth rate: Number of births to women ages 15–19 per 1,000 women ages 15–19.

Gross enrolment ratio, female: Total enrolment of girls in a given level of education (pre-primary, primary or secondary), regardless of age, expressed as a percentage of the official school-age female population for the same level of education.

Youth unemployment rate, female to male ratio: Ratio of the percentage of the female labour force population ages 15–24 that is not in paid employment or self-employed but is available for work and is actively seeking paid employment or self-employment to the percentage of the male labour force population ages 15–24 that is not in paid employment or self-employed but is available for work and is actively seeking paid employment or self-employment.

Maternal mortality ratio: Number of deaths due to pregnancy-related causes per 100,000 live births.

Population with at least some secondary education, female to male ratio: Ratio of the percentage of the female population ages 25 and older that has reached (but not necessarily completed) a secondary level of education to percentage of the male population ages 25 and older with the same level of education achievement.

Total unemployment rate, female to male ratio: Ratio of the percentage of the female labour force population ages 15 and older that is not in paid employment or self-employed but is available for work and is actively seeking paid employment or self-employment to the percentage of the male labour force population ages 15 and older that is not in paid employment or self-employed but is available for work and is actively seeking paid employment or self-employment.

Share of paid employment in nonagriculture, female: Share of women in paid employment in the nonagricultural sector, which comprises industry and services activities.

Female legislators, senior officials and managers: Share of legislators, senior officials and managers who are female.

Share of seats in parliament: Proportion of seats held by women in the national parliament, expressed as percentage of total seats. For countries with a bicameral legislative system, the share of seats is calculated based on both houses.

Life expectancy at age 50, female: Additional number of years that a 50-year-old woman could expect to live if prevailing patterns of female age-specific mortality rates stay the same throughout the rest of her life.

Old-age pension recipients, female to male ratio: Ratio of the percentage of women above the statutory pensionable age receiving an old-age pension (contributory, noncontributory or both) to the percentage of men above the statutory pensionable age receiving an old-age pension (contributory, noncontributory or both).

MAIN DATA SOURCES

Columns 1, 2, 13: UNDESA (2015s).

Columns 3–5: UNESCO Institute for Statistics (2016).

Columns 6 and 9: HDRO calculations based on ILO (2016a).

Column 7: UN Maternal Mortality Estimation Group (2016).

Column 8: HDRO calculations based on UNESCO Institute for Statistics (2016), Barro and Lee (2016), ICF Macro Demographic and Health Surveys and United Nations Children's Fund Multiple Indicator Cluster Surveys.

Column 10: ILO (2016b).

Column 11: World Bank (2016a).

Column 12: IPU (2016)

Column 14: HDRO calculations based on ILO (2016c).

Sustainable development

Country groupings (terciles)

| Top third | Middle third | Bottom third |

Three-colour coding is used to visualize partial grouping of countries by indicator. For each indicator countries are divided into three groups of approximately equal size (terciles): the top third, the middle third and the bottom third. See *Notes* after the table.

		Environmental sustainability						Economic sustainability					Social sustainability			
		Renewable energy consumption	Carbon dioxide emissions		Forest area		Fresh water withdrawals	Natural resource depletion	Adjusted net savings	External debt stock	Research and development expenditure	Concentration index (exports)	Income quintile ratio	Gender Inequality Index	Population in multi-dimensional poverty	Old-age (ages 65 and older) dependency ratio
		(% of total final energy consumption)	Per capita (tonnes)	Average annual change (%)	(% of total land area^a)	Change (%)	(% of total renewable water resources)	(% of GNI)	(% of GNI)	(% of GNI)	(% of GDP)	(value)	Average annual change (%)	Average annual change (%)	Average annual change (%)	(per 100 people ages 15–64)
HDI rank		2012^b	2013	1990/2013	2015	1990–2015	2005–2014^c	2010–2014^c	2005–2014^c	2005–2014^c	2005–2014^c	2014	2000/2014	2005/2015	2005/2014	2030^d
VERY HIGH HUMAN DEVELOPMENT																
1	Norway	58.0	11.7	2.0	33.2	−0.2	0.8	7.1	21.0	..	1.7	0.372	..	−3.8	..	32.2
2	Australia	8.4	16.3	0.2	16.2	−2.9	3.9	3.3	8.5	..	2.2	0.266	0.0	−1.4	..	31.3
2	Switzerland	22.7	5.0	−1.0	31.7	9.0	3.8	0.0	15.0	..	3.0	0.256	..	−5.1	..	38.3
4	Germany	12.4	9.2	..	32.8	1.2	21.4	0.0	13.3	..	2.9	0.097	..	−4.3	..	47.7
5	Denmark	27.6	6.8	−1.6	14.4	12.6	10.6	1.0	14.5	..	3.1	0.086	..	−3.7	..	37.1
5	Singapore	0.5	9.4	−2.1	23.1	−5.2	..	0.0	36.9	..	2.2	0.250	..	−5.3	..	36.5
7	Netherlands	4.7	10.1	−0.2	11.2	9.3	11.8	0.4	16.9	..	2.0	0.097	..	−4.3	..	41.9
8	Ireland	7.0	7.6	−0.7	10.9	62.2	1.5	0.1	16.1	..	1.5	0.241	..	−3.5	..	29.2
9	Iceland	78.1	6.1	−1.1	0.5	205.6	1.8	0.0	11.2	..	1.9	0.445	..	−5.9	..	32.5
10	Canada	20.6	13.5	−0.6	38.2	−0.3	1.3	2.1	7.0	..	1.6	0.179	−0.2	−3.1	..	38.5
10	United States	7.9	16.4	−0.7	33.9	2.7	13.6	0.7	6.4	..	2.7	0.095	0.4	−2.8	..	33.8
12	Hong Kong, China (SAR)	1.1	6.3	1.2	..	..	..	..	..	..	0.7	0.233	..	..	..	43.7
13	New Zealand	30.8	7.6	0.3	38.6	5.1	1.6	0.9	13.8	..	1.2	0.203	..	−1.0	..	34.9
14	Sweden	49.9	4.6	−1.2	68.9	0.8	1.6	0.2	18.8	..	3.2	0.091	..	−0.9	..	37.0
15	Liechtenstein	..	1.4	..	43.1	6.2	..	..	..	..	..	..	..	..	..	..
16	United Kingdom	4.4	7.1	−1.3	13.0	13.2	5.5	0.6	3.6	..	1.7	0.111	..	−3.8	..	35.0
17	Japan	4.5	9.8	0.4	68.5	0.0	18.9	0.0	3.4	..	3.6	0.128	..	−2.1	..	53.1
18	Korea (Republic of)	1.6	11.8	3.2	63.4	−3.9	41.9	0.0	18.7	..	4.3	0.148	..	−4.4	..	37.6
19	Israel	8.7	8.8	0.5	7.6	25.0	..	0.2	15.3	..	4.1	0.287	2.2	−4.0	..	22.9
20	Luxembourg	4.1	18.7	−1.5	33.5	..	1.2	0.0	12.5	..	1.3	0.107	..	−5.8	..	28.3
21	France	12.6	5.1	−1.0	31.0	17.7	14.1	0.0	6.6	..	2.3	0.092	..	−3.6	..	40.5
22	Belgium	7.4	8.4	−1.0	22.6	..	32.8	0.0	9.8	..	2.5	0.104	..	−2.9	..	38.1
23	Finland	39.1	8.5	−0.9	73.1	1.8	6.0	0.2	6.3	..	3.2	0.135	..	−3.6	..	43.3
24	Austria	34.5	7.4	−0.1	46.9	2.5	4.5	0.1	11.8	..	3.0	0.061	..	−3.9	..	40.5
25	Slovenia	19.3	7.0	..	62.0	5.1	3.6	0.5	10.8	..	2.4	0.158	−1.0	−6.4	..	42.7
26	Italy	12.1	5.7	−1.1	31.6	22.5	28.1	0.1	3.5	..	1.3	0.054	..	−5.2	..	48.6
27	Spain	15.7	5.1	−0.4	36.8	33.2	33.0	0.0	6.6	..	1.2	0.092	..	−3.3	..	41.4
28	Czech Republic	10.9	9.4	..	34.5	1.5	12.6	0.1	5.7	..	2.0	0.113	0.5	−1.6	..	36.1
29	Greece	13.9	6.3	−0.6	31.5	22.9	14.0	0.1	−5.8	..	0.8	0.339	..	−3.5	..	41.3
30	Brunei Darussalam	0.0	18.9	−1.0	72.1	−8.0	..	27.1	25.8	..	..	0.646	..	..	..	16.2
30	Estonia	24.9	15.1	..	52.7	1.2	13.4	0.8	16.5	..	1.4	0.118	−0.6	−4.6	..	37.9
32	Andorra	..	6.5	..	34.0	0.0	..	..	..	..	..	0.192	..	..	..	..
33	Cyprus	8.4	5.2	−0.4	18.7	7.2	26.5	0.0	0.3	..	0.5	0.209	..	−2.5	..	26.9
33	Malta	2.6	5.2	−0.7	1.1	0.0	44.4	..	..	..	0.8	0.375	..	−1.9	..	39.9
33	Qatar	..	40.5	2.2	0.0	..	374.1	13.8	29.6	..	0.5	0.519	..	..	..	5.1
36	Poland	11.1	7.9	−0.8	30.8	6.3	19.0	0.7	10.0	..	0.9	0.065	−0.6	−1.5	..	36.3
37	Lithuania	24.3	4.3	..	34.8	12.1	2.6	0.4	20.1	..	1.0	0.142	1.9	−3.2	..	36.0
38	Chile	30.3	4.7	2.8	23.9	16.2	3.8	8.0	4.1	..	0.4	0.334	−1.9	−1.9	..	27.0
38	Saudi Arabia	0.0	17.9	1.3	0.5	0.0	943.3	20.4	20.0	..	0.1	0.738	..	−6.2	..	9.5
40	Slovakia	10.5	6.2	..	40.3	1.0	1.1	0.5	1.3	..	0.9	0.175	0.1	−0.6	..	31.6
41	Portugal	25.6	4.4	0.2	34.7	−7.5	11.8	0.1	2.4	..	1.3	0.079	..	−4.9	..	44.7
42	United Arab Emirates	0.1	18.7	−1.8	3.9	31.7	1,867.0	9.2	..	..	0.7	0.405	..	−6.1	..	7.7
43	Hungary	10.2	4.2	−2.0	22.9	14.0	4.9	0.3	10.9	..	1.4	0.113	2.1	0.0	..	32.9
44	Latvia	40.4	3.5	..	54.0	5.8	0.7	1.0	0.2	..	0.7	0.096	0.9	−1.1	..	36.7
45	Argentina	8.8	4.5	1.1	9.9	−22.1	4.3	2.7	10.1	..	0.6	0.186	−3.8		..	20.3
45	Croatia	20.0	4.2	..	34.3	3.8	0.6	1.6	3.0	..	0.8	0.078	1.4	−2.0	..	39.7
47	Bahrain	..	23.7	−0.2	0.8	144.4	..	26.4	−2.0	..	0.1	0.369	..	−2.6	..	8.7
48	Montenegro	46.2	3.6	..	61.5	32.1	..	..	..	52.9	0.4	0.234	..		−23.4	30.0
49	Russian Federation	3.2	12.5	..	49.8	0.8	1.4	9.5	11.9	..	1.2	0.370	1.6	−2.3	..	29.5

		Environmental sustainability						Economic sustainability					Social sustainability			
		Renewable energy consumption	Carbon dioxide emissions		Forest area		Fresh water withdrawals	Natural resource depletion	Adjusted net savings	External debt stock	Research and development expenditure	Concentration index (exports)	Income quintile ratio	Gender Inequality Index	Population in multi-dimensional poverty	Old-age (ages 65 and older) dependency ratio
		(% of total final energy consumption)	Per capita (tonnes)	Average annual change (%)	(% of total land area[a])	Change (%)	(% of total renewable water resources)	(% of GNI)	(% of GNI)	(% of GNI)	(% of GDP)	(value)	Average annual change (%)	Average annual change (%)	Average annual change (%)	(per 100 people ages 15–64)
HDI rank		2012[b]	2013	1990/2013	2015	1990–2015	2005–2014[c]	2010–2014[c]	2005–2014[c]	2005–2014[c]	2005–2014[c]	2014	2000/2014	2005/2015	2005/2014	2030[d]
50	Romania	21.7	3.5	-2.8	29.8	7.4	3.0	1.0	21.6	57.0	0.4	0.099	-0.9	0.2	..	33.6
51	Kuwait	..	27.3	0.7	0.4	81.2	..	22.3	18.7	..	0.3	0.657	..	-1.0	..	6.8
HIGH HUMAN DEVELOPMENT																
52	Belarus	7.2	6.7	..	42.5	10.9	2.6	1.2	17.3	54.3	0.7	0.250	-1.1	..	..	30.3
52	Oman	..	15.7	4.1	0.0	0.0	..	34.9	-20.1	..	0.2	0.592	..	..	..	7.8
54	Barbados	9.5	5.1	0.9	14.7	0.0	87.5	0.7	-0.3	..	..	0.163	..	-1.2	..	35.6
54	Uruguay	46.4	2.2	2.4	10.5	131.3	..	2.6	8.1	..	0.3	0.215	-1.6	-2.8	..	26.8
56	Bulgaria	15.8	5.4	-2.0	35.2	17.1	25.7	0.8	10.7	90.1	0.8	0.105	1.6	-0.9	..	37.0
56	Kazakhstan	1.4	15.4	..	1.2	-3.3	18.4	13.7	3.0	83.3	0.2	0.668	-2.5	-4.5	-9.9	15.6
58	Bahamas	1.6	8.2	0.3	51.4	0.0	..	0.1	2.3	..	..	0.412	..	1.7	..	22.4
59	Malaysia	6.8	8.0	4.2	67.6	-0.8	1.9	5.5	12.0	66.8	1.3	0.178	-0.7	-0.1	..	14.5
60	Palau	2.7	10.7	-1.6	87.6							0.845				
60	Panama	22.9	2.7	3.9	62.1	-8.4	0.7	0.1	24.3	43.9	0.1	0.167	-2.4	-0.3	..	17.7
62	Antigua and Barbuda	..	5.8	0.8	22.3	-4.9	8.5	..	..	..	..	0.597	..	..	..	19.0
63	Seychelles	0.5	7.2	5.4	89.4	1.1	..	0.1	..	..	0.3	0.489	1.0	..	..	19.8
64	Mauritius	3.4	3.0	3.4	19.0	-6.1	..	0.0	2.7	90.9	0.2	0.219	..	0.5	..	25.9
65	Trinidad and Tobago	0.3	34.5	4.0	45.7	-2.6	8.8	13.4	-14.4	..	0.1	0.371	..	-0.7	..	21.9
66	Costa Rica	38.6	1.6	2.3	54.0	7.5	2.1	1.2	14.7	43.8	0.6	0.536	-1.5	-2.0	..	22.6
66	Serbia	19.6	6.3	..	31.1	9.9	2.6	..	..	78.7	0.8	0.105	-0.8	..	-21.6	32.7
68	Cuba	18.9	3.5	0.4	30.1	56.9	18.3	3.0	..	..	0.4	0.225	..	-2.0	..	36.2
69	Iran (Islamic Republic of)	0.9	0.0	3.3	6.6	17.0	..	12.6	..	1.3	0.3	0.671	-2.3	-0.2	..	13.4
70	Georgia	28.7	2.0	..	40.6	2.6	2.9	0.8	9.4	85.0	0.1	0.222	0.2	-1.1	..	29.7
71	Turkey	12.8	4.2	2.0	15.2	21.8	19.8	0.3	10.8	51.6	1.0	0.069	-0.3	-3.7	..	18.0
71	Venezuela (Bolivarian Republic of)	11.2	6.1	0.0	52.9	10.3	1.7	11.6	14.5	..	..	0.760	-1.7	-0.3	..	15.6
73	Sri Lanka	60.9	0.8	5.5	33.0	-9.4	24.5	0.5	17.3	59.7	0.1	0.204	-0.6	-1.3	..	23.7
74	Saint Kitts and Nevis	..	5.1	2.3	42.3	0.0	51.3	..	..	..	..	0.286	..	..	..	..
75	Albania	38.2	1.7	0.1	28.2	-2.2	4.3	3.8	-1.6	60.8	0.2	0.297	-0.8	-2.3	..	31.8
76	Lebanon	5.0	4.3	1.5	13.4	4.8	24.3	0.0	-7.7	68.0	..	0.122	..	..	..	21.1
77	Mexico	9.4	3.9	0.3	34.0	-5.3	17.2	5.0	7.9	34.7	0.5	0.131	-1.1	-1.9	-2.3	15.4
78	Azerbaijan	2.8	3.8	..	13.0	34.6	34.5	19.6	17.8	16.1	0.2	0.856	7.4	..	..	18.7
79	Brazil	43.6	2.5	2.5	59.0	-9.7	0.9	2.5	7.3	24.1	1.2	0.147	..	-1.4	6.2	19.9
79	Grenada	10.0	2.9	4.2	50.0	0.0	7.1	..	..	75.6	..	0.194	..	..	..	16.2
81	Bosnia and Herzegovina	15.3	5.7	..	42.7	-1.5	0.9	..	..	57.1	0.3	0.104	2.1	..	-11.2	37.3
82	The former Yugoslav Republic of Macedonia	16.5	4.0	..	39.6	10.3	8.6	2.2	13.5	65.7	0.4	0.189	1.9	-3.6	-9.2	27.7
83	Algeria	0.2	3.5	0.7	0.8	17.3	66.9	14.7	26.9	2.6	0.1	0.490	..	-2.1	..	14.0
84	Armenia	6.6	1.8	..	11.7	-0.9	37.9	1.8	0.4	74.8	0.2	0.223	-0.9	-2.6	..	28.7
84	Ukraine	2.8	6.0	..	16.7	4.1	8.5	3.2	-2.7	100.3	0.7	0.127	-1.7	-2.0	-8.8	30.8
86	Jordan	3.1	3.4	0.5	1.1	-0.6	92.4	0.5	15.7	68.5	0.4	0.156	..	-1.4	5.4	8.0
87	Peru	28.2	1.9	2.9	57.8	-5.1	0.7	4.8	13.3	34.3	..	0.227	-3.0	-1.6	-10.2	15.5
87	Thailand	23.0	4.5	4.6	32.1	17.1	13.1	3.4	12.0	38.2	0.5	0.076	-1.2	0.0	..	29.2
89	Ecuador	13.4	2.8	2.3	50.5	-4.4	2.2	7.8	11.2	26.6	0.3	0.500	-3.4	-1.8	-12.4	16.0
90	China	18.4	7.6	5.6	22.2	32.6	19.5	2.3	34.5	9.3	2.0	0.101	..	-2.7	-4.4	25.3
91	Fiji	12.2	1.9	2.4	55.7	6.7	0.3	0.8	4.7	21.6	..	0.255	0.8	-2.1	..	15.3
92	Mongolia	3.2	14.5	5.2	8.1	0.1	1.6	12.2	8.2	186.2	0.2	0.485	-0.6	-3.1	-9.4	11.8
92	Saint Lucia	2.3	2.2	2.8	33.3	-6.9	14.3	0.1	..	39.2	..	0.331	..	..	..	19.9
94	Jamaica	14.7	2.8	-0.4	31.0	-2.7	7.5	1.0	10.9	94.3	..	0.470	..	-0.9	-14.1	21.0
95	Colombia	26.3	1.9	0.5	52.7	-9.2	0.5	6.8	3.3	28.0	0.2	0.459	-1.7	-2.3	..	18.8
96	Dominica	11.6	1.8	3.5	57.8	-13.3	10.0	0.2	..	56.3	..	0.404	..	..	..	..
97	Suriname	19.4	3.9	-0.5	98.3	-0.6	0.6	9.8	-12.1	..	..	0.484	..	0.4	-4.7	16.2
97	Tunisia	13.0	2.5	2.0	6.7	61.9	69.7	3.8	-2.7	57.3	0.6	0.145	-1.4	-0.9	..	18.6
99	Dominican Republic	13.2	2.1	2.3	41.0	79.5	30.4	0.1	14.6	44.0	..	0.178	-1.9	-0.8	-0.7	15.6
99	Saint Vincent and the Grenadines	5.1	1.9	4.2	69.2	8.0	7.9	0.1	..	46.5	..	0.295	..	..	..	19.7
101	Tonga	1.1	2.0	4.0	12.5	0.0	..	0.1	..	44.2	..	0.296	-0.3	4.1	..	11.9
102	Libya	1.7	8.1	-0.1	0.1	0.0	822.9	16.2	34.1	..	..	0.765	..	-3.4	..	10.5
103	Belize	26.8	1.5	-0.4	59.9	-15.5	..	5.2	-5.5	82.9	..	0.158	..	-2.4	1.3	8.3

DASH BOARD 2

	Environmental sustainability						Economic sustainability					Social sustainability			
	Renewable energy consumption	Carbon dioxide emissions		Forest area		Fresh water withdrawals	Natural resource depletion	Adjusted net savings	External debt stock	Research and development expenditure	Concentration index (exports)	Income quintile ratio	Gender Inequality Index	Population in multi-dimensional poverty	Old-age (ages 65 and older) dependency ratio
	(% of total final energy consumption)	Per capita (tonnes)	Average annual change (%)	(% of total land area[a])	Change (%)	(% of total renewable water resources)	(% of GNI)	(% of GNI)	(% of GNI)	(% of GDP)	(value)	Average annual change (%)	Average annual change (%)	Average annual change (%)	(per 100 people ages 15–64)
HDI rank	2012[b]	2013	1990/ 2013	2015	1990– 2015	2005–2014[c]	2010– 2014[c]	2005– 2014[c]	2005– 2014[c]	2005–2014[c]	2014	2000/2014	2005/2015	2005/2014	2030[d]
104 Samoa	23.2	1.3	2.2	60.4	31.5	..	0.8	..	58.1	..	0.277	..	−1.0	..	13.7
105 Maldives	3.2	2.7	6.3	3.3	0.0	15.7	0.1	8.6	39.1	..	0.731	−0.1	−2.1	..	11.0
105 Uzbekistan	2.4	3.4	..	7.6	5.7	100.6	9.0	..	20.4	0.2	0.281	..	..	..	11.9
MEDIUM HUMAN DEVELOPMENT															
107 Moldova (Republic of)	4.7	1.4	..	12.4	28.2	8.7	0.4	13.8	74.0	0.4	0.146	−2.8	−1.5	−2.8	24.7
108 Botswana	23.9	2.5	1.1	19.1	−21.0	..	1.3	34.8	15.1	0.3	0.824	−1.8	−1.9	..	7.7
109 Gabon	69.6	2.9	−2.1	89.3	4.5	0.1	26.2	−2.1	28.6	0.6	0.628	..	−0.2	..	8.5
110 Paraguay	62.7	0.8	1.8	38.6	−27.6	0.6	5.3	10.0	47.9	0.1	0.335	−2.3	−1.3	..	13.2
111 Egypt	5.5	2.4	2.6	0.1	65.9	126.6	6.4	2.3	14.2	0.7	0.163	..	..	−11.9	10.5
111 Turkmenistan	..	12.8	..	8.8	0.0	..	35.7	..	1.0	..	0.756	..	..	..	11.0
113 Indonesia	37.1	1.9	3.7	50.2	−23.2	..	2.6	26.3	34.1	0.1	0.152	..	−1.4	−10.3	12.4
114 Palestine, State of	..	0.6	..	1.5	1.0	48.8	..	..	..	..	0.190	..	..	..	6.5
115 Viet Nam	35.6	1.7	7.5	47.6	65.6	9.3	4.0	15.0	40.6	0.2	0.143	0.8	0.7	..	18.3
116 Philippines	29.4	1.0	1.8	27.0	22.7	17.0	1.7	28.7	22.7	0.1	0.231	−1.0	−0.7	−2.7	10.3
117 El Salvador	34.0	1.0	3.5	12.8	−29.7	8.1	2.5	0.5	59.6	0.1	0.212	−3.7	−2.4	..	17.3
118 Bolivia (Plurinational State of)	28.0	1.9	3.8	50.6	−12.8	0.4	9.5	8.3	27.0	0.2	0.474	−4.7	−1.9	..	12.7
119 South Africa	16.9	8.9	−0.1	7.6	0.0	30.2	3.1	2.1	42.3	0.7	0.119	2.6	−1.3	2.5	10.5
120 Kyrgyzstan	22.5	1.7	..	3.3	−23.8	32.6	6.1	−5.8	101.1	0.1	0.175	−1.3	−4.2	−5.5	12.1
121 Iraq	1.6	4.9	2.2	1.9	3.3	..	18.5	−2.6	..	0.0	0.972	..	..	−6.3	6.0
122 Cabo Verde	21.2	0.9	5.1	22.3	55.7	..	0.5	20.3	86.4	0.1	0.411	−1.7	..	..	10.0
123 Morocco	11.3	1.8	2.7	12.6	13.7	35.7	1.0	16.6	41.1	0.7	0.157	−0.1	−1.3	..	16.1
124 Nicaragua	53.1	0.8	1.0	25.9	−31.0	0.9	7.4	11.7	88.8	..	0.221	−3.7	−1.0	−8.7	13.1
125 Guatemala	66.2	0.9	2.0	33.0	−25.4	2.6	4.6	2.6	33.1	0.0	0.132	−2.3	−1.6	..	9.5
125 Namibia	32.9	1.3	17.9	8.4	−21.0	..	1.2	16.9	..	0.1	0.212	..	..	1.1	7.4
127 Guyana	36.1	2.5	2.1	84.0	−0.8	0.5	10.8	−10.4	73.0	..	0.424	..	−0.2	−0.6	15.0
127 Micronesia (Federated States of)	..	1.4	..	91.8	..	..	0.1	..	..	..	0.426	−5.7	..	..	10.8
129 Tajikistan	58.0	0.4	..	2.9	1.0	51.1	1.1	14.3	44.3	0.1	0.406	−0.1	−1.2	−8.6	9.1
130 Honduras	53.4	1.2	3.5	41.0	−43.6	..	4.4	10.4	40.6	..	0.235	−3.9	−1.1	−6.7	11.0
131 India	39.0	1.6	3.6	23.8	10.5	33.9	2.9	19.0	22.7	0.8	0.175	..	−1.6	..	12.5
132 Bhutan	90.0	1.2	7.1	72.3	34.7	0.4	16.9	14.7	105.1	..	0.362	..	−1.1	..	10.8
133 Timor-Leste	43.1	0.4	..	46.1	−29.0	..	..	..	..	..	0.906	−2.0	..	..	8.2
134 Vanuatu	34.2	0.4	−0.3	36.1	0.0	..	0.0	..	17.2	..	0.638	..	..	..	9.9
135 Congo	48.2	0.6	0.6	65.4	−1.7	..	39.2	−69.8	33.3	..	0.788	..	−0.4	9.5	7.0
135 Equatorial Guinea	29.8	6.8	14.2	55.9	−15.7	..	67.2	..	..	..	0.698	..	..	..	9.4
137 Kiribati	2.9	0.6	2.8	15.0	0.0	..	0.0	..	..	..	0.897	..	..	..	9.5
138 Lao People's Democratic Republic	86.5	0.3	8.6	81.3	6.3	1.1	12.2	−4.1	95.9	..	0.285	1.3	..	−6.5	8.1
139 Bangladesh	38.3	0.4	4.9	11.0	−4.4	2.9	2.6	25.2	18.8	..	0.396	−0.4	−0.9	−5.3	10.6
139 Ghana	49.5	0.6	3.4	41.0	8.2	..	17.5	1.6	47.7	0.4	0.401	1.1	−0.7	−3.1	6.5
139 Zambia	88.2	0.3	−0.8	65.4	−7.9	..	8.9	3.5	28.9	0.3	0.612	7.2	−1.6	−2.0	4.8
142 Sao Tome and Principe	43.2	0.6	1.7	55.8	−4.3	..	1.6	..	63.9	..	0.624	−0.5	..	..	6.2
143 Cambodia	72.6	0.4	3.6	53.6	−26.9	0.5	2.3	3.1	42.9	..	0.317	..	−1.5	−5.8	10.4
144 Nepal	84.7	0.2	8.8	25.4	−24.7	4.5	5.8	32.7	20.0	0.3	0.145	−0.8	−2.2	−10.1	10.8
145 Myanmar	78.7	0.2	3.8	44.5	−25.9	..	3.9	..	10.2	..	0.273	..	..	..	12.5
146 Kenya	78.5	0.3	0.9	7.8	−6.6	10.5	2.8	4.0	26.7	0.8	0.194	1.3	−1.3	−5.6	6.1
147 Pakistan	45.5	0.8	1.2	1.9	−41.7	74.4	2.7	14.1	23.9	0.3	0.193	0.2	−0.9	0.8	8.6
LOW HUMAN DEVELOPMENT															
148 Swaziland	39.5	0.9	2.5	34.1	24.2	..	1.4	−1.6	13.8	..	0.272	0.6	−0.6	..	6.6
149 Syrian Arab Republic	2.4	1.9	−2.0	2.7	32.1	84.2	..	9.2	14.3	..	0.172	..	0.2	4.3	9.0
150 Angola	57.2	1.4	4.9	46.4	−5.1	0.5	24.5	3.0	23.9	..	0.958	−3.5	..	..	5.0
151 Tanzania (United Republic of)	88.2	0.2	3.9	52.0	−17.6	..	2.0	15.1	30.1	0.5	0.180	−0.4	−0.7	..	6.2
152 Nigeria	86.5	0.6	1.4	7.7	−59.4	4.6	6.6	11.0	4.9	0.2	0.758	−2.9	..	−1.1	5.1
153 Cameroon	78.1	0.3	3.3	39.8	−22.6	..	5.6	−2.3	16.4	..	0.442	3.1	−1.5	−1.5	5.8
154 Papua New Guinea	53.4	0.8	2.1	74.1	−0.2	0.1	15.0	..	147.6	..	0.280	−4.4	−1.3	..	6.4
154 Zimbabwe	75.6	0.9	−2.0	36.4	−36.6	17.9	3.8	..	84.2	..	0.312	..	−0.7	−4.7	5.0
156 Solomon Islands	67.2	0.4	−1.2	78.1	−6.0	..	36.0	−11.1	17.0	..	0.524	..	..	..	7.0
157 Mauritania	33.3	0.7	1.9	0.2	−45.9	11.8	20.7	−17.0	73.4	..	0.468	−2.0	..	−4.2	6.8
158 Madagascar	78.9	0.1	2.2	21.4	−8.9	..	4.3	−5.3	27.6	0.0	0.253	−1.5	..	..	6.4

HDI rank	Environmental sustainability — Renewable energy consumption (% of total final energy consumption) 2012[b]	Carbon dioxide emissions — Per capita (tonnes) 2013	Carbon dioxide emissions — Average annual change (%) 1990/2013	Forest area — (% of total land area[a]) 2015	Forest area — Change (%) 1990–2015	Fresh water withdrawals (% of total renewable water resources) 2005–2014[c]	Economic sustainability — Natural resource depletion (% of GNI) 2010–2014[c]	Adjusted net savings (% of GNI) 2005–2014[c]	External debt stock (% of GNI) 2005–2014[c]	Research and development expenditure (% of GDP) 2005–2014[c]	Concentration index (exports) (value) 2014	Social sustainability — Income quintile ratio — Average annual change (%) 2000/2014	Gender Inequality Index — Average annual change (%) 2005/2015	Population in multidimensional poverty — Average annual change (%) 2005/2014	Old-age (ages 65 and older) dependency ratio (per 100 people ages 15–64) 2030[d]
159 Rwanda	86.8	0.1	−0.2	19.5	50.9	..	5.7	4.8	26.1	..	0.439	0.3	−2.0	−4.6	7.0
160 Comoros	46.8	0.2	1.6	19.9	24.5	..	3.4	2.2	22.4	..	0.547				6.3
160 Lesotho	4.2	1.1	..	1.6	22.5	..	4.6	29.2	33.6	0.0	0.395	0.9	−0.3	..	6.1
162 Senegal	51.4	0.6	1.5	43.0	−11.5	..	1.1	12.4	36.6	0.5	0.222	0.4	−1.3	−3.4	5.6
163 Haiti	83.1	0.2	2.2	3.5	−16.4	10.3	3.1	16.6	22.2	..	0.499	1.4	0.2	−2.7	9.6
163 Uganda	90.3	0.1	5.0	10.4	−56.4	1.1	11.5	3.1	19.8	0.5	0.191	−1.0	−1.3	−1.1	4.3
165 Sudan	64.0	0.3	1.9	8.1	−37.5	71.2	3.6	6.1	30.6	0.3	..		−1.2	..	6.8
166 Togo	72.7	0.3	2.0	3.5	−72.6	..	7.8	−19.5	24.5	0.3	0.179		−1.3	−1.1	5.4
167 Benin	50.6	0.6	6.2	38.2	−25.2	..	1.4	12.3	22.8	..	0.283		−0.5	−1.4	5.8
168 Yemen	1.0	1.0	0.9	1.0	0.0	168.6	8.1	−11.5	22.0	..	0.531		−0.2	0.9	5.7
169 Afghanistan	10.8	0.7	5.2	2.1	0.0	..	1.6	−18.3	12.2	..	0.308		−1.0	..	5.0
170 Malawi	79.2	0.1	0.8	33.4	−19.2	7.9	10.8	1.8	40.1	..	0.482	−3.4	−0.5	−4.2	5.6
171 Côte d'Ivoire	74.4	0.4	−0.6	32.7	1.8	1.8	4.0	13.0	33.0	..	0.357	1.4	−0.2	2.5	5.6
172 Djibouti	31.4	0.7	1.1	0.2	0.0	..	..	..	62.5	..	0.173	2.2			9.1
173 Gambia	48.8	0.3	1.0	48.2	10.4	..	7.0	8.3	63.9	0.1	0.340		0.3	−0.9	4.9
174 Ethiopia	93.5	0.1	2.6	12.5	−17.8	..	11.2	14.5	30.4	0.6	0.313	1.4	..	..	6.6
175 Mali	83.9	0.1	1.0	3.9	−29.5	4.3	10.6	14.8	29.5	0.7	0.523	−2.2	−0.4	−1.2	4.5
176 Congo (Democratic Republic of the)	96.0	0.0	−4.7	67.3	−4.9	0.1	31.8	−26.6	19.1	0.1	0.400		−0.2	−0.6	5.8
177 Liberia	80.4	0.2	−0.1	43.4	15.2	..	27.4	−27.9	37.4	..	0.498		−0.3	−2.6	5.9
178 Guinea-Bissau	88.6	0.1	−0.5	70.1	−11.0	..	12.3	−19.3	26.6	..	0.936	8.0			6.1
179 Eritrea	80.4	0.1[e]	..	15.0	−6.8	..	15.1	..	23.8	..	0.366				4.9
179 Sierra Leone	80.3	0.2	1.9	42.7	−2.4	0.1	7.7	4.7	28.4	..	0.481		−0.1	−0.5	4.8
181 Mozambique	88.4	0.2	3.0	48.2	−12.5	..	1.8	8.5	47.6	0.4	0.260	0.0	−0.9	0.1	6.4
181 South Sudan	..	0.1	..			1.3	..	..	..	..	..				6.2
183 Guinea	76.3	0.2	0.4	25.9	−12.4	..	19.2	−47.8	22.9	..	0.491	−2.5		−2.2	6.1
184 Burundi	96.6	0.0	−2.7	10.7	−4.5	..	13.8	−8.6	22.3	0.1	0.350	−3.5	−1.1	−1.4	5.9
185 Burkina Faso	80.0	0.2	4.4	19.6	21.9	6.1	10.8	8.9	20.6	0.2	0.473	−3.7	..	−0.7	4.7
186 Chad	90.6	0.0	2.8	3.9	−27.3	1.9	13.0	..	21.6	..	0.905		−0.8	..	4.7
187 Niger	81.3	0.1	0.6	0.9	−41.3	2.9	13.7	5.7	32.1	..	0.426		−0.5	−0.6	5.8
188 Central African Republic	78.4	0.1	−0.3	35.6	−1.7	0.1	0.1	..	36.7	..	0.358			−1.3	6.8
OTHER COUNTRIES OR TERRITORIES															
Korea (Democratic People's Rep. of)	16.0	2.0	..	41.8	−38.7	11.2	..	..	..	..	0.341				17.8
Marshall Islands	..	1.9	2.9	70.2	..	..	..	..	..	..	0.760	..	..	..	..
Monaco	..	..	..	..	..	..	..	..	..	0.0	..				
Nauru	..	4.3	−4.8	0.0	..	..	..	..	..	..	0.819				
San Marino	..	..	..	0.0	..	..	..	..	..	..	..				
Somalia	94.2	0.1	14.1	10.1	−23.2	..	8.6	..	..	..	0.605				5.4
Tuvalu	..	..	..	33.3	0.0	..	..	..	..	..	0.752				
Human development groups															
Very high human development	9.1	10.9	−0.4	34.7	1.0	6.1	1.4	8.3	..	2.4	—	—	—	—	—
High human development	17.3	6.2	1.4	29.4	−0.9	5.1	3.5	25.1	19.4	1.6	—	—	—	—	—
Medium human development	35.6	1.6	1.1	29.2	−9.9	15.2	4.1	16.8	27.2	0.5	—	—	—	—	—
Low human development	78.5	0.4	0.3	25.0	−13.8	..	8.9	6.3	20.0	..	—	—	—	—	—
Developing countries	23.8	3.4	0.7	26.6	−6.7	7.2	4.6	21.9	21.0	1.2	—	—	—	—	—
Regions															
Arab States	3.6	4.8	0.5	3.0	−23.7	102.2	13.9	12.8	24.8	0.4	—	—	—	—	—
East Asia and the Pacific	20.1	5.8	−0.6	29.8	3.8	..	2.5	..	14.3	..	—	—	—	—	—
Europe and Central Asia	7.3	5.3	..	9.1	8.3	17.0	4.8	8.9	56.7	0.7	—	—	—	—	—
Latin America and the Caribbean	26.3	3.0	1.6	46.3	−9.4	1.7	4.5	8.4	30.1	..	—	—	—	—	—
South Asia	32.5	1.6	3.8	14.7	7.6	23.9	4.2	18.7	20.5	0.7	—	—	—	—	—
Sub-Saharan Africa	63.2	0.8	0.6	28.2	−11.7	..	8.3	5.7	24.7	0.4	—	—	—	—	—
Least developed countries	73.1	0.3	2.1	26.8	−12.4	..	8.8	9.0	25.3	..	—	—	—	—	—
Small island developing states	15.3	2.6	0.1	69.3	1.2	..	4.4	..	64.6	..	—	—	—	—	—
Organisation for Economic Co-operation and Development	10.4	9.7	−0.5	31.3	1.5	8.8	0.7	7.7	..	2.5	—	—	—	—	—
World	17.4	4.7	0.0	30.8	−3.2	6.9	2.2	13.0	21.4	2.0	—	—	—	—	—

NOTES

Three-colour coding is used to visualize partial grouping of countries by indicator. For each indicator countries are divided into three groups of approximately equal size (terciles): the top third, the middle third and the bottom third. See *Technical note 7* at http://hdr.undp.org/sites/default/files/hdr2016_technical_notes.pdf for details about partial grouping in this table.

a   This column is intentionally left without colour because it is meant to provide context for the indicator on change in forest area.

b   Data refer to 2012 or the most recent year available.

c   Data refer to the most recent year available during the period specified.

d   Projections based on medium-fertility variant.

e   Refers to 2011.

DEFINITIONS

Renewable energy consumption: Share of renewable energy in total final energy consumption. Renewable sources include hydroelectric, geothermal, solar, tides, wind, biomass and biofuels.

Carbon dioxide emissions per capita: Human-originated carbon dioxide emissions stemming from the burning of fossil fuels, gas flaring and the production of cement, divided by midyear population.

Includes carbon dioxide emitted by forest biomass through the depletion of forest areas.

Forest area: Land spanning more than 0.5 hectare with trees taller than 5 metres and a canopy cover of more than 10 percent or trees able to reach these thresholds in situ. Excludes land predominantly under agricultural or urban land use, tree stands in agricultural production systems (for example, in fruit plantations and agroforestry systems) and trees in urban parks and gardens. Areas under reforestation that have not yet reached but are expected to reach a canopy cover of 10 percent and a tree height of 5 metres are included, as are temporarily unstocked areas resulting from human intervention or natural causes that are expected to regenerate.

Fresh water withdrawals: Total fresh water withdrawn, expressed as a percentage of total renewable water resources.

Natural resource depletion: Monetary expression of energy, mineral and forest depletion, expressed as a percentage of gross national income (GNI).

Adjusted net savings: Net national savings plus education expenditure and minus energy depletion, mineral depletion, net forest depletion, and carbon dioxide and particulate emissions damage. Net national savings are equal to gross national savings less the value of consumption of fixed capital.

External debt stock: Debt owed to nonresidents repayable in foreign currency, goods or services, expressed as a percentage of gross national income (GNI).

Research and development expenditure: Current and capital expenditures (both public and private) on creative work undertaken systematically to increase knowledge, including knowledge of humanity, culture, and society, and the use of knowledge for new applications. Research and development covers basic research, applied research and experimental development.

Concentration index (exports): A measure of the degree of product concentration in exports from a country (also referred to as the Herfindahl-Hirschmann Index). A value closer to 0 indicates that a country's exports are more homogeneously distributed among a series of products (reflecting a well diversified economy); a value closer to 1 indicates that a country's exports are concentrated highly among a few products.

Income quintile ratio, average annual change: Change in the ratio of the average income of the richest 20 percent of the population to the average income of the poorest 20 percent of the population over 2000–2014, divided by the respective number of years.

Gender Inequality Index, average annual change: Change in Gender Inequality Index value over 2005–2015, divided by the respective number of years.

Population in multidimensional poverty, average annual change: Change in the percentage of the population in multidimensional poverty over 2005–2014, divided by respective number of years.

Old-age dependency ratio: Projected ratio of the population ages 65 and older to the population ages 15–64, expressed as the number of dependants per 100 people of working age (ages 15–64).

MAIN DATA SOURCES

Columns 1–4 and 7–10: World Bank (2016a).

Column 5: HDRO calculations based on data on forest area from World Bank (2016a).

Column 6: FAO (2016b).

Column 11: UNCTAD (2016).

Column 12: HDRO calculations based on data from World Bank (2016a).

Column 13: HDRO calculations based on the Gender Inequality Index time series.

Column 14: HDRO calculations based on the Multidimensional Poverty Index time series.

Column 15: UNDESA (2015a).

Regions

Arab States (20 countries or territories)
Algeria, Bahrain, Djibouti, Egypt, Iraq, Jordan, Kuwait, Lebanon, Libya, Morocco, Oman, State of Palestine, Qatar, Saudi Arabia, Somalia, Sudan, Syrian Arab Republic, Tunisia, United Arab Emirates, Yemen

East Asia and the Pacific (24 countries)
Cambodia, China, Fiji, Indonesia, Kiribati, Democratic People's Republic of Korea, Lao People's Democratic Republic, Malaysia, Marshall Islands, Federated States of Micronesia, Mongolia, Myanmar, Nauru, Palau, Papua New Guinea, Philippines, Samoa, Solomon Islands, Thailand, Timor-Leste, Tonga, Tuvalu, Vanuatu, Viet Nam

Europe and Central Asia (17 countries)
Albania, Armenia, Azerbaijan, Belarus, Bosnia and Herzegovina, Georgia, Kazakhstan, Kyrgyzstan, Republic of Moldova, Montenegro, Serbia, Tajikistan, The former Yugoslav Republic of Macedonia, Turkey, Turkmenistan, Ukraine, Uzbekistan

Latin America and the Caribbean (33 countries)
Antigua and Barbuda, Argentina, Bahamas, Barbados, Belize, Plurinational State of Bolivia, Brazil, Chile, Colombia, Costa Rica, Cuba, Dominica, Dominican Republic, Ecuador, El Salvador, Grenada, Guatemala, Guyana, Haiti, Honduras, Jamaica, Mexico, Nicaragua, Panama, Paraguay, Peru, Saint Kitts and Nevis, Saint Lucia, Saint Vincent and the Grenadines, Suriname, Trinidad and Tobago, Uruguay, Bolivarian Republic of Venezuela

South Asia (9 countries)
Afghanistan, Bangladesh, Bhutan, India, Islamic Republic of Iran, Maldives, Nepal, Pakistan, Sri Lanka

Sub-Saharan Africa (46 countries)
Angola, Benin, Botswana, Burkina Faso, Burundi, Cabo Verde, Cameroon, Central African Republic, Chad, Comoros, Congo, Democratic Republic of the Congo, Côte d'Ivoire, Equatorial Guinea, Eritrea, Ethiopia, Gabon, Gambia, Ghana, Guinea, Guinea-Bissau, Kenya, Lesotho, Liberia, Madagascar, Malawi, Mali, Mauritania, Mauritius, Mozambique, Namibia, Niger, Nigeria, Rwanda, São Tomé and Príncipe, Senegal, Seychelles, Sierra Leone, South Africa, South Sudan, Swaziland, United Republic of Tanzania, Togo, Uganda, Zambia, Zimbabwe

Note: Countries included in aggregates for Least Developed Countries and Small Island Developing States follow UN classifications, which are available at www.unohrlls.org.

Statistical references

Barro, R.J., and J.-W. Lee. 2016. Dataset of Educational Attainment, February 2016 Revision. www.barrolee.com. Accessed 8 June 2016.

CRED EM-DAT (Centre for Research on the Epidemiology of Disasters). 2016. The International Disaster Database. www.emdat.be. Accessed 7 July 2016.

Eurostat. 2016. European Union Statistics on Income and Living Conditions (EUSILC). Brussels. http://ec.europa.eu/eurostat/web/microdata/european-union-statistics-on-income-and-living-conditions. EUSILC UDB 2014—version 2 of August 2016.

FAO (Food and Agriculture Organization). 2016a. FAOSTAT database. http://faostat3.fao.org. Accessed 25 May 2016.

———. 2016b. AQUASTAT database. www..fao.org/nr/water/aquastat/main/index.stm. Accessed 23 June 2016.

Gallup. 2016. Gallup World Poll Analytics database. www.gallup.com/products/170987/gallup-analytics.aspx. Accessed 25 January 2016.

ICF Macro. Various years. Demographic and Health Surveys. www.measuredhs.com. Accessed 15 July 2016.

ICPS (International Centre for Prison Studies). 2016. "World Prison Population List (11th edition)." London. www.prisonstudies.org. Accessed 7 June 2016.

IDMC (Internal Displacement Monitoring Centre). 2016. Global Report on Internal Displacement. www.internal-displacement.org. Accessed 7 June 2016.

ILO (International Labour Organization). 2016a. Key Indicators of the Labour Market: 9th edition. Geneva. www.ilo.org/kilm. Accessed 9 June 2016.

———. 2016b. ILOSTAT database. www..ilo.org/ilostat. Accessed 24 October 2016.

———. 2016c. World Social Protection Report 2014–15. Geneva. www..social-protection.org/gimi/gess/ShowTheme.do?tid=3985. Accessed 7 June 2016.

IMF (International Monetary Fund). 2016. World Economic Outlook database. Washington, DC. www.imf.org/external/pubs/ft/weo/2016/02/. Accessed 10 October 2016.

IPU (Inter-Parliamentary Union). 2016. Women in national parliaments. www.ipu.org/wmn-e/classif-arc.htm. Accessed 19 July 2016.

ITU (International Telecommunication Union). 2016. ICT Facts and Figures 2016. www.itu.int/en/ITU-D/Statistics/Pages/stat/. Accessed 2 August 2016.

LIS (Luxembourg Income Study). 2016. Luxembourg Income Study Project. www.lisdatacenter.org/data-access. Accessed 15 July 2016.

Palma, J.G. 2011. "Homogeneous Middles vs. Heterogeneous Tails, and the End of the 'Inverted-U': The Share of the Rich is What it's All About." Cambridge Working Papers in Economics, 1111. Cambridge University, UK. www..econ.cam.ac.uk/dae/repec/cam/pdf/cwpe1111.pdf. Accessed 15 September 2013.

Syrian Centre for Policy Research. 2016. Confronting Fragmentation! Impact of Syrian Crisis Report. http://scpr-syria.org/publications/confronting-fragmentation/. Accessed 15 March 2016.

UNCTAD (United Nations Conference on Trade and Development). 2016. Data Center. http://unctadstat.unctad.org/EN/. Accessed 15 October 2016.

UNDESA (United Nations Department of Economic and Social Affairs). 2011. World Population Prospects: The 2010 Revision. New York. www.un.org/en/development/desa/population/publications/trends/population-prospects_2010_revision.shtml. Accessed 15 October 2013.

———. 2014. World Urbanization Prospects: The 2014 Revision, CD-ROM Edition. http://esa.un.org/unpd/wup/. CD-ROM. Accessed 20 July 2016.

———. 2015a. World Population Prospects: The 2015 Revision. New York. https://esa.un.org/unpd/wpp/. Accessed 19 July 2016.

———. 2015b. Trends in International Migrant Stock: The 2015 Revision. www..un.org/en/development/desa/population/migration/data/estimates2/estimates15.shtml. Accessed 1 August 2016.

UNECLAC (United Nations Economic Commission for Latin America and the Caribbean). 2016. Preliminary Overview of the Economies of Latin America and the Caribbean, 2015. Santiago. www..cepal.org/en/publications/type/preliminary-overview-economies-latin-america-and-caribbean. Accessed 15 March 2016.

UNESCO (United Nations Educational, Scientific and Cultural Organization) Institute for Statistics. 2016. Data Centre. http://data.uis.unesco.org. Accessed 10 June 2016.

UNESCWA (United Nations Economic and Social Commission for Western Asia). 2016. Survey of Economic and Social Developments in the Arab Region 2015–2016. Beirut. https://www.unescwa.org/publications/survey-economic-social-development-arab-region-2015-2016. Accessed 15 May 2016.

UNHCR (Office of the United Nations High Commissioner for Refugees). 2016. UNHCR Global Trends 2015. www..unhcr.org/global-trends-2015.html. Accessed 7 July 2016.

UNICEF (United Nations Children's Fund). 2016. The State of the World's Children 2016: A fair chance for every child. New York. www..unicef.org/publications/files/UNICEF_SOWC_2016.pdf. Accessed 22 July 2016.

———. Various years. Multiple Indicator Cluster Surveys. New York. http://mics.unicef.org. Accessed 15 July 2016.

UN Inter-agency Group for Child Mortality Estimation. 2015. www..childmortality.org. Accessed 25 July 2016.

United Nations Statistics Division. 2016a. National Accounts Main Aggregates Database. http://unstats.un.org/unsd/snaama. Accessed 15 October 2016.

———. 2016b. Millennium Development Goals Indicators Database. http://data.un.org. Accessed 5 August 2016.

———. 2016c. Sustainable Development Goals Indicators Database. http://data.un.org. Accessed 5 August 2016.

UN Maternal Mortality Estimation Group (World Health Organization, United Nations Children's Fund, United Nations Population Fund and World Bank). 2016. Maternal mortality data. http://data.unicef.org/topic/maternal-health/maternal-mortality/. Accessed 28 April 2016.

UNODC (United Nations Office on Drugs and Crime). 2016. UNODC Statistics. https://data.unodc.org. Accessed 7 July 2016.

UNOHCHR (United Nations Office of the High Commissioner for Human Rights). 2016. Human rights treaties. https://treaties.un.org/Pages/Treaties.aspx?id=4&subid=A&clang=_en. Accessed 1 May 2016.

UN Women (United Nations Entity for Gender Equality and the Empowerment of Women). 2016. "UN Women Global Database on Violence against Women." New York. http://evaw-global-database.unwomen.org. Accessed 4 August 2016.

WHO (World Health Organization). 2016. Global Health Observatory. www.who.int/gho/. Accessed 25 July 2016.

WHO (World Health Organization) and UNICEF (United Nations Children's Fund). 2016. Estimates of National Routine Immunization Coverage: 2014 Revision. www..who.int/immunization/monitoring_surveillance/routine/coverage/en/index4.html. Accessed 22 July 2016.

World Bank. 2016a. World Development Indicators database. Washington, DC. http://data.worldbank.org. Accessed 14 October 2016.

———. 2016b. Gender Statistics database. Washington, DC. http://data.worldbank.org. Accessed 1 August 2016.